ENCYCLOPEDIA OF
Community
CORRECTIONS

ENCYCLOPEDIA OF

Community
CORRECTIONS

Shannon M. Barton-Bellessa
Indiana State University

EDITOR

Los Angeles | London | New Delhi
Singapore | Washington DC

SSAGE

Los Angeles | London | New Delhi
Singapore | Washington DC

FOR INFORMATION:

SAGE Publications, Inc.
2455 Teller Road
Thousand Oaks, California 91320
E-mail: order@sagepub.com

SAGE Publications Ltd.
1 Oliver's Yard
55 City Road
London, EC1Y 1SP
United Kingdom

SAGE Publications India Pvt. Ltd.
B 1/I 1 Mohan Cooperative Industrial Area
Mathura Road, New Delhi 110 044
India

SAGE Publications Asia-Pacific Pte. Ltd.
3 Church Street
#10-04 Samsung Hub
Singapore 049483

Publisher: Rolf A. Janke
Acquisitions Editor: Jim Brace-Thompson
Assistant to the Publisher: Michele Thompson
Managing Editors: Susan Moskowitz,
                  Lisbeth Rogers
Reference Systems Manager: Leticia M. Gutierrez
Reference Systems Coordinator: Laura Notton
Production Editor: Jane Haenel
Typesetter: Hurix Systems Pvt. Ltd.
Proofreader: Emily Bakely
Indexer: Terri Corry
Cover Designer: Candice Harman
Marketing Manager: Kristi Ward

Printed in the United States of America.

Library of Congress Cataloging-in-Publication Data

Encyclopedia of community corrections / editor,
Shannon M. Barton-Bellessa.

p. cm.
Includes bibliographical references and index.

ISBN 978-1-4129-9083-7 (cloth)

1. Community-based corrections. 2. Criminals—
Rehabilitation. I. Barton-Bellessa, Shannon M.

HV9279.E46 2012

365'.603—dc23

2011049057

MIX
Paper from
responsible sources
FSC® C014174

12 13 14 15 16 10 9 8 7 6 5 4 3 2 1

Contents

List of Entries

Reader's Guide

Classification and Risk Assessment

Actuarial Risk Assessment
Classification Systems
COMPASS Program
Firearms Charges, Offenders With
Hare Psychopathy Checklist
Level of Service Inventory
Offender Needs
Offender Responsivity
Offender Risks
Prediction Instruments
Predispositional Reports for Juveniles
Risk and Needs Assessment Instruments
Risk Assessment Instruments: Three Generations
Wisconsin Risk Assessment Instrument

Diversion and Probation

Absconding
Augustus, John
Benefit of Clergy
Boston's Operation Night Light
Case Management
Caseload and Workload Standards
Circle Sentencing
Conditional Sentencing and Release
Conditions of Community Corrections
Continuum of Sanctions
Crime Control Model of Corrections
Curfews
Diversion Programs
Drug Courts
Faith-Based Initiatives
False Negatives and False Positives
Family Courts
Family Group Conferencing
Family Therapy
Felony Probation
Field Visits
Investigative Reports

Juvenile Probation Officers
Manhattan Bail Project
Mediation
Mental Health Courts
Neighborhood Probation
Offender Supervision
Pre-Sentence Investigation Reports
Pretrial Detention
Pretrial Supervision
Probation
Probation: Administration Models
Probation: Early Termination
Probation: Organization of Services
Probation: Private
Probation and Judicial Reprieve
Probation and Parole: Intensive Supervision
Probation and Parole Fees
Probation Mentor Home Program
Probation Officers
Probation Officers: Job Stress
Project Safeway
Recognizance
Reparation Boards
Restorative Justice
Revocation
Sanctuary
Shock Probation
SMART Partnership
Specialized Caseload Models
Teen Courts
Victim-Offender Reconciliation Programs
Wilderness Experience

History, Development, and Definitions

Attitudes and Myths About Punishment
Attitudes of Offenders Toward Community
   Corrections
Bail Reform Act of 1984
Banishment

Theory and Treatment in the Community

About the Editor

Shannon M. Barton-Bellessa is an associate professor of criminology and criminal justice at Indiana State University. She earned her B.A. (1991) in criminal justice from Kentucky Wesleyan College, her M.S. (1992) in juvenile and correctional services from Eastern Kentucky University, and her Ph.D. (2000) in criminal justice from the University of Cincinnati. Her numerous journal publications have been in the area of community corrections, correctional officer job satisfaction, and the juvenile justice system. She is the co-author of *Community-Based Corrections: A Text/Reader* (2012) and *Juvenile Justice: Theory, Systems, and Organization* (2005). She has been a co-investigator on a National Institute of Justice grant assessing the effectiveness of a cognitive-based program in a medium security prison and many small grants on various criminal justice system issues.

List of Contributors

Howard Abadinsky
St. John's University

Joseph Allen
Chaminade University

Gaylene S. Armstrong
Sam Houston State University

Thomas E. Baker
University of Scranton

J. C. Barnes
University of Texas, Dallas

Shannon M. Barton-Bellessa
Indiana State University

Julie A. Beck
California State University, East Bay

Christopher M. Bellas
Youngstown State University

Lindsey Bergeron-Vigesaa
Nova Southeastern University

Phyllis E. Berry
Washburn University

James M. Binnall
University of California, Irvine

Kristie R. Blevins
Eastern Kentucky University

Lauren M. Block
Washington State University

Sarah E. Boslaugh
Kennesaw State University

J. Michael Botts
Belmont Abbey College

Scott Wm. Bowman
Texas State University, San Marcos

James A. Brecher
Nova Southeastern University

Taylor Brickley
University of South Carolina

Chester L. Britt
Northeastern University

Jeannie S. Brooks
Psychology Gerena and Associates, Inc.

Deborah J. Brydon
Mount Mercy University

Christopher M. Campbell
Washington State University

Kimberlee Candela
California State University, Chico

Nigel J. Cohen
Independent Scholar

Kendell L. Coker
Chicago School of Professional Psychology

Charles J. Corley
Michigan State University

Beverly R. Crank
Georgia State University

Christian Dane
Georgia State University

Nicola Davis Bivens
Johnson C. Smith University

Aimée Delaney Lutz
University of New Hampshire

Rhonda R. Dobbs
University of Texas, Arlington

Brenda Donelan
Northern State University

Ellen Dwyer
Indiana University, Bloomington

Dula J. Espinosa
University of Houston, Clear Lake

Douglas N. Evans
Indiana University, Bloomington

Jamie J. Fader
State University of New York, Albany

Sean M. Falconer
Washington State University

Noelle E. Fearn
Saint Louis University

Charles B. Fields
Eastern Kentucky University

Erica L. Fields
Rutgers University

Farah Focquaert
Ghent University

Brett Garland
Missouri State University

Kimberley Garth-James
California State University, Sonoma

Tony Gaskew
University of Pittsburgh, Bradford

L. Kris Gowen
Portland State University

Richard M. Gray
Fairleigh Dickinson University

Marie L. Griffin
Arizona State University

Elaine Gunnison
Seattle University

Neil Guzy
University of Pittsburgh, Greensburg

Kenneth C. Haas
University of Delaware

Timothy Hare
Morehead State University

Nick Harpster
Sam Houston State University

Kay Harris
Temple University

Aida Y. Hass
Missouri State University

Francis Frederick Hawley
Western Carolina University

Todd C. Hiestand
MidAmerica Nazarene University

Michelle Hoy-Watkins
Chicago School of Professional Psychology

Jason R. Jolicoeur
Cincinnati State Technical and Community College

Linda Keena
University of Mississippi

Clive D. Kennedy
Chicago School of Professional Psychology, Los Angeles

Neha Khetrapal
Macquarie University

Janine Kremling
California State University, San Bernardino

Jennifer L. Lanterman
University of South Florida

Edward J. Latessa
University of Cincinnati

JiHee Lee
Indiana State University

Keith Gregory Logan
Kutztown University of Pennsylvania

Nathan C. Lowe
American Probation and Parole Association

Liz Marie Marciniak
University of Pittsburgh, Greensburg

Rande W. Matteson
Saint Leo University

Adam K. Matz
American Probation and Parole Association

Tana M. McCoy
Roosevelt University

Robert F. Meier
University of Nebraska, Omaha

Kevin I. Minor
Eastern Kentucky University

Junseob Moon
Kean University

Lisa R. Muftić
Georgia State University

Anne M. Nurse
College of Wooster

James C. Oleson
University of Auckland

Jeremy Olson
Seton Hill University

Mark N. Pettigrew
University of Manchester

Wm. C. Plouffe Jr.
Independent Scholar

Nahanni Pollard
Simon Fraser University

John Prevost
Georgia State University

Michael J. Puniskis
Middlesex University

Cara Rabe-Hemp
Illinois State University

Adrian Raine
University of Pennsylvania

Blake M. Randol
Washington State University

Laura A. Rapp
University of Delaware

Shamir Ratansi
Central Connecticut State University

Pili J. Robinson
Independent Scholar

Michael D. Royster
Prairie View A&M University

Meghan Sacks
Fairleigh Dickinson University

Patti Ross Salinas
Missouri State University

Stephen M. Schnebly
University of Illinois, Springfield

Pamela J. Schram
California State University, San Bernardino

Christine S. Scott-Hayward
New York University

Eric S. See
Methodist University

Ronak Shah
Indiana University, Bloomington

Derrick Shapley
Mississippi State University

Christopher Sharp
Valdosta State University

Casey Sharpe
Chicago School of Professional Psychology

James E. Shaw
*Chicago School of Professional
    Psychology*

Matthew J. Sheridan
Georgian Court University

Martha L. Shockey-Eckles
Saint Louis University

Edward W. Sieh
Lasell College

Kamesha Spates
Colorado State University, Pueblo

William Stadler
*University of Missouri, Kansas
    City*

Paul D. Steele
Morehead State University

Leonard A. Steverson
South Georgia College

Cheryl G. Swanson
University of West Florida

Christine Tartaro
*Richard Stockton College of
    New Jersey*

Caitlin J. Taylor
Temple University

Tracy Faye Tolbert
*California State University,
    Long Beach*

Jillian J. Turanovic
Arizona State University

John Turner
Indiana State University

Lisa Marie Vasquez
*John Jay College of Criminal
    Justice, City University of
    New York*

Yvonne Vissing
Salem State University

Robert F. Vodde
Fairleigh Dickinson University

Brenda Vose
University of North Florida

Patricia Bergum Wagner
Youngstown State University

Courtney A. Waid
North Dakota State University

Harrison Watts
Washburn University

Jalika Rivera Waugh
Saint Leo University

Stan C. Weeber
McNeese State University

W. Jesse Weins
Dakota Wesleyan University

Henriikka Weir
University of Texas, Dallas

Norman A. White
Saint Louis University

William R. Wood
University of Auckland

Miranda Young
Roosevelt University

Nancy Zarse
*Chicago School of Professional
    Psychology*

Introduction

At the end of 2009, the United States continued to experience unprecedented growth in the number of individuals under some form of correctional supervision. This number included 1.6 million persons incarcerated in state and federal systems and more than 5.6 million supervised in the community. Of those supervised in the community, more than 5 million individuals are placed on either probation or parole, as L. E. Glaze reports in *Correctional Populations in the United States, 2009*, a study prepared for the U.S. Bureau of Justice Statistics. Of those incarcerated, 97 percent will reenter society at some point. As states and the federal government continue to experience the realities of dwindling resources during these difficult economic times, the use of community-based alternatives has become a necessity rather than an indulgence.

Unlike many other facets of correctional-based sanctions, community-based alternatives are designed to minimize the penetration of offenders into the system. The study of community corrections as a discipline has experienced limited attention despite its increased use in the system. Few college curriculums require a course specifically designed to address the role of community-based alternatives, despite the fact that most probation and parole officers as well as other personnel are required to obtain four-year degrees for employment. Likewise, the role of community safety is of the utmost importance for supervision; therefore, an understanding of the components, evolution, and effectiveness of these alternatives is critical.

The concept of community-based corrections as an alternative to incarceration has a rather short history. Although some of the options can be traced back to the use of halfway houses during the early 1800s, the increase in community-based alternatives really began during the late 1960s and early 1970s. Examples of increasing prison populations,

the demise of rehabilitation, and the evolution of the "get tough on crime" movement further illustrate the use of community alternatives as less based on the concept of humanitarianism than on the need for individual accountability. Thus, the movement to enhance penalties that include a community component was born and grew. These alternatives to incarceration allow communities to continue to get tough on crime while balancing diminished resources with the need for punishment and reformation.

Community Corrections Defined and Studied

Community corrections conjure a multitude of images, depending on an individual's experience with the system or even as a community member. For the purposes of this encyclopedia, the term *community corrections*, or *community-based corrections*, includes all nonincarcerative sanctions, ranging from the least restrictive, fines, to the most restrictive, intermediate-sanction boot camps.

Although there may be a set definition used for alternative methods of supervision, the purpose of these options elicits different meanings and views. For example, some may view the purpose of these sanctions as coddling offenders and being "easy" on crime with those who have violated the law. This negative image has far-reaching implications, particularly from a political vantage point. More positive views of alternative sanctions include the use of mechanisms for probation and parole providing appropriate, "just" punishment while allowing the offenders opportunities to remain engaged and be contributing members of society. Regardless of one's perspective on community-based alternatives, the benefits of keeping an offender in, or reintegrating him or her back into, the community are endless. For example, offenders who remain in the community have the ability either to maintain or to seek employment. Gainful employment not only provides monetary support for the offender and his or her family but also provides a tool for repayment of fines or restitution. Similarly, offenders may take advantage of community treatment programs that address the underlying causes of their behaviors or provide service to the community that is otherwise not being provided. A growing body of literature assessing the effectiveness of these options indicates that offenders can successfully reintegrate back into their communities. Additionally, as researchers begin to assess the effectiveness of assessment tools for placement and needs, communities can best determine which offenders are most appropriate for a community-based option and which programs are best supported, particularly with limited resources.

The Encyclopedia

The purpose of the *Encyclopedia of Community Corrections* is to provide a comprehensive reference resource that reviews the topic of community-based alternatives to incarceration. This academic, multi-author reference work serves as a general and non-technical resource for students and instructors to help them understand the importance of community corrections. The encyclopedia also serves as a guide for readers to appreciate the requirements of the various alternatives, as a reference on the historical development of these options, and as a tool for facilitating discussions generated by the specific social and topical articles presented in the work. Although the history of community-based alternatives dates back to the mid-1800s, until now no reference work bringing together materials on the topic has existed. As the United States has experienced a surge in its focus on and the importance of community-based alternatives over the past 40 years, it is now time to bring together resource materials that are usable not only for academicians and students but also for those working in the field of criminal justice.

The encyclopedia is a compilation of nearly 200 carefully selected entries on the various community-based alternatives representing not only the options available but also the mechanisms used for selection, the effectiveness of these options, their philosophical purposes, and the historical evolution of the alternatives. In order to cover these topics, the encyclopedia has brought together a group of internationally recognized scholars to contribute to the understanding and advancement of the field of community-based corrections. This one-volume resource is essential for any person entering the field of criminal justice. It is intended not only to be used as a primer for the topic but also to inform individuals of the existence of alternatives to incarceration.

Topics covered in the encyclopedia range widely, including a discussion of the historical development of community-based alternatives, an overview of the philosophical underpinnings of punishment and how they apply to alternative sanctions in the community, theoretical approaches to reintegration and treatment, and new developments in legislation that have directly impacted how offenders are supervised and released. Entries on various options for diversion from incarceration are also included. These topics include a review of some of the more innovative approaches to dealing with specialized offender populations, such as drug courts, mental health courts, and reentry courts. The encyclopedia also includes information on the use of restorative justice programs as a mechanism for reducing costs while managing less serious offenders in the system and recognizing the rights of the victim; these include family conferences, teen courts, reintegrative shaming, community justice, and victim-offender mediation. Topics on the viability of treatment include a review of the impact of Robert Martinson and his "nothing works" proposition; a review of the role of treatment staff; and some of the more frequently used alternatives in the community. One of the growing areas in the field of community-based corrections continues to be the use of risk/needs assessments and classification. Entries in this reference work address the various types and historical development of these tools for offender management. Within this context, for example, the use of the pre-sentence investigation report is covered. Information on the evolution of probation, including recognizance and suspended sentences, is provided. The various ways to administer probation and parole are reviewed. Additionally, revocation procedures for both probation and parole are included. The move toward using intermediate sanctions with a residential component, including halfway houses, community residential treatment centers, shock incarceration, and boot camps, also warrants and receives coverage in this encyclopedia.

Likewise, intermediate sanctions that do not have a residential component—including both restrictive and financial options, such as fines, fees, forfeiture and restitution, community service, intensive supervision, electronic monitoring, home detention, day reporting centers, and testing technologies—receive individual attention. Once offenders are released from institutionalization, they are placed under supervision in the community (parole). Like the several entries covering probation, several entries on parole document its many facets, from its historical evolution to the various sentencing strategies used to administer parole and the use of parole boards.

In the 21st century, with its legal, political, and economic challenges, it is more imperative than ever that correctional systems seek corrections methods that are alternative to and more effective than incarceration. The *Encyclopedia of Community Corrections* will assist readers—from students to scholars to corrections professionals—in understanding the evolution, options, and effectiveness of community-based corrections as a viable alternative to incarcerating suitable offenders by supervising and treating them in the community.

Shannon M. Barton-Bellessa
Editor

Chronology

1789

William Rogers, a clergyman, begins offering instruction to inmates of the Walnut Street Jail in Philadelphia, starting what is often cited as the beginning of the correctional education movement.

1816

Elizabeth Fry begins teaching literacy to women and children in London's Newgate Jail, providing a model for later American women prison reformers.

1821

Elam Lynds is made warden of the recently opened Auburn Prison, where he develops the congregate system, which incorporates a rule of silence, use of striped clothing, and a requirement that prisoners move in lockstep.

1825

The New York House of Refuge, the first U.S. institution for juvenile offenders, opens.

1838

Ex parte Crouse, a decision by the Pennsylvania Supreme Court, establishes the doctrine of *parens patriae*: the principle that the state has the right to remove children from households in which they are not being properly cared for.

1841

Massachusetts becomes the first U.S. state to grant juveniles probation; by 1927, all states but one have enacted juvenile probation laws.

1844

In New York, the Women's Prison Association is founded with the purpose of improving the treatment of female inmates and creating separate facilities to house them.

1856

The first reform school for girls is established in Massachusetts.

1860s

Dorothea Dix surveys more than 300 poorhouses and penal institutions on the East Coast and reports that extensive reform is required.

1867

The New York Prison Association commissions a nationwide survey and evaluation of penal methods. The resulting *Report on the Prisons and Reformatories of the United States and Canada*, by Enoch Wines and Theodore Dwight, calls for changes to the current prison system.

The first statute allowing reduction of the sentences of federal prisoners in recognition of good behavior is passed.

1870

The National Prison Association (now called the American Correctional Association) is founded, making it the oldest organization in the world for people employed in the correctional profession; it publishes its *Declaration of Principles* in the same year.

1873

Indiana establishes the first woman's prison in the United States, the Indiana Women's Prison in Indianapolis.

1874

Fort Leavenworth opens in Leavenworth, Kansas, as a prison for military offenders.

1880

Massachusetts establishes the first statewide probation system in the United States.

1891

The federal prison system is established by passage of the Three Prisons Act, which establishes three prisons—in Atlanta, Georgia, in Leavenworth, Kansas, and on McNeil Island in Washington State—that operate with limited oversight from the U.S. Department of Justice.

1899

Illinois establishes the first juvenile court in the United States in Chicago, to supervise the treatment of children aged 16 and younger who were delinquent, dependent, or neglected; by 1925 every U.S. state but two has established separate courts for juveniles.

1910

Parole boards are established at each of the three federal prisons; the boards are made up of the warden and the physician from each institution and the superintendent of prisons from the Department of Justice in Washington, D.C.

1914

Katherine Bement Davis becomes the first woman to head the New York City Department of Correction. In her previous job as superintendent of the Bedford Hills Reformatory for Women, Davis was noted for her efforts to adapt school education to serve the needs of the incarcerated population.

1920s

Separate institutions are created in the federal prison system, through the leadership of Assistant Attorney General Mabel Walker Willebrandt, for younger offenders and women.

1927

The Norfolk State Prison Colony, conceived by sociologist Howard Bedding Gill, is founded in Norfolk, Massachusetts, as a "model prison community."

1928

James V. Bennett conducts a study of the federal prison system highlighting problems including overcrowding and the lack of meaningful programs for the inmates.

1929

Passage of the Hawes-Cooper Act places restrictions on the sale of goods made in prisons, primarily to protect private manufacturers and labor organizations from what they considered to be unfair competition.

1930

The Federal Bureau of Prisons is established in the United States to provide more humane care for inmates of federal prisons (11 were in operation at the time) and to professionalize the prison services.

A single parole board, the U.S. Board of Parole (later renamed the U.S. Parole Commission), is established for all federal prisons; originally it consisted of three members but was increased to five in 1948 and to eight in 1950.

The first training school for federal prison guards is opened in New York City.

1931

The Correctional Education Association, an international professional organization for educators working in adult and juvenile correctional and justice facilities, is founded in the United States.

The criminologist and reformer Austin H. MacCormick publishes *The Education of Adult Prisoners: A Survey and a Program*, which reflects the results of a 1928 survey of 110 adult correctional programs.

1932

A federal prison in Lewisburg, Pennsylvania, incorporates new concepts in corrections, including housing different security levels in the same institution.

1934

UNICOR, also known as Federal Prison Industries, is established by an act of Congress as a government corporation with the purpose of helping offenders acquire useful work skills that will help them transition to life outside prison.

The first maximum-security prison in the federal system, designed to house the most violent, disruptive, and escape-prone inmates, opens on Alcatraz Island in California.

The Chicago Area Project (CAP), a delinquency prevention program focused on the poorest neighborhoods within Chicago, is founded by Clifford R. Shaw.

1938

Approval of the Federal Juvenile Delinquency Act removes any minimum term of imprisonment for juveniles; they can be paroled at any time after commitment.

1942

Executive Order 8641 allows the U.S. attorney general to grant parole to federal prisoners who can be useful to the war effort, a measure prompted in part by the addition of large numbers of conscientious objectors (who were resisting the draft for World War II) to the federal prison system.

1950

The Youth Corrections Act allows federal sentencing of persons younger than 22 (at time of conviction) to indeterminate sentences with a maximum length of six years, with the exception of a few serious crimes. In 1958, provisions of the act are extended, in some cases to people younger than 26.

1954

The American Prison Association changes its name to the American Correctional Association and encourages members to use the term *correctional institution* rather than *prison* in referring to such facilities.

1955

The United Nations issues its *Standard Minimum Rules for the Treatment of Prisoners*, emphasizing rehabilitation.

1956

The Narcotics Control Act provides mandatory terms of imprisonment for some drug offenses and makes offenders ineligible for parole.

1960s

In California, the Chino Experiment applies a therapeutic community method in the attempt to change the antisocial behavior of offenders, incorporating work release, family contacts, and special training into the prison system.

1965

The National Council on Crime and Delinquency releases its *Survey for the President's Commission on Law Enforcement and Administration of Justice*, concluding that many institutions are brutal and degrading, failing to prepare prisoners for reentry into society.

1967

The Court Employment Project (CEP) is created by the Vera Institute of Justice in New York City; in 1989, it is combined with another Vera Institute initiative, the Community Service Sentencing Project (created in 1979), to form the Center for Alternative Sentencing and Employment Services (CASES).

1970s

The Bureau of Prisons opens Metropolitan Correctional Centers in New York City, Chicago, and San Diego to meet the need for additional pretrial detention facilities.

1970

The National Advisory Commission on Criminal Justice Standards and Goals publishes national goals and standards for prisons and jails.

1971

Lee Jett becomes the first African American to serve as a federal warden, at the Federal Correctional Institution in Englewood, Colorado.

Attorney General John Mitchell convenes a National Conference on Corrections, in part in response to a much-publicized riot at the prison in Attica, New York; one outcome is the founding of the National Institute of Corrections in 1974 to encourage professionalism, research, and exchange of ideas within the field of corrections.

1972

The U.S. Board of Parole is reorganized to create five regional boards with explicit guidelines for decision making, a requirement for written justification for parole decisions, and an administrative appeal process.

The American Civil Liberties Union creates the National Prison Project to safeguard the rights of prisoners in jails, prisons, immigration detention centers, and juvenile facilities.

Marvin Wolfgang and Associates publish a study (based on cases in Philadelphia, Pennsylvania) that claims that a small proportion of juvenile offenders, dubbed "the chronic six percent," are responsible for most delinquent acts, while most juvenile delinquents commit only a few offenses.

1973

New York State adopts the Rockefeller drug laws (named after then-governor Nelson Rockefeller), which increase penalties for a number of drug-related offenses, including sale and possession of marijuana, cocaine, heroin, and morphine; the laws provide for mandatory minimum sentencing.

The U.S. Supreme Court's decision in *Gagnon v. Scarpelli* provides legal protection to prisoners on probation or parole; elements of due process must be observed before probation can be revoked.

1974

The Juvenile Justice and Delinquency Prevention Act establishes four core protections for juveniles in the legal system: deinstitutionalization of status offenders, separation between juvenile and adult offenders, prohibition of placing juveniles in adult jails (with a very few exceptions), and a requirement that states address the disproportionate number of nonwhite juveniles in the justice system.

1975

The University of Michigan's Institute of Social Research begins conducting the Monitoring the Future survey, which collects information about drug use, juvenile delinquency, and related topics.

The National Institute of Corrections begins operation, with the goals of providing technical assistance to state and local corrections agencies and judicial, parole, probation, and law-enforcement staff; conducting research on corrections; maintaining an information center; and developing national corrections standards and goals.

1976

The Commission on Accreditation for Corrections publishes its first manual of standards, addressing the entire field of corrections for both juveniles and adults, including jails, prisons, probation, parole, and community residential centers.

The Parole Commission and Reorganization Act makes significant revisions to the U.S. Parole Commission (formerly the Board of Parole), including reducing years served before eligibility for parole for prisoners with life sentences, giving parole applicants the right to examine their own case files and bring a representative to their hearings, and mandating explicit guidelines for making parole decisions.

1977

The first National Conference on Correctional Health Care is held.

1980

The Civil Rights of Institutionalized Persons Act established that inmates have constitutional rights and authorizes the U.S. attorney general to seek relief on behalf of those confined in public institutions whose conditions deprive them of those rights.

1980–89

The number of inmates in U.S. federal prisons more than doubles—from approximately 24,000 to almost 58,000—due in part to changes in sentencing.

1982

James Q. Wilson and George L. Kelling introduce the "broken windows theory," which asserts that visible signs of vandalism encourage further vandalism and possibly more serious crime as well; this theory provides the basis for "zero tolerance" policies (basically, that any infraction of stated policies will be punished), which were first applied to gun possession on school campuses and later were expanded to include behaviors such as drug use, fighting, and bullying.

1983

The National Commission on Correctional Health Care is established to articulate national standards for healthcare in prisons.

Georgia and Oklahoma establish the first correctional boot camps in the United States; by 1995, about two thirds of the states are operating boot camps.

Corrections Corporation of America, a private company that owns, manages, and provides concessions for prisons and detentions centers, is founded in Nashville, Tennessee.

1984

The U.S. Supreme Court declares, in *Schall v. Martin*, that preventive detention of juveniles prior to their trials does not violate the due process clause of the Fourteenth Amendment.

The Comprehensive Crime Control Act of 1984 reinstitutes the federal death penalty, introduces mandatory sentencing, and defines many new federal crimes.

1988

The Rochester Youth Development Study conducts its first interviews investigating the correlates of juvenile antisocial behavior.

1989

Florida creates the first drug court in the United States, in part to deal with the large increase of offenders due to the prevalent use of crack cocaine; it allows nonviolent offenders to receive treatment rather than enter the criminal justice system.

1990–99

The inmate population in federal prisons more than doubles again, due in part to increased efforts to fight drug trafficking and illegal immigration, reaching almost 136,000 by the end of 1999.

1992

New Jersey passes the first Megan's law, which requires public release of information about known sex offenders; the impetus for the law was the rape and murder of Megan Kanka, a 7-year-old girl, by Jesse Timmendequas, a convicted sex offender living in her neighborhood.

1993

Kathleen Hawk becomes the first female director of the Federal Bureau of Prisons.

1994

The Violent Crime Conduct and Law Enforcement Act provides for the reduction of sentences for inmates who participate in drug treatment programs.

1997

In response to the growing number of drug courts established in the states, the National Drug Court Institute is established to conduct training and disseminate research.

The National Capital Revitalization and Self-Government Improvement Act gives the U.S. Parole Commission additional responsibilities, including jurisdiction over prisoners confined under District of Columbia felony sentences.

2001

Timothy McVeigh, the Oklahoma City Bomber, becomes the first federal prisoner to be executed since 1963.

The case of Nathaniel Brazill, convicted of a second-degree murder for a crime committed when he was 13, draws international attention when he is tried in an adult court and sentenced to 28 years without parole.

Following the September 11 terrorist attacks on the World Trade Center and the Pentagon, the Federal Bureau of Prisons adds counterterrorism to its list of goals.

2002

A residential, multi-faith-based program, the Life Corrections Program, is established within the federal prison system.

2003

The Inmate Skills Development Branch (now called the National Reentry Affairs Branch) is created in the federal prison system to coordinate release preparation and reentry efforts.

2006

The Federal Bureau of Prisons establishes a counterterrorism unit to investigate activities of inmates suspected of terrorist activities, monitor and analyze their communications, coordinate translation services, and collaborate with the intelligence community and other correctional and law-enforcement agencies.

The Adam Walsh Child Protection and Safety Act becomes federal law: It creates a national registry of sex offenders with different requirements for three tiers of offenders, depending on the severity of their crimes.

2007

According to the Bureau of Justice Statistics, 7.4 percent of U.S. federal and state prisoners are housed in private prisons.

2009

The Rockefeller drug laws are revised in New York State, including the removal of mandatory minimum sentences, a reform that is made retroactive.

2010

In January, California establishes a Community Corrections Program to manage initiatives for reducing recidivism and promoting public safety.

2011

In February, the federal Department of Justice releases its 2012 budget request. It includes a plan to reduce expenses by adopting a more generous "good-time credit" system, which is intended to result in earlier release of some prisoners.

In May, the U.S. Supreme Court rules that overcrowding in the California Prison System violates the Eighth Amendment to the Constitution (against cruel and unusual punishment). This ruling requires California to make plans for the early release of about 32,000 prisoners over the next two years.

2012

In March, the U.S. Supreme Court hears oral arguments in *Jackson v. Hobbs* and *Miller v. Alabama*, cases that address the constitutionality of sentencing juveniles (the defendants in both cases were 14 at the time of their crimes) to life without parole.

Sarah E. Boslaugh
Kennesaw State University

A

ABSCONDING

The term *absconding* is used to describe the behavior of someone who is in hiding to avoid arrest. In community corrections, absconding refers to the conduct of a person who, while under probation or parole supervision, fails to comply with the requirement to report periodically and otherwise maintain contact with the supervising agency. An offender who fails to report in person to the agency office as directed, who is no longer residing at his or her approved residence, and whose whereabouts are unknown is declared an absconder. Of the more than 5 million persons on community supervision (about 85 percent of whom are on probation), there are an estimated 250,000 probation absconders and about 55,000 parole absconders.

A person under community supervision signs an agreement requiring him or her to report periodically—usually once a week at first and subsequently less often when he or she appears to be conforming to supervision requirements. During the office report, the community supervision officer has an opportunity to discuss the offender's progress, his or her employment situation, and any substance abuse problems, as well as to make referrals and to provide advice and counseling.

The failure to locate and arrest absconders expeditiously poses a potential danger to the community and encourages other probationers and parolees to follow their example. In addition to no longer being monitored (checked for drug usage, for example), absconders have difficulty gaining lawful employment.

When a probationer or parolee fails to report as required, the supervising officer will attempt to contact him or her by telephone or a visit to the offender's residence or place of employment. If the officer confirms that the offender is no longer residing at his or her approved residence and the offender's whereabouts are unknown, a violation of probation/parole warrant will be issued. The enforcement of this warrant varies from agency to agency.

Incidents of probationers or parolees failing to report to their parole officer as scheduled will result in the officer visiting the offender's residence and/or place of employment. (Photos.com)

Some agencies rely on the police or sheriff to search for absconders; others employ warrant officers to carry out this task. Because police agencies in many jurisdictions, particularly in high-crime urban areas, have other priorities, they may be unwilling or unable to provide sufficient warrant enforcement services, so it is unlikely that anyone will actually pursue an absconder, and the warrant is likely to remain dormant until he or she is arrested for a new crime.

Thus, if the community supervision agency does not enforce its own warrants, they often go unattended; the potential danger to the public is obvious, as hundreds (or in larger jurisdictions, thousands) of probation and parole warrants go unenforced. Warrants turned over to outside law-enforcement agencies are occasionally used to coerce absconders into becoming informants, and community supervision agencies usually have rules against using their clients as informants because it would require them to associate with known criminals in violation of the rules of probation and parole.

Some community supervision agencies have a unit of specially trained probation or parole officers who search for absconders and who may also have other responsibilities, such as conducting surveillances or accompanying officers on field visits to high-risk offenders or to high-crime areas. The Pennsylvania Board of Probation and Parole's Fugitive Apprehension Search Team and the New York State Division of Parole's Absconder Search Unit receive cases in which the supervising agent or officer has been unsuccessful in locating the offender. Unit members work full time searching for and arresting absconders, and their expertise results in a high degree of success. These specialized units also develop a close working relationship with other law-enforcement agencies, enhancing community safety through the discovery of evidence of new criminal behavior.

Community supervision agencies whose officers receive law-enforcement training and are authorized to carry firearms and make arrests usually require supervising officers to search for their absconders. (Probation and parole officers' ability to make and carry firearms is a controversial issue.) The officer, accompanied by other armed colleagues, will visit the absconder's last known address—usually very early in the morning—and may conduct surveillance if it is believed that the offender is still living at the residence.

Community supervision officers will visit the local police or sheriff's agency that has responsibility for the area in which the absconder's last known address is located; it is not unusual for local police officers to be familiar with the subject. The community supervision officer may distribute photographs and other identifying information along with a contact number to police officers, who in the course of their responsibilities may encounter the absconder.

If initial efforts to locate and apprehend the absconder have failed, officers will carefully examine the offender's case folder for investigative leads, such as the names and addresses of codefendants, relatives, friends, former employers, and persons with whom he or she may have communicated while in prison. These persons, as well as neighbors from a last known or previous address, will be interviewed.

The officer will request a "rap sheet," the arrest record of the absconder that is maintained by a law-enforcement agency, such as the state police or the Federal Bureau of Investigation's National Crime Information Center. The rap sheet will reveal any recent arrests and will contain an entry submitted by the community supervision agency notifying law-enforcement agencies of the subject's fugitive status. The entry will contain the warrant number and date of issue, authorizing law-enforcement officers to hold the absconder pending notification of the community supervision agency.

Additional investigative efforts will include an examination of the absconder's credit record for recent purchases, a check of motor vehicle department records, and inquiries with public utility providers (such as electric and gas companies), the welfare department, the unemployment office, and school officials if the absconder has school-age children.

If the investigation reveals that the absconder has probably left the state, the community supervision agency will request that a federal warrant be issued for "unlawful flight to avoid confinement" and the fugitive division of the U.S. Marshals Service will join the search for the absconder. Some community supervision agencies team with U.S. Marshals in an effort to track down absconders.

When an absconder is apprehended as a probation or parole violator or arrested for a new crime, the violation of supervision warrant will be filed. The warrant usually precludes release on bail and the offender is entitled to two hearings, per *Gagnon v. Scarpelli* (411 U.S. 778, 1973), in cases of probation violation, and *Morrissey v. Brewer* (408 U.S. 471, 1972), in cases of parole violation. At the first hearing, known as a preliminary or probable cause hearing, a judge (in the case of a probationer) or a representative of the parole board (in parole cases) will hear evidence in the form of documents and sworn testimony from the supervising officer, any witnesses, and the offender. If the judge or parole board hearing officer finds probable cause—a very low level of evidence—to believe that the subject violated one or more of the conditions of supervision, the offender will be held in custody pending a second (a revocation) hearing, at which it will be decided if he or she will begin serving a prison sentence (for probationers) or will be returned to prison (for parolees) in order to complete his or her sentence. If there are mitigating circumstances, the offender can be released back into the community under supervision, often with additional restrictions, such as a curfew or more frequent reporting requirements.

Howard Abadinsky
St. John's University

See also Parole Officers; Probation Officers; Revocation

Further Readings

Abadinsky, Howard. *Probation and Parole: Theory and Practice*, 11th ed. Upper Saddle River, NJ: Pearson, 2011.

Brown, B. J., N. R. Bruce, and C. E. Sawyer. "Individual Differences and Absconding Behavior." *British Journal of Criminology*, v.18 (January 1978).

Schwaner, Shawn L., Deanna McGaughey, and Richard Tewksbury. "Situational Constraints and Absconding Behavior: Toward a Typology of Parole Fugitives." *Journal of Offender Rehabilitation*, v.27/1–2 (1998).

Williams, Frank P., M. McShane, and M. Dolny. "Predicting Parole Absconders." *The Prison Journal*, v.80/1 (2000).

ACTUARIAL RISK ASSESSMENT

Administered on offenders at various stages throughout the criminal justice system, risk assessments serve a range of purposes, such as granting early release or parole or determining an appropriate treatment or follow-up plan. The use of such instruments has become increasingly relevant in recent decades because of the increasing number of interventions aimed at violent or sexual offenders and the need to protect the public, particularly when community release is considered or mandated. Generally, these instruments estimate an individual's risk of reoffending or resuming other criminal behaviors in the future.

Risk assessments fall into one of two broad categories: clinical risk assessments and actuarial risk assessments. Whereas the former involves a close examination of an offender and relies on a trained clinician's in-depth knowledge and experience, the latter relies on statistical models to estimate an individual's probability of reoffending based on his or her similarity to other groups deemed high risk. While assessments incorporating both approaches are becoming more common, actuarial risk assessments have flourished since the 1990s.

Clinical Risk Assessments

Prior to the development of the actuarial approach, clinicians made determinations of risk on an individual basis. These clinical risk assessments used detailed interviews and extensive observation of an offender to form judgments about the offender's likelihood of reoffending. The information extracted from these sources included the social, environmental, personality, and behavioral factors that contributed to the offender's antisocial or criminal behavior in the past. This assisted the clinician in making a determination of whether he or she felt that those factors were still present and therefore posed a risk that the offender would engage in similar violent or criminal behaviors in the future. The clinician, using this information, would often also diagnose and classify the offender into mental health or offending risk categories. Although this process considered a more holistic inventory of traits and circumstances than some early actuarial approaches, the predictions arising from the clinical method were subject to criticism concerning their interclinician agreement, accuracy, and overall reliability. Actuarial assessments were developed to overcome some of these limitations of the clinical approach.

Actuarial Risk Assessments

Actuarial risk assessments (ARAs) have been in use in various realms for decades, notably in the insurance industry to develop, price, and evaluate products such as life and health insurance. Emerging in the field of criminal justice in the 1930s, predictions of risk using statistical probabilities began to estimate who would violate parole and who would not. This led to the further expansion of this approach and the further refinement of the methodology and techniques for developing reliable instruments. Although varying in the type of information gathered, all instruments share a similar methodological basis. By studying a large number of prior offenders' cases, certain factors related to risk could be extracted. These factors were then retrospectively validated using cases with both a low expectation of recidivism (or risk), and those with a high expectation of recidivism. This empirical validation is the distinguishing feature between clinical risk assessments and actuarial risk assessments. The use of this statistical approach claimed to increase the accuracy and efficiency of predictions over clinical approaches.

Often these instruments will combine numerous factors, both static (unchanging) and dynamic (changing). Static factors related to violence or recidivism may include age at the time of offense, number of prior convictions, or relationship to the victim. Dynamic factors include evidence of community support, response to treatment, and peer relationships. In addition to single static or dynamic factors, constructs such as scores for personality or other mental disorders identified in the American Psychiatric Association's *Diagnostic and Statistical Manual of Mental Disorders* (DSM), or theoretical constructs such as psychopathy, commonly show up in many actuarial risk assessment instruments (ARAIs). These factors, when assessed together, form a probability of future risk or recidivism of an offender, validated by comparing that offender to previous groups of individuals who displayed similar traits.

Four Generations of Risk Assessments

The development of risk assessments can be divided into four primary categories or developmental generations. Clinical risk assessments, as outlined above, form the first generation, focusing on a professional's judgment about whether a particular offender may reoffend. Second- and third-generation risk assessment came to be dominated by the statistical approach to risk, and the use of statistically validated instruments. The second generation of assessments first brought the actuarial approach into the instruments, forming judgments on empirically based estimates of risk, albeit generally from static

personal or background factors. This led to further development of the actuarial approach, as it was felt that static factors did not provide a clear picture of risk. The developers realized that although static factors were unchangeable, the offenders' probability of recidivating was not.

Therefore, the third generation of actuarial assessments incorporated dynamic risk factors and were better able to consider the changing situations and realities of the offender. The incorporation of dynamic factors was important in terms of their ability to predict recidivism accurately, along with their ability to assess changes in an offender's risk, such as following participation in a rehabilitation or treatment program in prison, or note if social or familial support systems increased or decreased over time. These third-generation instruments functioned not only for classification but also for intervention planning for offenders.

The fourth generation, which is relatively new in development, sees intake assessments linked with reassessments and considers treatment plans, services, and outcomes in the overall assessment of the offender.

Types of Actuarial Risk Assessment Instruments

There are several well-known and extensively researched actuarial risk assessment instruments (ARAIs) in use by clinicians and academics. Some of the more common instruments include the Violence Risk Assessment Guide, the Static-99, and the Sex Offender Risk Appraisal Guide. While not an exhaustive description of the instruments currently used, the following is a brief examination of a few of these more common actuarial guides.

Violence Risk Assessment Guide

A widely used actuarial tool for violence recidivism, the Violence Risk Assessment Guide (VRAG) was developed using patients detained in secure hospitals in the 1960s. The guide assesses 12 items, including scores on other scales such as the offender's Psychopathy Checklist–Revised (PCL–R) score, Elementary School Maladjustment score, Cormier-Lang scale score for nonviolent offense history, and alcohol abuse score. In addition being assessed on these scores, individuals are assessed with regard to whether they meet the criteria for any DSM-III (referring to the third edition) personality disorder, and whether they meet the criteria for schizophrenia.

Other factors—such as their age at the time of the offense, early childhood separation from a parent, prior failure on conditional release, marital history, the nature of the most serious injury they inflicted, and whether the victim was female—are also incorporated into the overall VRAG score.

Static-99

This brief actuarial instrument consists of 10 static risk factors, used for adult sexual offenders in determining their risk of both sexual and violent recidivism. The Static-99 is a derivative of two previously developed risk assessment instruments: the Rapid Risk Assessment for Sex Offense Recidivism (RRASOR) and the Structured Anchored Clinical Judgment scale (SAC-J). The factors assessed include the age at which the offender was exposed to risk, evidence of any live-in intimate relationship of two or more years, the individual's offending history for both nonsexual violence and sexual violence, convictions for noncontact sexual offenses, and sentencing history. The Static-99 also examines the victim-offender relationship, with particular note of whether the offender had any unrelated victims, any stranger victims, and any male victims. The summation of the presence or absence of any of the static factors can result in a maximum score of 12, with a score of 6 or more being considered a high risk for recidivism.

Static-2002

Building on the Static-99, the Static 2002 evaluates 14 items grouped into five conceptual categories, with scores ranging from 0 to 14. The Static-2002 maintains eight of the same items from the Static-99, although four of those items were adapted by modifying the coding rules in the original instrument. In addition to bringing in six new items, the Static-2002 removed two items from the Static-99, single and index nonsexual violence. The Static-2002 is considered more theoretically based than the Static-99 and has clarified coding rules, making coding consistent and reliable between users of the instrument.

Sex Offender Risk Appraisal Guide

The Sex Offender Risk Appraisal Guide (SORAG) is a modification of the VRAG and assesses the risk of recidivism for sexual offenders. The instrument consists of 14 weighted items: whether the offender lived with his or her biological parents up to age 16, elementary school maladjustment, history of alcohol problems, marital status, criminal history for nonviolent offenses, criminal history for violent offenses, previous convictions for sexual offenses, sexual offenses against girls under age 14 only, failure on prior conditional releases, age at index offense, meeting criteria for personality disorder under the DSM-III, DSM-III criteria for schizophrenia, phallometric test results indicating pedophilia or sexual sadism, and PCL–R score.

Psychopathy Checklist–Revised

Although the developers of the Psychopathy Checklist–Revised (PCL–R) adhere to the notion that it is for diagnosis only, further research discovered that the PCL–R was reasonably accurate at predicting both general and specific recidivism for varied populations. The PCL–R requires an in-depth review of an offender's personal and criminal history, along with a semistructured interview. The clinician then assesses the offender based on traits present and identifiable, such as glibness or superficial charm, grandiose sense of self-worth, lack of remorse or guilt, shallow affect, need for stimulation, being conning and manipulative, pathological lying, lack of empathy, parasitic lifestyle, promiscuous sexual behavior, lack of long-term goals, impulsivity, poor behavioral control, irresponsibility, failure to accept responsibility, juvenile delinquency, criminal versatility, and revocation of conditional release. As is shown above, the PCL–R often becomes a key component in other ARAIs, such as the VRAG.

Efficacy of Actuarial Risk Assessment Instruments

Although actuarial risk assessments have yielded more reliable predictions of recidivism than clinical risk assessments, they have not escaped criticism. Some studies have found that particular popular ARAIs actually have poor precision in terms of the margins of error for predicting who would be a high-risk individual and who would not. Others have found that there is little difference in the prediction accuracy of actuarial instruments as opposed to clinical judgments. However, in general, most studies and meta-analyses point to the increased reliability of the actuarial approach and the reduction of clinician error. The consensus regarding the preferred approach to risk assessment appears to be one of integration, asserting that the accuracy and reliability of risk assessment is enhanced by incorporating actuarial tools and probabilities into detailed clinical assessments. Incorporating both static and dynamic factors of risk also buoys the consistency of this approach, which can then be more reliable when assessing risk of recidivism upon release, or the design of treatment and intervention programs.

Nahanni Pollard
Simon Fraser University

See also Case Management; Classification Systems; Conditional Sentencing and Release; Offender Risks; Prediction Instruments; Risk and Needs Assessment Instruments

Further Readings

Bonta, J. "Risk-Needs Assessment and Treatment." In *Choosing Correctional Options That Work: Defining the Demand and Evaluating the Supply*, A. T. Harland, ed. Thousand Oaks, CA: Sage, 1996.

Ditchfield, J. "Actuarial Prediction and Risk Assessment." *Prison Service Journal*, v.113 (1997).

Hanson, R. K. and D. M. Thornton. "Improving Risk Assessments for Sex Offenders: A Comparison of Three Actuarial Scales." *Law and Human Behavior*, v.24/1 (2000).

Harris, G. T., M. E. Rice, and V. L. Quinsey. "Violent Recidivism of Mentally Disordered Offenders: The Development of a Statistical Prediction Instrument." *Criminal Justice and Behavior*, v.20 (1993).

Hart, S. D., R. D. Hare, and A. E. Forth. "Psychopathy as a Risk Marker for Violence: Development and Validation of a Screening Version of the Revised Psychopathy Checklist." In *Violence and Mental Disorder: Developments in Risk Assessment*, J. Monahan and H. Steadman, eds. Chicago: University of Chicago Press, 1994.

Moore, B. *Risk Assessment: A Practitioner's Guide to Predicting Harmful Behaviour*. London: Whiting and Birch, 1996.

Quinsey, L., G. T. Harris, M. E. Rice, and C. A. Cormier. *Violent Offenders: Appraising and Managing the Risk*. Washington, DC: American Psychological Association, 1998.

ADDICTION-SPECIFIC SUPPORT GROUPS

Addiction-specific support groups consist of groups of people who meet on a regular basis to facilitate and maintain their recovery from substance abuse. Also known as self-help groups, peer-based recovery groups, and mutual-aid support groups, they have voluntary members and are based on the notion that those who have experienced addiction and recovered from it are in a unique position to help those who are suffering from drug and alcohol dependence. The best-known addiction-specific support group is Alcoholics Anonymous (AA), which uses 12 steps to recovery. Other popular 12-step programs include Narcotics Anonymous (NA), Cocaine Anonymous (CA), and Gamblers Anonymous (GA). The 12-step groups are spiritually based but do not adhere to religious doctrine. In contrast, some faith-based groups have developed recovery support groups focused on their particular religious beliefs. For example, The Most Excellent Way offers Christian solutions for addictions. Non-faith-based groups also exist, such as Secular Organizations for Sobriety (SOS) and SMART Recovery. Women for Sobriety (WFS) is based on the New Life Program and includes a spiritual dimension. Some women who attend WFS also attend AA meetings, but many of the WFS attendees interviewed in one study said they like the opportunity afforded them in a gender-based group to focus on women's issues.

Studies have shown that active involvement in an addiction support group correlates with higher rates of sobriety, and that addicts are more like to heed advice from those who share their illness. (Photos.com)

Although the terms *support group* and *self-help group* are often used interchangeably, Linda Farris Kurtz notes that self-help groups are a larger and more complex form of group, with a clear mission of helping members change some aspects of themselves. Support groups are smaller and less complicated, and they seek to comfort rather than to change their members. Based on this distinction, 12-step programs, such as AA and NA, and other groups designed to bring about change in addictive behaviors would be classified as self-help groups. For purposes of this discussion, however, the terms self-help and support group are used equivalently.

History

There is a long history of addiction-specific support groups in the United States, going back to the 18th century. William White locates early peer-based recovery groups in Native American recovery circles. A precursor to AA, the Oxford Group had an international following in the 1920s and 1930s, receding in popularity in the 1940s. AA, founded in 1935, was influenced by many of the simple principles of the Oxford Group but has enjoyed considerably more longevity. Although the organization does not keep membership lists, U.S. membership is estimated at 1.3 million, with 39,700 of those members in correctional facilities. Membership overseas is estimated at 704,200. AA and other 12-step programs are based on self-examination and self-honesty, particularly about one's addiction, the identification and acknowledgment of one's character defects, one's effort to make restitution for harms done, and working with others. NA was founded in 1953 and remained relatively small until the 1970s and 1980s, when drug abuse became more prominent in American society. In 2004, it was estimated that 2.1 million people in the United States received assistance from a variety of addiction-specific support groups.

Contribution to Recovery

Addiction-specific support groups were developed, in part, as a response to the failures of professionally directed treatments. Advantages of the addiction-specific support groups are their accessibility (for example, AA's traditions dictate that the only requirement for membership is a desire to stop drinking), affordability (AA groups are self-supporting through members' voluntary contributions, often amounting to donations of as little as $1 to $2 per member per meeting), and continuity and sustained support (members are encouraged to attend meetings for the rest of their lives and can call on support of fellow members 24 hours per day). Substance abuse treatment programs and drug courts often encourage their clients to connect with support groups during treatment and following its completion. In the treatment vernacular, support groups become a form of aftercare.

White describes the "natural," "enduring," and "reciprocal" nature of relationships in support groups as superior to the "hierarchical," "transient," and "commercial" nature of relationships associated with professional treatment alone. While treatment staff in therapeutic communities are often former substance abusers, their relationships with clients differ substantially from those found in peer-based programs, where fellow substance abusers serve as guides, sharing their own experiences rather than engaging in directive behavior. Founding members of AA observed that practicing alcoholics are more likely to listen to recovery advice from someone who shares their illness. Group members also believe that because of their own involvement with addictions, they are more skilled at recognizing and confronting denial, dishonest behaviors, and tendencies toward relapse.

Twelve-step programs take a holistic approach to addiction, emphasizing that substance abuse is a symptom of the person's problems. Through self-examination, individuals are encouraged to change their way of living and their attitude toward life, substituting honesty and helping others with dishonest and self-centered behaviors. Support group members are encouraged to change their thinking, habits, and friendships moving from a culture of addiction to a culture of recovery. Addiction-specific support groups and professionally run treatment programs are not considered to be in competition, but rather complementary. Treatment programs may help jump-start individuals who have difficulty with recovery. Studies show that alcohol-dependent persons benefit from treatment and that co-occurring psychiatric problems may be better addressed in treatment settings.

Prisons often host addiction-specific support groups facilitated by inmates themselves as well as free world volunteers. At the same time, prisons also run drug treatment programs managed by paid professionals. Offenders sentenced to community corrections may have treatment or attendance at addition-specific support groups included as specific conditions of probation.

Evaluation

While there is logic to the recovery principles of addiction-specific support groups, they are difficult to evaluate. AA has been evaluated more than any other group, and there is considerable empirical evidence supporting its efficacy. However, data collected by AA shows that 64 percent of attendees drop out the first year. Those who remain sober for five years tend to have successful long-term recoveries. However, because membership is anonymous, it is very difficult to conduct follow-up studies. People who attend support group meetings, unless they are ordered to do so by a court, self-select into the programs, making random assignment for experimental purposes impossible. Research on heavy drug users suggests that self-help groups by themselves are not effective. There is no evidence indicating that any one type of support group is more effective than any other, and there is a lack of studies comparing different types of addiction-specific support groups. One of the few studies done in this regard compared personal and emotional changes among drug-addicted inmates in an Israeli prison in an NA-type meeting, without the 12-step, spiritually based program, and in an NA meeting based on the 12 steps. Inmates in the latter group had a higher sense of meaning and coherence in life and a greater reduction in intense negative emotions, such as anxiety, depression, and anger.

In spite of the difficulty in evaluating self-help groups, numerous studies have examined different aspects of recovery. A study of 200 members of NA who stayed off drugs for three years indicated that they had no more anxiety and no lower self-esteem than those who had never been drug addicts. Research on male alcohol and drug abusers found that those classified as higher attendees of AA and NA meetings after treatment significantly reduced their drug intake, after a seven-month follow-up period, to half as much as those classified as low attendees. These findings stood regardless of whether subjects had previously completed a hospitable rehabilitation program, suggesting that the effects of self-help groups were independent of the motivation of attendees. Another study found that for those

discharged from hospital treatment, attendance at AA meetings improved abstinence considerably more than adhering to prescribed medication. In a meta-analysis of more than 50 studies, the authors found that AA members stayed sober longer if they had a sponsor, worked the 12-step program, led a meeting, increased their participation in the program over time, and sponsored other AA members. Thus, program involvement, which cannot be mandated, was a key variable in improved outcomes. Additional research shows that those who are engaged in helping others recover had better abstinence records, supporting the helping principle and clarifying the process of 12-step programs. Also, both general and alcohol-specific support networks are related to short-term post-treatment abstinence, but only alcohol-specific support networks are positively associated with longer-term post-treatment abstinence.

Spirituality

Addiction-specific support groups are both spiritually based and secular. The better-known and more available groups are 12-step programs that are spiritual in nature and link spiritual growth with successful recovery. The second and third steps of these programs say, "We came to believe that a power greater than ourselves could restore us to sanity" and "We made a decision to turn our will and our lives over to the care of God as we understood him." The programs also prescribe prayer and meditation. Eight state and federal courts have ruled that a parolee has the right to be assigned to a secular treatment program. While not organized religion, the courts view the religious overtones of 12-step programs as sufficiently substantial to warrant prohibiting government from coercing parolees to attend them. Typically, when a judge orders a probationer to attend a 12-step meeting, the understanding is that the offender must attend some type of self-help program. Offenders often choose 12-step programs because they are the best known and most widely available. If alternatives are not available in a community, the probationer may see the choice as one between going to prison and attending a 12-step meeting, making the latter the only viable alternative. From the late 1980s through the mid-1990s, E. M. Read, with the U.S. Probation Office, wrote several articles and a book urging fellow probation officers to understand alcohol abuse within the context of the disease concept and specifically recommended that probation officers refer their clients to AA.

Surveys of members of secular support groups suggest that spiritual pathways to recovery may be contraindicated for them. Among secular addiction support groups, SOS uses cognitive tools to support recovery. SMART uses a four-point program based on rational emotive behavioral therapy. A substantial proportion of members of these groups do not like the references to God and "powerlessness" that are features of 12-step programs. Because participation in support groups improves recovery outcomes, it is important that individuals are well matched with the philosophy of the recovery groups to which they are referred. Thus, nonreligious people are less likely to participate in 12-step programs, and the converse is true for people who score higher on a measure of religiosity. In a study of New York clinicians, treatment professionals cited obstacles to participation in 12-step programs as a lack of motivation on the part of the client, a lack of readiness for change, and a lack of perceived need for help as more important than aspects of the programs themselves such as spirituality and admitting powerlessness over drugs and/or alcohol. A study of substance abuse treatment programs in the Department of Veterans Affairs showed that, in accordance with American Psychiatric Association guidelines, the majority of clinicians refer substance abuse patients to self-help groups after treatment, and that clinicians are less likely to make a 12-step referral if the client is an atheist.

Possible Dangers of Support Groups

Because professionals such as judges, probation officers, doctors, and other treatment specialists often refer addicted clients to peer support groups, it is important to address concerns that may arise about them. These include the fear that nonprofessionally directed groups may give misguided information to substance abusers, that group members may attempt to act as therapists when they have no professional training, that the expression of intense feelings and emotions in some group may overwhelm new members, and that group members may pressure newcomers into cultlike beliefs and stigmatized identities. Long-established groups often have guidelines in their literature that direct members to refrain from giving advice beyond their own experience with addiction recovery. A study of more than 1,300 medical trainees in Australia identified AA as an approach well supported by the research literature and therefore did not perceive this particular method of recovery as doing more harm than good. The new evidence-based case management advocated by the American Probation and Parole Association suggests that officers should be cognizant of the issues related to addiction-specific support groups and successful recovery.

Cheryl G. Swanson
University of West Florida

See also Case Management; Drug- and Alcohol-Abusing Offenders and Treatment; Drug Courts; Drug Testing in Community Corrections; Offender Needs; Temperance Movement; Therapeutic Communities

Further Readings

Atkins, Randolph G. and James E. Hawdon. "Religiosity and Participation in Mutual-Aid Support Groups for Addiction." *Journal of Substance Abuse and Treatment*, v.33/3 (2007).

Kurtz, Linda F. *Self-Help and Support Groups: A Handbook for Practitioners*. Thousand Oaks, CA: Sage, 1997.

Laudet, Alexandre B. "Attitudes and Beliefs About 12-Step Groups Among Addiction Treatment Clients and Clinicians Toward Identifying Obstacles to Participation." *Substance Use and Misuse*, v.38/14 (2003).

Read, E. M. "Twelve Steps to Sobriety: Probation Officers 'Working the Program.'" *Federal Probation: A Journal of Correctional Philosophy and Practice*, v.54 (1990).

Tonigan, J. S., E. Toscova, and W. R. Miller. "Meta-Analysis of the Literature on Alcoholics Anonymous: Sample and Study Characteristics Moderate Findings." *Alcoholism Treatment Quarterly*, v.14 (1996).

White, William L. "The History and Future of Peer-Based Addiction Recovery Support Services." Paper presented at the SAMHSA Consumer and Family Direction Initiative 2004 Summit, March 22–23, Washington, DC. http://www.bhrm.org/P-BRSSConcPaper.pdf (Accessed February 10, 2011).

ATTITUDES AND MYTHS ABOUT PUNISHMENT

The issue of crime and justice permeates the minds of the American populace on a daily basis through personal experiences or the media via what they see, read, or hear. In general, the American public has a sense about how much crime there is in the United

States and who is responsible for committing these offenses. Ask people about the causes of crime, and they are certain to delve into a discussion about their perceptions and beliefs about its existence, causes, and proper responses. Even though information is disseminated at a higher rate of speed than ever before, this information is typically mired by some political agenda or focus unbeknownst to consumers. The images provided by the media typically portray crime and the worst perpetrators as young, black, male, and poor. Despite these images, the real picture of crime is much different, particularly where race is concerned. Attitudes and myths about crime and punishment shape our views in such a way as to deceive the American public into supporting responses to behavior based upon extreme cases.

Myths about crime and punishment are propagated in a variety of ways. Most compelling for the maintenance of the myths are the ever-increasing discrepancies between the reality of crime and the political agendas that support increased punishment. Fortunately, since 2008, according to the Federal Bureau of Investigation, the United States has experienced a continual decline in crime rates. Even with the trend, efforts to focus on crime control initiatives still exist. As E. Currie notes, crime control policies constitute big business. Communities benefit economically from building more prisons, hiring more law enforcement personnel, and enhancing mechanisms of control. From a political perspective, therefore, the creation and maintenance of views toward crime that increase fear and offer support for harsher punishments are fruitful for reelection. Furthermore, as D. A. Green notes, these myths support the argument that crime and criminals are something to be feared, potentially even "evil." By dividing the culture into two distinct categories—us (law-abiding citizens) and them (offenders)—society can inevitably support responses to behavior that limit individual freedom and enhance the mechanisms for control by the government. Often, according to A. King and S. Maruna, these policies result in overcrowded correctional institutions with little or no reductions in recidivism.

Despite these differences in perceptions, more recent research suggests that individuals are inclined to support mechanisms for prevention, rehabilitation, and reentry more than strict emphasis on mandatory punishments. The problems associated with perpetuating crimes begin, according to

J. D. Unnever and F. T. Cullen, with the myths, as opposed to the reality, of how much crime exists in the United States and the proper responses to these behaviors.

As F. E. Hagan contends, myths about crime range from the likely victim to the perpetrators. For example, studies asking individuals to describe offenders reveal the following:

- Females and the elderly fear crime because they are the most heavily victimized of all groups.
- Victims of crime seldom know or recognize their offenders.
- Crime is rising by leaps and bounds and is at an all-time high.
- The larger the city, the greater the likelihood that its residents will be victims of crime.
- In general, residents of large cities believe that their police are doing a poor job.
- African Americans and Hispanics are less likely than the population as a whole to report personal crimes to the police.
- Most residents of large cities think that their neighborhoods are not safe.
- African Americans are overrepresented on death rows across the nation; however, this overrepresentation is more pronounced in the south than in other regions.
- Crime is an inevitable product of complex, populous, and industrialized societies.
- White-collar crime is nonviolent.
- Regulatory agencies prevent white-collar crime.
- The insanity defense allows many dangerous offenders to escape conviction.

Reality, however, paints quite a different picture from perceptions. As Hagan notes, for example:

- Rates of victimization are higher for males than for females and for younger rather than for older people.
- In a large percentage of violent crimes, particularly domestic violence, victims know and recognize their offenders.
- Beginning in the early 1990s, crime has been declining in the United States.
- The residents of smaller cities experience higher rates than those of larger cities for certain crimes, such as assault, personal or household larceny, and residential burglary.

- The opinions of residents of numerous cities across the national indicate that the vast majority are satisfied with the performance of their police; four out of five residents of 26 cities surveyed gave ratings of good or average.
- Crimes committed against African Americans and Hispanics are just about as apt to be reported as are crimes against victims in general.
- Nine out of 10 persons living in 26 large cities surveyed felt very or reasonably safe when out alone in their neighborhoods during daytime. A majority (54 percent) felt the same at night.
- African American overrepresentation on death row is less pronounced in the south than in other major regions of the country.
- Crime is not a major concern in some developed countries, and in Japan it has actually decreased in the post–World War II period.
- Unsafe working conditions and products kill and maim more Americans each year than do street muggers and assailants.
- Regulatory agencies have been understaffed, underfinanced, and inadequate in controlling white-collar crime.
- Despite media attention, insanity defense cases are rare; successful ones are even rarer.

Although reality is quite different from the myths that have been perpetuated, the perceptions of crime and safety matter, particularly when communities confront the very real need to make the best use of diminishing resources. As noted by Joan Petersilia, the shift toward punitiveness has resulted in a reduction in treatment and work programs behind institutional walls that may, in fact, best serve offenders upon their release. This includes opportunities for government support for higher education, such as the elimination of Pell grants for prison inmates in 1994. Given these vast discrepancies between myths and reality, it is imperative that the public view on crime and punishment be understood and that it should guide the process of disseminating information and responses to criminal offending.

The paradigm shifts in guiding philosophies of punishment and the overall "get tough on crime" approach have been well documented by Unnever and Cullen, C. Mancini and D. P. Mears, and S. Fass and Pi Chung-Ron. Despite the loss of faith in the government's ability to ensure public safety and the movement toward a justice model, the American public has still asserted the desire for offenders, once exposed to the system, to be better off when they leave supervision (whether confined or in the community) than before being exposed. Studies assessing the public support for punitive sanctions have varied in results. Regardless, since 2002, according to Peter D. Hart Research Associates, the public support for punitive sanctions has decreased. Instead, the public sentiment includes support for efforts to prevent offenses and to rehabilitate both violent and nonviolent offenders. Most recently, these efforts include combining forms of institutional corrections with reentry initiatives.

In 2009, the National Council on Crime and Delinquency sponsored a random survey, conducted by C. Hartney and S. Marchinna, of 1,049 households in the United States containing likely voters. The purpose of this study was to ascertain voter perceptions and attitudes toward punishment. Results from this study revealed that the majority of respondents believe that the current punishment strategy is too harsh, meaning the majority of nonviolent offenders should not be incarcerated. The majority (77 percent) further reported that probation is the best sanction for nonserious, nonviolent offenders, and 77 percent believe supervising offenders in the community does not threaten public safety. More than half (55 percent) believed that alternatives to imprisonment are more cost-effective to governments than is incarceration.

A larger question may concern what constitutes *punitiveness*. As Maruna and King contend, the mere construct of this term elicits different responses based on personal belief systems and attributes of respondents. Historically, studies of punitiveness have focused on the effects of specific attributes of respondents. For example, an individual viewing crime as a result of rational choices (taking a classical view) is more likely to support harsher punishments than an individual who explains the cause of crime as a result of factors outside his or her control (a positivist view). Despite these efforts to explain ideology in a diametrically opposite way, these studies failed to include circumstances such as the redeemable quality that a person may possess that makes that person more or less worthy of forgiveness or rehabilitation. In their analysis of 941 respondents to the Cambridge University Public Opinion Project (CUPOP), Maruna and King found that respondents placed offenders in one of four distinct groups or views: (1) offenders as "victims of society"; (2) offenders as "permanently damaged by society"; (3) offenders as "people who made bad choices"; or (4) offenders as "evil." The first two categories of offenders are reflective of the positivist school of thought, whereas the last two support the classical school. Those viewing offenders as "victims of society" purported that crime was a result of factors external to the individual. Offenders thus have redeemable qualities worthy of rehabilitation. Individuals classifying offenders as "permanently damaged by society" held similar beliefs to those who saw offenders as victims on how individuals began criminal activities; but, however, they argued that sustained offender behavior was a result of the hardening process and that, therefore, these individuals were unable to be treated in a manner that promoted redeemability. Similarly, those offenders classified as "people who made bad choices" were characterized as individuals who committed crime as a personal choice. Because of the ability to distinguish right from wrong, they too could choose not to commit crime as easily as they could choose to commit crime. Finally, those viewing offenders as "evil" similarly argued that crime is a choice; however, the choice was seen as a "one time only" process, and therefore no opportunity existed for going "straight."

Other researchers have categorized attitudes and responses to punishment as individual, by nature stemming from either personal experiences (instrumental) or a shared sense of anxiety (expressive) that occurs because of societal conditions that force increased residential mobility and a diminished sense of social certainty, as noted by T. R. Tyler and R. J. Boeckmann and by King and Maruna. A variety of background characteristics have been shown to predict punitiveness. "Men, older individuals and citizens with lower levels of educational attainment generally seem to hold more punitive views than others," according to King and Maruna. Views of the role of punishment are mired in arguments ranging from the efficacy of religious beliefs to instances of victimization. In a test of the "mugging thesis," whereby political conservatives argue that a liberal is someone who has not been mugged, Unnever, Cullen, and B. S. Fisher found a lack of support for this contention, and instead instances of fearing crime and racial-social animus (or a "heightened racial polarization") accounted for the majority of differences in views.

One explanation for the way people form their attitudes is offered by attribution theory. The processes of attitude formation are inherent within this theoretical framework. More specifically, attribution theory purports that an individual's attitudes are a direct reflection of his or her experiences. Thus, it is hypothesized that personal victimizations should result in more punitive attitudes toward crime and punishment. Furthermore, individuals supporting the rational choice view of crime, whereby they believe a person chooses crime willingly, are more inclined to support punitive responses to behavior, according to Maruna and King.

The role of punitiveness, Unnever and Cullen note, may also be attributed to the extent to which an individual relates to the offender. For example, when an individual knows the offender and the circumstances contributing to the behavior, that individual is less likely to support harsher penalties. Similarly, when given case-based scenarios in which less punitive options are offered, many individuals choose those options that support rehabilitation, according to Cullen, Fisher, and B. K. Applegate. These options contradict the sentiment espoused by the get-tough movement: that harsher penalties should be applied in all circumstances.

More recent research has examined three competing models of understanding the origins of punitiveness: (1) the escalating crime-distrust model, (2) the moral decline model, and (3) the racial-animus model. The escalating crime-distrust model asserts that individuals are willing to support the tough-on-crime movement because of their increased fear of crime and their lack of trust in the government to ensure their safety through other, less punitive mechanisms, according to Unnever and Cullen. The moral decline model focuses on the relative diminished capacity for society to uphold the morality of its citizens. This moral decay thus results in a lack of trust and social cohesiveness; therefore, support for harsher punitive responses to behavior increases. Finally, the racial-animus model contends that crime control policies are motivated by a racial bias. Despite the decline in overt vigilante justice, the existence of racial bias in perceptions of crime and offenders permeates the political environment and the creation of and responses to crime and punishment. In their test of these three models, Unnever and Cullen, using data from the 2000 National Election Study, found support for the racial-animus model. As Unnever and Cullen note, prejudiced members of the dominant group have their animus reaffirmed when being "criminal" is attached to those whom they already do not like, and their animus is justified even more when political officials "give them permission" to dislike "others" because of their superpredator status.

To summarize, the issue of crime and punishment and the myths that cause crime are important for both institutional and community-based corrections. The dissemination of incorrect information regarding recidivism rates and success of programs has led to a decrease in opportunities for offenders both behind institutional walls and in the community. Although holding individuals responsible for their actions is important, it is imperative that governments understand the myths and realities of crime if they are to respond with appropriate, politically supported initiatives. Similarly, as myths continue to be perpetuated, information targeting realistic responses to the causes of crime may be overlooked and in some instances may actually contribute to an increase in criminality. Society must therefore be concerned with uncovering myths and should seek better mechanisms for disseminating reality.

Shannon M. Barton-Bellessa
JiHee Lee
Indiana State University

See also Attitudes of Offenders Toward Community Corrections; Community Corrections and Sanctions; History of Community Corrections; Net Widening; Philosophy of Community Corrections; Public Opinion of Community Corrections

Further Readings

Adler, F. *Nations Not Obsessed by Crime.* Littleton, CO: F. B. Rothman, 1983.

Clinard, M. B. *Cities With Little Crime: The Case of Switzerland.* Cambridge: Cambridge University Press, 1978.

Clinard, M. B. and P. C. Yeager. *Illegal Corporate Behavior.* Washington, DC: Law Enforcement Assistance Administration, 1979.

Cullen, F. T., B. S. Fisher, and B. K. Applegate. "Public Opinion About Punishment and Corrections." In *Crime and Justice: A Review of Research*, Michael H. Tonry, ed. Chicago: University of Chicago Press, 2000.

Currie, E. *Crime and Punishment in America: Why the Solutions to America's Most Stubborn Social Crisis Have Not Worked—and What Will.* New York: Metropolitan Books, 1998.

Fass, S. and Pi Chung-Ron. "Getting Tough on Juvenile Crime: Costs and Benefits." *Journal of Research in Crime and Delinquency*, v.39/4 (2002).

Federal Bureau of Investigation. *Crime in the United States.* Washington, DC: U.S. Department of Justice, 2010.

http://www.fbi.gov/about-us/cjis/ucr/crime-in-the-u.s/2010/crime-in-the-u.s.-2010

Green, D. A. "Feeding Wolves: Punitiveness and Culture." *European Journal of Criminology*, v.6/6 (2009).

Hagan, F. E. *Research Methods in Criminal Justice and Criminology*, 8th ed. Upper Saddle River, NJ: Prentice Hall, 2010.

Hartney, C. and S. Marchinna. *Attitudes of U.S. Voters Toward Nonserious Offenders and Alternatives to Incarceration.* Oakland, CA: National Council on Crime and Delinquency, 2009.

Hills, S. L. *Corporate Violence: Injury and Death for Profit.* Totowa, NJ: Rowman and Littlefield, 1987.

King, A. and S. Maruna. "Is a Conservative Just a Liberal Who Has Been Mugged? Exploring the Origins of Punitive Views." *Punishment and Society*, v.11/2 (2009).

Mancini, C. and D. P. Mears. "To Execute or Not to Execute? Examining Public Support for Capital Punishment of Sex Offenders." *Journal of Criminal Justice*, v.38/5 (2010).

Maruna, S. and A. King. "Once a Criminal, Always a Criminal? 'Redeemability' and the Psychology of Punitive Public Attitudes." *European Journal on Criminal Policy and Research*, v.15/1–2 (2009).

Morris, N. *Insanity Defense: Crime File.* Washington, DC: National Institute of Justice, 1987.

Peter D. Hart Research Associates. *Changing Public Attitudes Toward the Criminal Justice System: Summary of Findings.* Washington, DC: Open Society Institute, 2002.

Petersilia, J. *When Prisoners Come Home: Parole and Prisoner Reentry.* New York: Oxford University Press, 2003.

Tyler, T. R. and R. J. Boeckmann. "Three Strikes and You Are Out, but Why? The Psychology of Public Support for Punishing Rule Breakers." *Law and Society Review*, v.31/2 (1997).

Unnever, J. D. and F. T. Cullen. "The Social Sources of Americans Punitiveness: A Test of Three Competing Models." *Criminology*, v.48/1 (2010).

Unnever, J. D., F. T. Cullen, and B. K. Applegate. "The Pragmatic American: Attributions of Crime and the Hydraulic Relation Hypothesis." *Justice Quarterly*, v.27/3 (2010).

Unnever, J. D., F. T. Cullen, and B. K. Applegate. "Turning the Other Cheek: Reassessing the Impact of Religion on Punitive Ideology." *Justice Quarterly*, v.22 (2005).

Unnever, J. D., F. T. Cullen, and B. S. Fisher. "'A Liberal Is Someone Who Has Not Been Mugged': Criminal Victimization and Political Beliefs." *Justice Quarterly*, v.24/2 (2007).

Walker, S. *Sense and Non-Sense About Crime, Drugs, and Communities*, 7th ed. Belmont, CA: Wadsworth, 2011.

ATTITUDES OF OFFENDERS TOWARD COMMUNITY CORRECTIONS

In the United States, criminal offenders can face a host of potential penalties. Many scholars refer to these varying sanctions as the punishment continuum. Occupying space on this punishment continuum are incarceration and various alternatives to incarceration. Many alternatives to incarceration are programs that exist in a community setting. For this reason, alternative sanctions are often collectively termed *community corrections*. Under the rubric of community corrections are such programs as parole, probation, intensive (or intense) supervision probation, boot camp, electronic monitoring, house arrest, drug treatment, and community service.

For those who espouse the use of community corrections and alternative sanctions, such penalties offer a number of advantages to imprisonment. First, community corrections can alleviate correctional costs, because typically community corrections programs are less expensive than incarceration. Second, sanctions that are alternative to incarceration can curb prison overcrowding. Keeping offenders in the community does not stress penal systems, many of which are currently at or above capacity. Finally, proponents of community corrections and alternative sanctions argue that these options better serve rehabilitative goals. Specifically, advocates contend that by individualizing programs that do not include a term of confinement, authorities address the specific needs of offenders while avoiding the criminogenic effects of prison. Drug treatment programs are an often cited example of an alternative sanction that targets offenders' risks while eliminating the potentially negative impacts of incarceration.

Although community corrections and alternative sanctions seem to offer jurisdictions viable punishment options, many oppose their implementation. Specifically, opponents of community corrections argue that such programs do not deter criminal conduct, fail to provide an adequate measure of retribution, and overlook the need to incapacitate those who have violated the law. In sum, those who contest the use of alternative sanctions often dispute the efficacy of penalties they view as lenient.

Perhaps understandably, research on criminal justice policy and corrections traditionally portrayed the continuum of criminal penalties as moving from less severe (community corrections) to most severe (incarceration). However, recent research on offenders' perceptions of punishment has revealed that many do not categorize criminal penalties accordingly. Instead, research shows that many criminal offenders, under certain circumstances, would prefer to serve a term of imprisonment rather than participate in an alternative form of punishment. Studies also have shown that offenders routinely devalue the rehabilitative aspects of community corrections programs. These revelations have led some to question the advantages of community corrections and to rethink their position with regard to such programs.

Community Corrections

Typically, alternative sanctions or community corrections are criminal punishments imposed on an offender in lieu of or in additional to a term of imprisonment. These sanctions take on several forms and operate in various ways. For example, probation is the most common category of community corrections and is often used by jurisdictions as an alternative to incarceration in both misdemeanor and felony criminal cases. As of 2011, there were more than 4 million probationers in the United States, half of whom had committed a felony. Probation is a period of state or federal supervision during which offenders must abide by rules and regulations that both proscribe and prohibit certain behaviors. If an offender fails to abide by probation mandates, he or she can be resentenced to a period of imprisonment. Other alternative sanctions—such as parole, boot camp, electronic monitoring, house arrest, drug treatment programs, and community service—also require offenders to comply with delineated restrictions. Like probation, these alternative sanctions dictate imprisonment as a potential consequence for those offenders who do not abide by their respective program guidelines.

Offender Perceptions

Although many scholars have long believed that community corrections and alternative sanctions are less severe than imprisonment, recent research has perhaps altered those beliefs. This research has shown that many offenders view community corrections as comparatively harsh forms of punishment.

Additionally, offenders who have experienced some form of alternative sanctions often question the rehabilitative impact of community corrections, noting that, in practice, community corrections programs fail to attend to offender risks.

The Perceived Severity of Community Corrections

Several studies have compared offenders' perceptions of intense supervision probation to their perceptions of prison. In these studies, researchers found that roughly one third of participating offenders reported a willingness to serve a term of incarceration in lieu of taking part in intense supervision probation. In one study, offenders ranked five years of intense supervision probation as a severer form of punishment than one year in prison. Research has also demonstrated that offenders routinely characterize boot camp as a more stringent penalty than prison. Similarly, in another study, when offenders were asked about their perceptions of standard probation, they consistently described probation as a punitive experience.

Notably, research has also shown that certain demographic variables influence an offender's perceptions of community corrections. For instance, in a study done by David May and Peter Wood, offenders' education level correlated with a willingness to serve a term of probation rather then a term of imprisonment. However, May and Wood also found that when asked how much probation an offender was willing to serve to avoid a year of imprisonment, offenders with higher levels of education consistently indicated shorter terms of probation than offenders with less education. May and Wood concluded that this suggests that offenders with higher levels of education have a more "conservative cost-benefit analysis" that accounts for the "gamble" of probation.

In that same study, May and Wood discovered that older offenders and offenders who had served relatively more time in prison were less likely to choose alternative sanctions over imprisonment. In addition, they found that females and married offenders were more willing to take part in alternative sanctions to avoid prison time. Again, May and Wood reasoned that older offenders and offenders who had experienced a lengthy prison term calculated the risks of probation to be higher than did younger, less experienced offenders.

The Perceived Effectiveness of Community Corrections

As noted, proponents of community corrections programs laud such programs for their rehabilitative potential. Nevertheless, research shows that many offenders do not experience community corrections as rehabilitative. Instead, offenders report feeling suffocated by the rules associated with community corrections programs. Although some note that the program structure is beneficial, far more question the effectiveness of programs that impose impossible burdens on those enrolled.

For offenders, community corrections can represent significant barriers to reintegration. In *Making It in the Free World: Women in Transition From Prison*, Patricia O'Brien presents research done with females subject to various levels of state and federal supervision. Relaying their experiences, O'Brien describes how various women attempt to reconnect with family, to find work, and to secure suitable housing. She describes the disempowerment felt by women subjected to the rules of state or federal supervision. One recurring theme in O'Brien's work is the parolees' and probationers' sentiment that supervision restrictions defeat reentry efforts. Specifically, many of the women in O'Brien's work note that supervising agents demand that parolees and probationers act autonomously to repair their lives but also enforce numerous regulations perceived as petty and juvenile. For example, various women interviewed by O'Brien describe incidents during which community corrections agents admonished them for going to work or attending parenting skills classes at a time when agents sought to conduct a surprise home inspection. These women uniformly characterize probation and parole officers as suspicious and unyielding. Moreover, O'Brien's subjects described feeling helpless and overwhelmed by the rules of supervision and the lack of meaningful assistance provided by community corrections agents.

James M. Binnall
University of California, Irvine

See also Prisoner's Family and Reentry; Reentry Programs and Initiatives; Reintegration Into Communities

Further Readings

Applegate, Brandon K. et al. "From the Inside: The Meaning of Probation to Probationers." *Criminal Justice Review*, v.34/1 (2009).

May, David C. and Peter B. Wood. "What Influences Offenders' Willingness to Serve Alternative Sanctions?" *The Prison Journal*, v.85/2 (2005).

O'Brien, Patricia. *Making It in the Free World: Women in Transition From Prison.* Albany: State University of New York Press, 2001.

AUGUSTUS, JOHN

John Augustus (1784/1785–1859), a successful shoemaker, a prominent citizen in Boston, and the acknowledged "father of probation," was born in Woburn, Massachusetts. He was known primarily for his pioneering efforts to divert drunkards and other minor offenders from incarceration, and it is estimated that at the time of his death, he had helped almost 2,000 prisoners at a personal cost of $243,234. He is also credited with coining the word *probation*, from the Latin word *probare* (meaning to test or to prove).

Little is known of Augustus's background or early years. At the age of 21, he moved to Lexington, Massachusetts, and became a cordwainer (shoemaker), eventually owning his own business. One indication of his prosperity occurred in 1819, when he deeded a large tract of land to the Lexington Academy to establish a school where he became a trustee. He moved to Boston in 1827 and continued his work as shoemaker. In 1841, Augustus was an active member of the Washington Total Abstinence Society and became increasingly concerned that poor drunks and petty criminals were receiving harsh mandatory sentences that were not warranted by the nature of the crime and the offenders' backgrounds. He felt that first-time offenders could best be rehabilitated if spared the sometimes horrendous experience of a prison sentence.

Later that same year, while attending a session of the Boston Police Court, Augustus witnessed a case involving a drunkard. He petitioned the court to defer the offender's sentence for three weeks and to release him under Augustus's supervision. He took the man into his home and found him a job. At the end of this probationary period, the man returned to court completely sober with a dramatically improved appearance, having signed a pledge with Augustus that he would stop drinking and stay out

John Augustus, considered the "father of probation" for his efforts in the mid-1800s to persuade the Boston Police Court to release offenders into his supervision rather than jailing them. (Public Domain via Wikimedia)

of trouble. The judge was astonished and persuaded of the sincerity of the man's reformation, and he waived the usual 30-day incarceration in the House of Correction, instead imposing a nominal fine of one cent plus court costs of $3.76.

Augustus continued to visit various Boston courts almost on a daily basis, sometimes acting as counsel for offenders, furnishing bail, and even finding homes for some juvenile miscreants. He was selective in choosing those to help, taking into consideration the age of the prospective probationer and his character, among other criteria. In 1843, Augustus expanded his interests to include children, both girls and boys, eventually supervising about 30 children whose ages ranged from 9 to 16. He continued to work as a shoemaker until 1846, when he had accumulated enough money to support himself and his endeavors without working.

Augustus's seemingly strange and unorthodox practices periodically brought him into conflict with some court officials and the police. At that time, police and other officers could receive payment of less than a dollar if there was a conviction in a case in which they had testified. An extra fee was also available for a warrant or writ resulting in incarceration. Augustus would bail out many defendants who would otherwise have been imprisoned, and some police officers obviously suffered financially from this practice. There were reports that officers would often wait until Augustus was outside the courtroom before calling a case in whose defendant Augustus was likely to take an interest. The officers would then hurry the offender before the judge and, after he was convicted, would be able to collect their fees.

In 1852, the 104-page *A Report of the Labors of John Augustus* was published in Boston, perhaps the only firsthand account of his work. The book contains no information about his family or his personal life, except that relating to his work. In 1858, an anonymous nine-page letter, *The Labors of Mr. John Augustus, the Well-Known Philanthropist, From One Who Knows Him*, was circulated in Boston. According to the author and acquaintance of Augustus, it was hoped that it would garner more public support for Augustus's work. After reading the letter himself, Augustus acknowledged the truth and unbiased nature of the observations contained within it.

Augustus died in Boston on June 21, 1859, at the age of 75. His legacy continued after his death, and by 1869 the Massachusetts legislature had passed a law requiring a state agent to be present in court if the process could result in the placement of a child in a reformatory. In 1878, a law was enacted that assigned a regular probation officer to the criminal courts of Boston and a probation statute establishing an official state probation system with salaried probation officers. Other states quickly followed. Even today, there are numerous examples of Augustus's continued influence. Several state and national professional probation and parole associations have named one of their prestigious awards in memory of John Augustus. For example, the Order of Augustus, presented annually by the Probation Officers Advisory Board of the Judicial Conference of Indiana, is awarded to an outstanding probation officer who exemplifies the ideals of John Augustus.

Charles B. Fields
Eastern Kentucky University

See also Beccaria, Cesare; Bentham, Jeremy; Brockway, Zebulon; Community Corrections and Sanctions; Elmira System; History of Community Corrections; Irish Marks System; Maconochie, Alexander; Parole; Probation; Probation and Judicial Reprieve

Further Readings

Anonymous. *The Labors of Mr. John Augustus, the Well-Known Philanthropist, From One Who Knows Him.* Boston: [s.n.], 1858. Available from the New York Historical Society.

Augustus, John. *John Augustus: First Probation Officer.* Montclair, NJ: Patterson Smith, 1972.

Augustus, John. *A Report of the Labors of John Augustus.* Boston: Wright and Hasty, Printers, 1852. Reprint. Lexington, KY: American Probation and Parole Association, 1984.

BAIL REFORM ACT OF 1984

The Bail Reform Act of 1984, which was part of the Comprehensive Crime Control Act of 1984 that was passed by Congress and signed into law by President Ronald Reagan, fundamentally altered pretrial release rules for individuals charged with committing certain types of crimes. Although the new law included bail provisions that had appeared in federal law before, such as freeing defendants on their own recognizance and setting limits on their release, the new law permitted them to remain in custody prior to, and in the absence of, any conviction if they were determined to pose a danger to another individual or to others living in the local area. Prior to the 1984 Bail Reform Act, defendants were ineligible for bail only if they had been adjudicated unlikely to be able to keep their promise to appear in court to answer the criminal charges that had been made against them. The pretrial detention provisions of this law were upheld by the U.S. Supreme Court in *United States v. Salerno* (1987). The Bail Reform Act of 1984 is germane to community corrections because it seeks to protect community members from crimes by people who have been arrested and because it represents a fundamental shift in corrections, as individuals who have been charged with a crime may now be incarcerated indefinitely in the absence of a guilty verdict for the sole purpose of preventing them from committing future crimes.

There are several types of crimes for which bail can be withheld, as a result of a special court proceeding held for such purpose, under the 1984 act.

Among them are violent crimes that can result in the death penalty or a life sentence and specific drug charges that can result in a minimum of 10 years' incarceration. Bail can also be denied to defendants who have already been found guilty of at least two felonies and are currently being charged with another felony that meets any of the aforementioned criteria. It can also be refused to anyone considered unlikely to appear at trial, likely to engage in obstruction of justice, or likely to become involved in jury tampering.

The 1984 act constitutes a significant departure from earlier law, since bail has historically been used in the United States to assure that individuals who have been arrested appear at their own trials. Early references to bail in federal law can be found in the Judiciary Act of 1789, which permits bail in all cases except those involving the death penalty, and the Eighth Amendment of the U.S. Constitution, which bars unreasonably high bail. It was the Bail Reform Act of 1966 that expanded bail, which had long been financially based, to include personal recognizance where money is not exchanged, set conditions for bail release, and withheld bail to allow pretrial detention for defendants deemed unreliable in their ability to make their own court dates.

At issue in *United States v. Salerno* was whether the Bail Reform Act violated the due process clause of the Fifth Amendment as well as the excessive bail clause of the Eighth Amendment. In a 6–3 decision, the U.S. Supreme Court, overturning an earlier decision in the case by the Second Circuit U.S. Court of Appeals, found the act constitutional under both amendments. The majority opinion, which was written by Chief Justice William Rehnquist, explained, among other things, that the Fifth Amendment permits a person to be placed in police custody prior to trial to prevent criminal action by that person. Doing so is not the same as punishing that person for those actions. He also specified that the Eighth Amendment does not mandate bail for any defendant—it merely limits the amount of bail that can be imposed in a criminal case. Justice Thurgood Marshall, who was joined in dissent by Justice William Brennan, noted that the ruling had the effect of allowing individuals who have not been convicted of any crime to be incarcerated on a continual basis just because the possibility exists that they might commit a crime at some later date. Also dissenting in the case was Justice John Paul Stevens, who questioned the issues addressed by the Bail Reform Act of 1984 with respect to the protection of innocent third parties. He stated that it was not likely that they would become safer if the person being held for their protection was found not guilty of the charge for which he or she had been arrested. Justice Stevens also agreed with Justice Marshall that the 1984 act contradicts the presumption of innocence standard, which has long been a feature of the U.S. criminal justice system.

Despite the U.S. Supreme Court's ruling in *Salerno*, the Bail Reform Act of 1984 remains highly controversial because it extended federal law in three new directions. First, it appears to allow individuals who have been charged with, but not convicted of, a crime to be held indefinitely without bail. Second, it seeks to prevent future crimes by jailing potential wrongdoers, although all humans have that potential. Finally, this law seems to undermine presumption of innocence and due process by subjecting those innocent of crimes, but who have not yet been adjudicated, to the same punishment (deprivation of liberty) given to convicted criminals.

Dula J. Espinosa
University of Houston, Clear Lake

See also Manhattan Bail Project; Pretrial Detention; Recognizance

Further Readings

Bail Reform Act of 1966, 80 Stat. 214.

Bail Reform Act of 1984, 98 Stat. 1976.

Golash, Deirdre. *The Bail Reform Act*. Washington, DC: Federal Judicial Center, 1987.

Serr, Brian James. *The Federal Bail Reform Act of 1984: The First Wave of Case Law*. Thesis/Dissertation. University of Illinois at Urbana-Champaign, 1985.

United States v. Salerno, 481 U.S. 739 (1987).

Weinberg, John L. *Federal Bail and Detention Handbook 2012*. New York: Practising Law Institute, 2012.

BANISHMENT

Throughout recorded history, various human societies and governments have moved to isolate offenders or those who have offended the collectivity. Although noted several times in the Old Testament and used by the Romans (several Roman rulers exiled political enemies and their own irritating children), it is most commonly known in modern times through the example of British penal transportation to the New World and Australia. Although the English Crown resorted to banishment in earlier times, its use was formalized only by the Transportation Act of 1718. British prisons, jails, and gallows were overtaxed at this time, and it was thought that this would relieve pressure on that system and provide much-needed labor to the colonies, primarily those in the New World. Between 1718 and 1775, 50,000 prisoners were sent to the New World British colonies.

This sentencing option was widely used, especially in London, as judges were increasingly reluctant to impose the death penalty on the wide range of even minor offenses that the law then prescribed. Terms for penal servitude in the colonies ranged generally from seven to 14 years. Returning to Britain before one's term was finished could result in a death penalty, although many who could, did, in fact, return. Those who could not return to England often absconded to the western frontiers, where labor was needed and few questions were asked about their past. Quite a few of those transported were recent Irish immigrants to England who had fallen on lean times; most were English, and relatively few were Scots. The most common ports for export were London and Bristol. Prisoners were subject to ritualized humiliation in an 18th-century version of a "perp walk," which occurred when they were marched from the port city's jail to the transport ships. Occasionally, gang members would successfully help a comrade escape during the stage between the city jail and the transport stage.

Conditions on board the convict transport ships were grim, and death rates were high during the six- to eight-week transatlantic journey. Convicts' working and living conditions in the New World colonies were often bestial. Women convicts were frequently sexually molested, and both sexes were worked harder than slaves. Slaves were considered property, and as such they were a valuable commodity; it would have been foolish to abuse them gratuitously. Transported prisoners were more like rental items and were subject to hard use. The writings of former transports are full of tales of hard use and woe, and there were few success stories, largely because of the extremely low status that they enjoyed in New World society. When the British began to transport prisoners to Australia in 1776 (during the American Revolution), the shipboard conditions were far worse, given the length of the journey and the tropical conditions encountered along the route. In the next 80 years, more than 180,000 British and Irish prisoners were sent to Australia. Prisoners were sometimes staked to the ground after landing on that "fatal shore" and had to contend with numerous poisonous spiders and snakes and hostile aboriginal inhabitants.

Conviction and transportation were seen by the British lower class as worse than a death penalty, and this belief was immortalized in folklore and broadside ballads. Those sent to the New World, and later to Van Dieman's Land (Tasmania) and Australia, were being sent to the literal end of the known world, and most never returned, even after their terms were up.

Not only did the British lower class fear transportation but some even asked for the death penalty rather than leave family and Old England. Noncriminal colonists in the New World were incensed by the policy and essentially expressed a "not in my backyard" reaction to this practice. Until the American Revolution itself, this issue was the chief irritant in American-British relations. Benjamin Franklin remonstrated against it numerous times.

The Russian czarist regime used Siberian exile quite frequently as a way to deal with both common criminals and intellectual opponents of its autocratic rule. The acclaimed writer Fyodor Dostoevsky was confined there for his part in the subversive activity of a group of young revolutionaries. Generally, many intellectuals while in Siberia were allowed to work in fulfilling occupations, such as teacher or administrator, but others had to go to prison and endure harassment from common criminals. Members of the intelligentsia who were sent to Siberia often supported one another and were well treated while there. Under czarist rule, many Bolshevik revolutionaries were also banished there for limited terms; it was an intellectual badge of honor to have been sent to Siberia. Ironically, when those formerly exiled established their own regime in 1917 (the Soviet Union), they continued to use Siberia as a place of exile for royalists and counterrevolutionaries. The esteemed writer Alexander Solzhenitsyn was banished to prison, and then to residential exile, there for making a sarcastic reference to Soviet premier Joseph Stalin in a letter from the front during World War II. Solzhenitsyn immortalized the extent and manifestations of Soviet penal practices in his monumental *Gulag Archipelago*.

Francis Frederick Hawley
Western Carolina University

See also Community Corrections as an Alternative to Imprisonment; Offenders With Mental Illness; Punishment

Further Readings

Ekirch, A. *Bound for America: The Transportation of British Convicts to the Colonies, 1718–1775.* New York: Oxford University Press, 1987.

Hughes, R. *The Fatal Shore: The Epic of Australia's Founding.* New York: Vintage, 1988.

Solzhenitsyn, A. *The Gulag Archipelago.* New York: Harper and Row, 1973.

Willis, J. "Transportation Versus Imprisonment in Eighteenth- and Nineteenth-Century Britain: Penal Power, Liberty, and the State." *Law and Society Review,* v.39/1 (March 2005).

BECCARIA, CESARE

Cesare Bonesana Beccaria (1738–94) was an Italian economist and politician best known for his brief but justly celebrated pioneering essay on penology, *Dei delitti e delle penne* (*On Crimes and Punishments*). This essay colored the views of many successive legal reformers and became incorporated into the penal codes of Europe and the United States. Although Beccaria lived before criminology emerged as a scientific discipline, his influence on criminology generally, and on the classical school of criminology in particular, was profound. His work remains relevant even today.

Born in Milan to an aristocratic family, Beccaria studied at the Jesuit college in Parma before graduating from the University of Pavia in 1758. Then, under the intellectual influence of the brothers Alessandro and Pietro Verri, Beccaria helped to organize a society, l'Accademia dei Pugni (the Academy of Fists), which was committed to political and economic reform. After reading works by Montesquieu, Helvetius, Thomas Hobbes, and David Hume, Beccaria produced a treatise in 1762 about remedies for the monetary disorders of Milan. However, it was only after collaborating closely with the Verri brothers (while Alessandro was a prison official in Milan and Pietro was writing a history of torture) that Beccaria produced his magnum opus of 1764, *On Crimes and Punishments*.

On Crimes and Punishments was initially published anonymously for fear of reprisals in response to the book's attack on the legal and prison systems then in place. Only when it became clear that authorities accepted the views contained therein did Beccaria dare to attach his name. The essay, however, became immediately famous. It was translated into French in 1766 and passed through six editions, all within 18 months. It was translated into English in 1767 and was read by statesmen such as John Adams and Thomas Jefferson.

Beccaria's essay was noteworthy not for its use of the social and political concepts that were in vogue at the time—ideas of social contract, utilitarianism, rationalism, and hedonism—but for the manner in which he combined these concepts. *On Crimes and Punishments* is not a desiccated exegesis of legal scholarship but an ardent, urgent call for legal and penal reform, written with great clarity and deep humanity. Building upon the concept of the social contract, Beccaria argued that each person sacrifices to the community just enough liberty to induce others to defend it. He then argued that those who commit crimes are in breach of the social contract and must be punished. Because he assumed that people are rational actors who are motivated by the pursuit of pleasure and the avoidance of pain, he believed that a properly ordered system of punishments would deter criminal conduct. Any punishment beyond this, Beccaria argued, is unnecessary and unjust.

Beccaria suggested that laws should be clear in defining crime and that judges should merely determine whether the law has been broken. He argued that punishments should be proportionate to the seriousness of the crimes for which they are imposed. Minor crimes should be punished little, whereas serious crimes that threaten the very existence of society should be punished severely.

Beccaria believed that the justifying rationale for punishment was deterrence, in the sense of both deterring the offender from future crime (specific deterrence) and deterring others (general deterrence). Effective punishments, he reasoned, were public, swift, and certain. The certainty of a punishment was more important than its severity, and swift imposition after offending would ensure that ideas of crime and punishment would remain firmly associated. Thus, for Beccaria, legal systems characterized by discretionary judgments, disproportionality, and delay were unlikely to reduce crime.

Beccaria opposed the use of torture, reasoning that confessions extracted under torture would compel defendants to implicate themselves, thereby leading to further suffering and harm. This was inconsistent with the individual's natural right to self-preservation.

Beccaria also repudiated the death penalty, reasoning that life imprisonment was sufficient to deter and noting that individuals entering into the social contract did not abrogate the right to their lives. He argued that corporal punishments were less desirable than fines or, when fines could not be paid, imprisonment.

On Crimes and Punishments proved to be an incredibly influential and enduring work. It was frequently invoked by intellectuals such as Voltaire (who used Beccaria's book in propounding his own views on legal reform until his death) and Jeremy Bentham (who drew heavily upon Beccaria's work in extrapolating a full-scale doctrine of utilitarianism). Provisions from his work were incorporated into the U.S. Constitution, and Beccaria's conclusion was adopted in near-verbatim fashion into Article 8 of the 1789 French Declaration of the Rights of Man and of the Citizen.

In 1768, Beccaria was appointed to the chair of law and economy at the Palatine School of Milan, an institution that trained individuals for government service. In 1771, he was made a member of the Supreme Economic Council of Milan, and in 1791 he was appointed to the board responsible for reforming the Italian penal code.

Later in life, Beccaria wrote rather little. He produced a brief work on literary style, although his treatise, *Elements of Public Economy*, was published posthumously in 1804.

James C. Oleson
University of Auckland

See also Attitudes and Myths About Punishment; Bentham, Jeremy; Philosophy of Community Corrections

Further Readings

Beccaria, Cesare. *On Crimes and Punishments*, Henry Paolucci, trans. Upper Saddle River, NJ: Prentice-Hall, 1963.

Maestro, Marcello T. *Cesare Beccaria and the Origins of Penal Reform*. Philadelphia: Temple University Press, 1973.

Phillipson, Coleman. *Three Criminal Law Reformers: Beccaria, Bentham, Romilly*. Montclair, NJ: Patterson Smith, 1970.

BENEFIT OF CLERGY

The term *benefit of clergy*, as a form of community corrections, has its roots in England during the Middle Ages. Following its inception, the benefit of clergy had quite a complex and changing history (Sawyer, 1990). As noted by Cross (1917), laws during this time favored the upper classes, who subsequently dominated Parliament. Because of a desire to protect personal property, crimes such as petty theft and arson carried sentences of death. The harshness of these penalties disrupted the fair administration of justice.

During this same period, the Holy Roman Catholic Church was very powerful. A struggle for power ensued between the Church and the sitting ruler in England at the time, King Henry II. His efforts to diminish the power of the Church became evident in his attempt to secularize all courts. More specifically, he focused on diminishing the power of the ecclesiastical courts by trying priests, monks, clerics, and nuns in the secular court system. In response to these efforts, the Holy Roman Catholic Church instituted its own variation on the administration of justice by the creation of the benefit of clergy. Priests, monks, clerics, and nuns accused of violating the law were to have their cases heard by the ecclesiastical court, thus altering the role of the Church to being one of an administrator of justice. The most compelling difference between the two court systems was that the Church viewed negative behavior as sinful as opposed to a violation against mankind. The punishments administered by the Church served the purposes of reformation and forgiveness as opposed to simply being punitive. Regardless, the origins of the benefit of clergy were based less on compassion and were more indicative of the Roman Catholic Church's effort to thwart the secular court movement and King Henry II's attempts to consolidate power in England.

Although this court arrangement at first mediated injustices for members of the clergy, the ability of the Church to effectively function in the role of law enforcement was questionable. Eventually, the religious court system began to mirror the injustices occurring in the secular system. Historical documents reveal an attempt to mitigate the severity of capital sanctions by juries, who would commit perjury to do so. Mitigation was accomplished by acquitting individuals accused of less serious felonies such as petty theft, in spite of clear evidence of guilt. Those juries not willing to fully acquit, however, would often find offenders guilty of misdemeanors in lieu of the more serious felony. Finally, the ability of the criminal court to enforce the laws diminished, whereas the power of civil court to regulate individual behavior increased.

Simultaneously, a combination of higher literacy rates, the proliferation of slavery, the use of pardons, and an increase in transportation prompted Parliament to develop exceptions to the legal protocol, resulting in the benefit of clergy being available to the general public. By 1603, the English benefit of clergy was expanded to the public as a mechanism for courts to mitigate the harshness of penalties (death) for felony offenses deemed "clergyable." Felonies such as murder, horse stealing, and certain arson, religious, and robbery offenses were omitted from this list and so remained punishable by death. Other felonies such as manslaughter, murder without malice, and larceny were considered "clergyable" and eligible for exemption from death.

Later, the benefit was additionally offered to individuals who had no prior history of exemption and possessed acceptable literacy. The determination of acceptable literacy was decided in two ways. First, one had to prove their absolute belief in the Bible, as well as an ability to live a life accordingly. Second, the individual was required to recite Psalm 51 from memory. The passage eventually received the nickname "neck verse," because the accused who successfully recited the verse was often spared death by hanging. Should the accused be able to satisfactorily pass both these test, he was granted benefit of clergy.

By 1623, the law again expanded to include women convicted of theft of merchandise under the value of 10 shillings. Women were fully included by 1691 and considered on equal terms with men. This allowed all women to seek a more lenient punishment by attempting to invoke the benefit of clergy. In support of Cross's (1917) argument about preferential treatment for the upper class, the literacy standard often excluded those who lacked formal education and a disproportionate number of women.

In 1706, the benefit of clergy omitted the literacy requirement, though it remained available only for the same set of offenses. From 1706 to 1718, hard labor was used as a means of punishment in lieu of the death penalty. English convicts pleading benefit of clergy became subject to seven years of indentured servitude and were transported to North America in shackles. Efforts to amend the benefit of clergy coincided with the passage of the Transportation Act of 1718 and an increased use of pardons. Because the American colonies adopted English common law as its premise for justice, both countries began practicing similar pardoning techniques within the same era.

By 1732, the benefit of clergy in America was again broadened, and Virginia slaves became legally eligible. Manslaughter, theft, and repeat offenses joined the list of excluded offenses. Other slave states, such as Alabama, also extended this benefit to slaves in 1805. In an effort to prevent repeat offenders from unjustly claiming the benefit, in 1779 criminals began to be branded on the thumb as an outward sign of having already received this ecclesiastic exemption. Later, branding was often combined with a term of confinement in jail as a means of incorporating somewhat more punitive measures.

In the case of slaves, physical punishment rather than death was preferred by the court because the slave's death meant considerable loss of valuable labor and vital property to the owner. Often these slaves would receive bareback lashings in lieu of death. In 1705, all slaves in Virginia were legally classified as property; as a result, stealing slaves became a felony. According to the benefit of clergy law at the time, this felony was ineligible for the benefit of clergy. In reaction to an increase in attempted slave escapes, a law was passed by the House in 1732 that made any accomplice to attempted slave escapes also a felon and without benefit of clergy.

In the early 19th century, criminal law began to undergo significant reforms. The benefit of clergy was officially abolished in 1827 in England, although as noted by Sawyer (1990) it had not actually been used since 1779. Despite being abolished in England, the benefit of clergy continued to be used in Massachusetts and Virginia during trials for slaves until 1848. Its long-term impact on the Western justice system was in providing first-time offenders alternative sanctions and greater leniency.

Michael D. Royster
Prairie View A&M University
Shannon M. Barton-Bellessa
Indiana State University
William Mackey
Indiana State University

See also Faith-Based Initiatives; Second Chance Act

Further Readings

Barton-Bellessa, Shannon M. and Robert D. Hanser. *Community-Based Corrections: A Text/Reader.* Thousand Oaks, CA: Sage, 2012.

Boyd, William K. "Documents and Comments on Benefit of Clergy as Applied to Slaves." *Journal of Negro History*, v.8/4 (1923).

Byrne, James M., Arthur J. Lurigio, and Joan Petersilia. *Smart Sentencing: The Emergence of Intermediate Sanctions.* Thousand Oaks, CA: Sage, 1992.

Cross, Arthur Lyon. "The English Criminal Law and Benefit of Clergy During the Eighteenth and Early Nineteenth Century." *American Historical Review*, v.22/3 (1917).

Ekirch, A. Roger. "The Transportation of Scottish Criminals to America During the Eighteenth Century." *Journal of British Studies*, v.24/3 (1985).

Morgan, Kenneth. "Convict Transportation to Colonial America." *Reviews in American History*, v.17/1 (1989).

Roberts, John W. *Reform and Retribution: An Illustrated History of American Prisons.* Lanham, MD: American Correctional Association, 1997.

Sawyer, Jeffrey K. "Benefit of Clergy in Maryland and Virginia." *American Journal of Legal History*, v.34/1 (1990).

BENTHAM, JEREMY

Jeremy Bentham (1748–1832) was an English jurist and philosopher whose name has become synonymous with the doctrine of utilitarianism. A prolific writer, Bentham produced many thousands of pages in an effort to codify a rational system of civil and penal jurisprudence. However, he was interested in many additional topics. For example, Bentham wrote extensively in the fields of moral and political philosophy, conceived the idea of the "hedonic calculus," and proposed a well-known model prison premised upon total surveillance: the Panopticon.

Bentham was born in London and was recognized as a precocious child. He entered Queen's College, Oxford, in 1760, when he was only 12 years old. He earned his bachelor's degree in 1763, achieved his master's degree in 1766, and was called to the bar in 1769. Nonetheless, Bentham was disgusted with the brutality, opacity, and inefficiency of the law and thought little of those commentators who attempted to justify the state of the existing law. Indeed, Bentham never practiced law, although he spent a great deal of time writing numerous pamphlets on legal issues (such as the packing of juries, the law of libel, and the extortions of the legal profession). He produced a detailed, critical *Comment* on William Blackstone's *Commentaries on the Laws of England*, although this was not published until nearly 150 years later. In much of his writing, Bentham struggled to simplify and clarify the law, reserving the use of punishment (an evil) for those cases where it would improve the net human condition.

This maximization of net human happiness (the greatest good for the greatest number of people) lies at the heart of utilitarianism. In his best known work, *The Principles of Morals and Legislation*, Bentham elaborated upon the principles of utility outlined in Cesare Beccaria's *On Crimes and Punishments*. Bentham argued that mankind is governed by pleasure (which, for him, was synonymous with benefit and good) and pain (synonymous with cost, expense, and evil), and he proposed a comprehensive system of classification for pleasures and pains. He cataloged 14 different basic pleasures, 12 different basic pains, and seven different dimensions by which these pleasures and pains can be measured. In this way, he reasoned, the happiness value of any given action could be evaluated. Bentham rejected Beccaria's humanism but believed that a scientific utilitarianism (founded in objective measures of pleasure and pain) would liberate people from suffering under laws established by superstition and prejudice.

Bentham identified 11 different properties of punishment: variability (the punishment is producible

in a range of severity or duration), equability (the punishment is proportional to the crime), commensurability (the punishment is proportional to other punishments, encouraging lawbreakers to choose less serious offenses), characteristicalness (the punishment is analogous to the offense, helping lawbreakers to remember it prior to offending), exemplarity (the idea of the punishment is enhanced, since it is the idea that deters), frugality (the punishment does not create any unnecessary pain), subserviency to reformation (the punishment tends to rehabilitate), efficacy in disabling (the punishment tends to incapacitate), subserviency to compensation (the punishment allows for restitution), popularity (the punishment is not unacceptable to the public), and remissibility (the punishment allows injustices to be redressed). These properties could be applied to various categories of punishments (such as corporal punishment, financial penalties, and incarceration), producing an analytic grid for the relative advantages of different punishments. While judges are unlikely to assess Bentham's 11 properties of punishment in an explicit manner, many of these properties are central to the imposition of punishment and are regularly incorporated into sentencing decisions.

Within criminology, Bentham is perhaps best known for his design of the circular prison that he called the Panopticon. From an observation tower at the center of the Panopticon, an observer would be able to gaze into all of the brightly illuminated cells that would line the outer walls. None of the prisoners would know when they were being watched, however, which would allow one guard to control hundreds or thousands of men. Bentham believed that the Panopticon's minimal staffing would decrease the cost of the prison, and he invested significant time and money in the promotion of the Panopticon. Bentham recuperated some of his investment in 1831, but the design was never implemented during his lifetime. Later prisons constructed around the world, however, featured elements of Bentham's panoptic design. Bentham's Panopticon was cited by Michel Foucault in *Discipline and Punish* as a metaphor for modern, disciplinary society and its tendency to transform individuals into docile bodies through observation and normalization.

Bentham exercised considerable influence in political and philosophical circles, serving as leader of the Philosophical Radicals (a group of disciples committed to the principles of utilitarianism). Along with James Mill, Bentham founded a journal, *The Westminster Review*, and published on a number of contentious subjects. The Philosophical Radicals even founded a university—University College, London—the first English university to admit students regardless of their race, creed, or political viewpoint. Although Bentham was 78 years old when the university opened, he is considered a father of the institution. He is still there: After Bentham's death, he was embalmed and placed on display at UCL as an "auto-icon."

James C. Oleson
University of Auckland

See also Attitudes and Myths About Punishment; Beccaria, Cesare; Philosophy of Community Corrections

Further Readings

Bentham, Jeremy. *The Principles of Morals and Legislation.* New York: Hafner Press, 1948.

Foucault, Michel. *Discipline and Punish,* Alan Sheridan, trans. New York: Pantheon Books, 1977.

Schofield, Philip. *Utility and Democracy: The Political Thought of Jeremy Bentham.* Oxford: Oxford University Press, 2009.

Boot Camps

Boot camps are residential institutions designed to correct the problematic behavior of delinquents or adult criminals. There is significant variability in what is considered a boot camp and in types of boot camps. While often referred to as one form of shock incarceration, boot camp programs traditionally include the following components: education and job training, community service, mental and physical healthcare, substance abuse counseling, case management, and aftercare services. Camps have the goals of deterrence, incapacitation, rehabilitation, punishment, and cost containment. Use of a military model was designed to make the treatment so unpleasant that people would be "scared straight" and shocked into better behavior as the staff attempted to break old habits and attitudes in favor of compliant and more positive ones. Boot camps are highly structured, with strict rules, routines, requirements for obedience to orders, and discipline for those who fail to comply. There is an emphasis on physical exertion as both rehabilitation and punishment. Some focus

on therapeutic, self-reflective processes. Others use step programs that give privileges once youths have adhered to the challenges of the previous level.

Use of penal boot camps as a correctional model began in the United States during the 1980s to provide an alternative to jail. The first adult boot camp opened in 1983 in Georgia; Louisiana opened the nation's first juvenile boot camp in 1985. They were hoped to result in keeping youths away from adult offenders, decreasing recidivism, lessening institutional crowding, shortening sentences in comparison to conventional detention, and as a result lowering costs. As of 1993, boot camp programs had been established by 30 states, 10 local jurisdictions, and the federal government. In 2003, there were more than 96,000 juvenile offenders in residential placements in the United States, and about 3,000 were serving their time in 54 boot camps in 17 states.

Boot camps may be state- or privately operated. The Violent Crime Control and Law Enforcement Act of 1994 called for appropriations of $150 million for state funding of alternatives to traditional incarceration, including boot camps. The Juvenile Justice and Delinquency Prevention Act of 1993 called for converting 10 closed military bases into boot camps. State-operated boot camps may be subject to more rules, regulations, policies, oversight, staff scrutiny, and monitoring than private ones. Private boot camps are targeted at worried parents with the means to send their children away to military-type programs to instill greater compliance. Costs to run boot camps are usually less than other forms of detention, ranging from $3,500 per month to $50,000 for a multimonth program. Cost containment is one of the perceived benefits of boot camp programs.

Boot camps are controversial. Advocates promote them as effective ways to transform aggressive, belligerent, hard-to-manage youths. Parents may seek them to deal with their children. Courts may mandate their use to prevent future bad behavior and protect the community. Advocates assert that a strict, "tough love" approach is necessary to help problematic youths to get "on track." Inherent in this approach is the idea that troubled youths have previously been treated too "softly" and need to have firm rules, boundaries, and consequences for their actions. Research indicates that some of the people sent to boot camp have violations that are not overly serious, such as shoplifting and bad attitudes, although some have enacted more serious

An alternative to jail, boot camps have been a controversial method of reform, with some claiming that U.S. recidivism rates of participants are no lower than the rates of prisoners. (Photos.com)

behaviors. Staff members may demand compliance with orders and discipline those who fail to comply, hoping such actions will result in long-term benefits to the inmate or camper. Because boot camps cost substantially less than other types of detention programs, they have become widely utilized. There is a general public sentiment that boot camps work.

Critics argue that boot campers may be subject to inhumane corporal punishment; mental and physical abuse; denial of water, food, or sleep; and extreme risks that can lead to injury or death. This harsh approach is criticized as antithetical to humane treatment and personal integrity, as a form of cruel and unusual punishment that violates Americans' Eighth Amendment constitutional rights. The Government Accountability Office (GAO) found a series of juvenile deaths that resulted from therapeutic regimes used. Deaths have occurred from dehydration, physical assault, neglect, and overexertion. Humiliation, fear, retaliation, and harsh confrontations are other forms of abuse. Critics allege that boot camps fail to incorporate social learning theory. Reasons for failure have included military models that promote aggression; an assumption that troubled youths and adults need structure, discipline, and order when these factors may not influence criminal behavior;

an assumption that most problematic behaviors are learned; wide variability in programs and staff competence; and a lack of community supports to reinforce positive behaviors when the program is completed. Because many campers may come from families in which dysfunction, abuse, crime, or other problems have been present, the behaviors that caused them to get into trouble may have been a result of coping with the abuses. Defiance, substance abuse, and aggression may be symptoms of underlying emotional or mental disorders, which a militaristic model may make worse. Failure to provide counseling to the youth and family may result in short- and long-term problems. Campers who witness staff screaming and using harsh penalties to gain respect and compliance may internalize and imitate the same behaviors. There is wide variability in the training used by boot camp staff members and their authority to decide how to treat campers. Some have therapeutic training, while others come from military or prison guard backgrounds. The result is that the boot camp approach may be counterproductive and encourage violence and hostility.

In their early stages, boot camps captivated the public's emotional support; they are now increasingly subject to evaluation and accountability. Research thus far has often cast doubt on the practical ability of boot camps to fulfill expectations. While some studies indicate that boot camps are effective in changing attitudes and perceptions, their success seems to depend on the type of program and the extent to which the facility employs specific legitimacy-building characteristics. Research indicates that boot camps in general have failed to live up to their expectations. Critics argue that correctional boot camps will continue to be ineffective, because the military model is not conducive to the rehabilitation of offenders and should be eliminated from the correctional repertoire in favor of more promising intermediate interventions. The hypermasculine attitudes and behaviors that characterize boot camps may be counterproductive to instilling more corrective and therapeutic ones. Investigators have found that few boot camps collect data or conduct comparative studies that can link the programs to success or recidivism, and they often discount intervening variables. Data from national juvenile justice organizations and the National Institutes of Health have supported a conclusion that boot camps do not decrease recidivism, although other studies argue to the contrary. There seems, however, to be no overall significant difference in recidivism between boot camp participants and comparison samples. Most studies have relied on nonrandomized comparison groups, if any. Early 1990s studies indicated that boot camps did not work and that some attendees committed more serious crimes after boot camp because they had learned techniques from their contact with more experienced offenders. Later studies indicate more positive results, especially if programs include therapeutic components. However, in general, studies indicate little difference between recipients of boot camp programs and other types of detention programs. In exploring variables beyond program participation that might contribute to recidivism, relationships between the likelihood of being rearrested and race, type of release, number of prior felonies, age, and criminal history are all worthy of consideration. Some studies indicate that boot camps may even make problems worse.

What seems clear is that boot camp programs require ongoing evaluation to determine whether such programs are effective. Good boot camp programs include excellent academics, opportunities for success, positive discipline methods, individual and family counseling, clear goals and priorities, careful eligibility criteria and screening processes, clear policies and procedures, closely monitored compliance with procedures, policies for handling failures, and investment in aftercare services. Such programs can improve inmates' perceptions of the justice system's legitimacy by increasing positive experiences, decreasing negative experiences, and limiting environmental deprivation.

Yvonne Vissing
Salem State University

See also Community Corrections and Sanctions; Community Corrections as an Alternative to Imprisonment; Community Service Order; Community-Based Centers; Continuum of Sanctions; Group Homes; Halfway Houses and Residential Centers; Residential Correctional Programs; Shock Probation; "What Works" Approach and Evidence-Based Practices

Further Readings

Arena, Michael. "Is That the Sound of 'Taps' Playing in the Distance for Correctional Boot Camps?" *Journal of Forensic Psychology Practice*, v.2/4 (2002).

Austin, James. *The Growing Use of Jail Boot Camps: The Current State of the Art.* Washington, DC: U.S. Department of Justice, 1993.

Bierie, David. "Cost Matters: A Randomized Experiment Comparing Recidivism Between Two Styles of Prison." *Journal of Experimental Criminology*, v.5 (2009).

Bottcheri, Jean and Michael Ezell. "Examining the Effectiveness of Boot Camps: A Randomized Experiment With a Long-Term Follow Up." *Journal of Research in Crime and Delinquency*, v.42 (August 2005).

DeMuro, Paul. "Boot Camps Revisited." *Journal of Juvenile Justice*, v.22/1 (2008).

Deuwe, Grant and Deborah Kerschner. "Removing a Nail From the Boot Camp Coffin: An Outcome Evaluation of Minnesota's Challenge Incarceration Program." *Crime and Delinquency*, v.54/4 (2008).

Franke, Derrick, David Bierie, and Doris Layton MacKenzie. "Legitimacy in Corrections: A Randomized Experiment Comparing a Boot Camp With a Prison." *Criminology and Public Policy*, v.9/1 (2010).

Henggeler, Scott and Sonja Schoenwald. "Boot Camps for Juvenile Offenders: Just Say No." *Journal of Child and Family Studies*, v.3/3 (2007).

Lutz, Faith and Courtney Bell. "Boot Camp Prisons as Masculine Organizations: Rethinking Recidivism and Program Design." *Journal of Offender Rehabilitation*, v.40/3–4 (2005).

MacKenzie, D., D. Wilson, and S. Kider. "Effects of Correctional Boot Camps on Offending." *Annals of the American Academy of Political and Social Science*, v.578/1 (November 2001).

Ravenell, Teressa. "Left, Left, Left, Right, Left: The Search for Rights and Remedies in Juvenile Boot Camps." *Columbia Journal of Law and Social Problems* (Summer 2002).

Russell, Keith. "Brat Camp, Boot Camp, Or . . . ?" *Journal of Adventure Education and Outdoor Learning*, v.6/1 (2006).

Simon, Jonathan. "They Died With Their Boots On: The Boot Camps and Limits of Modern Penalty." *Social Justice*, v.22 (1995).

Stinchcomb, Jeanne B. and W. Clinton Terry III. "Predicting the Likelihood of Rearrest Among Shock Incarceration Graduates: Moving Beyond Another Nail in the Boot Camp Coffin." *Crime and Delinquency*, v.47/2 (2001).

BOSTON'S OPERATION NIGHT LIGHT

In the early 1990s, Boston experienced a dramatic growth in gang-related violence and youth victimization. Boston's Operation Night Light, an enhanced supervision program, is considered one of the first formalized partnerships between police and probation officers in the United States. The goal of the program was to reduce juvenile recidivism and gang violence through increased enforcement of curfews, geographic restrictions, gang association restrictions, and other probation conditions.

The partnership was born from a chance encounter in 1990 between probation officers of Dorchester, Massachusetts, District Court and police officers of the Boston Police Department Anti-Gang Violence Unit. The officers realized that they were often dealing with the same offenders, and, as a result, a series of brainstorming sessions were organized to promote interagency collaboration. Operation Night Light was officially formed on November 12, 1992, when two probation officers, Bill Stewart and Rich Skinner, got in the backseat of a police car with two police officers, Bobby Merner and Bobby Fratalia, to perform the first of many joint patrols. Probation officer Stewart later stated, "We never used to leave the office or talk to the police . . . but in the early 1990s the probation office looked like a MASH unit and we were seeing these officers in the courthouse all the time, and we realized we were all dealing with the same kids. And one day they said, do you want to ride together?"

Operation Night Light is a component of a larger intervention known as Operation Ceasefire (Boston's Gun Project). In Night Light, probation officers were matched with officers of the Boston Police Department. The probation officers selected 10 to 15 of their most high-risk youths, typically

ages 17–25, and known for their gang affiliations. The team used unmarked cruisers and wore plain clothes while visiting each probationer at his home, school, or workplace while also driving through locations known for criminal activity and youthful congregation. Officers would also discuss substance abuse prevention and treatment options with youths and their families. The program focused on conducting supervision visits between 7:00 P.M. and midnight, when the youths were known to be more active on the streets. This required that probation officers alter their normal business hours, sending a greater message of accountability to probationers. Probationers possess diminished privacy rights and can be apprehended for a variety of noncriminal offenses. Under state law, probation officers have unrestricted rights to search for contraband and to visit their clients at any time. The Night Light program provided Boston police officers with information about who was on probation and about their conditions of supervision. As a result, police officers on the street could function as additional eyes for probation outside the joint patrols.

A large portion of the partnership involved intelligence sharing. In one example, the probation officers used the gang unit's intelligence to justify to judges the need for curfews and area restrictions as conditions of gang-affiliated offenders' probation. Officers also shared information concerning gang members with other local, state, and federal agencies, including the Drug Enforcement Administration (DEA) and the Bureau of Alcohol, Tobacco, and Firearms (ATF).

Since Night Light's inception, the program has led to more than 5,000 contacts with gang-affiliated probationers in the community. No independent evaluation has been conducted to establish the extent to which Night Light may have contributed to the drop in serious crimes in Boston during the 1990s. Many initiatives were in operation that targeted at-risk youths, and it should be noted that crime declined across many cities across the country during the same time period. Despite these caveats, the number of homicides, homicides with firearms, and assaults with firearms showed substantial reductions. For example, there were 93 homicides in 1993 as compared with 39 in 1997 (through November); there were 65 firearm-related homicides in 1993, compared with 21 in 1997 (again, through November). The number of firearm-related assaults dropped from 799 in 1995 to 126 in 1997 (through

Targeting juveniles and youths on probation, Operation Night Light was launched in 1992. The program uses a coalition of probation officers and the Boston Police department to conduct unannounced visits to the homes, schools, and worksites of high-risk youths. (Photos.com)

November). Additionally, from 1995 to 1997 there were no juvenile firearm-related homicides. The rate of curfew compliance of youths reportedly doubled to 70 percent from 1990 to 1997. More recent findings show that from 2006 to 2007, youth arrests declined 26 percent, from 971 to 718.

Although research is lacking to demonstrate the program's effectiveness, Night Light officials assert the program has had a substantial impact on gang members in Boston by showing probationers that the criminal justice system is serious about supervisory conditions. It is reported by offenders, police, family members, and other community members that youths take their conditions of supervision more seriously than in the past. Additionally, police and probation officers have reportedly developed greater respect for each other and recognize the unique powers of authority each group possesses. On the other hand, common criticisms of police-probation partnerships such as Night Light include issues of mission distortion, organizational lag, the "stalking horse" (the expansion of law-enforcement authority through probation), and an overreliance on suppression and deterrence. It is believed that more than 20 other jurisdictions in the United States have adopted similar partnerships, including, for example, the Kentucky Department of Juvenile Justice's Juvenile Intensive Supervision Team program and Texas's Project Spotlight.

Kevin I. Minor
Eastern Kentucky University
Adam K. Matz
American Probation and Parole Association

See also Curfews; Neighborhood Probation; Offender Supervision; Probation: Early Termination; Recidivism

Further Readings

Corbett, R. P., Jr. "Probation Blue? The Promise (and Perils) of Probation-Police Partnerships." *Corrections Management Quarterly*, v.2/3 (1998).

Corbett, R. P., Jr., B. L. Fitzgerald, and J. Jordan. "Operation Night Light: An Emerging Model for Police-Probation Partnership." In *Community Corrections: Probation, Parole, and Intermediate Sanctions*, Joan Petersilia, ed. New York: Oxford University Press, 1996.

Jordan, J. T. "Boston's Operation Night Light." *FBI Law Enforcement Bulletin*, v.67/8 (1998).

Kim, B., J. Gerber, and D. R. Beto. "Listening to Law Enforcement Officers: The Promises and Problems of Police-Probation Partnerships." *Journal of Criminal Justice*, v.38/4 (2010).

Worrall, J. L. and L. K. Gaines. "The Effect of Police-Probation Partnerships on Juvenile Arrests." *Journal of Criminal Justice*, v.34/8 (2006).

BROCKWAY, ZEBULON

In the years immediately following the Civil War, crime and violence were widespread as a new, urban-based elite established its dominance over the country. Those who did not accept the legitimacy of the ascendant American nation-state, often immigrants and the urban poor, were seen by elites as needing control and training to aid their assimilation. Chief among the efforts at "reforming" the urban poor were institutions in which they would be subject to intense attempts to redefine their reality and behavior to make them more acceptable to the middle-class- and elite-dominated world that was swiftly evolving. The ultimate goal, according to most contemporary experts, was to mold obedient citizen-workers. The premier institution in this process was the Elmira Reformatory, and its superintendent was Zebulon Reed Brockway (1827–1920).

Brockway had been involved in correctional reform from the mid-1800s. Starting as a guard in a Connecticut jail, he moved up, quickly becoming warden of the Monroe County Penitentiary in Rochester, New York, by 1854. After that assignment, he became warden of a house of correction in Detroit, Michigan, where he tried to introduce "indeterminate sentences." This pioneering attempt was nullified by state courts. Later, he became a prime mover of the reform concept at the Cincinnati meeting of the National Prison Association in 1870. Shortly thereafter, he was appointed warden of the new Elmira Prison, taking office in 1876. In 1880, he began a reform regime, starting with male first-time offenders between the ages of 16 and 25. It was widely felt that this age group would be more amenable to education, vocational training, and moral suasion. The training was often very rudimentary, sometimes focusing on repetitive molding of fine motor skills and rote learning of mathematical principles and tables. Prisoners also had to work in various prison industries, such as a farm, a foundry, and the prison itself. For a brief period when prison industry was banned, Brockway had prisoners drilling with dummy rifles for hours during the day. All this was done to promote discipline and blind obedience. If prisoners made a good adjustment, they were raised a grade and given a parole hearing after a period of time. If prisoners did not respond, they could be demoted a grade and not be eligible for a parole hearing. If they were obdurately recalcitrant, they could be beaten with a strap, have ice-cold water dumped on them while strapped to a chair, be marooned in solitary confinement for months, or even be slapped in the face by the warden himself. Brockway justified all this brutality in his writings and in testimony, which seem strangely at odds with the goal of education and reform as forms of therapy.

Brockway was a master of self-promotion and wrote numerous essays and several books expounding his philosophy and justifying his methods. It is only fair to point out that he popularized and basically originated the humane concept of indeterminate sentence and parole in the United States. The former involved a prisoner being held in a reformatory until he reformed and became qualified for parole. Parole was a strategy of managing prisoners and preparing them for reentry into the outside community. Prisoners who behaved while in prison and progressed according to a three-part system of grades were allowed to have a parole hearing. Paroled inmates remained under state jurisdiction for a period of six months on the outside. Brockway believed that a longer probation was demoralizing and counterproductive. The parolee also had to report to a volunteer guardian each month and provide full particulars concerning his situation and conduct.

Later the guardian role evolved into parole officers employed by the state. This was the foundation of modern parole, which even today retains many of these characteristics. The attempt to prepare the young, impressionable inmate for the outside was very attractive. The notion of having to report after release to a supervising authority figure who would help him find and keep a job was appealing to the patriarchal spirit of the day. The profound hope was that the parolee, having made a satisfactory institutional adjustment and having worked his way through the grade system, would find a good job and become a good, conformist American worker. In the process, the parolee would leave his criminal family, associations, and subcultures behind. In that fond hope, Brockway was profoundly naïve.

After long service in the correctional field, Brockway ran afoul of the prison's correctional supervisors and was forced out as superintendent in 1900. He continued to lecture and write, publishing *Fifty Years of Prison Service* in 1912, when he was 85. His legacy includes classification systems, indeterminate sentencing, parole, and creating the first modern reformatory-style prison. It became a model for subsequent American prisons and those in many other counties, which, in a flush of enthusiasm, adopted this general model for their own prisons in the late 19th and early 20th centuries.

Francis Frederick Hawley
Western Carolina University

See also Classification Systems; Elmira System; Indeterminate Sentencing; Probation and Parole: Intensive Supervision

Further Readings

Abadinsky, Howard. *Probation and Parole: Theory and Practice*, 11th ed. Upper Saddle River, NJ: Pearson, 2011.

Brockway, Zebulon. *Fifty Years of Prison Service*. Montclair, NJ: Patterson Smith, 1989.

Pisciotta, A. W. *Benevolent Repression: Social Control and the American Reformatory-Prison Movement*. New York: New York University Press, 1994.

Putney, S. and G. Putney. "Origins of the Reformatory." *Journal of Criminal Law, Criminology, and Police Science*, v.53/4 (December 1962).

CASE MANAGEMENT

The term *case management* began to appear in the clinical literature in the 1970s. Some of the concepts associated with case management, such as self-help and support networks, have been around for many years and are associated with core values in American society. The practice of case management has its origins in the deinstitutionalization of mental healthcare, which began in earnest in the 1970s. The transfer of large numbers of mentally ill individuals from highly structured institutional settings to the community required a different management strategy. Likewise, the community corrections movement identified a need for the treatment and supervision of offenders in the community to render treatment more effective and less costly than what could be realized in jails and prisons.

While case management in criminal justice includes enforcing the limits and standards of behavior that are required by the courts, the case management perspective is based on the rehabilitative model of offender behavioral change. Case management in corrections is defined as a systematic process that involves identifying the needs of offenders and matching them with selected services in the community. The process includes distinct activities, which together are designed to prevent recidivism, reintegrate offenders into the community, and monitor individual progress and program outcomes. Limitations on state budgets, the costs of incarceration, and the annual release of approximately 650,000 offenders from prison each year are factors that render case management a particularly important topic in the 21st century.

After prisoners are released, case managers may assist them with everything from basic life skills like finding employment and housing to treating disease or addiction. (Photos.com)

Core Values and Criminal Justice Theory

The idea of providing clients with supportive networks is a key element of case management. While rugged individualism and personal responsibility are core values in American society, using support networks—whether families, neighbors, faith organizations, schools, or other kinship groups—to solve problems has long been a part of American culture. French political thinker and historian Alexis de Tocqueville recognized the rich associational life in 19th-century America as supporting a thriving democracy. With respect to individual self-help, the compensatory perspective on case management recognizes that many offenders are the product of socially disadvantaged families or environments and need assistance. Nevertheless, they are responsible for using the resources provided to them and are ultimately accountable for resolving their own problems. Thus, core aspects of case management are not contradictory with the American experience. In 1935, the Social Security Act expanded the notion of helping networks to include formal (governmental and institutional) as well as informal networks of social support.

In criminal justice, Walter Reckless's theory of outer and inner containment is important to understanding the function of case management. When comprehensive case management and supervision are combined, limits are placed on the offender's behavior, the offender is involved in meaningful roles and activities, and complementary factors are in place, such as reinforcement by groups. Inner containment is realized when the offender can ultimately operate with few regulations as the individual achieves greater connection and attachment to society.

Deinstitutionalization

Although there are a number of contributors to the concept of case management, dating back to the mid-19th century, case management as a profession is associated with the deinstitutionalization of mental health institutions, which began as a movement in the 1950s and resulted two decades later in large numbers of clients with biological, psychological, and social problems being released from long-term care in state institutions to community settings. Case management developed to bridge the gap between institutional care and the community by developing a framework to help clients meet their needs in an unstructured environment. At the heart of case management was the concept of service delivery.

In their discussion of the history of the mental health deinstitutionalization movement, Richard Enos and Stephen Southern note that, after the end of World War II, popular depictions of mistreatment of mental patients aroused public criticism concerning their care. A number of scholars depicted mental institutions as antitherapeutic places where patients were managed and controlled rather than treated for their illnesses. In addition, clients often spent more time with poorly trained orderlies than they did with the treatment community of psychiatrists and psychologists. Some reformers advocated for the creation of a treatment community within mental hospitals that was more responsive to patient needs.

In the 1960s, community health centers began to appear in cities throughout the United States, and by the end of the decade the move from institutionalization to community treatment became a reality. This change required a new mechanism for delivering services, and case management became associated with meeting this need. In addition to treatment, mentally ill offenders needed assistance with housing, employment, and other services. Meeting these needs did not require professionals with advanced training in psychiatry and psychology. A new group of paraprofessionals were assigned to work with clients. Originally these paraprofessionals were tasked with assisting staff professionals, but gradually these case managers became professionals in their own right. The goal of case managers was to help those who needed assistance managing their lives and to support them with needed expertise when a crisis or emergency occurred. In some cases, case managers provided services directly though activities such as counseling. In many cases the case manager acted as a broker, connecting clients with available services in a particular locale. Over time, case management included activities that required additional training, such as classification and risk assessment.

Offenders who have been released from prison share similarities with deinstitutionalized populations from mental institutions. Many offenders have serious biological, psychological, and social problems and are unknowledgeable or otherwise disadvantaged with respect to access to medical and other social services. When released from prison, offenders often lack proper identification to obtain a driver's license, do not know how to apply for employment, lack housing opportunities, or suffer from acquired immune deficiency syndrome (AIDS), hepatitis C, and other debilitating diseases; in other words, they may not have the social and educational skills to participate successfully in society. Just as the mental health caseworker's goal is to prevent clients from harming themselves and others and being institutionalized, the goal of the correctional case manager is to assist the offender in ways that will contribute to reduced recidivism and greater public safety. For those offenders who are sentenced directly to alternatives to incarceration, the goal of case management is essentially the same, although these offenders may have fewer disabilities than those who have been incarcerated.

Federal Legislation

Federal legislation contributed to how case management developed. In 1963, Congress passed Public Law 88-164, which contributed to the deinstitutionalization of mental health services by funding the construction of mental health centers. A subsequent amendment provided for the staffing of these centers. Congress also passed Public Law 89-749, which established the framework for case management as a systematic planning process. The law provided grants to develop comprehensive plans for those with physical and mental health issues. In 1966, Congress authorized additional funding for mental health center staffs and expanded services available for support. Of particular importance for corrections case management was the passage of Public Law 89-793 in 1964. The legislation allowed for rehabilitation of drug addicts, emphasizing community treatment rather than imprisonment. The Public Health Service Act Amendments and Special Revenue Sharing Act of 1975 cemented the deinstitutionalized approach in mental health, stating that community mental health was preferable to institutional treatment.

Another contribution to the case management perspective was the passage of the Welfare Reform Act in 1988. The legislation focused on education and training for employment and specifically said that states could use funding to assign a case manager to each client participating in the program. The notion of case management as providing comprehensive services to those in need was underscored in a provision of the law that additional services be provided to allow family members to take part in job training and education. In 1977, clarification of the case management approach was provided by the National Institute of Mental Health in setting guidelines for its Community Support Program. Several necessary activities were identified for the program's case manager role. These included, among others, identifying the client base and providing outreach services; helping clients apply for various types of social welfare and medical programs; providing psychosocial and other types of services; providing mental, dental, and health services; and arranging for transportation to access services. In corrections, the Second Chance Act of 2008 provided funds to state and local governments for services to formerly incarcerated persons. In some states, funds have been used to enhance case management and case planning.

Case Management in Corrections

The case management of offenders is most likely to be assumed by probation and parole officers. With renewed emphasis on reintegration in the late 1990s and early 21st century, case management tasks have been assigned to prison personnel in some jurisdictions. The basic tasks of case management for offenders include (1) assessing client needs, (2) classification, (3) developing a service plan, (4) linking the client with appropriate services, (5) monitoring client progress, and (6) advocating for the client when needed. Some case management professionals identify the need to monitor the quality of service provision if time and resources permit. Criminal justice case management takes on additional tasks beyond those associated with traditional social service case management. These include risk assessment and intervening with appropriate sanctions when necessary. Unlike their counterparts in the social services, criminal justice caseworkers must enforce court-imposed requirements. Judicial requirements are frequently incorporated into the client's service plan. Correctional case management takes on considerably more law-enforcement functions than social service management, and these tasks must be balanced with the social service function. Explaining legal limits placed on probationers and parolees may be viewed as a counseling function, intended to assist offenders with successful completion of their sentences. Correctional case managers see their ability to impose graduated sanctions for those who fail to comply with treatment plans as a necessary component of effective case management.

The correctional case management perspective takes a holistic approach, addressing as many problems as possible that might contribute to relapse and recidivism. Kerry Murphy Healey found that many correctional case managers identified the need to move beyond the traditional case manager role of brokering services. They pointed out the need for cross training between case managers and mental health providers, drug treatment counselors, domestic violence personnel, and personnel in other treatment programs. For these practitioners, the line between broker and treatment roles was blurred.

Case Management Models

The original model of case management limited the role of the practitioner to that of broker and precluded active involvement as a client or treatment provider. While the generalist role still predominates, additional models have evolved. Two examples are assertive case management and strength-based case management.

Assertive case management requires the practitioner to actively assess client needs through field visits to their homes, work sites, or other community settings, rather than passively offering services from the central office. This corresponds with the movement on the enforcement side of probation and parole that advocates greater supervision in the field. Assertive case management is facilitated when corrections branch offices are located in neighborhoods where clients reside.

Strength-based case management identifies the strengths of the offender during the assessment phase and incorporates these strengths into a treatment plan. This model requires positive regard for the offender and the ability to move beyond easily identified strengths, such as training or experience in a particular occupation, to less concrete strengths related to attitudes, motivations, and other inner resources that can be linked to prosocial behaviors. A major challenge to this approach is the need to disapprove of offenders' negative behaviors while still focusing on client potential.

Case Management of Sex Offenders

Case management of sex offenders is challenging because of the need to focus on surveillance and public safety while maintaining the rehabilitative function of case management. Containment-focused case management is a model that focuses on three components: (1) surveillance, (2) treatment, and (3) verification. Assessment in the case of sex offenders is challenging because of the need to identify the offender's deviant arousal and behavior patterns and design supervision and treatment specific to the offender's characteristics and needs. Verification may include moving beyond compliance to more controversial methods, such as polygraph examinations. The threat of sanctions is seen as crucial to successful case management, even for the most motivated offenders.

Increasingly, case management has embraced the role that informal networks can play in successful reintegration. As an example, Circles of Support and Accountability (COSA), a prisoner-reentry program for sex offenders, was developed in Canada in 1994. A group of trained volunteers from the community meet regularly with the offender to provide practical, emotional, and spiritual support. In the Canadian model, case managers are not included as Circle participants, and Circle participants do not supervise or report back to them on the offender's status. However, this does not preclude case managers from referring offenders to a COSA. A 2007 Canadian study found that COSA participants had an 83 percent lower recidivism rate than a matched comparison group.

Challenges in Case Management

There are numerous challenges to effective correctional case management; two major ones are (1) relationships between correctional case managers and service providers and (2) overburdened case managers and limited resources. Tension between correctional case managers and those providing treatment may occur over perceived effectiveness of treatment and conflicting perspectives on the use of sanctions. Correctional case managers may view treatment specialists as insufficiently strict when enforcing conditions of supervision. Treatment professionals, on the other hand, may look at success in less black-and-white terms, seeing reduced drug use over time and the increased ability to maintain a job and participate in family life as indicators of program success. Cross training among criminal justice and treatment professionals, clear communication of program goals, the use of evidence-based programs, and the opportunity for case managers to have input into the evaluation of service providers can address problems that stem from coordinating the work of multiple service providers.

Overburdened case managers and insufficient resources to address client problems are issues that are much more difficult to address. Excessive caseloads limit the ability of case managers to address client needs effectively and holistically. Fewer resources in the community, including the availability of job opportunities, compound the problem. In some communities, reentry courts have been established to provide offenders with additional support. Typically, probation or parole officers who supervise offenders are included as participants.

Cheryl G. Swanson
University of West Florida

See also Caseload and Workload Standards; Correctional Case Managers; Offender Needs; Offender Responsivity; Reintegration Into Communities; Second Chance Act; Specialized Caseload Models

Further Readings

English, Kim. "The Containment Approach." *Psychology, Public Policy, and Law*, v.4/1–2 (1988).

Enos, Richard and Stephen Southern. *Correctional Case Management*. Cincinnati, OH: Anderson, 1996.

Hanser, Robert D. *Community Corrections*. Thousand Oaks, CA: Sage, 2010.

Healey, Kerry Murphy. *Case Management in the Criminal Justice System*. Washington, DC: National Institute of Justice, 1999.

Wilson, Robin, Franca Cortoni, and Veronica Vermani. "Circles of Support and Accountability: A National Replication of Outcome Findings." http://www.csc-Scc.9c.ca/text/rsrch/reports/r185/r185-Eng.pdf (Accessed December 2010).

Woodside, Marianne and Tricia McClam. *Generalist Case Management*, 3rd ed. Belmont, CA: Brooks/Cole, 2006.

CASELOAD AND WORKLOAD STANDARDS

Finding the "optimum" or "ideal" caseloads for parole and probation officers has long been a central concern for corrections agencies. According to the U.S. Department of Justice (DOJ), dramatic increases in the overall number of offenders entering local community corrections systems and a higher proportion of high-risk offenders placed under community supervision, coupled with the increasing number of correctional requirements placed on offenders, have led to increasing concerns over workload allocations for parole and probation officers. A caseload is the total number of offenders assigned to a probation or parole officer for supervision. A workload is the total amount of time that it takes an officer to perform the supervision tasks stemming from the caseload. Historically, the caseload standard has been the predominant model used by state and local corrections agencies to make caseload and workload allocation decisions. The caseload standard uses a formulaic method to establish a set number of clients who are assigned to each officer. Although the caseload standard has traditionally been accepted by officers and administrators, the model is increasingly being criticized for failing to account for the increased workload demands that officers have experienced in the past few decades.

Since the 1950s, corrections professionals have explored alternative models for allocating caseloads to parole and probation officers; however, caseload standards continue to be the predominant model. Workload standards have become the most viable alternative model, which allocates caseloads based on workload measures. Workload standards estimate the amount of time that it takes an officer to complete each task, accounts for workload discrepancies between different types of clients, and assigns caseloads accordingly. Workload standards offer a number of benefits, such as enabling an agency to allocate resources more appropriately and efficiently, providing data for budget justification and modification, and enhancing the overall effectiveness and accountability of corrections agencies. An increasing number of local corrections agencies are adopting the workload model because it offers many advantages over traditional caseload standards; however, most agencies continue to use the traditional caseload model.

Caseload Model

The caseload standard has long been the predominant model used by state and local corrections administrators to make caseload and workload allocation decisions. The traditional caseload model uses a uniform standard to establish caseload sizes for officers. In the process of establishing caseload standards, corrections administrators and funding authorities assess the community's corrections goals (including protecting the community and rehabilitating clients) and establish a caseload standard that meets their goals within given resource constraints. In some cases, corrections administrators rely on the caseload standard recommendations from authorities such as the American Correctional Association, the American Probation and Parole Association, the American Bar Association, and the Department of Justice's National Institute of Corrections when developing caseload standards. Unfortunately, according to the DOJ, caseload standards and workload allocation decisions are often not established from an evidential base but are instead produced through a contentious and political budgetary process. This process explains why some jurisdictions develop unusually high caseloads that substantially exceed professional standards and recommendations.

Many corrections administrators and funding bodies acknowledge that arbitrary caseload standards are imperfect because all clients do not require the same amount of agency resources (for example, high-risk clients require more monitoring and supervision than do low-risk clients). Despite this knowledge, many agency administrators and funding bodies continue to use traditional caseload standards. According to the DOJ, the caseload model has been heavily criticized for "arbitrarily" assigning caseloads to parole and probation officers irrespective of workload demands. The assumption underlying the use of caseload standards is that officers will budget their own time according to the varying levels of risks and supervision demands of clients within their caseload. To assure that the caseloads are distributed equitably, many agencies randomly assign clients to officers.

Although the caseload model has been traditionally accepted by officers and administrators, the model has been criticized because it fails to account for the rise in workload demands that officers have experienced in the past few decades. Dramatic increases in the overall number of offenders entering local community corrections systems and a higher proportion of high-risk offenders placed under community supervision, coupled with the increasing number of correctional requirements placed on offenders by judges and legislation, have led to greater concerns over workload allocations for parole and probation officers.

According to the U.S. Department of Justice's Bureau of Justice Statistics, the total number of adults in the United States under community corrections supervision tripled between 1980 and 2004, thus increasing from 1.7 million to 5 million (from 1,132 per 100,000 residents to 3,175 per 100,000 residents). This overall increase resulted from a variety of factors, including a growing number of adults entering the U.S. correctional system, an increasing number of prisoners being released for good time or mandatory releases (from 45 percent entering parole in 1995 to 52 percent in 2004), and an increasing number of probationers receiving direct sentences to community probation (from 48 percent in 1995 to 56 percent in 2004).

In addition to an increasing probationer population, evidence indicates that an increasing percentage of high-level offenders are being placed under community supervision as a result of mandatory releases and other policies aimed at reducing jail and prison overcrowding. According to F. Taxman, E. Shephardson, and J. Byrne, the probation population is increasingly mirroring the prison population, and more than half of all offenders under community supervision are convicted felons. These increasing supervision demands placed on corrections agencies are augmented by increased corrections requirements and conditions that are placed on offenders by judges, releasing authorities, and legislation. For example, an increasing number of jurisdictions are requiring mandatory drug screens regardless of the offender's substance abuse history. K. Lucken refers to this process as the "piling up of sanctions." As a result of this process, a growing number of punitive and rehabilitative controls are being placed on probationers, which increase workloads for parole and probation officers and increase the overall number of violations and offenders returning to the correctional system. As a result of these developments, caseloads and workload allocation issues are a growing concern among practitioners, communities, and policy makers.

Workload Model

Since the 1950s, community corrections professionals have explored alternatives to the traditional caseload model for assigning caseloads and allocating workloads for parole and probation officers. Workload standards, which allocate caseloads based on workload measures, have become the most viable alternative model. Workload standards estimate the amount of time that it takes the officer to complete each task and assign caseloads accordingly. The workload model offers many advantages over the caseload model, enabling an agency to allocate resources more appropriately and efficiently, providing data for budget justification and modification, and enhancing the overall effectiveness and accountability of the corrections agency.

The workload model consists of three core elements: classification, workload measurement, and workload reporting. The appropriate classification of offenders during intake is a critically important task for every community corrections agency. In the process of classification, offenders are categorized according to risk of reoffending (from low to high risk), offense type, criminogenic and rehabilitation needs, and other criteria. Community corrections professionals, including the President's Commission on Law Enforcement and Administration of Justice and the American Bar Association, have long recognized that the classification and differential treatment of offenders based on individual needs are fundamental tasks for community corrections professionals. Some agencies do not have specified classification criteria, whereas most agencies today have a standardized classification system. A variety of classification systems are used throughout the states. For example, Florida traditionally used a classification system that was based on the length of time that the offender was on supervision. For the past few decades, Ohio, Wisconsin, and a number of other states have used risk assessment instruments as tools to help assess each client's needs.

Workload measurement helps agencies determine how much time it takes to supervise each parolee or probationer and determine the "optimum" or "ideal" caseload. Time studies are a common form of workload measurement, estimating how much time it takes to complete each task that is involved with supervising a client. Two basic methods of workload measurement include descriptive and prescriptive methods. The descriptive method observes and measures the average amount of time that it takes an officer to complete each task or activity. The prescriptive method establishes standards for performance and compares the actual time that it takes to perform each task with the expected standard. Prescriptive studies are ultimately used to determine the minimum amount of time that it takes an officer to perform the task or activity based upon the minimally acceptable level of performance. The accompanying table provides a set of recommended caseload standards, which follow the logic of the workload model.

According to B. Bemus, G. Arling, and P. Quigley, workload reporting is an important component of the workload model because it provides data that assist the agency in monitoring and improving the performance of the model. Arguably, a workload model will not perform very well without the reporting component. Data collected from workload reporting assist the corrections agency in accurately budgeting for staff, allocating resources, auditing performance, and compiling additional data that can be used to justify agency budgets.

Cases-to-Staff Ratios by Type

Case Type	Cases-to-Staff Ratio
Adults	
Intensive	20:1
Moderate to high risk	50:1
Low risk	200:1
Administrative (e.g., bench probation, unsupervised probation)	No limit
Juveniles	
Intensive	15:1
Moderate to high risk	30:1
Low risk	100:1
Administrative (e.g., bench probation, unsupervised probation)	Not recommended

Source: Bill Burrell, "Caseload Standards for Probation and Parole," 2006.

In theory, the workload model has existed for several decades, but its adoption has taken some time. In 1990, Donald Evans, the president of the American Probation and Parole Association, advocated the adoption of a workload model that allocates cases based on the priority and varying supervision demands of clients within each caseload. Similarly, the National Institute of Corrections has advocated a movement toward the workload model. An increasing number of local corrections agencies are adopting the workload model because it offers many advantages over traditional caseload standards; however, a number of impediments prevent its widespread adoption. A national study conducted by the American Probation and Parole Association in 2006, which surveyed 228 corrections professionals, found that 24 percent of the respondents worked for corrections agencies that use some form of a workload standards model. The survey also found that a majority of the respondents, 58 percent, worked for agencies that use the traditional caseload model, and 17 percent of the respondents reported working for agencies that use other models for caseload allocation decisions.

Blake M. Randol
Washington State University

See also Community Corrections as an Alternative to Imprisonment; Parole Officers; Probation: Administration Models; Probation: Early Termination; Probation and Parole: Intensive Supervision; Probation Officers

Further Readings

American Probation and Parole Administration. "Facts from the Field." http://www.appa-net.org/eweb/DynamicPage .aspx?WebCode=VB_Facts (Accessed July 2011).

Bemus, B., G. Arling, and P. Quigley. *Workload Measures for Probation and Parole.* Washington, DC: National Institute of Corrections, U.S. Department of Justice, Office of Justice Programs, 1983.

Burrell, B. "Caseload Standards for Probation and Parole." 2006. http://www.appa-net.org/eweb/docs/appa/pubs/ SMDM.pdf (Accessed July 2011).

DeMichele, M. T. *Probation and Parole's Growing Caseloads and Workload Allocation: Strategies for Managerial Decision Making.* American Probation and Parole Association, 2007. http://www.appa-net.org/ eweb/docs/appa/pubs/SMDM.pdf (Accessed July 2011).

Lucken, K. "The Dynamics of Penal Reform." *Crime, Law, and Social Change,* v.26 (1997).

Taxman, F., E. Shepardson, and J. Byrne. *Tools of the Trade: A Guide to Incorporating Service Into Practice.* Washington, DC: National Institute of Corrections, U.S. Department of Justice, Office of Justice Programs, 2004.

U.S. Bureau of Justice Statistics. "Probation and Parole in the United States, 2004." November 2005, NCJ 210676. http://bjs.ojp.usdoj.gov/content/pub/pdf/ ppus04.pdf (Accessed July 2011).

CERTIFIED CRIMINAL JUSTICE PROFESSIONAL

The debate in America continues over whether law-enforcement officers will routinely have a college degree in the future. As early as the 1920s, Berkeley police chief August Vollmer was considered a visionary pioneer who advocated educating criminal justice practitioners. Since Vollmer's crusade to promote educating law enforcement, there has been improvement, but far from what he envisioned. At the same time, rank, title, and education do not necessarily equate with competence in any career field, including law enforcement. Generally, the political landscape found within law enforcement organizations has a far greater impact as a predictor of success in the career field than does education. In this discussion, we distinguish police and crime-scene investigators from corrections personnel, with the focus on law enforcement.

The U.S. Federal Bureau of Investigation (FBI), along with other federal law enforcement agencies, has strict standards regarding eligibility for hire, professional codes of conduct while employed in the agency, and adherence to FBI policies. (Federal Bureau of Investigation)

The Profession in General

A review of the federal law-enforcement officers' corps will dispel the notion that the college-degreed officer is not problematic. The Federal Bureau of Investigation (FBI) is one of several federal law-enforcement agencies with strict hiring standards, codes of conduct, internal agency policies, and relatively good employee benefits and salaries. The career journeyman (nonsupervisory) federal agent earns more than $140,000 per year, which represents an average salary of $50,000 more than the national median for a chief of police in the United States. However, none of these benefits has deterred FBI employees from engaging in unethical, immoral, and illegal conduct. If the conversation takes a focus on ethics and integrity, there is little evidence to support that the college-educated law-enforcement officer is devoid of these temptations.

Although it is unpopular to note, cronyism and most-favored status have a far greater influence on most law-enforcement careers than does a college degree. Some candidates for law-enforcement employment or career officers may ask the critical question: Should they pursue an academic degree or a series of certifications directly related to the career? Costs and time, as well as return on investment, suggest that these discussions are appropriate in today's complex world.

Nationwide, it is generally found that, in order to be considered for employment as a law-enforcement officer, the candidate is required to have completed a high school education or general equivalency diploma, be free from felony convictions, and pass a series of internal assessments. If the applicant successfully completes these assessments, he or she can attend a certified police academy training program that generally takes 16 weeks. After a candidate completes the police academy training program, some agencies require prospective officers to complete a field training apprentice program with a senior officer acting as a mentor. Upon successful completion of the training program, the officer is released to his or her assigned duties. Throughout their career, officers attend nonacademic, specialized training programs to comply with various mandates generally driven by legal precedent and policy mandates.

Overall, an officer can complete assigned duties with a general educational background and applied field training, along with experience provided by the agency. Given the status of the economy in 2010, most agencies must find ways to reduce their expenses, and funding for education and training are frequently targets for fiscal reduction measures. Agency-paid college education programs are likely to be reduced or altogether phased out because of costs.

On the other hand, civilian positions in law-enforcement agencies—such as fingerprint technicians, crime-scene investigators, and property and evidence personnel—have different standards. Whereas some agencies still employ certified law-enforcement officers for evidence-collection duties, many, because of fiscal issues, have made the change to hiring civilian employees. Additionally, with discussions surrounding the lack of science involved in criminalistics, more stringent requirements for identifying specialists are leaning toward a formalized education. Nevertheless, while some agencies may decide that a degreed employee is often helpful, a degree is not required for many positions. Overall, most civilian positions require a combination of experience and education, and certificates represent one method of acquiring and citing an acceptable education.

Formal Education

For the active-duty law-enforcement officer to attend college, a considerable investment of time and money must be made for an extended period. Moreover, prospective officers must make this decision not knowing whether the education will allow them to realize their career opportunities fully and without understanding how their decision could be impacted by the political landscape within the agency.

If a promotion opportunity exists and competition among applicants ends with promoting a candidate without a formalized college degree over a college-educated employee, candidates will receive the message that education is not a required qualification. Repeated promotion preferences generally lead candidates to conclude their college degrees are not a factor. Those who have considered attending college will likely choose another use of their off-duty time and savings, and that choice will not have any impact on their retirement income.

Another consideration is that an advanced degree is often viewed as a challenge by agency leadership and management. Most law-enforcement officers and supervisors may be skeptical or insecure about hiring an officer with a Ph.D., a J.D., an M.B.A., or another professional degree from a reputable institution; such personal and professional insecurities are not unique to law enforcement.

For the most part, the larger law-enforcement agencies offer attractive benefits and retirement programs to their workforces. However, the economy, again, has negatively affected those benefits. While the "20-year-and-out" retirement plans still exist, the law-enforcement officer who is considering attending college may be presented with a difficult argument. That is, at age 42, an officer with 20 years of service who is eligible for retirement in essence could retire and transition into a second career, regardless of whether he or she holds a college degree. Today, with the economy and job markets being understaffed and underutilized, many positions do not require a college degree.

From a criminalistics perspective, job announcements with many law-enforcement agencies require crime scene and identification specialists to hold at least an associate's degree; dependent on the level of involvement with evidence collection and crime lab submission, some agencies require a four-year science degree. After the most current findings of the National Research Council (in concert with the National Academy of Sciences), which identified that there is little "uniformity in the certification of forensic practitioners, or in the accreditation of crime laboratories" as well as the fact that "most jurisdictions do not require forensic practitioners to be certified, and most forensic science disciplines have no mandatory certification programs," it has become much more important for those interested in pursuing this line of work to achieve certification rather than a four-year degree as the most cost-effective way to achieve a position.

Certification

The certification system in education is found in many occupations, from service industries to medical billing and many others. Certifications may or may not be important to a particular job. However, an argument is that much of what is taught in the certification process can be taught on the job by vocational mentors. Both for-profit and not-for-profit educational institutions have been actively involved in creating certification programs for a vast number of people in many sectors, some almost guaranteeing

employment with their programs. Critics would say these programs have been overrated and oversold to prospective students, who in the current economy may have little chance of securing employment after completion.

In law enforcement, graduation from a police academy is traditionally very similar to securing a certification, and it is mandated by government legislation. Add-on certifications may offer benefits, but only if specifically designed to meet a particular occupation or need.

The self-paced electronic learning system affords almost anybody an opportunity to pursue certifications at his or her own pace and schedule. Costs can be bundled together in discount pricing structures and group rates. Additionally, many community colleges and universities offer flexible, blended programs that cater to officers and support personnel, allowing them to complete the certification while continuing to be employed full time.

A series of certifications can lead to a master certification that covers virtually all career-related educational material found in the general criminal justice curriculum at colleges. It would seem logical that officers would prefer to attend courses they know directly apply to their jobs, rather than other classes believed to improve their individual professional skills. For criminalistics positions, there are certifications available through annual conferences as well as professional organizations that cater to the many specialties within the forensic science discipline.

Of the local, state, and federal law-enforcement agencies (approximately 17,500), which employ around 800,000 active-duty law-enforcement officers and support personnel nationwide, approximately 1 percent have mandates to hire college-educated law-enforcement officers and support personnel.

Conclusion

Courses in economics, business, marketing, strategic planning, business technology systems, and global policy making most likely are not of interest to active-duty law-enforcement officers. For a crime-scene investigator or identification specialist, an advanced degree may cost more and require more time than the position calls for. An alternative to the formal college degree, therefore, can be a certification program, which assists personnel in reducing costs and managing their time in ways that target their careers better than can be accomplished through a formal academic degree program.

Jalika Rivera Waugh
Rande W. Matteson
Saint Leo University

See also Correctional Case Managers; Juvenile Probation Officers; Parole Officers; Probation Officers

Further Readings

Committee on Identifying the Needs of the Forensic Sciences Community, National Research Council. "Strengthening Forensic Science in the United States: A Path Forward." Washington, DC: Author, 2009. http:// www.ncjrs.gov/pdffiles1/nij/grants/228091.pdf (Accessed July 2011).

Crime Scene Investigator Network. "Expired Openings: Job Descriptions." 2011. http://www.crime-Scene -Investigator.net/employment.html (Accessed July 2011).

Crime Scene Investigator Network. "How to Become a Crime Scene Investigator." 2011. http://www.crime -Scene-Investigator.net/becomeone.html (Accessed July 2011).

Dixon, A. "Law Enforcement Certification Programs." July 7, 2010. http://www.ehow.com/list_6708090_law -Enforcement-Certificate-Programs.html (Accessed July 2011).

Fradella, H. F., S. S. Owen, and T. W. Burke. "Building Bridges Between Criminal Justice and the Forensic Sciences to Create Forensic Studies Programs." *Journal of Criminal Justice Education*, v.18/2 (July 2007).

International Association of Crime Analysts. "IACA Certification." 2010. http://www.iaca.net/Certification .asp (Accessed July 2011).

St. Petersburg College. "Crime Scene Technology Certificate Program." 2006. http://www.spcollege.edu/program/ CST-CT (Accessed July 2011).

U.S. News University Connection. Law Enforcement Certificates. 2011. http://www.usnewsuniversity directory.com/certificates/criminal-Justice/law- Enforcement.aspx (Accessed July 2011).

CIRCLE SENTENCING

Circle sentencing is part of a worldwide restorative justice movement that encourages the joint involvement of victims and offenders in determining how offenders will repay their debts to society. It is an old indigenous justice and healing practice common to aboriginal peoples in North America that was reintroduced in 1991 by judges and community justice committees in northern Canada. Minnesota authorities brought the practice to America when a pilot project was begun there in 1996.

The exact procedures of circle sentencing may demonstrate wide regional or cultural variation. However, in general there is a format for the circles that includes, initially, an application by an offender who wants to participate in a circle. Second, there is the victim's healing circle. This circle is attended by the victim and family, an elder who serves as mentor and discussion leader, volunteer members of the community, and representatives from social services and the legal system. The offender's family and friends may attend upon invitation from the victim. Participants in this circle initially discuss what happened, the event's impact on both victim and community, and what kinds of punishments are warranted. Everyone in the circle has an opportunity to speak without being interrupted. This promotes openness and respect for others' points of view, even if those views may be at odds or in conflict with one another. Typically, the speaker holds a symbolic object of some kind until he or she has completed all remarks. Then, the object is passed to the next person. Third, there is a similar healing circle for the offender and the offender's friends, family, and support group. It is likely that the victim and his or her friends, family, and support group will attend this circle as well. The fourth step takes place in a sentencing circle, where the involved parties come to a consensus on what should be included in the sentencing plan. This detailed plan clarifies what exactly is expected of the offender. The plan may also spell out what is required of family members, the community at large, and the formal justice system. Fifth, a series of follow-up circles are arranged to track the offender's progress. If the offender does not comply with what is asked of him or her, the offender is sent back to the judicial system for sentencing.

In a circle sentencing, the participants are more concerned about the offender's rehabilitation and reintegration into society than they are with the idea of general deterrence. Such concern was demonstrated in the first recent use of circle sentencing in 1992. When Philip Moses appeared in Judge Barry Stuart's Yukon Territorial Court, he arrived with 43 prior convictions. Justice Stuart saw his case as symptomatic of a failed system. He also knew that more than half of Canada's inmates serve time for nonviolent crimes, with indigenous people imprisoned at more than eight times the national rate. Thus, he opted to use circle sentencing. He utilized several principles of Yukon's Native culture in this case; for example, he asked for and received advice from the family and friends of Moses, who had threatened a Royal Canadian Mounted Police officer with a baseball bat.

It is not definitively known how effective sentencing circles are in preventing offenders from reoffending. Judge Stuart conducted his own study, in which he compared the experiences of offenders who had participated in sentencing circles with those who were processed by standard criminal justice practices. Veterans of the circle experience, in Stuart's study, told him that the circles were powerful experiences that pointed out the shared responsibility for the offender's behavior. The circles also produced more constructive relationships, enhanced respect and understanding among all who participated, and fostered innovative solutions that worked in the long term.

Some studies concur with Stuart's findings. However, results of other studies report a wide variety of outcomes, including one in which the evidence suggested that circle sentencing had no effect at all on the frequency, timing, or seriousness of a participant's future offending.

Critics of circle sentencing argue that the whole process works only if a human violation is easily identifiable. Thus, assault cases and especially sexual assault cases are the best candidates for circle sentencing. Other kinds of crimes, in which the victim is not readily apparent, make poor candidates for circle sentencing. Critics also contend that more empirical studies are needed before circle sentencing can be applied to every crime punishable under a state or providence's criminal code. Some of the strongest criticisms come from aboriginal peoples themselves. They assert that circle sentencing that is dominated by a Western-oriented judge can simply become another form of domination of indigenous peoples. According to this view, Indian justice, in its purest aboriginal form, should stand on its own.

Circle sentencing is a relatively new alternative method of criminal justice practice, and as such it is best viewed as a work in progress. More needs to be done to encourage victims to participate. More information needs to be supplied to the community so that it can confidently buy into the circles and what they accomplish. Additional community-based programs could be developed to supplement circle

sentencing. Finally, objective, comprehensive evaluations of circle sentencing by people not connected with the process are needed to determine how effective the circles are in reshaping lives and reducing recidivism.

Stan C. Weeber
McNeese State University

See also Family Group Conferencing; Reintegration Into Communities; Restorative Justice

Further Readings

Fitzgerald, Jacqueline. *Does Circle Sentencing Reduce Aboriginal Offending?* Sydney, Australia: New South Wales Bureau of Crime Statistics and Research, 2008.

Libin, Kevin. "Sentencing Circles for Aboriginals: Good Justice?" *National Post* (February 27, 2009).

Rekhari, Suneeti. "'People's Law' and Restorative Justice: The Success of Circle Sentencing in New South Wales." *Connections*, v.3 (2006).

Schwartz, Melanie. "Opening a Circle of Hope: The NSW Government Review of Circle Sentencing." *Indigenous Law Bulletin*, v.5 (2004).

Stuart, Barry. *Building Community Justice Partnerships: Community Peacemaking Circles*. Ottawa, ON: Aboriginal Justice Section, Department of Justice of Canada, 1997.

CIVIL AND POLITICAL RIGHTS AFFECTED BY CONVICTION

In the United States, a criminal conviction can drastically impact an individual's civil and political rights. Criminal convictions roughly divide into two categories, misdemeanor and felony convictions. A misdemeanor conviction normally carries a minimum sentence of less than one year in prison and rarely affects one's civil or political rights. Conversely, a felony conviction is punishable by at least one year of confinement and, in virtually every U.S. jurisdiction, will trigger the statutory diminishment or loss of an individual's civil or political rights.

Generally, civil and political rights are protections and benefits afforded citizens of a democracy. Specifically, civil rights insulate citizens from oppression or discrimination, guaranteeing fair and equal treatment. Political rights are rights that define certain aspects of American citizenship. In particular, formal and informal political rights ensure that all citizens have an equal opportunity to participate in democratic processes. The U.S. Constitution codifies many civil and political rights and generally discourages the infringement of such rights. Nevertheless, the Supreme Court has upheld federal and state legislation limiting or eliminating many of the civil and political rights of convicted felons.

The legislative mechanisms that impact the civil and political rights of convicted felons usually operate categorically. A felony conviction triggers certain federal and state statutes that curb or destroy one's civil and political rights. Sweeping federal restrictions of this sort impact almost every convicted felon in the United States. State statutes targeting convicted felons' rights vary jurisdictionally. Thus, both federal and state statutes delineate the contours of convicted felons' civil and political rights, impacting several areas of their lives. In most cases, convicted felons are exempt from all statutes impacting their civil and political rights only if or until they receive a pardon or a restoration of rights.

Civil Rights and Access to Resources

Federal and state legislation has a significant negative affect on convicted felons' civil rights. Many federal and state statutes deny convicted felons benefits widely available to the general public, seemingly discriminating against those who have once deviated from recognized law. However, the Supreme

Some U.S. states allow convicted felons to apply for a pardon, which will relieve them from further punishment and discrimination for their criminal offense. Felons are often discriminated against and face substantial obstacles when searching for employment. (Photos.com)

Court has held that such statutes do not offend the Constitution. Instead, the Supreme Court has consistently upheld federal and state laws that limit a convicted felon's access to occupational opportunities, public financial assistance, public housing, student loans, and parental privileges.

Convicted felons also face significant occupational obstacles as a result of their status. State legislation commonly limits convicted felons' job prospects by permitting employers to inquire about an applicant's history of arrest and/or conviction. Such legislation also routinely allows an employer to reject an applicant because of an arrest and/or conviction if the employer can show that a business justification or a business necessity spawned the rejection. The Civil Rights Act of 1964 suggests that convicted felons do enjoy limited constitutional protection from employers who deny occupation to convicted felons without adequate business grounds. Even so, the legal standards of business necessity and business justification are malleable concepts, potentially manipulated by employers who seek to discriminate against certain citizens solely on the basis of their legal status as convicted felons.

Federal legislation determines convicted felons' access to public financial assistance as well. In 1996, Congress passed the Personal Responsibility and Work Opportunity Reconciliation Act. The act restructured the requirements for federal financial assistance. Specifically, the act bars those convicted of felony drug offenses from receiving federal cash assistance or food stamps. The act also gives states the choice to enact legislation that would eliminate the categorical prohibition on federal assistance for convicted felony drug offenders. Nineteen states adhere to the prohibition; only 11 states eliminated the categorical prohibition in its entirety. The remaining jurisdictions modified the federal mandate but still require convicted felony drug offenders to conform to several other requirements prior to or while receiving federal assistance.

For convicted felons, securing suitable housing is perhaps the most formidable obstacle to successful reintegration. Upon release, convicted felons rarely have the financial capability of securing housing at market prices. Thus, many convicted felons have historically chosen to pursue public housing options or return to live with family members, many of whom already occupy public housing.

In recent years, however, federal legislation has made public housing an impossible option for convicted felons. In the 1990s, Congress passed the Housing Opportunity Program Extension Act of 1996 and the Quality Housing and Work Responsibility Act of 1998. These statutes authorize public housing authorities to deny convicted felons federally funded housing on the basis of a criminal conviction. Such measures, however, do not operate unconditionally. Housing authorities are free to consider evidence of rehabilitation and to allow convicted felons access to federally funded housing. Still, the exceedingly high demand for public housing and the scarce number of units make federally authorized, record-based eligibility criteria an effective way for housing authorities to whittle down lengthy waiting lists.

Federal legislation also limits the availability of student loans commonly secured by students in the United States. For instance, the Higher Education Act of 1998 bars convicted felony drug offenders from receiving federally funded student loans. The federal student loan restriction requires that states honor a graduated scale of ineligibility. Depending on the severity of the relevant drug offense, convicted felons may be ineligible for federal student loans for a number of years. Under a limited number of circumstances, convicted felons who have committed a drug offense can be eligible for student loans. However, such circumstances are rare and normally involve a lengthy and arduous process.

Parental Privileges

Federal and state guidelines regarding prospective adoptive or foster parents significantly affect convicted felons' civil rights in the area of parental privileges. In certain circumstances, the Federal Adoption and Safe Families Act of 1997 prohibits a convicted felon from adopting a child or acting as a foster parent. Specifically, the act denies convicted felons parental privileges when certain convictions are at issue. The act, however, allows states to overlook such restrictions and to substitute their own relevant guidelines. Currently, 15 states adhere to the federal structure, whereas 35 states have implemented their own standards. Notably, in some cases, state standards are far more restrictive than their federal counterparts.

Political Rights

Federal and state legislation dictates the extent of convicted felons' political rights. In many cases, federal and state statutes restrict convicted felons' opportunities to vote, hold public office, or sit on a jury. Again, the Supreme Court has consistently authorized legislation that curtails convicted felons' formal and informal political rights. Customarily, the Court has held that the U.S. Constitution implicitly or explicitly authorizes certain restrictions on political participation and that the Constitution simply does not protect convicted felons' opportunities to participate in other essential democratic practices. Thus, the Court has reasoned that the federal government and states are free to bar convicted felons from several essential democratic procedures.

Perhaps the most visible restriction on convicted felons' political rights are those statutes that hinder convicted felons' ability to cast a ballot. Felon disenfranchisement laws garnered nationwide attention following the contested 2000 presidential election, from which Florida barred thousands of convicted felons. Soon thereafter, legal scholars and social scientists spotlighted state statutes that bar convicted felons from voting. Currently, a convicted felon can forever lose the right to vote in 12 states, depending on a number of variables, such as the crime committed and the date of conviction. Comparatively, only two states, Maine and Vermont, allow convicted felons to vote without restriction. The remaining jurisdictions burden convicted felons' right to vote by making voter eligibility contingent on waiting periods or pardon requirements.

Like voter eligibility statutes, candidacy eligibility requirements vary jurisdictionally. In 17 states and the District of Columbia, convicted felons' opportunity to hold public office intimately links to voting restrictions. For example, in these jurisdictions, to be an eligible candidate a convicted felon must also be an eligible voter. Five states do not restrict the candidacy of those with a felony conviction. The remaining jurisdictions place time restraints on convicted felons' candidacy or require that a convicted felon secure a pardon or restoration of rights prior to running for office.

The exclusion of convicted felons from jury service is more prevalent than felon voter or candidacy disenfranchisement. Thirty-one states and the federal government statutorily prohibit convicted felons from serving as jurors in either civil or criminal litigation permanently. The remaining jurisdictions adhere to less drastic restrictions that ban convicted felons from the deliberation room for a period of years. Only one state, Maine, imposes no restriction on a convicted felon's opportunity to serve as a juror.

James M. Binnall
University of California, Irvine

See also Loss of Individual Rights; Pardon and Restoration of Rights; Reintegration Into Communities

Further Readings

Manza, Jeff and Christopher Uggen. *Locked Out: Felon Disenfranchisement and American Democracy.* Oxford: Oxford University Press, 2006.

Mukamal, Debbie A. and Paul N. Samuels. "Statutory Limitations on Civil Rights of People With Criminal Records." *Fordham Urban Law Journal,* v.30/1501 (2003).

Travis, Jeremy. *But They All Come Back: Facing the Challenges of Prisoner Reentry.* Washington, DC: The Urban Institute Press, 2005.

CLASSIFICATION SYSTEMS

Classification systems are primary management processes used by both correctional institutions and community corrections to determine appropriate security and custody status for adult and juvenile offenders. Classification is necessary in order to ensure correctional facility safety, efficient operations, fiscal responsibility, and appropriate levels of risk for community protection. When an offender is placed in confinement or in a community corrections program, by the courts as a probationer or as a parolee, custody and professional staff evaluate the offender by performing a risk assessment as well as determining the offender's needs. This process initiates the classification folder: a collection of files, both paper and electronic, that are secured and maintained by a classification officer and from which management and supervisors create a plan to minimize the risks and meet the offender's needs.

Information is collected from the offender, court documents, probation records (pre-sentence investigation reports), and other sources that minimally include medical, social, psychological, criminal (current and prior), religious, and academic or vocational training histories. This information is evaluated in order to assign the individual within a structure of security, custody, and programming. The committing offense and the sentence are often insufficient indicators with which to determine custody and security or necessary services for addressing risks to and needs in the community. Legal strategies and plea bargaining may have resulted in changes to the final offense for which a sentence is handed down; thus, the nature of the offender within the context of his or her security status and hence the interventions needed to ensure community safety and the appropriate level of offender treatment must be thoroughly considered for the purposes of classification.

The growth of correctional populations since the 1960s has amplified the pressure on community corrections resources, which are the recipients of increasing numbers of offenders who are returning from correctional institutions. Likewise, a greater emphasis has been placed on community corrections to provide a wider range of services as alternatives to incarceration. More effective classification is essential to this process. Pushed by "what works" (evidence-based practices), community corrections

Prison classification is essential for the safe operation of a prison facility. The offender will be assessed for dangerousness or risk and is classified to a corresponding level of confinement. (Wikimedia)

programs, like correctional facilities, have turned to more effective management tools, including instruments such as the Level of Services Inventory–Revised (LSI–R). Since 1982, other instruments have been developed. Subsequently, a greater emphasis has been placed on community corrections to achieve public safety through effective risk/needs assessments and to attain reductions in recidivism.

Classification processes are generally referred to as external or internal, and the type of systemic approach as subjective or objective.

External Classification

External classification is concerned with the custody and security needs of the correctional institution and seeks to protect both the facility and the offender, usually in that order: The security of the correctional institution assumes primacy. External classification takes place when the offender first arrives at a jail or correctional system reception center. There are two primary tasks: first, to determine whether to place the offender in the general population, and second, to establish the offender's custody level. Using the current offense, sentence, and prior offense history (which includes any escape history), the offender is assessed for dangerousness or risk and is classified to a corresponding level of the institution. These decisions are fundamental to maintaining a safe and efficient operating facility. Additional criteria for consideration may include age, gender, education and skill training, substance abuse patterns, history of violence, gang involvement, detainers, and disciplinary history. Initial programming assignments (such as psychiatric review or inclusion in a security threat group) may be made at this time, especially if the offender is perceived to represent a threat from the standpoint of security or custody. Custody designations take into account the aforementioned characteristics of the offender and may also be tempered by perceptions of the offender's personal strength. For example, placing younger and weaker offenders with older and more aggressive offenders can initiate incidents of mayhem and injury, and thus these placements are avoided.

Internal Classification

Internal classification occurs at the specific institutional setting. It is used to determine more detailed programming needs and definitive custody concerns,

such as cell placement, work assignments, and privileges that are appropriate to the offender and that meet a specific correctional facility's security standards. In this manner, the needs of the facility are addressed by focusing on the management issues of the offender. The internal classification process will assess the skill level of the offender for work and rehabilitation assignments that align with security mandates. Similarly, the process identifies who is at risk for inclusion in special populations that require a level of supervision different from that appropriate for the general population. Appropriate classification leads to appropriate housing and programming (treatment) upon arrival, thus both enhancing the offender's adjustment and increasing the possibility that he or she can in the future be reassigned to a less restrictive, general population or community program, which in turn improves management efficiency. Internal classification conducts periodic reviews to assess adjustment, to determine programmatic changes (treatment, work, and custody level), and to make release recommendations. Classification, at this juncture, takes into account the security of or risk to the community. That assessment influences decisions to release, deny, or implement special conditions (such as recommending civil commitment).

Subjective Versus Objective Classification

Historically, the first uses of classification involved the separation of women and children from adult male offenders. The classification process next came to rely on subjective evaluations.

Subjective classification commonly consisted of clinical interpretations, professional judgments, and experiences of staff members from representative departments. This information resulted in predictive attempts to place offenders in facilities and programs that would produce the best available management of the person with programming that met his or her needs. This model of classification has generally been inconsistent, arbitrary, and unreliable, frequently resulting in overclassification.

Recidivism rates—or what might otherwise be referred to as failure when offenders return to the community—resulted in the development of evidence-based risk/needs assessment instruments to be utilized in objective classification systems for assigning community controls for enhanced public safety. Subjective classification, used during early periods of the nation's prisons, has not entirely disappeared from the newer correctional classification landscape. Administrators will exercise their authority to supersede or override objective classification scoring and assign offenders as they wish. This is not necessarily a problem, inasmuch as objective classification scoring has its own flaws.

Objective classification systems have been implemented since the 1980s. These systems of evidence-based classification reduce the unreliability commonly associated with subjective classification. Prior to 1980, the only use of objective classification was by the Federal Bureau of Prisons and the California Department of Corrections. Objective classification processes rely on evidence-based instruments that, through research by states, federal agencies, and scholars, have been shown to be both reliable and valid. The instruments are administered, scored, and interpreted by trained professional personnel. Primary uses of the instruments include risk assessment for institutional placement and risk/needs assessments for community release and for community corrections placement. These assessments identify individual or "criminogenic" factors (such as addictions, escape, or violence) that should be addressed to minimize risk and thus result in either more efficient correctional operations or a reduction in recidivism (through improvements in such areas as medical, social, and academic or vocational deficiencies). Moreover, greater credibility has been achieved through the use of risk/needs assessment instruments.

Reliability of Assessment, Overclassification, and Reclassification

Initial assessment and scoring occur during intake and examine established criteria, such as current offense, length of sentence, previous offenses (including escape history), suicide risk, and age of the offender. The interpretations of the scoring influence whether a custody status is increased, decreased, or remains unchanged. Corrections have come under court review for overclassification, that is, for assigning excessive custody status. The courts have emphasized that classification must not be subjective or impulsive. Objective classification scoring justifies placement and minimizes the assignment of an unwarranted custody status. Both the decisions and scoring will be maintained in the classification folder and reviewed at different points during confinement to suggest when changes in custody status are most appropriate.

During confinement, reclassifications will occur. These reviews are often conducted annually, when an offender reaches certain stages, such as eligibility for promotion within the institution, periods when eligibility for community corrections placement are determined, or release from confinement. The assessment of risk during reclassification retains primacy for maintaining security within the institution and for consideration of reassignment to community corrections programs. Security risk increases as custodial assignment declines. The identification of dynamic criminogenic risk factors that may be addressed and mitigated following release to the community will minimize but not negate the likelihood of failure.

Classification for community corrections, whether emanating from an institution or from the courts as an alternative to confinement, involves more critical assessments, as it attempts to predict not only who is best served but also which is the more protective option. Objective classification decision making for community corrections placement and how best to serve the offender depend on evidence-based tools. These are used to identify less expensive options that maximize the predictability of community safety through both the mitigation of dynamic criminogenic factors and the control of static criminogenic factors. The objective nature of evidence-based classification tools moderates subjective administrative opinions and helps ensure objective determinations.

A primary change in decision making between the 1970s and the 1990s regarded which community resources take precedence. That primarily entailed determining officer caseloads to meet supervisory criteria based on static factors. Objective classification, since that time, has altered that perspective to address risk by instituting controls such as intensive supervision or day reporting programs to manage crime-causing conditions, concentrate on needs, mandate specific treatment strategies (such as aggression reduction training for anger or the New Freedom Curriculum for substance abuse, which are also evidence-based methodologies), and address dynamic criminogenic factors. Evidence-based practices (such as the Phoenix Program for gang intervention) used for classification in community corrections are on the rise. Results from such objective classification scoring frees officers by allowing them to turn attention from those requiring lower levels of supervision and focus on those who represent a greater risk, at the same time providing more effective tools with which to manage offenders in the community.

Objective, evidence-based classification systems for community corrections have changed the paradigm from one with a primary focus on preventing recidivism to one identifying resources that meet offender needs while minimizing risk. Management of offenders has become more efficient and effective through interventions that are measured and whose progress is assessed and adjusted to obtain essential outcomes, specifically addressing risk and needs to reduce recidivism and improve the likelihood of community safety.

Matthew J. Sheridan
Georgian Court University

See also Actuarial Risk Assessment; Brockway, Zebulon; Caseload and Workload Standards; False Negatives and False Positives; Hare Psychopathy Checklist; Level of Service Inventory; Offender Needs; Offender Risks; Risk and Needs Assessment Instruments; Risk Assessment Instruments: Three Generations; Wisconsin Risk Assessment Instrument

Further Readings

Austin, James. *Findings in Prison Classification and Risk Assessment.* Washington, DC: National Institute of Corrections, 2003.

Bonta, James. "Offender Risk Assessment: Guidelines for Selection and Use." *Criminal Justice and Behavior*, v.29 (2002).

Carlson, Peter and Judith Simon, eds. *Prison and Jail Administration: Practice and Theory.* Sudbury, MA: Jones and Bartlett, 2008.

Clear, Todd R., George F. Cole, and Michael D. Reisig. *American Corrections*, 9th ed. Belmont, CA: Thomson Wadsworth, 2010.

Handyman, Patricia, James Austin, and Owen Tulloch. *Revalidating External Prison Classification Systems.* Washington, DC: National Institute of Corrections, 2002.

Kane, Thomas. "The Validity of Prison Classification: An Introduction to Practical Considerations and Research Issues." *Crime and Delinquency*, v.32 (July 1986).

Van Voorhis, Patricia. *Psychological Classification of the Adult Male Prison Inmate.* Albany: State University of New York Press, 1994.

COMMUNITY CORRECTIONS ACTS

Beginning in the 1970s, many state governments in the United States, hoping to decrease reliance on state institutions, passed community corrections acts. The intent was to utilize more local and community correctional programs as alternatives to increasingly overcrowded state institutions. In addition, these legislative acts reflected the optimistic view of the community corrections era of the 1970s, according to which community treatment would be truly rehabilitative, in sharp contrast to incarceration in state prisons. The drive to set up community corrections centers closely followed the drive to set up community mental health centers. Unfortunately, lacking adequate financial support and under strong political attack from several quarters, community corrections programs began to decline in the 1980s, scarcely a decade after they had begun.

Community Corrections Acts in the 1970s

In the 1960s and 1970s, the American correctional system was undergoing a period of crisis. Resources were running thin, prisons were oppressive, and state correctional institutions were unable to provide programs and services that effectively met the needs of their charges. Alongside these difficulties were a series of reports demonstrating that crime rates consistently showed strong correlations with poverty, unemployment, population density, and other socioeconomic factors. It was becoming clear that criminality could not be separated from its structural and cultural origins and triggers, and that reducing crime would require addressing those factors holistically. Alternatives to incarceration, such as community corrections, could provide this, but traditionally such alternatives had been available only to the wealthier classes who could afford them. The poor and disenfranchised were confined to cells without access to services that might help to alleviate their poverty and unemployment and thus that might increase their chance of reducing crime. Their plight began to change, however, in the 1970s.

During this decade, numerous states began forming partnerships with community organizations, integrating their efforts with the civil society sector at the county and local levels. Although such collaborations varied greatly in their philosophies, their programs, their memberships, their resources, and their scope, many operated on three main premises: first, that the goal of corrections should be to restore an individual to his or her community; second, that this is best-achieved through sentences that are community-based and integrated into local programs; and third, that the majority of incarcerated offenders do not require imprisonment and are not well served by the isolation of prison.

Some states outsourced community corrections to nonprofit community organizations in only a few counties; others turned the bulk of their entire community corrections programming over to local communities. This second approach was especially common in many midwestern states, such as Minnesota, Indiana, Michigan, Iowa, and Ohio. Kansas, Virginia, Oregon, Colorado, Connecticut, and Tennessee also passed community corrections acts (although they occasionally used slightly different wording for these laws). Still other states increased their funding of community corrections through indirect means, such as reallocations and the expansion of preexisting programs.

How Community Corrections Worked

Although some community corrections organizations were religiously based, many were secular. The complex of community corrections tended to be composed of smaller, nimbler organizations centered in the communities of the offenders who utilized the service. In many cases, therefore, offenders were able to continue living at home while making use of the services provided for them in civil society community corrections. These sentences thus functioned much like an intensive probation, although frequently the offender would meet with a private individual overseeing his or her program, rather than a probation officer.

Most services were aimed at reducing recidivism rates by assisting offenders in engaging with their communities. Others focused more on surveillance and monitoring as a method of security and control. Frequently, organizations would interlock and integrate their services to better meet the needs of offenders. The state provided millions of dollars of grant money in support. Some scholars have critiqued community corrections acts for increasing the severity and punitiveness of community corrections organizations, even as these organizations

were expanded because of grant funding during this era. The state mandates of reports and surveillance occasionally required these organizations to be more stringent in whom they accepted into their programs and how offenders were managed, lest the organizations lose their funding.

Overall, however, county and local community corrections organizations were able to provide services at a much lower cost than the institutions of the state. Vocational training, work release, spiritual guidance, drug and alcohol rehabilitation, psychological treatment, family reunification, childcare, and education were all among the services offered by such organizations.

Decline in the 1980s

The community corrections era began to wane in the 1980s. Fear of crime continued to rise, and the so-called war on drugs ushered in a new era of crime control, with harsher sentences, mandatory minimums, and the wide-scale construction of high-security "supermax" (super maximum-security) prisons. This era of mass incarceration has been characterized by what scholars call the prison-industrial complex. As coal towns and farming communities saw their industries decline, rural unemployment skyrocketed, and rural towns began looking to prisons as a source of jobs for their communities.

Meanwhile, many of the civil society organizations that had served as community-based corrections alternatives to incarceration began to be replaced by for-profit, private-sector corrections facilities, including private prisons. Overburdened states began contracting public-private partnerships to relieve their own institutions, creating an incentive for correctional enterprises to acquire offenders to house for profit.

In the crime control era that began in the 1980s and continues today, we thus have seen a complete reversal of the three premises of the community corrections organizations established under community corrections acts. First, to the motivation to restore offenders to their community in order to facilitate their reintegration has been added a powerful profit incentive. Second, offenders have increasingly tended to be incarcerated in rural communities far away from their homes and families. Finally, prison rates have skyrocketed, as offenders have received longer sentences at higher rates in increasingly repressive institutions.

Conclusion

Despite such obstacles, a number of organizations of community corrections act counties—such as the Minnesota Association of Community Corrections Act Counties and the Indiana Association of Community Corrections Act Counties—persist. Although significantly diminished, grant money is still available for community corrections, both from the state and from a variety of foundations and organizations. These organizations are among the more influential lobbies for increasing community corrections programs, regularly proposing policy initiatives to encourage alternative sentencing programs, rehabilitation services, and community residency.

Ellen Dwyer
Ronak Shah
Indiana University, Bloomington

See also Community Corrections as an Alternative to Imprisonment; Conditions of Community Corrections; Crime Control Model of Corrections

Further Readings

Carey, M. "Restorative Justice in Community Corrections." *Corrections Today*, v.58/5 (1996).

Center for Community Corrections. http://centerforcommunitycorrections.org/?page_id=78 (Accessed July 2011).

Harris, M. K. "Key Differences Among Community Corrections Acts in the United States: An Overview." *The Prison Journal*, v.76/2 (1996).

Musheno, M. C. et al. "Community Corrections as Organizational Innovation: What Works and Why." *Journal of Research in Crime and Delinquency*, v.26/2 (1989).

Palumbo, D. J. et al. *Implementation of Community Corrections in Oregon, Colorado, and Connecticut.* Washington, DC: National Institute of Justice, 1984.

Petersilia, Joan. "What Works in Community Corrections: An Interview With Dr. Joan Petersilia," *Expert Q&A*, n.2 (November 2007). http://www.pewtrusts.org/uploadedFiles/wwwpewtrustsorg/Reports/sentencing_and_corrections/QA_Community_Corrections.pdf (Accessed July 2011).

Schoen, K. F. "The Community Corrections Act." *Crime and Delinquency*, v.24/4 (October 1978).

Shilton, Mary K. *Community Corrections Acts for State and Local Partnerships.* Laurel, MD: American Correctional Association, 1992.

COMMUNITY CORRECTIONS AND SANCTIONS

The concept of community corrections consists of both nonincarcerative alternatives to prison and intermediate sanctions that utilize community resources in official responses to criminal behavior. Nonincarcerative alternative sanctions include various forms of probation, parole, day reporting centers, monetary restitution, fines, fees, electronic monitoring, house arrest, intensive supervision programs, halfway houses, community service, residential programs, and boot camps, generally embracing a "rehabilitative ideal."

Probation and Parole

The two cornerstones of community corrections, probation and parole, provide supervision and limited control of offenders outside jail and prison facilities. Probation has it origins in medieval practices whereby fines or various forms of suspended sentences (some with and some without supervision) were imposed.

A Boston shoemaker named John Augustus, who in 1841 provided bail for an offender charged with public drunkenness, established initial precepts for probation in the United States. Augustus provided supervision and guidance for the offender, who returned to court three weeks later for sentencing. The court was so impressed with the reformation that had occurred that it fined the man only one penny plus court costs. Augustus continued working in this manner, and by 1858 had assisted more than 1,900 persons. Probation as an alternative sanction grew in popularity and became a favored means to address deviant behaviors committed by youths.

Probation not only monitors probationers but also makes recommendations to the court regarding appropriate dispositions. The objectives of probation are to protect the public, provide assistance to courts via recommendations and enforcement of court orders, provide assistance and guidance to offenders (such as access to treatment), and assist the offender in becoming a law-abiding citizen.

Over the years, probation has evolved and taken on various other forms. One such form is intensive supervision probation (ISP). ISP consists of persons who were once deemed too much of a risk to public safety to experience regular probation. These probationers typically have more supervisory and behavioral restrictions imposed upon them while reporting to their assigned probation officers more frequently.

Deferred adjudication probationers are generally ordered to some form of community service, treatment, or restitution (following a plea of guilty or no contest) whereby charges are often dropped upon successful completion of assigned tasks. Pretrial diversion probation, similar to deferred adjudication probation, enables offenders to experience community supervision without a finding of guilt. To that end, offenders are diverted or pulled away from further formal processing and are supervised in the community until court-assigned tasks are completed.

Split sentencing has allowed probation to be combined with other intermediate forms of punishment. That is, offenders may be required to spend a certain amount of time within a jail facility and/or pay fees, fines, or make restitution prior to receiving probation. Under split sentencing, once certain court-ordered preconditions are met, qualifying offenders can be placed on probation.

Parole

Parole—although somewhat similar to probation in terms of supervisory, guidance, and counseling practices—differs in that persons experiencing parole have been incarcerated. Earlier forms of parole enabled European inmates to receive "tickets of leave" that could grant them travel to newer colonies, thereby fulfilling labor needs. Once these convicted and sentenced felons served a certain amount of their prison sentence and met required preconditions, many became eligible for parole. These preconditions also consisted of displaying appropriate behaviors reflective of a reformed life. More intensive forms of parole exist for offenders who require stricter supervisory standards (such as frequent urine testing) along with an increase in the frequency of contact with a parole officer.

The primary purpose and objectives of parole have changed over time. Once steeped in the medical model, the primary objective was to assist in the reintegration of offenders into the community and reduce recidivism. However, Frank P. Williams, M. McShane, and M. Dolny suggest that the primary objective of parole is to protect the public from released offenders through monitoring, strict supervision, assisting offenders to reintegrate into the community, and bolstering the public's confidence in parole services.

Probation and Parole: Uses and Outcomes

Increases in the utilization of probation and parole reflect both dissatisfaction with the results of incarceration and the higher cost of incarceration. Imprisonment disrupts offenders' connections with family and community, thereby making reentry a greater challenge. In terms of cost, the Bureau of Justice Statistics reports that in 2001 states spent an average $22,650 per year, or $62.05 per day, for each inmate incarcerated. However, the Pew Charitable Trusts report that, among 33 states examined in 2009, "the average cost of managing an offender in the community ranged from $3.42 per day for probationers to $7.47 per day for parolees, or about $1,250 to $2,750 a year." Additionally, it should be noted that these costs are offset in some states where the probationer and/or parolee contributes or makes payments toward supervision.

Although the United States has the highest incarceration rate in the world, probation has become the most commonly used form of punishment, as 60 percent of convicted offenders are under some form of probation. More specifically, with more than three quarters of a billion persons under some form of the corrections umbrella, the Bureau of Justice Statistics notes that in 2007 slightly fewer than 4.5 million were on some form of probation, while another 800,000 experienced parole. Hence, the two cornerstones of community corrections—probation and parole—are the more viable options used as both alternatives to prison and sanctions for criminal behaviors.

Although the majority of convicted offenders are supervised in the community, significant numbers of those on probation and parole fail. While fewer probationers than parolees fail, this is often because more stringent requirements are placed on parolees. Moreover, Kevin Gray and colleagues note that most probationers experience revocation for technical violations (a failure to meet conditions of probation) rather than new criminal charges, while Joan Petersilia notes that parole failures account for a significant number of new prison admissions. Moreover, research has shown that rearrests of both probationers and parolees occur most often within the first three to six months of their experience. However, success varies by type of release among parolees. More specifically, as T. Hughes and colleagues note, parolees who receive a discretionary release via parole boards have higher success rates than parolees released through mandatory parole.

In an effort to curtail failure, both probation and parole have developed scientifically based prediction tools to assist in describing characteristics of offenders who are more likely to complete their programs successfully. Research shows that persons who are female, older, married, better educated, employable, and have fewer previous criminal convictions are more likely to complete probation. Similarly, it has been noted that parole success is mediated by sex, number of prior arrests, and supervision. Women, persons with fewer convictions, and individuals who are supervised upon release are better candidates for parole than persons who do not meet such criteria.

While reintegration and rehabilitation remain objectives of both probation and parole, supervision has become a primary function. Statistically based prediction scales are employed to calculate an offender's potential for reoffending and his or her likelihood of success. This trend will likely continue, as incarceration costs compel governments to seek alternative forms of punishment that protect society and provide a cost-effective means of retribution.

Day Reporting Centers

Day reporting centers (DRCs) evolved out of the British criminal justice system in the 1970s but soon were received as a valuable addition to community corrections within the United States. Dale Parent notes that current usage of DRCs parallels their development and utilization within the juvenile justice system in America. Juveniles in the past often reported daily to such centers for supervision and treatment. Primary objectives of DRCs are to provide higher levels of supervision and treatment and to reduce jail as well as prison overcrowding. In general, it is believed that offenders are more likely to stay out of trouble if their days are filled with constructive activities. While at the DRC, offenders may seek educational opportunities, explore employment options, access treatment programs, and participate in drug testing. Patrick Coleman and colleagues note that these centers have become popular as cost-effective means of maintaining

offender accountability and services, with fewer government staff needed to operate them. In fact, many DRCs are privately operated with contracts offered to local municipalities to supervise or provide various treatment options for offenders.

Parent notes that daily costs per offender in DRCs average approximately $35.00. While this is higher than traditional forms of probation and parole, it is less costly than incarceration and residential programs. Moreover, it is not uncommon for offenders to contribute monetarily to offset program and treatment costs.

Rates of completion in DRCs vary in terms of length and program orientation. Specifically, clients assigned to DRCs for more than six months have not fared as well as offenders assigned for shorter periods. Moreover, offenders who reported for supervision purposes were more successful than offenders assigned to service-oriented DRCs. Jack McDevitt and R. Miliano observed that it was not uncommon for failure rates to remain as high as 50 percent for offenders assigned to DRCs. However, it should be noted that these failure rates reflect the fact that DRCs generally accept more high-risk offenders than other types of programs. DRCs provide monitoring of and accounting for an offender's time and presence. Thus, DRCs supplement intensive supervision programs and stricter monitoring practices wherein offenders appear daily for specified periods of time. Persons most likely to complete a DRC program successfully are individuals who are older, have fewer prior arrests, and spend more time involved with the DRC program.

House Arrest

House arrest is an intermediate sanction that restricts a person's movement or confines the person to his or her home during specific periods when the individual is not at work, in school, or attending a treatment program. This measure has also been referred to as home detention or home confinement. This particular sanction has been used with pretrial detainees and convicted offenders. It has further been received as a jail or prison reduction strategy and an alternative sanction that enables an offender to remain in the community. House arrest is often a condition stipulated in conjunction with probation, parole, and electronic monitoring.

The primary objective of house arrest is to restrict movement. Among detainees awaiting trial, it serves to ensure a court appearance. Moreover, when coupled with electronic monitoring it enables correctional agents to verify and confirm that participants are adhering to the conditions of remaining at home during specified times. Thus, reduced recidivism is not a primary objective of house arrest.

Although initiated in the United States during the 1960s, house arrest grew in popularity in the 1980s. Legal issues surrounding use of house arrest challenge privacy rights. Privacy issues may impact detainees awaiting trial when their homes may be occupied by persons other than the detainee, whose rights to privacy are perceived as intruded upon. Another issue concerns the ability to deter criminal behavior, which may still occur within the home. It is not uncommon for persons under house arrest to be rearrested for such crimes as the possession and selling of drugs from their place of confinement.

While house arrest is less costly than jail and prison confinement (but more expensive than traditional probation), its effectiveness varies. For instance, detainees tend to be more successful at completion than probationers and parolees. Moreover, success is conditioned by employment status for probationers and parolees. That is, persons who maintain employment are more successful at completing the program. Nonetheless, results have been conflicting. Paul Gendreau and colleagues noted that persons who experienced house arrest were more likely to recidivate, whereas James Bonta and colleagues reported that house arrest lowered recidivism among both probationers and parolees. However, the ability afforded by house arrest to more successfully assess and assign risk level indicates that house arrest as an alternative detention strategy will likely remain a viable option, as supervision and restriction remain its primary objectives.

Electronic Monitoring

Electronic monitoring supplements various forms of community-based corrections in which higher levels of supervision are needed to support a court-ordered intermediate sanction. Electronic monitoring has been used in conjunction with probation, parole, house arrest, day reporting centers, and pretrial services for detainees awaiting trial. Originally designed for use with mentally ill patients released from institutions during the 1960s, electronic monitoring devices, which transmit signals and are worn on the

wrist, were introduced into the realm of criminal justice in the early 1980s. Earlier home-based devices required offenders to have a land-based telephone line, and the wrist transmitter detected distance from the telephone. This radio-frequency-based technology could confirm an offender's whereabouts only at specific times. Land-line telephones were usually placed in the offender's home, and costs of supervision were assumed by the offender. This transfer of costs may partially explain the initial application of electronic monitoring to persons convicted of driving under the influence and white-collar offenders. Petersilia would note that this practice led to charges of discrimination and net widening, such that many jurisdictions developed sliding payment tables to enable more offenders to experience electronic monitoring.

Technological advancements soon allowed the courts to track offenders on electronic monitoring through remote paging and global positioning satellites. Ankle bracelets replaced wrist-attached devices, and satellite monitoring and remote tracking (SMART) programs expanded the pool of offender candidates to include sex offenders. The SMART tracking devices could signal supervisory agencies when an offender entered an area (such as a school, park, or specific street) that had been labeled off limits. While this newer technology was more expensive than the radio-frequency-based wrist devices, it was still less expensive than the costs associated with jail, prison, or residential placement. Moreover, offenders still contributed to the costs of electronic monitoring. Hence, electronic monitoring continues to be used as an alternative sanction and overcrowding strategy.

The Center for Criminology and Public Policy Research at Florida State University notes that during 2000, more than 30,000 offenders had experienced electronic monitoring. Moreover, states have passed laws enabling wider usage, despite allegations of privacy intrusions. These legislated approvals reflect both citizen approval and empirical studies that show electronic monitoring to have increased offenders' likelihood of completing their programs and avoiding recidivism. Given these findings and the cost-effectiveness of electronic monitoring, its usage will likely continue, and adaptations allowing video-level surveillance as well as surgically implanted monitors may become realities in the not-too-distant future.

Halfway Houses

Halfway houses are residential facilities that vary in focus and permit offenders in need of stricter supervision to remain in the community while pursuing opportunities for employment, treatment, restitution, community service, and life-skills enhancement. Halfway houses have provided more structured environments for parolees, probationers, and detainees who may be required to make restitution or provide a service as a condition of having charges dismissed.

Although halfway houses existed in the early 18th century in the United States, it was not until the 19th century that these facilities became widely accepted and did more than provide shelter and food. During the decade of the 1950s, private halfway houses offered supervision, transitional services, and treatment to newly paroled inmates in an effort to lower recidivism. The Safe Streets Act of 1968 furthered the development of halfway houses at both federal and state levels, with an emphasis on reintegration. Although government-based funding for halfway houses decreased during the 1980s, private halfway houses continue to offer an array of services to eligible offenders referred by correctional entities. The referring state-level agency assumes much of the cost, but participating offenders may be required to defray 25 percent of the cost. Although less expensive than incarceration, halfway houses are more expensive than traditional forms of probation and parole.

Charles J. Corley
Michigan State University

See also Boot Camps; Community Service Order; Day Reporting Centers; Electronic Monitoring; Fine Options Programs; Halfway Houses and Residential Centers; Home Confinement and House Arrest; Parole; Probation; Probation and Parole: Intensive Supervision; Probation and Parole Fees; Restitution; Work/Study Release Programs

Further Readings

Andrews, D. A. and J. Bonta. *The Psychology of Criminal Conduct*, 5th ed. Cincinnati, OH: Anderson, 2010.

Bales, William et al. *A Quantitative and Qualitative Assessment of Electronic Monitoring*. Washington, DC: National Institute of Justice, 2010.

Coleman, Patrick, J. F. Green, and G. Oliver. *Connecticut's Alternative Sanctions Program: $619 Million Saved in Estimated and Capital Operating Costs*. Washington,

DC: U.S. Bureau of Justice Assistance Practitioner Perspectives, 1998.

Cullen, F. and P. Gendreau. "Assessing Correctional Rehabilitation: Policy, Practice, and Prospects." In *NIJ Criminal Justice 2000: Vol. 3, Changes in Decision Making and Discretion in the Criminal Justice System*. Washington, DC: U.S. Department of Justice, National Institute of Justice, 2000.

Gendreau, P., C. Goggin, F. Cullen, and D. Andrews. "The Effects of Community Sanctions and Incarceration on Recidivism." *Forum on Corrections Research*, v.12/2 (2000).

Gendreau, P., T. Little, and C. Goggin. "A Meta-Analysis of the Predictors of Adult Offender Recidivism: What Works!" *Criminology*, v.34/4 (1996).

Gray, Kevin, M. Fields, and S. R. Maxwell. "Examining Probation Violations: Who, What and When." *Crime and Delinquency*, v.47/4 (2001).

Hughes, T., D. J. Wilson, and A. J. Beck. *Trends in State Parole, 1990–2000*. Washington, DC: U.S. Department of Justice, 2001.

Latessa, E. and H. Allen. *Corrections in the Community*. Cincinnati, OH: Anderson, 1997.

McDevitt, Jack and R. Miliano. "Day Reporting Centers: An Innovative Concept in Intermediate Sanctions." In *Smart Sentencing: The Emergence of Intermediate Sanctions*, James Byrne, A. Lurigio, and J. Petersilia, eds. Thousand Oaks, CA: Sage, 1992.

Parent, Dale. *Correctional Boot Camps: Lessons From a Decade of Research*. Washington, DC: National Institute of Justice, 2003.

Parent, Dale. "Day Reporting Centers." In *Intermediate Sanctions in Overcrowded Times*, Michael Tonry and K. Hamilton, eds. Lebanon, NH: Northeastern University Press, 1995.

Petersilia, Joan. *Expanding Options for Criminal Sentencing*. Santa Monica, CA: Rand, 1987.

Petersilia, Joan. *Reforming Probation and Parole in the 21st Century*. Lanham, MD: American Correctional Association, 2002.

Petersilia, Joan. *When Prisoners Come Home*. New York: Oxford University Press, 2003.

Petersilia, Joan. "When Prisoners Return to the Community: Political, Economic, and Social Consequences in Sentencing and Corrections Issues for the 21st Century." Paper 9 in *The Executive Sessions on Sentencing and Corrections*. Washington, DC: U.S. Department of Justice, 2000.

Riordan, Jessica and Andrew McDonald. *One in 31 U.S. Adults Are Behind Bars, on Parole, or Probation*. Washington, DC: Pew Center on the States, 2009.

Sabol, William et al. *Offenders Returning to Federal Prison 1986–1997*. Washington, DC: U.S. Department of Justice, Bureau of Justice Statistics, 2000.

U.S. Bureau of Justice Statistics. "Expenditures/ Employment." http://bjs.ojp.usdoj.gov/index .cfm?ty=tp&tid=16 (Accessed December 2009).

Williams, Frank P., M. McShane, and M. Dolny. "Developing a Parole Classification Instrument for Use as a Management Tool." *Management Quarterly*, v.4/4 (2000).

COMMUNITY CORRECTIONS AS AN ADD-ON TO IMPRISONMENT

Designed to make use of community resources to aid in integrating convicted offenders back into society, community-based corrections can include programs such as diversion or pretrial release. Although these methods are examples of community corrections used as an intermediate sanction or punishment *alternative* to imprisonment, many if not most others are used or implemented *in addition* to incarceration. These may include halfway houses, therapeutic communities, and some work release programs. Such community corrections programs, therefore, are used and understood as add-ons to imprisonment. Furthermore, the concepts of the net-widening effect and extending supervision of ex-offenders relate heavily to the implementation of added supervision following imprisonment.

Post-Prison Supervision and Sentencing

Generally speaking, post-prison or post-release supervision is virtually any method whereby a corrections or court institution maintains control over individuals recently released from incarceration. This can be accomplished in a number of ways, each depending largely on a state's position on sentencing. Since the 1980s and 1990s, many states have taken a political, "tough-on-crime" stance in election platforms and resulting crime control policy. During this time, state philosophies on sentencing shifted from indeterminate to determinate policies, whereby legislatures began to mandate the lengths of sentences for certain crimes. Several states established sentencing commissions that would deliberate on and then justify certain sentencing guidelines, which were to be followed by judges and prosecutors in sentencing and plea-bargaining phases.

Under the indeterminate sentencing system, judges sentence offenders to a range of months or years in prison. For instance, for a case of robbery a judge might sentence someone to a minimum of three years and a maximum of seven. Within this range, the time of release from incapacitation is typically determined by a discretionary parole board. The board bases its decision to grant a release that is either before or up to the maximum date of the person's original sentence. As a result, the use of parole and other methods of community corrections in an indeterminate sentencing system is not normally understood as an add-on to imprisonment.

With the shift toward determinate sentencing, two decision-making power structures were substantially diminished, and some were even eliminated. The first was the discretionary power of the courtroom, which shifted from the judges to the prosecutors, as judges were forced to abide by sentencing mandates such as mandatory minimums (the forcible nature of which was struck down by the U.S. Supreme Court in 2004, though strict guidelines still remain), three-strikes legislation, and truth-in-sentencing laws. Subsequently, the practice of plea bargaining became the primary tool in sentencing. Along with the prescribed sentencing guidelines, the length and conditions of post-release supervision became a common element of the bargaining and general sentencing phases.

The second structure to be diminished was the discretionary parole board. It was largely necessary for the indeterminate sentencing systems to have a discretionary parole board because of the fluid nature of a person's sentence; however, abolishment of sentence fluidity subsequently eliminated the need for a parole board to determine the duration and intensity of post-release control. Instead, in determinate sentencing systems the post-release supervision is set by the judge during the initial sentencing and often is also based on a set of legislatively mandated guidelines. In such a system, post-release supervision can take the form of virtually any community corrections conditions and framework, ranging from simple parole officer supervision to halfway houses and even therapeutic communities. The implementation of mandatory community corrections clauses in the sentencing phase thus makes community corrections an add-on to imprisonment. Many emphasize that this use of community corrections constitutes more of an additional penalty (overincarceration) than a method of reducing recidivism.

Social Discipline

Although the purpose for using community corrections in any capacity and system is ultimately to achieve the successful reestablishment of positive social ties between the offender and the community, many programs may be used to maintain and extend state control, with the focus of diminishing the probability of recidivism and minimizing potential harm to law-abiding citizens. Put simply, one of the major uses of community corrections is to further control of released offenders in the community as a form of social discipline. Community corrections in this perspective can be understood through a social disciplinary model, whereby the individual is disciplined in plain view of the community to stigmatize the offender and thus potentially deter others.

As a result, the use of community corrections as a sanction to someone who has first been incarcerated would be recognized as an additional penalty, a punishment essentially tacked onto the original sentence of imprisonment. From the viewpoint of social discipline, a formal sanction such as a sentence of community service incorporates a level of informal control by assuming that the bonds between the offender and the society are strong enough essentially to shame the offender into conforming to conventional rules and law. Some states have even adopted the term "community punishment" as another way to refer to post-release supervision, further engaging the philosophy and practice of relying on the community members to aid in the implementation of punishment following incarceration.

Net Widening

As prisoners are released from imprisonment, the basic question of any system is "Who should be supervised?" Many states, even those with discretionary parole boards, rely on a method known as universal supervision, whereby virtually all offenders are required to have some form of post-release supervision. This is exemplified in the fact that only a fraction of prisoners, approximately one fifth, are actually released unconditionally or without required supervision. With such blanket policies as this, many argue that this is a method of net widening: the use of intermediate sanctions as additional penalties for those who were previously incarcerated and were eligible for basic supervision or unconditional release instead. In this sense, community corrections are used to increase the size of, or "widen," the criminal justice system's "net" of formal control.

An example of a net-widening practice in an indeterminate sentencing system could occur when an offender's opportunity for parole comes up

during the time he or she is serving a sentence. Upon meeting with the discretionary parole board, the individual, who might otherwise be eligible subject to a provision of intensive supervision by a parole officer and conditional release, is instead told that he or she must reside in a therapeutic community or a residential community corrections facility for a predetermined amount of time. In this case, the individual effectively has been handed a harsher penalty than (1) that suited to the offense and (2) that which another, very similar, case might have received.

In a determinate sentencing system, the universal supervision tactic is much more visible, as the individual is often sentenced to post-release supervision before any good time and programming may be accounted for. Subsequently, a large number of people sentenced will receive supervision, as the judge and prosecutors must assume that many if not most offenders will need a form of supervision. If there are community corrections resources available, the sentence will likely include a method of intermediate sanctions whereby the individual will be assigned a form of community corrections based on the type of offense that was committed.

This argument is often found in the literature regarding intensive supervision probation or parole (ISP). ISP is a method of control that subjects the recently released individual to more conditions, closer surveillance, and potentially more treatment, as in the case of halfway houses or therapeutic communities. Used as a more punitive technique of community corrections, ISP is viewed by the public and many practitioners as an effective and favorable way to control offenders upon release, with some empirical support. However, critics of ISP argue that its implementation is a mechanism of net widening, with other scholarly support finding that more offenders than those of just high risk or high need, as originally prescribed by the general ISP objectives, would as a result increase the population of those who are under ISP.

Advantages and Disadvantages

One potential advantage to the use of community corrections as an add-on to imprisonment is the impact on prison populations. With overcrowding becoming a serious issue for most states, the use of community corrections in the aforementioned capacities allows for a way to alleviate that problem. This is particularly true for indeterminate sentencing systems, wherein people may be granted release well before the sentence-prescribed max-out date. Through this practice, another advantage is created in terms of economic cost. As more prisoners are released into community corrections supervision, leaving fewer people in prison, there are inevitably fewer people to feed, house, and supervise. Considering that the majority of community corrections methods are cheaper than incarceration, this allows departments of corrections and states in general to save large sums of money.

On the other hand, critics of this practice would argue that the use of community corrections under this presumption is merely treating the symptom of a larger sentencing problem. As people are released from prison into community corrections, more beds become available to fill in prisons and jails, as a result allowing for judges to incarcerate more people. Thus, the net is widened, increasing the populations of both those incarcerated and those under criminal justice supervision in community corrections. In terms of fiscal savings, if in actuality the prison populations are not decreasing, then there is an increase in cost to the state as the price of imprisonment remains constant and the costs of community corrections supplement, rather than replace, the costs of incarceration.

Christopher M. Campbell
Washington State University

See also Probation and Parole: Intensive Supervision; Reducing Prison Populations; Sentencing Guidelines; Truth-in-Sentencing Provisions

Further Readings

Abadinsky, Howard. *Probation and Parole: Theory and Practice*, 11th ed. Upper Saddle River, NJ: Pearson, 2011.

Alarid, Leanne Fiftal and Rolando V. del Carmen. *Community-Based Corrections*, 8th ed. Belmont, CA: Thomson Wadsworth, 2011.

Morris, Norval and Michael Tonry. *Between Prison and Probation: Intermediate Punishments in a Rational Sentencing System*. New York: Oxford University Press, 1990.

Travis, Jeremy. *But They All Come Back: Facing the Challenges of Prisoner Reentry*. Washington, DC: Urban Institute Press, 2005.

Travis, Jeremy and Christy Visher. *Prisoner Reentry and Crime in America*. New York: Cambridge University Press, 2005.

COMMUNITY CORRECTIONS AS AN ALTERNATIVE TO IMPRISONMENT

Community corrections enable local treatment of offenders through nonincarcerative official responses to crime. Community corrections mobilize local resources such that qualifying offenders serve their sentences within the community, under the supervision of local correctional agencies, programs, and staff. These nonincarcerative alternative and intermediate sanctions include probation, day reporting centers, fines, electronic monitoring, house arrest, intensive supervision programs, halfway houses, community service, residential programs, and boot camps generally embracing a "rehabilitative ideal."

It is within the context of this rehabilitative ideal that treatment plans are developed whereby restorative justice principles of offender accountability and the resolution and restoration of balance can be attained for offenders as well as victims, and whereby the reintegration of offenders can be attempted.

History

Community corrections have evolved as an integral component of both the criminal justice and corrections systems. However, many elements of community corrections—such as restitution, retribution, and compensation—have origins in ancient and medieval eras, even noted in the Bible in Exodus 22:1–11. During the Middle Ages, King Æthelstane (895–940) prohibited the execution of anyone under 15 years of age and introduced a form of supervised released to a responsible party who would monitor the offender's behavior.

Banishment of offenders was a fairly common practice in England during the 17th century. In fact, it was not uncommon for England to transfer convicted criminals to the American colonies as a means of providing much-needed labor. This policy gave way to a forerunner of parole known as "tickets of leave," whereby convicted offenders were transported by the government to Australia after serving a portion of their sentence as indentured servants. Passage of the Penal Servitude Act in 1853 enabled Sir Walter Crofton of the Irish penal system to require that inmates display desirable attitudes and reform efforts as a prerequisite for securing a ticket of leave.

The two cornerstones of community corrections in the U.S. system of probation and parole parallel growth and experiences with the prison system. Punishment, not corrections, was the initial objective of justice. Throughout the Middle Ages, banishment and death were the more commonly used methods of punishment. Banishment was the punishment inflicted upon Adam and Eve, as described in the biblical book of Genesis. Public executions as well as horrific forms of noncapital punishment (the use of stocks and pillars, brandings, maimings, and floggings) were commonplace, and justice was based on retributive principles of *lex talionis*, or the law of retaliation, whereby the law seeks to compensate the offended party with punishment deemed equitable with the crime. These public displays were also used as a form of deterrence.

Hence, prisons were initially received as a more humane response to criminal behavior. The writings of Cesare Beccaria and Jeremy Bentham moved penology away from its retributive approach toward a doctrine of utility whereupon the greatest happiness for the greatest number was espoused. Utilitarianism suggests that, among other goals, the primary objectives of punishment are deterrence and proportionality. Offenders are punished to the extent that general deterrence and proportionality relative to the offense are observed. Moreover, it was believed that prisons enabled punishment to occur away from public view and specific deterrence would inhibit a released offender from reoffending.

Nonetheless, the ideal of prison as an appropriate response to crime soon dissipated, and the rise of alternative sanctions reflects disillusionment with prison response. While prisons in the United States reflected humanitarian efforts set forth by the Quakers in 1790 and were less harsh than their English predecessors, it had become clear that these penal institutions were not producing intended results. Moreover, prisons were expensive to build, staff, and operate.

The Rehabilitative Ideal

The emergence of community corrections reflects the diminishing belief that prison was an effective method of crime control and that released offenders had been adequately punished and reformed. Moreover, it coincides with the rise of the rehabilitative ideal and, infused within it, a medical model as an approach to corrections.

Prisoners' aid societies, such as the John Howard Society and the Philadelphia Society for Alleviating the Miseries of the Public Prisons, emerged during the latter part of the 18th century and helped propel the rehabilitative response. This rehabilitative response shifted the focus toward treatment of offenders whereby assessment of offender needs and crime control through curbing an offenders' desire to commit crime became primary objectives.

Treatment objectives were sought through alternative sanctions coupled with indeterminate sentencing as well as the acquisition of "good time," whereby offenders could impact their length of incarceration through achievement and by displaying appropriate behavior. To that end, community corrections evolved not as a complete alternative to prison but instead as a supplemental component reflecting diverse treatment modalities. Reformatories, such as the one in Elmira under warden Zebulon Brockway, embraced this new rehabilitative ideal and promoted treatment through comprehensive diagnosis and monitored progress. Correctional treatment staff sought new identities as correctional professionals entrusted with public safety through proper diagnosis and treatment of sentenced offenders.

About this same time, seeds of a parole system were planted in Europe. Around 1840, Englishman and former prisoner of war Alexander Maconochie became superintendent of the British penal colony at Norfolk Island. Maconochie, a deeply religious person, believed that one objective of imprisonment was prisoner reform. Maconochie thought harsh and brutal prisons produced hardened and brutal individuals who had little reason to observe social constraints upon release. Recidivism was quite high among released offenders at that time. Maconochie reasoned that a more humane prison environment, coupled with a "marks system" of release through graduated confinement stages, would enable inmates to experience levels of freedom that were earned while they were incarcerated. This marks system was instituted at Norfolk Island, where some 1,400 inmates were released upon qualifying and granted tickets of leave by the governor. These tickets of leave required released offenders to remain in the area unsupervised but imposed no further requirements. Although early release through attainment of good time was not a component of Maconochie's system, as offenders served their full sentences, it was reported that recidivism decreased. Thus, a system of release from confinement comparable to parole emerged through European experiences, whereas probation reflects a more American ideal.

The aforementioned model offered indeterminate sentencing along with opportunities for parole upon demonstration of acceptable values and behavior. The concept of the reformatory coincided with the rehabilitative ideal, and numerous states opened various forms of reformatories where education and training in a trade were offered as alternatives to traditional prisons. Still other states offered a form of suspended sentence as an alternative to prison, thereby reducing incarceration rates for qualified offenders. Massachusetts was the first state to hire a probation officer, and other states soon followed. Missouri enacted probationary legislation in 1897, followed by Vermont in 1898 and Rhode Island, Minnesota, and Illinois in 1899.

Acceptance and growth of probation were enhanced with the establishment of the first juvenile court in Cook County, Illinois, which encouraged probation as an official response to juvenile delinquency. In fact, probation was such a welcome alternative for juveniles that by 1925 most states had adopted it as a sanction for juvenile offenders. The federal probation system emanated from the Federal Probation Act, signed into law in 1925. Similar to practices initiated by John Augustus, persons currently granted probation must undergo a screening process, receive a suspended sentence, adhere to prescribed conditions of release, submit to supervision, and avoid behaviors that can lead to revocation. However, it was not until 1956 that probation existed in all 50 states and was extended to qualified adult offenders.

It should be noted that incarceration rates during most of the 20th century (as noted by Alfred Blumstein and A. J. Beck) fluctuated from a low of approximately 93 inmates per 100,000 persons in the population in 1930 to a high of 137 in 1939. It was not until 1975 that incarceration rates in the United States began to increase significantly. Institutionalization of the rehabilitative ideal and prison alternatives were factors that significantly impacted incarceration rates during most of the 20th century. Prisons remained crowded, however, and many states needed additional beds.

California was the first state to institute legislation supporting intermediate sanctions as a method of curtailing prison growth. The California Subsidy Program, established in 1965, reimbursed counties that diverted offenders to local programs as a sanction. While California was the first state to enact a community-corrections-based subsidy program, Minnesota has the distinction of legislating the first comprehensive community corrections act, which sought integration and standardization of community-based services. Since then, a majority of states have enacted community corrections acts to provide intermediate sanctions for convicted offenders.

Probation and Parole

The cornerstones of community corrections, probation and parole, flourished over the next several decades as reformers institutionalized individual treatment options that paralleled punishment. Probation provided a direct means to alleviate prison overcrowding and avert the prisonization process, or hardening of offenders, enabling offenders to maintain family and community ties while under supervision. This was seen as a viable response to crime, in that indeterminate sentences enabled inmates to progress at their own pace through treatment while incarcerated and to receive parole upon completion and assessment.

Probation in the aforementioned capacity serves at least two purposes supportive of elements of the criminal justice system. First, it provides support for prosecutors seeking plea bargains, whereby an alleged offender pleads guilty to an offense with the promise of probation as a sentence. Second, probation is supportive of judges desiring decreased court dockets of persons seeking trials, and it is subsequently supportive of defense attorneys, whose goals are to keep clients out of prison.

Similarly, prison wardens championed the ideals of parole, as it provided another tool for managing inmate behavior. That is, inmates know that to qualify for parole they must exhibit appropriate behavior during incarceration. Thus, prisoners conform to institutional and societal expectations while anticipating qualification for parole and conditional release.

Moreover, probation and parole have furthered the efforts of criminal justice professionals to establish a medical model for responses to crime, whereby indeterminate sentencing allows various treatment options in accordance with individual offender assessment and treatment modalities. While the medical model instituted during this period enabled halfway houses and furlough programs to evolve as reintegrative community-based tools, criticisms arouse during the 1970s and 1980s regarding reform efforts that challenged the rehabilitative ideal and efficacy of such programs. Amid rising crime rates and prison overcrowding, different philosophies of punishment emerged, which suggest incapacitation and just deserts as more appropriate modes of punishment.

Discretionary aspects of indeterminate sentencing also came under attack as disparities in sentencing were noted pursuant to nonlegal variables such as social class, race, and gender. This lack of uniformity would encourage justice advocates, such as Andrew von Hirsch, to propose punishment models whereby fairness or uniformity in sentencing was attained and sentenced offenders received the type of punishment deserved. To that end, numerous states instituted more determinate forms of sentencing (just deserts) and adopted sentencing guidelines, thereby limiting discretionary powers of judges such that more uniformity in sentencing exists while simultaneously curtailing abilities of parole boards to effect conditioned releases.

It was during this period, particularly during the 1980s, that the prison population soared as a new era bolstered retributive ideals that empowered legislators to "get tough on crime." More punitive responses to crime—such as mandatory minimums, three-strikes laws, enhanced drug laws, and zero-tolerance policies—provided more confinement options and longer sentences for convicted offenders. More specifically, the *Sourcebook of Criminal Justice Statistics* notes that by 1985 the incarceration rate had been raised to 202 per every 100,000 persons in the population. This was more than double the 93 per 100,000 persons reported in 1930 by Blumstein and Beck.

Higher recidivism rates also supported an incapacitation model whereby crime was projected to decrease as incarceration was perceived as a means both to protect society and to keep sentenced offenders from reoffending. However, as Dale Parent asserts, "incapacitation only works as long as offenders are incapacitated."

Given the more conservative and punitive responses to crime, one might have expected community-based corrections models to decline during this period.

Although that did happen in terms of funds committed to community corrections, actual usage of community-based responses to crime increased. As a case in point, the *Sourcebook of Criminal Justice Statistics* observes that, between 1980 and 1997, probation utilization grew 191 percent while parole grew 213 percent. Although more inmates were serving longer sentences than in the history of the country, numbers of offenders placed within community corrections alternatives also grew.

This growth was in part due to financial burdens associated with mass incarceration practices that further strained federal and state systems. For instance, the *Sourcebook of Criminal Justice Statistics* denotes that "direct expenditures for correctional activities by state governments grew from $4.26 billion in 1980 to $21.27 billion in 1994." In an effort to decrease expenditures for corrections, community-based alternatives that increased supervisory and monitoring functions were sought. One such alternative was "intensive supervision probation." While this marked something of a shift from the rehabilitative ideal originally practiced within community-based alternatives, it was a welcome change that placed a greater priority on monitoring offenders and public safety. Until this period in history, probation was perceived as an alternative to punishment more than a punishment that actually restricted freedoms with retributive elements. Thus the use of treatment modalities in the community became more aligned and complemented traditional supervisory functions of community corrections. The use of treatment while an offender was on probation served to meet the needs of both punishment and rehabilitation for qualifying offenders.

The U.S. Bureau of Justice Statistics reported that as of the end of 2009, there were 7,225,800 persons in U.S. jails, prisons, and probation/parole systems. Of those in the system, 2,297,400 were incarcerated. This represents the largest number of documented persons behind prison or jail bars throughout the world. However, the majority of convicted offenders are currently supervised in the community. H. West and W. Sabol noted that during 2007 more than a half million offenders were released from prison back into the community, while another 12 million were released from local jails.

Legislators continue to explore methods to decrease corrections budgets pursuant to high levels of incarceration and prison overcrowding. Many states, such as Kansas, are pursuing correctional methods that focus on reducing recidivism and providing rehabilitative options through support for community-based corrections. Similarly, Pennsylvania has introduced a four-phase intermediate correctional program whereby a sentenced offender spends an initial 11 months in prison, inclusive of substance abuse counseling, followed by two months of therapeutic community treatment programming, then six months of outpatient treatment, and finally a supervised reentry experience.

Current rehabilitative efforts have focused on the reintegration of offenders into society. Data repeatedly confirm that more than 80 percent of incarcerated offenders will be released to the community. Given high costs of incarceration, high rates of incarceration, and high rates of recidivism, assisting released inmates to reenter society successfully has the potential to decrease a state's prison population. These reentry programs generally consist of three phases. Phase one entails preparation for release through institutionally based programs such as risk assessment, education, mentoring, substance abuse counseling, and job training. Phase two consists of transitional support components: monitoring, reporting, life skills training, and various forms of counseling, incorporated into the released offender's daily or weekly routine. The final phase encompasses long-term support mechanisms enabling released offenders to receive the support determined necessary to keep them from reoffending or at least decrease the level of seriousness of offenses, should subsequent offenses occur. While utilization of the global positioning system (GPS) to facilitate monitoring devices enables greater surveillance, parole agents note that the resources and services provided during reentry are what moves the process along. Some of these direct and indirect resources include transitional housing, employment opportunities, and education; services may include substance abuse counseling, job skills training, and anger management classes.

Reentry programs have become numerous and diverse. While most programs are oriented around the three aforementioned phases, programs vary greatly in implementation and focus. For instance, with passage of the Second Chance Act by Congress in 2007, a growing number of states enacted reentry court initiatives (RCIs), whereby a seamless system of accountability and support is established and monitored by this particular court. The RCI provides assessment and planning, active oversight, management of support services, accountability to the community, graduated and parsimonious sanctions, and rewards for success.

Moreover, assistance with reentry enables corrections to utilize one of its more underutilized resources, the community. Research consistently shows that informal agents of social control are more powerful than formal agents of control in achieving and maintaining behavioral change. To that end, Jeremy Travis and Joan Petersilia champion a change that would compel inmates to conform to prison and societal standards through the rewarding of "good time" that reduces sentence length for appropriate behavior. Inmates who qualify for release would then participate in a pre-release program that focuses on the acquisition of skills that could move them toward independence.

Travis and Petersilia suggest that inmates should be released to a community-based intermediary agency that orchestrates community agencies such as churches, small businesses, schools, service providers, and civic institutions to operate collaboratively with criminal justice agencies supportive of reintegration. This intermediary agency could reflect a model similar to that of the Center for Alternative Sentencing and Employment Services, established in New York City. This agency serves in a brokering capacity pursuant to housing, employment opportunities, and economic growth between various levels of government and criminal-justice-related entities. Hence, the offender is more closely monitored, supervised, and supported by an empowered community equipped to provide necessary assistance.

In summary, reintegration of offenders into society has become a major focus of criminal justice agencies. In many ways that focus reflects dissatisfaction with the prison system and higher costs associated with imprisonment. However, when one considers that most inmates will eventually return to the community, it seems reasonable that efforts be taken beyond the prison to decrease their probability of recidivating. Reentry programs that prepare inmates and provide them with long-term support for release into the community reflect something of a paradigm shift, further embracing a rehabilitative model.

Charles J. Corley
Michigan State University

See also Community Corrections and Sanctions; Community Corrections as an Add-On to Imprisonment; Conditions of Community Corrections;

Diversion Programs; Drug Courts; Family Courts; Mental Health Courts; Teen Courts

Further Readings

Allen, Harry E. et al. *Corrections in America: An Introduction*, 12th ed. Saddle River, NJ: Pearson Prentice Hall, 2010.

Blumstein, Alfred and A. J. Beck. "Population Growth in U.S. Prisons, 1980–1996." In *Prisons*, M. Tonry and J. Petersilia, eds. Chicago: University of Chicago Press, 1999.

Cromwell, Paul et al. *Community-Based Corrections*, 6th ed. Belmont, CA: Thomson Wadsworth, 2005.

Glaze, L. and T. Bonczar. *Probation and Parole in the United States, 2006*. Washington, DC: U.S. Department of Justice, 2007.

Harrison, P. and A. Beck. *Prison and Jail Inmates at Midyear 2004*. Washington, DC: U.S. Bureau of Justice Statistics, 2005.

Lynch, J. P. and W. Sabol. *Prisoner Reentry in Perspective*. Washington, DC: Urban Institute, 2001.

MacKenzie, D. L. *Sentencing in the 21st Century: Setting the Stage for the Future*. Washington, DC: National Institute of Justice, 2000.

Morris, Norval. *Maconochie's Gentlemen: The Story of Norfolk Island and the Roots of Modern Prison Reform*. New York: Oxford University Press, 2002.

Parent, Dale. *Residential Community Corrections: Developing an Integrated Corrections Policy*. Washington, DC: National Institute of Corrections, 1990.

Petersilia, Joan. "A Decade of Experimenting With Intermediate Sanctions: What Have We Learned?" *Federal Probation*, v.62/2 (1998).

Petersilia, Joan. "Probation in the United States (Part I)." *Perspectives* (Spring 1998). http://www.appar-net.org/eweb/Resources/PPCSW_10/docs/sp98pers30.pdf (Accessed February 2012).

Seiter, R. P. *Corrections: An Introduction*. Upper Saddle River, NJ: Prentice Hall, 2005.

Tonry, M. *Malign Neglect: Race, Crime and Punishment in America*. New York: Oxford University Press, 1995.

Travis, J. and S. Lawrence. *Beyond the Prison Gates: The State of Parole in America*. Washington, DC: Urban Institute, 2002.

Travis, J. and J. Petersilia. "Reentry Reconsidered: A New Look at an Old Question." *Crime and Delinquency*, v.47/3 (2001).

U.S. Bureau of Justice Statistics. *Sourcebook of Criminal Justice Statistics*. Washington, DC: U.S. Department of Justice, 1998.

West, H. and W. Sabol. *Prisoners in 2007*. Washington, DC: U.S. Bureau of Justice Statistics, 2008.

Wodhal, Eric J. and Brett Garland. "The Evolution of Community Corrections: The Enduring Influence of the Prison." *The Prison Journal*, v.89/1 (2009).

Zimring, F. E. and G. Hawkins. *Incapacitation: Penal Confinement and the Restraint of Crime*. New York: Oxford University Press, 1995.

COMMUNITY PARTNERSHIPS

Community partnerships offer noninstitutional approaches to correctional service that have been found to be effective for the delivery of methods of prevention, treatment, and rehabilitation services for criminal justice offenders. Millions of people are released from prisons and jails each year, and government agencies alone cannot fully address the myriad challenges that individuals face after incarceration. Penal institutions cannot treat and rehabilitate the offender entirely; these processes must also occur when an offender returns to the community. Community rehabilitation may be less costly and more effective in preventing future crime.

When many different organizations in a community work together, they share common values and goals that can be mobilized to enhance offender, family, and community well-being. As intervention strategies, objectives, processes, and programs are created, shared, and implemented, community groups become partners. Partnerships allow for the creation of collective goals, identification of shared objectives, development of strategic plans, improved

A community partnership involves a variety of players to assist a recently released prisoner, including probation and parole officers, counselors, family therapists, and employment advisors. (Photos.com)

monitoring, evaluation of outcomes, and recommendations for changes. They continually improve both the process and structure so that success can become more feasible.

Greater funding possibilities may occur when agencies partner together, as may better program designs and increased opportunities for teamwork and leadership. Partnerships include the offenders, who may work to help support their community, which they see engaged in a process of trying to help them. This may send a message of mutual concern and respect. Where there are partnerships, everyone shares a responsibility for the outcomes of programs as well as the outcomes of offenders. By contrast, when agencies and individuals act as silos, they are the ones seen as responsible for the success or failure.

Understanding and utilizing the social environment of the offender and his or her family, community systems can be of particular use in developing correctional solutions. Offenders require a great deal of social support from multiple systems in order to rehabilitate. Studies suggest that the presence of support is a better predictor of outcome than the offender's condition at discharge or the severity of problems at the time of treatment. These studies suggest that work at the family, friend, group, and community levels helps mitigate the effects of the prison institution while supporting the offender through the transition to community living. Partnerships may provide the support necessary to help the offender deal with concrete needs such as housing, food, and employment, as well as the social and emotional challenges of transitioning out of incarceration. Studies indicate that offenders with few social supports face more difficulty once released.

Community partnerships have a multidimensional focus. Multiple players are involved, including the offender, the victim, their families, their friends, their social groups, and the community as a whole. Partnerships could focus on prevention, treatment, or rehabilitation. Community partnerships build upon the resources that naturally exist in the community, such as education, housing and welfare assistance, substance abuse treatment, job training and mentoring, and counseling. By connecting with other state agencies (such as state departments of labor, health, education, and social services), local government officials, intermediary organizations, and criminal justice and corrections officials can greatly expand the network of partners. They may be a central part of Homeland Security and community policing, where members of the community are encouraged to let authorities know when someone's behavior is atypical. They can also incorporate profit, nonprofit, governmental, and faith-based community organizations. They may be simple or complex, program-specific or communitywide, focused on actions at the individual or macro level (such as large-scale organizational and institutional actions). They can be as specific as gun buy-back programs or as extensive as systemwide approaches to prevention.

The use of community partnerships as a correction strategy is based on an open-systems perspective that values the old-time view of communities working together, where people know and can help one another. An open-systems approach holds that social systems and institutions are interrelated; a change in one part of one system inevitably influences the other parts. This approach assumes that no institution can act successfully in isolation from others. It also assumes that when multiple social institutions work together in a collaborative manner, the chances of rehabilitative success are increased. The open-systems approach continues to be embraced because it builds connections and communal ownership.

On the other hand, community organizations have come to exist in closed systems or silos—isolated units with their own funding streams, services, boards of directors, and clients. Closed systems are organized to be self-contained; they provide all services themselves and tend to view their clients as their exclusive responsibility. In closed systems, organizations even within the same community may find themselves in competition with one another for scarce resources, market share, and clients. There may be duplication of services, whereas some areas of need may remain unaddressed. Both agencies and individuals may not know what other organizations are providing, how they operate, or how best to access them. This is especially the case in large communities, where there are more agencies, more bureaucracies, and larger populations.

As this pertains to corrections, a closed-system approach would hold that the prisoner is served exclusively by the jail; when the prisoner is released, he or she is thrust back into a former life with no other supports. An open-systems, community partnership approach would view the release of the prisoner quite differently. For instance, while the prisoner was incarcerated, he or she would receive a variety of services, perhaps including education, counseling, and other forms of rehabilitation. Upon the prisoner's release to the community, a variety of partners would join in a case-planning process to ensure that the full range of services the prisoner needs to survive will be provided. These may include monitoring by probation and parole officers, educational assistance, individual counseling, family therapy, recreational outlets, career planning, and employment, to name but a few.

Successful community partnerships are more likely to occur when they have certain components. An advocacy and referral system should be in place to act on behalf of the offender and his or her family to ensure that they receive the assistance they need to avoid future problems. Services may include healthcare, education and training, counseling, housing, food assistance, substance abuse programs, newsletters, and outreach efforts. Particular areas of concern are assistance for basic needs and help in crisis situations. The needs of this population and the obstacles to changing behaviors are much larger than those faced by most other service populations. The referral process should be made easy. People often require guidance to navigate application processes. To encourage them to pursue statewide reentry opportunities, state agencies may need to work with community partners to simplify application procedures. The use of multilingual application forms may be important in communities where English is not spoken by large segments of the population. Resources may need to be tailored to meet the needs of the offender and the community.

In order for partnerships to be effective, it is essential to build a network of relationships among provider agencies. Partner organizations could work together on a regular basis through contracts with individual program silos or could function collectively in a collaborative meeting schedule through a new organizational structure or advisory system.

The creation of a database of community services and programs can serve multiple purposes and audiences. The database system can help to identify existing services and programs. It can also be used for communication, monitoring, and reporting activities, and it can help identify client needs, facilitate the tracking of client progress, and provide information on the effectiveness of referrals. Agencies can use their networks as a vehicle for sharing and accessing information with relevant agencies about the offender and programs. This data system can

facilitate effective case management. A data system can also help identify predictors for success and recidivism, such as static or dynamic predictors. Static predictors are those issues rooted in the past that cannot be changed, such as criminal history, variables related to family of origin, socioeconomic variables, race, and intellectual functioning. These variables have been heavily used by traditional corrections approaches for assessing risk. Dynamic predictors include such variables as attitudes and beliefs about criminal behavior, education, employment, substance abuse, and interpersonal conflict. Studies have found them to be as good as static factors in predicting recidivism.

When multiple agencies and programs are involved with assisting the offender, careful monitoring and coordination efforts must be in place to make sure needed services are accessible. Case management is particularly important so that valuable information is not lost and to ensure that clients' needs are being met. Offenders may not know how to access services, because they may not know what is available or even what they need. Case managers can help significantly in this process and may be pivotal in the successful long-term rehabilitation of the offender.

The community partnership process needs to be continually evaluated and changed when data so indicate. Outcome evaluation is important for both the offender and the partnership. Many programs do not document their processes and outcomes using strong research designs, so this is an area of possible improvement.

Community and faith-based organizations (CFBOs) can be valuable partners in correctional programs, but bridging the gap between large government bureaucracies and small, nonprofit service providers can be challenging. There is some documentation that unless they are carefully crafted, community partnerships may be blamed when serious criminals are put back into the community without sufficient monitoring and support. As a result, they may pose a risk to the community, which may withdraw its support for community correctional programs. The programs may also result in disempowered professionals if it is unclear who has ultimate responsibility and ownership. If community-based programs are to become a recognized alternative, research on their development and effectiveness is needed. Training programs in criminal justice must move toward a community-based approach to the academic, professional, geographic, social, and cultural contexts. Community organizations must communicate and partner together in practice, not just on paper, in order to be truly effective.

Yvonne Vissing
Salem State University

See also Community-Based Centers; Community-Based Vocational Networks; COMPASS Program; Faith-Based Initiatives; Neighborhood Probation; Project Safeway; SMART Partnership

Further Readings

Clear, T. and R. Corbett. "The Community Corrections of Place." *National Institute of Justice Journal*, v.23/1 (Winter 1999). http://ncjrs.gov/pdffiles/168618 .pdf#page=73 (Accessed July 2011).

Dolce, Philip C. "Building a Criminal Justice Program as an Educational, Community, and Professional Resource." *Community College Journal of Research and Practice*, v.28/2 (February 2004).

Epstein, J. et al. *School, Family and Community Partnerships: Your Handbook for Action*. Thousand Oaks, CA: Corwin, 2008.

Gendreau, P. "Offender Rehabilitation: What We Know and What Needs to Be Done." *Criminal Justice and Behavior*, v.23/1 (1996).

Johnson, T., K. Selber, and M. Lauderdale. "Developing Quality Services for Offenders and Families: An Innovative Partnership." *Child Welfare*, v.77/5 (September/October 1998).

Kane, Leah. "Partnerships Between States and CFBOs: Challenges and Opportunities." *Corrections Today*, v.71/6 (December 2009).

Mayo, Marjorie. "Partnerships for Regeneration and Community Development." *Critical Social Policy*, v.17/52 (August 1997).

Petersilia, J. *Community Corrections: Probation, Parole and Intermediate Sanctions*. New York: Oxford University Press, 1998.

Pranis, K. "Peacemaking Circles." *Corrections Today*, v.59/7 (1997). http://www.doc.mn.gov/rj/documents/ Peacemakingcircles.pdf (Accessed July 2011).

Rhine, E., J. R. Matthews II, L. A. Sampson, and H. Daley. "Citizens' Circles: Community Collaboration in Reentry." *Corrections Today*, v.65/5 (2003).

Rumgay, Judith and Sharon Cowan. "Pitfalls and Prospects in Partnership: Probation Programmes for Substance Misusing Offenders." *Journal of Criminal Justice*, v.37/2 (May 1998).

Whittaker, J., S. Schinke, and L. Gilchrest. "The Ecological Paradigm in Child, Youth, and Family Services: Implications for Policy and Practice." *Social Service Review*, v.60/4 (June 1986).

Wolfe, Alan. *Whose Keeper? Social Change and Moral Obligation*. Berkeley: University of California Press, 1989.

Yoon, J. and J. Nickel. *Reentry Partnerships: A Guide for States and Faith-Based and Community Organizations*. New York: Council of State Governments Justice Center, 2008.

COMMUNITY SERVICE ORDER

As used in both adult and juvenile justice systems in the United States and abroad, community service orders are sanctions that require convicted, adjudicated, or diverted offenders to work (usually unpaid) for a specified number of hours for governmental or nonprofit agencies. Service programs vary in the forms of work required from offenders, as well as the duration of service obligations. Common forms of service work include physical labor as well as semiskilled and skilled work performed for public or nonprofit agencies. The duration of service obligations may vary by offense as well as by municipality, from a few hours to hundreds of hours. Since their initial use as alternative programs for traffic offenders in the 1960s, community service orders (often referred to as "community service") have become one of the most frequently used types of sanctions in both juvenile and adult justice.

History

First employed in Alameda County, California, in 1966, community service orders were designed as an alternative for female traffic violators who faced jail time as a consequence of unpaid fines. According to M. Tonry and M. Lynch, this program received "widespread interest" and was influential in the implementation of similar programs in the United States. By the late 1970s, community service orders were being used regularly in many juvenile and adult criminal courts.

Public support for community service in the United States has remained strong since its inception. However, reasons for this support have shifted over time, as the goals and justifications for community service have been adapted to meet changing justice philosophies. In the 1970s and early 1980s, for example, community service programs were supported as cost-effective and potentially rehabilitative alternatives to incarceration. Organizations such as the Law Enforcement Assistance Administration (LEAA) provided millions of dollars in assistance to jurisdictions in order to establish community service programs in support of these goals.

By the mid-1980s, however, research on community service had found only small or no net reductions of recidivism for both youth and adult offenders. Other research found cases that suggested a net-widening effect on offenders sentenced to community service. Its rehabilitative promise waned, as did support and funding for its use as an alternative to incarceration. Nevertheless, throughout the 1980s the use of community service orders remained popular within juvenile and adult criminal courts, less as a means of rehabilitation or alternative to incarceration than as one of a growing number of punitive sanctions popular within the growing "tough on crime" turn in criminal and juvenile justice practices. The purpose of community service itself was thus largely reframed as one of retribution or deterrence, and along with other sanctions, such as boot camps, house arrest, and intensive supervision, community service came to be seen as an "intermediate" form of punishment, somewhere between community supervision and incarceration.

Community service has also gained substantial, although not unanimous, support within the field of restorative justice. As early as the 1970s, supporters of restorative justice argued that community service could be used to reintegrate offenders back into their communities. More recent work in restorative applications of community service have focused on its use as a "symbolic" or even literal type of restitution to the community and on its usefulness in forging interactions between community members and offenders. Others have been more critical of the use of community service in restorative justice, however, both in principle and in practice. Several critics have suggested that whatever are the benefits of community service, this approach fails to meet the basic definition of "restorative justice" insofar as it is not directed at meeting victims' needs. Other problems identified by critics and even some supporters include the tendency of justice organizations to hijack or merely relabel their community service programs as "restorative."

Community Service Outcomes

Much of the research that has been done on community service for both adult and youth offenders has focused on whether or not such programs decrease recidivism. G. Bazemore and D. R. Karp argue that most studies of youth community service have found either a small reduction or no net increase in reoffending, and this is in line with other research on the use of community service (not distinguishing between adult and juvenile offenders) that also has found no significant differences in recidivism between community service and other sanctions.

Community service programs have been assessed in dimensions other than recidivism, however, including individual indicators (such as rates of completion) and community indicators (such as total hours and/or monetary value of service work). The best known of these studies was Douglas McDonald's research on the Vera Institute service program in New York City in 1986. This study found that community service at the very least did not increase recidivism, and it also functioned to divert offenders from prison and provide substantial cost savings to the city in the form of more than 60,000 hours of free labor in 1984 alone. Later studies of service agencies, such as those used by Vermont Reparative Probationers, have found high rates of program completion (91 percent) and high rates of agency satisfaction (94 percent).

Survey and assessment research on participant satisfaction in community service programs has been cautiously positive. One study on 19 adult community service programs within the United States found that both offenders and victims believed the requirements of such programs were "fair," and offenders who completed the programs by and large viewed their experience as "useful." Another study, on the use of youth restorative community service in Deschutes County, Oregon, found that this program effectively served immediate community needs, such as the building of low-income housing, and these projects were supported through both time and money from community volunteers and organizations. Outside of the United States, research on the use of community service has also found high levels of offender satisfaction with service work in both

New Zealand and Scotland. Research from the latter also drew an important link between reduced recidivism and offender satisfaction with service assignments—noteworthy in that it suggests how offenders perceive the quality and purpose of their service work, which may influence rates of reoffending.

William R. Wood
University of Auckland

See also Community Corrections and Sanctions; Community Corrections as an Alternative to Imprisonment; Effectiveness of Community Corrections; Net Widening; Public Opinion of Community Corrections; Recidivism; Restorative Justice

Further Readings

Bazemore, G. and D. R. Karp. "A Civic Justice Corps: Community Service as a Means of Reintegration." *Justice Policy Journal*, v.1 (2004).

Bouffard, Jeffrey A. and Lisa R. Muftić. "The Effectiveness of Community Service Sentences Compared to Traditional Fines for Low-Level Offenders." *The Prison Journal*, v.87/2 (2007).

Harris, Robert J. and T. Wing Lo. "Community Service: Its Use in Criminal Justice." *International Journal of Offender Therapy and Comparative Criminology*, v.46/4 (2002).

McDonald, Douglas Corry. *Punishment Without Walls: Community Service Sentences in New York City*. New Brunswick, NJ: Rutgers University Press, 1986.

Tonry, M. and M. Lynch. "Intermediate Sanctions." *Crime and Justice: A Review of Research*, v.20 (1996).

COMMUNITY-BASED CENTERS

Community corrections agencies employ a large number of centers that are located in various neighborhoods. These centers have various missions, objectives, rehabilitative philosophies, punitive modalities, and techniques, and they serve a diverse array of offenders under different forms of community corrections supervision. Therefore, a number of community-oriented community corrections programs exist; some of these are residential, whereas others are nonresidential programs that fill a variety of needs regarding effective offender supervision in the community.

Community-based programs form a component of the correctional system termed intermediate sanctions, to denote punishments that are more stringent than basic probation or parole but less restrictive than prison. Intermediate sanctions have their roots in arrangements that resemble halfway houses, which were started by the Quakers in the 19th century. These programs were created to assist people just released from prison to become reintegrated into society. In the 1980s, intermediate sanction programs became very popular as courts and parole boards sought options to overcrowded prison systems. These programs exist because straight incarceration is too severe a punishment for many

Community-based centers can provide a cost-effective rehabilitation facility in or near residential areas that are convenient to offenders. These centers can reduce the likelihood of return to crime and imprisonment while improving community safety. (Photos.com)

low need/low risk offenders and basic probation with parole field supervision is often not sufficiently rigorous or effective for some high need/high risk offenders. Community-based centers represent an appropriate punishment philosophy because they comprise a "happy medium" of offender sanctions, especially when the costs of incarceration in prison settings are too high for most jurisdictions to support. While some intermediate sanctions—such as intensive probation supervision, house arrest, home confinement, electronic monitoring, and community service work—are not what are termed community-based centers, others—such as community residential centers (including halfway houses and transitional centers), diversion and restitution programs, shock-based programs, day reporting centers, and a variety of adjunct community programs (including substance abuse treatment centers that cater heavily to community corrections populations)—do constitute what are known as community-based centers.

Characteristics and Goals

Although community-based centers are extremely diverse, four basic characteristics can be distinguished. First, all of the programs are housed in buildings located in or near residential areas that can easily be accessed by offenders under supervision. Second, there are a number of practitioners—such as professional and paraprofessional correctional staff (officers or agents), counseling personnel, social workers, and medical personnel—who provide services to the offenders. Another characteristic is that there is a well-defined system of accountability to sentencing courts, parole boards, or juvenile authorities; this accountability is maintained and reported to officials by community corrections personnel working in these programs. Fourth, community-based centers are aligned with community resources, and staff members act as liaisons between the centers and community resources. Last, the management of these programs is assumed by administrators who are available for crisis and special needs assistance, should crisis situations arise.

The goals of these community-based programs vary by type, mission, and philosophy but generally exist to assist persons under community corrections supervision with four main objectives: (1) to reintegrate offenders back into society, (2) to facilitate rehabilitation of these offenders, (3) to provide sentencing and punishment options (particularly when

overcrowding in institutional correctional facilities exists), and (4) to assist offenders in becoming more accountable for their actions. Reintegration, in which criminal offenders who have been institutionalized attempt to resume normal activities with their communities, has been a goal in recent decades for the correctional system generally, and this responsibility has particularly fallen to the community-based centers. Rehabilitation has long been a goal of the correctional system, and helping offenders with problem solving and issues such as addiction is addressed in these centers. Sentencing and punishment options for courts and parole boards are extremely important, especially when overcrowding in correctional institutions occurs and alternatives to incarceration are needed. Community-based centers are particularly useful when graduated sanctions (increased or decreased punitive and restrictive sanctions that are imposed in accordance with offender behavior) are deemed beneficial. Community-based centers also provide such high levels of supervision that offender accountability is much greater than in regular community corrections facilities.

Although much of the supervision in community corrections is performed in the form of basic field supervision that takes place at offenders' places of residence or employment and that requires offenders to make office, phone, and other contacts with a probation or parole officer, many programs require offenders to participate in programs and sometimes reside in facilities that involve more than basic at-home monitoring. These programs are often termed "intermediate sanctions" programs and can be utilized through volunteer involvement, sentencing through a probation or parole process (normally through a revocation proceeding), or direct sentencing by a court. Again, these options require varying degrees of engagement, from a few required meetings to full residential placement.

Types of Centers

One type of community-based program is the community residential center (CRC). There are many types of CRCs, which can be publicly or privately operated and serve either probationers or parolees, males or females, and adult or juvenile offenders. They often focus on special needs and risk offenders, such as substance abusers, the mentally ill, or those with employment problems. Many programs fall under the CRC category, including halfway houses and transitional centers. The halfway house gets its name from the fact that the program is halfway between prison and the community. In these centers, offenders live under close probation or parole supervision in preparation for returning fully to the community. They are provided with living accommodations, food, counseling services, medical resources, and vocational training. Strict monitoring by community corrections personnel ensures compliance with all court- or parole-ordered conditions. These programs have a long history in the United States and reflect the current trend toward offender reintegration into the community.

Diversion and restitution centers are community corrections programs designed to help probationers and parolees to maintain employment and abide by conditions ordered by the sentencing courts or parole boards. These nonconfining residential programs offer substance abuse counseling, life skills training, and other services. Offenders in these programs work in the community, and the money received from their employment goes to court-ordered financial obligations, such as restitution, court costs, and child support. Like CRCs, diversion and restitution centers are designed to reintegrate offenders back into the community after a short period of residence at the center. Diversion and restitution centers also help satisfy another key focus in corrections: the idea of restorative justice. Restorative justice emphasizes the reparation of harm to a victim by an offender; these centers require the violator to provide restitution to those who have suffered monetary losses as a result of their actions.

Shock-based programs occur in another type of community-based center. The primary purpose of these programs is to shock or scare offenders—often juveniles, youthful adults, situational offenders, and first-time nonviolent felony offenders—into obeying the law. They often take a military, or "boot camp," approach involving rigid military drills, intense physical training, high levels of regimentation and military discipline, and submission to authority in order to reinforce the scare tactics. The hope is that these programs will have more permanent effects than those emerging from straight incarceration. Despite inconclusive and sometimes contradictory program evaluation findings, the programs are often sought out and promoted by politicians because of their perceived beneficial effects by the general public.

There are nonresidential centers that service community corrections offenders as well. Day reporting centers are programs that are in operation during normal business hours (during the day) and closely supervise probationers and parolees by requiring them to report in for monitoring for substance abuse or other needs and risks. These centers also assist with employment, family, educational, and other needs. The programs have elements of intensive probation supervision, home confinement, house arrest, electronic monitoring, early release programs, and community residential centers (albeit in a nonresidential environment). These programs are sometimes called "invisible prisons" or "halfway houses without houses" and are normally located in areas that can allow correctional staff to easily monitor offender behavior. Often offenders who are housed in area jails are allowed to finish out the last few weeks or months at home as long as they report to the personnel at these centers at prescribed times.

Although not always connected to an official community corrections agency, community treatment programs of different types are often used by persons on probation or parole or under juvenile supervision. Perhaps the most frequently utilized programs of this type are substance abuse programs, because of the high number of community corrections offenders with problems in this area. Locales that have drug courts especially utilize the services of substance abuse treatment programs. These programs consist of inpatient and outpatient treatment in an array of different modalities, many of them structured according to the 12-step model of substance abuse treatment. A special type of drug program is called a therapeutic community; it exists in both institutional settings and community, or "free world," environments and takes a holistic approach to substance abuse treatment services. Other community-based programs are those that focus on mental illness, gang activity, sex offenses (providing individual and group counseling), educational services, vocational training, health classes, parental skills, and life skills.

NIMBY

One of the problems associated with community-based centers involves the "not in my backyard," or NIMBY, syndrome. This term references the fact that many programs that house or serve persons convicted of criminal offenses are located in residential or mixed-use areas but are not welcome by citizens who live in the area. There are some benefits, however, to locating these programs in the "backyard": Some programs benefit communities by providing a limited number of jobs in the areas in which the community-based centers are formed; there is also the possibility of a deterrent effect in that the high visibility of correctional personnel in the area can drive potential offenders from the area. However, many community residents are wary of or downright averse to the housing (or frequent visits) of community corrections offenders in their neighborhoods.

Many centers and community facilities serve persons under some form of community corrections supervision. These programs provide a broad variety of resources to adult and juvenile probation and parole offenders; they are sometimes directly connected to community corrections agencies and sometimes simply an adjunct. Some programs are state-affiliated, while others are run by private enterprises. They address various offender needs and risks, such as substance abuse, mental illness, sex offenses, and gang-related behavior. Some programs are residential (over short periods of time), some are semi-residential, and others are completely based in the community. All operate to meet the requirements of effective supervision of offenders in the community.

Leonard A. Steverson
South Georgia College

See also Boot Camps; Day Reporting Centers; Group Homes; Halfway Houses and Residential Centers; Residential Correctional Programs; Residential Programs for Juveniles; Restitution Centers; Therapeutic Communities

Further Readings

Champion, Dean John. *Corrections in the United States: A Contemporary Perspective*, 4th ed. Upper Saddle River, NJ: Pearson Prentice Hall, 2005.

Champion, Dean John. *Probation, Parole, and Community Corrections in the United States*, 6th ed. Upper Saddle River, NJ: Pearson Prentice Hall, 2008.

Clear, Todd R. and Harry R. Dammer. *The Offender in the Community*, 2nd ed. Belmont, CA: Thomson Wadsworth, 2003.

Federal Bureau of Prisons. *Community Corrections Faqs*. http://www.bop.gov/locations/cc/ccc_faqs.jsp (Accessed June 2011).

Stevens, Dennis J. *Community Corrections: An Applied Approach*. Upper Saddle River, NJ: Pearson Prentice Hall, 2006.

COMMUNITY-BASED VOCATIONAL NETWORKS

Human behavior has traditionally been attributed to a series of adaptations to various stimuli within the surrounding environment. Studies continue to indicate that we as individuals will tend to gravitate toward that to which our minds and bodies have become accustomed as everyday patterns of experiences and expectations. The same concept is applied to individuals who have been incarcerated for a period of time and who must one day face the turmoil and confusion of returning back to free society after a long-standing absence from the norms, guidelines, and obligations that govern interactions within their new setting. The empirical literature is clear and compelling: Approximately 30 to 70 percent of offenders released from jail or prison fail within three years of release. This failure is evidence of two key problems: the inability of jails and prisons to adequately address the risk factors that increase likelihood of failure upon release, and the lack of prosocial networks and resources available to offenders during the community reintegration, or "reentry," process. Offenders who are unprepared to meet the demands, structural constraints, and normative patterns of society, after leaving prison, will undoubtedly return to their previous lifestyle of deviance and criminality, rendering their prison experience but a mere and temporary break in a vicious cycle of arrest, incarceration, release, and rearrest.

The toll this cycle takes on our social and economic structure is seldom examined in public circles, as both citizens and politicians continue to resolve the debate over crime and punishment in the direction of stricter punishment, longer sentences, more imprisonment (necessitating the building of more prisons), and generally "getting tougher" on criminals. The untold story, however, is that the overwhelming majority of offenders who are in prison will eventually be released into the community—with harsher laws, after longer periods of separation, and with very little preparation to deal with the struggles and conflicts that are posed by reentry.

These individuals will return to our society, move into our communities, occupy our neighborhoods, and live down the street from us. It would be beneficial to every individual in society to ensure that these offenders are well equipped with the structures necessary for their positive reintegration into the norms and values of productive citizens. The implementation of community-based vocational networks as a component of reintegration is a step in that direction and, therefore, a critical topic of debate and discussion within academic and professional circles in the field of community corrections.

The task of community correctional supervision agencies is to invest in programming that allows offenders to reintegrate positively into society and become productive, law-abiding citizens. One source of funding for such programming has traditionally focused on the concept of transitional intervention for offenders who are being released from prison into the community. The hallmark of this approach is the successful integration of offenders into the community through increased accountability and social support. An essential component of this structure has been the development of partnerships within the community to provide offenders with the services needed to bridge the gap between law enforcement and community and to assist offenders in becoming productive, law-abiding citizens. It is a well-documented fact in criminal justice research that the overwhelming majority of offenders released into the community after an extended period of incarceration experience tremendous difficulty in adjusting to life outside prison. This difficulty manifests itself in the ex-offender's inability to become stabilized with regard to housing, employment, family relationships, and other social responsibilities and obligations. Positive intervention on behalf of this population is essential to the successful goal of a reduction in recidivism.

What Are Community-Based Vocational Networks?

Community-based vocational networks are built on the notion that individuals placed in a situation of uncertainty, anxiety, and confusion need the support mechanisms necessary for positive integration. To better serve clients, these networks take a research-based approach that is tailored to the treatment needs of the particular offender population as well as the availability of resources within that community. In the effort to support and sustain formal intervention within a correctional setting, community-based vocational networks employ a proactive approach that directly addresses the struggles of reentry. Drawing on resources available within the community is a growing strategy used within community corrections to address the problem of offender reentry.

Immediately upon release from prison or jail, offenders are faced with a host of issues that must be addressed to ensure successful reentry. Many offenders must find stable housing, educational or vocational opportunities, substance abuse and mental health treatment, and other vital services while remaining compliant with all community supervision regulations. Gaps in service delivery therefore increase the chances of an offender's failing while on community supervision. Community-based vocational networks represent a strategy for filling in these gaps by providing career-planning services and support structures that increase accountability and encourage offenders to become more responsible. These neighborhood-based resources are designed to provide services that are more readily available and easily accessible to offenders throughout the community.

The goal of community-based vocational networks is to offer former inmates the tools, resources, and structured environments that support the learning of new behavior patterns geared toward strengthening ties with the local community, developing bonds and attachments to the workforce, and encouraging a crime-free lifestyle. In addition, the offender's family benefits by accessing a network of support and resources. Some of the stress is eased, and this increases the likelihood that family relationships damaged by criminal behavior will be mended and preserved. This is particularly beneficial to offenders' children. Although each program is designed to work on an individual level, the community as a whole is also a primary beneficiary. The community receives an infusion of services and resources for offenders and is thus better prepared to receive these offenders and assist them in avoiding breaking the law.

The Case for Community-Based Vocational Networks

According to research, securing and sustaining employment is one of the biggest challenges facing offenders returning to the community. Assessment instruments continue to show that offenders have significant deficits in the areas of education, vocational training, and employability. Moreover, experts note that education alone is not sufficient to break the cycle of reoffending. For educational programming to be effective, it must be paired with vocational and job skills training that is tailored to the specific needs of the offender. Integrating employment as a component of wraparound correctional intervention has proven to be a best practice within the field of community corrections.

Community-based vocational networks provide offenders within the community a critical framework for avoiding negative influences and staying focused on the process of reintegration. By increasing employment opportunities for offenders, community-based vocational networks help offenders become more self-sufficient, have access to a legitimate source of income, and become involved in a conventional, crime-free lifestyle. Moreover, through the various components of community-based vocational networks, offenders are more likely to be matched with employment that is suitable with their type and level of skill, as well as their personal goals and interests. This is a key to increasing the probability of job retention, as well as a successful relationship between the employer and employee. Studies show that offenders on community supervision who have stable employment and earn higher wages have more family stability and social ties to the community, as well as lower rates of recidivism. In the long run, therefore, community-based vocational networks contribute to an overall cost savings for the correctional system.

Components of Community-Based Vocational Networks

The various components of community-based vocational networks are designed to help ex-offenders not only find suitable, meaningful employment but also develop a framework of thinking that will ensure their success in the job market and in their daily lives. The community-based vocational network model provides a broad range of employment services, including employment history and skills assessment, vocational training, job readiness programming, employment placement opportunities, and job support resources.

A key to successful employment is the ability of vocational programming staff to be able to capitalize on the skills of each individual offender when conducting job placement services. This is done through the administration of assessment tests to each individual offender that includes an evaluation of work history, education, vocational aptitude, personal skills, individual interests, and long-term career goals, as well as deficits and barriers to success. Based on this assessment, goals are established and a long-range plan is developed that is customized to the particular program participant.

As technology has taken over the major industries within the labor market, the need for specialized skills to keep up with the demands of the workplace has become a major obstacle for offenders seeking employment. Vocational training has thus become an integral component of the community-based vocational network model. Vocational training coincides with educational programming to provide job seekers with classroom instruction that focuses on developing technical skills. Preparing offenders for the workplace goes beyond the acquisition of specialized training to include an awareness of job opportunities, as well as an understanding of workplace dynamics involving expectations and interpersonal interactions.

The job-readiness programming component of community-based vocational networks focuses on the specific demands and expectations of a prospective employer. Job-readiness programming takes on the form a specific workshop or apprenticeship opportunity, whereby the participant is able to gain an interactive understanding of the demands and expectations of the job. This allows program participants to become more aware of their own skills and potential, set positive work goals, and learn how to become successful in a particular job.

Employment placement relies on establishing partnerships with various community agencies to expand the network of opportunities to develop business relationships. It seeks to match jobs with program participants who have achieved certain skills and a certain level of job readiness. Employment placement takes a case management approach whereby the employment needs of the client are provided, as well as the specific performance needs of the prospective employer.

A final component of community-based vocational networks includes the provision of support staff who can offer clients access to "hands-on" assistance. These services focus on résumé development or enhancement, mock interviews, role-play in conflict management, and extensive job searches. This is essential to offender success in terms of developing the necessary skills to build positive relationships between prospective employers and coworkers. Moreover, job support resources also allow clients the opportunity to obtain assistance with logistical job readiness needs, such as having the proper clothing for the workplace, as well as transportation to a job site for an interview. Job support resources also address the areas of retention with follow-up assessments and reevaluations.

Aida Y. Hass
Missouri State University

See also Community Partnerships; Community-Based Centers; Reentry Programs and Initiatives; Reintegration Into Communities

Further Readings

Cnaan, Ram A., Jeffrey Draine, Beverly Frazier, and Jill W. Sinha. "Ex-Prisoners' Re-Entry: An Emerging Frontier and a Social Work Challenge." *Journal of Policy Practice*, v.7/2–3 (2008).

Pavis, Ross. "Preparing Federal Prison Inmates for Employment After Release: An Innovation at the Federal Bureau of Prisons." *Journal of Correctional Education*, v.53/4 (2002).

Urban Institute, Justice Policy Center. "Prisoner Re-Entry in Houston: Community Perspectives." 2009. http://www.urban.org/UploadedPDF/411901_prisoner_reentry_houston.pdf (Accessed July 2011).

Zweig, Janine, Jennifer Yahner, and Cindy Redcross. *Recidivism Effects of the Center for Employment Opportunities (CEO) Program Vary by Former Prisoners' Risk of Reoffending.* Oakland, CA: MDRC, 2010.

COMPASS PROGRAM

Since the 1990s, Rhode Island, among several other states, has developed new programs designed to improve successful community reentry of inmates following incarceration. With assistance from federal funding, such as that available through the Serious and Violent Offender Reentry Initiative (SVORI), one such program, COMPASS—Challenging Offenders to Maintain Positive Associations and Social Stability—integrates transitional services, focusing on return to the community with a long-term goal of decreasing the high rate of recidivism.

With more than 600,000 prisoners released into the community nationwide each year, large cities are especially impacted by the challenges of increased risk to public safety and a limited availability of jobs, housing, and social services for the returning ex-offender. In 2003, the United States made $100 million available in grant funds to develop, enhance, or expand programs to facilitate the entry of adults and juvenile offenders returning to communities. The National Institute of Corrections has provided guidance for these programs in the Transition from Prison to Community Initiative, which utilizes institutional program plans (IPPs) during incarceration and transitional accountability plans (TAPs) following release. TAPs include specified goals for each participant and a graduated imposition of sanctions when these goals are not met.

Monitoring of participants following release will also be accomplished by coordination with local law enforcement. Inmate records are accessible by local police through a computer system integrated into the Rhode Island Department of Corrections archives. Other services are synchronized through a community facility referred to as the Family Life Center (FLC), staffed by personnel especially sensitive to the needs of the offender population. FLC services include family reunification and counseling, faith-based mentoring, and linkages with other community resources designed to evaluate and meet the needs of the parolee. In addition, the FLC

Programs like COMPASS (Challenging Offenders to Maintain Positive Associations and Social Stability) are generally associated with better outcomes for ex-prisoners in obtaining housing and employment and an easier transitional return to the community. (Photos.com)

incorporates a restorative justice emphasis that coordinates victim services (such as restitution and the selection of a victims' advisory board). In addition to crime avoidance as a central aim of COMPASS, FLC encourages embracing prosocial activities that include familial responsibilities.

In addition to the post-release feature of COMPASS, equally important is the focus on inmates' rehabilitation early in the prison term. Inmates selected for COMPASS participation must have an IPP that addresses rehabilitative programming throughout their sentence. This IPP must include assessment procedures that provide for testing during several important time periods, including sentencing, release, at six months following release, and again at twelve months after release. Such procedures are designed to provide risk and needs information useful in developing the IPP and TAP.

Federal guidelines detail objectives in the COMPASS mission, including a priority of preventing reoffending and a second goal of maintaining public safety. Nationwide, a multisite evaluation was designed to determine how effective the SVORI-supported programs were in accomplishing these goals. Results from the study indicated that SVORI programs were successful in increasing access to services and programming related to employment, education, skill development, and substance abuse treatment. For example, 75 percent of participants in SVORI programs such as COMPASS were involved in these specialized services while incarcerated, as compared to 51 percent of ex-offenders who were not identified as SVORI participants. However, while the SVORI-funded programs were effective in providing more access to such services while inmates were incarcerated, it was also clear that the availability of prison services was not sufficient to meet the expressed needs of prisoners. Therefore, SVORI inmates reported needing more than half of available services (54 percent) while receiving 34 percent, as compared to only 22 percent of non-SVORI inmates. Authors concluded that these programs were still in developing and implementation phases, requiring several years to reach full implementation.

It was also found that service delivery declined substantially, on average, following release into the community, indicating that the services were not sustained during the most critical, high-risk time of need, when the inmate returned to the home community. For example, 51 percent of SVORI participants (as compared to 44 percent of non-SVORI participants) reported receiving educational services in prison, with a precipitous drop to 11 percent SVORI (compared to 8 percent non-SVORI) participants during the three months following release. That remained unchanged during the 12 months following return to the community.

Although programs such as COMPASS were generally associated with better outcomes in housing, employment, substance use, and self-reported criminal behavior, there were only slight differences in abstinence from illegal drugs for the SVORI participants (46 percent) as compared to the non-SVORI participants (43 percent). Similarly, rearrest rates were high for both groups at 24-month follow-up, with 68 percent of SVORI participants being arrested, compared to 71 percent of non-SVORI participants.

The study authors concluded that programs such as COMPASS will need to be given sufficient time to implement their multicomponent, multiphase programs before it is possible to determine their effectiveness. The overall multisite research did result in an extensive SVORI dataset that the authors conclude provides an opportunity for future research to explore questions about what works, independent of local programming and participant characteristics.

Clive D. Kennedy
Chicago School of Professional Psychology,
Los Angeles

See also Effectiveness of Community Corrections; Probation and Parole: Intensive Supervision; Reentry Courts; Reentry Programs and Initiatives; Reintegration Into Communities

Further Readings

Lattimore, P. K., D. M. Steffey, and C. A. Visher. *Prisoner Reentry Experiences of Adult Males: Characteristics, Service Receipt, and Outcomes of Participants in the SVORI Multi-Site Evaluation.* Research Triangle Park, NC: RTI International, 2009.

Lattimore, P. K., C. A. Visher, L. Winterfield, C. Lindquist, and S. Brumbaugh. "Implementation of Prisoner Reentry Programs: Findings From the Serious and Violent Offender Reentry Initiative Multi-Site Evaluation." *Justice Research and Policy*, v.7/2 (2005).

Rhode Island Department of Corrections. *The COMPASS Project: Challenging Offenders to Maintain Positive Associations and Social Stability.* http://www.doc.ri.gov/index.php (Accessed July 2011).

CONDITIONAL SENTENCING AND RELEASE

Conditional sentencing, commonly referred to as "informal probation," is also known as summary probation, court probation, or bench probation. Like all probation, this form of probation requires that an offender abide by certain conditions while on release in the community. The granting of this type of probation is at the discretion of the sentencing judge and is generally reserved for adults who commit misdemeanor offenses or for juvenile offenders. Unlike formal probation, informal probation is less stringent in terms of monitoring in the community and the length of the term. However, like formal probation, informal probation may come with various conditions. If these conditions are abided by without further incident or arrest, then the offender avoids a jail sentence for his or her crime.

Conditional release, more commonly known as parole, allows the offender to be released into the community to serve out the remainder of a prison sentence. This release is often determined by a parole board and requires strict monitoring of the offender, typically by a parole officer, for the duration of the conditional release. If the offender violates any of the terms of the release, he or she is subject to the revocation of parole and may be returned to prison to serve out the remainder of the sentence.

Conditional Sentencing (Informal Probation)

With informal probation, the judge orders the offender to a revocable release into the community as that person's primary sentence, often following a guilty plea. This sentence will usually come with mandatory conditions to which the offender must adhere, such as attending drug or alcohol treatment, paying fines, or completing community service. The primary condition that must be met is that the offender must not commit any further crimes. Unlike formal probation, which involves close supervision by a probation officer and often follows a term in jail, informal probation is more typically used in lieu of prison time altogether.

This type of probation is often offered to juvenile offenders if they confess to a relatively minor crime and/or as a diversionary sentencing option. If the sentencing judge determines that an incarceration term may be detrimental to the offender's rehabilitation or place the offender at higher risk of recidivism, then the use of informal probation may be a viable option. Not limited to juveniles, this type of probation may also be offered to adults who have pleaded guilty to a misdemeanor offense, such as driving under the influence, possession of drug paraphernalia, or vandalism. In many jurisdictions, the use of informal probation is formally prohibited for individuals who have committed a felony. Generally, informal probation may be substituted at the judge's discretion whenever the state's legislation permits the use of probation as a sentencing option for the particular offense committed.

Far more lenient than incarceration, informal probation is also considered less stringent than formal probation, both in reporting and in monitoring and the duration of the term. Unlike formal probation, informal probation generally does not involve the offender being assigned to a probation officer, and the offender is therefore not closely monitored while on probation. Rather, he or she is typically responsible for reporting directly to the court regarding adherence to the conditions set by the judge and maintenance of good behavior. Informal probation terms also tend to be shorter than formal probation terms, at times only as long as a month, as opposed to the possibility of years under a formal probation term. However, placing an individual on informal probation does not erase or negate a criminal conviction, as that person's admission of guilt will remain on his or her criminal record, much as it would if jail or formal probation were ordered.

The judge's decision to sentence an offender to a term of informal probation, rather than formal probation or incarceration, depends on numerous circumstances. These may include the nature of the offense, or whether there are particular circumstances, such as drug and alcohol addiction issues, mental health issues, or other treatment needs that would be better provided outside the formal incarceration or probation system. For juveniles, the judge may also consider the offender's family situation, performance in school, the peer network, and other means of support. In general, the decision to place an individual on informal probation will rely as well on the emotional stability of the individual and the judge's determination of whether there is a good likelihood of success for the individual on informal probation.

Although the individual on informal probation is not required to meet with a probation officer and thus is not as closely monitored as someone on formal probation, the court will be advised if the individual misses an important deadline, does not attend counseling or program sessions, or is arrested for another offense. If it is found that the individual has violated the terms of informal probation, he or she will often report to the court in a separate hearing to undergo a sentence adjustment by the judge. The sentence adjustment is at the discretion of the sentencing judge and will depend heavily on the nature and severity of the violation. Outcomes may include being sent to jail, the revocation of the informal probation sentence and its replacement with a term of formal probation, or a reinstatement of the informal probation on the same terms.

Conditional Release

Conditional release is more commonly known as parole, wherein an offender may be released into the community prior to the expiration of his or her term of imprisonment. Parole was first used in New York in 1876 and became prevalent in most states in the following years. However, many states have since abolished parole, opting instead for "truth in sentencing," whereby the amount of time handed down to an offender by the sentencing judge is the amount of time the offender must remain in custody.

For those states still utilizing a parole system, the terms and conditions of parole may vary. Generally, a parole board is charged with reviewing case histories of those eligible for parole, deciding upon the conditions should parole be granted, and ultimately approving or denying the conditional release into the community. The time line for parole eligibility is often governed by statute and may vary, depending on the nature and severity of the crime the offender committed. For lesser offenses, the parole board may have the discretion to decide when an offender may be eligible for parole.

Supervision of those on parole, while less expensive than housing offenders in custody, is intensive and closely monitored for the remainder of the term the offender would have spent in prison. This allows the offender to start contributing to society through active employment and to continue rehabilitation in the hope of preventing any relapse back into crime. The consistent supervision and monitoring of the offender serve as protections for the community,

while allowing the offender, under strict conditions, to reintegrate into that community. Often these conditions will involve securing employment, abstaining from drugs and alcohol, and avoiding certain areas or acquaintances who the court feels would be detrimental to the parolee's success.

If an offender, while on conditional release, violates a term of parole or commits a new offense, he or she may be subject to a revocation of the conditional release and can be ordered to return to prison to serve out the remainder of the original sentence.

Nahanni Pollard
Simon Fraser University

See also Community Corrections as an Add-On to Imprisonment; Community Corrections as an Alternative to Imprisonment; Discretionary Release; Good Time and Merit Time; Juvenile and Youth Offenders; Offender Supervision; Probation: Early Termination; Probation and Judicial Reprieve; Probation and Parole: Intensive Supervision; Reintegration Into Communities

Further Readings

Petersilia, Joan. *Reforming Probation and Parole in the 21st Century*. Lanham, MD: American Correctional Association, 2002.

Roberts, Julian V. and Allan Manson. *The Future of Conditional Sentencing: Perspectives of Appellate Judges*. Ottawa, ON: Department of Justice Canada, Research and Statistics, 2004.

Siegel, Larry J. and Joseph J. Senna. *Essentials of Criminal Justice*. Belmont, CA: Wadsworth Cengage Learning, 2009.

U.S. Bureau of Justice Statistics. *Probation and Parole in the United States, 2009*. Washington, DC: U.S. Department of Justice, 2010.

West Group. *West's Encyclopedia of American Law*. St. Paul, MN: Author, 1998.

CONDITIONS OF COMMUNITY CORRECTIONS

The main purpose of community-based correctional programs is to allow offenders to reside within their community and maintain daily responsibilities while serving out their punishment for the crimes committed, rather than removing offenders from society and placing them into a correctional institution.

These programs often require the offender to abide by specific conditions while in the community in order to achieve three main goals: maintain public safety, reduce the likelihood of the offender violating the law, and allow the offender to improve his or her circumstances through educational training and treatment programs. The philosophy underlying these unique programs is that some offenders will be better served by remaining in their community while being sanctioned, rather than being detained in a harsh correctional institution that could do more harm than good. However, because the offender violated the law, conditions are used as a means of controlling his or her behavior while he or she resides within the community. If the offender violates the conditions of the program, further penalties and sanctions may be imposed.

Role of Conditions

Community-based correctional programs hold offenders accountable for their crimes while allowing them to remain within the community. The majority of offenders in the United States do not pose a threat to their communities or to themselves, and there are many benefits to keeping offenders in their own communities while they receive their punishment.

Offenders participating in community-based correctional programs are able to keep their employment and maintain family responsibilities. They will have more opportunity to participate in treatment, educational, or vocational programs that will strengthen their future as law-abiding citizens. Offenders remaining in the community will also be more likely to give back to the victims and the community they harmed through restitution and community services. Last, by remaining in the community for the course of their punishment, the offenders will also avoid exposure to the violent subculture and stigma associated with correctional institutions.

Community-based correctional programs typically serve one of three main purposes: as a diversion from prosecution, as a sentence alternative to incarceration, or as assistance for the transition from incarceration back to the community. There are also a variety of factors that determine which offenders are eligible for participation in a community-based correctional program, such as the seriousness of the offense, prior criminal history, potential risk to the community, and personal characteristics of the offender.

Then, once an offender has been determined eligible for a community-based correctional program, decisions will be made by the supervising agency about the types of conditions that should be placed on the offender during the course of the sanction. The conditions imposed on an offender will vary, depending on the type of program, circumstances of the case, and the offender's personal characteristics, but general guidelines can be followed when determining appropriate and inappropriate conditions.

Over the last few decades, multiple agencies, associations, and commissions have created recommendations for what are appropriate considerations and conditions for an individual participating in a community-based correctional program. Typically, the focus of these recommendations has been on probation; however, these standards have been used by many practitioners when determining appropriate conditions for people participating in a variety of programs. When examining the recommendations set forth by the American Bar Association's Standards for Criminal Justice and the Model Penal

The conditions placed on an offender while participating in a community-based correctional program vary. The offender may need to attend educational or vocational training, receive substance abuse treatment, or undergo psychiatric treatment. (Photos.com)

Code, by the National Advisory Commission on Criminal Justice Standards and Goals, and by the American Probation and Parole Association, there tends to be general agreement on what constitutes appropriate and inappropriate conditions.

The standards recommended by these entities for appropriate conditions of probation generally start with a provision that the probationer should receive written notice of the conditions of probation from the sentencing court, and also have the conditions explained to him or her, either by the court or by the probation officer. This protects the probationer from being penalized for violating conditions of which he or she might be unaware or ambiguous conditions that were not understood.

In terms of what conditions would be appropriate for probation, the American Bar Association (ABA) recommended that the only condition that should be required by statute is that the probationer lead a law-abiding life while released. Generally, this is considered the most important condition of probation, and any subsequent conditions should be related to helping the probationer accomplish this goal or be related to rehabilitation. Furthermore, many agree that these additional conditions should be determined on a case-by-case basis and should never restrict one's liberty without reasonable justification for doing so. This protects the probationer from receiving conditions that are arbitrary, unrelated to the probationer's individual situation, or considered to be unconstitutional.

General Considerations for Conditions

The exact conditions imposed on an offender will often vary, depending on the specific community-based correctional program, circumstances and characteristics of the offender, and the jurisdiction. The supervising agency will often have great discretion in deciding what conditions to impose on an offender. However, generally there are two main categories of conditions offenders have to follow while participating in a program: control-oriented conditions and reform-oriented conditions.

Control-oriented conditions are aimed at making sure the offender refrains from harming another person or committing a new crime while participating in the program. Risk assessments will often be conducted by diversion program staff, a probation

officer, or a parole board to determine the type of restrictions needed for an offender to maintain community safety. For example, offenders participating in a community-based correctional program will often be required to remain within the jurisdiction of the sentencing court unless granted permission to leave and to report to those overseeing their supervision when requested. Those supervising the offender will also need to be notified of any changes in address or employment and sometimes must be allowed to perform home visits. Offenders will also be required to refrain from associating with disreputable persons and places. Restrictions will sometimes be placed on possessing a firearm and consuming alcohol, and any use of illegal substances will be prohibited. The basis for enforcing these control-oriented conditions is that they help decrease the likelihood of recidivism by forcing the offender to refrain from repeating previous delinquent behaviors.

Reform-oriented conditions are also aimed at reducing the likelihood of recidivism but do so by helping the offender improve current circumstances. In addition to risk assessments, needs assessments may be performed in order to determine what assistance, treatment, or programs would benefit the offender and help him or her to avoid reoffending. For example, while participating in the community-based correctional program, an offender may be required to attend educational or vocational training, receive substance abuse treatment, or undergo psychiatric treatment. Enforcing these conditions not only may reduce the likelihood of recidivism but also may make it more likely that offenders will become productive members of society in the future. Furthermore, offenders who participate in these programs while in the community are able to maintain ties to family and friends, who can lend support to their efforts and increase their chances of success. In addition to honoring control- and reform-oriented conditions, an offender may be required to pay fines, provide restitution to victims, or engage in community service as part of a community-based correctional program.

Depending on the specific purpose of the community-based correctional program, conditions may be more or less restrictive in some aspects. For example, drug courts advance a popular type of diversion program. The offenders participating in a drug court program will likely be given more conditions related to attending treatment and refraining from using illicit substances. Similarly, probation, a common alternative sentence to incarceration, often varies in the level of intensity of supervision. Offenders receiving unsupervised probation may only have to report to the probation officer via telephone, whereas an offender receiving intensive supervision may have to meet face to face with the probation officer on a weekly basis. Although probationers and parolees will often be subject to similar conditions, parolees may have more stringent conditions placed on them, because they have spent an extended period of time incarcerated and their offenses may be of a more serious nature.

Violating Conditions

In most cases, whether it is a diversion program such as that assigned by a drug court or an alternative sanction such as probation, community-based correctional programs have given offenders a second chance, allowing them to avoid severer punishments if they successfully adhere to their programs. However, offenders who fail to abide by the required conditions may receive further sanctions or be removed from the program.

Upon entry into the program, the offender should be notified by the supervising agency of the possible consequences for violating any of the program's conditions. Generally, there are two ways in which an offender can violate the conditions of the program: by committing law violations and by performing a technical violation. For example, an offender could violate the law by committing a new misdemeanor or felony crime while participating in a community-based correctional program. A technical violation would not involve criminal conduct but rather a violation of the conditions of the offender's program, such as failure to report to the supervisor or failure to attend required substance abuse treatment.

If an offender violates the conditions of the community-based correctional program (commits a technical violation), it is often left up to the discretion of those in charge of supervising the offender, such as a probation or parole officer, to decide on a course of action. For example, if an offender fails to report to the probation officer, the officer can determine whether to ignore the violation, institute more conditions on the offender, or take formal action and report the violation to the court. Because of their seriousness, law violations are more likely to result in formal action against the offender than are technical violations. In some cases, law violations may result in a mandatory revocation.

For those offenders on probation or parole, a formal revocation process can take place when violations occur. The probation or parole officer will make the decision to take formal action and report the violation to the court. Then, the decision whether to revoke an offender's probation or parole is up to the discretion of the judge who sentenced the offender. The U.S. Supreme Court has ruled that probationers and parolees are entitled to due process during revocation proceedings, including the right to notice of the hearing, the right to written notice of the charges, the right to be present at the hearing, the right to present evidence and witnesses, the right to confront witnesses, and the right to judgment by a neutral body.

Special Populations and Related Conditions

Many researchers and practitioners agree that conditions imposed during a community-based correctional program should be tailored to the individual offender's needs and characteristics. Therefore, there are certain populations within offenders that require specialized conditions related to their unique situation. For example, offenders with substance abuse problems will require medical treatment in order to overcome their addictions. Offenders accused or convicted of domestic violence will often be required to abide by any restraining orders against them as a condition of their specific program, and they may need to attend anger management courses or receive psychiatric treatment. Offenders accused or convicted of the sexual assault of a child will often be required to avoid certain locations where children will be, such as playgrounds and schools, and to register their address, and they will likely be required to undergo some form of psychiatric treatment. Juvenile offenders will also likely receive unique conditions, in this case because of their age. For example, juveniles are typically required to attend school regularly and may be subject to a curfew during the course of their program. All of these specialized conditions, and any others, could be enforced by the supervising agency at its discretion if the conditions are related to attaining the goals of maintaining public safety, helping the offender lead a law-abiding life, and rehabilitation.

Lauren M. Block
Washington State University

See also Goals and Objectives of Community Corrections; Offender Needs; Offender Risks

Further Readings

Abadinsky, Howard. *Probation and Parole: Theory and Practice,* 11th ed. Upper Saddle River, NJ: Pearson, 2011.

Alarid, Leanne Fiftal and Rolando V. del Carmen. *Community-Based Corrections,* 8th ed. Belmont, CA: Thomson Wadsworth, 2011.

American Bar Association. *Standards for Criminal Justice, Probation.* Chicago: Author, 1970.

Cromwell, Paul F., George G. Killinger, Hazel B. Kerper, and Charles Walker. *Probation and Parole in the Criminal Justice System,* 2nd ed. St. Paul, MN: West, 1985.

Continuum of Sanctions

The consequence for violating society's criminal law calls for a sanction proportionate to the seriousness of the offense. Over time, society has developed a wide range of consequences, which more recently have been used in a continuum. Because the philosophy or goal of punishment is intended to serve singular or multiple concurrent objectives, such as retribution, reform, deterrence, incapacitation, restoration, and rehabilitation, employing a continuum of sanctions serves to provide an array of pragmatic options and alternatives.

Notwithstanding the purpose and appropriateness of imprisonment for offenders who commit serious crimes or are deemed incorrigible recidivists, most criminal behavior does not warrant incapacitation. Beyond the overcrowded, violent, and harsh conditions of life behind bars, which can contribute to recidivist tendencies, a prison sentence may be considered too severe a punishment for lower-level crimes, which can also adversely impact a defendant's family and the community at large. Additionally, because of the inherent costs associated with incarceration in having to provide for food, shelter, clothing, medical care, supervision, and other necessities of life, the economic impact of incarceration proves counterproductive, particularly considering the systemic overcrowding of prisons nationwide.

Alternatively, while probation serves as a pragmatic alternative in diverting offenders away from prison and is widely used for providing some degree of supervision for first-time, low-level offenders, there are inherent limitations to its efficacy for offenders who require a greater degree of supervision, control, and resources.

Consequently, while incarceration may prove to be too severe a sentence and probation is limited in providing a greater degree of control and supervision, a pragmatic and effective alternative is the use of a continuum of sanctions vis-à-vis intermediate sanctions.

A continuum of sanctions represents a range or a combination of correctional strategies that provide judges or sentencing officers with a host of alternatives that may be used independently or in concert with one another to address the needs and interests of the defendant, as well as those of the victim and society at large. Considering that the use of these sanctions may be progressively employed, either singularly or in concert with one another, a degree of flexibility and adjustment in their application is possible, with the ultimate goal of achieving retribution, deterrence, reform, restoration, and rehabilitation. Contingent upon any number of factors—including the nature and seriousness of the offense, mitigating or aggravating circumstances, harm to the victim and society, the offender's criminal history, and society's expectation for retribution—the range or continuum of sanctions that may be employed includes fines, forfeiture, restitution, community service, counseling, participation in drug and alcohol treatment programs, house arrest or electronic monitoring, day reporting, intensive probation, stays at residential centers, participation in boot camp, shock incarceration, and split sentences.

Fines are monetary sanctions that require the offender to pay an amount of money that is used to compensate the victim and the state for the offender's violation of criminal law. The amount assessed is typically determined by the seriousness of the offense and the defendant's ability to pay. Approximately $1 billion in fines are collected annually in the United States.

Forfeiture involves the seizure by the government of property derived from or used in criminal activity.

Following a criminal conviction, legal forfeiture proceedings commence and can lead to a defendant's having to relinquish goods and property associated with the crime (such as cars, boats, and cash seized during the commission of illegal trafficking in drugs).

Restitution represents monetary compensation to the victim or to a public fund (such as victims' compensation boards) for financial, physical, or emotional loss. Compensation can be made in the form of monies and paid directly by the offender (in the case of an affluent offender) or from monies derived by performing public work or community service.

Community service, also referred to as a work order program, represents unpaid work that offenders must perform for a specified number of hours. Such activities may involve working at hospitals, working in recycling centers, cleaning streets, painting, or (in the case of professionals such as accountants, attorneys, and physicians) performing pro bono work. Community service, which is employed in varying degrees within all fifty states, provides offenders a means of contributing to, and a way of repaying, society for their transgressions.

Counseling provides education and coping measures for addressing the cause or causes of the offender's criminal behavior (such as substance abuse or uncontrolled anger).

Drug and alcohol treatment programs focus on providing services to treat defendants for their physiological and psychological dependencies on alcohol and drugs, which are often the root cause of criminality.

House arrest and electronic monitoring is a court-ordered sentence that requires an offender to remain confined to his or her residence for a specified amount of time. Home confinement can range from designated hours or days to weeks, months, or years. Ensuring that defendants comply with home confinement can include unannounced visits by a probation officer, telephonic reporting, or the use of electronic monitoring, which requires offenders to wear secure electronic devices around their wrists, ankles, or necks that either send a signal to a control office or are equipped with global positioning systems (GPS) to identify the exact location of the offender.

Day reporting centers are facilities where offenders report on a daily basis to receive designated intervention, counseling, and treatment.

Intensive probation represents a form of probation designed to provide strict control, surveillance, and supervision to the extent that it restricts and monitors an offender's movements and activities.

Residential centers, similar in concept to halfway houses for parolees, provide services for offenders typically in need of rehabilitative counseling, drug and alcohol treatment, outpatient psychiatric services, and prospective employment. By providing a stable environment where residents can share recreation and dining facilities, these facilities create an atmosphere conducive to community life.

Boot camps, most often used for first-time offenders in their late teens and early twenties, are military-style facilities used as an alternative to prison. With an emphasis on rigorous physical training and discipline, boot camps are designed to give offenders a sense of personal responsibility and teach them to recognize the ill effects of criminal behavior.

Shock incarceration and split sentencing involve exposing offenders for an abbreviated period of time to the harsh reality of prison life. Designed to shock the offender with an unadulterated insight into the ill effects of criminality and the harshness of prison life, these techniques underscore the importance for law-abiding behavior and the consequences of violations.

The strategic use of a continuum of sanctions can serve as an effective and pragmatic alternative to probation and prison. The advantages realized, when strategically employed, can reduce prison overcrowding, lower costs associated with imprisonment, minimize recidivism, provide restitution, make reparations to the victim and society, and restore and reintegrate the offender as a productive, law-abiding member of the community.

Robert F. Vodde
Fairleigh Dickinson University

See also Attitudes of Offenders Toward Community Corrections; Graduated Sanctions for Juvenile Offenders; Punishment Units

Further Readings

Alarid, Leanne Fiftal and Rolando V. del Carmen. *Community-Based Corrections*, 8th ed. Belmont, CA: Thomson Wadsworth, 2011.

Allen, H. E., C. E. Simonsen, and E. J. Latessa. *Corrections in America*, 10th ed. Upper Saddle River, NJ: Pearson Prentice Hall, 2004.

Clear, T. R., G. F. Cole, and M. D. Reisig. *American Corrections*, 9th ed. Belmont, CA: Thomson Wadsworth, 2010.

Gaines, L. K. and R. L. Miller. *Criminal Justice in Action*, 6th ed. Belmont, CA: Thomson Wadsworth, 2011.

Siegal, L. and C. Bartollas. *Corrections Today*. Belmont, CA: Thomson Wadsworth, 2011.

COOK COUNTY JUVENILE COURT

The first juvenile court was established in Cook County, Illinois, in 1899. After many social and legal organizations pushed for reform, children who were dependent or neglected as well as being delinquent were treated with a more rehabilitative rather than punitive approach. Although this first juvenile court has been criticized as becoming overly bureaucratic and straying from its central mission of rehabilitation, the Cook County Juvenile Court has more recently restructured to adhere to its mission of doing what is in the best interest of the child.

The first juvenile court was born out of the Progressive Era, which saw a need to save children from the ills of urbanization and social poverty. Often referred to as the Child Savers Movement, it involved many social and legal agencies, primarily in Chicago, that began to lobby for reform in the way that children were handled by the criminal justice system. It was believed that if parents could not take care of their children, then the state should take on that role. Homes were established in an effort to correct the behavior of youths and provide them with a structured and disciplined life. These homes were called houses of refuge, and the first was established in New York. They later spread to other cities, including Chicago and Philadelphia.

While these houses of refuge provided safe havens for children, separate legislation for dealing with delinquency and child victims was lacking. The notion that the government should assume responsibility for the supervision and protection of children, a philosophy known as *parens patriae*, was already well established in England. Two very influential organizations heavily involved in the passage of child reform legislation were the Chicago Women's Club and Hull House. Whereas the Chicago Women's Club worked within the already existing penal system for juvenile reform, Hull House devoted much of its attention to delinquency prevention. Both organizations lobbied members of the Illinois legislature as well as the governor before a bill was passed in 1899. The first juvenile law, titled An Act to Regulate the Treatment and Control of Dependent, Neglected, and Delinquent Children—also known as the Juvenile Court Act of 1899—established the first juvenile court in Cook County. The court opened its doors on July 5, 1899, under the direction of the Honorable R. S. Tuthill.

The juvenile court philosophy remains the same today as when the first court was established: that children in trouble should be helped or treated rather than punished. The court's mission was to make sure that children were provided with the care and protection owed to them by their parents and to do what was in the "best interest of the child." The presiding judge made clear from the outset that the court was not a place of mere convenience for parents who no longer wanted to handle their children, but rather a place where children could be saved from abuse and neglect or rehabilitated from delinquent behavior.

The court initially suffered from several problems. First, the 1899 legislation, which created the court, provided little guidance on how to pay for its most valuable staff, probation officers. Second, there was a great debate over the juvenile court's jurisdiction. The Chicago Criminal Court argued that, under the Illinois Constitution, it retained ultimate jurisdiction over juveniles, whereas the 1899 law gave such authority to the new court. Third, there was a tense relationship between social service agencies and courtroom actors such as the prosecutor and judge. The former viewed their role as more important, stressing a rehabilitative philosophy, while the latter began to shift their goals toward a more punitive remedy. This was first recognized in the 1950s, when there was no evidence to support an increase in juvenile crime, yet the number of juveniles sentenced to reformatories doubled. In 1961, the Cook County Juvenile Court underwent its first evaluation. The findings suggested that the court had failed to distinguish adequately between cases of neglect, dependency, and delinquency and that it was too political and bureaucratic.

A juvenile court can be administratively housed in three ways: as a separate court, as part of the family court, or as a subdivision of the trial court. Currently, the Cook County Juvenile Court is a separate, stand-alone court. With respect to subject matter, juvenile courts hear cases in three areas: delinquency, status offenses, and child neglect/dependency. Delinquency involves criminal conduct by juveniles (the same as if committed by adults). Status offenses are crimes that are illegal only for juveniles and not adults, such as curfew violations and truancy. In Illinois, the juvenile court hears delinquency cases involving those under the age of 17. Juvenile cases also historically differed in terminology from adult criminal cases. For example, the term *adjudication* was used instead of *trial*, and *disposition* was used instead of *sentencing*. However, as a result of the Juvenile Court Reform Act of 1998, Cook County currently uses the traditional criminal terms. Those deemed delinquent may be sentenced to the Illinois Department of Corrections Juvenile Division until they reach the age of 21.

During the first 10 years that the court was open, it held 190 sessions and processed 3,181 hearings. In 1902, the Chicago Juvenile Court Committee was created; it established a court staff, primarily of probation officers. By 1990, status offenders represented less that 0.1 percent of the court's caseload. The court reorganized in 1995, creating the Juvenile Justice and Child Protection Department, which handles delinquency cases for those under the age of 17; the Child Protection Division, which examines cases of child neglect, abuse, and dependency; and the Child Protection Department Resource Section, which seeks assistance from business, educational, and social service agencies to meet the needs of juveniles. In 2011, 15 judges were assigned to the court. The county probation department is under the umbrella of the Administrative Office of the Illinois Court Probation Division.

Christopher M. Bellas
Youngstown State University

See also Family Courts; Juvenile and Youth Offenders; Juvenile Probation Officers; Residential Programs for Juveniles

Further Readings

Applegate, Brandon, Robin King Davis, and Francis T. Cullen. "Reconsidering Child Saving: The Extent and Correlates of Public Support for Excluding Youths From the Juvenile Court." *Crime and Delinquency*, v.55/1 (2009).

Dodge, Mara. "Our Juvenile Court Has Become More Like a Criminal Court: A Century of Reform at the Cook County (Chicago) Juvenile Court." *Michigan Historical Review*, v.26/2 (2000).

Parker, Graham. "The Juvenile Court Movement: The Illinois Experience." *University of Toronto Law Journal*, v.26 (1976).

Platt, Anthony. *Child Savers: The Invention of Delinquency*. New Brunswick, NJ: Rutgers University Press, 2009.

CORRECTIONAL CASE MANAGERS

Correctional case managers or caseworkers are typically assigned to a living unit within a correctional facility. Both the adult and juvenile correctional systems employ case managers. These positions support community corrections in a variety of ways. These are normally professional positions within an agency and require a baccalaureate degree. The main duty of a case manager is to manage the progress of incarcerated individuals assigned to their caseloads, from initial entry into the correctional system through the period following release. Case managers are responsible for keeping community corrections involved in the progress of an inmate's individual case plan (ICP) prior to release. Much of the job of a case manager is to facilitate a successful transition of newly incarcerated individuals from civilian life to life in the institution and back to civilian life again.

Juvenile Correctional Case Managers

Daily duties of a juvenile case manager consist of counseling of juvenile offenders who have been placed in a form of administrative segregation. In some facilities, this is designated as a "security" unit and is in essence a jail inside the jail. The case manager will counsel youths who have violated program rules and thus have been assigned to the case manager's caseload. Examples of violations that may lead a juvenile to being placed in a security unit include cursing at staff, fighting, stealing from staff members, assaulting staff members, lying, being in possession of contraband, escaping or attempting an escape, masturbating, and indecent exposure. While the youth is in security, it is the case manager's responsibility to review incident reports on the youth to determine whether he or she needs to be admitted into the security unit or sent back to the dormitory or educational setting. Many security units have a full-time case manager who solely works admissions into the unit. If a youth is admitted into the security unit, the case manager will be responsible for conducting administrative hearings on the youth. An administrative hearing is a process whereby the youth goes through a hearing and is assessed consequences for whatever rule violation put him or her in the security unit. Along with the administrative hearings, the case manager is responsible for all the paperwork that ensures the youth's due process rights.

Case managers are responsible for conducting certain administrative hearings. These hearings are conducted with youths who participated in major rule violations. The case manager is responsible for conducting the investigation of the allegation of the rule violation, preparing the paperwork on the hearing, contacting family members to inform them of the hearing, contacting attorneys, and at times advocating for youths during a hearing. Moreover, a case manager serves as the hearing manager, somewhat like a judge. Following the conclusion of a hearing, the case manager prepares a hearing summary to send to the central agency office for review. After a youth is released from a correctional setting, if he or she continues to violate parole rules or commit crimes, community corrections will be responsible for conducting administrative hearings to recommit the youth back into state custody.

Caseworkers in Texas, for example, are responsible for developing ICPs for each youth assigned to their caseloads. This plan focuses on education, behavior, and correctional therapy. The ICP is a 30-day plan that focuses on areas of improvement and requires signatures of the youth, the case manager, and community corrections. If the youth does not meet the goals of the objectives in the plan, he or she is not promoted to the next level of the rehabilitation cycle.

Case managers are also responsible for conducting daily core group counseling sessions. Although different states take similar approaches, each state may use a different variation of a rehabilitation program for the youth that therefore requires a different counseling method. Counseling is central to the job of the case manager. Each month the case manager is required to spend a set number of minutes counseling youths assigned to their caseload. During these sessions, the case manager contacts family members, discusses the youth's incarceration and crime, goes over problems he may be having in the program, reviews education, and addresses plans for future release.

Adult Correctional Case Managers

Adult correctional case managers counsel demanding and noncompliant adult inmates who typically have adjustment issues when they are first incarcerated. Depending on the program of rehabilitation, many case managers are responsible for performing duties through a team approach to risk management. The team approach involves assessing risk factors in order to make a determination regarding the assignment of a facility or cell and the level or type of supervision required. This process is called classification. In addition, the case manager handles referrals for inmates' services and work assignments and develops a thorough release strategy for inmates who are close to release. The case manager reviews the inmates' work within the prison. Case managers maintain records of all assigned offenders to determine their progress and whether there is a necessity to change assignments or security classifications.

The position of case manager requires continuing and proactive interactions with inmates that are intended to effect cognitive programming to interrupt, rather than support, antisocial conduct and unacceptable reactions to situations that arise in the inmates' lives. The case manager presents a variety of programs to offenders, which are intended to aid in their successful reentry into the community following release from incarceration. These programs include substance abuse treatment, anger management, life skills, and job skills, to name a few. Once released, inmates have to work with community corrections regarding these programs. Their participation is documented and modifications are made if deemed necessary by community corrections.

Case managers serve as administrative staff, usually on both a treatment team and a management team. Case managers participate as members of a team that provides a range of case management services for inmates, from initial incarceration through post-release. The case manager assists with and prepares written or electronic reports, such as parole summaries or court-ordered presentencing investigations. Case managers work with community outreach and establish collaborative networks with appropriate partners to offer support and both pre- and post-release services for offenders that involve family members, community resources, and social service agencies.

Harrison Watts
Washburn University

See also Case Management; Juvenile Probation Officers; Parole Boards and Hearings; Parole Officers; Probation Officers

Further Readings

Jordan, D. "Transition Program: Part II." *American Jails*, v.22/3 (July 2008).

Park, J. and M. Huser. *Promising Life Skills Educational Programs for Incarcerated Audiences*. Madison: University of Wisconsin Extension, Family Living Programs, 2005. http://www.uwex.edu/ces/flp/families/promisingprograms.pdf (Accessed January 2011).

Sedlak, A. "Surveying Youths in Custody." *Corrections Today*, v.71/6 (December 2009).

COSTS OF COMMUNITY CORRECTIONS

Individuals who are in charge of creating and paying for community corrections programs and policies need to be aware of the economic costs of these programs and the potential benefits that society will enjoy as a result. In traditional community corrections, there are three types of fiscal sanctions: restitution, community service, and fines. However, in recent times, the economic benefits of community corrections have gone far beyond court-mandated sanctions to include treatment programs, services, education, employment training, and more. To estimate the costs of these programs, researchers must use different statistical techniques. The three main techniques are cost-benefit analysis, which weighs the price of a program compared to the benefit or the economic return; cost-effectiveness analysis, which determines whether a program is working in a fiscally responsible way; and cost-savings analysis, which determines whether a program is saving costs and, if so, how much.

Institutional corrections have been expensive for several decades now, and their costs continue to increase. Criminal justice spending on correctional facilities is outpacing the amount of money being spent on education, healthcare, and natural resources. Therefore, increased incarceration does not seem like the long-term fiscal answer to managing these rising costs.

In order to determine the economic costs of community corrections accurately, it is necessary to determine the annual cost of institutional corrections. In 2001, the United States spent nearly $30 billion on adult correctional systems. The average daily cost was $22,650 per offender. This amount constituted approximately 77 percent of states' correctional budgets. The remaining 23 percent was spent on juveniles, administration, and finally community corrections. The amount of money being spent each year on corrections, mainly prisons and jails, is increasing. Now more than ever, it is necessary to determine the economic costs and benefits of community corrections.

A few major evaluation studies have been conducted on the economic benefits of community corrections programs. The first is the Serious and Violent Offender Reentry Initiative (SVORI). Ironically, this program found no significant cost difference between the treatment group and the comparison group. This finding may result from the fact that more services, costing more money, were given to the treatment group. However, in each of the other studies there was a financial return of at least $1.13 for every dollar spent, with the highest return being $7.14 for every dollar spent. A new form of economical community corrections program has been created at restitution centers. These centers combine traditional community corrections with more modern methods. Restitution centers are designed to allow individuals to be gainfully employed but reside at the center until their debt is paid in full.

Economic Analysis

It is estimated that each year in the United States, victims of crimes suffer $105 billion in losses. Some of this is repaid by the individuals who commit the crimes. Restitution is the court-ordered repayment by the offender to the victim or victim's family for losses that occurred during the crime. Restitution has two purposes: First, it helps the victim rehabilitate financially; second, it serves as punishment of the offender. The number of items for which a victim can recuperate losses has expanded. Victims can gain restitution for time in court, medical expenses, court expenses, and burial expenses, for example.

Restitution can be given only in the amount of the direct or actual losses, not for indirect losses such as attorney's fees.

A second form of repayment to the community from offenders is through community service. Although in this case the offender is not directly repaying the victim, he or she is working off the debt by helping society as a whole. Community service is one of the largest economic benefits of community corrections. In many cases the state receives free labor and is able to save money, which in turn saves the taxpayer money.

The third form of economic repayment is in the form of fines. Fines differ from restitution; whereas restitution is paid to the victim directly, a fine is repayment to the government. Fines are used in only about 25 percent of felony cases. Fines come in three forms: fixed fines, set amounts of money that must be paid (such as $1,000); forfeiture, whereby the government seizes illegally obtained property, such as cars or houses; and day fines, which are based on the amount of money the offender makes. In the third case, a wealthy offender would have to pay more for the same crime than a poor person would.

These forms of repayment do not, however, offset the costs of community corrections. Ultimately, taxpayers and public policy makers need to know that community corrections programs are working both effectively and at a price that is affordable. Three types of economic analyses must be undertaken to make that determination. The first is cost-benefit analysis, which is basically weighing the amount of money it will take to implement a community corrections program against the benefit of implementing that program. For example, if the state believes that it will save money by having offenders participate in additional treatment upon release, it will be more inclined to spend money on such services. The second type of analysis is cost-effectiveness analysis. This analysis differs slightly from cost-benefit analysis, in that a determination of cost-effectiveness measures programs that have already been implemented and shows whether the program is indeed saving money, that is, whether it is more cost-effective than an alternative. The third and final analysis is cost-savings analysis. Cost-savings analysis shows how much money is actually being saved by a specific program.

Cost-Benefit Analyses

There are numerous challenges that need to be overcome to predict the economic cost of community corrections accurately. These programs are often spread across different providers. Few data measure the monetary value of these programs and services, and it is difficult to determine the indirect benefits these programs create. For example, it is difficult to measure the economic benefit to families when a member of their household has been given extra employment and education or training. It is hard to quantify how much more money that family will have, based on the idea that the offender from the family has the opportunity to get a better job as a result of his or her treatment.

The main strategy used when conducting an economic evaluation of a criminal justice–based community corrections program is the bottom-up approach. This approach uses the idea of estimating the cost of services for each individual and then totaling all the individuals together. However, studies like this are rare. Cost-benefit analyses of programs are uncommon; generally the studies focus on recidivism outcomes and other, more tangible public safety factors.

Program Evaluations

In 2003, the U.S. government implemented a program to develop new community corrections techniques. This program conducted a cost-benefit analysis to determine the reductions in economic costs to the criminal justice system (arrests plus incarceration) through the use of community corrections instead. The results from this study showed that at no point following the release of these offenders was there a significant difference in the cost between the enhanced community corrections programs group and the comparison group. The community corrections group had more access to services but averaged $97 per month more than the comparison group to participate in these community corrections services. Three months after release, the community corrections group saved an average of $6 per month, as opposed to the comparison group. However, by the 15-month mark, the community corrections group was spending, on average, $248 more than the comparison group. This could have resulted from the fact that more services were being offered and used by the community corrections group than by the comparison group.

These findings need to be taken with a grain of salt. Although they show that SVORI was not necessarily a cost-effective program when compared to regular community corrections programs, that does not mean that SVORI is not an effective community corrections tool. The recidivism rates for this program may be low enough to justify its spending, and furthermore SVORI may be cost-effective when compared to incarceration. This second scenario would suggest that community corrections programs are fiscally responsible when measured against incarceration.

Another program evaluation, a study conducted on the Maryland Reentry Partnership Initiative (REP), found that offenders in the treatment group were less likely to commit a new crime during the study period, from 2001 to 2005. Because of this reduction in new crimes, the program had a return of approximately $3 for every $1 invested. The total net benefit to the city of Baltimore was close to $7.2 million, or $21,500 per treatment group participant.

Subsequently, another study conducted found, after reviewing seven different community corrections programs, that all of them had some form of cost-benefit to the community. The benefit ranged from 1.13 to a high of 7.14, meaning that for each dollar spent a return of $1.13 up to $7.14 was being made.

Restitution centers represent another interesting approach to community corrections. These facilities are targeted at first-time offenders who owe restitution to the victim or victim's family. These facilities may offer some treatment, but generally the focus is on offenders finding stable employment and paying off their debts. Some of these centers will allow the offender to leave when the restitution is paid in full. Restitution centers offer a good alternative to prison for first-time offenders, allowing them to stay in the community and not increase the populations of already crowded prisons and jails.

Cost of Community Corrections

Although there are differences in the evaluations of community corrections programs, the consensus seems to be that community corrections treatment groups are more economically beneficial than comparison groups. There are a number of different concerns that need to be addressed in future evaluation studies.

First, almost none of the studies consider costs to the victims of crimes. There are a number of reasons for this. It is extremely difficult to quantify the intangible costs of crime to victims, and the actual losses, such as losses from property crimes

and medical expenses, are often already included in some of the other economic figures. Furthermore, many researchers are hesitant to estimate the costs incurred by victims, fearing unreliable results.

A sometimes overlooked economic benefit of increased community corrections programs is the ability for offenders to stay employed and to be a functioning part of society. In many instances, offenders are unable to secure employment, and therefore they either file for unemployment benefits or seek some other form of social support or assistance. This creates an unintended or indirect economic cost to society or the community, which ultimately leads to increased costs for taxpayers.

According to data gathered by the state of North Carolina, the cost of community corrections supervision is approximately $3.44 per offender per day, or $1,256 per year. However, this is only the cost of supervision. This cost is greater when one includes the cost of supervision for sex offenders or individuals with electronic anklets or global positioning system monitoring devices. The daily cost for these individuals is $11.07, for a yearly cost of $4,041. The amount it costs per day for treatment programs and other services varies from $0.97 per day for community service to $47.34 per day for substance abuse treatment for male probationers and parolees to $78.79 per day for private treatment beds. Although North Carolina is only one state, these statistics indicate that community corrections may be a cheaper alternative, at least from a supervision standpoint. However, from a services standpoint, it may be easier to supply treatment to offenders who are institutionalized.

Conclusion

The results from different studies are somewhat inconclusive, and this could be for a number of reasons. In the SVORI study, survey data were used rather than administrative data. For future research, administrative data may be better at predicting possible costs and benefits. Another problem with the current research is that it does not accurately say which programs or services are the most economically beneficial. Specifically, the evaluations do not show which services are the most economically efficient and whether the programs are more economically beneficial in an institutional or community setting. Until more research is done on this subject, it will be difficult to determine how much savings can be gained from community corrections programming. Moreover, the savings could vary from state to state and even city to city, depending on the program and implementation.

Ultimately, therefore, more research needs to be done on this topic to understand the full scope of the costs of community corrections. More focus is needed on the costs to victims, on the benefits of increased employment opportunities, and on a comparison of institutional correctional practices and their costs with community correctional practices and their costs. From the data shown in this article, it is clear that community corrections have a place in the correctional field. It is just a matter of time before more research and data determine just how beneficial community corrections are.

Sean M. Falconer
Washington State University

See also Effectiveness of Community Corrections; Evaluation of Programs; Fine Options Programs; Reentry Programs and Initiatives; Restitution; Serious and Violent Offender Reentry Initiative; "What Works" Approach and Evidence-Based Practices

Further Readings

Alarid, Leanne Fiftal and Rolando V. del Carmen. *Community-Based Corrections*, 8th ed. Belmont, CA: Thomson Wadsworth, 2011.

Cowell, Alexander J., Pamela K. Lattimore, and John Roman. *An Economic Evaluation of the Serious and Violent Offender Reentry Initiative*. Rockville, MD: National Institute of Justice, 2009.

Siegel, Lary J. and Joseph J. Senna. *Introduction to Criminal Justice*, 10th ed. Belmont, CA: Thomson Wadsworth, 2005.

Stephan, James. "State Prison Expenditures, 2001." Bureau of Justice Statistics, 2004.

Welsh, Brandon C. and David P. Farrington. "Correctional Intervention Programs and Cost-Benefit Analysis." *Criminal Justice and Behavior*, v.27 (2000).

COUNSELING

Community corrections have a long history of providing counseling and guidance to offenders released to the community. John Augustus, the "father of probation," provided counseling and employment assistance to the misdemeanants released to his care and reported on their progress to the courts. This followed a general cultural concern for correction, reform, and rehabilitation. Early proponents of juvenile justice and diversion counseled juveniles and sought to provide them with better opportunities. A strong focus on the needs of female offenders early in the 20th century provided a significant counseling emphasis.

In the context of community corrections, counseling has typically taken three forms: surveillance-based counseling, intended to determine whether the offender has been fulfilling his or her commitments to the court and the community; rehabilitative counseling, aimed at helping the offender to make positive decisions about his or her life choices and personal direction; and therapeutic counseling, aimed at discovering and modifying the root causes of criminal behavior. These kinds of counseling have also been provided in three contexts: as offered by the community corrections official on a one-to-one basis; as group interventions, either in house or by contractors; and as provided by contract agencies.

The early history of community corrections was marked by a powerful rehabilitative emphasis that continued until the period of civil unrest in the 1960s and 1970s. During this early period, covering about half a century (from the establishment of the first probation departments in the 1920s and 1930s), probationers were typically first-time offenders or

Offenders can be counseled on a one-on-one basis or in a group setting, and treatment can be conducted at an offender's home or at facilities involving substance abuse treatment agencies, community mental health centers, private mental health professionals, or social service organizations. (Photos.com)

minor misdemeanants in need of assistance more than surveillance. Even parolees—persons released early from prison to complete their remaining time on the streets—although viewed as more dangerous and more in need of surveillance than probationers, were provided with counseling in the hope that their lifestyles could be amended.

Community Corrections Officers as Counselors

During the 1950s and early 1960s, rehabilitative counseling became a mainstay of community corrections and was often based on either Rogerian or depth psychological techniques. Rogerian (named for humanistic psychologist Carl Rogers) techniques were nondirective. They provided little or no actual direction but focused on active listening; assuring the client that he or she was being understood and seeking to build a sense of positive self-worth in the offender. Such techniques were centered in the client's supposed need to be heard. Freudian or depth psychological approaches focused on allowing offenders to discover the roots of their problem behaviors through a process of self-discovery. As manifested in community corrections, such efforts often resulted in clear suggestions for action. Because the providers of such counseling often were neither qualified social workers nor trained psychotherapists, the value of such interventions was often questioned.

By the mid-1960s, during a period of growing concern for the due process rights of most defendants and a rising awareness of the social and psychological consequences of arrest and imprisonment, there were further concerted efforts to remove juveniles from the criminal justice system. A large number of probation and parole officers were trained social workers and there was a recommendation from the national government that probation officers have a master's degree in social work as an educational qualification.

Throughout the history of community corrections, there has been controversy over the propriety of probation and parole officers providing counseling and therapy. It was often argued that most of the staff was unqualified to provide counseling, let alone therapy, and that the more important duties associated with community corrections were to ensure that the offender did not reoffend, that the conditions of supervision were fulfilled, and that the community was protected. It was further argued that the two

roles would interfere with each other. The counseling perspective would prevent the officer from appropriately enforcing the conditions of supervision, and the law-enforcement approach would make a therapeutic alliance impossible. As the officer was always bound to enforce the conditions of supervision, the assumed need for confidentiality and trust was unreasonable.

During the 1980s, a strong reaction against rehabilitation, often echoing the tentative findings of Robert Martinson that no rehabilitation strategy had universal efficacy—nothing works—came together with an increasing intolerance for nonpunitive sanctions and the "justice as fairness" movement, to deemphasize counseling by community corrections officers and to focus on enforcement and surveillance. This also led to a devaluing of parole and its surveillance role in the community. As a result of this shifting emphasis, a great deal of the service provision and counseling in community corrections was shifted to contract agencies.

A middle way found by some officers was to identify the specific needs of each offender. This came to be known as the consumer-based approach, which was often paraphrased as "some need bread, others need Shakespeare, and still others needed to be apprehended and incarcerated." It was the community corrections officer who needed to make that determination. One of the more important impacts of the consumer-based approach was a focus on case management that was imported directly from social work. In case management, as a counseling style, the community corrections professional and the offender identify specific needs and tasks and collaboratively develop plans for their realization. While viewed as a commonsense implementation by those familiar with client-centered social work, the approach provided a significant set of tools for often overworked and undertrained probation and parole officers. Furthermore, because the approach is task-driven, it provided a significant means of integrating needs-based counseling with the surveillance and compliance monitoring duties of the community corrections officer. Both kinds of tasks could be integrated into the same case management scheme. One of the results of the approach was a transparent sense of the expectations and needs of the officer, the courts, and the offender.

Individual counseling with offenders, sometimes within a case management structure, has also focused on various psychotherapeutic approaches.

More recently, the National Institute of Corrections has promulgated a counseling strategy based on motivational interviewing, a style of counseling that is client-centered and moves toward discovering the offender's own motivations and capacities for change. The technique and its theoretical basis have been used across multiple disciplines and have received strong empirical support.

Motivational interviewing grows directly from the "stages of change" model that came to public attention with the publication in 1994 of James O. Prochaska, John C. Norcross, and Carlo C. DiClementi's *Changing for Good*. The stages of change model outlines a series of stages through which any change or decision process must pass and identifies specific means for passing from precontemplation (roughly equivalent to denial) to completion, at which stage the change has been realized and is relatively self-maintaining. Motivational interviewing works with the offender or client to identify goals that are meaningful to the client, as well as those that are obligatory, and gently guides the client in constructing a strategy to attain those goals. The approach is compatible with a strengths-based approach and assumes that clients, including offenders, can identify meaningful outcomes and the resources to attain them. In this case, the counselor's main responsibility is to guide the process subtly rather than to impose direction.

Group Counseling

Among noncontractual counseling efforts, usually provided by community corrections officers in an office context, are various modes of group counseling and therapy. These are preferred because they tend to be cost-effective and relatively easy to implement, but their efficacy is questionable. In-house implementations have included drug and alcohol counseling, anger management, supervision adjustment groups, and employment preparation groups. Because such groups cost very little, they are often used to provide mandated treatment for persons who, on a clinical basis, have few problems.

A significant part of the logic of group interactions is that they rely heavily on the experience of offenders to provide support, motivation, and feedback to others in the same situation. This is understood to be particularly valuable because the members of the group, understanding that the information comes from the personal experience of those in situations similar to their own, are likely to give credence to the information.

Apropos of the classical duties of surveillance counseling, groups have also been established to orient offenders to community supervision, provide information about community reintegration, and work to readjust criminal attitudes. In many agencies, newly released or sentenced offenders are assigned to orientation groups to ensure their understanding of the conditions of supervision and the services available to them in the agency. Parole agencies at various governmental levels have instituted transitional programs for new releasees that include orientation to supervision and work-readiness programs. Offenders who have received substance abuse counseling or treatment are also provided with links to outpatient treatment providers.

Contractual Services

Concurrently with whatever style of counseling the community corrections officers provide themselves, there has always been a range of contractual services used to fulfill the conditions of supervision. Most important, these have been provided by substance abuse treatment agencies, community mental health centers, private mental health providers, and social service organizations. A range of these services has been made available by both inpatient and outpatient providers. In some cases, these agencies have included halfway houses and day reporting centers.

In the federal system, these services are let out to bid on a contractual basis, and payment for them is included in the agency's annual budget. Some states follow suit, but others require the offender to pay for his or her own treatment or rely on state-funded agencies for services.

Typically, the service provider works in concert with the community corrections officer. There are generally regular contacts between the agencies and a fairly free flow of information to ensure that the offender is compliant and that appropriate services are being rendered.

With the institution of the 1996 legislation known as the Health Insurance Portability and Accountability Act (HIPAA), monitoring of contract medical services, with special regard to drug and mental health treatment, became more complex because of the requirement that even mandated patients have a right to privacy and must sign release forms in order for community corrections officers and treatment providers to communicate about the offender's progress. For most supervisees, this presents little problem and is understood to be a necessary part of the supervision process.

In those cases where substance abuse treatment has required medically supervised detoxification or when, in the opinion of the court or the community correctional agency, the services needed were beyond the capacities of staff, drug treatment has been provided across a range of treatment possibilities. The least restrictive drug treatment counseling may include evaluation, weekly individual and group counseling sessions, and a not atypical demand that the offenders attend some minimal number of 12-step meetings.

While not understood as treatment or counseling per se, the 12-step protocols—as provided by Alcoholics Anonymous, Narcotics Anonymous, and similar organizations—have been a mainstay of many community corrections efforts. These have extended beyond substance abuse to anger management, overeating, family violence, and other kinds of personal problems. In general, the 12-step organizations are viewed as supportive or adjunctive treatments.

More restrictively, offenders with long-term addictions and histories of relapse may be referred for inpatient drug treatment. Often preceded by medically supervised detoxification, inpatient treatment may last from 45 days to 18 months or more. Longer treatments typically include staged reentry with continuing counseling, job assistance, and family counseling. Traditionally, most such treatments have included a mandatory 12-step component.

Many correctional communities have endorsed the drug methadone and its variants as the treatment of choice for heroin and opiate abusers. More recently, naltrexone and buprenorphine (medications that block the pleasurable effects of opiates) have also been approved for addiction treatment. Methadone is ideally provided on a time-limited basis with both group and individual outpatient counseling (methadone-to-abstinence programs). However, in many instances it is provided as a simple replacement for the opiate with little consideration of termination.

Classical inpatient drug treatment developed out of the Synanon model that emerged in New York during the 1960s. It emphasizes group and individual counseling, strict conformity to community regulations, and involvement in a long-term restructuring of values, directions, and motivations. Special emphasis is also placed on personal responsibility for past and present actions.

More recently, inpatient and outpatient counseling for substance abuse issues, as well as more general antirecidivism counseling, has focused on cognitive behavioral and relapse prevention models. Cognitive behavioral models address thinking patterns, associations, and patterns of behavior that lead to substance use or offending. They often rely heavily on educational materials. Relapse prevention seeks to build cognitive behavioral strategies to avoid relapse and recidivism. Both involve understanding how and when the offending behavior occurs and learning to make other choices.

Mental health treatment and counseling are often provided by community mental health centers that have psychiatrists, psychologists, and therapists on staff. Under court order, the offender is referred to treatment at the center and his or her progress is monitored by center personnel, who make regular reports and conduct conferences with the community corrections officer. Increasingly these services are managed by community corrections officers with specialized caseloads and specialized training.

Specific services provided in the community often include sexual offender treatment, anger management, and treatment for perpetrators of family violence. Like drug treatment, these services may include both individual and group counseling. For batterers, violent offenders, and sexual offenders, empathy-based treatments—treatments aimed at teaching the offender how to appreciate the damage that has been done to the victim—are a popular, if unproven, treatment modality.

Within the community there exist a large variety of counseling agencies and service providers that are privately funded or supported by grants and charitable donations. These are often sources of educational and vocational counseling. Adult education classes and literacy programs typically operate at no charge to the offender and without the need for special contracts with the community corrections agency.

Finally, there are a variety of for-profit day reporting centers, halfway houses, and private prisons that can provide a variety of services for the offender who has returned or is returning to the community.

Richard M. Gray
Fairleigh Dickinson University

See also Addiction-Specific Support Groups; Case Management; Drug- and Alcohol-Abusing Offenders and Treatment; Drug Courts; Family Group Conferencing; Family Therapy; Motivational Interviewing; Offender Needs; Offenders With Mental Illness; Probation and Parole: Intensive Supervision; Sex Offenders in the Community; Specialized Caseload Models; Therapeutic Communities; Victim-Offender Reconciliation Programs; Violent Offender Reconciliation Programs

Further Readings

Bauman, S. and T. Gregory Kopp. "Integrating a Humanistic Approach in Outpatient Sex Offender Groups." *Journal for Specialists in Group Work*, v.31/3 (2006).

Brownell, P. and A. R. Roberts. "A Century of Social Work in Criminal Justice and Correctional Settings." *Journal of Offender Rehabilitation*, v.35/2 (2002).

Cahn, Edmond N. *Confronting Injustice: The Edmond Cahn Reader*. Boston: Little, Brown, 1966.

Fogel, David. *We Are Living Proof: The Justice Model for Corrections*. Cincinnati, OH: Anderson, 1977.

Friedmann, P. D. et al. "Collaborative Behavioral Management: Integration and Intensification of Parole and Outpatient Addiction Treatment Services in the Step'n Out Study." *Journal of Experimental Criminology*, v.5/3 (2009).

Kimora. "The Emerging Paradigm in Probation and Parole in the United States." *Journal of Offender Rehabilitation*, v.46/3–4 (2008).

Marlowe, D. B. "When 'What Works' Never Did: Dodging the 'Scarlet M' in Correctional Rehabilitation." *Criminology and Public Policy*, v.5/2 (2006).

Martinson, R. "What Works? Questions and Answers About Prison Reform." *The Public Interest*, v.35 (Spring 1974).

Prochaska, James O., John C. Norcross, and Carlo C. DiClementi. *Changing for Good*. New York: William Morrow, 1994.

Seiter, R. P. and A. D. West "Supervision Styles in Probation and Parole: An Analysis of Activities." *Journal of Offender Rehabilitation*, v.38/2 (2003).

Taxman, F. S. "To Be or Not to Be: Community Supervision Déjà Vu." *Journal of Offender Rehabilitation*, v.47/3 (2008).

Walters, Scott T. et al. *Motivating Offenders to Change: A Guide for Probation and Parole*. Washington, DC: National Institute of Corrections, 2007. http://nicic.gov/Library/022253 (Accessed July 2011).

CRIME CONTROL MODEL OF CORRECTIONS

The crime control model was developed by Herbert Packer (1925–72) as one of two competing models that explain the criminal process. The crime control and due process models are based on different value systems. The crime control model emphasizes punishment, keeping order, and victims' rights over the rights of the accused, whereas the due process model focuses on the protection of individual rights. The key component of Packer's crime control model is the repression of crime by efficiently disposing cases. The criminal justice system should operate like an assembly-line conveyor belt; cases should move quickly from one stage to the next, as a result swiftly convicting criminals. There is an ongoing debate over which model should prevail.

Currently the criminal justice system is based on the crime control model. This philosophy is reflected in corrections policies, including tough-on-crime policies, mandatory sentences, three-strikes laws, and truth in sentencing. The main criticism of the crime control model is that it promotes an assembly-line justice that emphasizes efficiency and assumes suspects' guilt as soon as the police determine that the suspect probably committed the crime. This is problematic, because the focus on efficiency and the presumption of guilt may lead to the violation of individual liberties and, more important, the conviction of innocent people.

Packer's Crime Control Model

Packer developed the crime control model during the 1960s, when crime was rising and the U.S. Supreme Court under Chief Justice Earl Warren had made several decisions that protected the rights of defendants, such as the exclusionary rule, the right to counsel, the Miranda warning, the expansion of post-conviction review, and other due process rights. Critics claimed that the courts were handcuffing the criminal justice system and that guilty defendants went free because of technicalities. Critics believed that crime would decrease only by focusing on deterrence and retribution, which are the main sentencing philosophies underlying the crime control model.

The crime control model proposes several values focusing on the efficiency of the criminal justice system. First, the most important goal of the criminal justice system is crime suppression. If crime is not suppressed, public order will break down, and if the law is not enforced efficiently, people will disregard the law. *Efficient* in this context means that criminals must be arrested and prosecuted as quickly as possible. Efficiency is the most important factor because the more time goes by the less likely a conviction. In order to accomplish this goal, Packer advocated for expanding the powers of the police by removing procedures that make it more difficult to establish the guilt of the suspect. Furthermore, policy makers who believe in the crime control model advocate for the greater use of plea bargaining, because it quickly disposes of cases and punishes offenders. About 90 percent of criminal cases are settled via plea bargaining.

Second, to be efficient, the criminal justice system should operate as an assembly-line conveyer belt, moving cases quickly from one stage to the next. This is accomplished through a system that relies on informality and uniformity. Packer sees formal processes meant to protect the due process rights of suspects as "clutter." For instance, court proceedings such as the examination and cross-examination of witnesses constitute an inefficient and costly way to determine the guilt of an offender. They are inefficient and unnecessary, because the police are fully capable of establishing guilt. There must also be uniformity in handling cases, because the large number of criminal cases can be handled only if there are routine procedures to be followed by everyone. Packer's assembly-line conveyor belt consists of seven steps, starting with pre-arrest investigation and ending with disposition. After the conviction of the offender the case is over, because people who are innocent will be screened out during the process. Thus, there is no need for a post-conviction appellate process.

Third, the "presumption of guilt" is a key concept in Packer's model because it guarantees the efficiency of assembly-line justice. Once a defendant is brought to trial, he or she should be presumed guilty. Police and prosecutors are responsible for establishing probable guilt of an offender. Probable guilt is not simply the opposite of the presumption of innocence. Rather, it refers to the confidence that a suspect is probably guilty and that the outcome of the case will be a guilty verdict. This is based on factual guilt, which can be established by police, contrary to legal guilt, which is established by the prosecutor. For instance, a police officer witnesses a crime and arrests the offender. The police officer establishes factual guilt because he saw the crime. In comparison, the presumption of innocence is not a prediction of the outcome of a certain case but rather a guideline for how the police and prosecutors should proceed in the case; it focuses on the rights of the individual and the determination of legal guilt. Determining legal guilt is difficult and time-consuming, because the prosecutor must prove in court that the suspect committed the crime. If the police officer violated the rights of the offender, it is possible that important facts will not be admissible in court and prosecutors may not be able to establish legal guilt. According to the crime control model, the concept of legal guilt and the presumption of innocence are very inefficient, and assembly-line justice can work only under the presumption of guilt.

Implications of the Crime Control Model for Community Corrections

As of 2009, there were about 5 million offenders on probation or parole in the United States, or one out of every 47 adults. Of these 5 million offenders, 84 percent were on probation and 16 percent were on parole. With the shift to the crime control model and the associated "tough-on-crime" attitude in the 1980s, the number of offenders who are on probation increased from about 1.1 million in 1980 to 4.1 million in 2009, and the number of offenders on parole increased from approximately 150,000 to 880,000 during the same period. The increase in the revocation rates has greatly contributed to the rise of the prison population over the past 30 years. The crime control model contributes to these high revocation rates, especially revocation for technical violations, because it asserts that offenders must be supervised closely and punished with incarceration because rehabilitation does not work.

Since the implementation of the crime control model the number of probation and parole revocations has increased by about 30 percent. Specifically, in 1985, about 80 percent of probationers successfully completed their probation terms. In 2009, only about 49 percent of probationers left their programs after successful completion. Also, more offenders (about 75 percent) are sent to prison for technical violations rather than serious new crimes. Only about 25 percent of offenders receive a new sentence for a new crime. The fact that the vast majority of offenders are being sent to prison for technical violations and minor crimes is consistent with the crime control approach of getting tough on criminals. The belief that minor violations should be punished harshly is rooted in a belief that minor violations will lead to bigger violations and new crimes. By contrast, many researchers believe that rehabilitation and treatment are more effective measures with regard to successful reintegration, especially for nonviolent offenders with drug abuse or mental health problems.

Criticisms

There are several criticisms on Packer's crime control model. First, Packer's model emphasizes crime repression via informal procedures and the assumption of guilt. Individual rights are not as important as efficiency and thus the model can lead to the violation of civil liberties and the conviction of innocent people. Packer argues that people who are innocent will be selected out during the process, but research, such as that conducted by the Innocence Project in 2009, has demonstrated that innocents have been convicted and executed for crimes they did not commit. The conviction of innocent persons poses a problem not only for those who are wrongly convicted, who end up spending many years in prison, but also for the community at large, because the real offender was not apprehended and trust in the justice system is eroded. Similarly, the crime control model does not include post-conviction appeals, giving the innocent little chance of overturning the wrongful conviction.

Second, the crime control model can be efficient only if police and prosecutors play the major role in the system. Packer states that police and prosecution would need wide discretion and power in arresting suspects and establishing guilt. This, however, is problematic, because research has consistently shown that the decisions of police, prosecutors, and judges are influenced by discriminatory stereotypes. Discrimination may perpetuate hostility and diminish cooperation with police, as occurred during the Los Angeles riots in 1992.

Third, the crime control model states that an efficient system will necessarily repress crime, but there is little evidence to support this contention. Crime rates have fluctuated considerably during the last decades and appear to be influenced by economic and social factors rather than policing methods.

Janine Kremling
California State University, San Bernardino

See also Attitudes and Myths About Punishment; Philosophy of Community Corrections

Further Readings

Bushway, Shawn D. and Anne Morrison Piehl. "Judging Judicial Discretion: Legal Factors and Racial Discrimination in Sentencing." *Law and Society Review*, v.35/4 (2001).

Glaze, Lauren E., Thomas P. Bonczar, and Fan Zhang. *Probation and Parole in the United States, 2009.* Washington, DC: U.S. Bureau of Justice Statistics, U.S. Department of Justice, 2009.

Greenberg, David F. "Time Series Analysis of Crime Rates." *Journal of Quantitative Criminology*, v.17/4 (2001).

Innocence Project. *Innocence Project Annual Report.* New York: Benjamin E. Cardozo School of Law, Yeshiva University, 2009. http://www.innocenceproject.org/news/AnnualReport2009.php (Accessed January 2011).

Lynch, Timothy. "The Case Against Plea Bargaining." *Regulation*, v.26/3 (Fall 2003). http://www.cato.org/pubs/regulation/regv26n3/v26n3-7.pdf (Accessed July 2011).

Packer, Herbert L. "Two Models of the Criminal Process: An Organizational Perspective." *University of Pennsylvania Law Review*, v.113/1 (1964).

Wodahl, Eric J., Robbin Ogle, and C. Heck. "Revocation Trends: A Threat to the Legitimacy of Community-Based Corrections." *The Prison Journal*, v.91 (2011).

CRIME VICTIMS' CONCERNS

Victimization occurs when an individual is directly harmed in some way by an individual or individuals acting outside the boundaries of criminal law. When victimization is reported, identifying the direct victim of a crime is relatively easy and appears to be a commonsense process. What is often misunderstood, however, is the fact that a crime committed against a victim is concomitantly viewed as a crime against society at large. In the act of committing a crime, the perpetrator not only harms the individual but also assaults society's overarching sense of morality by flagrantly violating the codified norms set in place to promote and sustain social order. Hence, following the identification and arrest of the alleged offender, the state, as opposed to the individual, files charges against the suspect and assumes responsibility for trying the case in criminal court.

The Uniform Crime Reports (UCR), which annually collects arrest statistics reported to the Federal Bureau of Investigation (FBI) by more than 17,000 law enforcement agencies across the United States, quantitatively tracks national crime rates and trends on an annual basis. Although considered by many to be the best available measure of crime and changes in criminal activity, the UCR is far from fully accurate. Most crime goes unreported, and the inaccuracies associated with the UCR are exacerbated by the fact that even those crimes that are reported often remain unsolved. Statistics alone fall short in telling the victim's story, because of their ability to provide only limited, if any, information about those acting as perpetrators and those who are victimized. Thus, valuable information that could help society serve the victim is all too often lost. This is especially true in consideration of the lasting effects of victimization.

In response to the shortcomings associated with the UCR, social scientists developed the National Crime Victimization Survey (NCVS), a qualitative research tool intended to solicit self-report data on both the demographics and the experiences of those victimized at the hands of another. Largely as a result of the yearly analysis of approximately 134,000 representative individuals, the NCVS is now officially recognized as a robust source of information on the initial experiences and consequences of victimization—information lacking in the statistical analyses that serve as the backbone of the UCR. The NCVS, combined with victim-based television shows such as *America's Most Wanted*, has led to renewed attention to victimization on the part of the general public.

The Reality of Reported Crimes

As the 1960s ushered in an era of legislation aimed at rendering equal rights to racial minorities and women, the criminal justice system turned its focus toward victims' needs. Although full awareness and reform remain lacking in 2010, prior to the latter half of the 20th century the victimized were truly background players following the commission of a crime. Law enforcement has historically served as the gatekeeper to the criminal justice process. In reality, however, it is the victim who has power and the capacity to transform the "law on the books" into the "law in action" by reporting the criminal act. All too often this does not occur, however, for a plethora of reasons. Paramount among these is the fear of what has been called double victimization at the hands of society and the criminal justice system itself. Although all too often remaining a background player as the criminal justice process plays itself out, the victim can report the crime to local officials, witness the successful apprehension and conviction of the offender, and feel justice has been served. At worst, especially in the case of rape perpetrated on women and girls, the victim herself faces undue scrutiny by the general public, those in law enforcement, and the courts, whose responsibility is to ensure that laws are upheld and unbiased verdicts are rendered.

Following the civil unrest and resulting legislation of the 1960s two major changes occurred that were intended to aid the victims of crime. First, both public and private programs emerged whose stated intent was to aid victims as they recovered from and rebuilt their lives following victimization. It was hoped this change alone would result in an increased willingness to report crime, thus leading to more arrests and removing more perpetrators from mainstream society. Second, research efforts began to use self-report studies in order to assess crime rates more accurately and to determine the public's overall fear of crime and citizens' level of trust in law enforcement and the criminal justice system as a whole. While both efforts are to be lauded and, at the time, represented innovative attempts to bring much needed change, crime victims today continue to face many of the same concerns that were commonplace more than 40 years ago.

Victimization, Fear, and Unreported Crime

Fear represents the primary barrier to the reporting of crime. This fear emanates from many sources—concrete threats leveled at the victim by the perpetrator, fear of retaliation from both the offender and society at large, previously witnessed unjust media exposure intended to question similar victims' credibility, and horror stories of less-than-professional treatment by those in law enforcement.

While important in and of themselves, the fears discussed above represent only the tip of the iceberg when considering why most crime goes unreported. Heretofore unaddressed, but of particular import, is the fear that victim will be viewed as somehow culpable for her or his own victimization. This particular fear has been exacerbated by the extensive media coverage of those who attempt to seek justice after having allegedly been harmed by a celebrity.

The 2003 charges brought against basketball player Kobe Bryant by the state of Colorado exemplify the power of the media in perpetuating victims' fears. Following a young woman's claims of having been raped by Bryant, she was next victimized by both the media and the criminal justice system itself. As the case against Bryant unfolded, flagrant loopholes in Colorado laws specifically designed to protect alleged victims came to light, thus allowing the young woman's prior behaviors and sexual history to be entered into the court proceedings. Via media coverage, highly sensitive and personal information about the young woman became public knowledge. The defense attorneys' successful utilization of the aforementioned legal loopholes, combined with the overexposure of the plaintiff's personal history, played to Bryant's advantage. Following the alleged victim's withdrawal of all allegations initially brought against Bryant, the case was fully dismissed.

Although damaging to the young woman who claimed to have been raped by Bryant, the Colorado events managed to bring a modicum of success in an unexpected manner. Following the events of 2003, many states have begun the arduous task of evaluating and, when needed, modifying their own laws aimed at protecting rape victims from such double victimization. However, unanswered questions remain. While individual states work to rectify the problems arising from poorly written legislation it is impossible to surmise the numbers of unreported rapes directly traceable to the treatment received by one young woman at the hands of both the Colorado criminal justice system and the overly zealous media.

Perception, Policy, and Practice

Names such as Willie Horton, Adam Walsh, Elizabeth Smart, and Megan Kanka both invoke and evoke visceral reactions from many in society—and well they should, albeit for different reasons.

Each touches on the issue of community corrections, policy changes aimed at safeguarding mainstream society, and shortcomings in contemporary efforts to achieve these goals.

When considering community corrections and its desired outcomes, one typically envisions the practices of probation and parole. While similar in nature—with each recognizing the culpability of the offender—differences exist between the two. Probation, while acknowledging the misconduct of the offender, allows the perpetrator to avoid incarceration while remaining in mainstream society. Parole is granted to the incarcerated offender who, after a period of time in prison, appears capable of effectively functioning outside the prison walls. While these are the most common forms of community corrections, many are unaware of a third possibility: the furlough system. During the U.S. presidential campaign of 1988, pitting the Democratic candidate Michael Dukakis, former governor of Massachusetts, against his Republican opponent, George H. W. Bush, the furlough came to Americans' attention through the case of Willie Horton.

While on furlough from the Massachusetts penal system, Horton brutally raped a woman after pistol-whipping, gagging, and ultimately killing her fiancé. Repeatedly airing campaign ads portraying Horton as the ultimate failure of the entire furlough practice, Bush overwhelmingly defeated Dukakis for the presidential bid—a victory that undoubtedly took advantage of the fear of crime as portrayed by the Horton incident.

In contrast to the brutality displayed by Horton, an incarcerated offender, the experiences of Adam Walsh, Megan Kanka, and Elizabeth Smart fueled fear among the general public. Kidnapped, sexually molested, and eventually murdered, Walsh and Kanka served as the basis for the introduction of new laws specifically intended to protect children from known pedophiles. Smart's kidnapping and nine-month torture at the hands of Brian David Mitchell and Wanda Ileen Barzee once again introduced fear among those wanting to do whatever was necessary to protect America's children from victimization.

Megan's law, named in honor of Kanka, passed at the federal level, attempted to introduce mandates that would inform parents of the location and reported residences of pedophiles living among the general public. Adam's law, named in honor of Walsh, expanded the previously enacted provisions by introducing a three-tiered level of sex offender reporting based on the crime committed and the threat of recidivism. Citing a lack of standardization across jurisdictions, the overload placed on probation and parole officers, and a tendency to release the incarcerated early to make room for new offenders, the laws passed have prompted mixed reactions from the American public. Regardless of public reaction, these laws, which conferred the ability of community corrections to monitor identified offenders, are indicative of the value Americans place on childhood and collectively represent an attempt to provide an added layer of protection for society's youth.

The Reality of Victimization

The primary legacy of victimization—among children and adults—is an ongoing and often lifelong fear of revictimization. This fear is not entirely unwarranted and need not be entirely counterproductive. Rational concern results in increased awareness among the general public and an increased tendency for would-be victims to protect themselves from the predators in society. However, a fine line exists between productive concern and uncontrollable, life-altering fear. The fear of victimization can dominate a victim's thinking and life patterns, becoming a phobia—a condition oftentimes requiring psychotherapy that may continue for years. Especially in the case of female rape it is not unusual for the woman's fear to become so pervasive she alters her entire life in ways that often seem unreasonable to the one who has not shared her experience. A deep-seated fear of others may lead the victim to go so far as to relocate her place of residence, refuse to reveal her address and/or telephone number to anyone, avoid interpersonal relationships altogether, or, at worst develop agoraphobia thus leaving the victim a prisoner of her own fears.

Although most scholarly research and the resultant literature tend to focus on the negative effects of female victimization, particularly with regard to rape, both genders are prone to experience the lasting physical and emotional effects that come with victimization. Among these are increased feelings of vulnerability and an altered view of self and society. All too often, victims view themselves as somehow deserving of the treatment received at the hands of a perpetrator. Unfortunately, members of law enforcement—the gatekeepers to the criminal justice process—may initially, and often unknowingly, affect the outcomes of victimization. Although law-enforcement officers may interact with victims without malice or intent, they are often ill equipped and untrained to deal with the psychological effects of victimization; nevertheless, the effects of their interaction with a victim can last a lifetime. The lack of appropriate training and understanding among many in law enforcement can plant the seeds of and exacerbate the already developing feelings of helplessness and worthlessness reported by many victims.

Change is needed if we are to help victims heal from and move beyond the damage done by the perpetrator's act. The first change must come from within the criminal justice system itself. Enhanced and ongoing education regarding how best to provide immediate aid—both physical and emotional—to the victim is the first step toward this needed change. Armed with the ability to empathize with the victim, law-enforcement officers must also have at their disposal the names and addresses of victims' advocates who can be on call to come to the scene of the crime. Healing must be given a chance through the earliest possible intervention. Just as it has been claimed that "it takes a village" to raise a child, so, too, does it take a collaborative effort to respond fully to the victims' needs and concerns.

Conclusion

The U.S. criminal justice system has a long history of turning the proverbial blind eye toward the needs of victims. Instead it has focused on apprehending the offender, securing and preserving crime-scene evidence, and building a case that will bring a guilty verdict against the alleged perpetrator. It was not until the mid-20th century that victims' concerns also became the concerns of those with the authority to enact, enforce, and uphold the laws of our country. While some needed changes have already occurred, many victims' needs remain unmet by a social institution specifically designed to focus its attention on the offender as opposed to the victim.

Each and every law-enforcement agency should have its own highly trained crisis intervention team whose expertise can help victims begin the healing process at the earliest point possible—when those in uniform respond to the initial call for help. Individual officers must also be well trained in the skill and art of assessing the individual's needs in order to ensure positive, nonincriminating interactions at first contact with the victim. Finally, each and every community needs to have psychological professionals available to respond to both the immediate and the ongoing mental health needs of the victim, regardless of his or her age or his or her ability to pay for services rendered.

Just as crime reduction requires a collaborative effort between law enforcement and the community it serves, so too is collaboration required to meet the individual needs of the victimized. All too often the full onus of responsibility for recovery is placed on the victim, who, highly vulnerable and ruled by fear, is ill equipped to take the steps necessary to begin the healing process. If the victim's life is to be fully restored, the criminal justice system must recognize and respond to its responsibility to treat that individual with respect and dignity. Concomitantly, the victim must be offered help in navigating the system—the maze of social service agencies—to begin, continue, and reap the benefits of the assistance needed for full restoration of his or her life. This requires extensive collaboration between agencies. It furthermore requires an educated citizenry willing to demand that victims' rights become a priority in the eyes and actions of legislators, law enforcement, and the courts, which must function collectively under the umbrella of the criminal justice system.

Martha L. Shockey-Eckles
Saint Louis University

See also Community-Based Centers; Counseling; Humanitarianism; Restorative Justice; Victim Impact Statements; Victim Services; Victims of Crime Act of 1984

Further Readings

Clements, C. B. et al. "The Measurement of Concern About Victims: Empathy Victim Advocacy and the Victim Concern Scale (VCS)." *Legal and Criminological Psychology*, v.11 (2006).

Dowler, K. "Media Consumption and Public Attitudes Toward Crime and Justice: The Relationship Between Fear of Crime, Punitive Attitudes, and Perceived Police Effectiveness." *Journal of Criminal Justice and Popular Culture*, v.10/2 (2003).

Geis, G. "Victims: Distinguishing Victims and Offenders, the Emergence of Victim Concerns, National Crime Victimization Survey." http://www.jrank.org/pages/2276/Victims.html (Accessed September 2010).

Harden, B. "Bryant Case Is Called a Setback: Recent Rape Victims Cite Confidentiality Breach, Advocates Say." *Washington Post* (September 3, 2004).

"Kobe's Accuser Hospitalized Last Winter as a Danger to Herself." http://www.foxnews.com/story/0,2933, 92892,00.html (Accessed October 2010).

Light, J. S. "The Effects of Privatization on Public Services: A Historical Evaluation Approach." *New Directions for Evaluation*, v.90 (Summer 2001).

Montaldo, C. "Rape Shield Law: The Kobe Bryant Case." http://www.crime.about.com/od/current/a/kobe040723 .htm (Accessed October 2010).

Moore, M. H. and R. C. Trojanowicx. "Policing and the Fear of Crime." *Perspectives on Policing*, v.3 (June 1988).

Shelton, Hon. D. E. "The 'CSI Effect': Does It Really Exist?" *NIJ Journal*, v.259 (March 2008).

CULTURAL COMPETENCE

Cultural competence is defined as a set of behaviors, attitudes, policies, and practices that enable and empower a practitioner or organization to provide culturally maximizing service to a culturally complex clientele. Cultural competence goes beyond simply acknowledging cultural diversity or a conglomeration of groups. In practice, culturally competent practitioners and organizations should acknowledge the influence that culture plays in communication and action, recognize the dynamics within cross-cultural relations, enhance their cultural competence through the acquisition of additional knowledge, and amend and adapt existing knowledge and practice with accompanying shifts in cultural competence.

Throughout most of the history of the American criminal justice system, practitioners used a "one size fits all" approach to community corrections. This philosophy assumed that criminal justice services and interactions should cater to groups of offenders *as offenders* rather than recognizing their varying cultures and backgrounds. The shift toward a more culturally competent criminal justice system began taking shape through the larger social changes and challenges of the 1950s and 1960s and the resulting value placed on diversities of culture. Consequently, criminal justice officials have recognized the role that cultural competence plays in both the improvement of services and interactions and the improved outcomes for offenders.

The cultural expansion of both offenders and practitioners in the criminal justice system has intensified the need for and value of cultural competence systems and practices. Increases in the numbers of women, people of color, juveniles, elderly, openly gay (or lesbian, bisexual, or transgender), international, disabled, lower-socioeconomic-status, and mentally challenged offenders have produced a more culturally diverse criminal justice system than at any other point in recent history. For community corrections practitioners, the value of cultural competence has additionally expanded, as they are interacting with diverse offenders, families, and communities. Contemporary efforts toward cultural competence have further expanded the traditional definitions of culture to include age, disability, religion, and sexual orientation, although most work in cultural competence in community corrections remains focused on race, ethnicity, nationality, gender, and class.

Race, Ethnicity, and Nationality

The need for cultural competence to manage offenders of different racial, ethnic, and national backgrounds is both essential and complex. Although these categories are presented together and are often used interchangeably, distinctions among these classifications are necessary. *Race* refers to biological or genetic variations in skin and/or hair color and facial shape, whereas *ethnicity* refers to a conception of cultural identity through learned behaviors, common heritage, geographic origins, and mutual language, and *nationality* refers to place of legal birth or citizenship status. Collectively, there are both an expected growth in the population numbers for racial and ethnic minorities in the United States and distinct overrepresentations in the criminal justice system of some racial and ethnic offenders.

The underlying characteristics of race, ethnicity, and nationality can produce language barriers, cultural misinterpretations and conflicts, mistrust, and nonmaximizing outcomes for community corrections practitioners that directly affect offenders, family members, and community members. Systems and practices in community corrections that support cultural competence for racial, ethnic, and national groups include policies for addressing linguistic challenges; training in recognizing subtle differences in cultural interactions; personal and organizational accountability for the historical, implicit, and pervasive stereotypes associated with race, ethnicity, and nationality; and offender, family, and community involvement in shaping culturally competent offender expectations.

Gender

The majority of criminal justice offenders in the United States are males; however, recent decades have seen dramatic increases in the number of female offenders. Because of these increases, the importance of establishing culturally competent systems and practices according to gender has grown. Similar to race, ethnicity, and nationality, cultural competence for gender goes beyond the recognition of gender differences. The challenge in achieving a gendered cultural competence is to acknowledge and understand existing systems and policies that have created gender-separate practices, yet even this understanding cannot ensure that culturally competent practices will be effected.

Community corrections practitioners who are both directly and indirectly involved in provided women with services—such as same-gender counseling, job assistance, or childcare assistance—can supply gender-specific services without providing culturally competent services. Gendered services that include family organization and relational strengthening, the rejection of long-standing gender stereotypes in work and education, empathy in response to victimization, and the acknowledgment of valued differences in assessments, service plans, and treatment options will produce culturally competent community corrections for women.

Socioeconomic Status

Socioeconomic status is the least formally recognized arena of cultural competence in criminal justice and community corrections, yet the need for conscientious systems and practices is essential in constructing a socioeconomically based, culturally competent system. The overwhelming majority of offenders who enter the U.S. criminal justice system are unemployed or underemployed, are uneducated or undereducated, and share structural difficulties meeting the expectations of community corrections. Living in a capitalist, meritorious society creates difficulties for socioeconomically challenged offenders, who often have been perceived as inherently criminal and dangerous or as deserving of harsher punishments or treatment solely as a result of their socioeconomic status. Offenders have to manage meeting the correctional expectations from practitioners who, if not properly trained, may consciously or unconsciously treat them adversarially based on their socioeconomic inferiority alone. Community corrections practitioners face significant challenges in overcoming numerous stereotypical beliefs about lower-socioeconomic-status offenders.

When interacting with offenders of a lower socioeconomic status, a culturally competent community corrections practitioner will recognize the *real*, structural challenges to obtaining employment and/or education and the structural limitations to socioeconomic meritocracy and mobility, provide empathetic patience for offenders falling short of expectations beyond the control of their socioeconomic conditions, and identify the apparent relationship between an offender's socioeconomic status and his or her self-concept.

Strengths of Culturally Competent Community Corrections

The proper training of community corrections practitioners to ensure culturally competent interactions with offenders produces practitioners who are better educated and better prepared for interacting with diverse populations, improves offender interactions and client-to-service connections, and strengthens community relations. In many ways, cultural competence allows offenders to be treated according to their personal and correctional goals and allows practitioners to bridge real, rather than stereotypical, obstacles to goal achievement.

Culturally competent community corrections practices additionally allow for a more accurate conceptualization of the offender that provides unique and culture-specific treatment and services. Through effective assessments and community correction plans, a practitioner and an offender can cooperatively address cultural challenges according to race, gender, religion, disability, sexual orientation, or other culturally specific traits. With the offender, the practitioner can create strategies that are specific and maximizing. Culturally competent community corrections, while challenging for the practitioner, ultimately provides a greater opportunity for the

long-term efficacy and success of offenders. It is a practice that supports valued offenders, knowledgeable practitioners, and diverse communities.

Challenges for Culturally Competent Community Corrections

The provision of culturally competent community corrections options that are specifically designed for appropriate groups is associated with personal and structural challenges. One significant challenge to providing culturally competent community corrections consists of the numerous intersections of culture for individuals. For a practitioner, difficulties arise when attempting to facilitate culturally competent services or assistance for offenders belonging to multiple cultures. Multiracial, multiethnic, or multinational individuals, as well as individuals who belong to multiple cultural backgrounds (such as those who are also poor, gay or lesbian, disabled, or female), provide challenges for practitioners in facilitating effective and accurate, yet potentially overlapping and contradictory, services. A strong gender component may not be effective for a woman from a particular ethnicity or nationality whose culture places a lower value on gender equity. Cultural competence is traditionally valued, yet it may not consistently be applicable to all individuals who fall into a particular culture.

A well-trained, culturally competent practitioner can distinguish times when cultural competence is important; it may prove exceedingly difficult, however, for a beginner or even a practitioner who is moderately trained in cultural competence to make such a determination. There are also challenges when cultural differences specifically contrast with correctional policy and procedure. Issues and challenges of religion, disability, or nationality may present circumstances under which the practitioner is left with minimal options in addressing the offender. While it may seem ideal to cater to a particular cultural practice of an individual, it may not be essential to that person's growth or program completion.

Practitioners who implement culturally consistent, inclusive systems and practices may also face challenges. An essential aspect of community corrections is the involvement of various aspects of the community. An effectively trained community corrections department cannot expect similar competencies from community employers, rental agencies, and other community-based correctional facilitators. As a society, we collectively struggle with practicing cultural competence. Therefore, having the expectation that offenders in community corrections will receive a unified approach to cultural competence may be unrealistic.

Scott Wm. Bowman
Texas State University, San Marcos

See also Disabled Offenders; Diversity in Community Corrections; Elderly Offenders; Female Offenders and Special Needs; Offenders With Mental Illness

Further Readings

Leavitt, R. *Cultural Competence: A Lifelong Journey to Cultural Proficiency*. Thorofare, NJ: SLACK, 2010.

O'Hagan, K. *Cultural Competence in the Caring Professions*. Philadelphia: Jessica Kingsley, 2001.

Reiman, J. and P. Leighton. *The Rich Get Richer and the Poor Get Prison: Ideology, Class and Criminal Justice*, 9th ed. Boston: Allyn & Bacon, 2007.

Sydney, L. M. *Gender-Responsive Strategies for Women Offenders*. Washington, DC: U.S. Department of Justice, National Institute of Corrections, 2003.

Walker, S., C. Spohn, and M. Delone. *The Color of Justice: Race, Ethnicity and Crime in America*, 4th ed. Belmont, CA: Thomson Wadsworth, 2007.

CURFEWS

Curfews are rules or laws that require people to remain indoors within a certain span of hours; these hours are almost always at night. Curfews are often temporarily imposed in times of disaster, riot, or emergency to reduce looting, accidents, and sabotage and to keep roads clear for emergency vehicles or the military. During the Middle Ages, daily curfews were enforced between the hours of sunset and sunrise and were announced by the tolling of church bells. At the sound of the bell, the city gates were locked, fires were extinguished, and citizens were expected to be in or close to their homes. A primary purpose of this practice was to prevent fires in the largely wooden, congested housing of the typical medieval city or town. However, the curfew also functioned to prevent drunken brawls in taverns and inns and to save local nobles the expense and trouble of law enforcement. Curfews also limited the movement and activities of certain denigrated classes of people, such as Jews and Gypsies (Roma).

During the period of slavery in the United States, all African Americans, slave or free, were required to have passes or manumission papers whenever off the plantation, especially at night. These curfews were rigorously enforced by "patrollers," who were generally local slaveholders, their political allies, and free employees.

More recently, curfews have been imposed on youth in order to keep them off the streets and, by extension, to keep the streets safe. The argument behind these restrictions is that they prevent youth crime and victimization. This appeals to common-sense thinking about parents assuming more responsibility for young people's actions and behavior and the idea that young people really have no legitimate business being out and about beyond school, work, and normal recreational hours. The state, then, has assumed the obligation to define and dictate what constitutes normal hours for young people's comings and goings. Stringent driver's license regulations that restrict the hours during which young people can drive constitute yet another form of state intervention in the lives of young people, as they indirectly impose a curfew (and were intended to do so by state legislatures). It should be noted that many in the minority community tend to view curfews as poorly disguised attempts at controlling their youth. Libertarians see such laws as enforcing a dubious strategy of social control at the expense of individual freedom. Since such laws generally do not work, criminologists have been highly critical of them and the complacency that they produce.

Curfew laws were first widely applied to American youth in the 1890s. Before that period, many youths were expected to work long hours and were on the street at all hours going to and from various workplaces. As the workplace changed and child labor laws came into being, redundant youth thronged the streets, and the problem of gangs and controlling them came to the fore. Curfews became popular as a way to regulate young, aggressive males and to keep young girls from being "ruined" by questionable associations. The hope was that curfews would help parents regain control of their offspring. As concerns with ungovernable youth escalated during the 1950s, the popularity of curfews grew. Today, as many as 75 percent of American cities have curfew laws, and law enforcement sees them as self-evidently useful tools.

One reason for the popularity and utility of curfews is that they help identify at-risk children within the younger range of offenders. Young children who are out at night are obviously poorly supervised, and an intervention of some sort is required. Law enforcement also approves of the ability that curfews afford them to stop and question all young people. Moreover, it is assumed that the likelihood that they will be stopped by law officers has at least some deterrent effect on youths who consider breaking curfew laws. Another attractive feature to law enforcement is that curfew laws usually require no additional resources or expenditures; they essentially afford police the discretionary power to detain young persons.

Curfew law sanctions may apply to youth, parents, or both. Fines can range from low, symbolic fees to thousands of dollars. Curfew laws operate under questionable commonsense assumptions. An important issue is that of parental involvement. That is, do the parents even care enough to use the laws to enforce discipline over their children's movements? Are the parents motivated and are they even present and not disabled by circumstance, distance, incarceration, disease, or substance abuse? Finally, another problematic assumption is that delinquents will simply stop conducting delinquent acts altogether if their nocturnal movements are subject to police intervention. The possibility that they will simply shift their delinquency to times not delineated by the curfew seems an inescapable outcome, however—one that is not much discussed by curfew advocates.

In surveys, parents and juveniles have both agreed that curfews could reduce juvenile delinquency. Most mayors share this belief, according to research. However, some truly laughable claims have been made to support the deterrent effects of curfews, and however popular they may be, research based on a dozen studies does not indicate that such regulations reduce juvenile crime and victimization. Their impact has been found to be small and limited to burglary, larceny, and simple assault. In some jurisdictions, serious crime has increased after curfew laws were strictly enforced. Moreover, because only one in five violent juvenile crimes occurs during curfew hours, it is clear that the impact of curfew laws must be limited.

Francis Frederick Hawley
Western Carolina University

See also Conditions of Community Corrections; Cook County Juvenile Court; Graduated Sanctions for Juvenile Offenders; Probation and Parole: Intensive Supervision; Public Safety and Collaborative Prevention

Further Readings

Adams, K. "The Effectiveness of Juvenile Curfews at Crime Prevention." *Annals of the American Academy of Political and Social Science*, v.587 (May 2003).

Howell, J. *Preventing and Reducing Juvenile Delinquency: A Comprehensive Framework*, 2nd ed. Thousand Oaks, CA: Sage, 2009.

Mays, G. L. and L. Winfree. *Juvenile Justice*. New York: McGraw-Hill, 2000.

DAY REPORTING CENTERS

Day reporting centers (DRCs), also referred to as day treatment centers, community treatment centers, and community resource centers, function as one form of intermediate sanction. DRCs provide enhanced supervision compared to regular probation and a focus on community-based treatment options. Ultimately, as an alternative to incarceration, the successful operation and function of a DRC should result in a cost savings to a state, county, or other governmental agency.

History

DRCs were first developed in Great Britain in the 1970s. British DRCs were intended to serve non-violent, chronic offenders. The theory behind the creation of British DRCs was that these low-level chronic offenders, who were often substance abusers and had mental health problems, did not pose a threat to public safety. Rather, they committed petty crimes to support addictions or because they simply lacked the basic life skills necessary to function in a law-abiding manner. Prior to the creation of DRCs, these offenders were subject to incarceration at a significant cost to the government. Probation officials persuaded the government to establish the DRCs to address the needs of these offenders in a community setting rather than sentencing them to periods of confinement in an effort to reduce costs and recidivism.

The British experience contributed to the establishment of DRCs in the United States in the 1970s.

These first American DRCs were used for juvenile offenders and the mentally ill, who returned to the community during the process of deinstitutionalization that was occurring during that period. DRCs were used for juvenile offenders as part of an effort to reduce the unnecessary incarceration of juveniles and its deleterious effects, while fostering the rehabilitative ideal. DRCs were also helpful in assisting and managing the mentally ill in the community. In the mid-1980s, officials in both Connecticut and Massachusetts developed DRCs for adult offenders. Growth was slow until the 1990s, when the number of DRCs significantly increased.

It is often argued that the rapid growth of DRCs, along with other intermediate sanctions and alternatives to incarceration, is attributable to skyrocketing prison populations and overcrowding in jails in the 1990s. Politicians and government officials turned to DRCs as a mechanism to manage offenders in the community in efforts to reduce the size of incarcerated populations and the attendant costs of incarceration.

Eligibility

Eligibility for DRCs varies substantially. DRCs vary by age-group, sex, criminal justice system status, and criminal history eligibility criteria. Some DRCs serve juvenile offenders, some serve adult offenders, and others serve both populations. DRCs that serve both juveniles and adults locate the groups either in separate areas of the same building or at separate locations. DRCs usually separate offenders by sex. Some DRCs that serve both males and females will assign them to coeducational groups, but many separate males and females and assign them to same-sex groups. Still other DRCs exclusively treat one sex. There is some evidence to support the separation of offenders by sex, as they may have different risks and needs and, therefore, require different treatment styles and management techniques.

DRCs also target individuals from different parts of the criminal justice system. DRCs may serve individuals in the pretrial phase, as well as those who have been convicted of an offense and who are on probation or parole. Individuals who are in the pretrial phase of the criminal case process have not been convicted of the current charges. Instead, judges use DRCs to engage and manage defendants in efforts to reduce failures to appear at court proceedings. Defendants participating in DRCs during the pretrial phase are often participating in some sort of treatment or service, such as drug treatment, designed to increase the likelihood of attendance at court proceedings.

Probationers and parolees also attend DRCs. DRCs are used in a variety of ways for convicted offenders. In some cases, offenders are mandated by a judge to attend the DRC as part of the sentence. For example, an offender may receive a split sentence, whereby the individual serves a period of time in jail and then a period on probation. The judge may require the offender to attend the DRC after he or she is released from jail and begins probation under supervision. Some parole authorities also include mandatory DRC participation on the parole certification as a condition of community supervision. In these cases, failure to attend the DRC is viewed as a parole violation and may result in revocation and confinement. Probation and parole officers sometimes use DRCs as an adjunct mode of supervision and treatment for offenders who they believe require more supervision or treatment than typically offered by standard probation or parole supervision, respectively. Finally, DRC referrals are used as an alternative to incarceration for probationers or parolees who have violated the terms of their community supervision and may otherwise be incarcerated for their violations. Thus, DRCs can serve as a step-down or step-up form of supervision and service delivery for pretrial defendants, offenders who have treatment or service needs, or offenders who have trouble abiding by the terms of their community supervision.

DRCs also determine eligibility based on the charges or criminal history. Some are geared toward first-time offenders, while others will serve any offender without a violent criminal history. Some DRCs specifically preclude participation by sex offenders or arsonists, while others cater to these dangerous or difficult-to-manage populations.

Services

DRCs provide both surveillance and services. DRC participants are required to make a certain number of contacts with the DRC every week, based on their phase of participation, in addition to reporting to their probation or parole officers. In some cases, probation and parole officers may be located in the same building as the DRC to increase surveillance, as well as facilitate successful participation in both the DRC and community supervision.

DRCs also serve as a locus for service delivery. DRCs vary in the types of treatment and services they provide but may include life skills training, training in job-readiness and job-seeking skills, job placement, educational services (such as preparation for earning a general equivalency diploma), drug treatment, and individual and group counseling. DRCs may provide these services on-site or serve as the central referral hub to community service providers.

Levels

Many DRCs use a system of graduated levels of supervision. The systems often feature three or four phases of decreasing degrees of supervision and program participation. The strictest level of supervision is the first phase. If participants successfully complete this phase, they can move to the next phase of supervision. Participants can also be sanctioned with return to higher levels of supervision if they fail to meet the terms of their current level of supervision.

Progression through the levels of supervision may be impacted by the length of stay. The length of stay can range from a few days for pretrial defendants to a year for offenders on probation or parole. Most participants attend the DRC for three to six months.

Evaluation

The existing evaluations of DRCs make it difficult to determine whether they are effective at increasing public safety, reducing recidivism, and reducing costs. There is no clear determination of effectiveness, because these evaluations are impacted by the populations targeted by different DRCs, the tolerance for program violations at individual DRCs, and the length of stay. Furthermore, all of the existing research utilizes a quasi-experimental design. The quasi-experimental design makes it difficult for researchers to rule out confounding variables, introduces threats to the internal validity of the study design, and severely impedes researchers' abilities to make conclusions about causal relationships.

Jennifer L. Lanterman
University of South Florida

See also Case Management; Community Corrections as an Add-On to Imprisonment; Community Corrections as an Alternative to Imprisonment

Further Readings

Craddock, Amy. "Day Reporting Center Completion: Comparison of Individual and Multilevel Models." *Crime and Delinquency*, v.55/1 (2009).

Craddock, Amy and Laura A. Graham. "Recidivism as a Function of Day Reporting Center Participation." *Journal of Offender Rehabilitation*, v.34/1 (2001).

Marciniak, Liz M. "The Use of Day Reporting as an Intermediate Sanction: A Study of Offender Targeting and Program Termination." *The Prison Journal*, v.79/2 (1999).

Parent, Dale. *Day Reporting Centers for Criminal Offenders: A Descriptive Analysis of Existing Programs*. Washington, DC: U.S. Department of Justice, 1990.

Parent, Dale et al. *Day Reporting Centers*. Washington, DC: U.S. Department of Justice, 1995.

Tonry, Michael and Kate Hamilton, eds. *Intermediate Sanctions in Overcrowded Times*. Boston: Northeastern University Press, 1995.

DETERMINATE SENTENCING

Determinate sentencing refers to the use of a predetermined range of punishments for criminal offenses, generally set forth by legislative action. It is distinguished from indeterminate sentencing, which gives judges broad discretion in imposing a variety of possible punishments, including fines, probation, restitution, and incarceration.

Definition and Characteristics

The two primary differences between determinate and indeterminate sentencing involve (1) the allocation of authority over sentencing decisions, and (2) in the case of incarceration the point at which the length of a sentence is determined. In determinate sentencing, the allocation of authority over the type and degree of punishment rests with legislatures or with sentencing commissions working under the auspices of legislatures. The effect of this approach is twofold. Primarily, it fundamentally alters *who* makes decisions regarding punishments for criminal offenses. Compared to indeterminate sentencing, determinate approaches restrict judicial discretion on the front end of sentencing as well as correctional discretion on the back end. For example, throughout much of the 20th century it was not uncommon for a judge to be able to choose from among a wide number of punishments for a variety of offenses. When choosing incarceration, however, the length of the sentence was normally later determined by correctional authorities—in particular parole boards, which were chartered with the power to determine when an inmate was fit to reenter society. In this regard, determinate sentencing also shifts the *when* of decisions regarding the length of confinement, from the back end of correctional decisions regarding release to the front end of discrete sentences imposed more immediately after conviction.

When contrasted against indeterminate sentencing, determinate sentencing frequently requires judges to adhere to the use of sentencing "guidelines" that generally take into account the seriousness of the offense and the criminal history of the offender. Many guidelines utilize a type of "sentencing grid," with one axis involving the type of offense and the other axis the criminal history or other factors, each specific possible combination requiring a specific fixed or fixed-range punishment. Not all guidelines within the 20 or so states that use them are determinate, however; some states use only "advisory" guidelines. Moreover, whereas determinate sentencing frequently relies on "presumptive" or "fixed" sentencing guidelines, it is often lumped together with other sentencing legislation, such as mandatory minimum sentences, sentencing enhancements, and three-strikes laws, all of which also limit judicial discretion. Strictly defined, however, determinate sentencing refers only to the use of predetermined sentences with fixed or fixed-range punishments. Because these other types of laws may or may not be "determinate"—for example, they may have no fixed upper range of punishment, or they may be added on to determinate-range punishments—it is not always accurate to define them as such.

History of Determinate Sentencing

Indeterminate sentencing was standard for state and federal criminal courts prior to the 1970s. This approach was rooted in pathological or medical explanations of criminal offending, which assumed that under the right conditions most criminals could be rehabilitated. Indeterminate sentencing was a reflection of this assumption, where criminal court judges in effect "turned over" offenders to correctional systems for an indeterminate period of time as needed for their successful rehabilitation. There was little challenge to this model prior to the late 1960s, largely for the reason that prison and crime rates had generally remained stable throughout most of the 20th century, with the exception of the Great Depression during the 1930s.

Criticisms of the use of indeterminate sentencing emerged in the late 1960s and early 1970s in response to changing social and political factors. During this time, the United States saw a marked increase in reported violent crimes. This increase was coupled with the social unrest of the civil rights and other protest movements, to the effect of a growing public and political perception that crime was out of control and the criminal justice system was not working to maintain law and order. The question of why the criminal justice system was not working had different answers for conservatives and liberals; the former generally saw the system as too lenient, whereas the latter saw it as too inequitable. However, there was a shared belief between these two positions that the use of indeterminate sentencing was problematic, with conservatives arguing that the system was too "soft" on violent or habitual offenders and liberals contending that indeterminate sentencing frequently resulted in radically different punishments for similar crimes committed by white and minority offenders.

The rehabilitative logic of indeterminate sentencing was itself also coming under scrutiny. Robert Martinson's 1974 study of 231 correctional rehabilitative programs argued that "nothing works"—meaning that prison rehabilitation programs demonstrated meager efficacy in reducing reoffending—and the political impact of this report was substantial. It also coincided with a growing and influential body of criminological work that viewed punishment as the primary legitimate function of the criminal justice system. James Q. Wilson's 1975 *Thinking About Crime* cast doubt on the assumed relationship between criminal offending and social factors such as poverty, and Wilson advocated the use of punishment—as opposed to rehabilitation—as the most effective form of deterrence and crime control. Wilson's work was influential on policy makers (notably Ronald Reagan), but equally influential was the work of Norval Morris and Andrew von Hirsch. Like Wilson, both Morris and von Hirsch advocated for a return to an emphasis on punishment, but unlike Wilson they viewed punishment as justified for reasons of social equity, not deterrence, arguing that the primary function of the criminal justice system should be to ensure that criminals received their "just deserts" for their offenses.

On the whole, however, the philosophical differences between deterrence and just deserts arguments was less problematic for policy makers, many of whom saw little contradiction between the two within the growing conservative climate of the late 1970s and early 1980s. Moreover, conservative policy makers found common ground with liberals regarding the failures of the criminal justice system, to the degree that they shared a perception of judicial excess and correctional capriciousness. It is unlikely, however, that determinate sentencing would have emerged in the manner and scope that it did without the work of Marvin Frankel, whose 1973 work *Criminal Sentences: Law Without Order* effectively conceptualized the problems of indeterminate sentencing and judicial discretion as a type of "lawlessness" that was neither effective in controlling crime nor equitable for criminal offenders. His solution to this problem involved removing judicial discretion away from individual judges into expert commissions, and providing these commissions with the legal authority to set binding recommendations regarding sentencing regulations, with the goal of achieving both greater uniformity in sentencing and less capricious use of incarceration.

As a result of Frankel's work in particular, several state legislatures modified their sentencing statues in order to limit the discretion of judges and parole boards in favor of determinate sentences for criminal offenders. In the late 1970s, Arizona, California, Colorado, Illinois, Indiana, Maine, and North Carolina passed determinate sentencing laws.

The "determinate scope" of these laws varied in their degree of limits to judicial and correctional discretion. California's Uniform Determinate Sentencing Act in 1976, for example, set forth discrete sentencing integers of minimum, middle, and maximum penalties for four categories of offenses, with the expectation that judges would impose middle penalties unless they could cite adequate reasons otherwise. On the other end of the continuum, Illinois's 1977 determinate sentencing law allowed for a much broader range of determinate sentencing discretion on the part of judges, with no fixed integers and substantially broader ranges of possible punishments.

Other states followed suit in passing determinate sentencing laws in the 1980s, notably Minnesota in 1980. Minnesota's determinate sentencing laws emerged out of the recommendations of an established sentencing commission that would later be used as a model by the federal government in its passing of the 1984 Sentencing Reform Act. The purpose for this legislation was, according to Congress, to provide for "truth in sentencing" as well as to ameliorate the "unjustifiably wide" disparities in federal sentences. The act abolished the use of parole at the federal level and created the U.S. Sentencing Commission. Following the directives set forth by Congress in the act, the commission in 1987 developed and implemented the use of determinate sentencing guidelines for all federal felony and Class A misdemeanor crimes. The guidelines consisted of 43 separate offense levels and six categories of criminal history, with the intent that offenses would be matched with criminal history to achieve a standardized sentence for each possible combination.

Effectiveness, Outcomes, and Trends

By 2002, comprehensive determinate sentencing legislation was being used in at least 17 states and at the federal level. However, by the early 2000s, its wide appeal as a panacea for both sentencing disparity and effective crime control had begun to wane for several reasons. Most significant, determinate sentencing laws on both the federal and state levels suffered serious legal challenges that restricted or barred their use. Beginning with *Apprendi v. New Jersey* in 2000, the Supreme Court issued a series of rulings that effectively found that the use of judicial sentencing beyond statutory maximums based on facts other than those decided by the jury was in

violation of the Sixth Amendment. While *Apprendi* did not involve determinate sentencing guidelines, its precedent informed *Blakely v. Washington* in 2004, where the Supreme Court applied the same argument to Washington State's determinate sentencing laws, which allowed judges to impose sentences beyond those set forth in the state's presumptive guidelines. In *United States v. Booker* in 2005, and most recently in *Cunningham v. California* in 2007, the same logic was applied respectively to the U.S. Federal Sentencing Guidelines and to California's use of determinate sentencing.

A second problem with comprehensive determinate sentencing legislation that began to temper its popularity was research in the 1990s suggesting that these laws had not proven to reduce crime in a manner proposed by their advocates. Throughout the 1980s, states with determinate sentencing laws had seen increases in crime on a rate similar to those with indeterminate sentencing, and the long and protracted crime decline that began in the mid-1990s was similarly equal among these states. Equally problematic was the growing evidence that this approach did not substantially reduce incarceration—an argument that had been made by Frankel and others as a primary justification for its use. While Washington State and Minnesota had seen smaller than average growth rates in their prison populations, most of the other states that employed determinate sentencing had seen either no marked difference or increases when compared to states that did not use determinate sentencing.

Third, by the late 1990s there was growing criticism aimed at the fact that the overrepresentation of incarcerated minority offenders had not markedly changed under the use of determinate sentencing. Several studies did find a decrease in sentencing disparities in states that used determinate sentencing, but these findings were overshadowed by the proliferation of state and federal criminal laws that appeared to target minorities. The most notable example of this was the federal sentencing guidelines for possession or distribution of crack and powder cocaine, which set similar sentences at a disparity of 100:1 (5 grams of crack versus 500 grams of powder cocaine) and resulted in a substantial increase in the rate of incarcerated African Americans.

Arguably however, the fact that no states have passed new comprehensive determinate sentencing laws for more than 20 years is less an indictment of the pervasiveness of this approach to sentencing than might first appear. In response to a variety of factors—legal challenges and rulings, academic findings, innovations in corrections and penology, and financial constraints—state legislatures have increasingly moved away from the broad and blunt instrument of comprehensive determinate sentencing legislation toward the use of mandatory minimums, sentencing enhancements, and three-strikes legislation. Like comprehensive determinate sentencing laws, these newer sentencing approaches restrict judicial discretion on the front end and correctional discretion on the back end. In some cases, they may indeed be "determinate" to the degree that they utilize mandatory minimum and maximum penalties. However, the popularity of such laws today, where every state and the federal government has some form of mandatory minimum sentencing and at least 40 states have some type of "habitual offender" law (three-strikes and similar laws), reflects the fact that they do not require a significant reworking of entire sentencing structures in order to achieve many of the same objectives. Rather, these laws can be applied piecemeal to one type of offense or to one category of offender (particularly habitual offenders). Compared to comprehensive determinate sentencing legislation, these laws have been more successful in withstanding legal challenges; more politically expedient in terms of aiming sentencing laws at specific types of offenses (violent crimes, sex offenses, and drug offenses); and more easily adapted to existing sentencing structures.

In this regard, while the use of comprehensive determinate sentencing legislation has waned, its impetus toward restricting judicial and correctional discretion has not. Rather, what has emerged in the place of comprehensive determinate sentencing legislation is the growth of a variety of hybrid sentencing approaches that have largely retained the punitive focus of fixed or mandatory sentencing but have largely jettisoned the promise that such approaches can effectively reduce crime or incarceration. Given the public support for such laws, coupled with the reticence of legislators to appear "soft on crime," it seems unlikely that policy makers will shift away from these types of sentencing laws in the near future.

William R. Wood
University of Auckland

See also Attitudes and Myths About Punishment; Indeterminate Sentencing; Martinson, Robert; Parole Boards and Hearings; Probation and Parole: Intensive Supervision; Reducing Prison Populations; Sentencing Guidelines; Three Strikes and You're Out; Truth-in-Sentencing Provisions

Further Readings

Engen, R. "Assessing Determinate and Presumptive Sentencing: Making Research Relevant." *Criminology and Public Policy*, v.8/2 (2009).

Frankel, M. *Criminal Sentences: Law Without Order*. New York: Hill and Wang, 1973.

Griset, P. *Determinate Sentencing: The Promise and the Reality of Retributive Justice*. Albany: State University of New York Press, 1991.

Martinson, Robert. "What Works? Questions and Answers About Prison Reform." *The Public Interest*, v.35 (Spring 1974).

Morris, Norval and Michael Tonry. *Between Prison and Probation: Intermediate Punishments in a Rational Sentencing System*. New York: Oxford University Press, 1990.

von Hirsch, Andrew. *Censure and Sanctions*. New York: Oxford University Press, 1993.

Wilson, James Q. *Thinking About Crime*. New York: Basic Books, 1975.

DISABLED OFFENDERS

Disabled offenders are subject to the manipulation of those who would take advantage of their disabilities. Many intellectually disabled offenders have diminished insight as to how their exploitation unfolded and few options to protect themselves from additional mistreatment. Therefore, disabled offenders necessitate advocacy, intervention, education, and specialized case management.

Defining Disabled Offenders

The definition of *disabled offender* includes broad categories of the disability community. Disability offenders include individuals who have disabilities related to one or more of the following areas: (1) physical, (2) mental, (3) aging, or (4) additional disabilities. Basic categories include (1) severe psychological disability, (2) mental retardation, (3) neurological impairment, and (4) substance abuse problems. These individuals may suffer multiple handicaps, mental disorders, and drug abuse problems.

Offenders with severe social limitations, learning disabilities, language barriers, and educational

Disabled offenders may suffer several handicaps, like neurological disorders, mental retardation, or drug abuse problems, and their specialized needs and problems require individualized attention and solutions. (Photos.com)

deficiencies present a major dilemma. The aging inmate population and mandated sentences impact correctional communities with an assortment of infirmities, including Alzheimer's disease and other forms of dementia. Sex offenders, considered treatable, may also be included in the disabled category. This entry will emphasize intellectually disabled offenders.

Intellectually disabled offenders have difficulty when attempting to verbalize their needs and express themselves. Therefore, disabled individuals are particularly vulnerable to abuses from the criminal justice system; however, most of their crimes are less violent. Many disabled offenders have a profound need for acceptance. They have the capacity to be easily motivated or manipulated into engaging in criminal behaviors. Their goal is to achieve approval or friendship. This offender is especially vulnerable when dependent personality disorder is added to the intellectual disability.

Encounters With Law Enforcement and the Criminal Justice System

The intellectually disadvantaged population is particularly susceptible during police interviews and interrogations. Disabled offenders may be inclined to accommodate the police at some point in the interrogation. Because of their disability, they are more likely to confess to crimes they did not commit. In addition, they are less likely to understand their constitutional rights under the *Miranda* decision and thus are less likely to withhold statements pending an attorney's counsel.

The intellectually disadvantaged may desire to please those in authority, leading to inadequate legal counsel and speedy plea bargains. They are more likely to plead guilty and not necessarily receive a lesser sentence or reduced charges. The legal disadvantages at predetermined stages of the criminal justice system create a double standard for achieving justice for the disabled offender.

Inmates with intellectual disabilities are at constitutional risk and legal disadvantage during their experience with the criminal justice system. Pretrial and trial processes present conflict for disadvantaged offender populations. Their status creates the need for an individualized effort to meet the constitutional mandates of the Fourteenth Amendment (the due process clause and equal protection clause requirements). Immediate assistance from an attorney may help disabled individuals receive equal justice under the law.

The intellectually disabled are especially defenseless and open to exploitation when incarcerated with hardened criminals. There is approximately one intellectually disadvantaged prisoner for every 20 prisoners. Once incarcerated, the disabled prisoner is very likely to become victim to sexual exploitation, which leads to additional emotional problems.

Moreover, this population has difficulty remembering prison rules. Therefore, they are frequently cited for infractions. Rule infringements can lead to prison disciplinary actions and longer periods of incarceration for failure to earn release time for "good time" served. The secondary results of their noncompliance with prison rules can result in fewer opportunities for parole.

Advocacy, Intervention, and Education

The disabled offender population requires advocacy to protect their rights when they encounter the criminal justice system. Advocacy programs are important to support fairness, due process, and equal protection under the law. Opportunities for disabled persons to participate in alternatives to incarceration and specialized correctional programs offer appropriate opportunities for treatment. Advocates encourage support for the proper legislation and protection of the disabled population's fundamental human rights.

The identification of the intellectually disabled offender population takes professional effort and programmed strategies. The primary goal of providing assistance to disabled offenders must target the preliminary stages of the criminal justice system. This initial process starts with educating police officers and judges to respond appropriately during early encounters. Police officers and investigators risk the suppression of any confession when taking advantage of the disabled offender.

The central theme of educational programs requires emphasis on eliminating social stigma and discrimination. Disabled offenders become adept at concealing their disabilities to avoid stigma and discrimination. Criminal justice education requires accessing the court system concerning disabled offenders' possible adjustment to community placements. Community education programs emphasize the needs of disabled offenders and their accountability in community-based programs. These disabled offenders require education concerning citizenship and the law. Disabled offenders need information concerning relevant community support services to alleviate social pressures and reduce criminal behaviors.

Case Management

The probation officer or correctional counselor emphasizes counseling and treatment modalities and applies a specialized caseload model. The approach is individual and strives for excellent rapport with the offender. The purpose is to establish the changes necessary for adjustment to community life.

The probation officer or correctional counselor applies social work strategies and individualized casework methods to provide the necessary support for the social or physical adjustment for the disabled offender. A personalized plan is encouraged and developed to help facilitate the improvement of the disabled offender's behavior. The plan identifies relevant criminal justice and community services.

The primary issues with the intellectually disabled offender stem from poor self-esteem, impulse-control issues, developmental disabilities, and an inadequate educational foundation. Counseling and treatment programs seek to reduce vulnerabilities that place the disabled person at risk. The treatment program requires excellent assessment and evaluation. Caseworkers and counselors may well discover that these offenders' criminal behaviors are based on an array of intellectual, emotional, and physical difficulties.

Conclusion

Disabled offenders are a growing population in the criminal justice system, and incarceration is increasingly the incorrect solution. No simple solution is available for disabled criminal offenders; their special problems require complex solutions: superior counseling and excellent individualized programming. The recognition that this population requires a specialized caseload model offers a pragmatic start to improving support and identifying effective solutions for disabled offenders.

Thomas E. Baker
University of Scranton

See also Cultural Competence; Diversity in Community Corrections; Employment-Related Rights of Offenders; Offenders With Mental Illness; Specialized Caseload Models

Further Readings

Bolin, Sheila A., R. A. Flesch, and Fanchon A. Funk. *Disabled Offenders: (Stop, Search and Arrest)*. Longwood, FL: Gould, 1997.

Camilleri, J. A. and V. L. Quinsey. "Appraising the Risk of Sexual and Violent Recidivism Among Intellectually Disabled Offenders." *Psychology, Crime and Law*, v.17/1 (2011).

Lindsay, William R., John L. Taylor, and Peter Sturmey, eds. *Offenders With Developmental Disabilities*. Hoboken, NJ: Wiley, 2004.

Mawhorr, T. L. "Disabled Offenders and Work Release: An Exploratory Examination." *Criminal Justice Review*, v.22/1 (1997).

Springer, David W. and Albert R. Roberts, eds. *Handbook of Forensic Mental Health With Victims and Offenders: Assessment, Treatment, and Research*. New York: Springer, 2007.

DISCRETIONARY RELEASE

Discretionary release is the key feature of the indeterminate sentencing system. The indeterminate sentencing system allows individualized measures of incarceration for offenders sent to prison and gives parole boards discretion to determine when an offender is ready to be released, under supervision, back into the community. Each year, approximately one quarter of those released from imprisonment are released through the discretionary mechanism.

The uses of indeterminate sentencing and its counter-system, determinate sentencing, vary across the United States. Historically, however, indeterminate sentencing was dominant until the rehabilitative ideal came under attack in the 1970s. With disillusionment in the successes of rehabilitation schemes, followed by the implementation of "get tough" or "tough-on-crime" policies in the 1980s and later, determinate sentencing schemes, whereby the parameters of an offender's prison term are dictated by legislation, steadily began to replace indeterminate systems. As those systems were replaced, parole boards steadily lost much of their discretionary power of release. Discretionary release had been, and still is, the primary mechanism by which to reduce overcrowding in prisons and alleviate associated costs. As it was scaled back, however, the correctional system grew and prisons were, and still are, often to be found running far beyond their intended capacities.

The use of discretionary release will often be tempered by two variables: cost and the political climate. An offender will be released back into the community only after a parole board is satisfied that he or she has served a suitable length of the sentence term and no longer poses a threat to the public. General support for such releases, however, has historically been susceptible to change stemming from both public and political attitudes, and parole boards are not fully immune to those influences. In 1980, while determinate sentencing was still gathering favor among states, more than half of prisoners who were released were done so with the discretion of parole boards. Today, however, that number has been reduced to approximately half; the political climate has been less hospitable to the early release of convicted offenders. In addition, the general public has grown to be less deferential to a parole board's decision making and is more supportive of offender terms being dictated by legislation. The other factor, cost, which works in conjunction with or is even born of the political climate, also exercises influence over the use of discretionary release. Recent pressures on state budgets mean that, for many states, corrections is no longer protected from fiscal cuts. As budgets have been curtailed, prisons are expected to spend less, and one way of freeing up space, and reducing cost, is to invoke discretionary release. States may therefore turn to this mechanism to relieve pressure on the prison system.

The repeal of indeterminate sentencing, and consequentially the scaling back of discretionary release, was a hallmark of the change in crime policies and attitudes toward criminal offenders after the collapse in the belief of rehabilitation. In the mid-1970s, the rehabilitative ideal was widely judged to have been a failure, and indeterminate sentencing was deemed, by all along the political spectrum, to have been poorly utilized. As indeterminate sentencing came under attack, so too came the attack on parole boards, which were criticized for arbitrary and poorly calculated decision making. For decades, parole boards had been relied upon to determine when an offender was ready to be released from prison. However, just as the "treatment" given to those incarcerated was judged as having failed, as a corollary, so too was the insight and power of parole boards to judge an offender's early release back into the community. By 1978, six states had passed determinate sentencing laws, and that number increased to 14 by 1996. By 2000, four states had abolished discretionary release for certain categories of offenders, and 16 states had abolished discretionary release for all offenders.

Even where indeterminate sentencing schemes are still in operation, an offender is not guaranteed parole—or even an appearance before the parole board. Contrary to popular belief, an offender does not decide to apply for parole; the decision on whether an offender is eligible for early release is made for that person. In *Greenholtz v. Inmates of the Nebraska Penal and Correctional Complex* (1979), the U.S. Supreme Court held that inmates do not have a constitutional right to expect parole. In light of the decision, states have been free to determine what standards an inmate must meet in order to be considered for discretionary release. Some offenders, by virtue of the offense for which they were incarcerated, have been deemed ineligible for release back into the community. Generally, those offenders released under the discretion of parole boards are those whose offenses are relatively minor; sex offenders and those convicted of violent crime, for example, are most often expected to remain incarcerated for the length of their term.

Mark N. Pettigrew
University of Manchester

See also Determinate Sentencing; Indeterminate Sentencing; Parole Boards and Hearings; Probation and Parole: Intensive Supervision

Further Readings

Barton-Bellessa, Shannon M. and Robert D. Hanser. *Community Based Corrections: A Reader*. London: Sage, 2011.

Champion, Dean J. *Probation, Parole and Community Corrections*. Upper Saddle River, NJ: Prentice Hall, 2007.

Kuziemko, Ilyana. *Going Off Parole: How the Elimination of Discretionary Prison Release Affects the Social Cost of Crime*. Cambridge, MA: National Bureau of Economic Research, 2007.

DIVERSION PROGRAMS

Society has developed a wide array of ideological and pragmatic sanctions in response to crime; these include retribution, reform, deterrence, incapacitation, restoration, and rehabilitation. Although any of these sanctions, whether employed singularly or concurrently, may be deemed appropriate and proportionate to the seriousness of certain offenses, there are many times when alternative and more productive means for addressing and remediating criminal behavior are preferred. This has led to the introduction and popular use of diversion programs, which ostensibly involve diverting offenders away from the criminal justice system toward some form

An offender processed through a diversion program participates in a community-based treatment and supervision program that will often lead to a reduced charge and will relieve overburdened court systems, police departments, and probation officers. (Photos.com)

of treatment, remediation, and prevention of further criminal behavior.

Diversion programs (also referred to as diversionary programs) typically are applied to first-time offenders involved in minor offenses or nonviolent crimes, such as criminal mischief, fraud, theft, embezzlement, domestic violence, prostitution, low-level and nonviolent white-collar crimes, and criminal behavior related to substance (abuse such as the use and possession of controlled dangerous substance or driving while intoxicated). For such criminal behavior, the courts have deemed that diversion programs provide offenders a "second chance" by affording them the opportunity to participate in a community-based treatment and supervision program in lieu of being formally processed through the court and adjudication system. When the offender has satisfactorily completed the conditions of the program, criminal charges are dismissed, thus serving the needs and interests of the defendant and society at large.

History and Purpose

The concept of diversionary programs originated during the mid-1960s and involved juveniles who had committed first-time, minor criminal offenses. Taking into consideration their impressionable age, the negative internalization associated with being taken into custody, and the stigmatization often associated with being labeled a juvenile delinquent or criminal (which can reinforce negative associations with other delinquents and thus encourage further criminal behavior), the courts were interested in providing juvenile offenders a second chance. This was deemed to provide a more humane, sensitive, and a pragmatic approach to addressing the causes of the offending behavior, thus reducing recidivism. Other notable advantages to these juvenile diversionary programs were their ability to reduce caseloads, implement a more streamlined adjudication process, and, most important, provide the counseling, treatment, and support needed to assist the juvenile offender and his or her parents to address collaboratively the conditions and circumstances that lead to the delinquent behavior. This approach set the stage for similar diversionary programs to be implemented for adult offenders. Conceptually, diversionary programs have been lauded as less punitive and more rehabilitative, thus dealing with the causes of offending behavior and helping in the prevention of future criminal behavior.

In addition to relieving the courts and the greater criminal justice system from the impact of burgeoning caseloads and associated expenses, several other benefits are realized by diversionary programs involving adult offenders. First, they provide the offender the opportunity of avoiding criminal prosecution and conviction. Second, they help the offender to avoid the negative stigmatization associated with a criminal conviction. Third, they assist in the treatment and rehabilitation of the offender. Fourth, where applicable, they help facilitate restitution to the victim. Fifth, they reduce recidivism. Finally, they develop responsible and productive alternatives as opposed to taxing an otherwise strained criminal justice system. While the majority of diversion programs occur at the pretrial stage, because of their utility and efficacy they have been extended (where applicable) to offenders during the various stages of the criminal justice process.

L. Siegel and C. Bartollas, addressing diversionary programs, explain that they can be viewed either as those providing "true diversion" or as those that support what has been described as "minimization of system penetration." While true diversion is deemed to have occurred if offenders enter and successfully complete the conditions set forth by the court to avoid criminal prosecution, a minimization of system penetration is accomplished when the extent to which offenders interface with the criminal justice system has been reduced. In this regard, many factors and variables can influence an offender's eligibility for diversion and the extent to which such programs are employed. Some key considerations involve the defendant's criminal history, mental health, history of substance abuse, family and community ties, outcomes of an evaluation, and attitude toward and receptiveness to participating in a recommended diversionary program.

Diversionary programs, therefore, can be viewed as serving five main constituency groups: (1) first-time, low-level juvenile offenders whose arrest and conviction could lead to some form of stigma or negative labeling with long-term debilitating effects and recidivism; (2) first-time, low-level adult offenders who pose no threat to the community and are unlikely to commit future offenses; (3) offenders whose crime may be related to some form of psychological disability or mental impairment and who therefore require special needs programs and are best served by some form of treatment involving counseling and rehabilitative services; (4) offenders whose criminal behavior is related to some form of substance abuse (such as drug or alcohol abuse); and (5) offenders whose criminal behavior is related to some form of social pathology, such as prostitution, gambling, or domestic violence.

Types of Programs

Because any number of factors can contribute to the causes of delinquent, deviant, or criminal behavior, diversionary programs often involve educational and treatment components aimed at addressing the root causes of, or circumstances contributing to, the offending behavior and thus mitigating criminality, providing restitution to the victim, and restoring family and community ties. Such programs may also involve a host of other conditions that serve to prevent the offender from engaging in future criminal behavior. Three popular diversion programs are dispute and resolution programs, substance abuse treatment programs, and mental health treatment programs.

The goal of dispute and resolution programs (also known as mediation programs) is to mediate conflicts between citizens that have led to the filing of low-level criminal complaints, thus relieving the courts of having to reconcile such offenses. With an emphasis on mediation, the disputing parties agree to meet with a specially trained independent mediator in achieving a just and amiable resolution.

Substance abuse treatment programs (sometimes referred to as drug courts) provide counseling and treatment interventions for low-level, first-time drug offenses related to the illegal possession or use of drugs such as cannabis, cocaine, and opiates. Offenders are closely monitored to work with counselors and drug treatment specialists; this typically begins with an initial assessment of an offender's drug use history, to include the results of a drug screening test. The nature and frequency of drugs abused (whether marijuana, amphetamines, barbiturates, cocaine, or prescription medications) and any applicable physiological and psychological dependency will determine the nature and intensity of the treatment employed. It can include regular drug testing, individual and group counseling, and attending Narcotics Anonymous (or, in the case of alcoholics, Alcoholics Anonymous) meetings. Although overcoming addictions is challenging and difficult, these diversionary programs have served to mitigate recidivism and have relieved the courts, prisons, and the criminal justice system at large of offenders who would otherwise have burdened the system and not addressed the causes of their criminality.

Mental health treatment programs are designed for special populations. Disturbingly, many first-time, low-level, nonviolent offenders who enter the criminal justice system suffer from some form of mental illness or psychological impairment. Often indigent and without access to mental healthcare, these offenders are best served by diverting them from the criminal justice system and providing them professional mental health treatment and counseling. Because of the deinstitutionalization of the mentally ill and the lack of community health and social services, many indigent offenders suffering from some form of mental illness do not have access to the necessary counseling and treatment to address the root causes of their criminal behavior. Consequently, many of these offenders make their way into the criminal justice system. Hence, diversionary mental health treatment programs have been instrumental in filling a large void. Underscoring the extent to which juveniles are inflicted with some sort of mental health issue, L. F. Alarid and R. V. del Carmen, citing a report by the Council of State Governments (2008), observed that "nearly two-thirds of boys and three-quarters of girls detained in juvenile facilities were found to have at least one psychiatric disorder, with approximately 25 percent of these juveniles experiencing disorders so severe that their ability to function was significantly impaired." Similar to other diversion programs, mental health treatment programs (often working under the auspices of mental health courts) employ a team approach to treat the offender's disability, thus mitigating the offender's criminal behavior.

Notwithstanding the advantages of diversionary programs in being able to divert first-time, low-level criminal offenders from overburdening the criminal justice system, two notable shortcomings have been identified. The first deals with providing inadequate alternatives for those who fail to complete the requirements of a diversionary program, and the second deals with the issue of "net widening," a term used to describe a phenomenon that actually leads to more offenders being processed by the criminal justice system.

Robert F. Vodde
Fairleigh Dickinson University

See also Drug- and Alcohol-Abusing Offenders and Treatment; Drug Courts; Mediation; Mental Health Courts

Further Readings

Abadinsky, Howard. *Probation and Parole: Theory and Practice*, 11th ed. Upper Saddle River, NJ: Pearson, 2011.

Alarid, L. F. and R. V. del Carmen. *Community-Based Corrections*, 8th ed. Belmont, CA: Thomson Wadsworth, 2011.

Allen, H. E., C. E. Simonsen, and E. J. Latessa. *Corrections in America*, 10th ed. Upper Saddle River, NJ: Pearson Prentice Hall, 2004.

Clear, Todd R., George F. Cole, and Michael D. Reisig. *American Corrections*, 9th ed. Belmont, CA: Thomson Wadsworth, 2010.

Gaines, L. K. and R. L. Miller. *Criminal Justice in Action*, 6th ed. Belmont, CA: Thomson Wadsworth, 2011.

Gilbertson, Troy A. "Systems Modeling for Drug Courts: A Policy Research Note." *Criminal Justice Policy Review*, v.19/2 (2008).

Lightfoot, Elizabeth and Mark Umbreit. "An Analysis of State Statutory Provisions for Victim-Offender Mediation." *Criminal Justice Policy Review*, v.15/4 (2004).

Siegel, L. J. and C. Bartollas. *Corrections Today*. Belmont, CA: Thomson Wadsworth, 2011.

Siegel, L. J. and J. C. Worrall. *Introduction to Criminal Justice*, 13th ed. Belmont, CA: Thomson Wadsworth, 2011.

DIVERSITY IN COMMUNITY CORRECTIONS

Offenders who encounter community corrections are a diverse group of individuals, and numerous diversity variables must be considered when working with this population. Diversity represents differences or variations in class, culture, ethnicity, race, religious preference, gender, abilities, age, nationality, acculturation status, sexual orientation, language preferences, and more. These factors must be considered when working with any client. Community correctional staff need to consider culturally relevant delivery techniques and models to accommodate the unique needs of the individuals whom they serve. It is therefore important to understand the demographics of community corrections, acculturation factors that may affect reintegration, and other cultural considerations when working with individuals in community corrections.

Acculturation and Reintegration of the Offender Into the Community

The U.S. Supreme Court ruling in *Brown v. Plata* (2011) stated that overcrowding of prisoners in the California Department of Corrections was in violation of the Eighth Amendment protection against cruel and unusual punishment. Subsequently, the Supreme Court ordered the release of more than 40,000 inmates back into society. The reintegration process that an offender may experience in his or her transition from incarceration to community corrections may, in and of itself, present an interesting cultural shift. Jail and prison systems provide inmates with a rigid structure in daily operations and schedules. Institutional programs proscribe inmates from functioning independently. For example, inmates are informed when to eat, sleep, recreate, work, and visit. This type of structure provides inmates with a guided routine that increases organizational efficiency as well as inmate safety and security. Additionally, having a set daily routine decreases the risk of miscommunication, unsafe behaviors, violence, and elopement.

Thus, community reintegration is an acculturation process. The transition from the culture of prison to the culture of community corrections will require a paradigm shift for an offender, from a highly structured to a much less structured daily routine and greater degree of accountability. The lack of structure in daily routine may create opportunities for those with less discipline to engage in acts that may increase the risk of recidivism (behaviors, such as a technical violation of supervised release or even another crime, that could lead to rearrest). Offender oversight and risk management are of critical importance to the community corrections staff in order to protect the public. While community-based correctional personnel may provide some level of offender oversight, the responsibility for creating personal structure, developing a daily routine, and complying with the conditions of supervised release is the inmate's.

Cultural Awareness and Sensitivity

In order to facilitate effective community-based interventions, services must be delivered in a culturally competent manner. It is important that community corrections staff provide services that meet the needs of their diverse offender populations. Special accommodations may be needed to facilitate and increase compliance. Individual needs and adjustments in services ought to be broadly considered and culturally relevant. That is, every individual may have unique needs that require accommodation. Staff must feel comfortable inquiring about any cultural practices or special accommodations that may otherwise impact mandatory requirements. For example, a family- or group-oriented intervention model may be more effective than an individual approach for certain ethnic minority groups. Additionally, all services must be provided in the offender's language of preference. Thus, if the community correctional staff member who is assigned to work with an offender speaks a different language, someone who speaks the offender's language should be assigned to the case or an interpreter must be provided. Another consideration for community corrections employees is that individuals typically identify with and relate better to individuals with whom they are most similar. Therefore, when possible, agencies ought to provide diverse community correctional staff to work with a diverse offender population.

Community corrections staff should also consider how the offender's culture and world experiences influence his or her interactions with members of the legal system; these may involve such considerations as trust, ability to communicate, and nonverbal communication. Staff should be aware of their own biases about working with a specific group and proceed accordingly, either by altering their biases or by referring cases to more culturally attuned staff members. When staff do not have familiarity with a specific cultural group or its practices and how those may affect compliance, efforts should be made to obtain training, consultation, or education.

Population Demographics

In the United States, ethnic minorities represent a large number of individuals who are incarcerated. Most of these individuals will return to the community under some form of correctional supervision. Community corrections staff must be prepared to handle issues relevant to ethnic and racial diversity among the client population. Each racial group's historical experience within the realm of race relationships in the United States may affect its members' worldviews, perspectives on the legal system, and how they relate to correctional staff.

Robert Hanser, in *Community Corrections*, sets forth many important considerations for those providing community supervision. Recommendations include recognizing that racial disparities and forms of discrimination exist. Such issues may affect the dynamics of trust, communication, and comfort with correctional staff. Hanser also reminds his audience that within every culture are a variety of subcultures. For example, in the culture of *Hispanics* (the term used by the U.S. Census Bureau), there are four primary groups in the United States: those of Mexican, Central American, South American, and Caribbean descent. However, the terms *Latino* and *Latina* in reference to Americans are considered to be more encompassing than the term Hispanic. Offenders must be referred to in a manner based on self-identification within a specific ethnic group. Additionally, Hanser recommends that the acculturation level and acculturation process of individuals, groups, and families within an ethnic group be considered as they relate to these individuals' level of comfort and assimilation into mainstream society. This can be important, for example, when working with clients such as Asian Americans and Pacific Islanders.

According to the Bureau of Justice Statistics' *Bulletin on Probation and Parole in the United States*, in 2009 there were approximately 5,018,855 men and women under community supervision (namely on probation or parole). In terms of race, whites represented the largest number of individuals in community corrections. The Bureau of Justice Statistics indicated that, of the probation population in 2009, 1,483,180 (55 percent) were white, 804,591 (30 percent) were black/African American, 362,156 (13 percent) were Hispanic/Latino, 25,981 (1 percent) were Asian, and 6,256 (1 percent) were American Indian/Alaskan Native. More than 13,000 inmates identified themselves as biracial. The parole population was somewhat smaller overall (819,308, including federal and state). Whites represented 330,004 (41 percent), blacks/African Americans 315,581 (39 percent), Hispanics/Latinos 145,436 (18 percent), American Indians/Alaskan Natives 8,366 (a bit more than 1 percent), Asians 5,529 (less than 1 percent), and Native Hawaiians/Other Pacific Islanders 1,219 (less than 1 percent).

Given the aforementioned data, blacks and Hispanics were overrepresented among parolees and probationers as compared to their numbers in the general population. That is, according to the 2009 Census Bureau, blacks represented 12.9 percent of the overall population and Hispanics/Latinos represented 15.9 percent. Whites represented a bit more than 65 percent of the general population, which is proportionate to their higher numbers in the community corrections system.

Working With Individuals With Special Needs

Clients with special needs require special services. Depending on an offender's physical limitation or disability, specific mandatory requirements may pose a challenge. For example, special audio devices or telephone equipment may be required for an individual who is deaf or hearing-impaired. Individuals with limited mobility may have unique transportation needs. Thus, community corrections personnel may need to use alternative means of communication, more convenient meeting locations, or assisted transportation. Regardless of the physical disability, however, correctional staff must be prepared to provide appropriate culturally specific services if they are to provide the best service to meet offender abilities.

Elderly Offenders

The National Institute of Corrections (2004) defines the elderly within the realm of corrections as inmates who are 50 years old or older. The base age of 50 is generally used by agencies because environmental factors in prison affect the aging process. These factors include situational stressors (related to finances, family, fear of harm, and so forth), lack of sufficient healthcare, and history of chronic substance abuse. The elder inmate population has grown since the 1990s, and many of these individuals require community-based correctional services. Correctional personnel need to consider the declining health of elderly offenders. These individuals may require assistance with obtaining medical funding or insurance benefits, medical services and care, dietary needs, assisted living or housing services, and special programs.

Women in Community Corrections

According to the Bureau of Justice Statistics, in 2009 males continued to represent the largest number of individuals on probation (76 percent) and parole (88 percent), as compared to women (24 percent and 12 percent, respectively). In 2007, it was estimated that 1.7 million children had an incarcerated parent, accounting for 65,600 mothers who were incarcerated in 2007, according to the February 2009 Sentencing Project.

A unique set of gender-specific considerations must be taken into account when working with female offenders. They are more likely to have histories of sexual and other physical abuse, domestic violence, and substance abuse. Women may experience separation issues, feelings of guilt related to periods of separation from their children, and attachment issues. Strength-based interventions or treatment approaches may be more effective when working with women. That is, an emphasis must be placed on assets, empowerment, and enhancement of personal strengths. If women offenders have a history of physical or sexual victimization, special precautions should be taken to ensure that the individuals are not continually subjected to victimization. Thus, community corrections staff must have adequate knowledge and training in the unique dynamics of the cycle of abuse. Staff must be prepared to provide a safety plan for the women and their children (if any) and consider unique issues related to privacy of information and confidentiality.

Gay, Lesbian, Bisexual, and Transgender Offenders

Just as ethnic minorities may experience negative effects from the cultural, historical, and environmental variables of mainstream society, members of the gay, lesbian, bisexual, and transgender (GLBT) community constitute a marginalized group and may have experienced similar discrimination. The lives and world experiences of members of the GLBT community may also affect their feeling of safety and their ability to communicate with certain correctional staff. It is important to establish a sense of trust and rapport with members of this population. While offenders are in prison, staff are required to protect prisoners from violence. Community corrections staff will have the same responsibility if an offender presents concerns about risk of safety in the community because of sexual or gender identity. Violence prevention, safety concerns, and special privacy issues must be regarded. Services for transgender offenders might include safe housing and possibly gender-specific programming. It is also critical that services be offered according to the offender's gender identity, as opposed to her or his biological gender.

Michelle Hoy-Watkins
Chicago School of Professional Psychology

See also Attitudes and Myths About Punishment; Cultural Competence; Disabled Offenders; Elderly Offenders; Employment-Related Rights of Offenders; Female Offenders and Special Needs; Offenders with Mental Illness

Further Readings

Bloom, Barbara and Anne McDiarmid. "Gender-Responsive Supervision and Programming for Women Offenders in the Community." In *Topics in Community Corrections: Annual Issue 2000 Responding to Women Offenders in the Community*. http://nicic.gov/Library/Files/period180.pdf (Accessed July 2011).

Brown v. Plata, 563 U.S. ___ (2011).

Center for Children and Families in the Justice System. "10 Principles of Service Delivery." 2004–10. http://www.lfcc.on.ca/HCT_SWASM_3.html (Accessed July 2011).

Gould, Laurie A. "Perceptions of Risk, Need, and Supervision Difficulty in the Community Corrections Setting." *Southwest Journal of Criminal Justice*, v.6/3 (2010).

Hanser, Robert D. *Community Corrections*. Thousand Oaks, CA: Sage, 2010.

National Institute of Justice, Office of Justice Programs. *Culture and Diversity Issues in Restorative Justice*. Washington, DC: Author, 2007.

The Sentencing Project. *Incarcerated Parents and Their Children: Trends 1991–2007*. http://www .sentencingproject.org/doc/publications/ publications/inc_incarceratedparents.pdf (Accessed July 2011).

Stevens, Kelli D. "Addressing Gender Issues Among Staff in Community Corrections." http://www.aca.org/ fileupload/177/ahaidar/Stevens.pdf (Accessed July 2011).

Tseng, Wen-Shing, Daryl Matthews, and Todd Elwyn. *Cultural Competence in Forensic Mental Health: A Guide for Psychiatrists, Psychologists, and Attorneys*. New York: Brunner-Routledge, 2004.

U.S. Bureau of Justice Statistics. *Bulletin on Probation and Parole in the United States, in 2009*. http://www .bjs.gov/content/pub/pdf/ppus09.pdf (Accessed July 2011).

U.S. Department of Justice National Institute of Corrections. *Correctional Health Care: Addressing the Needs of Elderly, Chronically Ill, and Terminally Ill Inmates*. Washington, DC: 2004.

Drug- and Alcohol-Abusing Offenders and Treatment

There is a great deal of interest in community corrections as a means of dealing with the problems of the abuse of illegal substances, pharmaceuticals, and alcohol. Much has been made of their link to crime, and there continues to be some debate about the propriety of treatment versus punishment, especially for drug offenders. In the context of community corrections, it is important to understand the relationship between substance use problems and crime, the impact of community treatment, some of the requisites for effective treatment (diagnosis and use monitoring), and some of the types of treatment available.

The Arrestee Drug Abuse Monitoring Program of 2009 (ADAM II) sampled adult males who were arrested in 10 different cities across the United States. Of the arrestees sampled, 31 to 51 percent had used marijuana in the previous 30 days, 17 to 44 percent tested positive for cocaine, and between 1 and 29 percent tested positive for heroin. The data from ADAM II underscore the problem of drugs in America, but they also show something else. The distribution of the drugs used at the time of arrest varies widely from city to city. Methamphetamine was used by 31 percent of arrestees in Sacramento, California, but was almost unknown in New York. Similarly, although heroin was used by 18 percent of Chicago arrestees, it was present for only 1 percent of arrestees in Charlotte, North Carolina. Drug abuse is a real problem, but it is not a uniform problem. Drug abuse is often a part of a local culture and economy; it is not a single phenomenon.

Violent crimes accounted for more than 15 percent of the arrests in nine out of the 10 ADAM cities and ranged from 17 percent in Atlanta to a high of 31 percent in Chicago. Property crimes accounted for 11 percent of arrests in Washington, D.C., and 34 percent in New York. Drug-related crimes, including simple possession, accounted for more than 20 percent of crimes in all sites and nearly 50 percent of arrests in Washington and Chicago. A final category, other crimes, made up more than 40 percent of all crimes in six of the 10 cities. The other crimes category included violations of community supervision (probation and parole), public order offenses, traffic offenses (including driving under the influence and driving while intoxicated), and other minor offenses. It is striking to note that the combined levels of the drug crimes and the other categories account for more than 60 percent of all crimes in nine of the 10 reporting cities and more than 75 percent of all arrests in half of the cities sampled. While this does not negate the fact that drug and alcohol use is associated with criminal activity, like broader patterns of criminality, the larger proportion of crimes reported are nonviolent.

Although using a different measure (the number of reported arrests, not individuals arrested), the Federal Bureau of Investigation (FBI) drug arrest statistics for 2009 indicate that 18.4 percent of drug arrests were for manufacturing or distribution, whereas 81.6 percent of those arrests were for possession, with the total number of drug-related arrests estimated at 1,663,582. Arrests for driving under the influence (of drugs or alcohol) were estimated at 1,440,409. As noted in the ADAM II report, the bulk of arrestees had been arrested multiple times in the previous year. According to the Bureau of Justice Statistics, in 2008, 19 percent of the victims of violent crime believed that the offender was under the influence of alcohol.

Treatment as an Answer to the Cost of Imprisonment

The Pew Charitable Trusts report that in April 2010 there were more than 1.6 million Americans in jail or prison. The National Center on Addiction and Substance Abuse at Columbia University (CASA) estimates that the cost of imprisonment for drug offenders at both state and federal levels amounts to $37 billion a year. Diversion of even 10 percent of that population to drug treatment would result in significant savings.

As a policy issue, drug-related crime has become a centerpiece of some of the commonsense approaches to the costs of imprisonment and the practical effects of drug treatment. In 2000, California's Proposition 36, by allowing for diversion or treatment for persons whose most serious offense was drug possession, set the tone for correctional treatment for drug offenses across the nation. According to the Campaign for New Drug Policies, in the year after its implementation, prison populations in California dropped by 20 percent, a reduction of 4,000 persons. This led to a spate of similar initiatives across the country that resulted in significant savings from both the long-term effects of treatment and the short-term savings in the direct costs of imprisonment.

While the move from a punishment regime to a treatment regime has been resisted in some quarters, both the National Institute on Drug Abuse (NIDA) and CASA agree that there is significant evidence that mandated treatment is as effective as voluntary treatment and that community supervision is as effective in its capacity to reduce recidivism as imprisonment. There is long-standing agreement that mandated treatment keeps people in treatment long enough to have a positive effect on both their substance use problems and the probability that they will return to crime. For persons under community supervision (probation, parole, supervised release, and pretrial diversion), drug and alcohol treatment represents a cost-effective means of providing a humane and effective measure of correctional control and rehabilitation.

Addiction Treatment: Assessment and Monitoring

According to NIDA, addictions come in many forms, and treatment needs to be tailored to the needs of the client; there is no "one size fits all" remedy. From the outset, it is important to determine the offender's level of drug or alcohol involvement. It is possible to differentiate between substance users (experimental or recreational users), abusers (persons who have had or risked significant trouble with family, employers, school, or the law because of ongoing drug or alcohol use), those who are physically dependent (those who display withdrawal symptoms, use more than they would like to use, or show an inability to quit), and those who are addicted (those who display the symptoms of dependence along with craving and obsessing about the problem substance or behavior). These basic levels are typically determined by instruments using criteria from the *Diagnostic and Statistical Manual* of the American Psychiatric Association. For this purpose, there are multiple scales and diagnostic services available to community corrections professionals.

Each level of problem calls for a different kind of response. Whether the problem is illegal drugs, prescription drugs, alcohol, or multiple substances, diagnosis of the level of the problem is an essential first step toward treating the problem. In the context of community corrections, diagnostic services can be provided by consultants and contract agencies, although some community corrections agencies do in-house assessments.

One of the important considerations for any drug treatment regimen is the accurate monitoring of continuing substance use during treatment. It is impossible to determine whether treatment is working if there is no objective measure. Although there are multiple ways of determining whether or not an offender assigned to substance abuse treatment is drinking or using drugs, the most common way of testing for drugs is urinalysis. Most programs test for the so-called NIDA–5 (cannabinoids, cocaine, amphetamines, opiates, and phencyclidine). Expanded panels also test for alcohol, barbiturates,

Ecstasy, and other substances. Ideally, offenders with treatment conditions should submit to random urinalysis on a weekly basis. The protocol for taking random weekly samples allows the sample to be taken on any day of the week; the client does not know on which day she or he will submit the sample. Other tests for substance use include sweat patches, blood testing, hair samples, and pupil responses.

Because alcohol is typically out of the system within 24 hours, urinalysis is often replaced with regular breathalyzer tests for those who abuse alcohol. According to a 2006 Substance Abuse and Mental Health Services Administration (SAMHSA) advisory, a relatively new urine test for alcohol, ethylgluconuride (EtG), may be used to detect the use of alcohol up to 80 hours after use, but it is insufficiently supported to sustain legal action.

Standard treatments for alcoholism and addiction include programs for long-term inpatients, short-term inpatients, and outpatients, as well as drug courts and any of these options accompanied by pharmacological aids. Pharmacological aids divide into two variants, those that block the effects of the substance and those that punish the use of the substance.

Following assessment, an appropriate level of treatment is assigned. A wide variety of treatments and supportive modalities are available. The most familiar approach to drug and alcohol problems is provided by the 12-step movement and is found in Alcoholics Anonymous, Narcotics Anonymous, Cocaine Anonymous, and similar groups. Although familiar to almost everyone, these are not treatment modalities but rather support groups. In and of themselves, without the application of a therapeutic regime, their worth is questionable. Nevertheless, NIDA reports that they are widely used to support treatment in the addictions and alcoholism community. Variants of the 12-step model have arisen with specific religious and nonreligious orientations: Jewish, Fundamentalist Christian, Rationalist, and others.

Inpatient Treatment

During the evolution of the disease model of addiction and alcoholism, the most consistent model of inpatient treatment became a medically assisted detoxification regimen, followed by either a 30-day (short-term) or 180-day or longer (long-term) inpatient treatment.

Because some drugs, including alcohol and benzodiazepines, have a potentially life-threatening withdrawal syndrome, their treatment is most frequently preceded with a medically assisted withdrawal or detoxification regime. Other drugs, including cocaine, heroin, and methamphetamines, do not have dangerous withdrawal syndromes, but medical assistance may be used to ensure the comfort of the patient and encourage completion of the process.

After detoxification, inpatient programs begin a regimen of strict discipline, usually incorporating a component of addiction education, an examination of thinking patterns. and a cognitive behavioral program designed to identify relapse cues and how to avoid them. Many such programs also include regular attendance at 12-step meetings, often several each day. As part of their bio-psycho-social approach to addiction treatment, such programs also provide employment assistance and family counseling. Both long-term and short-term treatments typically offer outpatient follow-up programs to provide continuing counseling and support for program graduates. Some provide aftercare at sober houses, where graduates can reenter the community in a supportive environment.

Whether a client is assigned to long-term or short-term treatment is often determined by the kind of substance he or she has been using, the length of the involvement with the substance, the length and depth of the involvement in an aberrant lifestyle, and the presence of comorbidities: co-occurring diagnoses and problems.

The more complex the defining problems and the longer the addictive pattern, the more likely it is that the client will be in need of long-term treatment. NIDA suggests that treatment must be long enough to effect change in the offender. This is often as little as 30 days and rarely longer than 18 months.

Outpatient Treatment

Outpatient programs vary in composition, emphasis, and number of sessions. Intensive outpatient treatment often requires multiple group sessions, with individual counseling, employment, and family counseling and attendance at 12-step meetings. Less intensive programming may include groups and individual counseling, with other kinds of treatment added as necessary. While there are state-level certifications for alcohol and substance abuse treatment counselors, the quality of services can vary widely from program to program.

Three main approaches to outpatient drug and alcohol treatment have been developed and subjected to significant testing by the federal government and are increasingly used throughout the country. All were manualized and subject to significant testing during and since the Project Match study of the effect of treatment matching on drinking behaviors in alcoholism. In the time since their original publication, all three have been applied to all manner of substance abuse treatments beyond alcohol. These treatments are 12-step facilitation therapy, motivational enhancement therapy, and cognitive behavioral therapy.

The goal of 12-step facilitation therapy is to engage the client in the philosophy and discipline of the 12-step community. This therapy focuses on encouraging the client to take responsibility for his or her problems, to surrender to a higher power, and to build a lifestyle free of substance abuse. The program has had success with alcoholics and has been used with opiate, cocaine, and methamphetamine addicts.

Motivational enhancement therapy (MET) has found a great deal of application and validation both within and outside addiction treatment. It grows directly from the "stages of change" model that came to public attention with the publication of James O. Prochaska, John C. Norcross, and Carlo C. DiClementi's *Changing for Good*. The stages of change model outlines a series of stages through which any change or decision process must pass and identifies specific means for passing from precontemplation (roughly equivalent to denial) to completion, in which the change has been realized and is relatively self-maintaining. Motivational enhancement therapy begins with diagnosis and a description of the problem and works with the offender to identify treatment outcomes. A central part of the approach attempts to have the client understand the inconsistencies between his or her behavior and stated desired outcomes. MET has been shown to be most effective in creating and maintaining the motivation to enter and complete treatment. Combined with cognitive approaches, it has been very effective with alcohol and marijuana addictions.

Cognitive behavioral therapy has already been described and has become one of the most commonly used approaches to drug treatment. It includes addiction education, an examination of thinking patterns, and a cognitive behavioral program designed to identify relapse cues and how to avoid them. It is useful across the range of substance abuse disorders and is often combined with other approaches.

Drug Courts

Drug courts are a significant source of effective community treatment for drug-impacted offenders of all varieties. Drug courts combine the impact of lower caseloads, immediate reinforcement for compliance, and punishments for noncompliance with intense treatment and case management.

Participants are typically enrolled in intensive outpatient treatment programs, accompanied by regular, often weekly (at the outset), reports to the court. In those sessions, their progress, including urinalysis results, is reported to the court by both community corrections officers and drug treatment providers. In the context of those meetings, the court has the authority to impose intermediate sanctions (including short-term imprisonment), relieve or increase reporting requirements, and provide positive reinforcement and encouragement. As the sessions are played out in open court, there is also a strong element of community reinforcement and social learning. Assignment to drug courts is made as part of the sentencing process.

Pharmacological Interventions

Pharmacological interventions are used in conjunction with therapy to block the action of addictive drugs, partially block and partially mimic their action, or cause discomfort when the problem substance is used. Methadone was the first chemical treatment to be approved by the Food and Drug Administration (FDA) for the treatment of opioid addiction and was cited as the treatment of choice for heroin addiction by the American Medical Association (AMA). Methadone blocks the euphoric effects of heroin, morphine, and other opioids while preventing withdrawal symptoms. In combination with counseling, it is held to be very effective in reducing the cravings and relapses that are characteristic of opioid addiction.

Buprenorphine is a drug that partially replaces the action of opioids and partially blocks their actions. It is relatively safe and has been approved for prescription by physicians. In otherwise well-motivated opioid addicts, for whom intensive treatment would be unproductive, it provides a positive alternative. Its efficacy, like that of other treatments, is enhanced by adequate counseling or therapy.

Unlike the other two drugs mentioned, which partially mimic the action of opioids, naltrexone completely blocks their action. Its impact on the nervous system is such that it has been used to eliminate the inebriant effects of alcohol and marijuana as well as heroin and morphine. It is most effective when combined with an adequate counseling regimen.

Two other drugs have been specifically designated for use with alcohol. Acamprosate is prescribed to mollify the symptoms of withdrawal from alcohol and has a positive effect on continuing abstinence. Disulfiram (Antabuse) has been in use for the treatment of alcoholism for many years. Unlike the other pharmacological agents listed, its effects focus not on the neurology of addiction but alcohol metabolism. By interfering with the processing of alcohol and its byproducts, by allowing their accumulation in the body, disulfuran can make persons who drink alcohol while taking this drug violently ill after only one drink. It is used to discourage drinking and to prevent drinking in high-risk situations.

Richard M. Gray
Fairleigh Dickinson University

See also Addiction-Specific Support Groups; Case Management; Community Corrections as an Alternative to Imprisonment; Costs of Community Corrections; Counseling; Drug Courts; Drug Testing in Community Corrections; Motivational Interviewing; Recidivism; Reducing Prison Populations; Specialized Caseload Models; Therapeutic Communities

Further Readings

American Psychiatric Association. *Diagnostic and Statistical Manual of Mental Disorders*, 4th ed. Washington, DC: Author, 1994.

Green, Roberta. "State Prison Population of Drug Users Dropped 20% in 1 Year After Prop. 36." Santa Monica, CA: Campaign for New Drug Policies, 2002. http://www.prop36.org/pdf/P36_drops_Prison_Pops.pdf (Accessed July 2011).

Kadden, R. et al. *Cognitive-Behavioral Coping Skills Therapy Manual: A Clinical Research Guide for Therapists Treating Individuals With Alcohol Abuse and Dependence*. Rockville, MD: U.S. Department of Health and Human Services, 1995.

Miller, W. R. *Motivational Enhancement Therapy Manual: A Clinical Research Guide for Therapists Treating Individuals With Alcohol Abuse and Dependence*. Rockville, MD: National Institute on Alcohol Abuse and Alcoholism, 1995.

National Center on Addiction and Substance Abuse at Columbia University. *Shoveling Up II: The Impact of Substance Abuse on Federal, State and Local Budgets*. 2010. http://www.casacolumbia.org/articlefiles/380-ShovelingUpII.pdf (Accessed July 2011).

National Institute on Alcohol Abuse and Alcoholism. *Cognitive-Behavioral Coping Skills Therapy Manual*. Project MATCH Monograph Series 3. DHHS Publication 94–3724. Rockville, MD: Author, 1994.

National Institute on Alcohol Abuse and Alcoholism. *Motivational Enhancement Therapy Manual*. Project MATCH Monograph Series 2, DHHS Publication 94–3723. Rockville, MD: Author, 1994.

National Institute on Drug Abuse. *Principles of Drug Abuse Treatment for Criminal Justice Populations: A Research-Based Guide*. NIH Publication 06–5316. Rockville, MD: U.S. Department of Health and Human Services, National Institutes of Health, National Institute on Drug Abuse, 2007.

National Institute on Drug Abuse. *Principles of Drug Addiction Treatment: A Research-Based Guide*. Rockville, MD: U.S. Department of Health and Human Services, National Institutes of Health, National Institute on Drug Abuse, 2000.

Nowinski, J., S. Baker, and K. M. Carroll. *Twelve Step Facilitation Therapy Manual: A Clinical Research Guide for Therapists Treating Individuals With Alcohol Abuse and Dependence*. Project MATCH Monograph Series 1. DHHS Publication 94–3722. Rockville, MD: National Institute on Alcohol Abuse and Alcoholism, 1994.

Office of National Drug Control Policy. *Arrestee Drug Abuse Monitoring Program II: ADAM II 2009 Annual Report*. Washington, DC: Executive Office of the President, 2010. http://www.whitehousedrugpolicy.gov/publications/pdf/adam2009.pdf (Accessed July 2011).

Pew Center on the States. "Prison Count 2010: State Population Declines for the First Time in 38 Years." April 2010. http://www.pewcenteronthestates.org/uploadedFiles/Prison_Count_2010.pdf (Accessed July 2011).

Prochaska, James O., John C. Norcross, and Carlo C. DiClementi. *Changing for Good*. New York: William Morrow, 1994.

Substance Abuse and Mental Health Services Administration. "ADVISORY: The Role of Biomarkers in the Treatment of Alcohol Use Disorders." *Substance Abuse Treatment News for the Treatment Field*, v.5/4 (September 2006). http://kap.samhsa.gov/products/

manuals/advisory/pdfs/0609_biomarkers.pdf (Accessed July 2011).

U.S. Bureau of Justice Statistics, Office of Justice Programs. *Alcohol and Crime: Data From 2002 to 2008.* Washington, DC: Author, 2010. http://bjs.ojp.usdoj.gov/content/acf/apt1_crimes_by_type.cfm (Accessed July 2011).

U.S. Department of Justice, Federal Bureau of Investigation. "Crime in the United States, 2009." http://www2.fbi.gov/ucr/cius2009/arrests/index.html (Accessed July 2011).

West, H. C. et al. *Prisoners in 2009.* Washington, DC: U.S. Bureau of Justice Statistics, 2010. http://bjs.ojp.usdoj.gov/content/pub/pdf/p09.pdf (Accessed July 2011).

DRUG COURTS

A drug court is a type of problem-solving court designed to reduce the demand for alcohol and other drugs by addressing offenders' addictions through judicially supervised legal processes whereby the judiciary, prosecution, defense, probation, and treatment providers all work collaboratively. Although drug courts were not developed until the late 1980s, they have proved to be an exceptionally popular approach to the treatment of addiction: As of the end of 2007, there were 2,147 of these courts in the United States. They operate in all 50 states and have been introduced on a modest basis in the United Kingdom and Australia as well.

During the 1980s, as part of the "nothing works" disillusionment with rehabilitation, many U.S. jurisdictions adopted a zero-tolerance approach to drugs. Funding for treatment and prevention was diverted to enforcement and prosecution, and courts struggled to process their swelling dockets. In Dade County (Miami), Florida, criminal justice officials developed the first drug court program in 1989 to cope with large numbers of addicted offenders and growing jail populations. Alameda County, California, opened the second program in 1991.

Drug court proponents believe that addiction to alcohol and drugs is a treatable disease, but it is generally understood that addiction is difficult to overcome and that one or more relapses often occur prior to recovery, for those who do recover. Instead of responding to relapses or minor violations of program requirements with severe and punitive measures (long-term incarceration), many drug court programs employ a regime of graduated sanctions. Initial use of alcohol or drugs may trigger minor sanctions (a verbal reprimand or a requirement that the offender write an essay about the inappropriate behavior), whereas successive violations trigger more serious sanctions (such as community service or a weekend in jail). Conversely, many programs issue small rewards (such as candy bars or a certificate) for success and compliance with program requirements.

Some drug courts, also called diversion courts, operate prior to adjudication. If a defendant who is charged with a drug crime and has no prior convictions completes a preadjudication drug court program, the charge is dismissed and no criminal record is produced. On the other hand, if the defendant does not complete the program, the court records the arrest and the prosecutor files charges for the drug crime. In post-adjudication drug courts, the criminal record already exists, but successful completion of the drug court program may be sufficient to reduce the length of the sentence, sometimes requiring only probation and/or community service.

Key Components

The Drug Courts Standards Committee of the National Association of Drug Court Professionals, in coordination with the Bureau of Justice Assistance, issued a publication in which it identified 10 key features of drug courts. Drug courts are integrated (treatment for alcohol and drugs is combined with processing by the justice system), cooperative (the traditional adversarial relationship between prosecution and defense is replaced with a nonadversarial approach), timely (eligible participants are identified and enrolled quickly), comprehensive (programs provide access to a continuum of treatment services), monitored (abstinence is monitored with frequent drug and alcohol testing), coordinated (programs operate under a comprehensive strategy designed to address noncompliance), judge-led (the judge has ongoing involvement with program participants, not as an arbiter of disputes but as the leader of the nonadversarial team), evaluated (management, monitoring, and evaluation systems all allow program staff to adapt the program to emerging problems and to assess the program's efficacy), training-intensive (program staff are fully trained in drug court operations and issues, and they participate in ongoing interdisciplinary training), and partnership-based (programs operate as a partnership between public, private, and community-based organizations, and they foster the development of coalitions among justice system staff, community groups, and treatment groups).

Successes and Other Problem-Solving Courts

Empirical research of drug courts suggests that they are effective in treating drug and alcohol abuse and in reducing rates of recidivism. Several independent meta-analyses of drug courts have shown that drug courts significantly reduce recidivism rates by an average of 7 to 14 percent, compared to control groups. The U.S. Government Accountability Office (GAO) has issued three reports (1997, 2002, and 2005) on drug courts. Based on an assessment of 23 programs, the 2005 study concluded that offenders who completed drug court programs were significantly less likely than comparison group offenders to be rearrested or reconvicted. The GAO also indicated that, although the up-front costs of drug courts were greater than those associated with probation, drug courts are more cost-effective over time, principally because they reduce recidivism rates and thereby avoid the costs associated with victimization, investigation, prosecution, and corrections. Other researchers have reached similar results. The Washington State Institute for Public Policy found that drug courts cost the public an average of $4,333 per participant but produce savings of $4,705 for the public in recidivism-related expenses and save $4,395 for potential victims. Thus, each participant saves a net $4,767. A California study suggested that drug court programs cost approximately $3,000 per participant but save approximately $11,000 per participant over the long term.

Although drug courts are the most common form of problem-solving court, the key principles and the operational practices of drug courts have been adapted to a variety of other social problems as well, including teen offending, homelessness, prostitution, gun offenses, gambling, and community reentry after imprisonment. At the end of 2007, there were 1,057 problem-solving courts (that were not drug courts) in the United States. Truancy courts were the most common of these (304), although there were also substantial numbers of mental health courts (219), domestic violence courts (185), and child support courts (154).

James C. Oleson
University of Auckland

See also Drug- and Alcohol-Abusing Offenders and Treatment; Drug Testing in Community Corrections;
Family Courts; Mental Health Courts; Teen Courts; Therapeutic Jurisprudence

Further Readings

Belenko, Steven. "Research on Drug Courts: A Critical Review." *National Drug Court Institute Review*, v.1/1 (1998).

Berman, Greg and John Feinblatt. *Good Courts: The Case for Problem-Solving Justice*. New York: The New Press, 2005.

Collins, Lily A. and Jack B. Moyer. *Drug Courts*. Hauppauge, NY: Nova Science Publishers, 2011.

National Association of Drug Court Professionals. *Defining Drug Courts: The Key Components*. Washington, DC: U.S. Department of Justice, Office of Justice Programs, Bureau of Justice Assistance, 2004.

Roper, Glade F. *Drug Courts*. New York: Springer, 2010.

Drug Testing in Community Corrections

Drug testing is the method whereby drugs or the byproducts of drug metabolism in the body (metabolites) are detected through a chemical analysis of biological material (such as blood, hair, or urine) provided by an individual undergoing the test. This method of detection is commonly utilized by juvenile and adult community corrections agencies as an objective way of assessing whether an offender is complying with the terms of his or her supervision. Drug testing is necessary because supervision of an offender in the community is often conditional upon the offender's meeting specific behavioral expectations, such as refraining from the unlawful use of drugs. Probation, parole, halfway houses, and residential facilities are all community corrections agencies that utilize this method of assessment. Although these agencies can test hair and blood samples, the most common biological material used for drug testing is urine. Collecting urine samples is generally considered less intrusive and can provide quick, reliable results.

Administration

Although probation, parole, and residential supervision facilities may be the most recognizable community corrections settings in which drug testing occurs, specialized courts require that offenders be drug-tested on a more frequent and regular basis. For example, drug courts and "driving under the influence" (DUI) courts may mandate the drug testing of offenders several times per month, whereas an offender in a traditional community corrections setting may be tested once per month or at the discretion of the supervising agency. Regarding discretionary testing, the nature of the offense typically influences the frequency of drug tests. Offenders being supervised for drug and alcohol offenses, for offenses committed while under the influence of drugs and/or alcohol, or for a history of either are typically tested with the greatest frequency.

Offenders may be ordered to submit a biological sample for drug testing at a private laboratory, at the community corrections facility, or in the field (for example, at the offender's home). Hair and blood specimens are collected directly by community corrections officials or trained professionals such as nurses or laboratory technicians. Urine specimens are provided by the offender, typically under the direct supervision of a same-sex community

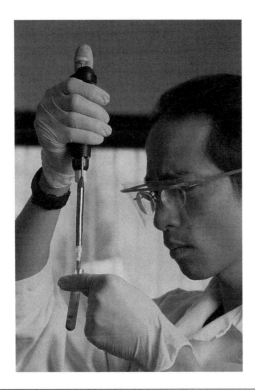

Correctional probation officers use drug tests to monitor offenders' drug and alcohol usage while on community supervision using a chemical analysis of a specimen of blood, hair, urine, sweat, or saliva collected from the offender. (Photos.com)

corrections official or one of the professionals mentioned above.

Supervised specimen collection is necessary to prevent the offender from providing a specimen from another person or intentionally altering the sample through the use of an adulterant or diluting agent. Adulterants, also referred to as masking agents, are meant to conceal the presence of a drug or drug metabolites in a person's urine. Some urine drug testing kits can also detect the presence of masking agents. Detection of a masking agent will, at minimum, result in the offender's being required to retake the test. Severer repercussions are also common and vary by agency and jurisdiction. Unlike the use of masking agents, the dilution of a urine sample will not hide the presence of a drug or drug metabolite. Instead, dilution reduces the concentration of the drug in the sample. This is commonly achieved through ingestion of large amounts of fluid or adding water to the sample. If urine is diluted sufficiently, the drug will not be detectable in large enough quantities to trigger a positive result on the test. This type of adulteration is detectable through visual inspection of the sample (clear urine signals dilution) and with some drug test kits. An offender who provides a diluted sample is typically required to repeat the test until a testable sample is provided.

Testing Methods

Once a testable sample is obtained, it is either tested immediately on site or sent to a laboratory for analysis. The advantages of on-site testing are that it produces immediate results and has a lower cost relative to lab testing. Immediate results are particularly desirable in the community corrections setting, because they expedite the provision of services (such as drug counseling and drug rehabilitation programs) or the criminal justice process (an admonishment, arrest, or court hearing) that can follow a positive test. This type of testing is commonly conducted through a noninstrument method, meaning the testing implement is directly observed by the administrator and results are indicated as either positive or negative. Laboratory tests can be more expensive and take several days to yield results. However, they are calculated through an instrumental process, which uses machinery to detect the presence of drugs or drug metabolites. In addition to providing a greater degree of sophistication, this method is associated with a greater degree of accuracy, because results are quantified rather than being provided in a simple positive or negative fashion. Some jurisdictions prefer accuracy to immediacy, because the results are less likely to be challenged in subsequent court hearings.

Whether on-site or conducted in a laboratory, immunoassay is currently the most utilized drug detection technology. The immunoassay process detects the concentration of a drug by measuring the reaction between antibodies and an antigen (drug or drug metabolite) in a person's bodily fluid, with larger reactions indicating larger concentrations of the drug. A second and less utilized method of drug detection is through gas chromatography/mass spectrometry, which analyzes the test sample at the atomic level. This method is considered the most accurate of all tests but is not used as frequently as immunoassay, because of its relative complexity and cost. Typically, gas chromatography/mass spectrometry is reserved for confirming or disconfirming an immunoassay test that has been challenged in court.

Drug Types

It is important to note the distinction between being prohibited from "using illegal drugs" and being prohibited from "the illegal use of drugs." Offenders under community corrections supervision are typically prohibited from the illegal use of drugs. This means not only the use of illegal drugs such as cocaine and heroin but also the abuse or unlawful use of prescription drugs. For instance, an offender cannot use prescription drugs unless specifically prescribed by a doctor, and only in accordance with the prescribed dosage amounts, while the prescription is valid. Accordingly, most drug tests in community corrections also detect prescription drugs, such as barbiturates and certain opiates and amphetamines. Common illegal and prescription drugs or drug metabolites screened for in drug tests include the following:

- Marijuana/THC
- Cocaine metabolite (from use of cocaine powder or crack cocaine)
- Amphetamines (such as Adderall and Benzedrine)
- Methamphetamine (also called meth, speed, and crank)
- Opiates (such as morphine, heroin, and opium)
- Barbiturates (such as Amobarbital "blues," Secobarbital "reds," and Phenobarbital "goofballs")

Taylor Brickley
University of South Carolina

See also Addiction-Specific Support Groups; Drug- and Alcohol-Abusing Offenders and Treatment; Drug Courts; Offender Risks; Specialized Caseload Models

Further Readings

Dupont, R. L., T. M. Mieczkowski, and R. M. Newel. *Drug Testing in Correctional Settings: Guidelines for Effective Use.* Center City, MN: Hazelden, 2005.

Petersilia, Joan. *Community Corrections: Probation, Parole, and Intermediate Sanctions.* New York: Oxford University Press, 1998.

Robinson, Jerome J. and James W. Jones. *Drug Testing in a Drug Court Environment: Common Issues to Address.* Washington, DC: U.S. Department of Justice, Office of Justice Programs, Drug Courts Program Office, 2000. http://www.ncjrs.gov/pdffiles/ojp/181103.pdf (Accessed July 2011).

Vito, G. F., S. T. Holmes, T. J. Keil, and D. G. Wilson. "Drug Testing in Community Corrections: A Comparative Program Analysis." *Journal of Crime and Justice,* v.15/1 (1992).

EFFECTIVENESS OF COMMUNITY CORRECTIONS

At first glance, many people would agree that America's criminal justice system is faced with numerous challenges, especially in terms of tackling overcrowding in correctional facilities and reducing recidivism. The United States experienced the highest incarceration rates in the world in the mid-1970s, as criminal justice policy shifted from a rehabilitative to a punitive model. The United States currently detains five to eight times more offenders than any western European country, and three quarters of offenders committed to state prisons are nonviolent offenders, whereas two thirds of these incarcerated individuals are racial and ethnic minorities. Thus, alternatives to incarceration appear to be in a state of flux, as professionals work toward developing programs and policies that attenuate the significant burdens that currently plague the criminal justice system.

Overview of Community Corrections

Prior to beginning a discussion on the effectiveness of community corrections, an operational definition of the term is needed. The term *community corrections* can be loosely defined as legal sanctions applied to either adult or juvenile offenders on their release from detention. These community corrections programs are typically operated under the supervision of probation or parole agencies and can include multiple components. In addition to providing supervision and monitoring functions within the community, these programs might include additional goals that are designed to facilitate increased accountability of one's actions while also providing offenders with rehabilitation services. There are various types of community corrections, such as diversion, restitution, probation, parole, and halfway houses.

Unfortunately, it appears as though research examining the effectiveness of community corrections programs is scarce. The majority of existing community corrections programs have not been scientifically evaluated, and consequently their effectiveness remains unclear. Promoting quality scientific research efforts that are geared toward assessing the effectiveness of community corrections could perhaps increase the public's overall level of confidence in the court system. Furthermore, these programs are at times delivered in a uniform fashion in which individual characteristics of the offender (such as his or her culture) might not be taken into account when determining the most appropriate community correctional placement. This is problematic, because such individualized care is critical to maximizing treatment efficacy. Decisions to place an offender in a community-based program should be based on careful analysis that is conducted scientifically on a case-by-case basis.

Balancing Community Engagement With Public Safety Concerns

The idea that communities can be more proactive in terms of engaging with the judicial system is growing in popularity. Specifically, the community can help the judicial system by working collaboratively to address increases in less serious, nonviolent offenders, repeat offenders, and overcrowding in correctional institutions. A review of the research reveals that, in the United States, the concept of community justice grew out of the public's awareness that society can do a better job of policing itself. The U.S. government worked to create community courts and various community-based correctional initiatives that are geared toward engaging communities in the battle against crime reduction. Sentencing reform efforts can focus on promoting the development of community-based alternatives to incarceration while reducing recidivism through increased application of evidence-based rehabilitative efforts. Such alternatives, however, have received a good deal of public criticism and raise the issue of the importance of considering the general public's view of maintaining offenders within society as opposed to the confines of a correctional setting. The public's reservations about community corrections are highlighted and exacerbated when news stories circulate about a repeat offender living in the community who has committed a heinous crime. Thus, although the idea of providing monitoring, supervision, and needed services to offenders within the community, as opposed to within correctional institutions, can address issues such as prison overcrowding, some people remain skeptical of whether community-based corrections can be effective in preventing recidivism.

For decades, heavy reliance was placed on the perceived need for incarceration as the most effective way to protect society. Tougher legal sanctions, such as the creation of mandatory minimum sentencing guidelines, have resulted in lengthier periods of incarceration for many offenders, which also has led to fiscal challenges as governments work to address the problem of prison overcrowding. Policy makers have begun to address such problems by examining the severity of offenders' violations when determining whether incarceration is a necessity. Many offenders are sentenced to confinement following the commission of their first offense, although many incarcerated individuals have committed nonviolent acts and/or are low-level drug offenders. Moreover, the U.S. Bureau of Justice Statistics has revealed that violent offenders comprise fewer than one third of all new admissions into state prisons. The Center for Community Corrections is seeking to help inform public policy to address matters pertaining to public safety, reentry, and recidivism by promoting

community-based sanctions and programs that are based on research.

At the federal level, the Bureau of Prisons (BOP) has developed connections with various entities—such as the federal courts, state and local corrections, and myriad community groups—to develop community-based correctional programs. For example, the BOP holds contracts with various residential reentry centers (RRCs), which are designed to provide housing, supervision, vocational assistance, and other services (such as extended substance abuse treatment services) to inmates who are nearing release from detention. Conversely, the BOP has indicated that some federal inmates released from prison are placed on home detention, which requires the released inmate to abide by a set schedule and curfew; this arrangement can also include electronic monitoring equipment to enable officers to detect any violations quickly. Accordingly, it seems as though the federal government has covered the bases in terms of providing supervision and monitoring of released offenders, although additional programming appears to be less emphasized for offenders who are not classified as mentally ill or suffering from substance-related disorders.

Mental Health Courts

For cases involving special needs offenders (those who suffer from psychiatric and substance-related disorders, for example), specialized services can be incorporated into various community corrections programs. An examination of the mental health court system appears warranted; such venues tend to serve as a gateway to community-based correctional services that are geared toward the mental health needs of offenders. The idea of a mental health court system stemmed from concerns that many mentally ill offenders who were arrested on so-called petty offenses suffered psychiatric decompensation on their admission to detention. It was suggested that, for at least some offenders, the underlying behavioral problem might stem from issues pertaining to mental health as opposed to criminality. It was thought that by assisting the offender with gaining access to mental health treatment, a more effective way of addressing the actual problems accounting for the criminal behavior could be identified.

A review of the literature regarding the efficacy of the mental health court system appears limited, although many experts would agree that the system appears promising. Mental health courts continue to bear the brunt of criticism, as they can be viewed as coercive, in violation of due process rights, and inadequate in terms of treatment quality. An important inquiry is whether defendants who suffer from significant psychiatric illness have the requisite mental capacity to make informed treatment decisions that would be in their best interest. Limited research on the efficacy and implications of the mental health court system hinders our ability to answer these questions.

Outpatient Commitment

Prior to the 1950s, psychiatric hospitals played a significant role in housing, treating, and managing individuals with severe psychiatric illness. Advances in psychopharmacological treatments contributed to a shift toward deinstitutionalization of the mentally ill, as many individuals were able to function either independently or with some form of assistance within the community. Outpatient commitment then appeared to develop as a means of preventing rehospitalization. Outpatient commitment is said to have initially developed as an extension to the civil rights movement, at a time when mental health law placed strong emphasis on maximizing an individual's rights and preserving freedoms. Outpatient commitment was seen as a viable way to maintain an individual's right to liberty by treating mentally ill offenders in the community as opposed to prison.

J. P. Hanlon and colleagues argued that preventive outpatient commitment raises some significant constitutional questions. According to the Hanlon group, such mandated treatment might be viewed as coercive, failing to bridge the gap between mandated treatment and therapeutic jurisprudence. Further empirical study of the effectiveness of outpatient commitment is necessary, given the inherent issues pertaining to constitutionality (that is, whether participation in such treatment violates an individual's informed consent). This also raises the question of whether or not such "treatment" simply constitutes an extension of incarceration and whether outpatient commitment can be called treatment at all.

Many opponents of court-mandated community-based treatment emphasize problems related to admission criteria. These problems include difficulty assessing an individual offender's level of dangerousness, determining the likelihood of compliance, and identifying what constitutes actual voluntary consent

to enter treatment. This also raises questions regarding the efficacy of existing assessment procedures that are used to determine the appropriateness of community corrections for some offenders, as well as what level of supervision and monitoring is needed. As many commentators would agree, the court system is already overburdened, and detention centers, jails, and prisons are suffering financial setbacks. Raising the question of whether or not the criminal justice system has sufficient resources to individually and thoroughly assess all offenders who are considered for placement within a community corrections program is critical to ascertain the most appropriate and beneficial sanctions and treatments.

Efficacy of Community Corrections for Adults

Current literature on community corrections for adult offenders appears to focus more on the general rationale for community placement than on differential treatment or rehabilitative efforts. At first glance, it appears as though adult offenders have limited access to community-based corrections as an alternative to incarceration. This is especially true when it comes to consideration for outpatient commitment in order to address difficulties related to criminality that are outside the scope of chronic and persistent mental illness.

Court-mandated outpatient treatment may be useful in cases in which a judge seeks to impose a less punitive sanction that is intended to foster rehabilitation. Offenders who are sentenced to community confinement may receive services in various facilities and are likely to be required to comply with other mandates, such as maintaining stable housing and income. Unfortunately, however, this may prove to be a rather daunting task for many offenders as they encounter barriers to autonomous functioning in the community. It appears as though some of these mandates might be viewed as unreasonable on initial sentencing imposition. For instance, in the case of a low-level drug offender who is committed to an outpatient substance abuse treatment program, it might prove challenging for the individual to engage in treatment while simultaneously working to become gainfully employed. Without first conducting an assessment of the individual offender's skills, education, and employment history, the court might fail to notice that the individual might be lacking the abilities needed to seek and obtain employment within the time period specified. This could, in some cases, lead to premature termination of services, as the offender could be found to be in violation of the less restrictive sanction and subsequently sent to a correctional facility where he or she might have access to increased supervision but decreased access to intervention services and community-based supports.

With regard to home detention as a component of community corrections, this type of sanction involves limiting an offender's access to the community in the interest of preserving public safety. Home detention might also serve a rehabilitative function in that it requires the offender to function autonomously within the community by mandating gainful employment. Again, this can prove to be quite a challenge for many offenders, especially those with additional criminal histories that might lead employers to be reluctant to hire them. It appears as though individualized assessment and service provision (such as vocational training) might assist offenders in complying with their community-based sanctions.

An additional, unanswered question concerns how the offender can work to regain his or her role as an autonomously functioning adult in society. Some might argue that previously incarcerated offenders might experience significant struggles as they work to function within society, lacking the structures, imposed by the court, to which they might have grown accustomed. Many repeat offenders might view incarceration as a "normal" way of life, as they struggle to regain—or sometimes to achieve for the first time—an adaptive role in society. This challenge might prove particularly difficult to meet for offenders who do not have access to additional social supports or vocational resources. Therefore, programs should also focus on helping offenders transition to being autonomous individuals as they reintegrate into society; such efforts might reduce recidivism. However, community corrections programs might not afford adult offenders access to needed services that would allow them to assume healthy and adaptive roles in today's society.

Efficacy of Community Corrections for Juvenile Offenders

The majority of research conducted on the efficacy of community corrections appears to focus on juvenile offenders. These efforts may emerge from research findings that emphasized the limited benefit

that could be derived from managing recidivism in juveniles via formal sanctions. However, many commentators would also argue that community corrections for juvenile offenders are not always effective at deterring future criminality. Alternatively, placement within residential treatment programs serves only as an extension of traditional incarceration. Furthermore, the quality of service delivery must be considered when evaluating the effectiveness of community corrections for juvenile offenders who are in need of specific types of interventions (such as sex-specific treatment, behavior modification, individual psychotherapy, and family therapy services).

A seminal study conducted by William S. Davidson and his colleagues in 1987 sought to examine the relative efficacy of various treatments longitudinally on a sample of 213 juvenile offenders from a medium-sized industrial city located in the midwestern United States. In this study, four interventions were performed by nonprofessionals and contrasted with an attention-placebo group and a treatment-as-usual control group. Within each treatment condition, a college-level student worked individually in a community setting with a participant. Within the action condition (AC), the model of intervention included an assessment of desired behavioral change and needed community resources, initiation of intervention efforts, assessment and revision of intervention efforts, and preparation for service termination. The second condition was referred to as the Action Condition–Family Focus (ACFF). Within this condition, principles of advocacy and behavioral contracting were employed exclusively with family members, and the primary emphasis within this condition was on a behavioral rather than a psychotherapeutic approach. The third condition was called the Action Condition–Court Setting (ACCS) to determine the extent to which independence of the diversion program from the court was a significant contributor to treatment outcome. In the fourth condition, the Relationship Condition (RC), the importance of interpersonal relationships was emphasized, and this condition focused on the development of unconditional positive regard, empathy, genuineness, and communication skills. Furthermore, the Attention Placebo Condition (APC) served as an attempt to control for the effects of nonspecific attention and consisted of lecture presentations on general delinquency topics. Within the Control Condition (CC), participants were returned to court for processing.

A three-part analysis of the experimental conditions in the aforementioned study revealed that the conditions involving specific treatment models (AC, RC, and ACFF) were found to be superior in terms of lowering recidivism in comparison to the CC. Furthermore, results suggested that when interventions were carried out beyond the direct influence of the court, the result was lower recidivism rates. However, self-reported delinquency data did not show any significant effects on recidivism. Accordingly, this study revealed that not only is the integrity of the individual treatment instrumental in determining outcome, but the organizational setting in which interventions are delivered also plays a pertinent role in determining outcome.

An additional seminal study conducted by Patricia Chamberlain and John B. Reid sought to compare the relative effectiveness of group care (GC) and multidimensional treatment foster care (MTFC) on a sample of 79 male adolescents with histories of chronic and severe delinquency. Within the MTFC condition, emphasis was placed on using behavioral management strategies to provide the juveniles with a structured daily living environment that included close supervision and clearly delineated rules. Caregivers were instructed on how to implement an individualized plan for each juvenile that included different levels of supervision and privileges based on each juvenile's level of compliance with program rules, adjustment to school, and overall progress. Within the GC condition, some variations in theoretical approach were incorporated. However, the underlying premise of the GC condition was that one's peer group can most strongly influence and motivate positive behavioral change through group-based therapy, where expectations for the development of prosocial norms, confrontation of each youth's problematic behavior, and participation in decision making and discipline served as the foundation for the condition.

Results of this study revealed that fewer juveniles in the MTFC condition, as opposed to those placed in the GC condition, absconded from their placements, and juveniles in the MTFC condition were more likely to complete their programs successfully. One year following referral for this study, it was found that those juveniles in the MTFC condition spent fewer days in detention and/or in state training schools. Collectively, it was determined that the MTFC condition proved to be more favorable in comparison to the GC condition. However, these benefits were applicable only for the short-term, and longer-term outcomes for chronic and serious juvenile offenders have yet to be determined.

Cultural Considerations in Community Corrections

Considerations regarding the roles of race, ethnicity, and culture in service provision in community-based sanctions are of paramount importance. While this matter can be important to consider for juvenile as well as adult offenders, it appears more salient when discussing the implications of community corrections for adult offenders—perhaps because juvenile offenders receive mental health and related services at a younger age, which consequently can shape their attitudes toward service provision, whereas adults likely have already developed cognitive schemas toward the meaning of actively seeking out needed services.

As our society grows to become more diverse, the emphasis placed on the importance of delivering services from a culturally sensitive perspective appears to be a primary focus of many professional training programs. When community sanctions are imposed through the court system, many offenders might find themselves feeling quite overwhelmed at the novelty of the programs they encounter and consequently may experience difficulties with adjustment and engagement in treatment. It remains unclear where the burden of ensuring the delivery of culturally sensitive care should be placed. Many experts would agree that the treatment provider should be held accountable for ensuring that individualized and culturally sensitive assessment and service delivery take place. Currently, many of our existing community corrections programs appear to be faced with administrative restrictions that could prevent them from ensuring that direct-care staff are properly trained and well versed in delivering rehabilitative services in a culturally sensitive fashion.

Racial disparities in community-based mental health treatment can increase the risk of incarceration because of a reluctance to receive preventive services. At the preincarceration level, African Americans are less likely than their Caucasian counterparts to seek community-based mental health services. However, one must consider the adaptive nature of seeking additional services while detained, as opposed to seeking such services in the community. In comparison to offenders in the community, who have limited knowledge about services that might be available to them, detained offenders are more likely to have greater access to information about the services available to them in detention. Thus, system barriers and an absence of necessary resources in the community might, at least to some degree, account for treatment disparities among Caucasian and African American offenders. Racial differences in mental illness could also explain why there are a significantly greater number of African Americans, as opposed to Caucasians, incarcerated in our correctional institutions, and focusing on a deinstitutionalizing perspective could reduce overall rates of incarceration.

The importance of culturally sensitive needs assessment and service delivery cannot be underestimated when considering the imposition of community-based legal sanctions, and better-informed treatment providers can more effectively work to engage diverse individuals in treatment. Taking an individualized approach to sanction imposition and service provision can also prove to be beneficial in terms of case management. Professionals can actively work to assess and eliminate an individual's perceived barriers to beneficial services that can be found in the community and prevent recidivism.

Summary and Conclusion

Currently, there appears to be a significant need for further scientific study of the effectiveness of various types of community corrections for both adult and juvenile offenders. Although issues regarding the provision of monitoring and supervision services in order to protect society as a whole are important, scientific evaluation of needed programs and how those services are administered is also imperative at this time. Preventive services that could essentially be delivered within the community as a diversionary strategy for adult offenders could prove to be promising. For example, although some courts might not consider imposing a sanction of community-based substance abuse treatment for an offender who is not actively dependent on substances or even using substances at the time he or she comes into contact with the criminal justice system, careful assessment of the individual's static and dynamic risk factors could indicate that such treatment would be beneficial in terms of preventing recidivism. This is particularly true for individuals identified to have

risk factors associated with future substance use. Furthermore, thorough needs assessments of many offenders could reveal deficiencies in social or vocational skills. These could help guide the court in determining appropriate service referrals to prevent recidivism and to increase the likelihood that the offender would gain needed insight into factors that contribute to recidivism.

With regard to existing community corrections programs that offer additional services to offenders, further research examining the efficacy of such programs appears warranted. Over the long term, scholarly efforts could prove to be more cost-effective for the judicial system as a whole, as programs that are not significantly beneficial can be eliminated and substituted with ones that are. In addition, scientific analysis of existing community corrections programs can inform administrators about necessary modifications that would improve the overall effectiveness of such programs. Without continuing research examining the efficacy of community corrections programs, society might run the risk of losing funding for programs that work, which in turn could exacerbate the problems that already burden our criminal justice system.

Kendell L. Coker
Chicago School of Professional Psychology
Jeannie S. Brooks
Psychology Gerena and Associates, Inc.

See also Costs of Community Corrections; Evaluation of Programs; False Negatives and False Positives; Goals and Objectives of Community Corrections; Prediction Instruments; Recidivism; Risk and Needs Assessment Instruments; Risk Assessment Instruments: Three Generations; "What Works" Approach and Evidence-Based Practices

Further Readings

Center for Community Corrections. "Reentry and Employment in St. Louis: A Model for Business, Community, and Workers." http://centerfor communitycorrections.org/?page_id=68 (Accessed February 2011).

Chamberlain, Patricia and John B. Reid. "Comparison of Two Community Alternatives to Incarceration for Chronic Juvenile Offenders." *Journal of Consulting and Clinical Psychology*, v.66/4 (1998).

Davidson, William S., II et al. "Diversion of Juvenile Offenders: An Experimental Comparison." *Journal of Consulting and Clinical Psychology*, v.55/1 (1987).

Federal Bureau of Prisons. "Community Corrections." http://www.bop.gov/locations/cc/index.jsp (Accessed February 2011).

Fischer, Donald G. and Richard Jeune. "Juvenile Diversion: A Process Analysis." *Canadian Psychology/ PsychologieCanadienne*, v.28/1 (1987).

Hanlon, J. P. et al. "Expanding the Zones: A Modest Proposal to Increase the Use of Alternatives to Incarceration in Federal Sentencing." *Criminal Justice*, v.24/4 (2010).

Hiday, Virginia A. "Outpatient Commitment: The State of Empirical Research on Its Outcomes." *Psychology, Public Policy, and Law*, v.9/1–2 (2003).

LaFond, John Q. and Mary Durham. *Back to Asylum*. New York: Oxford University Press, 1992.

National Institute on Corrections. "What Works in Community Corrections: An Interview With Dr. Joan Petersilia." http://nicic.gov/Library/022833 (Accessed January 2011).

Stefan, Susan and Bruce J. Winick. "A Dialogue on Mental Health Courts." *Psychology, Public Policy, and Law*, v.11/4 (2005).

Warren, Roger K. "The Most Promising Way Forward: Incorporating Evidence-Based Practice Into State Sentencing and Corrections Policies." *Federal Sentencing Reporter*, v.20/5 (2008).

Winick, Bruce, J. "Outpatient Commitment: A Therapeutic Jurisprudence Analysis." *Psychology, Public Policy, and Law*, v.9/1/2 (2003).

Wolf, Robert V. "Community Justice: An International Overview." *Judicature*, v.91/6 (2008).

Youman, Kerstin et al. "Race Differences in Psychopathology and Disparities in Treatment Seeking: Community and Jail-Based Treatment-Seeking Patterns." *Psychological Services*, v.7/1 (2010).

ELDERLY OFFENDERS

The United States has the highest incarceration rates in the world. Since 1980, the U.S. prison population has grown 290 percent. Such astronomical growth has resulted in a current U.S. prison population of more than 2 million. This overall increase in the offender population has led to the emergence of a complex special needs population within U.S. prisons: elderly inmates. Elderly inmates pose significant challenges to the U.S. criminal justice system.

Although the U.S. prison population has traditionally been young (the average inmate age is 38), as these inmates age, the elderly inmate population grows. The Bureau of Justice Statistics classifies any inmate over the age of 55 as elderly. Recent statistics revealed nearly a 75 percent increase in elderly offenders in U.S. prisons and jails. As of 2008, U.S. prisons and jails housed more than 74,000 offenders over the age of 55.

Elderly offenders can generally be divided into three categories. The first group typically consists of offenders who entered the system when they were young, but, because of lengthy sentences and no possibility of parole, they have joined the ranks of the elderly. Their crimes typically consist of brutal crimes such as murder or sexual assault. The second group includes inmates who entered prison at an old age and simply add to an already aging prison population. They were typically arrested for nonviolent crimes, such as financial crimes. Finally, career criminals make up the third group. Over the years, these inmates age as they cycle in and out of prisons.

Researchers claim that the aging of the prison population can be traced back to two general root causes. First, advances in medicine coupled with longer life spans have led to a larger elderly U.S. population. Current estimates claim that Americans over 50 make up 33 percent of the U.S. population. Similar demographic shifts among inmates have also been identified, and the U.S. Census Bureau predicts that by 2030, this population will make up more than 30

The numbers of elderly individuals breaking the law and being imprisoned is increasing. The cost of providing healthcare for inmates over age 60 is three times higher than a younger prisoner. (Photos.com)

percent of inmates. Second, policies associated with sentencing guidelines have changed. Mandatory sentencing and tougher sentencing guidelines have just about guaranteed that many inmates will spend the rest of their lives behind bars.

Mandatory sentencing guidelines surfaced in the 1980s as a direct response to the "war on drugs." Such laws were based on the premise that longer sentences would deter criminal behavior. The courts specifically sought to deter violent crimes, drug violations, and habitual offenders. However, research finds that mandatory sentencing laws do little to deter crime. Instead, these laws have triggered prison overcrowding and considerable aging of the prison population.

Health and the Aging Prison Population

Increased numbers of elderly offenders have resulted in various consequences. A noteworthy difference between younger offenders and elderly offenders is evident in health. Elderly offenders suffer from a host of health-related issues. Offenders not only suffer from health complications more frequently but also tend to do so earlier in life. For example, incarcerated individuals are said to have health problems similar to those in the general population who are 10 years older. Consequently, the health status of a 55-year-old inmate would be similar to that of a 65-year-old non-inmate. Classifying a 55-year-old inmate as "elderly" is therefore fitting.

All inmates upon their arrival to prison are required to undergo a complete physical. Contingent on the results, the individual will be categorized as a special needs inmate or a general population inmate. Special needs housing accommodations can vary from one institution to the next, but some institutions, such as the Pennsylvania Department of Corrections, house inmates based on need. For example, for housing purposes inmates are classified as part of the general population, as wheelchair-bound, as geriatric, or as those with long-term illnesses. All institutions within the Bureau of Prisons are accredited by the Joint Commission for the Accreditation of Healthcare Organizations (JCAHO).

According to a nationwide survey conducted by the Illinois Department of Corrections, 3.3 percent of the total inmate population suffers from a chronic illness. Of these inmates, at least 6 percent who are over the age of 50 reside in special-unit housing. Between 2001 and 2004, the leading cause of death among the inmate population was digestive diseases. The types of chronic illnesses that entitle one to special housing vary. However, the survey results reveal that inmates diagnosed with severe neurological problems or who suffer from renal failure constitute the majority of special-unit residents and infirmary patients.

The average cost of incarcerating an elderly prisoner is astonishing. It costs nearly three times more to imprison these individuals. Recent trends in state and federal prisons reveal that the approximate annual cost to house an elderly inmate runs about $69,000 per year per inmate, compared to $22,000 for a healthy, younger inmate. Explanations for disproportionate health expenditures between elderly and young offenders are complex, and the discussions in the literature focus mostly on three causes for the variation. First, elderly inmates generally require longer and more frequent hospital stays; second, they often require more repeated contact with healthcare providers; and third, as their lengths of stay and need for more attention increase, so do the costs.

Although the medical services provided to inmates are acquired at significantly discounted prices, chronic health problems, along with longer life expectancies of inmates, have placed an insurmountable burden on the criminal justice system. Institutional staffs within the health services division are allotted the task of ensuring that inmates receive proper medical, dental, and psychiatric care in agreement with proven healthcare standards. While prison officials concur that these costs are excessive, statistics reveal that they will continue to climb. Scholars recommend administering health prevention programs to ease financial burdens.

The Mounting Dilemma

The elderly inmate, to a greater extent than inmates of other age groups, faces an assortment of adversities that vary considerably from one inmate to the next. This places significant encumbrances on today's prisons, particularly in the areas of offender assessment, programming, planning, and monitoring. Therefore, in addition to the burden of rising healthcare costs in the prisons, the rising number of elderly offenders has also produced structural and programmatic issues.

Because elderly offenders often face issues similar to their counterparts in the free world, they also require age-appropriate accommodations. Thus, structural and building issues associated with elderly offender needs pose challenges to prison staff. Studies maintain that prisons are built with the young, healthy, and physically active in mind. Therefore, prison administrators are faced with constant dilemmas surrounding the fact that prisons are not designed for older inmates. It is estimated to cost more than $100,000 per cell to build a prison. Thus, it is not feasible to build new prisons designed specifically for this population, so prison staff members do their best to accommodate the aging population instead.

Prison staff accommodate elderly offenders through an assortment of prison programs. Geriatric inmate programs are restricted to elderly inmates and involve medical services, substance abuse and psychological services, employment programs, education programs, and religious programs. Modifications may involve accommodations for diet or employment activities. Such modifications typically require additional training among staff members to ensure that elderly offenders receive proper care.

The elderly inmate population is unique in its own right. Inmate risk classifications are based on age, severity of offense, and prior prison records. As a result, elderly offenders are often classified as low-risk. Many of these inmates no longer pose a danger, and they often occupy trusted positions within the prison. Dwindling budgets and overcrowded prisons cause one to wonder whether state and federal prisons should look at possible early release alternatives for elderly offenders.

The Bureau of Justice Statistics asserts that more than 95 percent of the U.S. prison population will eventually serve out their prison terms. Each year, more than 600,000 prisoners are released back into the community. A considerable number of these individuals will be released to parole supervision. One of the primary challenges in community corrections to date is the widespread release of elderly offenders. Ensuring that older offenders are able to transition back into the community successfully is critically important.

Until recently, post-release supervision programs were not structured to address specific social service needs of elderly offenders. However, federal and state geriatric release pilot programs have compelled researchers and policy makers to explore the unique needs of elderly inmates upon their release. Preliminary evidence has revealed that overburdened probation systems are regularly required to distribute the majority of their resources to younger and more dangerous inmates. As a result, many elderly offenders are often left to care for themselves.

Prisons, like other social institutions, must be prepared for America's aging population. Researchers claim that successful transitions into the community for offenders of all ages must include housing and financial assistance. However, reinstating such resources takes time. Policy makers argue that additional resources should be allocated to address geriatric issues in post-release supervision, in addition to training probation officers to deal with such issues. Further research is essential to aid correctional officials in their managerial processes and in the implementation of effective community corrections programs and facilities.

Kamesha Spates
Colorado State University, Pueblo

See also Diversity in Community Corrections; Humanitarianism

Further Readings

Chiu, T. *It's About Time: Aging Prisoners, Increasing Costs, and Geriatric Release.* New York: Vera Institute of Justice, 2010.

Clear, Todd R., George F. Cole, and Michael D. Reisig. *American Corrections*, 9th ed. Belmont, CA: Thomson Wadsworth, 2010.

Federal Bureau of Prisons. *About the Federal Bureau of Prisons.* Washington, DC: U.S. Department of Justice, 2007.

Federal Bureau of Prisons. *State of the Bureau 2008.* Washington, DC: U.S. Department of Justice, 2008. http://www.bop.gov/news/PDFs/sob08.pdf (Accessed September 2010).

Federal Bureau of Prisons. "2010 Quick Facts About the Bureau of Prisons." http://www.bop.gov/about/facts.jsp (Accessed March 2010).

Gallagher, Elaine M. "Elders in Prison: Health and Well-Being of Older Inmates." *International Journal of Law and Psychiatry*, v.24/2 (2001).

Maruschak, Laura and Allen Beck. *Bureau of Justice Statistics Special Report: Medical Problems of Inmates.* Washington, DC: U.S. Department of Justice, 1997.

Morton, Joann B. *An Administrative Overview of the Older Inmates.* Washington, DC: U.S. Department of Justice, 1992.

Stojkovic, Stan. "Elderly Prisoners: A Growing and Forgotten Group Within Correctional Systems Vulnerable to Elder Abuse." *Journal of Elder Abuse and Neglect*, v.19 (2007).

U.S. Census Bureau. "The Older Population in the United States: 2010–2050." http://www.census.gov/prod/2010pubs/p25-1138.pdf (Accessed September 2010).

West, Heather C. and William J. Sabol. "Prisoners in 2007." In *Bureau of Justice Statistics Bulletin*. Washington, DC: U.S. Department of Justice, Office of Justice Programs, 2008.

ELECTRONIC MONITORING

Electronic monitoring is a program or sentencing philosophy that uses advances in computer technology to monitor offenders under community supervision. Electronic monitoring can be applied under conditions of house arrest, or it could be used for location monitoring or for the detection of alcohol in an individual's body. It is widely accepted that electronic monitoring was proposed in 1964 by Ralph Schwitzgebel, who was a psychology professor at the University of California. Little interest was shown in electronic monitoring throughout the 1970s. However, as the prison and jail population of the late 1980s and 1990s grew, house arrest using electronic monitoring provided an economical alternative to incarceration in a state or local facility. The first formal electronic monitoring program was implemented in 1983 in Albuquerque, New Mexico. Judge Jack Love placed a probation violator on electronic monitoring for one month.

The methods of electronically monitoring offenders have seen recent advances in the use of global positioning system (GPS) and cellular technologies, which allow for more reliable and accurate tracking of offenders. As new technologies continue to develop, and as budgetary constraints continue to plague governmental entities, the possible options for electronic monitoring of offenders will continue to grow.

Types and Uses of Electronic Monitoring

Electronic monitoring comes in several forms and is used primarily in the contexts of house arrest, active monitoring, passive monitoring, and alcohol monitoring.

House arrest is a court-ordered home detention that allows an individual who is sentenced to a jail term to spend that time at his or her residence as an alternative to confinement to a jail cell. House arrest originated in the mid-1980s in the state of Florida. With the advent of electronic monitoring, house arrest now presents a less labor-intensive alternative for probation departments.

In active monitoring, offenders who are placed on community supervision wear an electronic device that is usually attached to the offender's ankle. This device contains a transmitter that sends signals to a monitor, which uses telecommunications to monitor the offender's location in the house or within a certain range. If the base monitoring device does not receive a signal, an automated call to a main computer (at a separate location) is made to notify law enforcement that the signaling device is out of range. This would then prompt a probation officer to investigate the offender for being out of range.

With passive monitoring, the individual under community supervision is required to wear a computerized device on the ankle or wrist. The offender receives a computerized telephone call instructing him or her to verify, by means of a device, that he or she is at the correct location. The computer telephones randomly during the hours that the supervised individual is supposed to be home (in the case of house arrest). If the offender is wearing a wristlet, for example, it would then be placed into a verification box located at the offender's home in response to the telephone call from the central computer. A second method employs voice verification. When the computer calls the residence of the offender he or she must repeat the words that the computer requests. The unit then analyzes the voice pattern and compares it with words previously recorded by the offender to see if the patterns match. If they do not match, a second test is made. If that test is failed, then the probation department is notified of a failed test and will arrange for follow-up with the offender.

Electronic monitoring is now being used to monitor individuals, both pre- and post-trial, for consumption of alcohol. One popular product is the SCRAM (secure continuous remote alcohol monitor) device. This device is worn by the offender as an ankle bracelet. About every half hour, the device conducts a transdermal alcohol analysis by sampling the insensible perspiration collected from the air above the skin of the person wearing the device.

The device then stores the data and, at predetermined times, transmits the data through radio-frequency signals to the base station. The base station then uses telecommunications to alert a company that manages the device. The company then issues a report to the court authority that has control or custody of the individual wearing the device. Alternatively, the individual wearing the bracelet travels to the location of the company that monitors the device. The device is plugged into a computer, which downloads and reads the data that are stored on the device. A report is then issued to the supervising authority.

Effectiveness

Electronic monitoring has not been without criticism. Offenders are charged with paying for the electronic monitoring devices, which can be quite expensive. With regard to their impact on recidivism, there have been inconclusive results. Electronic monitoring has aided offenders in completing their sentences, but reduced rates of recidivism have not been evident.

The National Council on Crime and Delinquency conducted an evaluation of Florida's house arrest program and found that the impact of electronic monitoring on prison overcrowding, offender behavior, and state correctional costs was positive. Electronic monitoring is a punitive sentence that is designed to reduce institutional overpopulation. In addition to surveilling offenders, electronic monitoring reduces costs, offers a front-end solution to correctional overcrowding, and provides a flexible option for particular offenders who are working and providing for a family. This type of system may allow the offender to keep his or her job and thus the ability to maintain the responsibilities that he or she has. Moreover, electronic monitoring can allow for a pregnant offender to serve time at home rather than in a correctional setting. Consequently, there is a substantial monetary savings for the government.

Harrison Watts
Washburn University

See also GPS Tracking; Home Confinement and House Arrest; Prison Overcrowding; Reducing Prison Populations; Work/Study Release Programs

Further Readings

Giles, J. "No Drinking: We've Got You Tagged." *New Scientist*, v.204 (2009).

Lewis, John Dufton. *Attitudes, Knowledge, and the Practice of Electronic Monitoring: Comparing the Opinions and Understanding of Citizens and Probation Officers.* Ottawa, ON: Library and Archives Canada, 2007.

Siegel, Larry J. and Joseph J. Senna. *Essentials of Criminal Justice.* Belmont, CA: Wadsworth Cengage Learning, 2009.

ELMIRA SYSTEM

Elmira refers to two distinct prison experiences in the American narrative. The first and less well-known episode involves the Elmira (New York) facility's function as a prison camp for Confederate prisoners of war. This facility was strictly a warehouse for enlisted personnel, as the practice of prisoner exchange had ceased. Built on flood-prone ground and poorly provisioned, Elmira's inmates experienced severe privation, exposure to extreme weather, starvation, disease, and indifference from the Lincoln administration. Access to abundant provisions, food, and transport existed, yet they were apparently purposely withheld. Consequently, this facility had the highest death rate of any Union prison: During its existence, from mid-1864 though mid-1865, one quarter of those confined there died. The building and maintenance of the prison and provisioning of the guards and its inmates proved a boon to local politicians and businesses, however. This led to enthusiasm for prisons as a community industry in the area.

After the war, the site and community languished until it became the first "modern" prison of its type built along the lines of a "reformatory." This new nomenclature and orientation were products of the National Prison Association meeting held in Cincinnati, Ohio, in 1870. The focus of that meeting was the creation of the Elmira Reformatory and the moral improvement of inmates through treatment. Through the use of discipline-enhancing vocational education, parole, and the indeterminate sentencing, the reformers expected inmates to return to society with the tools necessary for successful reintegration. Directly influenced by the Irish marks system advocated by Sir Walter Crofton, the facility was opened for reform efforts in 1876. Implementation of the reform agenda was delayed by an influx of unsuitable inmates who had been sent from other institutions. It was only in 1881, after a number of escapes and murders of staff members, that the warden, Zebulon Brockway, was able to restrict the population to first-time offenders between the ages of 16 and 30 and begin his reform-oriented regime.

Brockway created a three-tiered process in which he often conducted the intake interview himself. Next, new prisoners were generally assigned to the second grade. Students and faculty from nearby Elmira College provided classes for youthful inmates. These classes often featured repetitive mathematics and fine-muscle tuning exercises, which were intended to build logical thinking and make inmates more employable in the work environments of the late 1800s. To this latter end, inmates were assigned to work on the prison farm, at an iron foundry, or in various prison maintenance capacities. Long hours of military drill with wooden rifles were assigned to impart discipline and a sense of order and regularity.

Inmates who performed adequately and earned sufficient positive "marks" for six months were promoted to the next, or "first," grade. Inmates who were recalcitrant or lazy would lose marks and could be demoted to the third grade. The third grade was an almost solitary existence in which prisoners were kept isolated and allowed to interact only with prisoners of the same grade. Subsequently, they could be restored to the second grade only through a month of perfect behavior. Those inmates who performed to Brockway's satisfaction and earned full marks for a year could earn a parole hearing and possible release. It should be noted that a true indeterminate sentence—that is, one resulting in a prisoner's being held until the institutional staff deemed him fully ready for release, no matter how long—was never granted by the New York State legislature. Such conformity to the expectations of the treatment staff may well have represented only successful institutionalization and not necessarily readiness for life on the outside. Brockway believed that this was a major flaw in the logic of the program, but, ever the realist (and not wanting to antagonize the politicians and legislature), he accepted this as a political fact of life.

An indefatigable self-promoter, Brockway had four general rules for good correctional administration. The first was that custody should be so secure that prisoners would not waste time plotting escapes but instead would focus their energies on their reform. Second, he tried to exclude outsiders, both benevolent groups and family, from the prison

because the institution itself was, he believed, competent and did not require assistance or interference from those parties. A third pillar of Brockway's correctional philosophy was that the warden should have great latitude in discipline and administration. Finally, Brockway, like other Victorian thinkers, strongly supported keeping prisoners constantly occupied so that they would have no occasion for vice, mischief, or retrogressing. Thus, they were to be kept on the run and busy from sunup to sundown.

In several forums, Brockway reported that around 80 percent of ex-inmates on parole had succeeded in leading normal and productive lives. However, most contemporary criminologists reject this figure as grossly exaggerated. The failures of the system he attributed to the premature release of prisoners. Ultimately Brockway had a major conflict with the prison's board of supervisors, which forced his resignation in 1900.

Critics have pointed out that pseudoscience, brutality, and self-promotion, not reform, were Brockway's stock-in-trade. According to modern criminologists, the prison was a failure, not because inmates were released prematurely but because of the failure of total institutions generally. In addition, Brockway's real agenda was to control lower-class folk and to impose middle-class morality and then-extant Protestant notions about work; such efforts were bound to fail once prisoners returned to their predominantly lower-class milieus. Finally, Brockway's pseudoscientific medical-model treatment approach was ineffective and brutal. Ultimately, harsh physical coercion was frequently employed; he sometimes slapped prisoners in the face and justified his behavior as part of the treatment agenda. As one might expect, the custody staff did not accept treatment as the institution's transcendent goal but instead focused on security. Inmates continued to maintain their own subculture, which was in fundamental opposition to the reality that the institution and guards attempted to impose.

Most American reformatories and many prisons worldwide that were built after 1880 used the Elmira system as a model, to one extent or another. The terms "reformatory" and "training institute"—used even today in the names of both adult and youth prisons—reflect this societal disposition to accept "treatment" and vocational training as desirable, albeit superficial, goals. In most cases, this institutional nomenclature was meaningless; real efforts at reform were certainly abandoned by Elmira and other American prisons by the 1930s. The Elmira system was so diluted in its approach—and those copying it even more inclined to water down reform in order to focus on custodial goals—that real efforts at reform had little chance of success. As one might expect, the ongoing elaboration of a continuum between inmate institutional culture and criminal street culture served to frustrate and defeat the best efforts of reformers, not all of whom were as self-interested, deluded, and contemporarily influential as was Brockway.

Francis Frederick Hawley
Western Carolina University

See also Brockway, Zebulon; Indeterminate Sentencing

Further Readings

Gray, M. *The Business of Captivity: Elmira and Its Civil War Prison.* Kent, OH: Kent State University Press, 2001.

Pisciotta, A. W. *Benevolent Repression: Social Control and the American Reformatory-Prison Movement.* New York: New York University Press, 1994.

Putney, S. and G. Putney. "Origins of the Reformatory." *Journal of Criminal Law, Criminology, and Police Science,* v.53/4 (December 1962).

EMPLOYMENT-RELATED RIGHTS OF OFFENDERS

A collateral consequence of a criminal conviction is the barrier that exists when an ex-offender tries to enter the workforce. An employer may be unwilling to hire an ex-offender because of concerns about future crimes and the safety of other employees and clients. Additionally, an employer may have fears about facing a negligent hiring lawsuit that could hold an employer responsible for the criminal conduct of an employee. This is unfortunate; for offenders reintegrating into society, employment is key to success and may result in a reduced likelihood of recidivism. Some limited protections do exist to prevent employment discrimination on the basis of prior convictions. Nevertheless, because of the limited nature of these protections, employment discrimination in the private employment context remains relatively unchecked.

Generally speaking, offenders have no legally recognized right to withhold their status as a convicted felon from a potential employer. Moreover, some jurisdictions maintain a complete ban on public employment for ex-offenders. Some employers, such as those in childcare or healthcare fields, are legally required to obtain the criminal records of potential employees, as ex-offenders may be banned from employment in these fields. It is understandable that an applicant may wish to conceal his or her status as an ex-offender from an employer. However, if an ex-offender lies about that status during the hiring process and a hire results, subsequent termination for dishonesty could well be the consequence. Moreover, parole agencies may require that parole officers inform prospective employers about an individual's previous convictions.

Title 7 of the Civil Rights Act of 1964 provides limited protection for ex-offenders. Under Title 7, public and private employers are prevented from discriminating against people based on race, color, religion, sex, or national origin. Ex-offenders are not considered a protected class for purposes of Title 7. However, an employer may not adopt a hiring policy that has a disparate impact on a protected class. Courts have allowed Title 7 claims against private employers when the employer maintained a ban against hiring ex-offenders and the ban had a disparate impact against members of a protected class such as African Americans or Hispanics, even though there was no evidence of discriminatory intent. Based on this rationale, the U.S. Equal Employment Opportunity Commission maintains that it is an illegal practice for an employer to refuse to hire ex-offenders based solely upon previous convictions. Nevertheless, in the absence of a disparate impact on a protected class, Title 7 may not prevent employment discrimination against ex-offenders.

Employers do have a defense to a Title 7 disparate impact claim: They may refuse to hire ex-offenders if they can demonstrate a business necessity for the ban that is somehow related to job performance. In demonstrating a business necessity, employers must consider "the nature and gravity of the offense or offenses, the time that has passed since the conviction and/or completion of the sentence, and the nature of the job held or sought."

A minority of states and municipalities have provided additional protections for ex-offenders, beyond those recognized by Title 7. For example, Wisconsin's

Fair Employment Act and New York's Human Rights Law prevent a private employer from refusing to hire an individual solely on the basis of a prior conviction. Some municipalities may prevent a public employer from asking about an applicant's criminal record until after the employer has determined whether the applicant is sufficiently qualified for the job.

The requirement of occupational licensing may present another hurdle for ex-offenders attempting to enter the workforce. Several fields, ranging from barbering to legal practice, require that an individual obtain an occupational license before becoming eligible for employment. Licensing boards may flatly refuse to consider ex-offenders or may be required to consider an applicant's "moral character," which as a practical matter results in rejection for ex-offenders. Some overly broad licensing restrictions have been rejected by the courts based on constitutional due process and equal protection challenges, but courts have upheld licensing requirements that have shown a suitable connection between the license and the ex-offender's previous conviction. Some critics have claimed that courts have inconsistently applied this requirement. For example, the refusal to grant a license to an ex-offender who wanted to operate a dance hall was upheld because of concerns about attracting a certain clientele, whereas a refusal to grant an ex-offender a license to sell cars was struck down.

Under the Americans with Disabilities Act (ADA) of 1990, employers may not discriminate against disabled individuals and must make reasonable accommodations for disabled employees unless such accommodations would result in undue hardship for the employer. Drug addiction and alcoholism are recognized as disabilities under the ADA.

The ADA does not protect ex-offenders who currently use drugs, and only ex-offenders who have completed or are participating in a supervised drug treatment program are protected. Employers may not discriminate against an ex-offender struggling with alcoholism. An employer may discharge or decline to hire an ex-offender who is also an alcoholic if the ex-offender poses a substantial risk of harm that cannot be diminished by reasonable accommodations. Additionally, employers may prohibit the consumption of alcohol during work hours and may discharge an employee if he or she attempts to work under the influence of alcohol.

Todd C. Hiestand
MidAmerica Nazarene University

See also Community-Based Vocational Networks; Loss of Capacity to Be Bonded; Second Chance Act

Further Readings

Lucken, Karol and Lucille Ponte. "A Just Measure of Forgiveness: Reforming Occupational Licensing Regulations for Ex-Offenders Using BFOQ Analysis." *Law and Policy*, v.30 (2008).

Saxonhouse, Elena. "Unequal Protection: Comparing Former Felons' Challenges to Disenfranchisement and Employment Discrimination." *Stanford Law Review*, v.56 (2004).

Stoll, Michael A. "Offenders, Criminal Background Checks, and Racial Consequences in the Labor Market." In *Civil Rights and the Low-Wage Worker*. Chicago: University of Chicago Law School, 2009.

ENVIRONMENTAL CRIME PREVENTION

Environmental crime prevention is more commonly known as "crime prevention through environmental design" (CPTED). It is an approach to problem solving that places a heavy emphasis on modifying conditions of the community environment that may increase offending opportunities in a given area. CPTED approaches advocate that the proper design of a place can serve not only to reduce fear and encourage prosocial usage of an area but also to reduce both the opportunity and the incidence of criminal or antisocial behavior. CPTED assumes that offenders will generally weigh the pros and cons when considering whether to commit a crime. This assumption comes from "rational choice" and "routine activities" theories and was informed heavily by the development of environmental criminology. These theories and others surrounding geography and crime, together with pioneering work in the fields of urban planning and land use, all consider the physical environment's role in the maintenance or reduction of crime and disorder. Therefore, early and current advocates continue to propose that the design of an area can reduce fear and criminality by adhering to basic notions of territoriality, surveillance, and access control.

The ideas behind CPTED are commonly traced back to work done in the 1960s and 1970s. In the early 1960s, Jane Jacobs noted that urban design and community interaction could be pivotal in ensuring that informal social controls worked to reduce urban disorder. Her research emphasized the built environment's role in strengthening a sense of "community" and allowing residents and users the chance to interact and establish a more vibrant street life. Formalizing the tenets of CPTED, C. Ray Jeffrey focused on the importance of the physical environment when it came to ways of both explaining and preventing crime. Building on Jacobs's ideas, Jeffrey focused intently on social behaviorism when examining the complex relationship between psychological factors of both antisocial and prosocial users and the environments they occupy. Soon thereafter, Oscar Newman conducted his examination of design and space when conceptualizing the notion of "defensible space." Focusing intently on architectural and site design rather than high-level urban planning, Newman's work expanded on the concepts of territoriality, design-based surveillance, and "image and milieu."

Under the tenets of defensible space, the proper design for living environments as they relate to disorder and safety needs to incorporate strategies inherent in territoriality, natural surveillance, image, and milieu. Modern conceptions of CPTED have taken these original strategies and focused on variations on three common themes: territoriality, natural

Criminal behavior can be mitigated through the use of environmental design strategies, including using proper lighting and surveillance, selectively placing entrances and exits, and using fences and landscaping to define public, semi-public, and private spaces. (Photos.com)

surveillance, and access control. These themes focus on how the environment provides opportunities for unwanted behaviors such as crime. Through the analysis of how these design features may be supporting this undesirable behavior, strategies can be enacted to reduce these opportunities by changing aspects of building or community design, site layout, accessibility, and ways that users populate the space.

When examining territoriality, CPTED approaches focus on defining ownership of an area, be it a public or a private space, such as a commercial establishment or a residential building. Design features seek to provide formal and informal cues as to who has ownership over the space and how other users are expected either to use the space or to avoid infringing on it. This may be accomplished in subtle ways, by using such techniques as landscaping, fencing, and pathway construction, or in more overt ways, for example via the use of signage or gating.

The focus on natural surveillance comes from the adherence to the notion that if offenders are not seen, their antisocial activity cannot be reported or acted upon. Thus, in order to reduce the opportunities for unwanted behavior, the environment must provide the residents and prosocial users of the space the ability to survey their area and the users within it. Design features need to support this natural surveillance by incorporating clear lines of sight to and from buildings and common spaces. Often this surveillance is supported not only by reducing blind spots in the environment (such as in parking garages) but also with appropriate landscaping designs that maintain the attractiveness and territoriality of an area while not blocking views either to or from public spaces and user areas. The use of lighting is of central importance as well, as surveillance without the proper lighting support discourages users from becoming aware of their surroundings and impedes their ability both to be prosocial users of a space and to spot antisocial users of the space.

Access control has become central to CPTED approaches and holds some theoretical similarities to the notion of territoriality. The design of ingress and egress to an area, if envisioned properly, should balance the need for ease of access of legitimate users with the need to ensure that visitors to the space and their activities while using that space are known and legitimate. Proper design of access areas also allows potential observers the opportunity to assess those coming into the area, in order to support natural surveillance and territoriality.

Although variations on and additions to these approaches have developed over the years, CPTED maintains a focus on the broad goal of image in order to establish and maintain the aesthetic integrity of an area. CPTED therefore discourages unattractive design elements, such as large gates or bars for physical security, instead emphasizing that such elements should blend into the surroundings to make the environment attractive for potential prosocial users at the same time that criminal opportunities are subtly blocked.

The primary difference between CPTED and other criminal justice approaches is that CPTED focuses on proactive strategies to prevent crime before it happens. In addition, CPTED departs from some measures more akin to physical security, such as the installation of more traditional opportunity-blocking structures (locks, bars, cameras, and the like), as it considers design and the potential attractiveness to prosocial users in its prevention techniques.

Nahanni Pollard
Simon Fraser University

See also NIMBY Syndrome; Project Safeway; "What Works" Approach and Evidence-Based Practices

Further Readings

Brantingham, P. L. and P. J. Brantingham. *Patterns in Crime*. New York: Macmillan, 1984.

Cohen, Lawrence E. and Marcus Felson. "Social Change and Crime Rate Trends: A Routine Activity Approach." *American Sociological Review*, v.44/4 (1979).

Cornish, D. and R. V. Clarke. *The Reasoning Criminal: Rational Choice Perspectives on Offending*. New York: Springer, 1986.

Jacobs, J. *The Death and Life of Great American Cities*. Random House: New York, 1961.

Jeffery, C. Ray. *Crime Prevention Through Environmental Design*. Beverly Hills, CA: Sage, 1971.

Newman, Oscar. *Defensible Space: Crime Prevention Through Urban Design*. New York: Macmillan, 1972.

Zahm, D. *Using Crime Prevention Through Environmental Design in Problem Solving*. Washington, DC: U.S. Department of Justice, Office of Community Oriented Policing Services, 2007. http://www.popcenter.org/tools/cpted (Accessed July 2011).

Ethics of Community-Based Sanctions

A variety of ethical concerns are related to community-based sanctions, particularly moral arguments vis-à-vis community-based sanctions as an alternative to imprisonment. This overview first considers what it means to take a human rights and human dignity approach to community-based sanctions. Next, community-based sanctions are discussed within the wider framework of public health ethics and specific questions and moral arguments related to autonomy and mandatory treatment. Then, the concept of community-based sanctions is placed within the broader framework of restorative justice. Finally, the importance of proportionate community-based sanctions that are justifiable in themselves, and not merely as an alternative to imprisonment, is highlighted.

As the rates of imprisonment are on the rise worldwide and prisons get more and more overcrowded, society is faced with an ever-growing mix of ethical, financial, and safety concerns that urgently need our attention. A strong case can be made from an ethical and societal perspective that community-based sanctions are to be preferred for the majority of today's prisoners, especially for children, women, and prisoners with mental health and substance abuse issues. As exemplified by the Tokyo Rules (the United Nations Standard Minimum Rules for Non-Custodial Measures), experts have urged jurisdictions to take an approach to crime and criminal justice that views imprisonment as a last resort. If prisons were limited to individuals who are justifiably incarcerated, many of today's issues could have been prevented or at the very least contained. Indeed, little evidence exists that higher rates of imprisonment increase public safety. On the contrary, research indicates that imprisonment raises rather than diminishes recidivism. At the same time, several research studies show that alternative sanctions are successful in reducing recidivism and drug abuse.

For a substantially large part of the current prison population, a strong case can be made in favor of community-based sanctions. About 95 percent of prisoners are eventually released back into society. A major problem that prisoners face upon reentry is that their time spent in prison has eroded their lives both professionally (since they lack training, have lost skills, and have had limited or no employment opportunities) and privately (through loss of family and friends, emotional support networks in general, and housing opportunities). Moreover, stigmatization acts as an indirect, enduring form of punishment that aggravates the situation. Not surprisingly, then, recidivism rates are extremely high. In fact, research shows that imprisonment is counterproductive in terms of rehabilitation and reintegration in society for low-level offenders and for those in need of special care, notably for individuals with mental health and substance abuse problems. Although it is often argued that only the incapacitation of offenders (by means of imprisonment or residence in secure mental health facilities) can offer adequate security, in today's society, where prisons lack the necessary resources to provide adequate care and opportunities for rehabilitation, we need to admit that prison terms often aggravate recidivist behavior and thus raise, rather than diminish, crime rates.

Moreover, in many cases adequate control can also be administered through alternative sanctions (such as house arrest, electronic monitoring, and supervised community service). Prisons pose a huge cost to society in terms of buildings, staff, care, and consequential costs such as the risk of disease spread upon offenders' reentry into society. Also, the long-term costs of imprisonment for offenders' family members and communities are often ignored. Despite these issues, for a limited number of severe offenders incapacitation remains the only viable option. Provided that no human rights violations occur, incapacitation can be appropriate for offenders who pose a continuous high risk of committing serious offenses and for whom imprisonment provides the only acceptable risk-minimizing strategy. Unfortunately, the sheer fact of overcrowding and the shortage of available, effective alternatives gives rise to growing numbers of human rights violations, simply because prison systems lack the necessary resources to provide prisoners with adequate care: general healthcare, mental healthcare, privacy, and even light and air.

Current findings in cognitive neuroscience and genetics elucidate the nature and causes of human behavior; it has become important to rethink traditional notions of free will and criminal responsibility. At the very least, we must reconsider our notions of ethical and effective punishment. It is paramount that sanctions, whether constituting imprisonment or any type of alternative to imprisonment, be in no way inhumane, cruel, or degrading. From an ethical perspective, it can be forcefully argued that imprisonment should be limited to those cases in which no other effective alternatives exist. If less restrictive alternatives achieve the same level of effectiveness in reducing recidivism rates, then those alternative sanctions are to be preferred and need to be implemented. There are several strong moral reasons for promoting effective community-based sanctions as an alternative to imprisonment. These moral reasons hinge upon the (potentially) more humane nature of alternative sanctions.

Human Rights and Human Dignity

The rights of suspects and offenders and the rights and needs of victims and society as a whole need to be carefully balanced. To assure that the rights of victims are not infringed upon, it is necessary that community-based sanctions are prescribed by law, including appropriate reparations to victims and other relevant actors in society. Moreover, effective risk prevention and acceptable risk-minimizing measures are of the utmost importance.

Imprisonment involves a loss of individual liberty, which is regarded as one of the most fundamental human rights. In order to sanction offenders by incapacitating them, by taking away their individual liberty, governments need to make sure that no other sanctions that do not involve incapacitation would work equally well in addressing their goals. If the goal is to prevent future crime, then current research shows that community-based sanctions work, at the very least, as well as imprisonment does. In general, because of today's overcrowded prisons and the lack of available resources to provide adequate care, community-based sanctions are much less conducive to human rights violations than imprisonment and should therefore be the preferred option for most offenders, provided that the rights of victims are upheld and the safety and concerns of society at large are addressed. Similarly, imprisonment is much more likely to involve some type of infringement of human dignity than are community-based sanctions. If implemented, community-based sanctions, and civil rights restrictions in particular, need to be tailored to the offender and the crime in question, both to protect society and to maximize opportunities for effective rehabilitation. Unnecessarily intrusive or disproportionately harsh sanctions should be considered violations of an offender's basic human rights and dignity.

The United Nations Convention on the Rights of the Child states that the imprisonment of children should be used only as a last resort and should be kept to the shortest appropriate time span. Institutionalization of child offenders is often counterproductive in terms of reeducation and rehabilitation, and it can be considered inherently harmful to the child. Most child offenders are best sanctioned by means of community-based alternatives that include appropriate treatment and other needed services. It is in the best interests of both the child and the community that the child's support networks are not destroyed and that the whole community takes part in the child's reeducation and rehabilitation.

The United Nations Principles for the Protection of Persons with Mental Illness holds that all individuals who are mentally ill have a basic right to the best available healthcare and should be treated with humanity and respect for the inherent dignity of the human person. Substance abuse is often a symptom if not an instigator of a mental health disorder, and offenders who are suffering from substance abuse have a right to the best available treatment. In general, if incapacitation is necessary, offenders with mental health and substance abuse issues should not be held in prisons, but rather treated in secure mental health facilities. If adequate control can be achieved by means of community-based sanctions and mandated outpatient treatment, then this is to be preferred from a human rights perspective.

Public Health Ethics

Public health ethics is concerned with the health of populations and groups of individuals, rather than the health of a given individual, and it largely focuses on preventive measures that can be set in place by governments or can be demanded from private actors. Public health policies have a commitment to promote health generally and a commitment to improve the health of those who are systematically disadvantaged. Prisoners with mental health and substance abuse problems are, because of the lack of available care and in general inappropriate place of confinement (for example, drugs are often easily available inside prisons and adequate drug treatment options are lacking), a systematically disadvantaged group. Community-based sanctions that include adequate

treatment programs offer a better prospect for rehabilitation and reducing recidivism rates in offenders with mental health and substance abuse issues, compared to imprisonment. Hence, from a public health ethics perspective, society can benefit by establishing effective community-based sanctions.

The rates of mental illness among prisoners are higher compared to similar groups in the general population, and the overall incidence rate is high. Overcrowding, boredom, and inadequate care in prisons often lead to mental health problems or exacerbate existing ones. More than half of the prisoners in the United States and as many as two thirds of prisoners in the United Kingdom suffer from mental illness. Female prisoners in the United States have a higher prevalence of mental health disorders compared to male prisoners. In the United States, only one in three state prisoners, one in four federal prisoners, and one in six jail prisoners report receiving treatment during their incarceration. Research indicates that especially offenders with mental health and substance abuse issues are at risk of multiple incarcerations. Because mental health issues are a risk factor for criminal behavior and imprisonment of individuals with mental health issues exacerbates these issues, we have strong moral reasons to build and implement effective community-based sanctions that focus on mental health and substance abuse treatment for those offenders who suffer from mental illness and substance abuse. Moreover, treatment for mental illness should take other factors into account that may challenge or even prevent successful treatment. Broader issues—such as housing, employment, education, skills, and social and emotional support networks—need to be addressed. The availability of structural and emotional support networks is a necessary condition for the success of long-term treatment. It is therefore of the utmost importance that mental health and drug courts not only focus on treatment but also provide access to structural and emotional support networks. Many of these objectives can be achieved by incorporating the offender's family and wider community into the process of rehabilitation and reintegration.

Autonomy

If offenders with mental health and substance abuse problems are given the option of entering into a community-based corrections program that involves intensive mandatory treatment rather than sentencing to prison, then one could argue that treatment in this sense constitutes a quasi-coercive approach. The use of intensive mandatory treatment is a controversial issue for many experts, some even describing it as an abuse of human rights. Others view it as a solution to drug-related crime. A third possibility can be considered, however. Intensive mandatory treatment can be viewed as a more humane way of dealing with drug-related crime and with offenders who suffer from mental health and substance abuse problems. Although quasi-coercive to some, and thus negating an individual's right to autonomous decision making, it has been defended as potentially enhancing autonomy by others.

Autonomy is one of the most important concepts in contemporary medical ethics. It refers to an individual's capacity for self-determination or self-governance and implies that our choices are our own and do not result from any kind of external pressures. As bioethicist Arthur Caplan has convincingly argued, mandatory psychopharmacological treatment for substance abuse can be seen as a means of increasing the ability of individuals with substance abuse problems to function autonomously. Individuals who are severely addicted are coerced by their addiction, in the sense that addiction limits an individual's capacity for self-determination and, hence, autonomous choice. Through treatment for finite periods of time, addicted offenders' capacity for self-determination can be restored. Thus, treatment can be seen as augmenting or restoring autonomy rather than restricting or neglecting it. Rather than coercing an individual, the option of quasi-compulsory drug treatment endows the offender with a choice—a choice between, on one hand, accepting quasi-compulsory drug-treatment, as an alternative to imprisonment, and, on the other, serving time in prison. It is a restrained choice, and some would argue that one cannot autonomously choose between these options and will likely be pressured into choosing quasi-compulsory drug treatment to avoid spending time in prison. Similar arguments have been put forward about consenting to research in prison settings. However, it has been shown that even prisoners with mental health issues are capable of making an informed choice within prison settings. Even if we assume that a choice between imprisonment and quasi-compulsory outpatient drug treatment cannot be made fully autonomously, does this mean that we should not offer it? Are not many, if not most, of our choices heavily constrained by situational factors

and hence not fully autonomous? There is a huge and important difference between coercion, which is obviously morally problematic, and being able to choose between imprisonment and quasi-compulsory treatment. Indeed, rather than experiencing the option of quasi-compulsory drug treatment as coercive, many offenders have viewed it as an opportunity.

The philosopher John Rawls designed a thought experiment to determine the morality of certain issues and social institutions, such as slavery. The thought experiment runs as follows: If we had to re-create society without knowing which position we would have in that society—without, for example, knowing if we would end up being a judge, a victim, or a drug-related offender—what would we decide? Would we create a world in which imprisonment is the only option available or create a world in which we can choose between two options, imprisonment and mandated drug treatment? If we positioned ourselves behind this Rawlsian "veil of ignorance," would we prefer a world in which we have both options or a world in which the only option available for drug-related offenders is imprisonment? The same question can be asked with regard to community-based sanctions involving mandatory mental health or drug treatment in general. Would we prefer to have a choice or not? Although both imprisonment and community-based sanctions involve a restriction of liberty, many view the latter as a more humane type of punishment compared to the former.

It has been argued that quasi-compulsory treatment can be justified only if it indeed results in less harm to the person and to others. Recent studies suggest that quasi-compulsory treatment is as effective as voluntary treatment provided in the same facilities in reducing crime and substance use. A European study on quasi-compulsory treatment promisingly found that offering treatment to substance-dependent offenders is an effective alternative to imprisonment, in terms of both reducing substance abuse and crime and improving health and social integration, with better results even in the long run. Several U.S. studies involving drug courts show similar promising results in terms of reductions in drug use and crime.

Restorative Justice

It is important that community-based alternatives to imprisonment pay sufficient attention to the needs and concerns of the victims, as well as to the legitimate concerns of other relevant actors in society.

Compared to prison sentences, community-based sanctions are better suited to addressing reconciliation attempts. Effective community-based sanctions can thus complement the aims of restorative justice programs, in which the rights, needs, and interests of victims, offenders, and all other relevant actors are addressed while attempts to reconcile the parties involved are being made. Restorative justice approaches to crime are based on the belief that all the relevant parties need to be actively involved in resolving the existing conflict and addressing its consequences. Restorative justice programs have the broader aim of enhancing social capital and promoting tolerance through the implementation of a relational and peaceful approach to conflict resolution. The rising need for and potential benefits of a relational approach to ethical dilemmas is defended by several ethicists, both in the domain of criminal justice and in the domain of medical and global ethics.

Although community-based sanctions are potentially more humane compared to imprisonment, we should not forget that community-based sanctions are punishments. As should be the case for prison terms, community-based sanctions should not be unduly harsh or unnecessarily intrusive. The sanction's severity should be proportionate to the crime, and the level of intrusiveness of the sanction should not exceed what is necessary to achieve its goals. As is the case with imprisonment or any other type of sanction, community-based sanctions are prone to human rights and human dignity violations. As legal philosopher Andrew von Hirsch argued, community-based sanctions need to be justified in their own right, not merely in comparison to another, harsher type of sanction.

Farah Focquaert
Ghent University
Adrian Raine
University of Pennsylvania

See also Cultural Competence; Faith-Based Initiatives; Humanitarianism; Offenders With Mental Illness; Punishment; Restitution; Restorative Justice; Sanctuary

Further Readings

Caplan, Arthur. "Ethical Issues Surrounding Forced, Mandated, or Coerced Treatment." *Journal of Substance Abuse Treatment*, v.31 (2006).

Kleinig, John. *Ethics and Criminal Justice: An Introduction.* Cambridge: Cambridge University Press, 2008.

Kuehn, Bridget M. "Mental Health Courts Show Promise." *Journal of the American Medical Association*, v.297/15 (April 2007).

Schaub, Michael et al. "Comparing Outcomes of 'Voluntary' and 'Quasi-Compulsory' Treatment of Substance Abuse Dependence in Europe." *European Addiction Research*, v.16 (2010).

Stevens, Alex, Tim McSweeney, Marianne Van Ooyen, and Ambros Uchtenhagen. "On Coercion." *International Journal of Drug Policy*, v.16 (2005).

United Nations. *Handbook of Basic Principles and Promising Practices on Alternatives to Imprisonment.* New York: Author, 2007.

von Hirsch, Andrew. "The Ethics of Community-Based Sanctions." In *Community Corrections: Probation, Parole, and Intermediate Sanctions*, Joan Petersilia, ed. New York: Oxford University Press, 1996.

EVALUATION OF PROGRAMS

Program evaluation uses social science research methods to systematically investigate the consequences of social intervention programs. Evaluation of community corrections practices has become increasingly common, as justice administrators and other decision makers identify best practices and set performance standards in the attempt to eliminate ineffective supervision strategies and promote public safety. The success of a community corrections program depends on the validity of the theoretical perspective underlying the program, the logic of its design, the degree to which the design is actually implemented, and the social context in which the program is implemented. Evaluation research investigates these influences in a summative sense, up to a given program benchmark, such as the completion of the program or a program funding year. It also investigates programs in a formative sense, that is, in a continuous manner throughout the program's history, with the intention of refining the program's effectiveness on a continuous basis.

Community corrections evaluation studies are responsive to their many constituencies and stakeholders—notably, program sponsors and funders, agency administrators, offender clients, and others whose lives are directly and indirectly affected by the behaviors of offenders supervised in the community. Such studies should be designed to provide results in a timely and understandable manner in order to be of the greatest utility to stakeholders in pursuing their goals. The evaluation research literature confirms that the lack of sufficient program assessment impedes program performance. The following discussion focuses on the principal tasks of program evaluators: preevaluation activities, process assessments, and outcome evaluations. It concludes with some presentation of the role of program evaluation in promoting evidence-based practices in community corrections.

Preevaluation Activities

The first step in the assessment process is to determine if a community corrections program can be validly assessed. From a methodological standpoint, this includes determining if adequate information can be assembled to conduct a scientifically valid assessment. For example, an evaluation study designed to determine if release into a halfway house will provide a cost-effective alternative to intensive parole supervision is not feasible if sufficient financial information has not been collected for both. From a programmatic perspective, it might also be inappropriate to conduct a summative final outcome assessment for a complex community corrections program, such as a drug court, if the program has been in operation for only a year or two. In this instance, it is unlikely that the program is fully stable and performing up to its full potential, and the number of drug offenders who have completed the program is probably insufficient to determine if the impact on recidivism and relapse rates is significant, relative to other program approaches. Determining the possibility and appropriateness of evaluation research is called an "evaluability assessment" and should be considered prior to committing to a formal evaluation research study.

Designing Evaluation Research

Evaluation studies are more successful if the evaluation team is involved in the initial planning of the program. This ensures detailed documentation of important planning decisions, and the evaluation team can assist the program staff and other stakeholders in specifying the program goals, objectives, and activities in a measurable way. For example, a community-based sex offender treatment program might be created to promote public safety. To determine the relative success of the program, systematic thought must be given to what will be considered a threat to public safety: Is the program limited to future sexual offenses committed by those served by the program, or does it include other serious criminal offenses, risky behaviors such unauthorized contact with children, or other violations of supervisory conditions? For how long must an offender avoid unacceptable behaviors before he or she is considered a success? Must the entire program be completed before the offender is considered to have been influenced by the program intervention, or could partial completers also be considered? Is the proportion of successful clients two years after completing the program the most useful measure of the program's effectiveness, or should cumulative days of residence in the community completed by program recipients without inappropriate behaviors be used as the outcome measure?

A useful tool that the evaluation team can help develop with stakeholders during the preevaluation phase is a logic model. Logic models come in several forms, but they share a similar syntax:

> If (type of program recipient) is subjected to (type of program intervention) for (intensity or duration of the intervention) within (a particular context), then we expect that that person will change in his or her (attitudes, skills, behavior) in the short term, his or her (attitudes, skills, behavior) in the intermediate term, and his or her (attitudes, skills, behavior) over the long term.

For example, the logic model for a therapeutic halfway house might be:

> Offenders with histories of substance abuse released from prison who have limited familial and community support are eligible to live in the County Reintegration Facility, where they will receive weekly cognitive-behavioral treatment, employment counseling, social skills training, and daily monitoring for substance abuse, for not less than twelve months. At least 90 percent of these offenders will stay crime- and drug-free from their time of entrance into the program, 80 percent will successfully gain and maintain employment and/or admission into educational or vocational training programs within 90 days of admission, and 70 percent will fully reintegrate into the community with no further serious criminal incidents within three years after program completion.

While slightly awkward in its wording, a logic model such as this one provides information concerning the program type, target group, the social context, and intervention strategies of the program, as well as its specific short-, intermediate-, and long-term performance goals and program performance assessment criteria.

Process Evaluation

A process evaluation documents what has been done to implement the program and produce desired change among clients. It measures the resources invested in pursuing the program's goals and the manner in which those resources have been organized and administered. The evaluation team collects and analyzes information concerning the time, human, and financial investments in the program. Process evaluation measures the delivery of services to the client, how professionals develop the skills necessary to do their job, and how they are organized, supervised, and supported in their work. Since community corrections programs typically engage with a network of other service programs, their ability to coordinate effectively with other agencies becomes part of the process evaluation.

Social programs never turn out exactly as planned. This is not necessarily the fault of poorly trained or unmotivated program staff; it could be the result of institutional and community influences or client behaviors beyond the program's control. Assuming that even the best planned program will not be implemented exactly as envisioned at its start-up, it is important to continuously monitor program fidelity: the degree to which and manner whereby the program adheres to or deviates from the original plan. Ongoing process assessment will help in the early identification of unanticipated program barriers or facilitators, and to initiate program refinements that address problems and capitalize on opportunities. When significant and sustained deviation from the original program plan is documented through evaluation, administrators and other stakeholders can begin to refine the program plan and/or logic model in a deliberate, rather than ad hoc or crisis-driven, manner.

Outcome Evaluation

Outcome evaluations determine changes among service recipients, or some other targeted group of stakeholders, as a result of the program's activities. The simplest form of outcome evaluation is determining the gross effect of the program in question.

An example of a gross outcome is that 75 percent of those who complete a drug court program are not rearrested within three years. This might be an interesting finding, especially if compared from one year to the next, but it does not address the question of whether there might be a more effective program or to what degree attending the drug court is an improvement over recovery without receiving any program services at all. Thus, outcome evaluation is usually concerned with estimating the net effect of the program, relative to alternatives. Net outcomes also take into consideration the influence of other factors acting on the client while that person is engaged in the program under analysis. For example, some drug court participants might be receiving other services beyond those provided by the court, might be under different levels of monitoring, or might have other complicating conditions, such as cognitive disorders, that could affect their success in the program. While no evaluation research project can control for all possible influences on program outcomes, efforts to do so can produce a more realistic picture of the benefits of program participation and allow for fairer comparisons between programs.

The introduction of controls requires the use of some type of experimental or quasi-experimental research design, such as those described by Donald T. Campbell and Julian C. Stanley. The most rigorous and popular form of such research is the randomized group assignment design. While there are many variations of the randomized group assignment design, they all involve assigning subjects to at least one experimental group that receives the intervention and one control group that does not. It is assumed that if potential program clients are randomly assigned to the experimental and control groups, the groups, given large enough sample sizes, will be identical on other traits that might cause the outcomes to vary independent of the program intervention itself.

While useful in laboratory research, such a design is difficult to obtain and sustain throughout the course of a community corrections intervention, for many reasons. Many community corrections programs do not have a sufficient number of clients assigned to them in a given time period to justify the assumption that equality between control and experimental groups has been reached by random assignment. Even if there were sufficient numbers assigned to each group, attrition from either group during the course of a lengthy program would, by the time of program completion, result in a loss of group equivalency by those in the experimental group. Evaluators have used techniques such as propensity score matching to attempt to address these methodological concerns, but they are not a substitute for rigorously sustained group equivalency. Furthermore, clients not only must be matched in terms of personal characteristics at the time they enter into the experimental or control group but also must have similar experiences outside the program during the intervention. This is unlikely, particularly for offender clients who must attend other forms of treatment, have different experiences with employment, or suffer from unanticipated community situations that could affect their outcomes.

Finally, it is unlikely that the criminal justice system would be willing to assign a group of convicted offenders to a control group in which no services are provided; this option could be seen as placing the community at too great a risk. Rather, offenders might be assigned to a promising community corrections program that offers the possibility of greatly improved outcomes for the client and other stakeholders, while the control group would be assigned to some more traditional condition, such as regular parole supervision. If, however, there is strong reason to suspect that the promising program will in fact produce significantly better personal and community outcomes, some stakeholder groups or external observers might argue that it is immoral to withhold the best services to some offenders.

In summary, while methodologically rigorous designs including randomized group assignment will provide the most definitive estimation of a program's effectiveness, they might be viewed as impractical, illegal, or immoral, especially among those who are not fully committed to the virtues of evaluation research in the first place.

Cost Assessments

Program evaluators assess program costs for at least two major reasons. First, when policy makers have to make decisions on where and how to invest scarce economic resources in producing public safety, they are responsive to research findings that are cast in economic terms. Second, "bang-for-the-buck" estimates allow for comparison among very diverse social programs: Community corrections programs can be compared, at least in economic terms, to programs with similar public safety

goals, such as community drug sweeps or school prevention programs, if their costs for improving community safety can be reliably estimated.

Cost assessments are usually either descriptive estimates (of overall program costs and costs per client) or cost-efficiency estimates. The former requires that the evaluation team, in consultation with stakeholders, identify and assign fiscal value to all program costs, then agree on the number of clients by which those costs should be divided. Sometimes program costs are limited to the funding that has been appropriated for the program, be it a halfway house, a domestic violence diversion, or a drug court program. However, sometimes programs "leverage" additional resources, such as the involvement of volunteers, faith-based groups, or other social services and entitlements for which the program clients are eligible, and these also contribute to the program outcomes. A fair cost assessment includes all of these program investments. Overall program costs alone may influence policy decisions, in that there might be a maximum funding limit for any community corrections program. To determine the cost-per-client ratio, stakeholders must agree on which clients to count: Does the client group include everyone referred to a program, or only those who fully complete all or a major portion? It is useful to agree on these definitions in advance and make them explicit, to allow for cross-program comparisons.

Cost-efficiency estimates build on descriptive analyses. Once program costs are determined, program benefits must also be identified and valued. Cost-benefit analysis is complicated by difficulties in assigning value to program benefits that are not usually measured in economic units. For example, while we might relatively easily assign a cost to the investigation and prosecution of, and intervention resulting from, a violent criminal event committed by an offender under community supervision, it is difficult to estimate accurately the psychological cost to a victim or the cost associated with an increased fear of crime experienced by citizens as a result of the crime. Generally, some agreement is reached among stakeholders and/or decision makers on how to value the benefits associated with a successful program outcome, and the benefits accrued by the total number of program participants can be compared to the program costs. Like costs, all program benefits must be included in these assessments; omitting important costs will result in overly optimistic estimations of the program's efficiency, while omitting important benefits will result in overly conservative estimates.

While keeping in mind that some stakeholders might suffer the greater share of program costs and others enjoy most of the program's benefits, the most direct efficiency estimates merely indicate that a program shows a net economic benefit or loss. More nuanced analyses estimate the total program cost per program participant. For example, if in one year it cost $200,000 to operate a program that served 100 clients, the cost per client would be $2,000. However, a cost-effectiveness, or cost-benefit, analysis is used to estimate the cost per successful client outcome. If the same program had a 25 percent success ratio, then the cost per successful client outcome would be $8,000. When cost-effectiveness is calculated, comparisons can be made between different programs if their clients and goals are similar. Cost-effectiveness calculations also suggest that programs can be improved by finding ways to control unnecessary costs, serve more clients, or improve program effectiveness.

Evidence-Based Community Corrections

"Evidence-based," "results-based," or "best-practice," programs have become increasingly popular in the corrections field, to the point where states and the federal government expect that a substantial proportion of criminal justice program funding must be invested only in evidence-based programs. Designation of a program as a best practice usually requires that it has been assessed in a methodologically rigorous manner, ideally using the randomized group assignment design in several different community contexts, and that the results show significant effectiveness across those contexts. Community corrections programs that have been rated as best practices include job training programs, intensive supervision of high-risk juvenile and adult offenders, drug treatment programs that employ urine testing and cognitive-behavioral therapy, drug courts, community-based adult and juvenile sex-offender treatment programs, and adolescent diversion programs such as teen courts. Best practices can also be a critical component of different types of programs. Brad Bogue and colleagues have derived a set of system principles that they believe are most effective in reducing recidivism among offenders

under community supervision: (1) target high-risk offenders, (2) assess offender needs, (3) be flexible in designing individual responsivity into programming, (4) develop behavior management plans for offenders, (5) deliver treatment programs using cognitive-based strategies, (6) motivate and shape offender behaviors, (7) engender the broader community as a protective factor against recidivism and use it to support offender reentry and reintegration, and (8) identify outcomes and measure progress.

Paul D. Steele
Morehead State University

See also Costs of Community Corrections; Effectiveness of Community Corrections; False Negatives and False Positives; Goals and Objectives of Community Corrections; Prediction Instruments; Recidivism; Risk and Needs Assessment Instruments; Risk Assessment Instruments: Three Generations; "What Works" Approach and Evidence-Based Practices

Further Readings

Bogue, Brad et al. "Implementing Evidence-Based Practices in Community Corrections: The Principle of Effective Intervention." http://www.nicic.org/Library/019342 (Accessed December 2010).

Burrell, William. "Probation and Public Safety: Using Performance Measures to Demonstrate Public Value." *Corrections Management Quarterly*, v.2 (1998).

Campbell, Donald T. and Julian C. Stanley. *Experimental and Quasi-Experimental Designs for Research*. Dallas, TX: Houghton Mifflin, 1963.

Drake, Elizabeth K., Steve Aos, and Marna G. Miller. "Evidence-Based Public Policy Options to Reduce Crime and Criminal Justice Costs: Implications in Washington State." *Victims and Offenders*, v.4 (2009).

Lipton, Douglas S. et al. "Program Accreditation and Correctional Treatment." *Substance Use and Misuse*, v.35 (2000).

MacKenzie, Doris L. "Evidence-Based Corrections: Identifying What Works." *Crime and Delinquency*, v.46/4 (2000).

Rossi, Peter H., Mark W. Lipsey, and Howard E. Freeman. *Evaluation: A Systematic Approach*, 7th ed. Thousand Oaks, CA: Sage, 2004.

Sherman, Laurence et al. *Preventing Crime: What Works, What Doesn't, What's Promising*. Washington, DC: U.S. Department of Justice, National Institute of Justice, 1998.

FAITH-BASED INITIATIVES

In the community corrections context, the term *faith-based initiatives* refers to a collection of public policies that appropriate funds to faith-based organizations so they can increase their capacity to rid communities of their problems and ultimately curtail the dilemmas associated with the relative and absolute deprivation that can lead to criminality and recidivism.

Religious institutions collectively face the strain of maintaining a minimum overhead, because of the uncertainty of their fiscal status and the threat of unexpected operational expenses, while displaying evidence of concern and action regarding secular but social needs. As religious organizations, they often seek to meet societal needs as part of their mission, which lies beyond congregational maintenance. The social problems they work to address include mental illnesses, substance abuse, poverty, and their by-products, including criminality. Addressing such problems in the community, however, often requires significant financial resources that are beyond most faith-based organizations' internal means.

Public officials face two intersecting pressures: the demand to take a tough stance on crime and, at the same time, maximize economic efficiency. Faith-based initiatives have emerged from the core belief that religious institutions can reduce prison recidivism by rehabilitating offenders without public funding. However, shifting some responsibility for correctional treatment from the government to the private sector requires the public to support legislative action, and hence controversy surrounds the rhetoric and policies of faith-based initiatives. Government often criticizes religious institutions as abandoning "the social gospel" or the insufficiency in social activism and the inadequacy of faith-based organizations' aid to the needy, and this situation essentially empowers the state to define the mission and interpret the creeds of religious groups.

Politics plays a significant role in the existence of faith-based initiatives. State and municipal politicians typically face pressing interrogation about their positions and action plans for minimizing crime and managing criminal behavior. If political candidates are then elected or appointed, they often face significant pressure to follow through with their campaign promises. Tensions between competing ideologies greatly affect the degree to which faith-based initiatives can be implemented or repealed. This may result in legislation that regulates both public and private funding. As state and federal budgets shrink, existing secular programs and services are prone to drastic shifts in resources, which ultimately impact the receiving communities.

History

During the 1980s, under the presidential administration of Ronald Reagan, targeted reductions of the U.S. federal budget triggered the defunding of a host of social programs and services. However, the budgetary shift accompanied a drastic increase in prison construction and incarceration. In response, religious institutions and para-church organizations became the resources of last resort and were forced to fill the void in the social safety net on behalf of the marginalized. Evidence of increased faith-based efforts supported the belief that such organizations could become increasingly productive and instrumental in the services they provide; therefore, advocates could justify less reliance on the government for services.

The passing of the Welfare Reform Act of 1996 under the administration of President Bill Clinton accompanied the initiation of "charitable choice." At the time, Senator John Ashcroft, the leading congressional advocate of charitable choice, sought to make federally funded grant contracts accessible to faith-based organizations on equal terms with other private-sector organizations. Religiously affiliated organizations such as Catholic Charities, Lutheran Social Services, and the Jewish Federation had previously received federal grants, yet these nonprofit organizations existed as separate organizations from their respective denominations. However, charitable choice enabled explicitly sectarian institutions, such as mosques, synagogues, and churches, to compete for federal funds generated through tax revenues.

Charitable choice was criticized as not adhering to the establishment clause of the First Amendment to the Constitution, which proscribes the government's giving preference to any particular religion. The Anti-Defamation League has established several mildly arbitrary standards regarding regulatory criteria, which seek to protect religious liberties. Such standards include refraining from proselytizing and discriminatory hiring. However, the guidelines for public display of religious symbols remain subject to interpretation. Employment, promotions, terminations, and retaliation based on religious grounds remain difficult to prove, expensive to challenge in court, and time-consuming, often taking several years to settle legally. Groups regarded as hatemongering or favoring extreme dogmas, such as those that sanction terrorism, are ineligible to receive federal funds. However, religious groups collectively tend to contain implicit cultural biases and ethnocentric tendencies that can easily appear offensive or potentially threatening to some outside groups.

In January 2001, immediately after his inauguration, President George W. Bush established the White House Office of Faith-Based and Community Issues. Early in Barack Obama's presidency, Obama appointed Joshua DuBois as executive director of the White House Office of Faith-Based and Neighborhood Partnerships to recommend amendments to Executive Order 13199 under the auspices of establishing additional regulations intended to protect religious freedom. Such regulatory modifications entail the availability of like services from a secular organization. In addition to ensuring equality and fairness in the assessment of their performance outcomes, the federal government has the obligation to treat public- and private-sector organizations as coequals in terms of the criteria used in competing for grants.

Conservative Ideological Arguments

Conservative ideology typically approaches crime and poverty as associated with consequences of individual morality. Conservatives argue that criminal transgressions derive from individual choice, as reflected by having a flawed character. Governments lack the tools or means to cultivate virtues, and such attempts often overreach their authority and drain resources away from other much-needed functions. However, faith-based organizations have greater legal autonomy and are better equipped to assist individuals in shaping their moral conduct. As individuals collectively embrace high ethical standards, criminal behavior is likely to diminish. According to conservative ideology, ethically reformed individuals are more likely to make decisions that will improve their livelihoods and result in reducing poverty. As poverty declines, the crime rate decreases, since there is a positive correlation between economic need and the motive for committing a crime.

Conservatives seek to advance their argument through an appeal to taxpayers, noting that social services provided by faith-based organizations will help alleviate the burden for public funding through taxation. Also, because of political pressure to "get tough on crime," conservatives tend to label intermediate punishment and especially rehabilitative services as "lenient" and "ineffective" because they lack severe consequences that would deter criminals from engaging in crime.

Decades of empirical studies have identified a host of independent variables that predict criminal activity, including employment status, level of formal educational attainment, median household income, and criminal activity among family members. Conservatives tend to subscribe to the idea that, despite such circumstances, rational human creatures decide whether or not to engage in criminal behavior. Persons with high virtues are not exempt from the problems associated with scarcity in employment opportunities or limited access to advanced formal education. However, conservatives note that many who face these problems, including many of the working poor, whose impoverished status results from earnings significantly below those that provide a livable wage, have an increased likelihood of choosing alternatives to crime.

According to Ram Cnaan, U.S. congregations collectively have a surplus of untapped resources. Cnaan has estimated that congregations on average give $184,000 annually to social programs. Cnaan's studies indicated that approximately 23 percent of church budgets support social programs.

Liberal Ideological Arguments

A typical liberal ideology argues that faith-based initiatives contribute to the defunding and elimination of greatly needed government-supported social programs, particularly those needed by the economically disadvantaged. As public programs and services are privatized, social service funding begins to shift to private sources and leads to dependence on charitable contributions.

Additionally, liberals suggest that to avoid violating the U.S. Constitution, criteria for supporting faith-based initiatives must be established such that religious institutions receiving funds will strictly adhere to secularized programs. Liberals argue that faith-based initiatives contain fluid rather than concrete boundaries between the institutions' secular obligations and sectarian missions.

A liberal framework suggests that faith-based initiatives relieve the government from a significant portion of its obligations to those in society who rely on needed social services. Religious organizations have succeeded at the micro level in meeting societal needs, but such organizations lack the capacity and means to provide adequate services on a large scale. Moreover, faith-based organizations typically lack legal authorization for services, such as supervising ex-offenders who require monitoring while taking psychiatric medicine. Assuming these added responsibilities would increase faith-based institutions' liability risk, resulting in premium increases for additional insurance coverage.

Liberals also argue that, as needed services become scarce through privatization and delegation to religious entities, most marginalized and desperate members of society become pressured to compromise personal religious convictions in order to benefit from governmental grants controlled by religious institutions. Moreover, liberal ideology supports the premise that privatizing social programs contributes to mass disenfranchisement, which creates favorable conditions for incarceration and recidivism for those who have been released.

Government support for faith-based initiatives, liberals argue, also leads to taxpayers directly financing religious activities against their wills. Indirectly, tax revenues contribute to grants to religious organizations, allowing religious organizations to reallocate otherwise less available funds to religious worship and religious activities.

Stratification not only affects faith-based organizations; those organizations also reflect social inequality in their presence. Sociologist Mark Chaves argues against Cnaan's claim that faith-based organizations have an abundance of resources. Chaves references U.S. congregational studies of both Christianity and Judaism, which show that approximately 60 percent of all congregations have an active membership of fewer than one hundred. Chaves attributes Cnaan's overestimation to an inadequate sample in measuring the population of congregations, noting an overrepresentation of larger and more affluent churches and synagogues. In sharp contrast with Cnaan's findings, Chaves's findings indicated that approximately 3 percent of faith-based organizations' resources have been allocated to social programs and services.

Faith-based initiatives, moreover, necessitate intrusive measures on the part of government to regulate religious activities beyond those necessary to be in compliance with requirements for nonprofit organizations. Another political concern arises in applying the Civil Rights Act of 1964. The Civil Rights Act was intended to minimize discriminatory practices, but it provides for "exemptions for religious organizations from the ban against religious discrimination in employment" (42 U.S.C. §§ 2000e-1). The Civil Rights Act neither condones nor prohibits faith-based initiatives, but its provision with regard to religious institutions could divert taxpayer revenues to finance institutions that may lawfully practice discrimination.

Impact on Community Corrections

The United States has one of the world's most religiously diverse populations, with a significant amount of interfaith coexistence, though not complete toleration. As an unintended consequence of faith-based initiatives, religions themselves must now compete against one another to receive shrinking federal funding.

In 1998 in Wisconsin, the Joint Legislative Council's Special Committee on Faith-Based Approaches to Crime Prevention and Justice was created with the original purpose of reducing both crime and recidivism rates. The committee also advocated restorative justice as a necessary part of the corrections process. Such reform efforts began with redefining the prison chaplain's role, making the chaplain responsible for meeting an inmate's spiritual needs while also providing rehabilitative services without partiality favoring any distinct religious tradition. *Pitts v. Knowles* (1972) contributed to the advancement of the enforcement of "freedom of worship" such that inmates are legally entitled to have access to sacred literature and sacraments on equal terms. The committee further mandated that approved correctional, rehabilitative, or religious representatives who have proselytizing capabilities would serve as unpaid volunteers. Wisconsin's Department of Health and Family Services (DIIFS) funds religious organizations—including the Salvation Army, Lutheran Social Services, Catholic Social Services, Catholic Charities, Bethany Christian Services, Holy Cathedral Church of God in Christ, Word of Hope Ministries, and Community Enterprises of Greater Milwaukee—to create and administer programs that may contribute to crime reduction.

In April 1997, the Texas State legislature approved Prison Fellowship Ministries, based in Reston, Virginia, to financially sponsor the Christian-based rehabilitation program called the InnerChange Freedom Initiative (IFI), located at the Jester II unit in Sugar Land, Texas. The law aims to promote faith-based programs in correctional facilities on equal terms with secular services and programs. IFI contained elements of a proto-faith-based initiative because it functioned as a Christian correctional center and offered an alternative placement facility for nonviolent offenders nearing parole or release. The program embraces the restorative justice model of victim-offender reconciliation. The services are geared toward cultivating positive behavior and assisting in adequate reintegration into society after release. The Prison Fellowship Ministries pays the salaries of IFI staff. Activities in the first phase of the program include anger management, overcoming substance abuse, and goal setting. Phase two incorporates serving the community. The third phase, in the post-parole setting, includes support groups and mentorship provided by members of the Christian faith.

IFI's safeguard against violating the U.S. Constitution's principles of religious freedom lies in the facts that participants must first volunteer and inmates do not have a faith requirement; Christians and non-Christians alike can participate. Inmates interested in the pre-release program must have minimum security classification status. However, the fact that the facility received funding from public tax dollars was controversial.

In the 1990s, the U.S. Department of Justice issued grants to 16 community organizations targeting juvenile delinquency prevention in a collective effort called the Boston Strategy to Prevent Youth Violence, which emphasized law enforcement working in partnership with religious organizations as an additional but significant community resource. Additional strategies included assistance from the Ten Point Coalition, through which churches become directly involved in gang intervention through various outreach efforts, including evangelism.

Lemon v. Kurtzman (1991) functions as the basis of the so-called Lemon test, which measures whether or not a U.S. constitutional violation exists in terms of policies and programs involving a relationship between the state and religious institutions. The program's sole purpose must be secular, not targeted toward religion or any particular faith, with strict avoidance of "excessive government entanglement."

Michael D. Royster
Prairie View A&M University

See also Community Partnerships; COMPASS Program; Ethics of Community-Based Sanctions; Humanitarianism; Sanctuary; Volunteers and Community Corrections

Further Readings

Black, Amy E., Douglas L. Koopma, and David Ryden. *Of Little Faith: The Politics of George W. Bush's Faith-Based Initiatives*. Washington, DC: Georgetown University Press, 2004.

Chaves, Mark. *Congregations in America*. Cambridge, MA: Harvard University Press, 2004.

Cnaan, Ram A. *The Invisible Caring Hand: American Congregations and the Provision of Welfare*. New York: New York University Press, 2002.

Collett, Jessica L. et al. "Faith-Based Decisions? The Consequences of Heightened Religious Salience in Social Service Referral Decisions." *Journal for Social Scientific Studies*, v.45/1 (2006).

Donaldson, Dave and Stanley Carlson-Thies. *A Revolution of Compassion: Faith-Based Groups as Full Partners in Fighting America's Social Problems*. Grand Rapids, MI: Baker Books, 2003.

Franklin, Robert M. *Another Day's Journey: Black Churches Confronting the American Crisis*. Minneapolis: Fortress Press, 1997.

Horowitz, Daniel and Ruth Mitchell. "Safeguarding Religious Liberties in Charitable Choice and Faith-Based Initiatives." Washington, DC: Center for Inquiry, 2009. http://www.centerforinquiry.net/uploads/attachments/Safeguarding-Religious-Liberty-in-Charitable-Choice-and-Faith-Based-Initiatives.pdf (Accessed July 2011).

McClellan, Melissa. "Faith and Federalism: Do Charitable Choice Provisions Preempt State Nondiscrimination Laws?" *Washington and Lee Law Review*, v.61 (2004).

Smith, R. Drew, ed. *New Day Begun: African American Churches and Civil Culture in Post-Civil Rights America*. Durham, NC: Duke University Press, 2003.

Walker, Theodore, Jr. *Empower the People: Social Ethics for the African-American Church*. Maryknoll, NY: Orbis Books, 1991.

Wineburg, Bob. *A Limited Partnership: The Politics of Religion, Welfare, and Social Service*. New York: Columbia University Press, 2001.

Wuthnow, Roberts. *Saving America? Faith-Based Services and the Future of Civil Society*. Princeton, NJ: Princeton University Press, 2004.

FALSE NEGATIVES AND FALSE POSITIVES

A key component of community corrections programs is the ability to predict the level of risk that offenders pose once released back into the community. Assessments of offender risk (such as high risk versus low risk) are used by correctional authorities to determine proper levels of correctional supervision and treatment options. False positives and false negatives are two types of error that stem from efforts to assess and classify levels of offender risk. False positives occur when low-risk offenders are incorrectly labeled as belonging to the high-risk group. False negatives occur when high-risk offenders are incorrectly labeled as belonging to the low-risk group. Both types of error reduce the effectiveness of community corrections programs by limiting the extent to which correctional interventions can be matched to the characteristics and needs of individual offenders.

Various risks are associated with releasing convicted offenders back into the community under correctional supervision. Perhaps most important is the potential for the offender to recidivate (that is, reoffend). Because risk levels vary substantially across offenders, it is important to differentiate between low-risk and high-risk offenders. There are four goals associated with efforts to classify and assess levels of offender risk: ensuring community safety, matching offenders' needs with appropriate levels of supervision and programming, increasing correctional efficiency, and lowering cost.

Factors associated with offender risk generally are grouped into one of two categories: static risk factors and dynamic risk factors. Static risk factors consist of enduring characteristics of the offender that cannot be altered by correctional interventions. Examples include offender age, prior record, and social class. Dynamic risk factors comprise the attributes of offenders that are amenable to external influence. Examples of dynamic risk factors include education, interpersonal skills, and alcohol or drug addiction.

Correctional authorities utilize two basic methods for assessing offender risk: subjective classifications and objective classifications. Subjective classification methods rely on the experience and personal judgment of correctional officials to determine risk levels. Subjective methods utilize broadly defined information on offenders and are both person-centered and flexible. Objective classifications of risk (or structured objective assessments) involve the use of predetermined risk factors that are defined and measured systematically. The aim of objective assessment methods is to quantify the risk or likelihood of a specific outcome (such as recidivism). The most commonly utilized objective classification instrument in North America is the

Level of Service Inventory–Revised (LSI–R). This instrument includes 54 risk indicators that are divided into 10 subscales that include characteristics such as an offender's criminal history, education/employment, and finances. The total number of identified risk factors are summed to compute an LSI–R score, with higher scores indicating a higher risk of recidivism and criminal behavior. Scores are used to group offenders into ordinal scales of risk (such as high-, medium-, and low-risk) that can help officials determine appropriate levels of community supervision and correctional programming. Other common objective risk assessment instruments include the Hare Psychopathy Checklist–Revised (PCL–R), the Violence Risk Assessment Guide (VRAG), and the Historical, Clinical, and Risk Management Scheme (HCR-20). Research has demonstrated that objective assessment instruments are capable of accurately predicting levels of offender risk and identifying the correctional needs of offenders.

Unfortunately, attempts to assess and classify levels of offender risk sometimes produce erroneous results such as false positives and false negatives. False positives and false negatives also can result both from efforts to identify the correctional needs of offenders and from efforts to monitor compliance with court-ordered conditions (such as drug testing). For example, an assessment that determines that an illiterate offender does not have educational needs would be an example of a false negative. Similarly, a false positive on a drug test could lead to the unnecessary revocation of parole for a recently released inmate.

The causes of false positives and false negatives in offender classification and assessment are numerous and include risk cutoff scores that are too low (which create false positives) and the use of risk criteria that are too specific (which creates false negatives). Offender dishonesty can be an additional problem. For example, the failure of offenders to provide truthful responses to questions regarding current drug and alcohol use and abuse may lead to erroneous classifications of risk and needs.

Because risk levels vary substantially across offenders, it is important for correctional authorities to identify low-risk and high-risk offenders accurately and to tailor correctional interventions based on risk assessments. Errors resulting from the risk assessment process, false positives and false negatives, limit the ability of community corrections programs to provide for community safety, tailor correctional treatment to offenders' needs, and reduce costs while increasing the efficiency of correctional programming.

Stephen M. Schnebly
University of Illinois, Springfield

See also Actuarial Risk Assessment; Classification Systems; Hare Psychopathy Checklist; Level of Service Inventory; Prediction Instruments; Risk and Needs Assessment Instruments

Further Readings

Bonta, James. "Offender Risk Assessment: Guidelines for Selection and Use." *Criminal Justice and Behavior*, v.29/4 (2002).

Kroner, Daryl G. and Jeremy F. Mills. "The Accuracy of Five Risk Appraisal Instruments in Predicting Institutional Misconduct and New Convictions." *Criminal Justice and Behavior*, v.28/4 (2001).

Sun, Key. *Correctional Counseling: A Cognitive Growth Perspective*. Sudbury, MA: Jones and Bartlett, 2008.

Family Courts

Families have had a separate court in which to litigate their private problems since English common law, but the United States was slow to adopt this trend. Between 1900 and 1918, the Progressive Era brought forth advances in social consciousness and paved the way for a movement that would push for a family-centric court. In 1959, the Standard Family Court Act was put forth by several high-profile groups. This law stated that juvenile and family problems were best handled by nonadversarial tactics, and it put forth a number of proposed changes that it believed would best benefit families in crisis. However, although family courts have been accepted by the vast majority of states, there is still little consensus about what constitutes a family court or even how one is best run.

History

Prior to the Progressive Era, juveniles were treated mostly like adults, subject to the same punishments and treatments. Those who helped establish the first family courts focused on rehabilitation and treatment of juveniles and their families. In 1912, New Jersey granted juvenile courts the jurisdiction to hear all domestic disputes. In 1914, Ohio took a broader approach to family matters by creating the Division of Domestic Relations in the Hamilton County Court of Common Pleas. The court was granted jurisdiction over the domestic relations issues of divorce, alimony, contributing to delinquency of children, early forms of child support, and the juvenile issues of delinquency, dependency, and neglected and crippled children.

There was little development in this area until 1959, when the Standard Family Court Act was put forth. This act was championed by several well-regarded groups, such as the National Probation and Parole Association, the National Council of Juvenile Court Judges, and the U.S. Children's

The 800 Broadway building in Cincinnati, Ohio, houses the Hamilton County courts. In 1914, Ohio created a domestic relations division of the Hamilton County court with jurisdiction over issues of divorce, juvenile delinquency, dependency, and neglected and handicapped children. (Wikimedia/Derek Jensen)

Bureau. These groups called for a separate and distinct court in each state that dealt exclusively with family matters, and what it considered "family matters" covered a broad range of issues. The law stated that family courts should cover traditional areas, such as divorce, child support, and custody matters, but it also suggested that the family courts take on several criminal issues, such as crimes committed against a child by a parent and criminal charges against adults for abandoning or failing to provide support for children. The law also stated that these courts should take over mental health issues, such as involuntary commitment of both adults and juveniles, and areas tangential to family matters, such as the granting of permission for juveniles to marry and become employed.

The philosophy behind the Standard Family Court Act held that nonadversarial and therapeutic procedures were the best way to deal with juvenile and family problems. It suggested that the best way to help families was to use judges with specialized dispute resolution training and ensure that these judges would have complete records on all matters related to the family so as to be able to put forth the best suggestions for them. In 1980, the American Bar Association added its support, stating that each state should develop a unified family court.

While the support of these well-established organizations helped pave the way for a nationwide establishment of family courts, movement toward that goal was slow. By 2006, only 75 percent of states had variations on family courts—although up from 11 states (22 percent) with family courts in 1998. This is surprising, considering the percentage of family-related cases filed: nationwide, 41 percent annually. In Nebraska, 58 percent of all annual filings are related to juvenile or family law. Nevada and Maryland boast 49 percent and 46 percent of all cases, respectively, and 41 percent of New Jersey's annual cases are family related.

Problems in Establishing a Family Court

Because family courts are run on a state-by-state basis, there is no agreed-upon definition of what a family court is or which areas it should cover. Many retain exclusive jurisdiction over matrimonial issues such as adoption, paternity, divorce, alimony, and the custody, visitation, and support of children coinciding with the separation of families. Some family courts also adjudicate over domestic violence trials and punishments. Other family courts have expanded their jurisdiction to include quasi-criminal matters, such as abuse and neglect of children and juvenile delinquency, and a few address the other areas set forth in the Standard Family Court Act.

The confusion and disagreement over which matters should fall under the jurisdiction of a family court are partly responsible for the reluctance of several states to start unified courts. It is clearly sensible that interrelated matrimonial issues, such as divorce, alimony, and child custody and support, should be tried in the same court. This would streamline and speed up hearings, providing quick relief for the litigants and cutting down on strained judicial resources. However, to follow the Standard Family Court Act, the courts would need to be expanded to include criminal matters such as domestic violence and child abuse and neglect, as well as health matters such as involuntary commitments and guardianship cases. This puts an enormous burden on family court judges, demanding that they become experts in several disparate types of law.

Judicial tenure also varies among the states. Some family court judges spend only a few months or years in family court; others are given lifetime tenure in family courts. Both methods have drawbacks. Rotating judges through family court too quickly means that the judges do not have enough time to become experts in their field and thus render decisions that are truly in the best interest of the family. Moreover, new, untrained judges must be brought in to take the place of those rotating out, and these new judges must be retrained; families will undoubtedly suffer during a new judge's learning curve. Quick removal also means that judges are not able to become intimately acquainted with particular troubled families and individuals throughout ongoing cases, and thus they may tend to suggest only short-term solutions.

However, keeping judges in the same family court positions with the same cases for too long can quickly lead to burnout. Family cases are among the most emotionally draining, and judges quickly become fatigued. Spending too much time in the position can lead some judges to hardness and a lack of emotion that does not benefit family court litigants. Furthermore, judges who spend too much time on a specific family's case can end up involuntarily or inadvertently violating evidence laws. A judge who has been dealing with the same family over a protracted period may improperly consider past events when determining new hearings. For example, if a familiar family comes before a judge for a domestic violence hearing, the judge's awareness of past acts of violence or past threats, which may not otherwise have been admissible in trial, may play a role in the judge's decisions.

Family litigants may also have issues with the structure of family courts. One party may feel that the judge to whom it is assigned is unfair or has a particularly heavy-handed technique. The family randomly assigned to the judge would thus be stuck with him or her until retirement, which can sometimes be decades in the future. Families may also find some judges to be overreaching in their attempts to heal and help them. If a juvenile is found delinquent for a minor charge, such as stealing a candy bar, a judge, intending to help the child, may institute drastic measures, such as a full-scale family background investigation, the involvement of Child Protective Services, or even neglect charges against the parents.

Despite these daunting concerns, the sheer number and complexity of family law cases throughout the nation every year are legion, and it is likely that standardized family courts will eventually expand through all 50 states.

Erica L. Fields
Rutgers University

See also Family Group Conferencing; Family Therapy; Juvenile and Youth Offenders; Prisoner's Family and Reentry; Teen Courts

Further Readings

Babb, Barbara A. "Reevaluating Where We Stand: A Comprehensive Survey of America's Family Justice Systems." *Family Court Review* (April 2008).

Committee on the Standard Family Court Act of the National Council on Crime and Delinquency in Cooperation With the National Council of Juvenile and Family Court Judges and the U.S. Children's Bureau. *Standard Family Court Act*. New York: National Council on Crime and Delinquency, 1959.

Edwards, Leonard P. *The Juvenile Court and the Role of the Juvenile Court Judge.* Reno, NV: National Council of Juvenile and Family Court Judges, 1992.

Geraghty, Anne H. and Wallace J. Mlyniec. "United Family Courts: Tempering Enthusiasm With Caution." *Family Court Review* (October 2002).

Hawes, Joseph M. and Elizabeth F. Shores. *The Family in America: An Encyclopedia.* Santa Barbara, CA: ABC-CLIO, 2001.

Hill, Frances G. "What's a Family Court, and What's in It for the Lawyer?" *Res Gestae* (November 2000).

Katz, Sanford N. and Jeffrey A. Kuhn. *Recommendations for a Model Family Court: A Report From the National Family Court Symposium.* Reno, NV: National Council of Juvenile and Family Court Judges, 1991.

Liu, Irene Jay. "Report: Family Courts in Crisis: System Handling Emotional Domestic Cases Overwhelmed." *Albany Times Union* (October 25, 2009).

Page, R. W. "Family Courts: An Effective Judicial Approach to the Resolution of Family Disputes." *Juvenile and Family Court Journal*, v.44/1 (1993).

FAMILY GROUP CONFERENCING

Family conferencing provides an alternative to formal involvement in the juvenile justice system and the correctional system. It is a diversionary program for youth who engage in minor criminal behavior for the first time and uses community-based supports to prevent recidivism. Family conferencing involves a process that includes a meeting among the youth's family, the police, school officials, the victim, and other community members to respond to and address the youth's misconduct and criminal behavior. The victim, community members, and the youth's family each discuss the impact of the youth's offense, including sharing the youth's emotions surrounding the harm that he or she caused. The conferencing also addresses opportunities for the youth to make amends to those aggrieved and develops a plan to prevent the youth from reoffending.

Description

Initiated in New Zealand and Australia, family conferencing was introduced to the United States during the 1990s. It focuses on a discussion that supports both the victim and the young offender. The conference is facilitated by a professional case manager, independent of all parties. Both the victim and the offender may invite people to the conference as supports or representatives. Since family conferencing tends to operate under the restorative justice model, the focus of the discussion emphasizes victim-offender dialogue in order to restore the damages to the victim and address the specific offense the youth committed. All parties speak, one at a time, about their personal experiences and reactions. During this discussion, a clear distinction is made between the youth as a person and the youth's criminal behavior. Discussion of restitution is initiated by the parties through the facilitator. A written agreement among the conferencing participants, based on what the victim wants and the youth's response, is the last component of family conferencing. Thus, the purpose of family conferencing is to develop specific plans that address the issues leading toward the youth's involvement in illicit activity and set corrective behavioral goals for the youth to help the youth understand the impact of his or her behavior. Some proponents of family conferencing argue that this process teaches youths a sense of right and wrong by exposing them to the various perspectives of the conference participants.

Family conferencing encourages active participation by the community in order to prevent recidivism by the youth and in general promote the safety of the community. Family conferencing involves voluntary participation by the other parties: victim, offender, and families. The youth and the family may be offered the opportunity to engage in family conferencing as a diversion from the formal juvenile justice system, but the youth has the right to refuse participation. The victim may also refuse participation. The youth would then enter the juvenile justice system and risk entering some type of correctional program (such as residential placement or drug treatment) if adjudicated.

Benefits

Youths hear the direct impact of their behavior on the victim and community and are given the opportunity to recognize, acknowledge, and admit guilt for the offense. This discussion may help the youth to develop a better understanding of the broader impact of his or her behavior, and increase accountability for that behavior. Proponents of family conferencing claim that youth participation in these discussions is critical to preventing recidivism.

Victims are provided with the opportunity for closure. The victim expresses his or her feelings to the offender, hears the admission of guilt, and may gain an understanding that the offender is being held accountable for the offense. Furthermore, the community is involved much more so than traditional juvenile offender proceedings; members of the community directly involved in the incident are invited to participate in the family conferencing, as opposed to not being allowed into the courtroom during juvenile hearings because of the confidential nature of these proceedings. Family conferencing acknowledges the impact of the youth's offense on community members.

The participants, as a whole, may derive satisfaction with the informal process of family conferencing. The parties are avoiding the traditional juvenile justice system, which can be complex and challenging to understand. Instead, parties are actively involved in a decision-making process that is less formal and specified to the individual needs of the parties.

Risks

Family conferencing is offered only for specific types of offenses (such as property offenses). Most cases diverted to family conferencing are minor offenses that ultimately may not have been fully prosecuted or adjudicated in the juvenile justice system. Family conferencing typically does not involve a violent or more serious offense, even if it is the first such offense.

Since the conferencing involves multiple adults whose participation in the discussion involves expressing their disapproval of the offense to the juvenile, the environment of the conference may induce a sense of powerlessness in the youth rather than instill empathy and understanding. The conference could discount the youth's self-worth if the facilitator is unable to maintain neutrality or control the direction of the conversation. Furthermore, because a police officer may be one of the community members present during the conference, the environment may not be safe for the youth offender to make a full and honest disclosure, accepting responsibility for his or her behavior.

At the same time, since the conference tends to focus on the behavior of the offender, the victim may experience feelings of alienation. For the victim, the conference may provide no advantage over the traditional juvenile justice system, where services focus on the youth offender and not the victim.

Proponents of family conferencing tend to argue through theoretical perspectives on the effectiveness of reducing recidivism rather than utilizing the results of empirical research. More research is needed to measure not only the effects of family conferencing on recidivism but also the impact of diversionary programs on the community.

Aimée Delaney Lutz
University of New Hampshire

See also Diversion Programs; Juvenile and Youth Offenders; Restitution; Restorative Justice; Victim-Offender Reconciliation Programs

Further Readings

Bradshaw, William and David Roseborough. "An Empirical Review of Family Group Conferencing in Juvenile Offenses." *Juvenile and Family Court Journal*, v.56/4 (2005).

Hayes, Hennessey and Kathleen Daly. "Youth Justice Conferencing and Reoffending." *Justice Quarterly*, v.20/4 (2003).

Umbreit, Mark S. and Susan L. Stacey. "Family Group Conferencing Comes to the U.S.: A Comparison With Victim-Offender Mediation." *Juvenile and Family Court Journal*, v.47/2 (1996).

FAMILY THERAPY

One of the most significant support systems for a correctional inmate is his or her family. Positive family relationships offer substantial opportunities for successful inmate readjustment and reintegration back into the community. Inmates who enjoy the benefits of family support have increased opportunities for successful rehabilitation, in comparison to those who serve their sentences in isolation and loneliness. Unfortunately, other than periodic family visitations, the modest encouragement from correctional facility staff impedes motivation to seize valuable therapeutic and rehabilitative opportunities.

Defining Family Therapy

Positive family relationships support the development of healthy personal and social adjustments.

For families of released prisoners that can survive the disintegration of family relationships through lengthy sentences, the prelease stage of incarceration has proven to be the most successful time to attend family therapy sessions. (Photos.com)

One fundamental purpose of family therapy is to acknowledge the need to treat the prisoner and his or her immediate family as a unit. Family therapy involves the inmate, family members, and a family therapist who supports the exploration of frequently uncharted family dynamics. This therapeutic modality attempts to identify dysfunctional family issues and encourage improved communication patterns. The goal is to emphasize positive family relationships and identify the role of effective communication and feedback.

The objectives of structural family therapy include an analysis of family structure, the altering of family subsystem patterns, and the establishment of appropriate boundaries. The therapist's emphasis is on communication therapy, effective role expectations, stability, and tools for improved communication.

Successful family therapy programs seek to repair ineffective and sometimes irrational belief systems. Therapy sessions address self-defeating patterns of family interaction that have emerged as dysfunctional and repetitive. The strategy is to defeat detrimental styles of communication that are unwittingly passed from one generation to the next. Strengthening family relationships and alleviating faulty family interaction assist family members in building better relationships and improving communication skills.

Special Population Needs

Female inmates are at significant risk and often require family therapy. Research on female inmates indicates that they suffer serious consequences from family separation. Approximately 75 percent of female inmates represent expectant mothers and mothers who look forward to returning to their children. These children are likely to experience rejection and anger for being left behind and excluded from their mothers' lives. Inmate family backgrounds frequently include abuse, alcoholism, drug addiction, wide-ranging criminal behaviors, and incest. The failure to address unfavorable family dynamics is ill-fated. Ignoring the foundation for an inmate's dysfunctional family and psychological issues supports replication of similar consequences for the next generation.

Pre-Release and Immediate Post-Release Issues

For inmates about to be released or reintegrating into family life just after release, reemerging family demands and responsibilities may prove overwhelming. Resentment over fewer than expected family visits, as well as family hostilities, may surface in the former inmate. The cycle of family pain over the loss of children and the offender's ineptness and diminished status may increase family tension and anger. Family members may demonstrate resentment for financial losses, social stigma, and additional family readjustment difficulties that have materialized.

Role conflict from family members who assumed responsibilities for social and financial support during the inmate's absence may inflame arguments. Arguments may emerge over child-rearing practices or adjustments that the spouse and other family members must make after having performed the absent inmate's roles and responsibilities during the offender's imprisonment. This conflict may escalate to the point of violence, and the spouse or former inmate may flee the family relationship.

Community Corrections: Family Therapy Obstacles

Many correctional leaders view family therapy as impractical and present some reasonable arguments. Reasons for not implementing family counseling programs often relate to financial concerns. Prison programs are the last funded and the first to experience budget cuts. Other practical reasons are that family may have to travel long distances, may be able to make only short visits, or may visit infrequently.

In addition, finding qualified professionals willing to facilitate family therapy sessions in a prison setting, which is most often located in a distant rural area, can be problematic. These are real logistical and administrative concerns for correctional administrators. In addition, the financial strain on families struggling to survive the financial losses related to having a family member incarcerated limits meaningful participation.

Prison overcrowding rates continue to soar, placing more emphasis on security rather than treatment. The U.S. prison system population continues to grow in an environment of diminishing space and resources. The political pressures for harsher sentencing and less support for rehabilitation place prison officials in difficult positions and leave them less inclined to embrace experimental programs.

Moreover, correctional administrators face political pressure for improved substance abuse rehabilitation programs, which therefore tend to have first priority and are likely to take precedence. As the cost of incarceration increases, forces that drive such proposals may also fade. Family counseling programs remain a low priority because of overcrowding and budget limitations. These issues will continue to have an impact on future family therapy programs in correctional facilities.

Community Corrections: Family Therapy Issues

Inadequate family counseling programs affect both male and female inmates. Prisoners live in a world where relationships are important; daily isolation from family members and their community proves challenging. The treatment goal is to modify poor patterns of communication and improve family support systems. Inmate incarceration challenges the entire family unit, and family therapy can be decisive in restoring or preserving the inmate's relationship with his or her family as they negotiate the correctional process.

Lengthy prison sentences encourage inmate isolation, often resulting in divorce and eventual family disintegration. Family members may no longer trust the incarcerated individual, and hope dissipates over time. For those families who survive, the best opportunity for family therapy exists during the pre-release stage of incarceration. During this period,

there is often a considerable degree of residual anger that is now mixed with the joy of release. The inmate's children and spouse may harbor resentment for abandonment and having to face life without spousal support.

Conclusion

Most offenders are eventually released from prison; relatively few inmates serve life sentences. The American correctional system continues to pay the high costs of imprisonment. The economy suffers a second defeat from inmates' loss of productivity: the opportunity costs of their lost contributions to society. The inmate will eventually return to a family life, and inmates need to have family therapy assistance to make that transition possible. Reintegrating into society as a contributing citizen is not an easy task. Therefore, planning and treatment for that significant event should include family members.

Although the criminal offender population may continue to have limited access to family therapy as a correctional treatment modality, research has shown that success in parole and community adjustment largely correlated with positive family relationships. Furthermore, a positive adjustment increases with strong family ties while the inmate is incarcerated. Families may therefore represent the most important correctional asset in the rehabilitation process.

Thomas E. Baker
University of Scranton

See also Community-Based Vocational Networks; Family Group Conferencing; Female Offenders and Special Needs; Loss of Parental Rights

Further Readings

Goldenberg, Irene and Herbert Goldenberg. *Family Therapy: An Overview*. Belmont, CA: Brooks/Cole, 1991.

Kaslow, Florence W. "Couples or Family Therapy for Prisoners and Their Significant Others." *American Journal of Family Therapy*, v.15 (1987).

Phillips, Richard L. and Charles R. McConnell. *The Effective Corrections Manager: Correctional Supervision for the Future*. Boston: Jones and Bartlett, 2005.

Van Voorhis, Patricia and Michael Braswell. *Family Therapy: Correctional Counseling and Rehabilitation*, 3rd ed. Cincinnati, OH: Anderson, 1997.

Yaffe, Rebecca M. and Lonnie F. Hoade. *When a Parent Goes to Jail: A Comprehensive Guide for Counseling Children of Incarcerated Parents.* Windsor, CA: Rayve, 2000.

FELONY PROBATION

Felony probation refers to a probation sentence that has been granted to a person convicted of a felony offense (as opposed to a misdemeanor offense). Although it revolves around working with more serious offenders, felony probation is based on the same general tenet of traditional probation in that the sentence allows the offender to be supervised within the community as long as he or she abides by all of the probation terms and conditions mandated by the court. Felony probation does, however, differ from traditional probation in terms of its foundation, application, and implementation.

In its base form, the traditional argument for a sentence of probation was to rehabilitate offenders by integrating them into the community with minor restrictions, and it was originally intended and used for offenders who were thought be of little or no risk to the community. In large part because of the growth in the prison population, probation is now seen as a necessary alternative to deal with felons who would ordinarily have been incarcerated in the past. However, this shift does not correspond to the types of offenders whom probation was initially intended to serve—namely, less serious, nonviolent, and misdemeanant offenders who were judged to be amenable to rehabilitation. During the first half of the 20th century, the percentage of felons on probation rarely exceeded 10 percent of the total probation population; the majority of felony offenders were sentenced to a term of confinement. Today, the granting of probation to felons is much more common, with nearly one third of all felons being sentenced to felony probation exclusively and more than half serving at least part of their sentence in the community.

Compared to the typical probationers of the past, the application of felony probation sentences today means that probationers are more likely to be violent offenders, have substance abuse problems, live in unstable family environments, encounter dire employment prospects, suffer from emotional problems, and be diagnosed as mentally ill. With the increased usage of probation for felons, community protection and recidivism have become important issues of study. To this end, the classification of offenders in terms of risk to the general public and their individual needs has been emphasized.

The terms and conditions of felony probation differ from those typically found in nonfelony probation. These differences are implemented because of the more serious nature of the offense and the perceived increased risk of reoffending and recidivating. Felony probation sentences are typically three to five years in length, whereas misdemeanant probation ranges from one to three years. Although many of the conditions of probation are the same for felony probation as they are for regular probation, they often differ in terms of intensity and stringency; moreover, punitive and restitutive measures are more commonly applied to felony probationers.

Felony probationers typically have to comply with additional and stricter probation conditions than do their nonfelony counterparts. These conditions commonly include increased reporting to probation officers, completion of mandatory programs (such as those addressing substance abuse and anger management), required employment or vocational training, regular random drug testing, residence and workplace visitations, out-of-state travel restrictions, and limitations on the places the offender can visit and the people with whom the offender can come into contact.

Unlike those on regular probation, felony probationers are regularly dispensed a jail term as part of their probation sentence. Integrating jail time along with a probation sentence is often treated as serving the goals of punishment, blocking current criminal offending, or deterring an offender from crime upon release by exposing him or her to the potential consequences of probation violations. About one fourth of all felony probationers nationally fall under this sort of split-sentence structure. In such instances, the probationer will usually serve time in jail for up to a year and then complete the rest of his or her term in the community on probation.

If a felony probationer is convicted of a new offense or violates the terms and conditions of probation, his or her probation can be revoked, and this, in addition to a number of other consequences, could ultimately result in the probationer's being resentenced to prison. For a felony probationer, being resentenced to prison usually means a longer prison stay than that of a nonfelony probationer, since the felony probationer's initial offense was more serious. Revocation rates for felony probationers are higher than those of nonfelony probationers, but the reasons for this difference extend beyond the notion that these offenders are simply higher-risk than the others. One explanation is that felony probationers are monitored more closely and have to comply with more and stricter rules; besides increasing detection of new offenses, this produces a higher likelihood of probation being revoked for a technical violation of probation terms and conditions.

Even though felony probationers are generally free to move about the community like regular probationers (and unsanctioned citizens, for that matter), they differ from both in the respect that they are subject to the loss of or restrictions placed on their rights. In many jurisdictions, individuals convicted of a felony are usually prohibited from engaging in several activities, such as voting, working in positions requiring specific licenses (such as the legal professions, teaching professions, and other occupations that involve working with children), serving in the military services, holding public office, serving on a jury, and owning or possessing a gun or ammunition. Additionally, felons are often denied a number of forms of social support, including unemployment benefits, subsidized or affordable housing benefits, and student loans. Although felony probationers have the benefit of physical freedom, the application of these various sociolegal punishments and controls can impede an offender's ability to reintegrate back into the community.

Joseph Allen
Chaminade University

See also Probation; Probation: Early Termination; Probation: Organization of Services; Probation: Private; Probation and Parole: Intensive Supervision; Probation and Parole Fees; Probation Mentor Home Program

Further Readings

Champion, Dean J. *Felony Probation*. New York: Praeger Publishers, 1988.
Lindner, Charles J. "Probation's First 100 Years: Growth Through Failure." *Journal of Probation and Parole* (Spring 1993).
Petersilia, Joan, ed. *Community Corrections: Probation, Parole, and Intermediate Sanctions*. New York: Oxford University Press, 1998.

FEMALE OFFENDERS AND SPECIAL NEEDS

While female offenders represent only a fraction of the crime perpetrated in society, the numbers of female offenders appear to be growing. In considering female offenders, it is important to examine the extent to which they are arrested and the nature of female offenders in community corrections and institutions, as well as the special needs or challenges they face in their communities.

Female Arrests

The Uniform Crime Reporting (UCR) Program, operated by the Federal Bureau of Investigation (FBI), report crime and arrest data from more than 12,000 city, county, and state law-enforcement agencies in the United States. According to the UCR publication *Crime in the United States, 2009*, law enforcement, nationwide, made an estimated 13,687,241 arrests in 2009. Approximately 580,000 were for violent crimes, and about 1.7 million were for property crimes. Specifically, the highest arrest counts were for drug abuse violations (1,663,582), driving under the influence (1,440,409), and the property crime larceny-theft (1,334,933). Of total arrests, 26.3 percent were of females.

Female rates of arrest are highest for prostitution (disorderly conduct and vagrancy), property crimes (larceny, embezzlement, forgery, and fraud),

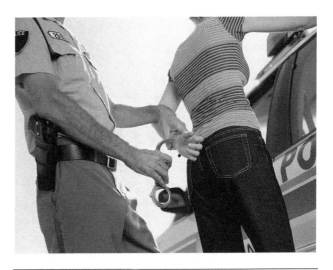

Correctional programs treat a predominantly male offender population and are often ill equipped to handle women's self-care, health, and mental health needs. (Photos.com)

substance abuse (driving under the influence, drugs, and liquor law violations), and simple assault. The offense category of simple assault includes mostly minor incidents of threat or physical attack against another person, such as scratching, biting, throwing objects, hitting, and kicking.

Although females are underrepresented in serious personal and property crimes, such as homicide, rape, robbery, and burglary, 10-year arrest trends, reported in UCR, indicate the female percentage of arrests has risen 11.4 percent. During the same time frame, the percentage of arrests for men has decreased 4.9 percent. The offense profiles of women have shifted toward greater involvement in robbery (up 40.8 percent), burglary (up 26.7 percent), and larceny (up 37.3 percent).

In 2009, 83 percent of female arrests in the United States were of women over the age of 18. One fourth (25 percent) of the female offenders were between the ages of 25 and 35. Five percent of women arrested were younger than 15, and the peak age for an act of juvenile delinquency was 16. In regard to age of female offenders, the 10-year arrests trends remain unchanged.

Females in Confinement

The Bureau of Justice Statistics (BJS) publication *Prison and Jail Inmates at Midyear, 2008* reported that state and federal correctional authorities had jurisdiction or legal authority over 1.6 million prisoners. Additionally, 785,556 inmates were held in custody in local jails. An estimated 207,700 women, or 9 percent of those incarcerated in 2008, were held in prisons or jails. That represents a 33 percent increase in female prisoners since 2000.

Female incarceration rates were considerably lower than male incarceration rates at every age. Black females (with an incarceration rate of 349 per 100,000) were more than twice as likely as Hispanic females (147 per 100,000) and more than 3.5 times more likely than white females (93 per 100,000) to have been in prison or jail on June 30, 2008.

According to a BJS survey of female prisoners, women in prison are, on average, 25 to 29 years old and single heads of household with an average of two dependent children. Two thirds of incarcerated women have children under the age of 18. In addition, a large proportion of incarcerated female offenders have histories of substance and sexual abuse. For example, nearly half (46 percent) of the

women in prison had been using drugs or alcohol or both at the time that the imprisonment offense occurred. Similarly, more than half (60 percent) of all female inmates were victims of physical abuse, and 36 percent reported having been sexually abused.

Females in Community Corrections

The Bureau of Justice Statistics' Annual Parole and Probation Surveys provide counts for the total number of persons supervised in the community and counts of the number entering and leaving supervision during the year in all 50 states, the District of Columbia, and the federal system. Survey data for 2008 revealed that one of every eight adults on parole (94,400) was a woman. Females represented one of every four adults on probation (957,600). The female parole and probation populations have experienced a modest increase since 1995. For instance, the female parole population increased from 10 percent in 1995 to 12 percent in 2000 and 2007. Correspondingly, the female probation population increased from 21 percent in 1995 to 22 percent in 2000 and 23 percent in 2007.

The effectiveness of community corrections varies by groups of probationers and parolees. Data suggest that more than three fourths of offenders placed on probation for a misdemeanor successfully complete their supervision. However, felons have considerably higher recidivism rates. (Recidivism occurs when an offender repeats criminal behavior after having been punished or disciplined.) In a 2004 report, 272,111 former inmates were tracked for three years after their release from confinement. Nearly 9 percent of the prisoners released were female. Of those released females, more than half (58 percent) were rearrested, and 40 percent were reconvicted within three years of their release. Of the released female prisoners, 17 percent returned to prison with a new conviction.

Overall, the recidivism rate for female offenders is lower than that for males. In comparison, women offenders are older, have achieved higher educational levels, and possess more employment experience and skills than male offenders. In addition, they have less extensive criminal histories and tend to enter prison for the first time at an older age than males.

Special Needs of Female Offenders

Historically, correctional programs, either in prison or in the community, have been unable to meet the needs of female offenders. Designed to serve the predominantly male offender population, correctional agencies have not addressed the multidimensional problems that form the framework for women's criminal behavior. The majority of female offenders are poor, disproportionately African American or Hispanic, undereducated, unemployed, and unskilled. Although those characteristics are similar to characteristics of male offenders, women are distinguished by their daily self-care, health, relationships, academic/employment, and mental health needs.

Women often enter and are released from correctional supervision without the tools to assist them in responsible daily self-care, such as safe housing, transportation, childcare, and money management skills. Female offenders need to be engaged in correctional programming that is designed to educate them in how to maintain a clean residence, develop a responsible budget, and sustain personal hygiene, appearance, and decorum. Women offenders need to be able to identify and access community resources for basic needs.

Many women offenders suffer from a variety of health problems, including tuberculosis, hepatitis, and sexually transmitted diseases. Pregnant offenders are at risk for child delivery problems because of poor health, drug abuse, and limited prenatal care. In addition, most female offenders are drug-dependent and need treatment. Treatment is less expensive and more effective in reducing recidivism than is incarceration. The treatment women need can be provided in the community.

In particular, female offenders are often young mothers who face the trauma of separation from their children. Women offenders need the criminal justice system to provide parenting classes and help them maintain relationships with their children. Strong connections with their children keep women alive and motivated to modify criminal behavior. Too often, women's correctional facilities are located at great distances from where their children live, making frequent visitations difficult. Empowering family ties is essential to creating an environment conducive to change and healing.

Significant numbers of female offenders are poorly educated, with insufficient employment histories. According to a recent survey, nearly one third of the female prisoners examined had never completed high school, and 39 percent quit because they were pregnant. Twenty-two percent had been unemployed in the three years prior to imprisonment, and only 29 percent had just one employer during that period. Female offenders need to be provided courses in basic education (to attain their general equivalency diplomas), and those who have graduated from high school need college-level instruction. In addition to needing opportunities to complete a formal education, women offenders need both traditional and nontraditional occupational training. While the community provides much training in traditional women's work such as nursing and paralegal fields, a criminal record may adversely impact women's ability to work in those disciplines.

Women offenders have higher rates of mood and psychiatric disorders than do women in the general population. Studies of women in prison confirm that treatment for personality, post-traumatic stress, anxiety, mood, and attention deficit disorders is needed to reduce recidivism. The most common disorders are drug and alcohol abuse, post-traumatic disorders, and borderline personality disorders. If a female offender is diagnosed with a post-traumatic stress disorder, she has by definition been exposed to a traumatic event. Conversely, a diagnosis of borderline personality disorder is associated with a childhood history of neglect, physical and sexual abuse, and early separation from family. It is well documented that physical and sexual abuse are disproportionately common among female offenders. Female offenders need correctional programming that offers supervision, assessment, and treatment for their mental health problems. Adequate mental health programs will empower them to develop a healthier level of personal responsibility and offer hope for rehabilitation.

Linda Keena
University of Mississippi

See also Diversity in Community Corrections; Effectiveness of Community Corrections; Offender Needs; Women in Community Service Programs

Further Readings

American Correctional Association. "Female Offenders: Meeting Needs of a Neglected Population." Laurel, MD: Author, 1993.

Edwards, Todd. "Female Offenders: Special Needs and Southern State Challenges." Atlanta, GA: Southern Office, the Council of State Governments, 2000.

Pederson, Elizabeth. *Providing Services to Female Offenders: Policy Perspectives on Sentencing and Parole*. Stanford, CA: Stanford Criminal Justice Center, 2006.

Shearer, Robert A. "Identifying the Special Needs of Female Offenders." *Federal Probation*, v.67/1 (June 2003).

Van Wormer, Katherine S. *Working With Female Offenders: A Gender-Sensitive Approach*. Hoboken, NJ: John Wiley, 2010.

FIELD VISITS

Field visits are an intrinsic component of community corrections and involve community corrections professionals supervising the offender in the community and visiting the offender at his or her residence, place of employment, school, or other agency setting (such as his substance abuse treatment meeting or anger management course) to ensure the offender's compliance with the terms and conditions of probation, parole, or other community-based sanctions.

Field visits have their origins in 19th-century practices of social services charitable organizations. Historically, social work posits that long-term change is accomplished by fostering relationships, teaching basic skills, and offering moral instruction, which are accomplished through visits to the residence (referred to as "friendly visitation"). The premise is that, through proper instruction (and not merely handouts) and established professional relationships, people can make effective change in their lives. Given the fact that many early community corrections professionals (that is, probation and parole officers) were recruited from the social work professions, field visits and friendly visitation were employed in early community corrections and continue today.

Field visits not only enable community corrections professionals to advance the various goals of community corrections (deterrence, incapacitation, retribution, and public safety) but also constitute a key supervision tool. During a field visit, the professional is able to verify the offender's residence, employment, or school enrollment and assess its suitability. A probation officer can determine if an offender is in compliance with the terms and conditions of his probation judgment by not living with or in the proximity of children (often required of those convicted of sex offenses involving children) or associating with other known felons. Field visits may

Field visits at an offender's residence, work site, school, or treatment center allow community corrections professionals to verify that an offender is maintaining the terms of his or her release and may reduce the likelihood of recidivism. (Photos.com)

assist in deterrence in that offenders may have negative views of the field contacts and opt to remain out of trouble to ensure that the offender is not subject to an intrusion of his or her privacy. In turn, verification and assessment of an offender's residence or employment promote public safety.

Ongoing visits to the employer, residence, or school may also serve as a deterrent, in that the supervision of the offender outside the office may include searches of his or her person or property, and thus the offender will refrain from possessing weapons and other contraband that violates the terms and conditions of probation. Field visits may serve as a means of incapacitation, in that they can reduce the likelihood that an offender may reoffend. Offenders who are subject to random and unannounced field visits will be unlikely to engage in criminal behavior in the residence, school, or workplace if they are uncertain when the community corrections professional may appear for a field visit. This surveillance of offenders may in turn promote public safety.

Field visits promote rehabilitation in that they allow community corrections professionals to develop trust and rapport with the offender in circumstances that are less intimidating than the courthouse or the professional's office. Field visits also promote rehabilitation in that community corrections professionals have the opportunity to conduct field visits at agencies (such as substance abuse facilities and school or training facilities), where people work with and develop rapport with the offender and the offender's family members, thus extending the support network of the offender in a rehabilitative context.

Finally, field visits promote overall effective supervision and monitoring of offenders subject to community corrections supervision, in that they can be conducted on nights and weekends and thus complement office visits by extending supervision of the offender beyond the confines of the office and typical daytime, weekday hours.

Given the types of offenders placed on probation today (violent offenders, felons, and those with mental, behavioral, and substance abuse issues)—as opposed to the nonviolent, first-time offenders typical of the era when friendly visitations were introduced to community corrections in the 19th century—the safety of community corrections professionals is a concern. Community corrections professionals are increasingly working in a law-enforcement capacity. Community corrections professionals often go into high-crime neighborhoods to visit their offenders (often with multiple offenders residing in the same neighborhood). Likewise, many offenders have communicable diseases (such as hepatitis, some types of meningitis, and tuberculosis), which can be transferred through airborne pathogens. Field visits may affect the length of exposure to an offender with a communicable disease or the physical proximity of a professional to an infected offender. Other factors that can affect the community corrections professional's safety is whether the field visits are conducted alone or in pairs, whether the community corrections professional is armed, whether he or she has a cell phone or radio, and whether she or he has protective gear, such as a bulletproof vest.

There are no nationwide minimum standards for the number of field visits or the manner in which they should be conducted. They may be reactive or proactive, and the required number of field visits varies from state to state. Traditionally, the level of supervision of the offender equates with the number of field contacts. Those offenders on electronic house arrest, electronic monitoring, or intensive supervision probation are subject to more frequent field visits; offenders on intensive supervision probation are subject to be supervised by two-person teams often consisting of a probation/parole officer and an surveillance officer.

Nicola Davis Bivens
Johnson C. Smith University

See also Philosophy of Community Corrections; Probation Officers: Job Stress

Further Readings

Alarid, Leanne Fiftal and Rolando V. del Carmen. *Community-Based Corrections*, 8th ed. Belmont, CA: Thomson Wadsworth, 2011.

Dolgoff, R. and R. Feldstein. *Understanding Social Welfare*. New York: Harper and Row, 1980.

Lindner, C. "Probation Field Visit and Office Report in New York State: Yesterday, Today, and Tomorrow." *Criminal Justice Review*, v.17/1 (Spring 1992).

FINANCIAL PENALTIES

Consisting of the distinct institutional agencies of policing (law enforcement), courts (adjudication), and corrections (prisons, jails, probation, and parole), the criminal justice system, under the rule of law, serves as the foundation for maintaining order in society. According to the U.S. Bureau of Justice Statistics, nationwide, more than 10 million people are arrested yearly. Within the framework of the criminal justice system, if an individual is convicted of a criminal offense, the court adjudicates a sentence, which may range from incarceration to a form of community corrections. Community corrections include a wide range of programs that offer alternatives to incarceration, which include pretrial release, boot camps, probation, and parole. The most common type of community corrections program is probation, whereby a person convicted of a criminal offense continues to live and work within the confines of the community but is placed under court-ordered supervision and must abide by a set of mandated behavioral rules and conditions for a specified period of time. If the person violates the terms of the court-ordered conditions, the court may order the person to serve a term of imprisonment. Today, almost 5 million Americans are on active supervised probation.

A significant component of a criminal sentence within community-based corrections is financial penalties. The use of these economic sanctions has been a steadfast court-imposed sentence since the creation of the criminal justice system. Financial penalties can include a number of sanctions, based on the type of jurisdiction: (1) fines, court costs, forfeiture, or restitution; (2) service fees; and (3) special assessments. It is estimated that financial penalties generate more than $20 billion in revenue annually for state and federal governments in the United States.

Restitution is a court-ordered monetary payment to compensate the victim of a crime for a loss or damages incurred. A fine is the traditional monetary penalty imposed on a defendant based on the severity of the crime. The fine is normally regulated by state or federal criminal statute. Court costs are fees imposed on people convicted of crimes in order to offset the costs that are incurred during the facilitation of the judicial process. Forfeiture is a civil judgment imposed against a person by the state or federal government and involves the confiscation of assets that are believed to have been used as instruments in, or gained in, the commission of a crime. Forfeiture can involve money, property, or any asset of value. Service fees cover a variety of monetary sanctions that are designed to offset specific service-related programs offered by the court—for example, pre-sentence report fees, public defender fees, restitution collection fees, alcohol or drug assessment fees, alcohol and drug collection fees, driver education fees, bail investigation fees, license revocation fees, urinalysis fees, counseling fees, deferred adjudication fees, domestic offender education fees, pretrial jail fees, postconviction jail fees, DNA bank fees, out-of-state fees, first-offender fees, work release fees, probation supervisor fees, parole supervisor fees, community service fees, and house arrest fees. Finally, special assessments cover any additional monetary sanctions imposed by the court for specialized programs not covered under service fees—for example, crime-stopper's fees, criminal justice planning fees, victim compensation funds, and victim advocate fees. Of course, there are residual economic sanctions, which are not court-ordered, such as attorney fees, insurance rate increases, bail bonds, and sanctions associated with loss of employment.

One of the most difficult and problematic issues concerning financial penalties is determining exactly how the monetary fee will be collected. Although collection methods are normally determined by state law or federal statute, it is estimated that more than 50 percent of all financial penalties go uncollected. The Executive Office for United States Attorneys (EOUSA) and the Offices of the United States Attorneys (OUSA) are responsible for establishing policies and procedures for the collection and enforcement of all monetary criminal judgments, fines, assessments, court costs, and forfeitures imposed by the court, under 18 U.S.C.A. § 1963. This includes, if necessary, the enforcement and collection of criminal monetary debts during the period of a defendant's federal incarceration.

Tony Gaskew
University of Pittsburgh, Bradford

See also Bail Reform Act of 1984; Community Corrections and Sanctions; Fine Options Programs; Probation and Parole Fees; Restitution

Further Readings

Criminal Penalties, 18 U.S.C.A. § 1963.
New York Criminal Procedure: Collection of Fines, Restitution or Reparation, Article 420, Section 420.10.
U.S. Bureau of Justice Statistics. *Sourcebook of Criminal Justice Statistics*. Washington, DC: U.S. Department of Justice. http://www.albany.edu/sourcebook (Accessed March 2011).
U.S. Department of Justice, Office of the United States Attorney. "Collection of Criminal Monetary Impositions (2011)." http://www.justice.gov/usao/eousa/foia_reading_room/usam/title3/12musa.htm (Accessed April 2011).

FINE OPTIONS PROGRAMS

Fines are one of the oldest types of penalties imposed on offenders. In the United States, fines are commonly used as intermediate sanctions. If an offender is ordered to pay a fine, he or she must pay a specific dollar amount to the court. Fines are utilized at both the federal and state levels and can be given as stand-alone penalties or in conjunction with other sanctions, such as community service, probation, or even incarceration. Offenders who are ordered to pay fines as their only punishment are typically low-risk, nonviolent offenders with little or no criminal history. Stand-alone fines are commonly associated with minor crimes, such as traffic violations, petty theft or shoplifting, and public order offenses. Fines are usually combined with other sanctions if the

Under fine options programs, participants who are unable to pay a sentenced fine are allowed to perform unpaid community work equal to the value of the fine instead of being imprisoned. Offenders who are punished with fines are typically low-risk, nonviolent offenders who have committed minor crimes such as traffic violations, petty theft, or shoplifting. (Photos.com)

crime is more serious, if the offender has a criminal history, or if the offender is deemed at high risk for recidivism. The amount of the fine is assessed by the judge and usually increases incrementally with the seriousness of the offense. For felony cases, fines are used in about 25 percent of state cases and 13 percent of federal cases. More than $1 billion in fines are collected in the United States each year.

There are two correctional philosophies guiding the use of fines. The primary purpose of a fine is retribution, with the monetary penalty serving as punishment for the crime that was committed. Second, fines are supposed to have a deterrent effect that will prevent offenders from committing future crimes. There is some evidence indicating that fines are at least as effective at preventing recidivism as incarceration. For example, research has shown that, controlling for offense and individual characteristics, the odds of additional arrest and incarceration are significantly lower for offenders who were given a fine, when compared to those sentenced to serve time in jail.

In the United States, there are two main types of fine programs. The first program is known as fixed fines, in which the amount of money to be paid is based only on the offense. Day fines, which consider both the offense and the offender's ability to pay, are the second option.

Fixed Fines

The traditional and most commonly used type of fine in the United States is the fixed fine. For fixed fines, judges sentence offenders to pay a certain amount of money based on the offense committed and without regard to the particular individual's ability to pay. Many jurisdictions have a published schedule of suggested or maximum fine amounts for various crimes. Judges use these guidelines in conjunction with their discretion to assign monetary amounts that fit the offense under consideration.

Theoretically, fixed fines will allow the courts to implement fines in a way that is consistent among offenders, because similar individuals who commit the same crime will receive the same financial penalty. For example, if a fine for a certain crime is set at $500, all offenders who commit that offense and are sentenced to pay a fine will have to pay the $500, regardless of their annual incomes. Judges and other criminal justice personnel, however, have realized that two offenders facing the same fine might experience it very differently. That is, a certain fine amount might be reasonable for one offender but impossible to pay for another offender. Consequently, many agents of the system are calling for a more graduated fine system that considers not only the offense committed but also the financial circumstances of the individual offender. Day fine programs are examples of this type of structured system.

Day Fines

Following the day fine models found in Europe and South America, several jurisdictions in the United States have implemented graduated fine structures. Day fines are different from fix fines in that they are based on both the offense and the offender's ability to pay. Within the day fine system, specific numbers of "punishment units" for certain crimes replace the dollar amounts associated with those crimes under the fixed fine system, and the number of punishment units increases with the severity of the crime. The consistency among offenders receiving day fines stems from the number of punishment units rather than the number of dollars.

To illustrate, consider a jurisdiction that has assigned a value of 10 percent to each day fine punishment unit. The structured fine schedule will indicate how many punishment units are assigned to each type of crime. If the guidelines show that shoplifting is associated with a fine of 15 punishment units, offenders who are convicted of shoplifting must pay 10 percent of their daily salaries for 15 days. If someone makes $100 per day, he or she will have to pay a fine of $10 per day for 15 days, or a total fine of $150. If someone makes $300 per day, he or she will have to pay a fine of $30 per day for 15 days, or a total fine of $450. While the dollar amount of the fine is different, the two offenders are each paying the same percentage of their salaries. Consequently, structured day fine programs might be more equitable than fixed fines because a fixed amount might be more punishing to those who earn less money that to those who have higher salaries.

Most jurisdictions in the United States use fixed fine structures and have not yet implemented day fine programs. Evidence indicates that day fines are a promising option for courts that wish to consider individual circumstances along with the offense. It is likely that the day fine approach will spread as more judges become familiar with it.

Kristie R. Blevins
Eastern Kentucky University

See also Attitudes and Myths About Punishment; Community Corrections and Sanctions

Further Readings

Gordon, Margaret A. and Daniel Glaser. "The Use and Effects of Financial Penalties in Municipal Courts." *Criminology*, v.29 (1991).

Ruback, R. Barry and Mark H. Bergstrom. "Economic Sanctions in Criminal Justice: Purposes, Effects, and Implications." *Criminal Justice and Behavior*, v.33 (2006).

Winterfield, Laura L. and Sally T. Hillsman. *The Staten Island Day-Fine Project*. Washington, DC: U.S. Department of Justice, 1993.

FIREARMS AND COMMUNITY CORRECTIONS PERSONNEL

Perceived and real threats of violence exist for those responsible for ensuring public safety in the community. To remedy these dangers, states have begun incorporating the use of both lethal and nonlethal measures for addressing safety concerns while on the job.

The Need for Protection

As of 2009, more than 5 million individuals were under some form of community-based sanction. The level and quality of offender supervision are paramount for those responsible for reducing recidivism and ensuring community safety. More specifically, public opinion polls conducted in Massachusetts during the latter half of the 1990s reveal that only 26 percent of respondents reported being confident that their probation system could adequately supervise offenders, and more than 50 percent reported that a probation sentence was too lenient.

At one point in history, the role of community correctional officers (CCOs) was to assist offenders in societal reintegration. CCOs had a more therapeutic role, similar to that of a social worker. After World War II, politicians found themselves more involved in the area of community corrections, creating legislation that would, over time, transform the therapeutic role of CCOs into that of a law-enforcement figure. Over the past 20 to 25 years, changes in philosophy have resulted in an increase in the workload allocation for the CCO. For example, increased responsibilities include making more frequent contacts both in the field and in the office, completing more detailed paperwork, meeting more stringent deadlines in shorter periods of time, and maintaining larger caseload sizes (the average caseload size for probation officers is 139). Officers have simultaneously been asked to perform the tasks of retribution (punishment), while ensuring the rehabilitation (treatment) of offenders.

In addition to increases in workload demands, courts have continued to place higher-risk offenders on community-based alternative sanctions. In 2009, for example, 51 percent of all persons on probation were convicted of felony offenses. These figures are particularly worrisome when research reveals that as many as 39 to 55 percent of all community-based officers report either being victims of or receiving threats of violence while on the job. Furthermore, between the years 2000 and 2009, more than one fifth of all homicides of law enforcement officers in the line of duty were committed by individuals who were on probation or parole at the time. The majority of homicides are committed between the hours of 9:00 P.M. and 10:00 P.M., which are typically the times CCOs complete their field visits. Despite this high number of reported violent victimizations, to date no one mechanism for tracking the number of CCO assaults exists.

CCOs' Use of Weapons

As these statistics suggest, the threat to CCOs continues to increase, and therefore so does the need for officers to protect themselves and the public. As a result, more CCOs are carrying weapons, both lethal and nonlethal, and increasing their use of safety training. The increased use of firearms by CCOs accompanies their growing authority in the lives of offenders.

For example, numerous probation officers in New York City are now authorized to carry firearms as a response to their work with high-risk dangerous offenders. Similarly, many probation departments in the state of California permit the utilization of firearms by their officers. West Virginia allows probation officers to carry firearms without a permit, while New Jersey's Probation Officer Community Safety Unit Act requires that no fewer than five officers in each county carry a firearm and enforce warrants. Other states, such as Florida, have begun to use dart-firing stun guns as nonlethal alternatives to firearms.

As a mechanism for improving community safety, agencies utilize training techniques to improve the mental preparedness of officers who confront multiple situations. These techniques include scenario-based training tools that allow officers to consider situational elements such as the continuum of force necessary to deescalate a situation, crisis rehearsal, and evidence-based safety practices.

The impact of carrying weapons on the safety of officers and the community is of utmost concern. To date, little research has been conducted specifically addressing this question. As R. T. Sigler and B. McGraw note, probation and parole officers who carry firearms while on the job report doing so without role conflict (such as treatment versus punishment). However, research assessing the impact of the perceived social distance between the offender and the armed supervising officer reveals a negative correlation. As J. Helfgott and E. Gunnison report, the social distance is greatest between offenders and officers when a firearm is present. One explanation for this difference is that armed officers tend to have attitudes indicative of law enforcement rather than treatment. This increased level of distance between the CCO and offender may arguably be based on social background (rather than the presence of the weapon) and the inability of the officer to address offender needs.

Overall, the debate regarding carrying firearms by CCOs persists. As agencies continue to address resource reductions, creativity becomes imperative. The use of agency partnerships between law enforcement officials and CCOs provides one such example. These relationships show promise as a tool to maintain public safety, reduce recidivism and duplication of effort, and enhance the working relationships among agency personnel.

Shannon M. Barton-Bellessa
John Turner
Indiana State University

See also Attitudes of Offenders Toward Community Corrections; Caseload and Workload Standards; Community Partnerships; Field Visits; Probation Officers; Probation Officers: Job Stress

Further Readings

Abadinsky, H. *Should Parole Officers Make Arrests and Carry Firearms?* Rockville, MD: National Criminal Justice Reference Service, 1975.

Anonymous. "Florida Eyes Training for Use of Stun Guns." *Crime Control Digest*, v.40/3 (2006).

Anonymous. "Legislature Can't Arm Courthouse Officers." *Corrections Digest*, v.37/4 (2006).

Anonymous. "West Virginia Expands Officer Gun Privilege." *Corrections Digest*, v.33/22 (2002).

Barton-Bellessa, S. and R. D. Hanser. *Community-Based Corrections: A Text/Reader.* Thousand Oaks, CA: Sage, 2012.

Brown, P. W. "Guns and Probation Officers: The Unspoken Reality." *Federal Probation*, v.54/2 (1990).

Brown, P. W. "Probation and Parole Officers Up in Arms Over the Gun Issue." *Corrections Today*, v.51/2 (1989).

Burrell, W. D. "Probation and Public Safety: Using Performance Measures to Demonstrate Public Value." *Corrections Management Quarterly*, v.2/3 (1998).

Burrell, W. D. *Trends in Probation and Parole in the States.* Lexington, KY: American Probation and Parole Association, n.d. http://www.appa-net.org/eweb/docs/appa/pubs/TPP.pdf (Accessed July 2011).

DeMichele, M. and B. Payne. "Probation and Parole Officers Peak Out: Caseload and Workload Allocation." *Federal Probation,* v.71/3 (2007).

Finn, P. and S. Kuck. *Stress Among Probation and Parole Officers and What Can Be Done About It.* Washington, DC: National Institute of Justice, 2005.

Glaze, L. E., T. P. Bonczar, and F. Zhang. *Probation and Parole in the United States, 2009.* Washington, DC: Bureau of Justice Statistics, 2010.

Gorman, K., M. Gregory, M. Hayles, and N. Parton. *Constructive Work With Offenders.* Philadelphia, PA: Jessica Kingsley, 2006.

Helfgott, J. and E. Gunnison. "The Influence of Social Distance on Community Corrections Officer Perceptions of Offender Reentry Needs." *Federal Probation,* v.72/1 (2008).

Sigler, R. T. and B. McGraw. "Adult Probation and Parole Officers: Influence of Their Weapons, Role Perceptions and Role Conflict." *Criminal Justice Review,* v.9 (1984).

FIREARMS CHARGES, OFFENDERS WITH

Like the overall crime rate, firearm-related offenses have declined in most jurisdictions since the mid-1990s. However, the number of violent or weapons-law offenders entering community corrections supervision has increased since the end of the 1990s. The justice system has responded to public concerns about firearm offenses by enacting new and tougher firearm legislation and increasing the level of federal involvement in these crimes. As a consequence of these changes, an increasing proportion of offenders who used a gun in the commission of a crime have been sent to prison and return to the community under parole supervision. Corrections officials have reacted to these changes by establishing community supervision programs and policies that focus on protecting the public.

Concern for Firearm Offenses Among Those Under Community Supervision

Professionals have targeted the prevention of firearm-related offenses among probationers and parolees convicted of violent and weapons-related offenses, since these individuals are becoming more numerous and are at high risk for violent offending and victimization. Even parolees and probationers who have not been convicted of firearm-related offenses have been the target of specialized community corrections firearm-reduction programs and policies, since they share social conditions with and are demographically similar to firearm offenders. Both groups disproportionately reside and spend time in high-crime urban areas, and in both groups there is an overrepresentation of males. The overrepresentation of minorities under community supervision is also striking. Minority overrepresentation is also evident with firearm-related offenders: Blacks are five times more likely than whites to be arrested on a weapons charge, and the gun homicide rate for young Hispanic males is about seven times the rate for young white males. Probationers and parolees are also at great risk for becoming victims of violent crime. Three quarters (75 percent) of young homicide victims in Boston had a prior criminal record, and in Philadelphia 93 percent of homicide victims had a prior criminal record. Nationally, males with a criminal record are 22 times more likely to incur a firearm-related injury than are males with no criminal record.

Preventing Firearm Offenses by Those Under Community Supervision

Community corrections agencies have become increasingly diverse in their strategies for supervising specific offender groups, and they have implemented several innovative programs to supervise firearm offenders and prevent subsequent crimes. One of the most replicated programs is lever pulling. Lever pulling is a process that utilizes the justice system's resources in a collective way to provide probationers and parolees with a "carrot" and "stick" message. At lever-pulling meetings, probationers and parolees are provided a choice: Officials suggest resources to help them lead law-abiding lives, but they are also informed that if they choose to continue their violent lifestyles, justice agencies will collaborate to ensure that they receive the maximum penalties under the law.

Community corrections officers have also been actively involved in preventing firearm-related offenses. One widely replicated prevention effort is Operation Night Light, which began as a partnership between Boston-area probation and police officers. It pairs one probation officer with two police officers to make surprise visits to high-risk youth probationers during the nontraditional work hours of 7:00 P.M. to midnight. In Boston, probationer new arrests declined 9.2 percent between January 1994 and June 1996, compared with a statewide increase of 14 percent.

Another firearm prevention program in which community corrections has played an integral part is the Chronic Violent Gun Offender Strategies program. The purpose of this program is to prevent firearm-related crimes by a select group of individuals who are perceived by criminal justice professionals to be most likely to commit a violent crime in the near future by increasing awareness of the identities of high-rate gun offenders, sharing information within and across agencies, and promoting officer safety when offenders are encountered in the community. Community corrections officers play a critical role in this program, since many of the targeted individuals may be currently or previously under community supervision.

Paul D. Steele
Morehead State University

See also Firearms and Community Corrections Personnel; Loss of Right to Possess Firearms; Offender Risks

Further Readings

Bilchik, Shay. *Promising Strategies to Reduce Gun Violence.* Washington, DC: U.S. Department of Justice, 1998.

Bynum, Tim and Scott H. Decker. *Project Safe Neighborhoods: Strategic Interventions.* Chronic Violent Offenders Lists, Case Study 4. Washington, DC: U.S. Department of Justice, 2006.

Cook, Phillip and Jens Ludwig. *Gun Violence: The Real Costs.* New York: Oxford University Press, 2000.

Glaze, Lauren E. and Thomas P. Bonczar. *Probation and Parole in the United States 2008.* Washington, DC: U.S. Department of Justice, 2009.

Greenfeld, Lawrence A. and Marilyn W. Zawitz. *Weapons Offenses and Offenders.* Washington, DC: U.S. Department of Justice, Office of Justice Programs, 1995.

Kennedy, David M. "Pulling Levers: Getting Deterrence Right." *National Institute of Justice Journal,* v.2/8 (1998).

Kennedy, David M., Anthony A. Braga, and Anne M. Piehl. "Youth Violence in Boston: Gun Markets, Serious Youth Offenders, and a Use-Reduction Strategy." *Law and Contemporary Problems,* v.59/1 (1996).

Raphael, Steven and Jens Ludwig. "Prison Sentence Enhancements: The Case of Project Exile." In *Evaluating Gun Policy: Effects on Crime and Violence,* Jens Ludwig and Phillip J. Cook, eds. Washington, DC: The Brookings Institution, 2003.

Reichert, Kent. *Police-Probation Partnerships: Boston's Operation Night Light.* Philadelphia: University of Pennsylvania, Jerry Lee Center of Criminology, 2002.

Steele, Paul D. and Lisa Broidy. *The Strategic Approaches to Community Safety Initiative in Albuquerque: Project Activities and Research Results.* Washington, DC: U.S. Department of Justice, 2005.

FLAT TIME

Flat time refers to the actual portion of a sentence that a defendant must serve, regardless of the administrative determination. The term was coined to reflect actual time that must be served in response to swings in sentencing philosophies. Throughout the history of U.S. criminal sentencing, time served has been affected by shifts between judicial determination and administrative determination based on guidelines.

In the early and mid-20th century, when a defendant was sentenced to a fixed term of incarceration, that defendant served that exact amount of time. For example, if a defendant was sentenced to 15 years in prison, the defendant would serve

While serving a flat-time sentence, the prisoner must serve each day of the sentence without the possibility of suspension, commutation of sentence, probation, pardon, parole, work furlough, or release on any basis. (Photos.com)

15 actual years and was released after the completion of the sentence to rejoin the community. In the late 20th century and early 21st century, there was a movement in state corrections toward administrative sentencing involving good-time credits, parole, pardons, and clemency. Consequently, the association between the judge's sentence and the actual time the defendant served diminished. Over time there has been a failure to address the problems of increasing prison overpopulation that is now resulting in administrative release compelled by this very prison overcrowding. The push of legislative bodies to enhance drug-related crime is one reason for this overcrowding. This problem, combined with state budget shortfalls, has led state legislatures to reexamine flat time and determinate sentencing.

Determinate Sentencing

A determinate sentence restricts parole boards from releasing inmates before their sentences have expired (minus good-time credits). These prison commitments cannot be modified to recognize a prisoner's development while in custody. Under the determinate sentencing philosophy, the term of imprisonment is determined at the actual sentencing of the defendant and not based on the conduct of the prisoner throughout the term of the sentence. Once the judgment is issued, the sentence then is absolute, with the primary exception being the loss of good-time credits for failure to follow the prison rules.

Flat-time sentencing would fall under this type of sentencing philosophy. The RAND Corporation studied flat-time sentencing in the late 1970s and concluded that a small number of felons committed a large percentage of crimes. Consequently, flat-time sentencing would incapacitate these criminals thus reducing the crime rate. This type of sentencing would be particularly favorable for repeat offenders. However, critics of flat time would argue that with flat-time sentencing the prison population does not respond well to correctional management techniques, since prisoners have no hope of early parole. Hence, flat-time prisoners could become a management problem.

The federal government established federal sentencing guidelines in the 1980s. These guidelines eliminated federal parole. The guideline system seeks to remedy the past problems of sentencing by generally requiring judges to sentence according to the guidelines and by eliminating parole so that offenders will serve real time sentences. The idea is to eliminate the deception that parole plays in a sentence. In addition, sentencing decisions based on calculated formulas on which judges could rely were thought to create uniformity in punishment. This sentencing formula takes into account the offense level and the criminal history category. These two factors are utilized to develop a sentencing table or matrix showing months of imprisonment to be applied to the sentence.

In theory, determinate sentencing seems advantageous. However, the guidelines significantly limit judges' discretion. A judge must provide written justification for any sentence that falls outside the guidelines, and indeed the guidelines have been challenged in court on the basis that they limit discretion of the sentencing judges. In spite of this challenge (*Mistretta v. United States*, 488 U.S. 361, 1989), the constitutionality of the sentencing guidelines has been upheld.

Indeterminate Sentencing

Courts using an indeterminate sentencing philosophy can establish minimum and maximum sentences within the sentencing guidelines; however, the actual length of the sentence is often left up to the administrators of the correctional system. In practice, indeterminate sentencing occurs when a judge announces that the defendant is consigned to prison for the term prescribed by statutory law of (for example) five to 10 years. However, the actual time the inmate spends in confinement is determined after an evaluation by correctional authorities and review by a parole board. In the foregoing example, that determination would take place after five years.

Indeterminate sentencing seeks to individualize each sentence by allowing for the offense and the offender, but to do so after the fact. The actual time served not only is based on conditions as they existed at the time of the judge's verdict but also takes into account the inmate's post-sentence conduct and behavior.

Harrison Watts
Washburn University

See also Determinate Sentencing; Indeterminate Sentencing

Further Readings

Fogel, David. *Flat-Time Prison Sentences: A Proposal for Swift, Certain, and Even-Handed Justice*. Chicago: Illinois Law Enforcement Commission, 1975.

Perren, S. "Indeterminate Sentencing Redux: A Return to Rational Sentencing." *Federal Sentencing Reporter*, v.22/3 (2010).

Webb, Vince. "Inmate Support for 'Flat-Time' Sentencing and Related Proposals: A Research Note." *Criminal Justice Review*, v.3/1 (Spring 1978).

FRONT-END AND BACK-END PROGRAMMING

Within the field of community corrections, the concept of both front-end and back-end programming for offenders is experiencing a resurgence of favor as states face increasing budgetary constraints. The ultimate goal for both is to select offenders to match with evidence-based programming for rehabilitation (whether it is vocational, educational, or treatment-based). Although the two are similar in theory, their implementation, and subsequently their outcomes, are very different.

Front-end programming involves proactively seeking alternatives to incarceration, prior to sentencing, in order to divert offenders from formal criminal justice proceedings. These alternatives involve several different aspects of intensive supervision, which include counseling, education, and a dynamic redirection of problematic behaviors to address and rectify underlying criminogenic factors. A major factor in the implementation of these programs is the assessment of often intangible factors, such as an offender's motivation for change and treatment readiness in order to effectively target criminal thinking and behavior patterns. This assessment becomes problematic with compulsory treatment orders, as is seen in the drug court movement. However, the dynamic factors of offender motivation and amenability are not the purview of only the drug court movement. Other specialized courts, such as mental health courts, have also risen throughout the country to handle the specific needs of special offender populations. Furthermore, as states experience an increase in prison overcrowding and a decrease in funding, an increasing number are looking for programs that divert offenders from

incarceration, and even more are utilizing sentencing impact studies.

Ultimately, with the rise of incarceration rates and the expense related to housing offenders, states have begun to concentrate on the front end of the criminal justice system to make determinations on who should be sentenced to prison in the first place. The result has been a reevaluation of the types of offenders who are admitted to prison, specifically focusing on low-level property and drug crimes. This move has been bolstered by decades' worth of research—although the highly politicized mantra of "getting tough on crime" continues to prove problematic, in that the general public's view of incarceration alternatives is largely negative. Often, these front-end sentencing alternatives are viewed as not punitive, and therefore illegitimate in meeting the stated goals of protecting the public. In fact, M. Vaughn's findings illustrate that the second largest factor that corrections administrators believe is contributing to prison overcrowding is a punitive public. The largest factor is longer sentences—a direct reflection of the punitive mind-set.

The question of whether or not front-end programming meets the intended goal of reducing offender populations has become the focus of several projects and has garnered a great deal of support. Researchers have found that pilot programs in Florida were often able to offer considerable cost savings, with no effect on service delivery and effectiveness. The cost savings are especially important to state governments that have experienced significant budget shortfalls as a result of the recession that began in 2008. This has forced a reanalysis of sentencing practices from a practical policy perspective. The result has been a reduction and reclassification of criminal offenses in several states, which has decreased sentence severity and reduced sentence length. Furthermore, states have committed to strengthening alternative sentencing programs, with a focus on substance abuse, specialty courts, and less expensive community-based supervision. Finally, for those offenders sentenced to prison, states also have begun to enhance back-end programs that accelerate successful sentence completion.

The result of the focus on front-end program directives has been an increase in evidence-based, community-oriented supervision. Conversely, back-end programming focuses heavily on the reentry of prisoners into the community. This focus is due, in large part, to the increasing number of offenders who have been resentenced to prison after a parole or probation violation. In a 20-year period, from 1980 to 2000, this number increased from 27,000 to 200,000, more than a sevenfold increase. Currently, this means that more than one third of prison admissions involve individuals being resentenced to prison. As a result, there has been a paradigm shift in the administration and supervision of parole and probation. Just as front-end sentencing programs increasingly use the risk/needs assessment matrix, back-end sentencing seeks to increase the use of indeterminate sentencing ideologies that focus on risks and needs in assessing release from incarceration. Along with an overhaul of appellate review, advocates have called for an increase in discretionary parole release.

However, the romanticized view of parole boards as convening authorities that fully assess the offender's future criminality often conflicts with the reality of a highly disorganized system that is subject to the same political "get tough" influences as is the rest of the criminal justice system. Furthermore, the parole authority is often disconnected from the judicial body that invoked the original sentence. This presents a significant problem, as the judge often has the greatest amount of information on the offender as a result of the pre-sentence investigation (if conducted). This communication "disconnect" is not only present within the various parts of the criminal justice system but also extends to the supervisory bodies outside the criminal justice system, resulting in a disjointed continuity of care and supervision for the offender. As a result, several states are gravitating toward a system of graduated release, whether it be in the form of halfway houses or transitional centers, that gradually reintroduce the offender to society through a system of decreasing supervisory intensity and increasing service and education placement. The result has been marked increases in successful reintegration and decreases in prison overcrowding. However, these back-end programs tend to be the exception instead of the preferred method of practice.

One of the greatest threats to successful back-end programming tends to be limited employment opportunities, even more so as the nation continues its recession and high unemployment rates. Moreover, the increase in public fear as a result of the September 11, 2001, terrorist attacks has increased the collateral consequence of nonacceptance and reintegration after incarceration. The public's perception of offender reintegration continues to be one of the biggest hurdles to successful programming, although no studies have been conducted to assess the impact of collateral consequences and the methods to overcome those consequences. The impact of this lack of research is a continued reliance on discretionary decision making that is often fueled by political positioning and negative media attention.

While an overarching reeducation of the public is probably unrealistic because of the length of time involved, policy makers are being forced to rethink and reevaluate processes in response to the increased fiscal constraints, and subsequent constituent anger, facing state governing bodies. This presents a unique possibility for an in-depth assessment of the legal system's barriers to successful reentry for specific offenders. Although most administrators agree that repeat felon offenders are inappropriate choices for reintegration, the majority agree that property and drug offenders present potentially ideal candidates for back-end programs. However, this paradigm shift does not preclude the necessity to reassess the continuity in service delivery and effectiveness from incarceration to community, which has often been overlooked.

Christopher Sharp
Valdosta State University

See also Determinate Sentencing; Diversion Programs; Drug Courts; Family Courts; Mental Health Courts; Prisoner's Family and Reentry; Reentry Courts; Reentry Programs and Initiatives; Serious and Violent Offender Reentry Initiative; Teen Courts

Further Readings

Austin, A. *Criminal Justice Trends: Key Legislative Changes in Sentencing Policy 2001–2010.* New York: Vera Institute of Justice, 2010.

Chanenson, S. "Guidance From Above and Beyond." *Stanford Law Review,* v.58 (2005).

Love, M. *Relief From the Collateral Consequences of a Criminal Conviction: A State-by-State Resource Guide.* Buffalo, NY: William S. Hein, 2006.

Travis, J. "Back-End Sentencing: A Practice in Search of a Rationale." *Social Research,* v.74/2 (2007).

Vaughn, M. "Listening to the Experts: A National Study of Correctional Administrators' Responses to Prison Overcrowding." *Criminal Justice Review,* v.18/1 (1993).

FURLOUGHS

Prison furloughs were originally intended to accomplish a variety of correctional goals. In addition to using furloughs to relieve overcrowding and assist in rehabilitation, correctional authorities used them to reward good behavior, to reintroduce an inmate back into society, to take advantage of educational and training opportunities, and to maintain family and community bonds. The extent to which furloughs actually facilitate any of these goals is questionable.

Spurred by recommendations from the 1967 President's Crime Commission, modern furlough programs were developed in the 1960s and expanded rapidly across the United States. It was relatively rare for inmates released under a furlough to commit a new crime, so furlough programs went mostly unnoticed. That ended on April 13, 1987, when Willie Horton, a Massachusetts inmate on furlough, raped a woman after restraining and brutalizing her fiancé. What happened next was a storm of controversy involving race, crime, criminal justice, and presidential politics, the effects of which can still be felt today. Although Horton's name lives on in discussions of criminal justice policy, the same cannot be said for inmate furlough programs.

Origins of Furlough Programs

The concept and goals of a prison furlough were relatively simple and straightforward. The United States seemed to be facing a crisis in the 1960s and 1970s, as incarceration rates started an upward climb that has yet to be reversed. In 1970, approximately 200,000 people were incarcerated in the United States; today, that number is more than 2.2 million. Looking for a way to relieve some of the pressure of the increase in the prison population, states began experimenting with furlough programs in the 1960s. An inmate would be released from the institution for a specific period of time, ranging from a few hours to days, to participate in planned activities such as family visits, educational programs, or work, and then return to the institution. While on furlough, the inmate would typically be unsupervised. The 1967 President's Crime Commission both praised these programs and called for their expanded use. By the mid- to late 1970s, virtually all states had some variation of a furlough program.

Furloughs were generally popular, noncontroversial, and unnoticed.

Massachusetts began its furlough program in 1972 with legislation signed by Republican governor Francis Sargent. Like many states, Massachusetts prohibited granting furloughs to inmates convicted of first-degree murder and sentenced to life without parole. This law was challenged, and the court determined that under the law, these inmates were eligible for furloughs. In 1976, the legislature passed a bill that would specifically deny furloughs to these inmates. However, Governor Michael Dukakis vetoed that bill because he believed in the rehabilitative potential of furloughs. The sequence of events leading to Horton was set in motion.

The 1988 Presidential Campaign

There is no question that Willie Horton, a convicted murderer released on furlough in 1986, raped a woman and brutalized her fiancé. Also undisputed is that the Horton furlough became a major issue for Governor Dukakis as the Democratic candidate for president in 1988. What is in question, however, is exactly who brought this event to the public's attention, transforming it from a state tragedy to a national obsession. While some evidence exists that fellow democratic candidate and rival Al Gore was the first to shine light on the Massachusetts furlough program during a 1988 primary presidential debate, the issue did not gain steam until Dukakis had won the Democratic nomination for president and George H. W. Bush had won the Republican nomination.

Not only did those supporting Bush introduce the name Willie Horton to the American people but they changed it as well. Horton's first name was William, but it was determined that the nickname, "Willie," produced a more frightening image than did William. Two campaign ads focusing on the Horton furlough were released during the 1988 presidential race: "Weekend Passes" and "Revolving Door." Horton was featured in "Weekend Passes," showing him to be an African American by way of a black and white booking photograph (popularly known as a mug shot), along with details of his original conviction for robbery and murder of a 17-year-old boy. The ad then describes the brutal assault and rape he committed while released on furlough. The victims were white. The ad presents Bush's and Dukakis's contrasting views on the death penalty and ends with the tagline: "Weekend Prison Passes. Dukakis on Crime."

"Revolving Door" avoided mentioning Horton by name but was obviously based on the Horton event. A long line of inmates are shown moving in and out of a prison through a revolving door. The ad notes that Dukakis vetoed both the death penalty and the bill limiting furloughs while he was governor of Massachusetts. The voice-over references that "many" of those furloughed committed new crimes, such as kidnapping and rape, and that "many" were still at large, while avoiding any statistical evidence. The ad ends with another powerful tag line: "Now Michael Dukakis says he wants to do for America what he has done for Massachusetts. America cannot afford that risk."

The ads were immediately accused of promoting racism. Critics charged that Horton's particular crime, committed by an African American against a white couple, was being used to incite fear of crime, African Americans, and Dukakis in middle-class white America. Although controversial during their initial release, these ads struck a chord with the American public and were aired repeatedly as they were discussed by various media outlets, civil rights leaders, and political pundits.

The Lasting Effects

Furlough programs were generally designed as a mechanism to assist the prison in its management of inmates while aiding an inmate's rehabilitation and reentry into society upon completion of his sentence. Over time, more emphasis was placed on utilizing inmate furloughs as a means of minimizing the burden of an increasing prison population. Furloughs were never designed for inmates serving a life sentence without the possibility of parole, as these inmates presented a greater risk to the community and would have little to lose by violating a furlough. Massachusetts, however, was unique in permitting furloughs for these inmates. The Horton case caused furlough programs to be disbanded across the country at a rapid rate. States are simply unwilling to risk the negative attention they would receive should one of their inmates commit a heinous crime while released on furlough.

In the political activities leading up to the 2012 presidential election, two Republicans with potential presidential ambitions faced the specter of Horton.

Mike Huckabee, former governor of Arkansas, and Tim Pawlenty, former governor of Minnesota, encountered questions and criticism concerning their involvement in the release of inmates who committed rape and murder while on parole. Although parole generally provides for more supervision than do furloughs, these cases were reminiscent of the Horton case and provided a similar test to determine the candidates' positions on crime.

As of 2011, Horton was currently serving two life sentences plus 85 years in a maximum-security facility in Maryland. The Horton case was made possible by the political expansion of furlough programs into areas they were never designed to go. What was once a tool to assist only those inmates destined to reenter society was transformed into a program that allowed all to participate. The last casualty of the Horton case was therefore the furlough system itself. Although still used at the federal level, furlough programs have all but vanished from state prison systems. What had the potential to be a useful tool of relatively low risk has been relegated to a mere footnote in the history of the correctional system.

Eric S. See
Methodist University

See also Crime Victims' Concerns; President's Task Force on Corrections

Further Readings

Carlson, Peter and Judith Garrett. *Prison and Jail Administration: Practice and Theory*, 2nd ed. Sudbury, MA: Jones and Bartlett, 2008.

JFA Institute. *Unlocking America: Why and How to Reduce America's Prison Population*. Washington, DC: Author, 2007. http://www.jfa-associates.com/publications/srs/UnlockingAmerica.pdf (Accessed December 2010).

Living Room Candidate. "Presidential Campaign Commercials 1952–2008." http://www.livingroomcandidate.org/commercials/1988/willie-horton#4123 (Accessed December 2010).

President's Commission on Law Enforcement and the Administration of Justice. *The Challenge of Crime in a Free Society: A Report by the President's Commission on Law Enforcement and the Administration of Justice*. Washington, DC: U.S. Government Printing Office, 1967. http://www.ncjrs.gov/pdffiles1/nij/42.pdf (Accessed December 14, 2010).

Goals and Objectives of Community Corrections

Due in large part to the massive prison overcrowding of the past several decades, as well as the expenses that have accompanied this growth, the demand for and provision of various community corrections programs are at an all-time high. Hence, specifying the primary goals and objectives of these programs is necessary to ensure that these community-based corrections programs can be evaluated on the fundamental bases of need, effectiveness, efficiency, and public safety and protection. The major goals and objectives of community corrections programs are (1) to reduce prison populations, (2) to protect the public (that is, provide public safety), (3) to keep offenders (under supervision) in the community, (4) to reduce offender recidivism, and (5) to generate cost savings.

Reducing Prison Populations

As of 2011, more than 2 million individuals were incarcerated in correctional institutions across the United States. Although a sentence to probation continues to be the most common (and likely) punishment imposed on those convicted of felony offenses, jail and prison sentences (or some combination of these sanctions) represent significant portions of criminal punishments: between 30 and 40 percent. Where to house this ever-expanding jail and prison population has been subject to ongoing debate, as issues related to facility overcrowding continue to

arise. Typically, however, building, expanding, and refurbishing correctional institutions have been the common responses of local, state, and the federal government to the correctional overcrowding issue. This leads us to one of the most dominant criticisms of incarceration and, at the same time, one of the

Prisons and jails cost U.S. states billions of dollars a year to maintain and operate. The state of Ohio has estimated that it has saved $11,000 per state resident by using community corrections practices in lieu of prison time. (Photos.com)

most attractive aspects of community corrections programs: the expense.

There are many expenses associated with incarcerating convicted offenders in correctional institutions. Not only are there the considerable financial costs of building, maintaining, and operating the facilities themselves, but there are also a multitude of social costs, for both communities and families. Prisons and jails are expensive to build; some price tags run to the tens of millions of dollars. Moreover, once these correctional facilities are built, it costs millions of dollars to operate and maintain them. In addition to these costs are other expenses that community corrections programs are particularly well suited to challenge: the social costs of incarceration. Removal of individuals from society (to placement in a correctional institution) results in various consequences for the communities and families left behind. Although too numerous to describe in detail here, these social consequences often include loss of a parent, child, or other family member; loss of income (in many cases the primary breadwinner); loss of family and a community support system; loss of a potential or actual contributing member of the community; and the ill effects from the incarceration experience itself.

Finally, it should also be noted that the reduction of prison populations as a main objective of community corrections programs does not necessitate the removal of dangerous, violent, or threatening offenders (or chronic or career criminals) from custody and placement back into the community. Rather, as is apparent from court records and from prison and jail population records, a significant portion of the incarcerated population (about 40 percent) consists of nonviolent offenders. Hence, the removal of these individuals from custody or, better yet, the initial sentencing of these offenders to community corrections programs instead of prison or jail may work to combat both the financial and social costs of incarceration. Research suggests that offenders, especially nonviolent ones, can be just as successful—if not more so—when placed in community corrections as they are in institutional correctional facilities.

Protecting the Public

Contrary to much popular belief, community corrections programs make concerted efforts to protect the public from becoming victims of crimes. Research and programmatic reports describe an array of new (or updated) supervision and monitoring techniques and tools aimed at ensuring the public's safety by carefully keeping track of individuals placed in community supervision programs. Not only do these efforts monitor the whereabouts of participants in community corrections programs; in some cases, they also assist officials in identifying offenders who may pose threats to public safety or those who are already engaging in criminal or potentially dangerous activities. Among the tools used to monitor offenders' whereabouts and activities are polygraph tests, drug and alcohol monitoring tools, and tracking devices such as those associated with the Geographical Information System (GIS) and the global positioning system (GPS). Furthermore, community corrections programs work to enhance public protection in the long run, assisting offenders, through use of program services, to change their attitudes and behaviors.

Some research also indicates that the use of a community-based sanction—as opposed to an institutional or custodial sentence—results in enhanced public safety, as offenders placed in the community do not have to deal with prisonization and reentry issues, which tend to hinder the ability of former inmates to successfully reacclimate to life outside prison and jail. More specifically, offenders initially placed on probation or other community-based options remain in the community to serve out their sentences. This situation, in and of itself, likely results in better societal protection, as these offenders are not exposed to the criminogenic prison or jail environments, and thus they are significantly less likely to pick up the additional "procrime" or "procriminal" attitudes and behaviors that can be found in correctional institutions. Moreover, as these folks remain in the community while under correctional supervision, they also do not need the reentry services that are critical for those sentenced to a custodial facility.

Keeping Offenders (Under Supervision) in the Community

There are numerous advantages associated with maintaining offender supervision, monitoring, rehabilitation, and accountability within the community, as opposed to placing these individuals in correctional institutions. The most obvious benefit is the significantly reduced cost of community, as compared to institutional, placement (this point is discussed in more detail later). In addition to the lowered costs of community corrections programs, there are other advantages. Contrary to critics' claims that community-based programs are ineffective or merely "slaps on the wrists" to offenders, research indicates that supervising, monitoring, and rehabilitating offenders in the community are at least as effective as prison and jail confinement at reducing recidivism and protecting the public. Furthermore, performing these tasks while offenders remain within the community means that offenders (and their families and communities) do not suffer the additional complications and negative consequences associated with the removal (for any length of time) of individuals from their homes and communities and the various effects that this loss has on the families and communities left behind. More specifically, individuals in community-based correctional programs not only have the opportunity to receive the monitoring, supervision, and access to rehabilitative treatment that they need but also are in a much better position to retain the family, community, and social support networks they have developed. Families of offenders can continue to benefit from the financial and other contributions and roles played by individuals under correctional supervision in the community—most of which disappear, or at least are greatly reduced, when these offenders are in prison or jail.

An important issue regarding community correctional programs concerns how offenders are "kept" under supervision and what this means exactly. First, it should be pointed out that there are many different kinds of community-based correctional programs, including, but not limited to, probation, intensive supervision probation (ISP), parole, halfway houses, house arrest (and electronic monitoring), day reporting centers (DRCs), residential community corrections centers (RCCs), and therapeutic communities (TCs). An offender given a community-based correctional sentence may be placed in any one of these programs or even a combination of two or more. An important exception is a parole sentence: Only offenders who are released from serving a prison sentence of some length may be placed on parole. All of these community correctional program options include, to some extent, supervision by a community corrections official and conditions (rules) associated with the offender and his or her sentence.

Generally, offenders sentenced to community corrections programs are subject to an array of conditions or rules to which they must adhere while under the supervision of a community corrections officer. In the case of residential (and day reporting) community-based programs, there are usually several different community corrections officers with whom an offender must interact, including the supervisory staff in the facility as well as rehabilitative or treatment-oriented staff. There is also a set of rules that govern the operation of residential community corrections centers, in addition to rules governing offenders' behaviors. More commonly, however, offenders are "kept" under supervision in the community by placement on some kind of probation program. Although these programs are not residential in nature (that is, these offenders live at home while under this and other kinds of community-based programs), offenders are typically "kept" under supervision by an assigned probation (or parole) officer responsible for monitoring their behavior, including their adherence to the conditions and rules set by the sentencing judge to ensure that they refrain from involvement in crime. Adequate monitoring and supervision by a community corrections officer ensure that offenders under community supervision will abide by the rules and provide a mechanism for holding offenders accountable for failing to do so. Thus, the process is set up to keep offenders in the community while they obey the rules, sparing taxpayers the enormous expenses associated with institutionalization, but also to identify when offenders have broken (or are at risk of breaking) the rules in order to protect the public and hold offenders accountable for their crimes and misbehaviors. This leads to the next major goal associated with all correctional programs, including those based in the community: reducing offender recidivism.

Reducing Offender Recidivism

Recidivism is defined simply as the recurrence of criminal behavior by an offender. Certainly, one of the primary objectives of all community corrections programs is to reduce, if not eliminate entirely, reoffending by previously identified, convicted, and punished/rehabilitated offenders. Community-based corrections programs attempt to reduce recidivism in several ways. Most important, reduced recidivism is sought by providing offenders with access to treatment and rehabilitation programs that respond directly to offenders' likelihood (and opportunity) to engage in criminal behaviors. More specifically, programs and services that address criminogenic risks of offenders are key components in many community-based correctional programs. These programs often target areas or needs, such as education, living skills, cognitive skills, drug or alcohol abuse, anger management, job training and skills, and mental health issues. Community corrections programs and officials can directly provide some of these services in addition to monitoring offenders to ensure that they access and take advantage of these provisions. More commonly, however, community corrections staff and officials identify needed treatment and rehabilitation services and then link their clients to these services in the community. By addressing the needs of offenders within the community and identifying and responding to offenders' risks, using community-based resources, community corrections programs aim to reduce reoffending by their clientele. It should also be noted, however, that even though most prisons and jails provide some types of treatment and rehabilitation services, research suggests that community-based programs and services tend to be much more extensive and effective (for a variety of reasons) than prison- or jail-based services.

Community corrections programs also seek to reduce recidivism by drawing on key correctional objectives and philosophies such as punishment, specific deterrence, and incapacitation. Community corrections programs punish offenders not only by subjecting them to supervision and monitoring their activities but also by using an array of graduated sanctions or punishments that correspond to violations of the rules and conditions of their sentences. Community corrections staff have the ability (in many circumstances) to impose additional restrictions on offenders if their behavior warrants it or if offenders fail to conform to the expectations of their sanctions. Additionally, offenders placed in community-based corrections programs are likely incapacitated (unable to commit criminal offenses) to some degree by virtue of the supervision and monitoring of their behaviors by community corrections officials and staff. This monitoring tends to result in a reduction in offending by these individuals as they realize that their behavior is being observed and violations will be punished. The philosophy of specific

deterrence comes into play here as well. More specifically, according to this philosophy, offenders who are placed in community corrections programs because of their prior misbehaviors will be significantly less likely to reoffend in the future precisely because of the inconveniences and consequences associated with their sentence to a community corrections program.

Finally, research indicates that recidivism reductions offered by community corrections programs are as large as, if not larger than, those produced by custodial sanctions. In fact, some research suggests that institutional sanctions actually increase subsequent offending rather than reduce it. Certainly, community corrections programs have not completely eliminated the occurrence of recidivism; however, it is quite clear that the rates of recidivism associated with community corrections program participation compare favorably with the rates of recidivism for those offenders sentenced to prison or jail. As discussed in more detail next, the reduction of recidivism generated by community corrections programs is even more promising because it reduces financial cost when contrasted with institutional corrections efforts.

Generating Cost Savings

There is no question that one of the main objectives of community corrections programs is to provide offender supervision, accountability, punishment, treatment, and rehabilitation, as well as other correctional services at a much lower cost than the very high expenses associated with imprisoning and jailing offenders. Studies that compare the costs of prisons and jails with the expenses of an array of community correctional programs overwhelmingly report that the community-based options are much cheaper than institutional options. In addition, it is important to note that a large proportion of offenders placed under supervision in the community are often ordered to pay fees, fines, or other monies in order to help pay for their particular program or service and offset taxpayers' financial responsibilities. While costs for the different community-based correctional programs vary substantially—from traditional probation at the low end to residential correctional centers and boot camps at the higher end—building, maintaining, and operating prisons remain very expensive (and ongoing) correctional efforts, and the expenses become even more problematic in economically troubled times.

Generally, comparative reports of jurisdictions within the United States indicate that the costs of probation, per probationer per day, range from $1.27 to $9.46, whereas jail and prison costs (combined per inmate per day) range from $44.00 to $125.00. The costs of other community corrections options (such as ISP programs, RCCs, and electronic monitoring) fall somewhere between these two extremes. Thus, it appears that community corrections programs strive for correctional goals and objectives similar to those of traditional institutional corrections—protecting the public; supervising, monitoring, and treating offenders; and reducing offender recidivism—while doing so at a much reduced cost to the taxpayer, community, family, and offender. Currently, however, approximately 90 percent of all correctional budgets are spent on costs associated with institutional corrections facilities, while the remaining 10 percent supports all community-based correctional programs. This issue of disproportionate financial support is just one of several important matters that should be considered in focusing on the future of community corrections.

Future Issues

Although it appears that the goals and objectives of community corrections are appropriate and promising, there remain many issues critical to improving and enhancing the future use of these correctional options. An important matter concerns taking steps to improve the public image of community corrections programs. It is quite clear that many in the public view certain community corrections programs as too lenient on offenders. It is also clear, however, that the public is very supportive of alternatives to prison and jail for offenders. Thus, clarifying exactly what certain community corrections programs are and how they work to protect the public, reduce offending, and hold offenders accountable is an important step in garnering public support for the use and expansion of these correctional options.

A second, complementary issue involves encouraging or mandating criminal justice officials and decision makers to use community corrections options appropriately, as they are meant to be used: as alternatives to custodial sanctions and not as add-ons to jail or prison sentences. Clearly, using community corrections programs as add-on sanctions likely undermines many of the benefits of these programs (such as improving cost-effectiveness, reducing the need for reentry/reintegration services, reducing prison and jail populations, and reducing recidivism).

A final challenge confronting the future of community corrections programs is the need for correctional practitioners, researchers, and communities to continue efforts to clarify and understand the underlying goals and objectives of these programs to improve our ability to provide and use community-based correctional programs whose value can be accurately and appropriately evaluated.

Noelle E. Fearn
Saint Louis University

See also Attitudes and Myths About Punishment; Costs of Community Corrections; Effectiveness of Community Corrections; Philosophy of Community Corrections; Prison Overcrowding; Recidivism; Reducing Prison Populations

Further Readings

Alarid, Leanne Fiftal and Rolando V. del Carmen. *Community-Based Corrections*, 8th ed. Belmont, CA: Thomson Wadsworth, 2011.

American Correctional Association. *Intermediate Punishment: Community-Based Sanctions*. Baltimore, MD: United Book Press, 1990.

Austin, James. "Prisoner Reentry: Current Trends, Practices, and Issues." *Crime and Delinquency*, v.47/3 (2001).

DeMichele, Matthew and Mario Paparozzi. "Community Corrections: A Powerful Field." *Corrections Today* (October 2008).

Fry, Russ. "Community Corrections' Core Mission." *Corrections Today* (April 14, 2007).

Greek, Cecil E. "The Cutting Edge: Tracking Probationers in Space and Time: The Convergence of GIS and GPS Systems." *Federal Probation*, v.66/1 (2002).

Hansen, Christopher. "The Cutting Edge: A Survey of Technological Innovation: Where Have All the Probation Officers Gone?" *Federal Probation*, v.65/1 (2001).

Karp, David R. and Todd R. Clear. *What Is Community Justice?* Thousand Oaks, CA: Pine Forge Press, 2002.

Latessa, Edward J. and Paula Smith. *Corrections in the Community*, 4th ed. Cincinnati, OH: Anderson/LexisNexis, 2007.

Lowenkamp, Christopher T., Edward J. Latessa, and Alexander M. Holsinger. "The Risk Principle in Action:

What Have We Learned From 13,676 Offenders and 97 Correctional Programs?" *Crime and Delinquency*, v.52/1 (2006).

Petersilia, Joan. *Community Corrections: Probation, Parole, and Intermediate Sanctions.* New York: Oxford University Press, 1998.

Petersilia, Joan. *When Prisoners Come Home.* New York: Oxford University Press, 2003.

Wodahl, Eric J. and Brett Garland. "The Evolution of Community Corrections: The Enduring Influence of the Prison." *The Prison Journal*, v.89/1 (2010).

GOOD TIME AND MERIT TIME

Good-time or merit-time credit, which is time credited to a prisoner's sentence for desired behavior or participation in prison programs, has historically been a means for corrections officials to control prison crowding, conserve resources, and provide incentives for prisoners to behave well while incarcerated, in the hope of transitioning that positive behavior into the community upon release. As the criminal justice system has evolved, such credits have remained useful to prison officials. In the modern era of crowded prisons and resource shortages, the use of these credits has grown increasingly important to running prison systems in ways that preserve public safety, meet offenders' needs, and maintain fiscal responsibility.

New York enacted the nation's first good-time laws in 1817, and 20 years later Massachusetts became the first state to implement a parole system. Use of parole did not become widespread, however, until New York adopted it concomitantly with implementation of indeterminate sentencing in 1876; this sentencing system established minimum and maximum prison terms for crimes and permitted early parole release of those who had served the minimum, minus good-time credits. This development led states to release prisoners early, based on good behavior, under the auspices of community supervision.

The system of indeterminate sentencing, good-time credits, and parole continued until the 1970s, when a movement to "get tough" on crime swept the nation. Some states replaced indeterminate sentences with sentences that were exclusively or primarily determinate in nature; instead of correctional authorities having discretion over release decisions, offenders served set periods. Whereas conservatives attacked indeterminate sentencing and parole as too lenient and compromising public safety, liberals believed correctional authorities, especially parole boards, had so much discretion over release decisions that gross disparities and abuses had occurred in many cases. Thus, many jurisdictions either curtailed or abolished parole release.

Prison populations exhibited steady growth after the mid-1970s because of laws that incarcerated more persons for longer terms. Faced with more restricted release options than before, and coupled in some states with court orders to reduce prison crowding, many jurisdictions began to rely on good-time/merit-time credits (or some version thereof) to reduce the terms offenders remained in prison and thereby contain rising prison populations. Methods of determining the amount of credit varied, and continue to vary, by jurisdiction, with some granting one day's credit for each day served with good behavior, in addition to the amount of merit-time credit given to an inmate who obtained a general equivalency diploma (GED) while in prison, for example. The federal government set the maximum good-time rate for federal inmates at 54 days per year for exemplary behavior.

These credits can be applied when a person leaves prison upon expiration of the sentence without any conditions or community supervision. For example, an individual sentenced to five years in prison who has acquired 12 months of good time for desired conduct and six months for completion of a GED could be released after serving three and a half years without any further correctional supervision. Alternatively, these credits may be applied when a person leaves prison at the discretion of some government entity, such as a parole board, with release conditional on compliance with the terms of community supervision. Using the example of a person sentenced to five years in prison, the individual may be released after serving only about three years, minus any good-time or merit-time credits, to complete correctional supervision in the community.

Good-time/merit-time credits have several purposes. When they are intended to deter such undesired prisoner behaviors as violence, credits are automatically awarded to prisoners but then deducted if prisoners are found to have engaged in misconduct. The U.S. Supreme Court has ruled that prisoners facing a loss of good-time credits may be entitled to due process protections. Research has found this method to be less successful at controlling prisoner behavior than the alternative of applying credits to reward desired behaviors, such as furthering education.

Correctional agencies will continue the use of good-time/merit-time credits. Some states have become more creative in rewarding offenders for positive behavior. For instance, those who abide by community supervision conditions for a certain time period may have that time applied to their sentences if they ultimately violate conditions and return to prison. Given that prisons house many recidivists, this use of such credits can help control crowding, conserve resources, and, more notably, assist in the development of prosocial lifestyles among people leaving prison.

Kevin I. Minor
Eastern Kentucky University
Nathan C. Lowe
American Probation and Parole Association

See also Offender Responsivity; Reducing Prison Populations; Sentencing Guidelines

Further Readings

Browning, Jane. "Coming to Terms With Prison Growth." *Corrections Today*, v.69/5 (2007).

Emshoff, James G. and William S. Davison. "The Effect of 'Good Time' Credit on Inmate Behavior." *Criminal Justice and Behavior*, v.14/3 (1987).

Greenfeld, Lawrence et al. "Prisons: Population Trends and Key Issues for Management." *Criminal Justice Review*, v.21/4 (1996).

Hepburn, John R. and Lynne Goodstein. "Organizational Imperatives and Sentencing Reform Implementation: The Impact of Prison Practices and Priorities on the Attainment of the Objective of Determinate Sentencing." *Crime and Delinquency*, v.32 (1986).

Mays, G. Larry and L. Thomas Winfree Jr. *Essentials of Corrections*, 4th ed. Belmont, CA: Thomson Wadsworth, 2009.

Parisi, Nicolette and Joseph A. Zillo. "Good Time: The Forgotten Issue." *Crime and Delinquency*, v.29 (1983).

Pew Center on the States. "Policy Framework to Strengthen Community Corrections: Earned Compliance Credits." http://www.pewcenteronthestates.org/uploadedFiles/Earned%20Compliance%20Credits.pdf (Accessed December 2010).

Schriro, Dora. "Is Good Time a Good Idea? A Practitioner's Perspective." *Federal Sentencing Reporter*, v.21/3 (2009).

Weisburd, David and Ellen S. Chayet. "Good Time: An Agenda for Research." *Criminal Justice and Behavior*, v.16/2 (1989).

GPS Tracking

Since the 1960s, the location of offenders under community supervision has been monitored with the assistance of electronic devices. Increasingly, electronic monitoring relies on technology that uses the global positioning system (GPS) to monitor offenders. The adoption of GPS monitoring has been facilitated by court decisions that find this form of surveillance can be employed without violating the offender's constitutional rights. In fact, some states now require the use of GPS for certain perceived high-risk offender groups, particularly sex offenders. GPS monitoring has also become more common in the supervision of domestic violence and drug offenders, as well as supervisees with gang affiliations. Although it has become an accepted part of community supervision, GPS monitoring is not without its complications.

GPS technology was created by the U.S. Department of Defense in the 1970s. Over time, GPS has been adapted for nonmilitary purposes and has become more affordable and portable. Usually combined with radio-frequency receivers, computer technology, and cell phone service, GPS utilizes satellites orbiting the earth to communicate information in real time (or near real time) about geographic location. In community corrections, offenders are generally required to wear a tamper-resistant, battery-operated radio-frequency transmitter around the ankle. They also must carry a portable GPS tracking unit with them, usually strapped around the waist or shoulder or carried by hand. If the offender fails to carry or attempts to disable the GPS tracking unit, enters a prohibited area, or leaves his or her home without authorization, an alert is issued to a central monitoring unit, overseen by corrections professionals or a private contractor. The offender's supervisor is then notified. Even if the offender has not acted in violation of his or her supervision conditions, the supervisor can track the offender's movements from stored data, which might be useful in identifying, or eliminating, the offender in reports of new crimes. Some newer GPS units can also determine alcohol consumption,

Offenders in community corrections programs are often required to carry a portable GPS tracking unit to monitor that they do not enter a prohibited area or leave their home without permission. Community corrections supervisors estimate that 70 percent of GPS alerts are false alarms. (Photos.com)

which makes them useful in monitoring those who have been convicted of driving under the influence (DUI) or other offenses in which alcohol has played a significant role.

Passive, active, and hybrid GPS monitoring systems are currently in use. Unlike active systems, which constantly relay real-time location information via cell phone service to a central monitoring system, passive systems relay information only when the offender connects the GPS tracking unit to a docking station, usually connected with a land-line telephone. Hybrid systems are also available; these report information every few hours, and if an alert is detected, the real-time active system is triggered.

GPS programs attempt to balance the integration of offenders into the community with public safety and security. GPS monitoring is significantly cheaper than incarceration. A cost analysis conducted in Florida estimated that enrolling all sex offenders in a GPS monitoring program would cost $8 million, but incarcerating them would cost $56 million. Also, to the degree that GPS monitoring diverts offenders from incarceration, it can lessen problems associated with overcrowding in jails and prisons.

While findings were mixed, the majority of early research has suggested that GPS monitoring increases public safety. These studies were flawed, in that they often mixed high- and low-risk offender groups, did not include adequate comparison populations, or studied programs in which monitoring was inconsistent. In 2010, however, a methodologically rigorous study by William Bale and his colleagues concluded that any electronic monitoring reduced recidivism by 31 percent and that recidivism was 6 percent less among those monitored by GPS rather than radio-frequency systems. Results were consistent across all offender groups, regardless of demographic characteristics or type of supervision, but were less marked for violent offenders.

GPS technology is not without its shortcomings, however. Technological failures can occur: Battery life, computer glitches, and obstructed cell phone service can render GPS monitoring inaccurate or inoperable. Location monitoring does not preclude reoffending, and some studies suggest that high-risk offenders are not deterred from crime even while being monitored. GPS monitoring can also have unanticipated negative effects on the offender's community adjustment and his or her ability to maintain employment, and monitoring can create complications for offenders' families.

While the cost of GPS monitoring is less than that of incarceration, it is more expensive than traditional community supervision in that it incurs equipment costs, as well as personnel training and offender supervision costs. In practice, cost comparison studies that claim that GPS monitoring is cheaper than incarceration are misleading, since it is not used exclusively as an alternative to incarceration; only about one third of the 5,034 cases studied by Bales and colleagues were diverted from prison. A principal reason for high GPS monitoring costs is that such monitoring produces a vast amount of information. Parole officers have noted that it takes about one hour to review the information produced the previous day for each offender under supervision. One officer stated that many of his supervisees did not require electronic monitoring but that mandatory laws or court-imposed conditions required that it be maintained. Many judges who impose monitoring are unfamiliar with the system, its capabilities and limitations, and its costs. For these and other reasons, the cost of managing a large-scale GPS network has become a problem in several states, resulting in fragmentary implementation of legislatively mandated offender monitoring. GPS is therefore not a substitute for effective personal supervision of offenders by probation and parole officers and other criminal justice professionals. GPS monitoring appears to have its greatest effect in reducing recidivism when coupled with effective personal supervision.

Paul D. Steele
Morehead State University
Deborah J. Brydon
Mount Mercy University
Timothy Hare
Morehead State University

See also Electronic Monitoring; Home Confinement and House Arrest; Prison Overcrowding; Reducing Prison Populations; Work/Study Release Programs

Further Readings

Bales, W. et al. *A Quantitative and Qualitative Assessment of Electronic Monitoring.* Washington, DC: U.S. Department of Justice, Office of Justice Programs, National Institute of Justice, 2010.

Brown, T., S. McCabe, and C. Welford. *Global Positioning System (GPS) Technology for Community Supervision: Lessons Learned.* Washington, DC: U.S. Department of Justice, Office of Justice Programs, National Institute of Justice, 2007.

Carpenter, C. L. "Legislative Epidemics: A Cautionary Tale of Criminal Laws That Have Swept the Country." *Buffalo Law Review*, v.58 (2010).

Padgett, K. G., W. D. Bales, and T. G. Blomberg. "Under Surveillance: An Empirical Test of the Effectiveness and Consequences of Electronic Monitoring." *Criminology and Public Policy*, v.5 (2006).

GRADUATED SANCTIONS FOR JUVENILE OFFENDERS

The term *graduated sanctions* refers to the establishment of a set of juvenile court interventions that become increasingly punitive and restrictive as offending behavior becomes more serious or repetitive. These sanctions developed as practitioners, judges, researchers, and legislators became aware of an inability of juvenile courts to address youth crime effectively. As juvenile courts began to see a significant increase of delinquency in the late 1980s, it became apparent that typical court responses were inadequate. At that time, most courts employed two intervention options for delinquent youth: traditional probation, with the youth living at home under formal supervision of juvenile authorities, and placement of the youth in some form of secure facility until he or she could be returned safely to the community. The increase of youth crime, combined with research showing that recidivism was not diminishing, brought about the need to establish intervention alternatives along a range of increasing formality and restrictiveness that could more effectively address delinquency. Because many of these alternatives were to be available in the community, graduated sanctions became associated with community corrections.

The idea of a continuum of restrictiveness suggests that as a youth exhibits more serious and repetitive delinquent behavior, he or she should be subject to decreasing privileges and freedoms. This continuum would allow the court to more appropriately address the needs of all youth committing recognized delinquent acts. The most common descriptions of this continuum include five stages of increasing restrictiveness. These can be summarized as warnings, informal interventions, formal probation, day treatment/intensive supervision, and residential placement.

Warnings typically include a stern verbal admonition from or a single counseling session with a juvenile officer or judge. Most appropriate to first-time nonviolent, nonserious offenders, warnings may be effective in redirecting youths from minor delinquent acts. Although documentation of the incident may be kept in a juvenile record, no adjudication to criminal charges occurs.

Informal interventions may include short-term supervision from a juvenile officer or agreement from the youth that she or he will complete a brief course of counseling, volunteer for a few hours of community service, or repay damages and write an apology letter to a victim. Still appropriate for nonserious, nonviolent offenses, informal interventions differ from warnings in that some future action is required of the offender. Documentation of the intervention is likely kept at least until the conditions imposed by the court and agreed to by the youth are met. Often, once the conditions are satisfied, all formal charges are dismissed. Again, no adjudication or conviction occurs.

Formal probation occurs after an adjudication or conviction to the delinquent charges. This intervention is typically applied to first-time or more serious offenders who are believed, after proper assessment, to be at relatively low risk of harming the community further. At this level, the youth is usually required to meet with a probation officer on a set schedule. Usually, departments will require the youth to see his or her probation officer at least one time per month, in person. Conditions for successful completion of the term of probation are set both by the court and by the probation department. These conditions may include completing a course of counseling, a skill development program, or a predetermined number of community service hours; paying a fine to the court or restitution to the victim; meeting a curfew to be at home every night by a set time; and/or regularly attending school with proper behavior. The primary goals of formal probation are generally both to punish the offender and to provide services (such as counseling) that are believed to benefit the youth so that he or she will not commit further delinquent acts. Although the youth's record will likely not be open to public inspection, a formal adjudication or conviction, along with the court-imposed requirements, will be placed in the youth's juvenile file.

Day treatment usually involves intensive supervision, but intensive supervision may not involve day treatment. Appropriate for more serious or repeat offenders or for youths who are believed to pose a moderate risk of harm to the community, day treatment requires the youth to visit a program during the day for a set number of hours and return to his or her home in the evening. The day treatment may be operated by professional staff or by probation officers. The youth will be required to attend academic classes; individual, family, or group counseling; competence and skill development programs; or other services deemed appropriate by the court. In some areas, the day treatment attendance may occur after the youth's return from public school, with hours set in the evening or on weekends. Intensive

probation follows many of the requirements of formal probation described above, but it involves reporting to the probation officer more often and may include electronic monitoring. These visits usually include both scheduled and unscheduled in-person visits, telephone calls, and letter reporting.

Residential placement involves facilities where delinquent youth will go to live. These may be near the youth's home or considerably distant, and they can be operated by the probation department, a state agency, or a private organization. Residential placement is usually reserved for youth who are not safe in their own homes or who pose a high risk of harm to the community. Residential placements also vary along a continuum of restrictiveness, from foster care, which is not secure, to a home or facility in the community secured by staff presence at all times to a locked facility that closely resembles an adult correctional institution. Once placed in such a facility, the youth must complete certain actions in order to be released; these are usually developed with the assistance of program staff and the probation department. In some cases, the court will prescribe that the youth serve a specific length of time. The youth's access to the outside world and visitation from family will vary greatly, depending on the location of the facility and the restrictiveness level. Once a youth completes the conditions of placement or serves the time set by the court, she or he may be returned home without supervision if the court has no further concerns. If the court feels there is a need for further service or there is perceived risk of harm to the community, the youth may return home under formal probation or intensive supervision.

Jeremy Olson
Seton Hill University

See also Case Management; Continuum of Sanctions; Juvenile and Youth Offenders

Further Readings

Butts, J. A. and D. P. Mears. "Reviving Juvenile Justice in a Get-Tough Era." *Youth and Society*, v.33 (2001).

Juvenile Sanctions Center. *Graduated Sanctions for Juvenile Offenders: A Program Model and Planning Guide.* Reno, NV: National Council of Juvenile and Family Court Judges, 2002. http://www.ncjfcj.org/content/view/1375/331.

Krisberg, B. B., E. E. Currie, D. D. Onek, and R. G. Wiebush. "Graduated Sanctions for Serious, Violent, and Chronic Juvenile Offenders." In *Serious, Violent, and Chronic Juvenile Offenders: A Sourcebook*, James C. Howell et al., eds. Thousand Oaks, CA: Sage, 1995.

GROUP HOMES

The group home is a relatively recent phenomenon in community corrections. Group homes came into prominence in the 1970s. Group homes replaced asylums, orphanages, and other institutions that were shut down either for abuse or lack of funds. There are many types of group homes for many different social problems, including alcohol and drug abuse, mental illness, juvenile delinquency, emotional abuse, and domestic violence. Group homes are primarily private, nonprofit entities even though a few public group homes exist. States may partially fund even private group homes through state programs, in an attempt to avoid incarceration of either the mentally ill or juveniles. There are both short-term group homes and long-term group homes that offer residential care. Costs for such facilities are usually covered through supplemental security income (SSI) payments, and the group home makes sure the person is fed, sheltered, and clothed adequately.

Although group homes vary in size and in types of individuals they allow, the largest group homes usually house no more than 12 persons. There are two main ways people are supervised in group homes: either through caregivers who work in shifts or by means of live-in caregivers. According to Jake Terpstra, shift care has been more successful than in-home residential care, because the intensity of the responsibility is easier for the caregiver to sustain if he or she can get away from the home and have time to rest. Live-in caregivers must maintain their professionalism constantly and have no place to go or to feel comfortable or vent the frustrations they may encounter on the job; hence, live-in caregivers are more prone to burnout as well as lapses of professionalism while on the job.

Group homes offer both benefits and risks. One benefit is that families of offenders may be relieved and comforted by no longer having to provide primary care for the offender, whose behavior they may not be able to handle physically, mentally, or both.

A group home is a less expensive option to placement in a correctional facility or mental institution; however, juveniles in group home settings often feel abandoned and isolated and experience low self esteem. (Photos.com)

Moreover, group homes tend to cost less than other options, such as housing in a correctional facility or mental institution. Group homes can also provide rehabilitation, allowing offenders to live their lives in the context of other persons with past difficulties; hence the former offender's problems are no longer a stigma, because a responsible group home ensures that all people living there are in a community environment.

According to a RAND Corporation study, in 1994 every dollar spent on treatment in group homes led to a 7.46 percent reduction in crime-related spending and lost productivity. However, a study done at the University of Illinois by Joseph Ryan and colleagues indicates that juveniles who are in group homes are 2.5 times more likely to enter the juvenile justice system than are children from similar backgrounds. Likewise, blacks tend to be placed in group homes at higher rates than whites. According to a study done by Lori Grubstein for Temple University in 2000, the recidivism rate for teens leaving group homes in Philadelphia was only 22 percent per year after leaving. She also found higher rates of self-esteem, a stronger attachment to teachers, and more community involvement.

This does not mean that group homes have no problems. In many states there are inadequate regulations of group homes, as well as inadequate oversight. For-profit group homes may cut costs in areas that are crucial to the care of the patients. Juveniles who are in group homes often suffer from low self-esteem and emotional problems, which may lead to higher rates of pregnancy and even suicide. Patients in group homes who are not visited by family and friends may develop a sense of abandonment and isolation.

A study done by Carl Li, Peter Johnson, and Kathleen Leopard in 2001 argued that depression is a rampant problem in group homes. Studying group homes in South Carolina, they found that roughly 75 percent of the adolescents were depressed or exhibited depressive symptoms. The authors also found that females were more likely to have these depressive symptoms than were males.

Often, group homes are opposed within communities for fear that they will lower property values. While these claims are rarely founded on fact, group homes have usually found it difficult to locate in certain wealthier neighborhoods. City governments have proposed and passed zoning restrictions that have stopped group homes from being placed in certain neighborhoods. Many group homes are therefore forced to locate in low-income neighborhoods where drug and crime problems are common; this gives the residents of group homes access to environments that produced many of the problems they already have.

Some group homes, especially those that deal with juveniles, can be very expensive. According to strugglingteen.net, costs vary but range from around to $30,000 to $50,000 per year. Costs may be able to be deferred using insurance or state funding, but for parents in low-income brackets, group homes may be too expensive.

Group homes can be successful, but one who is considering placing a relative in such a facility must first match the potential patient's needs with the right group home. One must also make sure that the personnel in the group home have adequate training. Licensing boards for group homes should be consulted to make sure no complaints have been filed against the potential group home. Finally, costs must be fully understood and considered in making the decision to use a group home.

Derrick Shapley
Mississippi State University

See also Addiction-Specific Support Groups; Boot Camps; Halfway Houses and Residential Centers; NIMBY Syndrome; Residential Programs for Juveniles; Therapeutic Communities

Further Readings

Altshuler, Sandra and John Poertner. *Assessment of the Well-Being of Adolescents in Three Substitute Care Placement Types*. Champaign: University of Illinois School of Social Work, 2001.

Grubstein, Lori. "Group Home Programs." Crime and Justice Research Institute, 2000. http://www.temple.edu/prodes/adobe/grouphomes.pdf (Accessed July 2011).

Levinson, Jack. *Making Life Work: Freedom and Disability in a Community Group Home*. Minneapolis: University of Minnesota Press, 2010.

Li, Carl, Peter Johnson, and Kathleen Leopard. "Risk Factors for Depression Among Adolescents Living in Group Homes in South Carolina." *Journal of Health and Social Policy*, v.13 (2000).

Ryan, J. P. et al. "Juvenile Delinquency in Child Welfare: Investigating Group Home Effects." *Children and Youth Services Review*, v.30 (2008).

Terpstra, Jake. "Group Homes for Children Types and Characteristics." 1979. http://www.temple.edu/prodes/adobe/grouphomes.pdf (Accessed July 2011).

Halfway Houses and Residential Centers

Halfway houses and residential programs for criminal offenders have a long history in the United States. In the past, the typical use of a community residential facility was as a halfway house. These programs were designed as transitional placements for offenders to ease the movement from incarceration to life in the free society. In time, some programs developed as alternatives to incarceration, so that the "halfway" aspect could mean either halfway into prison or halfway out of prison.

Between 1950 and 1980, the number and use of such halfway houses grew considerably. There was a setback in the 1980s, but since the 1990s residential placements for criminal offenders have undergone considerable role expansion. Increasingly, the population served by these programs has come to include large numbers of probationers and persons awaiting trial. In many jurisdictions, placement in a residential facility is available to judges as a direct sentencing option. These changes in the role and population of residential programs have supported the replacement of the traditional halfway house notion with the broader notion of a community corrections residential facility.

Until recently, community corrections residential programs were subsumed under the general rubric of halfway houses. This label, however, has proven to be inadequate as a description of the variety of residential programs used with correctional populations today.

The current name given to such programs, "community corrections residential facilities," reflects the role expansion of the traditional halfway house that has occurred in recent years. G. E. Rush defines a residential facility as "a correctional facility from which residents are regularly permitted to depart, unaccompanied by any official, for the purposes of using community resources, such as schools or treatment programs, and seeking or holding employment." This definition is free of any reference to incarceration that was implicit in the term *halfway*. Furthermore, the concept of a residential facility does not necessitate the direct provision of any services to residents within the facility and clearly identifies the program with a correctional mission. Thus, unlike the traditional halfway house, the community residential facility serves a more diverse population and plays a broader correctional role. Traditional halfway houses are included within the category of residential facilities, but their ranks are swelled by newer adaptations, such as community corrections centers, pre-release centers, and restitution centers.

Development of Community Residential Programs

Halfway houses as transitional programming for inmates released from prisons are not a new phenomenon. Their origins can be traced at least as far back as the early 19th century in England and Ireland. In the United States, the exact origin of halfway houses is not clear, but one such program, the Isaac T. Hooper Home, was started in New York City in 1845. A halfway house for released female prisoners was opened in Boston, Massachusetts, in

1864. For nearly 100 years, halfway houses tended to be operated by charitable organizations for the benefit of released inmates. Halfway house programs did not begin a period of expansion until after World War II.

In the 1950s, specialized residential programs to deal with substance-abusing offenders were added to the traditional halfway house programs. Residential programs for alcoholic or drug-addicted offenders opened and spread throughout this period and into the 1960s. For typical criminal offenders, halfway house placements were rare. In the mid-1960s, however, the President's Commission on Crime and Administration of Justice (1967) signaled a change in correctional philosophy toward the goal of reintegration. Reintegration placed increased emphasis on the role of the community in corrections and on the value of keeping offenders in the community, rather than in prison, whenever possible. This ideology of community corrections supported the notion of residential placements for convicted offenders, and halfway houses began a period of unprecedented expansion, supported by federal funding.

During the early 1980s, support for halfway house programs dwindled. The effects of recession, the demise of federal funding, and a general hardening of public attitudes toward offenders worked against the continued growth and development of halfway houses and other residential programs. This period of retrenchment was, however, short-lived. The same forces that temporarily halted the growth of residential programs soon added their weight to continued development.

Since the 1990s, community corrections residential facilities have grown in response to the crisis of prison crowding. H. E. Allen and colleagues attribute an increased use of halfway houses with parole populations to three factors: the philosophy of reintegration, the success of such programs in the mental health field, and the lower costs of halfway houses compared with prisons. To these was added the need to respond to the prison crowding that began in the 1980s.

In an era when both correctional costs and populations grow yearly, planners, practitioners, and policy makers have supported a wide range of correctional alternatives. As R. Guynes has observed, one effect of prison and jail crowding has been a dramatic increase in probation and parole populations. Furthermore, Joan Petersilia, among others,

suggests that these larger supervision populations are increasingly made up of more serious and more dangerous offenders. Community residential facilities have come to be seen as an important option for the management and control of these growing and more dangerous offender populations.

A result has been the redefinition of the role of community residential facilities. The traditional role of transitional placement for offenders, along with responses to special needs populations such as substance abusers, has been expanded. Residential placement has emerged as a correctional alternative in its own right.

Residential Facilities in Corrections

As the foregoing discussion illustrates, it is not possible to describe the "average" residential facility. Diversity in population, program, size, and structure is the rule. It is, unfortunately, also not possible to know for certain how many such facilities are in operation today or the number of offenders served by them. The National Institute of Corrections supported a survey that identified 641 community corrections residential facilities. The identification was based on the characteristics of residents as under correctional supervision, among other criteria. Although there are admittedly incomplete data, it is possible to estimate that there are in excess of 600 residential facilities in operation today. Furthermore, it appears that the number of facilities has grown as much as 50 percent since the beginning of the 21st century.

It is not possible to estimate the number of offenders served by these facilities with any certainty. Length of residence is typically short, on the order of three to four months, meaning that a facility with 50 beds may serve 150 to 200 individuals annually. Based on the probability that a halfway house would annually serve three to four times as many residents as it has beds, it is not unreasonable to estimate that many thousands of offenders are served by these programs each year.

Types of Facilities

Allen and colleagues developed a four-class typology of halfway houses, using two dimensions to yield four possible types of facilities. Halfway houses can be either public or private, and their programs can be either interventional or supportive. Public or private, of course, relates to the organization of the facility as either a government entity or not. Program types are based on whether the services of the facility are designed to intervene in problem areas of the residents' lives, such as substance abuse counseling, or to provide a supportive environment in which residents use community resources.

What Do We Know About the Effectiveness Question?

Despite the long tradition of residential community correctional programs, until recently the research literature concerned with them was sparse and inconclusive. In 2002, however, a large study of community correctional facilities was conducted by C. T. Lowenkamp and E. J. Latessa. This study included an examination of 38 halfway houses and more than 6,400 offenders (3,200 each in the treatment and comparison groups). Although results from this study showed that, overall, halfway houses did indeed reduce recidivism, not all programs were effective. Furthermore, programs had a much more pronounced effect on higher-risk offenders, and higher-quality programs performing better than lower-quality programs. A 2010 replication study conducted by Latessa, Lori Brusman Lovins, and P. Smith found similar results as the 2002 study.

The Future of Residential Facilities

Residential community correctional facilities that evolved from traditional halfway houses are now becoming multiservice agencies. These facilities will continue to grow and develop new programs. In large part, this will be a response to the crowding of local and state correctional institutions. Many traditional residential facilities will seize the opportunity to diversify and offer a wider range of programs and services, such as victim assistance programs, family and drug counseling, drunk driving programs, work release centers, and house arrest, electronic monitoring, and day programs for offenders.

Finally, although there has been an increase in public-sector operation of residential facilities, particularly pre-release and reintegration centers, it will be the private sector that will continue to play a dominant role in the development and operation of residential correctional programs. A number of arguments support private provision of community-based correctional services. Principal among these is cost-effectiveness. Proponents argue that the private sector will contain costs and thus, for the same dollar amount, provide more, or at least better, service.

Edward J. Latessa
University of Cincinnati

See also Addiction-Specific Support Groups; Boot Camps; Group Homes; NIMBY Syndrome; Residential Programs for Juveniles; Therapeutic Communities

Further Readings

Allen, H. E., E. W. Carlson, E. C. Parks, and R. P. Seiter. *Program Models: Halfway Houses*. Washington, DC: U.S. Department of Justice, 1978.

Beha, J. A. "Testing the Functions and Effects of the Parole Halfway House: One Case Study." *Journal of Criminal Law and Criminology*, v.67 (1977).

Guynes, R. *Difficult Clients, Large Caseloads Plague Probation, Parole Agencies*. Washington, DC: U.S. Department of Justice, 1988.

Keller, O. J. and G. Alper. *Halfway Houses: Community Centered Correction and Treatment*. Lexington, MA: D. C. Heath, 1970.

Latessa, Edward J., Lori Brusman Lovins, and P. Smith. *Follow-Up Evaluation of Ohio's Community Based Correctional Facility and Halfway House Programs—Outcome Study*. Cincinnati, OH: Center for Criminal Justice Research, University of Cincinnati, 2010.

Lowenkamp, C. T. and E. J. Latessa. *Evaluation of Ohio's Halfway Houses and Community-Based Correctional Facilities*. Cincinnati, OH: University of Cincinnati, 2002.

Petersilia, J. *Probation and Felon Offenders*. Washington, DC: U.S. Department of Justice, 1985.

President's Commission on Law Enforcement and Administration of Justice. *Taskforce Report: Corrections*. Washington, DC: U.S. Government Printing Office, 1967.

Rush, G. E. *The Dictionary of Criminal Justice*, 3rd ed. Guilford, CT: Dushkin, 1991.

HARE PSYCHOPATHY CHECKLIST

Psychopathy, or the disorder of empathy, is a developmental disorder characterized by high levels of instrumental antisocial behavior. The disorder is usually diagnosed by high scores on psychodiagnostic tools. The Antisocial Process Screening Device (APSD) is deployed for assessing psychopathic tendencies in childhood and adolescence, and the Psychopathy Checklist (PCL) is used for assessing adults. The instrument for adults was later published as the Psychopathy Checklist–Revised (PCL–R). PCL–R consists of 20 items (PCL contained 22 items). Each item in the newer version is scored on a three-point (0, 1, and 2) scale. A score of 0 signifies nonapplicability, 1 stands for somewhat applicable, and 2 signifies full applicability. PCL–R can be used in diverse settings (such as institutions, detention centers, and community and forensic psychiatric hospitals). Psychopaths score between 30 and 40, whereas typical individuals score between 0 and 5.

Factor analyses of behaviors rated on PCL–R reveal two independent factors: (1) an emotion dysfunction factor and (2) an antisocial behavior factor. Socioeconomic status and IQ are found to be correlated with scores on the antisocial factor, but neither is associated with scores on the emotion dysfunction factor. This happens because the scores on the emotion dysfunction factor seem to be determined by different influences from those that determine the scores on the antisocial behavior factor. Furthermore, scores on the antisocial behavior factor decline with age, but scores on the emotion dysfunction factor remain constant. The scale robustly predicts institutional adjustment, community violence among prisoners, reoffense rates, and treatment response.

The 20 traits assessed by the PCL–R scale are as follows:

Factor 1:

- Glib/superficial charm or the tendency to be charming, slick, and verbally facile
- Grandiose or a grossly inflated self-worth
- Pathological lying
- Cunning and manipulative tendencies
- Lack of remorse or guilt
- Shallow affect or superficial emotional responsiveness
- Callous attitude and lack of empathy
- Failure to accept responsibility for one's own actions

Factor 2:

- Prone toward boredom or the need for stimulation
- Parasitic dependence or lifestyle
- Poor control of behavior
- Promiscuous sexual activity
- Early onset of behavior problems (usually before 13 years of age)
- Lack of realistic long-term goal planning
- Impulsivity
- Irresponsibility
- Juvenile delinquency
- Revocation of conditional release

Traits not associated with either factor:

- Criminal versatility
- Numerous short-term marital relations

Factors 1 and 2 are highly correlated with each other, and this high correlation is indicative of a single underlying disorder. However, research has failed to provide support for the two-factor model in female samples, even though Factor 1 scores have been more important in measuring psychopathy in women. Furthermore, Factor 1 has been correlated with low empathy, low anxiety, low suicide risk, and low stress reaction, combined with high scores

The Hare Psychopathy Checklist–Revised is a diagnostic tool used to assess psychopathy and antisocial behavior. An individual's socioeconomic status and intelligence level have been correlated with antisocial traits. (Photos.com)

on scales of well-being and achievement. On the other hand, scores on Factor 2 have been correlated with sensation seeking, social deviance, high risk of suicide, and low socioeconomic status. A recent edition of PCL–R lists four factors covering the 20 traits.

Limitations of the Psychopathy Checklist

The PCL–R was aimed at representing 16 defining criteria of psychopathy initially identified by H. Cleckley in 1941, but it diverges considerably and skips nine features identified by Cleckley. This leads to speculations that PCL–R lacks an organized theoretical framework.

The cutoff separating psychopathic individuals from typicals has also invited controversy. The probability that actual psychopaths will be identified as psychopaths is .72, whereas the probability that nonpsychopaths will be identified as nonpsychopaths is .93, with this cutoff score.

An aggregate of scores on both the factors may not be an ideal approach to predicting violence. Consider a case in which two individuals both obtain high scores on the scale, but the first individual scores high because of high scores on Factor 1 and the second individual scores high because of high scores on Factor 2. The two assessed individuals may have varying probabilities to indulge in criminal behavior, because Factor 2 scores predict criminal behavior more effectively.

Finally, it is important to note that the forensic samples employed are usually from North America and Canada. The correlations between impulsive behavior and the psychopathy construct differ between African Americans and Anglo-Americans.

Neha Khetrapal
Macquarie University

See also Juvenile and Youth Offenders; Offender Needs; Offender Risks; Offenders With Mental Illness

Further Readings

Cleckley, H. *The Mask of Sanity*. St. Louis, MO: Mosby, 1941.

Cooke, D. J. and C. Michie. "Refining the Construct of Psychopathy: Towards a Hierarchical Model." *Psychological Assessment*, v.13 (2001).

Frick, P. J. and R. D. Hare. *The Antisocial Process Screening Device*. Toronto, ON: Multi-Health Systems, 2001.

Hare, R. D. *The Hare Psychopathy Checklist*, 2nd ed. Toronto, ON: Multi-Health Systems, 2003.

Hare, R. D. *The Hare Psychopathy Checklist–Revised*. Toronto, ON: Multi-Health Systems, 1991.

Hare, R. D. "A Research Scale for the Assessment of Psychopathy in Criminal Populations." *Personality and Individual Differences*, v.1 (1980).

Hare, R. D. *Without Conscience: The Disturbing World of the Psychopaths Among Us*. New York: Guilford Press, 1993.

Khetrapal, N. "SPAARS Approach: Implications for Psychopathy." *Poiesis and Praxis: International Journal of Technology Assessment and Ethics of Science*, v.6/3 (2008).

Kosson, D. S., S. S. Smith, and J. P. Newman. "Evaluating the Construct Validity of Psychopathy in Black and White Male Inmates: Three Preliminary Studies." *Journal of Abnormal Psychology*, 99 (1990).

HISTORY OF COMMUNITY CORRECTIONS

The current system of corrections in the United States emerged in the 20th century as an institution designed to incarcerate offenders, deter offenders from future crimes, and transform offenders into law-abiding citizens. However, for much of European-American history, punishment was the sole means of corrections, and little or no attention was given to the idea of deterrence or rehabilitation. The rehabilitation model emerged within the system of community corrections, which operates using a diverse array of programs and sanctions allowing offenders to serve out sentences within a community setting instead of a correctional institution. This essay explores the evolution of community corrections and the pathways through which the rehabilitative model advanced from abstract to concrete philosophies of crime and punishment.

Crime and Punishment

During the Middle Ages, punishments were gruesome affairs constructed mainly for revenge and retribution. Individuals accused of the act of heresy, for example, were tortured using an instrument called the heretic's fork. Heresy constitutes a denial of faith as defined by the Catholic Church, which implies that people of the period were not allowed to question church leaders or church doctrine regardless of the abstract nature of such doctrine. Individuals who did were considered heretics and therefore subjected to the heretic's fork. The instrument, which looks much like a modern dinner fork, was strapped to the neck by a belt and positioned under the soft pallet of the chin and the sternum. The accused was then bound to a pole with the fork in position. The accused was forced to stand for several hours while attempting to hold the head up straight. Once the accused was exhausted, the head would fall forward, and the fork would puncture the heart.

By the 14th and 15th centuries, definitions of crime and punishment had become so distorted that the state began to arrest people for the crime of witchcraft. This period, which is also known as the "burning season," eventually left several towns and villages empty of human life. Some individuals considered themselves practitioners of the dark arts. Given that many definitions of crime were grounded in superstition and mysticism, any act construed as witchcraft would be grounds for arrest.

Individuals who practiced early forms of holistic medicine fell under suspicion as well. In an attempt to ground the horror of witch burning, advice books of the times served to justify the charges and inevitable punishment. Yet despite the publication of books such as the *Malleus Maleficarum* (1486) of Heinrich Kramer and James Sprenger—which provided intricate details describing the cause, arrest, torture, and execution of witches—no human being was ever proven capable of flying on a broom, casting impotency spells that actually work, controlling thunder and lightning, communicating with or raising the dead, or vanishing into thin air. These activities are veritably impossible for humans to accomplish, yet thousands, mostly women, were arrested, tortured, burned at the stake, drowned, hanged, strangled, or otherwise murdered for being guilty of a crime they could not have committed.

By the 17th and 18th centuries, acts of public torture and execution had slowed to some degree, yet the definitive structure of crime remained somewhat abstract. Prior to 1820, for example, pickpockets were routinely sentenced to death by hanging. Pickpockets are individuals, usually male, who are highly skilled thieves who commit acts of larceny-theft by picking the pockets of unsuspecting victims. This crime was hardly worthy of the death penalty. Nevertheless, to ensure that the punishment had the

desired effect, authorities gathered large crowds to witness the execution.

It is interesting to note, however, that hangings and executions in general seldom had the desired effect. These events often evolved into social events more akin to entertainment than to methods of deterring people from committing crime. Musicians, acrobats, and court jesters entertained the crowd; food and strong drink were served; and a good time was had by all. The spectacle of punishment, in short, had a reverse, or negative, effect on the human psyche. Instead of manifesting as a deterrent to crime, the population en masse became more desensitized to the punishment, no matter how gruesome. Ironically, these violent executions drew great numbers of predators, including pickpockets and thieves. The authorities thought they could frighten an entire population into subservience and silence. In reality, the spectacle had little effect on criminal behavior, and crimes thrived.

The decline of public torture accompanied the advent of capitalism, which introduced a new market economy into European society. Up to this point, the social structure was organized around an agrarian order whereby people, mostly peasants, lived in communal arrangements and shared the goods and services made available through specialization and the individual objectification of labor. Within this order everyone worked for the common good, and individual identities were shaped by the land on which people worked for generations. Allegiance was given to the noble or lord, who owned or managed the land and who protected his people under a system of paternalism. The agrarian order declined, however, as the capitalist doctrine of private property gave rise to a new system of landownership, which had an impact on the manner in which survival was sustained among the peasant class. People who had worked the land were displaced from their homes and herded into small urban communities, where they were forced to live in close proximity with people with whom they previously had no association. As time progressed, relationships became more depersonalized and interpersonal ties that at one time bound people together dissipated.

Furthermore, the means whereby personal survival was attained under the old order changed. Much-needed goods and services, which were previously negotiated through a system of trade and barter, came to be administered through a new system of surplus exchange. This is where money or rare instruments of value, such as gold, were exchanged for a product of equal or lesser value. The problem in this exchange method, particularly for the peasant class, who were used to the agrarian method of payment, was that they had no means of participating in the market economy. Therefore, the growing disjunction between goods and services, and the money needed to attain them, may have had a significant impact on the way new survival strategies were developed. Without the means to take care of basic needs such as food and shelter, many people may have turned to crime as the only means of surviving.

With survival at stake for thousands, it is inevitable that crime rates spiraled out of control, particularly as people struggled to survive in an environment that was alien to their former way of life. Moreover, these new urban communities, which were experiencing a rapid growth cycle, were now overcrowded with people struggling to adapt to a new social order without the benefit of an institution charged with enforcing order. Without a functioning system of enforcement in place, criminal activity spiraled out of control. Therefore, the pressure to develop an institution designed specifically for the purpose of crime control increased.

Around this period, Italian jurist and economist Cesare Beccaria (1738–94) questioned the efficacy of torture as a legitimate form of punishment. This challenge is articulated in his publication of *On Crimes and Punishments* (1764), which became the cornerstone of the classical school of criminology. According to Beccaria, for punishment to serve as a deterrent to crime, it must (1) be dictated by law, (2) be proportionate to the crime committed, and (3) be certain, swift, and open to the public. These characteristics of punishment evolved into deterrence theory, which stands as one of the principal doctrines shaping modern studies of criminal justice.

Another figure during this period was Jeremy Bentham (1748–1832), an English philosopher, who proposed that criminal behavior was caused by the pleasure/pain principle, which is a calculation that a prospective offender makes when deciding whether or not to commit a crime. For example, if the potential for pleasure from the crime is higher than the risk of being caught and punished, then the potential for the crime to occur increases, and vice versa. Bentham set forth this theory in his *Principles*

of Morals and Legislation (1789), which became a major contribution to the classical school of criminology. Bentham was also responsible for the philosophy of utilitarianism, an ethical doctrine that focused on punishment as an essential element of social control.

Both Beccaria and Bentham believed that criminal behavior is the result of rational and conscious choices, which makes criminals responsible for their actions. Likewise, appropriate forms of punishment would deter future acts of crime. In short, the definitive structure of crime and punishment introduced through the classical school had a significant impact on the philosophy shaping a new institution of crime and control in Europe and America. It was not long, however, before a contravening school emerged to challenge the classical approach.

The positivist school of criminology challenged the prevailing concept of the thinking criminal with the concept of determinism, which proposes that criminal behavior is the product of biological, psychological, and social forces that emerge outside human control. The person best known for this work is Cesare Lombroso (1835–1909), the father of modern criminology.

Lombroso, who considered himself a criminal anthropologist, was one of the first researchers to apply the scientific method to the study of crime. The term *biological determinism* underscores his belief that criminal behavior is determined by the biology and genetics of the offender. In this sense, criminals are atavistic in nature, throwbacks to earlier periods of human evolution who suffer from inferior genetic traits. Lombroso may not have realized it at the time, but this thinking, and its emphasis on race, had a devastating impact on the development of a modern system of criminal justice and crime control.

Nevertheless, the positivist school played a significant role in reshaping the definitive structure of crime and punishment. Although the emphasis on the criminal offender gave room for future challenges to the theories and methods of biological determinism, the emphasis was on treatment as the key element in deterring offenders from future crimes. Lombroso proposed that treatment had to be drawn from a proven scientific method, with greater emphasis on the causes relationships that create crime. Furthermore, proponents of the positive school were staunch supporters of the rehabilitation model.

Community Corrections

By the 19th and 20th centuries, the rehabilitation model had emerged within the system of community corrections, which operated using a diverse array of programs and sanctions that allowed offenders to serve out sentences within a community setting instead of a correctional institution. This system is based on the rehabilitation and reintegration models, which are both grounded in the belief that criminals can be reformed with punishment as well as treatment. The most common systems of community corrections are probation and parole, which also have their origins in European-American history.

Probation

The purpose of probation is to provide the offender with a chance to rehabilitate outside the prison system. The term *probation* is derived from the Latin word meaning "to prove"; it is up to the probationer to prove himself or herself worthy of the opportunity to reintegrate into society. Probation is a privilege, not a right.

The origins of probation can be traced to the Middle Ages, when, according to English law, the right of rehabilitation was reserved for the nobility. Royal pardons, judicial reprieve, and the Church provided sanctuary and protection from harsh punishment for those of the privileged class. By the 14th century, the practice of "binding over for good behavior" was used as a temporary release in order to give the offender time to secure a pardon or lesser sentence. This practice of "binding over" was adopted by American courts, which had the power to suspend sentences and offer the accused the right of "recognizance" or obligation to the court.

The first case of probation in the United States can be traced to Massachusetts in 1830. At the time, a woman named Jerusha Chase pleaded guilty of theft in a house. Before she could be sentenced, several of her friends pleaded to the court to let her go, and the court obliged. The court released her on her own recognizance with the caveat that she return when requested. She was acquitted of a separate charge of larceny in 1831 but found guilty of the original charge. This case, which set the precedent for probation in the United States, also set the standard that the offender must not reoffend during the period of obligation.

The practice of probation evolved with the help of John Augustus (1784/1785–1859), a shoemaker,

who in 1841 asked a judge in a Boston court if the court would allow him to sponsor a man charged as a drunkard rather than sentence him to prison. The judge obliged, and Augustus, under the obligation imposed by the court, returned in the required three weeks with a reformed offender who was clean, sober, and rehabilitated. This episode arguably launched not only the system of probation in America but also the career of probation officer. Augustine served in this context for the next 18 years as a volunteer of the court. During this period, he established the methodology for the background investigation, which flourishes today as a common practice in probation. After Augustus's death in 1859, the first probation statute was passed in the state of Massachusetts and later throughout the United States.

In the American colony of Pennsylvania, the Quakers rejected the idea of torture and severe punishment, instead embracing the idea of reform as the principal means of deterrence. Led by William Penn, in 1682 the Quakers proposed a new penal code, grounded in concept of "utilitarianism," which they used as an ethical means of punishment. Thus the Great Law, as it became known, constituted a watershed moment in the growth of institutional and community corrections in America.

Parole

The purpose of parole is to provide offenders with the opportunity to leave prison after serving a portion of their sentence. The term *parole* is derived from the French word for "word" or "promise," which implies that the inmate is invested in a standard of honor once released into the population. Like probation, parole is a privilege, not a right. Parole involves a reward system developed for inmates who have adhered to prison rules and controlled their behavior to the satisfaction of prison authorities. Today it is also seen as a method of supervision that is more cost-effective than prison, does not compromise the safety of others in society, and at the same time transforms the offender into a law-abiding citizen.

There are two forms of parole. There is mandatory release, which the law requires after the prisoner has served a specified time, and discretionary release, whereby a parole board is charged with the responsibility of determining at which time the prisoner has met eligibility requirements for release. Although parole boards are responsible for setting the criteria for release, they are also given the authority to deny freedom if the rules of release are violated.

The development of the modern parole system is attributed to Alexander Maconochie, who was the governor of Norfolk Island prison, located off the coast of Australia. Around 1840, he instituted a system of "earned release credits" that were used to determine the length of time inmates had to serve before release from prison. Conditions in the penal colony in Australia at the time were such that inmates serving life sentences were subjected to brutal forms of punishment that did little to deter future acts of criminal behavior. Maconochie introduced a prison structure whereby newly incarcerated prisoners were first imprisoned under strict supervision and then, through conditional release, could achieve freedom. The movement from one stage to the other determined the number of credits inmates could earn, which then served as the calculus for parole. Walter Crofton, who was the governor of Ireland's prison system, instituted a similar model in 1854, in which "tickets of leave" served as the determinate factor for early release.

The system of parole in the United States began in 1867 with the establishment of the Department of Justice, which then created the first statute designed to administer the early release of inmates who demonstrated good behavior while incarcerated. The first American administrator to use this system is Zebulon Brockway, a Michigan penologist who is credited with devised a method of "good-time credits," which he instituted in 1876 at Elmira Reformatory in New York. Brockway employed a two-stage strategy for managing prison populations and preparing inmates for early release. The system was based on "indeterminate sentencing," whereby the release date is set by a governing body, coupled with "parole supervision." Brockway's ideas reflected the philosophy of the day, which held that criminals could be changed and that the supervision of the prisoner should be individualized. In keeping with current thinking, the sole purpose and function of community corrections is to transform offenders into law-abiding citizens.

Tracy Faye Tolbert
California State University, Long Beach

See also Attitudes and Myths About Punishment; Community Corrections Acts; Community Corrections and Sanctions; Community Corrections as an Add-On to Imprisonment; Community Corrections as an Alternative to Imprisonment; Philosophy of Community Corrections; Probation: Early Termination; Probation and Parole: Intensive Supervision

Further Readings

Anderson, David A. "The Deterrence Hypothesis and Picking Pockets at the Pickpocket's Hanging." *American Law and Economics Review*, v.4/2 (2002).

Barstow, Anne Llewellyn. *Witchcraze: A New History of the European Witch Hunts*. San Francisco: HarperCollins, 1994.

Beccaria, Cesare. *On Crimes and Punishments*, Henry Paolucci, trans. New York: Bobbs-Merrill, 1963.

Bentham, Jeremy. *An Introduction to the Principles of Morals and Legislation*. Oxford: Clarendon Press, 1823.

Clear, Todd R., George F. Cole, and Michael D. Reisig. *American Corrections*, 9th ed. Belmont, CA: Thomson Wadsworth, 2010.

Gottschalk, Marie. *The Prison and the Gallows: The Politics of Mass Incarceration in America*. New York: Cambridge University Press, 2006.

Grinnel, Frank W. "The Common Law History of Probation." *Journal of Law and Criminology*, v.32 (May/June 1941).

Kramer, Heinrich and James Sprenger. *The Malleus Maleficarum*. 1489. Reprint, Montague Sommers, trans. New York: Dover Publications, 1971.

Little Hoover Commission. *Back to the Community: Safe and Sound Parole Policies*. Sacramento, CA: Author, 2003.

Masters, Ruth E. *Counseling Criminal Justice Offenders*, 2nd ed. Thousand Oaks, CA: Sage, 2004.

Masters, Ruth E. et al. *CJ: Realities and Challenges*. New York: McGraw-Hill, 2010.

McLynn, Frank. *Crime and Punishment in Eighteenth-Century England*. New York: Routledge, 1989.

Montgomery, Reid, Jr. and Steven Dillingham. *Probation and Parole in Practice*. Cincinnati, OH: Pilgrimage, 1983.

Shaw, George Bernard. *The Crime of Imprisonment*. New York: Philosophical Library, 1946.

Trevor-Roper, H. R. *The European Witch-Craze of the Sixteenth and Seventeenth Centuries and Other Essays*. New York: HarperCollins, 1967.

Whitehead, Philip and Roger Statham. *The History of Probation: Politics, Power and Cultural Change 1876–2005*. Crayford, UK: Shaw and Sons, 2006.

Wilson, James Q. and Joan Petersilia. *Crime: Public Policies for Crime Control*. Oakland, CA: Institute for Contemporary Studies Press, 2002.

Wright, Bradley R. E., Avshalom Caspi, Terrie E. Moffitt, and Ray Paternoster. "Does the Perceived Risk of Punishment Deter Criminally Prone Individuals? Rational Choice, Self-Control, and Crime." *Journal of Research in Crime and Delinquency*, v.41/2 (May 2004).

HOME CONFINEMENT AND HOUSE ARREST

Home confinement and house arrest trace their origins to the New Testament of the Bible, to text (estimated to have been written between 59 and 63 C.E.) that describes the arrest of the apostle Paul for his teachings; he was ordered to remain in his residence, with a military guard ensuring that he would not leave. In the 17th century, the scientist Galileo was similarly arrested during the final years of his life for his writings and views. In contemporary community corrections, home confinement and house arrest reemerged around the 1970s and 1980s. Many states seeking to divert nonviolent offenders from costly jail and prison beds, to reduce jail and prison overcrowding, and to strengthen existing community-based sanctions such as probation or parole—yet still preserve punitive sanctions—implemented home confinement sanctions.

Today, home confinement and house arrest are part of both the pretrial and postconviction management of offenders. The terms *home confinement* and *house arrest* are often used interchangeably and allow the offender to serve a portion of his sentence within his or her residence. These sentencing and supervision options serve various goals and objectives in offender management and public safety. Home confinement and house arrest involve the offender's being restricted to his or her residence with minimal (if any) opportunity to leave the residence as an alternative to incarceration. The offender is not allowed to leave the residence, with the exception of approved absences, such as going to work, school, or treatment programs. These options also serve to punish the offender, protect the community from the offender, and serve as a supervision resource for community corrections and court personnel to monitor and enforce an offender's compliance with the terms and conditions of a release or suspended sentence.

In terms of pretrial management, offenders are given the opportunity to be released from custody while they are awaiting trial, often through posting bail and being placed on house arrest. Judges have the discretion to order various terms and conditions with which the offender must comply as a condition of release; noncompliance may result in the revocation of an offender's release. Often home confinement and house arrest are ordered, thereby allowing the offender to be closely supervised while awaiting trial, yet reducing jail overcrowding.

In terms of postconviction management, home confinement and house arrest are intermediate sanctions (punishments that are "midway" between community-based corrections and institutional corrections). They are often a condition of an offender's probation or parole supervision.

Home confinement and house arrest are often coupled with electronic monitoring. Electronic monitoring involves the use of electronic equipment to verify that the offender is complying with the terms and conditions of home confinement by transmitting a signal designating when an offender leaves or enters a residence or when the equipment has been tampered with. If an offender leaves the residence without permission or fails to return to the residence at the time designated by the court or probation officer, or if the offender removes or damages the equipment, an alarm signal is transmitted to an offsite monitoring location, which in turn notifies the probation officer or other professional designated to supervise the offender on house arrest. Whether the signal is for a nonapproved leave, a late return, or damaged equipment, the supervising officer or professional must then travel to the residence or otherwise attempt to locate the offender. In the 1960s, psychologist Ralph Schwitzgebel created an electronic collar that, among many tasks, could track an offender's movements. While tested and patented, the device was never used in corrections. New Mexico judge Jack Love, inspired by an *Amazing Spider-Man* comic, is often credited as the catalyst behind electronic monitoring (sometimes referred to as electronic house arrest). In the comic, one of the superhero's enemies created a tracking device that would allow him to track Spider-Man's whereabouts at all times. After an unsuccessful attempt to get the New Mexico Department of Corrections to use tracking devices that were already in use to track animals, Judge Love was able to get an engineer to create a tracking device that could be used on offenders. The device would register an alarm.

Judge Love sentenced the first person to electronic monitoring in 1983. Today, electronic monitoring can include satellite tracking of offenders (using the technology employed in global positioning devices used in motor vehicles). Electronic monitoring makes home confinement more practical in terms of monitoring the offender's compliance with the terms and conditions of house arrest.

Home confinement and house arrest have shown minimal promise in terms of effectiveness in reducing recidivism. Citing the findings of James Bonta, S. Wallace-Capretta, and J. Rooney, William D. Burrell, and Robert S. Gable (the latter the brother of Schwitzgebel) posit that home confinement, particularly electronic monitoring, is consistent with other forms of community-based supervision options in terms of reducing recidivism. However, Burrell and Gable, citing the findings of K. G. Padgett, W. D. Bales, and T. G. Blomberg, contend that while home confinement does little to impact recidivism, it does show promise for somewhat suppressing criminal behavior during the period of time the offender is being monitored or serving a period of home confinement. According to Burrell and Gable, the effectiveness of home confinement and house arrest is rooted in the fact that these sanctions communicate the seriousness of an offense and force an offender to think about his or her offending behaviors.

Nicola Davis Bivens
Johnson C. Smith University

See also Probation: Early Termination; Probation and Parole: Intensive Supervision

Further Readings

Burrell, William D. and Robert S. Gable. "From B. F. Skinner to Spiderman to Martha Stewart: The Past, Present and Future of Electronic Monitoring of Offenders." *Journal of Offender Rehabilitation*, v.46/3–4 (January 2008).

Caputo, Gail A. *Intermediate Sanctions in Corrections*. Denton: University of North Texas Press, 2004.

Champion, Dean J. *Probation, Parole, and Community Corrections*, 6th ed. Upper Saddle River, NJ: Pearson Prentice Hall, 2007.

Schmalleger, Frank and John Ortiz Smykla. *Corrections in the 21st Century*, 5th ed. Boston: McGraw-Hill, 2009.

Siegal, Larry and Clemens Bartollas. *Corrections Today*. Belmont, CA: Thomson Wadsworth, 2011.

HUMANITARIANISM

Humanitarianism is an ethical provision of kindness, benevolence, concern, empathy, moral obligation, and sympathy present in social welfare and spiritual pursuits. It holds that humane treatment of others should be given to everyone, irrespective of who they are or what they have done, because they are valued as human beings who have the capacity for goodness. The term *humanitarianism* is used as shorthand to encompass a complex set of currents of thought, actions, and institutions between which the boundaries are unclear. Essentially, humanitarianism embodies a view that all people have the right to receive respect, not because of what they do but simply because they exist.

History traces the belief in human equality back to the Greeks and Aristotle, This view was born out of a sense of spiritual connectedness with others. As a practical approach, it is often attributed to Christian influence, especially the parable of the Good Samaritan, whose actions demonstrated the belief that is important to help others because of their interconnectedness with other human beings and the divine. Although spiritual beliefs may vary from one religious group to another, the concept of humanitarianism unifies all religions.

The importance of humanitarian treatment of others was encouraged during the European period of the Enlightenment (in the 17th and 18th centuries). Political and social philosophers of this period advanced the idea that humanity could be improved through legal reforms and changes in social structure. This view was espoused by those who believed that the penal and criminal justice systems were harsh and that people who broke the law still deserved fair and kind treatment. The humanitarian ideal embraced the value of active compassion and had a compelling influence on social action from the 18th century on. It is also an important component in the delivery of human rights.

Humane treatment of others gained attention during the 1800s, when progressive individuals and religious leaders felt that criminals, the mentally ill, and others whose behavior was defined as "wrong" were being maltreated. It was generally believed that the behavior of such individuals—variously labeled as bad, sinners, deviants, deficient, or simply not thinking properly—could be changed through punishment and coercion. During this period of rising industrialism, humanitarians were appalled at the resulting brutality of the criminal justice system, not to mention the common exploitation of non-offending laborers, and how those in authority could sometimes justify torture as a necessary means to achieve social goals. Humanitarianism thus was a larger social movement—encompassing the need to reform not only the penal system but also labor (including slavery, which many regarded as immoral). Later manifestations of early 19th-century humanitarianism, for example, included abolitionism (which led to Emancipation during the Civil War) and the civil rights movement of the mid-20th century. Humanitarianism also laid the foundation for fair treatment of women, children, the elderly, the disabled, and those who were physically or mentally ill.

It is interesting that humane treatment of animals was ensconced in law before the humane treatment of children was. One case in the 1870s involved Mary Ellen, an abused little girl in New York. Few laws were in place to protect her; she received assistance from authorities only by arguing that she was a member of the animal kingdom and therefore should be protected under the jurisdiction of the Society for the Prevention of Cruelty to Animals, which had worked for animal protection laws.

Humanitarianism assumes that human values are important, that the way humans treat one another is important, and that certain human behaviors are appropriate while others are inappropriate. Humane

The humanitarian ideal established in the 18th century was an important foundation for the awareness of the need to treat the elderly, disabled, and physically or mentally ill population with care and compassion. (Photos.com)

action is rights-based and designed to alleviate suffering and save lives. Humanitarians value peace and actions that lead toward equality and prosperity. However, despite the many worthy ideals that humanitarians claim are important, there are limits to humanitarianism and compassion, especially toward those who have "wronged" others.

The issue of humanitarianism in criminal justice has shifted focus in recent years. Criminals were treated in ways that could be defined as inhumane over the long course of history, but today just and humane treatment of offenders has become more prominent. The issue of humane treatment has also arisen with respect to illegal immigrants, alleged terrorists, prisoners, and other marginalized peoples. The criminal justice community is confronted with the issue of how to protect the community while constructing an image and policies that are perceived by offenders as humane and just.

Nonetheless, there has been a resurgence in the impetus to penalize offenders. Some experts argue that American society is using the criminal justice system to scapegoat people who are perceived to be offenders, such as Muslims who have no relationship to terrorism. Crime and criminals may serve as scapegoats for anxieties about the solidarity of society. Indeed, many of the public's major crime obsessions of the 1980s and 1990s have proven to be gross distortions of reality; reports of child kidnapping, ritual satanic abuse, murders by serial killers, juvenile violence, and crack cocaine addiction have turned out to be more fiction than fact. Unfortunately, these fears have led to hyperpunitive strategies for dealing with crime, such as stripping judges their discretionary decisions in mitigating punishment. As a result, the interests of offenders have often become submerged in a discourse that focuses almost exclusively on the suffering of crime victims. This has resulted in a form of reasoning that sets one form of human welfare in opposition to another.

Yvonne Vissing
Salem State University

See also Cultural Competence; Ethics of Community-Based Sanctions; Faith-Based Initiatives; Punishment; Restitution; Restorative Justice; Sanctuary

Further Readings

American Immigration Law Center. "Humanitarian Parole." http://www.ailc.com/services/humanparole/index.htm (Accessed July 2011).

Andreopoulos, G. and L. Lantsman. "The Evolving Discourse on Human Protection." *Criminal Justice Ethics*, v.29/2 (August 2010).

Donini, Antonio. "The Far Side: The Meta Functions of Humanitarianism in a Globalised World." *Disasters*, v.34, supp. 2 (April 2010).

Gierycz, Dorota. "From Humanitarian Intervention to Responsibility to Protect." *Criminal Justice Ethics*, v.29 (August 2010).

Janzekovic, J. "Humanitarianism: What It Is and How to Get Some." *Social Alternatives*, v.24/3 (Third Quarter 2005).

Kennedy, J. "Crime, Punishment, and Perception." *Human Rights: Journal of the Section of Individual Rights and Responsibilities*, v.29/2 (Spring 2002).

Rieffer-Flanagan, B. "Is Neutral Humanitarianism Dead?" *Human Rights Quarterly*, v.31/4 (November 2009).

U.S. Citizenship and Immigration Services. "Humanitarian Parole." http://www.uscis.gov/portal/site/uscis/menuitem .eb1d4c2a3e5b9ac89243c6a7543f6d1a/?vgnextoid=accc 3e4d77d73210VgnVCM100000082ca60aRCRD&vgne xtchannel=accc3e4d77d73210VgnVCM100000082ca60 aRCRD (Accessed July 2011).

Watkins, S. A. "The Mary Ellen Myth: Correcting Child Welfare History." *Social Work*, v.35/6 (1990).

INDETERMINATE SENTENCING

Indeterminate sentencing emerged during the reformatory era, around 1870. It is based on the philosophies of individual justice and rehabilitation. Under indeterminate sentencing, there is no fixed time that an offender must spend in prison; rather, judges have much discretion in determining the appropriate minimum and maximum sentence. For instance, the judge may impose a sentence of three to five years for a drug offender. Depending on the behavior of the offender while in prison, he or she may be released after three years or later. How soon an offender is released is typically decided by a parole board, and upon return into the community the offender will be under supervision for a certain period of time.

In the United States, indeterminate sentencing was the prevailing philosophy between 1930 and 1970 in all state and federal jurisdictions. During the mid-1970s, the attitude toward offenders and rehabilitation changed. High crime and recidivism rates, disparities in sentencing, lack of fairness, and the belief that offenders were not punished harshly enough led to a rise of "tough-on-crime" policies and a shift toward determinate sentencing, such as mandatory sentence terms based on standard guidelines and "three-strikes" laws. There are, however, signs of a recent shift toward rehabilitation. This shift is reflected in the increasing popularity of drug courts and other programs that divert offenders away from prison and into treatment and rehabilitation programs. One of the main reasons appears to be the great increase in the cost associated with growing incarceration rates and overcrowding in prisons and jails.

Origins and Underlying Ideas

The idea of indeterminate sentencing emerged during the reformatory era of corrections, around 1870, with the meeting of the National Congress on Penitentiary and Reformatory Discipline in Cincinnati, Ohio. At the time, American penologists had become disillusioned with the idea that penitentiaries, such as Eastern State Penitentiary and Auburn Prison, focused on penitence, solitude, and silence as the best ways to correct the behavior of criminals. Many inmates in these penitentiaries became mentally ill because of the inhumane conditions they were forced to suffer.

As a result of the failure of the penitentiary, penologists started to emphasize reformation of offenders via rehabilitation and treatment. The underlying principles of indeterminate sentencing are individualized justice and rehabilitation of offenders. Individualized justice is based on the assumption that every offender is different and deserves a treatment and punishment tailored to his or her specific needs. Thus, judges consider a variety of offense and offender characteristics in their sentencing decisions. Proponents of indeterminate sentencing believe that offenders can be rehabilitated because they are malleable and, with the appropriate treatment, can become productive members of society.

Indeterminate Sentencing as the Prevailing Correctional Theory

Between 1930 and 1970, all states and the federal government used indeterminate sentencing laws. Under these laws, the states and the federal government established maximum (and sometimes minimum) sentences for certain offenses. Judges have wide discretion to decide whether to impose fines, probation, jail, prison, or community service as long as they did not impose a sentence greater than the predetermined maximum. Offenders sentenced to prison can apply for early release after serving a certain minimum sentence.

The decision of whether to grant early release is made by parole boards, which typically consist of experts on human behavior, including psychologists, criminologists, and judges. The idea is that the judgment of whether an offender is ready to return to society should be made by those who have the necessary knowledge and insight to assess the offender's state of mind. The time needed for rehabilitation varies for different offenders. Thus, offenders should be released from prison based on their behavior while incarcerated. Inmates who behave well and make progress toward becoming law-abiding citizens are released early. Offenders who continue to be obnoxious and troublesome and engage in criminal behaviors while incarcerated serve longer sentences, because they need more time to be reformed. It is believed that the possibility of early release will encourage rehabilitation because inmates will actively participate in treatment and vocational programs as a sign of reformation. The possibility of early release also offers some advantages for the prison administration, because offenders can earn "good time" for good behavior. Thus, there is an incentive to refrain from violent and disobedient behavior and comply with the prison rules. Similarly, there is an incentive to complete necessary work in the prison, including meal preparation, cleaning, and making reparations.

The Fall of Indeterminate Sentencing

During the mid-1970s, the popularity of indeterminate sentencing and rehabilitation began to decline for several reasons, including high crime and recidivism rates, disparities in sentencing, lack of fairness, and the belief that offenders were released from prison too early.

First, research demonstrated that there were apparent inconsistencies in sentencing. Critics argued that judges had too much discretion and that the lack of guidelines and standards led to great sentencing disparities; for example, two offenders who had committed the same crime under similar circumstances might receive very different punishments, depending on the judge. This type of arbitrary decision making was believed to increase discrimination against minorities and poor people. As a solution, many states implemented mandatory minimum sentencing guidelines that were meant to ensure that similar offenses receive similar punishments.

Second, during the mid-1970s the public became more concerned about high crime rates, especially high rates of violent crime and recidivism. Rehabilitation did not appear to be a solution to the crime problem. This perception by the public was supported by the 1974 report "What Works? Questions and Answers About Prison Reform," by Robert Martinson, in which he concluded that "nothing works" and that offenders cannot be rehabilitated. As a result of the growing criticism, politicians began to lobby for tough-on-crime policies. Many states and the federal government implemented sentencing laws that included predetermined minimum and maximum sentences. Under the new determinate sentencing laws, judges have much less discretion in their sentencing decisions and have less opportunity to take the circumstances of the crime and the offender into consideration when rendering decisions.

Third, people became dissatisfied with the parole system, which enabled parole boards to grant prisoners early release into the community. The public believed that the sentences served by offenders were too short and that punishment overall was too lenient. Another concern was that even the most vicious offenders had a chance of being released from prison and that offenders might manipulate parole boards into believing that they had changed and were no longer a danger to society. In response to these criticisms, many states implemented truth-in-sentencing laws that required offenders to serve at least 85 percent of their sentence. Additionally, 14 states and the federal government no longer use parole boards.

Even though one of the main arguments for determinate sentencing was to decrease sentencing disparities and the crime rate, especially the violent crime rate, research demonstrates that these goals have not been accomplished. Also, one of the unintended consequences of these laws is the great increase in the incarceration rate—from 330,000 in 1970 to 2.1 million in 2005—creating substantial strain on the corrections system and state budgets.

Current Status of Indeterminate Sentencing

Some evidence suggests a current shift toward rehabilitation and the reconsideration of indeterminate sentencing. In the past 20 years, drug courts have become increasingly popular as an alternative to incarceration for nonviolent drug offenders, but also increasingly for more serious offenders. Between 1989 and 2007, the number of drug courts grew from one (in Miami, Florida) to 2,140 throughout the country. Several other problem-solving courts have been established across the country. The problem-solving courts include driving while intoxicated (DWI) courts, co-occurring disorder courts, mental health courts, and community courts. The purpose of these problem-solving courts is to rehabilitate offenders in the community and help them to stay out of prison. Additionally, three-strikes laws have been abandoned by all states (with the exception of California), mainly because of the high cost and overcrowding issues. Several initiatives around the country provide better rehabilitation and reintegration programs for offenders. For instance, many states divert nonviolent offenders into restoration programs that emphasize paying the community back for the damages incurred by the crime. These restorative justice programs are also increasingly available to serious offenders.

Janine Kremling
California State University, San Bernardino

See also Determinate Sentencing; Irish Marks System; Probation and Parole: Intensive Supervision

Further Readings

Blumstein, Alfred. *Research on Sentencing: The Search for Reform*. Washington, DC: National Academy Press, 1983.

Huddleston, C. West, Douglas B. Marlowe, and Rachel Casebolt. *Painting the Current Picture: A National Report Card on Drug Courts and Other Problem-Solving Court Programs in the United States*. Alexandria, VA: National Drug Court Institute, 2008.

Lynch, Michael J. *Big Prisons, Big Dreams: Crime and the Failure of the American Penal System*. New Brunswick, NJ: Rutgers University Press, 2006.

Martinson, Robert. "What Works? Questions and Answers About Prison Reform." *The Public Interest*, v.35 (Spring 1974).

Miller, Martin B. "Indeterminate Sentence Paradigm: Resocialization or Social Control." *Issues in Criminology*, v.7/2 (1972).

Tonry, Michael. *Reconsidering Indeterminate and Structured Sentencing*. Washington, DC: U.S. Department of Justice, Office of Justice Statistics, National Institute of Justice, 1999.

U.S. Bureau of Justice Statistics, Council Panel on Sentencing Research, Office of Justice Assistance. *1996 National Survey of State Sentencing Structures*. http://www.ncjrs.gov/pdffiles/169270.pdf (Accessed January 2011).

Zalman, Marvin. "Rise and Fall of Indeterminate Sentencing." *Wayne Law Review*, v.24/1 (1977).

INVESTIGATIVE REPORTS

An investigative report or report of investigation (ROI) is the documentation of the collection of a series of facts and findings that answer the question posed as the purpose of the investigation. Contained in the report are the who, what, when, where, how, and why that tell the reader what happened. The key to writing an investigative report is ensuring that the writer, author, or investigator remains as neutral as possible while recording the facts. Investigative reports are often associated with the criminal justice system but are used throughout society, in one form or another, to meet the needs of businesses, agencies, governments, and other entities. Traditionally recorded on paper, the reports can also be videotaped or in digital formats; such formats, however, are more often used for interview reports than for a full ROI. An investigative report must be clear, concise, accurate, readable, reliable, thorough, and logically organized.

The format of the investigative report will depend on why the report is being prepared, that is, the question or issue that the report must resolve. Such reports can be intended to document a variety of events, such as a homicide, robbery, accident, fraud, rape, theft, drug sale, malpractice concern, securities violation, health study, whistleblower retaliation, or terrorist event. They can also document the results of a background investigation for a security clearance or access request, or a pre-sentence investigation (PSI) ordered of a probation officer by a trial judge to aid in sentencing of a convicted defendant.

Whether it relates to a criminal, civil, or administrative issue, the substance of the report will reflect documented facts that are relevant to the underlying purpose of the investigation. Different agencies, departments, and organizations may have their own formats or special software that must be used. The Nuclear Regulatory Commission, Drug Enforcement Administration, Federal Bureau of Investigation, and Immigration and Customs Enforcement, all federal agencies, use different forms and formats; those report styles will also differ among most state, county, and local police departments. However, all these agencies expect that the reports will contain reliable, relevant, and material facts.

Who, What, When, Where, and How

If the purpose of the investigation is to solve a criminal or civil case, then it is particularly important that

Investigative reports provide investigators and law enforcement with a detailed and reliable format to document facts related to criminal and civil cases. (Photos.com)

an investigative report answer the basic questions of who, what, when, where, and how—or, to state it another way, Who did what to whom, on what date (when), at what location (where), and how (in what manner)?

"Why" something happened may not be a conclusion that the report can reach, nor may the answer to that question be relevant to prove a criminal violation. In cases such as a first-degree murder (premeditated murder), why the person committed the murder is not an element of the crime, although if known, it makes proving or solving the crime much easier. Why a crime is committed may emerge as the result of a confession by the offender, or it may represent a conclusion drawn as the result of extensive direct and circumstantial evidence. Although a judge will not include the "why" in his or her instructions to the jury regarding the elements of the crime, it is likely that each person on the jury will want to know and will likely wish to discuss this point during jury deliberations. When the investigative report can provide sufficient facts from which to draw conclusions concerning the "why," it will help the jury to reach a verdict.

Formatting an Investigative Report

Every department, agency, company, or person requesting an investigation will most likely have a report format that best suits that entity's needs. Formats vary as a matter of preference as well as several practical factors, having to do with the following:

- Subject matter (background, security clearance, criminal/civil violation, and so forth)
- Purpose (whether related to pre-sentence, parole violation, prosecution, grand jury, or other issues)
- Type (criminal, civil, or administrative)
- Requestor (prosecutor, attorney, administrative official, private business, insurance company, court/judge, intelligence agency or national security, and so forth)
- Statute
- The proactive or reactive nature of the report

This list is not intended to be all-inclusive, but rather to present the reader with an understanding that numerous factors that can affect exactly how a report is structured and what purpose it is to serve. It is important to remember that the report format is intended to serve the needs of the person requesting the report. One basic format for an ROI includes the following subsections:

- Executive Summary (synopsis)
- Table of Contents
- List of Interviews (which may include a separate list of subjects or some other notation next to the names of the individuals; it may also be expanded to include a "List of Documents Reviewed")
- Details of the Investigation (a narrative of the facts)
  - Purpose of the Investigation (the issue or question to be addressed)
    - Legal Citations (listing the appropriate statutes and other legal documentation)
  - Methodology (depending on the nature of the investigation)
  - Background
  - Facts of the Investigation (the exact format of which will depend on the purpose or issue that is the subject of the investigation)
    - Based on a chronology of events
    - Based on the witness statements about the event
    - Based on the scientific or financial data
    - Based on the statute or methodology driving the investigation
    - There may also be a separate section within the Facts Section that lists or separates law enforcement, third agency, grand jury, or classified material
- Conclusion (although not all investigations ask for a conclusion by the investigator)
- Recommendations (if requested; this may address a programmatic remedy to ensure that this problem does not recur and whether to forward the matter for collection, prosecution, administrative action, or the like)
- List of Exhibits (to include copies and where the originals are located, whether laboratories, computer thumb drives, vaults, courts, case file cabinets, or elsewhere)

White-collar crime reports may be more complicated and include segments not associated with a simple "purse snatching" (robbery), drug sale, or theft of a television from a home (burglary). However, even the simplest crime may be complicated by such factors as the number of people involved, the value of the items, the sophistication

of the plot, scientific evidence, computer records, the length of time to complete the crime (or series of crimes), or the length of time to capture the suspects, just to mention only a few factors.

Generally, the Executive Summary or Synopsis should be no longer than a page in length. The summary will include a brief statement of the purpose of the investigation, as well as the conclusion. It will also include a brief factual statement to support the conclusion. The report will pass through several hands, and many people will never get past the summary. Therefore, a well-written summary will ensure that the report actually gets to those who need to use the results of the report.

The Details of the Investigation, or body, of the report should start with an opening paragraph that outlines the nature and purpose of the investigation. This could be an allegation of wrongdoing—such as a theft, copyright infringement, conspiracy, civil rights violation, or any number of other crimes—and a list of the code violations. If the purpose does not relate to the violation of a law, then this should be clearly stated; for example, the report may be a PSI or a background investigation. If there are multiple alleged crimes or issues, then each crime or issue will be stated or listed and a conclusion written to address that issue.

The author of the report may either attach exhibits to the original report, as appropriate, or list the location of each original exhibit. This is particularly important if the exhibits are in evidence lockers, laboratories, or even with other agencies. It is important to remember that interview reports are generally not considered evidence but rather a recording or notes of an interview, and thus hearsay. The person interviewed during the investigation will provide the testimonial evidence in court or at the hearing. Clearly, in a criminal proceeding a defendant has the right to confront an accuser and an interview report is not sufficient; one cannot cross-examine paper or a videotape.

The last thing that the investigator will do is sign the report.

Conclusion

The investigation report format described above is but one example of many formats that are used. Some departments use preprinted forms that permit the investigator or officer to check boxes and fill in blank areas. Others have their investigative reports preformatted on a computer screen so that the investigator can simply provide the requested information by completing the template or respond by answering a series of questions, the responses to which will be included in a completed report compiled by the software. In the end, the data points in the sample format listed above and the underlying issues (who, what, when, where, how, and, perhaps, why) will all have to be answered in some manner.

Keith Gregory Logan
Kutztown University of Pennsylvania

See also Case Management; Pre-Sentence Investigation Reports

Further Readings

Biggs, Michael. *Just the Facts: Investigative Report Writing.* Upper Saddle River, NJ: Prentice Hall, 2000.
Michael, A. S. *The Best Police Report Writing Book.* Seattle, WA: CreateSpace, 2009.
Rutledge, Devallis. *The New Police Report Manual.* Belmont, CA: Wadsworth, 2000.

IRISH MARKS SYSTEM

In the mid-1800s, Great Britain was overwhelmed by a crisis in corrections. The American colonies, having declared their independence in 1776, were henceforth unavailable for use as a destination for transported prisoners. Using Australia as a substitute thereafter proved to be expensive and ineffective. Hulks—disease-ridden, decommissioned ships moored in various rivers—were abandoned as a housing option as simply inhumane and archaic. These circumstances created fertile conditions for limited experimentation at various sites within Britain's far-flung colonial empire. Such was the case when Captain Alexander Maconochie tried something new at Norfolk Island in the South Pacific in 1854, a "marks system." Closer to home, Walter Crofton, employing some of the same concepts, is often credited with instituting reforms in Ireland in 1854. Accordingly, the system embodying these changes became known within the correctional community as the Irish marks system.

Some experts believe that Major Joshua Jebb, surveyor-general of the overall British prison system, was the real author of some of these reforms. In any case, he certainly allowed the "progressive stage system" to come into existence. The stages differed in various colonial locations and eventually led to their modification and use under the aegis of Zebulon Brockway, in the post–Civil War era at the Elmira Reformatory in upstate New York.

The Progressive Stage System in British Prisons

In the initial stage of the progressive stage system, the prisoner would be kept in isolation, as in the penitentiary system. In that earlier system, it was hoped that the prisoner would see the error of his ways, be suitably penitent, and reform. The prisoner would, however—even if suitably chastened and saved through the grace of God—remain in solitary for the remainder of his sentence. Although favored by religious leaders, this system was expensive, and the isolation imposed led to insanity among inmates.

Under the progressive stage system, isolation would last for only a short time. In the second stage, inmates would be sent to conduct public works within prison settings. It was thought that keeping prisoners employed would both build character and serve the public weal.

The final stage contained the most controversial elements of the day, involving a form of conditional release, or "ticket of leave," that was based on institutional adjustment. That is, prisoners who behaved well while in prison were released early. After some understandable hesitancy and opposition from the public and politicians, this policy, which gave prison administrators increased control over inmates, was implemented.

Maconochie on Norfolk Island

Alexander Maconochie, in a report written while secretary to the colonial governor of Van Diemen's Land (modern Tasmania), condemned convict labor as brutalizing in general. His critique, similar to that of American abolitionists, was that this system, in which absolute power was exercised by the few over the many, created a grossly distorted and pathological social nexus. His solution, which was to be implemented in isolated Norfolk Island, was a marks system. Convicts earned good marks for good behavior and lost them for violating rules.

Maconochie believed that this system would lead to the end of physical punishment and coercion.

Prisoners would learn to work cooperatively, and the cultivation of this cooperative behavior would ease their reentry into general society. Isolation and punishment should occur at the beginning of the sentence, but the avowed purpose of imprisonment should be reformative, not retributive.

Maconochie's tenure at Norfolk Island was marked by an assertion of moral power and the use of charismatic reform: He inspired prisoners and jailers through expressions and manifestations of faith in the possibility of reform. Ultimately, his reforms were seen as too radical and permissive, and he was recalled.

Crofton in Ireland

Maconochie's scheme, though rejected in England, was adopted by Walter Crofton in Ireland. An act of Parliament in 1853 gave prisons flexibility in instituting ticket-of-leave provisions in the final stage of imprisonment. In the late 1850s, Crofton developed the Irish convict system, which refined the earlier progressive stage system.

Convicts in Ireland initially served a stage of solitary confinement for eight or nine months—the length was dependent on the prisoner's conduct while imprisoned. He was kept on reduced rations for the first half of the sentence, then allowed more food and the opportunity to work. Work had formerly been punitive and meaningless to prisoners, which, reformers reasoned, had made prisoners work-averse. Under the new system, it was hoped that the prisoner would come to associate increased rations with productive labor and, in general, see work in a different light. To that end, work was regarded as a privilege, and idleness, with its associated boredom and monotony, would be avoided by prisoners. This insight was seen as the first stage of reform.

The second stage made heavy use of the marks system, as had been used by Maconochie. Inmates could accumulate positive points through work, school, and obedience. Additionally, there were four stages within the second stage through which the prisoner could advance or be demoted. When he ascended by dint of accumulation of marks though three classes to the A, or advanced, class, the prisoner could work and be kept apart from other inmates. It was assumed that he had learned the habits of self-discipline and hard work and was now ready for life in society. The reform was to be individual and

was not as collective an approach as that used by Maconochie. Those who did not advance beyond this stage simply were held until their sentences ended.

Those who completed the requisite number of months in the A class were sent to the final stage, or "intermediate prisons." Crofton saw this type of facility as a device to allow the inmate to gain more skills and get accustomed to the demands of freedom and dealing with discretionary time. Convicts who misbehaved or who could not deal with the lack of control were sent back to prison. In the intermediate prison stage, minimal coercion and restraint were used; officers were unarmed. It was essential to demonstrate that the convict was trusted and that the community at large could see him as worthy of trust and eventual freedom.

After a period of individualized attention and successful program participation, the prisoner was eligible for conditional release on a ticket of license. He had to register with police and maintain stability of residence. He would be subject to bimonthly supervisory visits by prison authorities. In addition, he was to work and not keep company with criminal associates. Being unemployed was grounds for revocation of the ticket of license. If a licensee's behavior was marginal, the totality of circumstances would be considered and the revocation was not finalized. Crofton noted that these individuals initially objected to such intensive supervision but learned to accept it as a reality of conditional release. Once the period of his original sentence had expired, the convict was fully restored to freedom in the community and was free of any lingering inherent supervisory disabilities.

Crofton attempted to make prison realistically reformative; punishment alone simply did not deter. The point of the Irish system was to make the prisoner view labor and self-restraint positively. The underlying assumption informing this regime was that the positive changes the inmate made within the progressive stages would inform his postconfinement adjustment and would remain lifelong features of his behavior and personality. Crofton knew that to effect such changes would take time and would not invariably meet with success.

This system was received with enthusiasm from progressive penologists in both Europe and America, and its primary import is that it served as a model and inspiration for the American reformatory movement. Early manifestations included the Ohio State Reform Farm, established in 1857, and, in Massachusetts, advocacy for reforms like those used by Crofton were sought in 1865. Dr. E. Wines was in correspondence with Crofton in the 1860s and clearly saw the Irish system as a model for reform in the United States. The reform-minded prison congress of 1870 in Cincinnati (the National Congress on Penitentiary and Reformatory Discipline) heard speakers specifically recommend that the Irish system, in its entirely, be adopted in the United States. Zebulon Brockway, speaking at the meeting, advocated similar ideas and called for holding prisoners in prison until reformed. The congress called for a society in which reform was the specific purpose of punishment. This notion was at odds with the idea that punishment existed primarily for the infliction of misery on the convict.

Ultimately, the 1870 congress and the spirit of reform it engendered led directly to the establishment of New York's Elmira Reformatory. This prison's regime contained a progressive stage system, conditional release, and supervised parole, which was an American adaptation of the ticket of license. It focused on work and institutional adjustment as prerequisites for obtaining parole. Thus, the reformatory movement set the foundation for American corrections into the first years of the 20th century.

Francis Frederick Hawley
Western Carolina University

See also Brockway, Zebulon; Elmira System; Maconochie, Alexander; Probation and Parole: Intensive Supervision

Further Readings

Abadinsky, Howard. *Probation and Parole: Theory and Practice*, 11th ed. Upper Saddle River, NJ: Pearson, 2011.

Morris, N. and D. Rothman. *The Oxford History of the Prison: The Practice of Punishment in Western Society.* New York: Oxford University Press, 1995.

Putney, S. and G. Putney. "Origins of the Reformatory." *Journal of Criminal Law, Criminology, and Police Science*, v.53/4 (December 1962).

Job Satisfaction in Community Corrections

While studies measuring job satisfaction for probation and parole officers, along with other persons working in community corrections, are infrequent, this issue has grown in importance (and interest) as the demand for and use of community-based corrections programs has expanded in recent decades. To be sure, much more research is needed in order for us to understand fully how to provide community corrections personnel with greater opportunities for experiencing satisfaction in their work environments. What we do know, however, is that job satisfaction is strongly related to performance expectations, access to needed resources and support, job-related stress, and burnout and turnover. Unfortunately, it appears that community corrections personnel, similar to police and prison staff, suffer from the same kinds of stress-related issues (such as dangerous clientele, lack of resources, and lack of community support) that tend to be associated with lower levels of job satisfaction and higher levels of burnout and turnover. The remainder of this entry highlights what we know about these issues and provides suggestions for enhancing retention and satisfaction for community corrections personnel in the future.

Factors Related to Decreased Levels of Job Satisfaction

Many components of community corrections work have been identified in the literature as contributing to increased stress, burnout, and turnover for employees. One particular issue is the role dichotomy that is inherent in most positions in community corrections agencies. Specifically, researchers and experts point to the fact that community corrections officers are tasked, fundamentally, with both assisting offenders and, at the same time, monitoring and supervising their behaviors in order to detect any criminal behavior for which the offender may be punished. Essentially, community corrections personnel are required to act, often at the same time, as both rehabilitative mentors and law-enforcement officers. This dual expectation is difficult for many officers and is compounded by the fact that many community corrections officers (and the agencies in which they work) lack access to the resources necessary for successfully fulfilling either of these core expectations. Generally, community corrections personnel and agencies do not have the financial (and other) resources needed to meet basic job-related responsibilities (such as optimal caseload assignments, adequate supervision/monitoring tools, and providing appropriate client referrals to community-based programs).

Additional factors that contribute to reduced job satisfaction, higher levels of stress, and increased burnout and turnover include the poor public image of community corrections personnel, low pay and benefits, low morale, and low and/or ambiguous recruitment standards, training protocols, and promotion criteria and opportunities. More specifically, some studies reveal that the public holds a negative view of community corrections programs that extends to the persons who hold positions in these agencies. Furthermore, the public tends to have

Community corrections workers and those in law enforcement suffer from the same stress-related issues, leading to lower levels of job satisfaction and higher levels of employee burnout. (Photos.com)

unclear and/or unrealistic expectations regarding the objectives of community corrections and the related responsibilities and tasks of community corrections officers (such as public safety, supervision, and social work roles).

By far one of the most commonly cited frustrations of community corrections personnel is the low pay. It is likely that low compensation rates, by themselves, increase stress and turnover. It is also quite likely that low pay serves to aggravate the other irritations discussed above (such as role conflict, role ambiguity, and poor public image) and that low pay and benefits, by themselves, would not be such a critical issue were it not for these other nuisances. Finally, unclear and less-than-optimal recruitment, training, retention, and promotion protocol and opportunities are additional work-related stressors that contribute to lower levels of job satisfaction for community corrections professionals. Most community corrections agencies now require that employees have a four-year college degree (although some still require only a high school diploma or two-year degree). Training protocol, retention strategies (if any), and promotion criteria and opportunities vary greatly across agencies and programs, leading to frustration and dissatisfaction on the part of community corrections personnel. However, the National Probation and Parole Association, along with other reports and works, increasingly recommends greater standardization in these areas in order to provide clearer guidelines and expectations for those employed in community corrections.

Increasing Job Satisfaction in Community Corrections Work

There appear to be several promising strategies for increasing reports and feelings of job satisfaction for those working in community corrections, most of which relate to clearly defining what community corrections work is and should be. To respond to the much discussed issue of role conflict and ambiguity, as well as the related problem of lack of sufficient resources, clarifying and prioritizing the primary objectives of community corrections programs is critical. Once clearly defined objectives are established, several other commonly cited negative issues may be more easily dealt with as well, such as improving recruitment, training, and retention strategies to correspond more closely to these stated objectives.

Additionally, a more clearly defined role for community corrections personnel may also lend itself to greater improvements and specificity in pay grades (commensurate with performance and experience) and promotion criteria and opportunities (for those meeting or exceeding objectives and goals).

Finally, enhancing the professional image of community corrections workers, through more clearly established goals and expectations, may also contribute to enhancing the public's understanding of and support for the efforts of these individuals.

Noelle E. Fearn
Saint Louis University

See also Parole Officers; Probation Officers; Probation Officers: Job Stress

Further Readings

Alarid, Leanne Fiftal and Rolando V. del Carmen. *Community-Based Corrections*, 8th ed. Belmont, CA: Thomson Wadsworth, 2011.

Cronin, Brian E., Ralph Kiessig, and William D. Sprenkle. "Recruiting and Retaining Staff Through Culture Change." *Corrections Today*, v.70/4 (August 2008).

Latessa, Edward J. and Paula Smith. *Corrections in the Community*, 4th ed. Cincinnati, OH: Anderson/ LexisNexis, 2007.

Lee, Won-Jae, James R. Phelps, and Dan Richard Beto. "Turnover Intention Among Probation Officers and Direct Care Staff: A Statewide Study." *Federal Probation*, v.73/3 (2009).

Shaner, L. "Recruitment and Retention in Community Corrections: Report From a National Institution of Corrections Conference." *Federal Probation*, v.58/4 (1994).

Slate, Risdon N., Terry L. Wells, and W. Wesley Johnson. "Opening the Manager's Door: State Probation Officer Stress and Perceptions of Participation in Workplace Decision Making." *Crime and Delinquency*, v.49/4 (2003).

Whiteacre, Kevin W. "Measuring Job Satisfaction and Stress at a Community Corrections Center: An Evidence-Based Study." *Corrections Today*, v.68/3 (June 2006).

Juvenile Aftercare

Juvenile aftercare consists of supervisory and support services provided to delinquent youth upon their release from residential facilities or juvenile correctional institutions. Aftercare programs and post-release supervision are designed to facilitate a smooth transition from facility to community during a period of time in which young people are particularly likely to encounter problems that place them at risk for reoffending. In preparation for this reintegration phase, aftercare workers and juvenile probation officers help youths become reenrolled in school, work with their families to ensure that there is a stable home environment, connect youths to employment opportunities, and locate other community-based services that fit their clients' individual needs. In addition to these support services, supervisory services require young people to meet conditions of their release, such as paying restitution, participating in community service activities, and passing regular drug screens.

Almost 100,000 youths are released from residential facilities each year, though this number is decreasing as youth confinement is utilized less frequently since the height of the juvenile get-tough-on-crime movement in the 1990s. Using the Census of Juveniles in Residential Placement, it is possible to develop an empirical portrait of returning youths. The vast majority are male (88 percent) and racial or ethnic minorities (39 percent are black, non-Hispanic and 17 percent are Hispanic). Nearly one fifth (19 percent) are 14 years old or younger, and more than one third (36 percent) are age 17 or older. The majority of returning youths (60 percent) were committed to facilities for nonviolent offenses such as property crimes (31 percent), drug offenses (9 percent), public order offenses (15 percent), and status offenses (4 percent). Although the average length of stay inside a facility is less than one year, most returning youths have been court-ordered to multiple facilities and spend a significant portion of their adolescence incarcerated.

Failure during the reentry phase is common. As many as two thirds of returning youths are rearrested, and up to one third are reincarcerated within a few years after release. Less than a third are either in school or employed a year after leaving facilities. Because young people inside residential placements present greater needs than their adolescent counterparts, they are an especially vulnerable population upon release. They encounter significant challenges in terms of family stability, educational attainment, mental health, and substance abuse. The majority (70 percent) are raised in (and return to) single-parent homes, and just over half (52 percent) have at least one family member who has also been incarcerated. These young people are also particularly likely to have children of their own already. Incarcerated youths are more than twice as likely as the general population of U.S. adolescents not to have completed the eighth grade (58 percent versus 24 percent). By the time they reach young adulthood, only 12 percent of formerly incarcerated youths have a high school diploma or general equivalency diploma (GED), compared to 74 percent of their cohorts. Special education needs are found among this population at three to five times the rate of other young people of the same age. One in eight is identified as mentally retarded. The majority of incarcerated youths have some sort of mental health problem, including disruptive behavioral disorders, anxiety disorders, or mood disorders. These young people are significantly more likely than their adolescent counterparts to consider, attempt, or complete suicide. Finally, they are also more likely to report being involved with drugs and/or alcohol and at earlier ages than are adolescents in the general population.

As some of these statistics suggest, youth reentry presents unique challenges for aftercare programs, because young people encounter a "dual transition" from facility to community and from adolescence into early adulthood. Developmental psychologists have recently exposed the harmful effects of youth confinement on the developmental processes leading adolescents into healthy adult roles. They point out that the successful transition to adulthood requires young people to develop a sense of social competence and mastery over their worlds, autonomy from parents and others, and self-direction.

These building blocks of maturity are compromised when young people are sent to residential placements and cut off from the support of positive role models and community institutions such as schools, resulting in what some have referred to as "arrested development." Months and even years spent inside juvenile correctional facilities can put youth "off time" in reaching important markers of adulthood, such as high school graduation or establishing a stable employment history. For all these reasons, youth reentry experts contend that aftercare programs need to employ a developmental lens, ensuring that services are targeted toward each youth's individual developmental level (regardless of chronological age).

Historically, juvenile aftercare services have been underfunded and have received little emphasis in most jurisdictions. Recently, several scholars have attempted to link youth reentry to the scholarly and funding momentum generated by research on adult prisoner reentry, with some success. Two initiatives, the Department of Justice's Going Home: Serious and Violent Offender Reentry Program and the collaborative Young Offender Initiative: Reentry Grant Program, represent the federal government's commitment to strengthening community-based efforts to improve outcomes for youths returning home from residential facilities.

Although rigorous evaluations of aftercare programs are rare, a number of programs have generated evidence of their promise for reducing recidivism among returning youths. One such model is the Intensive Aftercare Program (IAP), targeted toward high-risk offenders. At the heart of IAP is an overarching case management system that coordinates services of multiple providers from the point of admission to a residential facility through the end of the reentry phase. The five components of this case management system are (1) risk assessment and classification, (2) individualized case planning that incorporates family and community perspectives, (3) a mix of intensive surveillance and services, (4) a balance of graduated incentives and consequences, and (5) links with community resources and social networks. The IAP model has been implemented in Colorado, Nevada, and Virginia, where process evaluations have demonstrated some implementation problems but otherwise positive results. Outcome evaluations have found promising results for the Starr Commonwealth program in Michigan, Ohio, and Indiana; Multidimensional Treatment

Foster Care (MTFC) in Oregon; Specialized Foster Care for High Risk Delinquents in North Dakota; the Philadelphia Intensive Aftercare Project; the Thomas O'Farrell Youth Center in Maryland; Bethesda Day Treatment Center in Pennsylvania; the Florida Environmental Institute (FEI); Project CRAFT (Community Restitution and Apprenticeship Focused Training), implemented in multiple states; and the GROWTH program for high-risk female offenders in Alabama.

Research on these and other programs has identified a number of overarching principles that guide successful aftercare efforts and that are derived from the literature on successful delinquency interventions. This body of research, which has generated several meta-evaluations of delinquency treatment programs, has identified the following characteristics most commonly present in successful interventions. These efforts target specific dynamic and criminogenic characteristics, implement a plan that is strictly adhered to by trained personnel, require staff and offenders to make frequent contact, use cognitive and behavioral treatments, and target offenders with the highest risk of recidivism.

Across jurisdictions, juvenile aftercare may be delivered by aftercare workers (often in private, contracted aftercare programs), juvenile probation officers, or some combination of the two. Because juvenile probation departments are also often responsible for screening cases for processing, making detention decisions, preparing pre-sentence investigations, and supervising youths who have been adjudicated delinquent but remain in the community, reentry services are often delivered through a dedicated aftercare unit. In contrast to adult parole, aftercare probation combines supervision with support or treatment strategies.

In sum, heightened attention to the high rate of failure among delinquent youths upon their return to the community and the potentially damaging developmental effects of confinement in juvenile institutions have spurred increased funding for comprehensive aftercare programs and high-quality evaluations designed to identify what works in juvenile aftercare. Although much more needs to be done, we now know more about how best to address the many challenges presented by youthful offenders returning from residential facilities.

Jamie J. Fader
State University of New York, Albany

See also Actuarial Risk Assessment; Conditions of Community Corrections; Juvenile and Youth Offenders; Offender Supervision; Probation and Parole: Intensive Supervision; Residential Programs for Juveniles; Serious and Violent Offender Reentry Initiative; "What Works" Approach and Evidence-Based Practices

Further Readings

Armstrong, Troy L., ed. *Intensive Interventions With High-Risk Youths: Promising Approaches in Juvenile Probation and Parole.* Monsey, NY: Criminal Justice Press, 1991.

Byrnes, Michelle, Daniel Macallair, and Andrea D. Shorter. *Aftercare as Afterthought: Reentry and the California Youth Authority.* San Francisco: Center on Juvenile and Criminal Justice, 2002.

Gies, Steve V. *Aftercare Services.* Washington, DC: U.S. Department of Justice, Office of Justice Programs, Office of Juvenile Justice and Delinquency Prevention, 2000.

Snyder, Howard N. "An Empirical Portrait of the Youth Reentry Population." *Youth Violence and Juvenile Justice*, v.2/1 (2004).

Steinberg, Laurence, He Len Chung, and Michelle Little. "Reentry of Young Offenders From the Justice System: A Developmental Perspective." *Youth Violence and Juvenile Justice*, v.2/1 (2004).

JUVENILE AND YOUTH OFFENDERS

Treatment of youths in noninstitutional settings has become increasingly popular over the last 40 years because of policy changes, shifting perspectives on delinquency, and increasing financial strains at all levels of government. Community-based programs handle youths at all phases of processing, from preadjudicatory detention to postadjudication services. These programs include diversion, probation, specialized courts, day treatment, group homes, foster care, restorative justice, community service, and restitution, as well as prevention and intervention initiatives. While many see significant benefits in providing these choices, others view the broadening of preadjudicatory alternatives as widening the net within which youths can be snared.

Contextual History

From their inception, juvenile courts in the United States have been guided by the philosophy of *parens patriae*, meaning the state has the responsibility and obligation to act as parent to dependent, neglected, incorrigible, or delinquent youths. Benevolent judges and court personnel implement treatment decisions that foster the development of troubled youths into healthy adults. A basic assumption of court personnel is that youths require structured environments; structured environments enhance social, academic, and vocational skills and provide appropriate supervision, guidance, and discipline. It is believed that such programs help develop hardworking individuals who ultimately become productive citizens. Consistent with the social beliefs of the early juvenile court environment, personnel referred youths to residential institutions to receive such supportive foundations.

However, a shift occurred with regard to what constitutes an appropriate setting for providing benevolent treatment. Early institutions housed youths of all types, including those who were dependent or neglected, status offenders, and delinquents (criminal law-violating youths). Dependent and neglected youths are children who lack parental care. Status offenders are runaways, curfew violators, truants, or incorrigibles and appear to lack adequate supervision. Exposure of these nondelinquent youths to criminally involved youths was potentially harmful. Many believed that these early institutions were criminogenic, essentially training grounds for criminal behavior.

During the 1970s, Jerome Miller, commissioner of the Massachusetts Department of Youth Services, raised concerns regarding the placement of status offenders in institutions with delinquent youths. He argued that status offenders be treated in community-based settings. The effort to remove status offenders from institutions is known as deinstitutionalizing status offenders (DSO) and was the basis of the Office of Juvenile Justice and Delinquency Prevention Act of 1974 (OJJDP Act). Miller believed that the success of this initiative would be directly proportionate to the development of sufficient community-based alternatives to serve these youths.

Simultaneously, concerns began to arise about the disproportionate minority confinement (DMC) that existed in the juvenile justice system. This was an outgrowth of the OJJDP Act and its reauthorizations through the 1980s and 1990s. In 1992, the confinement focus expanded to include any

Early juvenile offender institutions housed neglected runaways, curfew violators, and truants and lacked the supervision needed to ensure a youth's well-being during his or her stay in custody. (Photos.com)

contact with law enforcement. Proponents of DMC initiatives showed that minority youths were overrepresented in the system's institutions and had significantly greater levels of contact across all decision points. The federal government mandated that states determine if DMC was present in their systems and required the development of a plan to address the problem.

These two policy initiatives, DSO and DMC, along with the belief that institutional care facilitated delinquency, have contributed to declining use of large institutions for juvenile treatment in favor of community-based alternatives. Community-based programming allows youths to maintain their ties with family, school, and community. Maintaining these ties supports and facilitates treatment and the transition and reintegration of youths back into the community upon program completion. Reports show that youths treated in community-based programs recidivate less than those institutionalized. Moreover, community-based care

costs substantially less than care in a large residential facility.

The American Correctional Association reports that the cost of institutional care averages approximately $88,000 per year nationally. The Justice Policy Institute reports that in 2007, 64,558 youths were in residential facilities at a cost of $5.7 billion. Two thirds of these youths came into the juvenile system as nonviolent offenders. A *New York Times* article reported that in 2010, New York State would spend $170 million on 21 juvenile institutions that would house fewer than 700 youths. Such newspaper coverage plays a significant role in shaping public views of the juvenile and criminal justice systems. Although citizens generally hold a belief that troubled youths deserve to be treated and rehabilitated, surveys show that an overwhelming majority do not believe that institutions are very successful. Evidence-based community alternatives with a proven record of success are a better investment of taxpayer dollars. Closing expensive facilities would have the added benefit for state and federal legislators of being responsive to constituents and allowing them to reduce the cost of treating juveniles in less expensive community-based programs.

Many states have realigned their budgets, allocating funds to local counties for community-based services from the savings accrued as the large facilities are closed. California, Illinois, New York, Ohio, Oregon, Rhode Island, and Washington have passed legislation redirecting funds saved by reduced use of institutions to local governments and organizations that provide alternative care at the community level. Further savings are obtained by using existing private agencies to offer some of the needed programming. This approach spreads resources further, representing a convergence of public and private dollars. Extant community organizations and programs can deliver services with funding augmented by public grant programs, reducing start-up costs, overhead, and ongoing facility maintenance.

In sum, community-based treatment appears to be more appropriate for nonviolent youths as well as some serious offenders and is more effective than traditional institutional placements. There is greater public support by citizens who are concerned with both youth crime and the cost of the care of juveniles needing services. Finally, the cost of care is less of a burden to taxpayer, state, and local communities.

Types of Programs

Community-based programs provide justice personnel with a variety of options that allow shorter-term custodial choices for processing and crafting treatment plans for youth. Preadjudicatory diversion is the least invasive approach that occurs with a youth. Upon review, law-enforcement officers or intake workers may essentially opt to remove the youth from the justice pipeline. This is what Miller envisioned with the DSO initiative, removing youths from the harm of formal juvenile court processing. There are three choices available to police and court officers when a youth comes to their attention: take no action, divert, and formal filing. Some have expressed concern with regard to the addition of diversion; youths who would previously have been sent home are now brought into a justice-related referral. These placements or referrals are known as net widening; they catch in the justice net youths who are marginally in need of intervention.

Youths coming into contact with the juvenile court are often processed informally, and even when they receive formal processing many are likely to be given some diversionary or community-based treatment program. Reportedly, even when informally processed, more than 50 percent of youths have some supervised outcome. The process of referral to a community-based program is often in the hands of an intake officer or juvenile officer. Of the youths who move forward in the court to formal case processing, nearly one third of the ones not found to be delinquent receive a supervised outcome.

Some youths previously detained in a juvenile facility while awaiting case processing are now diverted to alternatives to detention. The Annie E. Casey Foundation developed a program called the Juvenile Detention Alternatives Initiative (JDAI). Under JDAI, an assessment is made of the level of community threat a youth presents; if the threat level is low, an alternative is selected. These alternatives can include programs such as electronic monitoring, home detention, and evening reporting to ensure monitoring for community safety. One reason for the use of these alternatives is that detention was used punitively instead of ensuring appearance at hearings. Another reason was that research suggests detained youths will experience harsher outcomes when their cases are heard. Community-based processing has become more common across the United States, lowering the daily head counts at the nation's juvenile detention centers.

The youth court diversion program effectively metes out fair and firm punishments and has a low rate of recidivism. There are several models employed by youth courts, involving adult judges, youth judges, tribunals, and peer juries. While the deciding member of the court is the adult in the first of these models, the remaining court structures allow teenagers to hear and judge cases. Although it is not clear that the courts are successful in reducing recidivism, they enjoy support as a method of engaging young people in understanding the system and being accountable.

Diversion is viewed as a less costly and less stigmatizing process; however, there are indications that diversion is an entry point to having a juvenile record, since success or failure to complete the programs is monitored by court personnel or possibly probation officers. There are mixed findings regarding the effectiveness of diversion programming, which is expected given the wide variety of service providers and the lack of coordination among them. Research shows reductions in recidivism among diverted youths; however, other research shows no difference in the performance of diverted youths when compared to youths processed in traditional ways. There is no research reporting significantly worse performance. Finally, the argument has been made that diversion will improve when youth needs are appropriately matched to the programs to which they are referred.

Upon adjudication, the most common outcome is supervision under the jurisdiction of the juvenile probation officer. When supervision is recommended under the jurisdiction of the court or probation officer, various conditions and stipulations must be adhered to. Probation allows the youth to remain in the community, but he or she must meet the requirements or face custodial care. A youth will be required to meet with the officer as specified; follow all local, state, and federal laws; not possess firearms; remain in the local jurisdiction; attend school or work; and allow unannounced home visits by juvenile officers. Youths may also be referred to treatment programs based on risk and need assessments that identify their strengths and weaknesses.

The referrals may include programs such as school-based day treatment or alternative schools, attendance monitoring, drug treatment, aggression or violence prevention, work skills training, and restorative justice initiatives. Cases may be handled using less punitive and potentially harmful processing through youth or teen drug or gun courts. Youths may be required to attend gang suppression or intervention programs, drug programs, programs that offer academic and behavioral counseling, and family counseling. These programs may be privately or publicly managed.

Pros of Community-Based Programs

The juvenile court's primary function is to provide a response to troubled youths that enhances their transition to more successful development and life-course trajectories. Although some youths require severe sanctions and highly supervised treatment programs, many youths can be handled in less restrictive settings and programs without negative outcomes. Minimally, the latter group will do no worse than if they had been sent to a long-term treatment facility.

The use of the community-based programs also means that youths are not exposed to the full measure of the juvenile justice system and the negative stigma and labeling attached to such treatment. Without a formal finding, there is no official record of youthful indiscretion. With recent calls for the opening of juvenile records for purposes of handling cases in adult courts, not having a formal finding is a protection against the harm that a prior adjudication can have in such legal proceedings. The use of juvenile diversion programs also helps to maintain a youth's ties within the local community, which are often lost when a youth is placed in a long-term residential facility. Maintaining community ties allows work with families and schools to enhance adjustment within those institutions and provides an opportunity for a successful return home. Finally, the cost of community-based treatment is significantly less than institutional care, and in many instances the burden of cost is shared with the private sector. This savings may be appropriated to other social needs.

Cons of Community-Based Programs

Critics point out negative consequences associated with diversion for youth behavior and systemic

implications. It is suggested that one consequence of the use of diversion programs is that troubled youths will view the justice system as lenient. The failure to impose a punishment will obscure the seriousness of the circumstance in which they find themselves, and they will not comprehend the seriousness of becoming involved with the juvenile justice system. It is the mind-set of classical theorists that certain, swift, and proportionate punishment will extinguish delinquent behavior and deter such behavior in the future. It is believed that the failure of the system, therefore, is that the response does not help to deter juvenile crime.

Net widening is a significant concern. Diversion programs can lead to involving youths who previously would not have been selected to receive services. The inclusion of such youths in diversion services creates exposure to the social harm that program referral and involvement can bring. There is some degree of labeling and stigma associated with treatment referral. Additionally, the placement of a youth in an alternative program generates a record of the diversion; since the youth will not be repeatedly diverted, the court must know what the prior contact involved and whether or not it was successful. Hence, the desire to protect youths from harm may in fact expose them to some harm.

Summary

The use of community-based alternatives is a common practice at various stages of the juvenile justice process. These alternatives are utilized at the point of initial contact with police, at intake, during the initial court hearings, and following adjudication. They often include some form of supervision, such as electronic monitoring, home detention, appearances at reporting centers, meetings with court-appointed officials, or structured conditional probation. To complete the diversion process, youths may be required to participate in various counseling and treatment services.

There are mixed findings on the efficacy of community programs. However, evidence shows that some community-based programs produce improvements in the youth recidivism rates. More important, it is found that there are no poorer outcomes than there would be if youths were placed in facilities. The success or failure of community-based programs is also assessed in the context of cost. It can be argued the cost savings for community versus institutional care is an important consideration, lending support to community care when outcomes are at least no worse than those from institutional care. Ultimately, community-based programming represents a viable and less expensive alternative to custodial care in a long-term institution. With the concerns about the cost of treatment, the desire to maintain family and community ties, and efforts to reintegrate troubled youths back into the community, the use of these treatment alternatives will likely increase.

Norman A. White
Saint Louis University

See also Cook County Juvenile Court; Graduated Sanctions for Juvenile Offenders; Juvenile Aftercare; Juvenile Probation Officers; Predispositional Reports for Juveniles; Residential Programs for Juveniles; Teen Courts

Further Readings

Dembo, Richard, Jennifer Wareham, Thomas Chirikos, and James Schmeidler. "Economic Impact on the Justice System From Reductions in Diversion Program Funding." *Journal of Offender Rehabilitation*, v.41/3 (2005).

Mathur, Sarup R., Heather Griller Clark, and Naomi Schoenfeld. "Professional Development: A Capacity-Building Model for Juvenile Correctional Education Systems." *Journal of Correctional Education*, v.60/2 (2009).

Piquero, Alex and Laurence Steinberg. "Public Preferences for Rehabilitation Versus Incarceration of Juvenile Offenders." *Journal of Criminal Justice*, v.38/1 (2010).

Welsh, Wayne and Philip Harris. "Reducing Overrepresentation of Minorities in Juvenile Justice: Development of Community-Based Corrections." *Crime and Delinquency*, v.42/1 (1996).

JUVENILE PROBATION OFFICERS

Juvenile probation officers (JPOs) have been rightly called the workhorses of the juvenile justice system, because of the varied tasks that they are called to perform. Their jobs can include intake screening of cases for court, counseling, acting as a juvenile prosecutor or defense advocate, investigating a recently adjudicated delinquent and writing the predispositional report (PDR), and revoking the probation of a delinquent who has not fulfilled the conditions by which he or she has agreed to live. JPOs may be called upon to deal with volunteers for teen court or conduct home visits to check on the environment of a child taken into custody by the police. He or she may spend the day searching on the Internet for programs appropriate to the needs of a juvenile with unique issues or spend hours on the telephone doing much the same thing, talking with program directors and superintendents of juvenile facilities. It is the job of the JPO to know what programs exist, where they are located, and if they are available at any given time. The JPO may also be called upon to run group therapy sessions, anger management classes, classes in parenting for parents and guardians of a juvenile, and courses in drug treatment or prevention. In some states, JPOs serve as juvenile parole officers and oversee the aftercare of a juvenile who has been released from an institution. In some cases, they may even act as directors of halfway houses, restitution programs, or detention facilities (juvenile holding facilities or "jails"). As a juvenile court insider, the JPO has to work closely with judges, educating them tactfully regarding the newest developments and accepted practices in the juvenile justice field, and learning their idiosyncrasies with respect to dispositions. Finally, JPOs often get to supervise juvenile probationers in the field. This means that they go to the homes, schools, or workplaces of "delinquents" (those so labeled by the courts, that is, such as those who have been convicted in adult court) and investigate their progress, performance, and attitude. The job of a JPO is challenging and in most jurisdictions calls for a specialized degree in criminal justice, criminology, social work, or a related field. In order to advance beyond the lowest level, a master's degree is a necessity.

For a number of decades, JPOs have been focused on diversion efforts. These programs attempt to funnel the first-time or minor delinquent away from full court involvement and the effects of negative labeling that may occur there. Such efforts would normally begin at intake screening, when the JPO might conclude that a juvenile found with a marijuana joint in his pocket might benefit more from a drug resistance or substance abuse education program than from a formal juvenile court hearing. The JPO, acting as intake officer, would check openings and availability and then divert that youth to such a program. Upon successful conclusion of that program, the juvenile would have no record and would not have to go to court. However, if the youth chose not to participate, did not attend, or did not finish the prescribed course or treatment, he would return to the court and have an adjudication hearing. At that point, the youth is fully involved in the juvenile justice system.

There are many types of diversion programs, including anger management, substance abuse, parenting, gang resistance, and victim awareness programs, as well as programs aimed at building self-awareness and self-esteem. Some programs are aimed at sexually active teenage girls and involve providing sexual education to prevent pregnancy or further pregnancies; for those teenage girls who have had children, there are programs that teach effective parenting. Diversion programs may involve drug screening and often require school attendance. JPOs will also informally and individually counsel juveniles and perhaps also their parents or guardians and waive court hearings.

If a juvenile is adjudicated as delinquent, which is parallel to a conviction in adult criminal court, the JPO will usually be required to write a juvenile predispositional report (PDR). Using information gathered at intake, subsequently, and following the hearing, the JPO will conduct a thorough investigation covering the delinquent's social life, school performance, home life, and attitude toward the offense. Gang involvement or presence of a weapon will get special attention. At the conclusion of this process, the JPO will make certain recommendations based on the needs of the juvenile, the availability of treatment or services, and the judge's predisposition. This recommendation may in large part determine the juvenile's future in or out of the system. The JPO might recommend any of the many treatment modalities outlined earlier or might alternatively recommend incarceration or juvenile probation. Juvenile probation is a noncustodial status or process that occurs when a delinquent is released to the community in the care of his or her parents but has to submit to certain conditions, such as going to school, observing a curfew, refraining from alcohol and drug use, submitting to drug tests, accepting home visits, and desisting from involvement with gangs. The juvenile must also agree to visit a juvenile probation officer for status reports and counseling at certain intervals. Ideally, visits to the home by the JPO would always be a condition, but because of large caseloads that is not always feasible. Juveniles must also waive the expectation of privacy and agree that their rooms or persons can be searched at any time. Depending on other factors, they may also

have to attend a house of worship and keep a job. Of course, they are expected to obey all laws, not to leave the jurisdiction, not to possess a firearm, and to pay restitution and fines if so ordered. They must desist from criminal or delinquent associations.

Approximately 65 percent of adjudicated delinquents receive probation of one sort or another. Males constitute about 75 percent of probationers, females, 25 percent. The percentage of females is much higher than is the percentage of women in adult courts, which probably reflects the traditional and historically paternalistic stance of the court: that is, to protect young women from street life and associated temptations. Blacks make up about 30 percent of those on probation, whites 70 percent. It should be noted that juveniles who are placed in alternative community treatment programs are nominally under control of the facility's staff but remain under the legal supervision of a JPO.

In the 1980s, intensive supervision probation (ISP) was the order of the day. Juveniles who would normally have been sentenced to custodial facilities were often given probation in order to relieve overcrowding and not tax state budgets with the high costs of incarceration. As a result, many juveniles were supervised intensively within their home communities. Juvenile probation officers were given small caseloads (of about 25) and made as many as five personal contacts per week with offenders; youths often had to submit to electronic monitoring and house arrest to limit their movements or to keep track of their whereabouts at all times. This was essentially incarceration in the community, a money-saving expediency, and was not really probation at all, with JPOs operating as guards. Surprisingly, there was no substantive decrease in recidivism for youths on intensive supervision.

Residential treatment alternatives are numerous and can include any noninstitutional facility. Many of these are halfway houses where young offenders receive treatment and education while living in a highly structured environment. Some of these centers involve intensive work programs; others focus on educational outcomes. Almost all feature total immersion in a therapeutic milieu or at least have a therapeutic rationale. Typically, group therapy is a fact of life in group homes. Some people do not adjust well to group settings and present problems for the group facilitator and the facility itself: They may be deliberately disruptive or may use the group for inappropriate venting or reminiscing about "the good old days" when they were on the street. It is a challenge to keep these groups on task. A few of these programs involve very creative and unusual approaches, such as horse or animal therapy. The goal in programs of this type is to develop empathy, attachment, and a sense of responsibility for the animal's care and well-being.

Because probation officers are involved in supervising all juvenile court sanctions, the number of juveniles under probationary supervision is high. Some estimates range as high as 1 million when all the different sorts of juveniles in programs that fall under the aegis of the court are totaled. Some of the other programs that fall under juvenile probationary supervision include juvenile gun courts, intensive aftercare programs (corresponding to parole for adults), and restitution programs.

When juveniles fail to follow the conditions of their probation or abscond, it falls to the JPO to revoke their probation. In a revocation hearing, the juvenile must be afforded counsel, and the JPO must demonstrate that reasonable efforts were made to provide the delinquent with treatment. It must be shown that the youth did not complete his or her part of the agreement and that the interest of the community would be best served if the youth were confined to a custodial facility.

Francis Frederick Hawley
Western Carolina University

See also Juvenile Aftercare; Predispositional Reports for Juveniles; Pre-Sentence Investigation Reports

Further Readings

Martin, Gus. *Juvenile Justice: Process and Systems*. Thousand Oaks, CA: Sage, 2005.

Mays, G. L. and L. Winfree. *Juvenile Justice*. New York: McGraw-Hill, 2000.

Sanborn, J. and A. Salerno. *The Juvenile Justice System: Law and Process*. Los Angeles: Roxbury, 2005.

Torbet, Patricia M. *Juvenile Probation: The Workhorse of the Juvenile Justice System*. Washington, DC: U.S. Department of Justice, Office of Justice Programs, Office of Juvenile Justice and Delinquency Prevention, 1996.

Law Enforcement Administration Act Initiatives

In 1968, the U.S. Congress passed the Omnibus Crime Control and Safe Streets Act (OCCSSA). OCCSSA created the Law Enforcement Assistance Administration (LEAA), an agency within the U.S. Department of Justice. LEAA advanced crime control through a wide range of grants, mostly given to states and local governments. Some supported state and local anticrime programs; others were used to educate and train police officers. In 1974, LEAA also began to help fund community corrections. The first programs focused on juvenile status offenders, but over time, community correction initiatives for adult offenders emerged as well. Despite the success of some of these programs, their lives were short. The work of Robert Martinson and others—which argued that rehabilitation programs, whatever their format, did little to reduce offender recidivism rates—undercut LEAA. There also were many critics of its funding policies. In 1980, Congress abolished LEAA; its allocation expired in 1982.

History and Initiatives

The roots of the OCCSSA, and hence of the LEAA, lay in the bitter presidential campaign of 1964, during which George Wallace and Barry Goldwater attacked Lyndon Johnson as soft on crime. Once elected, Johnson created the President's Commission on Law Enforcement and the Administration of Justice. This commission then successfully recommended OCCSSA to Congress. As a result, in 1968, LEAA was born. Although LEAA lasted little more than a decade, it undertook an impressive number of initiatives, some of which continue to the present. Others have evolved and some have been disbanded. In the last category is the Law Enforcement Education Program (LEEP). Between 1968 and 1976, LEEP introduced significant funding for criminal justice higher education and eventually provided aid for more than 100,000 students of criminology, criminal justice, and law enforcement at more than 1,000 colleges and universities.

LEAA also focused more on state-level initiatives than had its predecessors. It encouraged the establishment of state planning agencies (SPAs) intended to allow states to target crime control strategies to their own needs. There was a perceived need to allow states to focus on particular types of offenders, or on social and structural factors particular to a given state. At the same time, LEAA played a role in developing standards for U.S. criminal justice institutions. For instance, with the financial support of the LEAA, the U.S. criminal justice system witnessed systemwide technological improvements in forensic science, DNA technology, and police officer tools and equipment.

Some LEAA initiatives were highly successful. For example, the Career Criminal Program, which encouraged prosecutors' offices to focus resources on major repeat offenders, still exists in cities across the United States. The associated Prosecutor's Management Information System (PROMIS) streamlined and automated case tracking and scheduling, and its technological infrastructure continues to be developed. A third example is the Treatment Alternatives to Street Crime (TASC). When the first TASC programs started in 1972, they focused on the pretrial diversion of first-time offenders with addiction problems to community facilities. Since then, TASC has expanded to cover a wide range of offenders, returning those who fail to comply with drug treatment programs to the legal system. Cost-benefit analyses suggest that TASC programs reduce recidivism rates at a lower cost than those associated with processing offenders through the traditional criminal justice system.

Problems and Critiques

In spite of these general successes, over time critics saw certain of the LEAA's policies and practices as either prohibitively costly or unsuccessful. LEAA's "block grants" gave organizations, especially states, onetime large sums to fund programs. This limited the number of grants LEAA could give. LEAA also provided few checks on how the money was spent and, at best, limited incentives to ensure that funded programs were efficient and efficacious. The criticism arose that the LEAA was giving blank checks when it could have been providing smaller seed grants, to be renewed or extended at the discretion of the LEAA based on program evaluations. While appropriations to the LEAA grew rapidly, from $63 million in 1969 to $886 million in 1975, this high cost did not seem to yield crime control returns. Rising crime rates made the LEAA increasingly unpopular. In response, grants eventually became more discretionary and categorical. However, this in turn required much more oversight to manage distribution of grant money, complicating and slowing the LEAA's operations. To add to the bureaucratic complexity of the LEAA, as the administration began to expand, the administration saw a frequent turnover of administrators, each of whom offered different priorities on crime control, with some focusing more on policing, others on courts, others on corrections, and still others on communities.

Between 1968 and 1982, the LEAA received more than $7.5 billion in congressional appropriations. While many of its programs were successful, former employees of the LEAA and officials of the current Office of Justice Programs have critiqued what they characterize as the LEAA's view of throwing money at problems as a useful crime prevention strategy. Policies such as block grants were viewed as optimistic but shortsighted, with limited ability to address the complexity of the crime problems being targeted. Much of the grant money went to the SPAs, which often lacked the power or ability to implement the strategic planning desired by the LEAA. State and local governments became more critical of the administration, describing it as a burdensome and imposing bureaucracy whose guidelines, programs, and services were not always relevant to the needs of lower governments.

Moreover, certain initiatives of the LEAA and the Omnibus Crime Bill as a whole invoked significant controversy. The Omnibus Crime Bill had emerged in a climate of rising crime rates, particularly in the realm of drug abuse. Social turbulence and protest characterized much of the political landscape. With its focus on law enforcement and crime control, the administration became closely characterized by "law and order" and "war on crime" rhetoric, which at the time was politically tethered to conservative politics. This emphasis was tied to a corresponding decrease in attention to crime prevention policies and corrections, such that the police increasingly became the most prominent face of justice.

1979 Justice System Improvement Act

As executive and legislative dissatisfaction with the LEAA grew, the 1979 Justice System Improvement Act was passed, which amended the Omnibus Crime Bill by transferring the National Institute of Law Enforcement and Criminal Justice from the LEAA to the National Institute of Justice. The act also led to the creation of the Bureau of Justice Statistics, further diminishing the duties of the LEAA. Finally, crime rates continued to rise during the existence of the LEAA, and the organization was disbanded in 1982, officially because of "failure of appropriations." The LEAA was replaced by the Office of Justice Assistance, Research, and Statistics, which in turn was replaced in 1984 by the current Office of Justice Programs.

Ellen Dwyer
Ronak Shah
Indiana University, Bloomington

See also Crime Control Model of Corrections; Political Determinants of Corrections Policy; Work/Study Release Programs

Further Readings

Feeley, M. and A. Sarat. *The Policy Dilemma: Federal Crime Policy and the Law Enforcement Assistance Administration*. Minneapolis: University of Minnesota Press, 1980.

National Archives. *Records of the Law Enforcement Assistance Administration (LEAA)*. http://www .archives.gov/research/guide-Fed-Records/groups/423 .html (Accessed July 2011).

U.S. Department of Justice, Office of Justice Programs. "LEAA/OJP Retrospective." 1996. http://www.ncjrs.gov/pdffiles1/nij/164509.pdf (Accessed July 2011).

LEVEL OF SERVICE INVENTORY

The Level of Supervision Inventory (LSI) is a theoretically driven and empirically supported offender classification instrument developed in the early 1980s by Canadian psychologists Don Andrews and James Bonta. The LSI was updated and renamed the Level of Service Inventory–Revised (LSI–R) in the 1990s. The purpose of the instrument is to help practitioners identify the risks/needs and responsivity factors of individual offenders so that the information can be used for case management planning. That is, the more accurate an assessment instrument is in identifying an offender's risks/needs and responsivity factors, the greater is the potential for matching the offender to a treatment program that will help reduce the offender's likelihood of recidivism.

Used by more than 900 agencies in North America, the LSI–R is among the most popular risk assessment instruments in use today. Its popularity may be attributed, in part, to the versatility of the instrument. Andrews and Bonta suggest that the LSI–R is appropriate for use in "identifying treatment targets and monitoring offender risk while under supervision and/or treatment services, making probation/supervision decisions, making decisions regarding placement into halfway houses, deciding appropriate security-level classification within institutions, and assessing the likelihood of recidivism." The LSI–R has also been the subject of more than 40 academic studies. Although the instrument has not received unanimous support across samples, the predictive validity of the instrument has been supported across categories of gender, race, age, and criminal justice populations.

The LSI–R is a third-generation risk assessment instrument that includes 54 questions falling into 10 domains, or categories. These include criminal history, education/employment, finances, family/marriage, accommodation, leisure/recreation, companions, alcohol/drug problems, emotional/personal problems, and attitudes/orientation. Although the LSI–R does include a few questions that are static in nature, the majority of questions address dynamic factors. The inclusion of dynamic factors on the assessment is one of the strengths of the instrument, because dynamic factors can be targeted for change through treatment, whereas static factors are not amenable to change through treatment. Therefore, the LSI–R may be more oriented toward treatment than instruments from the second generation, which relied heavily on static factors or the clinical judgment assessments used in the first generation of offender classification.

The assessment is designed to be administered by a criminal justice practitioner who has been trained on the LSI–R instrument. This practitioner administers the instrument in a semistructured interview with the offender that typically takes 45 minutes to an hour to complete. The 54 items on the assessment are scored either Yes or No or on a scale of 0 to 3, with 3 indicating a satisfactory situation with no need for improvement, 2 indicating a relatively satisfactory situation with some room for improvement evident, 1 indicating a relatively unsatisfactory situation with a need for improvement, and 0 indicating a very unsatisfactory situation with a very clear and strong need for improvement.

Upon completion of the interview, the criminal justice practitioner scores the offender on the 54 items. One point is awarded per item that is scored Yes, 1, or 0. The criminal practitioner tallies the points based on the offender's responses to the 54 questions to determine the total LSI–R score. The score is then compared against the range of scores that fall within each designated risk level: a score of 0 to 13 is low, a score of 14 to 23 is low/moderate, a score of 24 to 33 is moderate, a score of 34 to 40 is medium/high, and score of 41 to 54 is high. Based on the risk designation determined by the offender's total LSI–R score, the criminal justice practitioner is able to outline a case management plan most suitable for the offender based on his or her risks, needs, and responsivity factors.

The LSI–R is an important assessment tool that promotes effective correctional treatment. The instrument is theoretically driven and includes dynamic items that have been empirically proven to be the best predictors of crime. Moreover, the LSI–R is straightforward, is easy to administer and score, allows the criminal justice practitioner to exercise professional discretion during the semistructured interview and scoring, and provides practitioners with information necessary for risk management and case management planning. Because of the dynamic nature of the instrument, offenders may be reassessed after having received treatment to determine whether or not the offender's risks and needs have changed. If so, the offender's treatment plan may be modified to address his or her current risks and needs. In sum, use of the LSI–R by trained practitioners assists in offender risks/needs assessment and case management planning and helps ensure that practitioners are able to make case management decisions that place offenders in treatment programs that can address their risks/needs and therefore provide the best opportunity for reducing recidivism.

Brenda Vose
University of North Florida

See also Actuarial Risk Assessment; COMPASS Program; Hare Psychopathy Checklist; Offender Needs; Offender Responsivity; Offender Risks; Risk and Needs Assessment Instruments; Salient Factor Score; Wisconsin Risk Assessment Instrument

Further Readings

Andrews, Donald A. and James Bonta. *LSI–R: The Level of Service Inventory Revised User's Manual.* North Tonawanda, NY: Multi-Health Systems, 1995.

Flores, Anthony, Christopher T. Lowenkamp, Alexander M. Holsinger, and Edward J. Latessa. "Predicting Outcome With the Level of Service Inventory Revised: The Importance of Implementation Integrity." *Journal of Criminal Justice*, v.34 (2006).

Smith, Paula, Francis T. Cullen, and Edward J. Latessa. "Can 14,737 Women Be Wrong? A Meta-Analysis of the LSI–R and Recidivism for Female Offenders." *Criminology and Public Policy*, v.8 (2009).

Vose, Brenda, Paula Smith, and Francis T. Cullen. "The Empirical Status of the Level of Service Inventory." *Federal Probation*, v.72/3 (2008).

LIABILITY

Inmates serving sentences in institutions or within the community have some limited legal rights. An alleged violation of those rights may lead to civil or criminal cases at the state or federal level. From the plaintiff's perspective, prevailing in federal court in a civil rights lawsuit is preferable to a victory in a state court, since the former awards attorney fees, damages, and injunctive relief. State court tort lawsuits have the potential to result in a financial award for the plaintiff, but money to pay the plaintiff's attorney must be taken out of that award, and there is no possibility of injunctive relief. Cases in state court tend to be easier for plaintiffs to win, but the state laws concerning negligence do vary widely from state to state.

Prison inmates and offenders serving sentences in the community may name corrections personnel as defendants in federal court through civil rights actions. A civil rights suit involves Title 42 of the U.S. Code, Section 1983, and therefore these lawsuits are commonly referred to as Section 1983 cases. Offenders filing a Section 1983 case are alleging that their constitutional rights were violated by government action or inaction. A landmark case that outlined the criteria necessary for someone to allege that a civil rights violation was committed by a government entity is *Monell v. Department of Social Services* (436 U.S. 658, 1978). In *Monell*, the U.S. Supreme Court established that a civil rights violation under Section 1983 occurred when (1) a person was deprived of a right, privilege, or immunity guaranteed under the Constitution and federal laws, and (2) the deprivation resulted from official policy or custom of a local government entity. In *Brandon v. Holt* (469 U.S. 464, 1985), the Supreme Court clarified the extent to which organizations are held responsible for the actions of staff members who are performing their duties. According to the *Brandon* decision, offenders may choose to name specific correctional employees in their lawsuits, and if the activity or inactivity in question was committed by the staff member "in his official capacity," the organization that employs that staff member will be held liable.

Corrections liability issues in state courts are generally based on state tort law. A tort is a wrong or injury for which a court may award compensation. When individuals under the supervision of a corrections agency sue in state court, the lawsuit usually pertains to a claim of negligence. There are four general issues for courts to consider in cases where negligence of corrections personnel is alleged: the plaintiff was owed a legal duty; there was a breach of that duty because of action or inaction of the defendant; the plaintiff suffered an injury as a result of the breach of duty; and the defendant's actions or inactions were the proximate cause of that injury.

Officers are clearly in charge of providing some level of supervision for offenders on their caseloads, but the question that state courts have had to address is whether officers should be held responsible for the behavior of their clients. Corrections personnel are given a degree of protection from lawsuits in the form of immunity. Judges are given absolute immunity while performing their jobs, meaning that they cannot be sued for their judicial decisions. Corrections staff members, however, are not granted that level of protection. Some, but not all, states have ruled that parole boards should have quasi-judicial immunity, meaning that their release decisions cannot be used as the basis of a negligence claim. Probation and parole personnel, as well as officers who supervise offenders on home confinement, day reporting, and community service assignments, may be granted qualified immunity. Qualified immunity, also known as good-faith immunity, protects officials from civil actions. *Wood v. Strickland* (420 U.S. 308, 1975) is often referred to when determining when to grant qualified immunity. According to the *Wood* ruling, qualified immunity is appropriate when (1) the official did not know, and should not have had to know, that the action violated constitutional rights of individuals, and (2) the official was operating under good faith and the belief that his or her actions were constitutional. The U.S. Supreme Court clarified the conditions under which it is appropriate to grant qualified immunity to public officials. In *Harlow v. Fitzgerald* (457 U.S. 800, 1982), the Court ruled

that qualified immunity should be granted as long as officials' conduct did not violate the rights of others. Community corrections personnel tend to be granted qualified immunity in most states, provided that they can demonstrate that the action that is the subject of the lawsuit was discretionary rather than ministerial. Personnel performing discretionary functions are often protected by the courts, because subjecting every release, revocation, and sanction decision to litigation would damage the effectiveness of the criminal justice system and make it nearly impossible for staff members to perform their duties. Ministerial functions, however, are treated differently. Ministerial functions do not involve personnel having to use their judgment. Rather, they are tasks that are to be performed as part of each employee's job. Failure to carry out those tasks as defined either by law or an agency's policies will likely result in the awarding of damages for negligence, provided that the action or inaction was the proximate cause of the injury.

Offenders were granted the right to name specific correctional employees in lawsuits involving an activity or inactivity committed by a prison staff member acting in an official capacity under the *Brandon v. Holt* decision. (Photos.com)

State courts have sided with probation and parole agencies when they have been sued for the conduct of offenders, so long as the offenders' detrimental conduct was not foreseeable to the officers. For example, the Virginia Supreme Court found that a parole officer should not be held liable for the death of two women who were killed by a parolee. The plaintiff argued that the officer should have known of the danger, because the officer was aware of a few misdemeanors committed by the parolee and failed to revoke parole. The court ruled that evidence of some misdemeanors was not enough to foresee the murders and prevent them (*Fox v. Curtis*, 372 S.E. 2d 373, 1988). In situations in which the threat of danger is more apparent to the officer, the officer is legally obligated to act. In *Garcia v. Superior Court* (789 P. 2d 960, 1990), a parole officer was held liable for the death of a woman, Grace Morales, at the hands of a parolee. The officer was aware of a threat to kill Morales, but he assured Morales that the parolee would not act on the threat. Additionally, when Morales attempted to get a restraining order, the officer intervened and assured Morales that it would not be necessary.

Rolando del Carmen and Eve Trook-White wrote the first comprehensive report on liability in community corrections in the United States. They identified seven areas of agency and supervisor liability: negligent failure to train, negligent hiring, negligent assignment, negligent failure to supervise, negligent failure to direct, negligent entrustment, and negligent retention. Agencies that hire, retain, and continue to entrust an employee who is clearly inappropriate for the position may be held liable for the employee's actions. Even if the agency hires the appropriate personnel, failure to provide proper training and supervision can result in the employee's failing to provide the client with the appropriate level of care or supervision, and this can be the proximate cause of an injury to the client or a member of the community.

Government agencies that contract corrections work to private nonprofit or for-profit groups may not escape liability if the private organization is found to be negligent or violating the rights of clients under supervision. In such an instance, both the private agency and the government entity may be at risk for litigation. Government agencies can work to reduce such risk by being selective in choosing partnerships with private groups and by diligently monitoring the performance of those groups to ensure that they are properly handling the operations, supervision, and implementation of their policies and procedures.

Christine Tartaro
Richard Stockton College of New Jersey

See also Offender Supervision; Parole Boards and Hearings; Parole Officers; Probation Officers

Further Readings

Anderson, James F. and Laronistine Dyson. *Legal Rights of Prisoners.* Lanham, MD: University Press of America, 2001.

Brandon v. Holt, 469 U.S. 464 (1985).

del Carmen, Rolando V. and Eve Trook-White. *Liability Issues in Community Service Sanctions.* Washington, DC: U.S. Department of Justice, National Institute of Corrections, 1986.

Fox v. Curtis, 372 S.E. 2d 373 (1988).

Garcia v. Superior Court, 789 P. 2d 960 (1990).

Harlow v. Fitzgerald, 457 U.S. 800 (1982).

Monell v. Department of Social Services, 436 U.S. 658 (1978).

Morgan, Kathryn D., Barbara A. Belbot, and John Clark. "Liability Issues Affecting Probation and Parole Supervision." *Journal of Criminal Justice,* v.25/3 (1997).

Wallace, H. and C. Roberson. *Legal Aspects of Corrections.* Incline Village, NV: Copperhouse, 2000.

Wood v. Strickland, 420 U.S. 308 (1975).

LONG-TERM OFFENDER DESIGNATION

In the Canadian criminal justice system, certain offenders bear the label "long-term offender." According to Canadian public safety agencies, as of 2005 there were roughly 300 long-term offenders in Canada. Generally, Canadian courts affix the long-term offender designation to offenders who ostensibly show little promise for rehabilitation and who pose a significant risk to society. A number of procedural guidelines dictate when the Canadian criminal justice system employs the long-term offender designation. Proponents of the long-term offender designation argue that such a measure represents an effective effort to curb recidivism and protect the general public. Yet, those critical of the tag contend that the long-term offender designation, and its accompanying guidelines, make an offender's reintegration more difficult by constructing unnecessary reentry obstacles. In the United States, the criminal justice system does not recognize or utilize the long-term offender designation.

Created by Bill C-55, which became law on August 1, 1997, the long-term offender designation can apply to those who commit a "serious personal injury offense" or a host of other enumerated sexual offenses. Canadian criminal code defines a "serious personal injury offense" as one involving the use or attempted use of violence that results in threatened or actual physical or psychological harm. Although Canada's definition of a serious personal injury offense excludes first- or second-degree murder, it includes all other offenses that may carry a penalty of 10 years of imprisonment or more. In addition, the Canadian criminal justice system's definition of personal injury offense incorporates a variety of sexual assaults. Nevertheless, legislative guidelines governing the long-term offender designation expand the list of applicable crimes to include virtually all other offenses of a sexual nature. For instance, sexual interference, invitation to sexual touching, sexual exploitation, and exposure can warrant the long-term offender designation. Thus, most commentators opine that Canadian lawmakers targeted sex offenders when crafting the long-term offender designation.

Mechanically, the long-term offender designation requires Canadian prosecuting authorities, known as the Crown, to apply for long-term offender status after an offender's conviction but prior to sentencing. A court then hears evidence relating to the long-term offender application at a requisite hearing. The offender in question is required to appear at a long-term offender application hearing and may present character evidence otherwise inadmissible in criminal proceedings. At that time, to secure a long-term offender designation, prosecutorial agents, according to the Criminal Code of Canada (Part XXVI, Section 753.1[1] [a]-[c]), must show that (1) "it would be appropriate to impose a sentence of imprisonment of two years or more for the offense for which the offender has been convicted," (2) "there is a substantial risk that the offender will reoffend," and (3) "there is a reasonable possibility of eventual control of the risk in the community." If a prosecutorial agent proves each of these required elements, a Canadian judge has the option of affixing the long-term offender designation to the offender in question. An offender, however, has the option to appeal an unfavorable outcome of a long-term offender designation hearing.

Notably, the long-term offender designation requires Canadian courts to determine the likelihood that an offender will engage in future criminal activity that poses a risk to society. Under Canadian law, repeat offenders and those offenders who commit crimes of a sexual nature categorically satisfy this prerequisite of the long-term offender designation. However, for other offenders, Canadian judges frequently rely on actuarial assessments when calculating an individual's propensity for reoffending. Most commonly, Canadian courts employ the Hare Psychopathy Checklist, which assesses an offender's psychopathic tendencies and, in turn, his or her probability for recidivism. Critics of actuarial assessments, such as commentator David MacAlister, assert that such tests are difficult to refute and that such assessments make futile attempts to predict the behavior of individuals based on tested group characteristics. However, others note that actuarial assessments are the most accurate predictors available to Canadian courts.

Ultimately, if a Canadian court applies the long-term offender label to a convicted criminal, it must also impose a sentence of at least two years in prison and a period of supervision, of not more than 10 years, to follow that period of incarceration. This period of imposed supervision must comport with the guidelines set out in section 161 of Canada's Corrections and Conditional Release Act regulations. For example, while supervised, the offender must remain within territorial boundaries fixed by supervising agents, must report to supervising agents any change in address or employment, and must refrain from owning or possessing firearms. Moreover, supervising agents can impose any number of additional restrictions they deem necessary to ensure that an offender does not, once again, engage in criminal activity. If a long-term offender violates the rules of supervised release or commits a new crime while subject to supervision restrictions—both considered a breach of a long-term offender order—he or she is subject to a period of imprisonment of up to 10 years. A violation of long-term offender orders differs from Canadian parole in this respect, as parolees only face up to two years of confinement for violations of supervision restrictions that do not amount to new criminal acts.

Opponents of the long-term offender designation question the utility of an extended period of supervision. Many argue that restrictive supervision rules hamper an offender's reentry into the community by imposing unrealistic demands on many individuals who are already ill-equipped to deal with even basic reintegration pitfalls. Nevertheless, supporters of the long-term offender designation view it as a necessary tool to combat recidivism and to protect Canada's citizenry primarily from those who have committed sex crimes.

James M. Binnall
University of California, Irvine

See also Sex Offender Registration; Sex Offenders in the Community; Sexual Predators: Civil Commitment

Further Readings

Grant, Isabel. "Legislating Public Safety: The Business of Risk." *Canadian Criminal Law Review,* v.3/177 (1998).

Henry, Yukimi. "Psychiatric Gating: Questioning the Civil Committal of Convicted Sex Offenders." *University of Toronto Faculty Law Review,* v.59/229 (2001).

Law Commission of Canada. *Law and Risk.* Vancouver: University of British Columbia Press, v.15/10 (2005).

LOSS OF CAPACITY TO BE BONDED

Commercially available fidelity bonds may not be obtainable to cover potential employees who are also ex-offenders. Insurance companies may designate an individual as "not bondable" because of previous fraudulent behavior, criminal convictions, or a history of substance abuse. As a result, this loss of capacity to be bonded may prevent an employer from hiring an otherwise qualified ex-offender.

Loss of capacity to be bonded may create difficulty for ex-offenders searching for employment. Difficulty in obtaining employment, along with other issues, such as loss of voting rights, is commonly referred to as the "collateral consequences" of a conviction. It has been recognized, however, that the ability to gain and maintain employment may help prevent an ex-offender from reoffending and may play an important role in reducing recidivism. Policy makers have enacted reforms intended to reduce the barriers to employment for ex-offenders in an effort to reduce recidivism. The Federal Bonding Program,

sponsored by the U.S. Department of Labor, is one such policy.

As a regular course of good business practice, many employers purchase fidelity bonds from commercial insurance companies. A fidelity bond is like an insurance contract that protects the employer from the dishonest behavior of employees. If an employee is covered under a fidelity bond and that employee steals money or equipment from the employer, the employer will be reimbursed. An employer may require that all employees be covered by a fidelity bond and may refuse to hire individuals who are not bondable.

The U.S. Department of Labor took note of this issue and in 1966 instituted the Federal Bonding Program. This program is intended to provide an incentive for employers who would otherwise be predisposed to avoid hiring an ex-offender because of fears that the ex-offender might steal from the employer. The Federal Bonding Program provides a fidelity bond, at no cost to the employer or employee, which covers an ex-offender who would be designated as not bondable for purposes of commercially available bonding. This program is available to any ex-offender regardless of type or number of convictions.

The Federal Bonding Program also allows an employee who demonstrates trustworthiness to become bondable despite a past criminal record. Fidelity bonds provided through the Federal Bonding Program cover an employee for a six-month period. These fidelity bonds are policies currently issued by the Travelers Casualty and Surety Company of America. If an employee demonstrates honesty during this six-month period, the employer may purchase fidelity bonds as it would for any other employee through Travelers.

The fidelity bonds offered through the Federal Bonding Program are available in amounts from $5,000 to $25,000. The default amount covered is $5,000. If an employer demonstrates that an employee may steal more than $5,000 in equipment or cash at one time, then the bond amount may be increased in $5,000 increments, up to a ceiling of $25,000. If an employee covered under the Federal Bonding Program steals from an employer, the employer will be reimbursed to the extent of the loss, limited by the bond amount, without having to pay any deductible.

By most accounts, the Federal Bonding Program has proven to be successful. According to the U.S. Department of Labor, more than 42,000 individuals have taken advantage of the Federal Bonding Program, with only approximately 460 employees failing to demonstrate their trustworthiness. This allows the U.S. Department of Labor to claim a success rate of about 99 percent. Furthermore, according to a research study, only 12 percent of employers claimed they would hire an ex-offender, but this number jumped to 51 percent if the ex-offender were bonded.

Despite these successes, critics have pointed out several areas where the Federal Bonding Program could be improved. The coverage limit may be insufficient and could be increased. Additionally, the availability of the Federal Bonding Program may not be adequately publicized to ex-offenders or employers. Also, the program covers employee dishonesty related only to theft, including forgery and embezzlement. There is some indication that employers may avoid hiring ex-offenders because of the potential for negligent hiring liability. A negligent hiring claim arises when a third party is injured by an employee and that injury was foreseeable on the part of the employer. The Federal Bonding Program does not cover claims related to negligent hiring. Additionally, the program does not cover claims because of shoddy workmanship or employee injury. Finally, the program does not cover self-employed individuals who do not have federal taxes automatically deducted from their pay. This may prove to be an obstacle to temporary contract workers.

Todd C. Hiestand
MidAmerica Nazarene University

See also Community-Based Vocational Networks; Employment-Related Rights of Offenders; Reentry Programs and Initiatives; Work/Study Release Programs

Further Readings

Colorado Department of Labor and Employment, Workforce Center. *The Federal Bonding Program.* Denver, CO: Author, 2008.

Homeless Veterans Reintegration Program. "Ex-Offenders and Employment." http://www.worksupport.com/documents/HVRPFactsheet6.pdf (Accessed February 2011).

U.S. Department of Labor. "The Federal Bonding Program." http://www.bonds4jobs.com (Accessed February 2011).

LOSS OF INDIVIDUAL RIGHTS

In the United States, a criminal conviction spawns the permanent or temporary loss of some individual rights. Codified as the first 10 amendments of the U.S. Constitution, commonly known as the Bill of Rights, individual rights guarantee American citizens certain freedoms and protections. The U.S. Constitution generally forbids federal, state, or local action that infringes on citizens' individual rights. In some circumstances, however, courts have upheld legislation limiting or eliminating the individual rights of convicted criminals. Specifically, the Supreme Court has authorized federal legislation that permanently prohibits certain criminal offenders from possessing firearms or ammunition, effectively abolishing their Second Amendment individual rights. The Supreme Court has also upheld probation and parole regulations that require most convicted criminals to submit to suspicionless, warrantless searches of their homes or persons, temporarily eradicating their Fourth Amendment protections against unreasonable searches and seizures.

In 1789, James Madison introduced the Bill of Rights at the first U.S. Congress. Ratified on December 15, 1791, the Bill of Rights initially served as a check on the powers of the federal government, prohibiting federal actors from encroaching on citizens' individual rights. Nevertheless, at the time of their codification, the Bill of Rights did little to protect citizens from state or local government threats to individual rights. In 1833, the Supreme Court squarely addressed the breadth of protection offered by the Bill of Rights in *Barron v. the Mayor and City Council of Baltimore*. In *Barron*, the Court held that the Bill of Rights only stemmed the power of the federal government and did not forbid state or local authorities from impinging on the individual rights of its citizenry.

Following the Civil War, the United States again amended its Constitution. Commonly known as the Reconstruction Amendments or the Civil War Amendments, the Thirteenth, Fourteenth, and Fifteenth amendments were legislative attempts to halt widespread racial discrimination against African Americans at the federal, state, and local levels. Of these measures, the Fourteenth Amendment proved the most drastic constraint on state and local power. In relevant part, the Fourteenth Amendment states, "nor shall any State deprive any person of life, liberty, or property without due process of law." Through this due process clause of the Fourteenth Amendment, the Supreme Court has applied the Bill of Rights to state and local governments in a series of landmark decisions, protecting citizens from state or local action that eliminates or diminishes their individual rights.

Challenges to legislation affecting individual rights force courts to engage in rather complex constitutional analyses. Generally, in such cases, courts will scrutinize restrictive legislation by examining the purpose of the legislation and the legislation's relationship to its professed purpose. When legislation targets an individual right, the level of scrutiny a court applies depends entirely on the nature of the right at issue and the history and characteristics of the population affected. If federal, state, or local legislation impacts an individual right that is also a fundamental right or implicates a group that has historically suffered discrimination because of a common immutable trait, courts will employ a heightened level of scrutiny when reviewing such legislation. Courts may also defer to the text of the Constitution, conducting an analysis specific to the individual right at issue.

Second Amendment

The U.S. criminal justice system characterizes a criminal conviction as either a misdemeanor or a felony. A misdemeanor conviction normally carries a minimum sentence of less than one year in prison and will result in the loss of one's Second Amendment rights only if it involves the commission of certain crimes. Conversely, a felony conviction is punishable by at least one year of confinement, is typically associated with severer forms of lawlessness, and uniformly leads to the permanent loss of one's Second Amendment freedoms.

In relevant part, the Second Amendment reads, "The right of the people to keep and bear arms shall not be infringed." Since its drafting, the Second Amendment has protected citizens from

federal action that limits Second Amendment individual rights by requiring that such action withstand heightened constitutional scrutiny. In 2010, in *McDonald v. City of Chicago*, the Supreme Court held that certain Second Amendment protections also insulate citizens from some forms of intrusive state and local government action. Thus, at any level, certain legislation diminishing the Second Amendment rights of citizens receives heightened constitutional scrutiny.

Under federal statute, all felony criminal convictions trigger the permanent loss of a convicted felon's Second Amendment rights. Specifically, Section 922(g)(1) of the Gun Control Act of 1968 prohibits those "who have been convicted in any court of a crime punishable by imprisonment for a term exceeding one year" from owning or possessing a firearm or ammunition. In 1996, legislators amended the Gun Control Act of 1968 with the Lautenberg Amendment, in order to include misdemeanants convicted of domestic violence. Section 922(g)(9) of the Lautenberg Amendment permanently bans any person "who has been convicted in any court of a misdemeanor crime of domestic violence" from owning or possessing firearms or ammunition. Hence, federal legislation permanently bars all convicted felons and all misdemeanants convicted of domestic violence from owning or possessing firearms or ammunition.

In 2008, in *District of Columbia v. Heller*, the Supreme Court held that one's Second Amendment right to "keep and bear arms" is an individual right. In *McDonald*, the Court classified some Second Amendment rights as fundamental, which would trigger heightened constitutional scrutiny. Since *Heller*, several federal courts have upheld legislation that eviscerates the Second Amendment rights of convicted felons and misdemeanants convicted of domestic violence, even after applying heightened constitutional scrutiny. In these instances, federal courts found that legislation prohibiting convicted criminals from owning or possessing firearms bears a substantial relationship to an important state objective. Federal courts have uniformly held that crime prevention is an important state objective and that preventing certain convicted criminals from owning or possessing firearms bears a substantial relationship to such an objective. Courts arrived at this conclusion by noting that felons and some misdemeanants are far more likely to commit firearm-related crimes than nonfelons and nonmisdemeanants.

Fourth Amendment

A term of federal or state supervision, in the form of probation or parole, can accompany or replace a misdemeanor conviction or a felony conviction. Typically, probation is a term of supervision imposed in lieu of incarceration for misdemeanor convictions or lower-level felony convictions. Most often, parole is a term of supervision during which an offender serves the remainder of an imposed prison sentence outside prison. Both parole and probation normally require that those subject to supervision agree to submit to suspicionless, warrantless searches of their home or person, in essence waiving their Fourth Amendment individual rights.

The Fourth Amendment ensures "the right of the people to be secure in their persons, houses, papers, and effects, against unreasonable searches and seizures." At the time of its drafting, the Fourth Amendment protected citizens only from federal action amounting to unreasonable search and seizure. In 1963, in *Mapp v. Ohio*, the Supreme Court held that the Fourth Amendment applies to the states through the due process clause of the Fourteenth Amendment. Hence, all U.S. citizens currently enjoy protections from unreasonable searches and seizures levied by federal, state, or local officials.

When determining the constitutionality of federal, state, or local action that impinges on a citizen's Fourth Amendment protections, courts assess whether the search in question is reasonable. In such an instance, the courts look to the text of the Fourth Amendment, which only prohibits "unreasonable" searches. Courts assess the reasonableness of a search by examining the totality of the circumstances surrounding the search. In doing so, courts weigh the intrusion on an individual's privacy against the degree to which the search is necessary to promote a legitimate governmental interest.

In response to numerous challenges, courts have routinely upheld probation and parole regulations requiring convicted criminals to submit to suspicionless searches. Most recently, in 2006, in *Samson v. California*, a parolee challenged a California parole restriction that authorizes parole agents or other peace officers to conduct warrantless searches of parolees with or without cause. Holding that California's parole regulation did not violate the Fourth Amendment, the Supreme Court conducted the customary Fourth Amendment balancing test. Specifically, the Court held that parolees have a diminished expectation of privacy and that California has an "overwhelming interest" in closely supervising parolees, as they are very likely to commit future criminal offenses. The Supreme Court's holding in *Samson* authorizes federal, state, and local authorities temporarily to curtail the Fourth Amendment protections of those convicted criminals subject to probation or parole in any jurisdiction in the United States. Accordingly, when probationers and parolees complete an imposed term of supervised release, authorities can no longer infringe on their Fourth Amendment individual rights and protections.

James M. Binnall
University of California, Irvine

See also Civil and Political Rights Affected by Conviction; Pardon and Restoration of Rights

Further Readings

Binnall, James. "Released From Prison . . . but Placed in Solitary Confinement: A Parolee Reveals the Practical Ramifications of *Samson v. California*." *New England Journal on Criminal and Civil Confinement*, v.34/65 (2008).

Pinard, Michael. "An Integrated Perspective on the Collateral Consequences of Criminal Convictions and Reentry Issues Faced by Formerly Incarcerated Individuals." *Boston University Law Review*, v.86/623 (2006).

Rosenthal, Lawrence and Joyce Lee Malcolm. "*McDonald v. Chicago*: Which Standard of Scrutiny Should Apply to Gun Control Laws?" *Northwestern University Law Review Colloquy*, v.105/85 (2010).

LOSS OF PARENTAL RIGHTS

For many offenders, potentially one of the severest consequences of engaging in criminal behavior is the loss of parental rights. Every state in the United States has its own laws that dictate when a court may terminate parental rights. Depending on the type and length of sentence imposed on the offender, the law may require that the offender's parental bond be permanently severed. In other cases, termination of parental rights is not mandatory, but the underlying behavior, regardless of the sentence, may trigger a court action to assess and possibly intervene in the parent-child relationship. The rights of one parent can be terminated without negating the rights of the other parent, but if both parents lose their rights to the child, the child becomes a ward of the state and may be placed in a permanent adoptive family or guardianship.

The Adoption and Safe Families Act (ASFA), a federal statute passed in 1997, has had a major impact on the parental rights of offenders, particularly those who are incarcerated. According to the Bureau of Justice Statistics, the majority of inmates in the nation's prisons are parents of minor children. One goal of ASFA was to protect children from the instability of long-term foster care by streamlining adoption procedures. ASFA set strict timetables for terminating the rights of parents whose children are in foster care, so that the children could be quickly placed for permanent adoption. Under ASFA, state agencies are required to initiate proceedings to terminate a parent's rights to his or her child once the child has been in foster care for 15 of the previous 22 months. As a result, offenders who are sentenced to serve time for even low-level nonviolent felonies often run afoul of ASFA's 15-month time limit. If their child must be placed in foster care while they serve their sentence, the parent-child relationship will be legally severed before they get out of prison. For this reason, community correctional programs that allow offenders to reside with their young children have the effect of allowing families to remain unified, as opposed to being statutorily broken apart.

Laws implementing ASFA vary somewhat from state to state. Although ASFA only requires termination proceedings when the parent has been apart from the child for 15 months, some states have shortened this time period to as few as six months. On the other hand, when ASFA mandates the initiation of termination proceedings, roughly half of the states allow at least some exceptions to be made that would enable offenders to retain their parental rights. These exceptions include situations in which the child is placed in the custody of a family member while the offender is incarcerated, or where the state

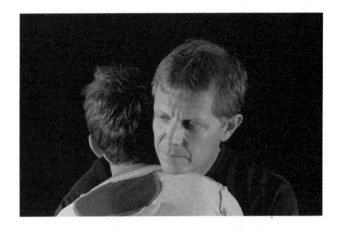

Parental rights may be terminated depending on the type and length of sentence imposed or the inability of the parent to provide for the child's needs. Each U.S. state is responsible for establishing its own statutory grounds. (Photos.com)

can document a compelling reason that severing the parent-child relationship would violate the child's best interests.

For those offenders who are able to maintain parental relationships while incarcerated, most correctional facilities provide for some visitation. While some facilities explicitly stress family unification and a child-friendly environment, others do not. Visitation is a privilege, not a right, and the U.S. Supreme Court has consistently held in cases such as *Overton v. Bazzetta* (539 U.S. 126, 2003) that penal institutions may restrict child visits as they deem appropriate.

Besides the loss of parental rights that stems simply from being incarcerated, laws throughout the U.S. provide numerous other grounds for terminating parental rights. Although each state is different, in general all states allow for the involuntary termination of the parent-child relationship when the parent is deemed unfit because he or she fails to provide for the child's basic needs, or creates some risk of harm to the child. The U.S. Supreme Court determined in *Santosky v. Kramer* (455 U.S. 745, 1982) that, in order to terminate an individual's parental rights permanently, the state must prove that the parent is unfit by clear and convincing evidence. This is a lower standard of proof than what is required to find someone guilty of a crime, which requires proof beyond a reasonable doubt.

States may prove that a parent is unfit by producing clear and convincing evidence of any of a variety of factors, depending on the jurisdiction. Some of the more common of these factors include a history of neglect, abuse, or abandonment of the child in question or of other children, failure to properly support the child, failure to maintain regular contact with the child, sustained mental illness, drug or alcohol abuse on the part of the parent, or conviction of a violent felony against a family member. Consequently, the same grounds used to convict the offender of a crime in the first place may in many cases also provide sufficient reason for him or her to lose his or her parental rights.

Patricia Bergum Wagner
Youngstown State University

See also Family Courts; Family Therapy; Female Offenders and Special Needs; Reintegration Into Communities

Further Readings

Adoption and Safe Families Act of 1997, Pub. L. No. 105-89, 42 U.S.C. § 1305.

Glaze, Lauren E. and Laura M. Maruschak. *Parents in Prison and Their Minor Children.* Washington, DC: U.S. Department of Justice, 2010. http://bjs.ojp.usdoj.gov/index.cfm?ty=pbdetail&iid=823 (Accessed July 2011).

Overton v. Bazzetta, 539 U.S. 126 (2003).

Santosky v. Kramer, 455 U.S. 745 (1982).

U.S. Department of Health and Human Services, Child Welfare Information Gateway. *Grounds for Involuntary Termination of Parental Rights: State Statutes*, 2010. http://www.childwelare.gov/systemwide/laws_policies/statutes/groundstermin.cfm (Accessed July 2011).

Loss of Right to Possess Firearms

Part of the Bill of Rights, the Second Amendment to the U.S. Constitution grants to individual citizens the fundamental right to keep and bear arms. The extent of the right to keep and bear arms has been the subject of heated debate in the United States. It was not until the U.S. Supreme Court decided two cases, *District of Columbia v. Heller* (2008) and *MacDonald v. City of Chicago* (2010), that the right was formally recognized as an individual fundamental right applicable to the federal government and all of the states. This acknowledgment is extremely important, as only fundamental rights are given the highest protection against intrusion by the government.

Usually, whenever a person is convicted of a crime, he or she is fined and/or sentenced to jail or prison for a term of months or years as punishment. Fines are usually imposed for misdemeanors; imprisonment is much more frequently imposed when the crime committed is a felony. As a general matter, a misdemeanor is a crime that is punishable by a year or less in jail, and a felony is a crime that is punishable by more than a year in prison. This distinction is important when it comes to the right to keep and bear arms.

Under U.S. law, it is generally known that it is a crime for a person who has been convicted of a felony to keep and bear arms, despite the Second Amendment. However, the law is a bit more complex: Under Title 18 of the U.S. Code, Section 924(g), it is unlawful for a person to possess a firearm that has been shipped through interstate or foreign commerce if the recipient (1) has a conviction of a crime punishable by more than a year in prison, (2) is a fugitive from justice, (3) is an unlawful user or addicted to controlled substances, (4) has been adjudicated as mentally defective or committed to a mental institution, (5) is an illegal alien or is not a lawful immigrant, (6) has been dishonorably discharged from the armed forces, (7) is a U.S. citizen who has renounced his or her citizenship, (8) is subject to a restraining order involving domestic relations that finds that the person is a credible threat, or (9) has been convicted of a misdemeanor involving domestic violence.

The issue of what constitutes a felony can raise problems. Under ancient English common law, a person convicted of a felony was considered a heinous person and of unsavory character. Indeed, the punishment for most felonies under English common law was death. Felons were considered to be the most dangerous persons in society. Once a person was branded as a felon, the only route to survival open to that person was a life of crime. This ancient common-law rule was the basic reason that felons were prohibited from possessing firearms. The foundations of the U.S. legal system lie in English common law. Thus, U.S. laws prohibiting felons from possessing firearms have a historical basis.

Most states classify felonies as crimes punishable by a year or more in prison. Some states define felonies differently. For example, in Massachusetts, crimes

Despite the Second Amendment, a felon is excluded from the right to possess firearms, which some authorities believe violates their constitutional rights. Noncompliance is a class C felony with a penalty of up to 10 years in prison. (Photos.com)

punishable by less than two and a half years in prison are considered misdemeanors. Thus, what might be a felony in another state is only a misdemeanor in Massachusetts. The issue is complicated by Title 18, Section 921(a)(20) of the U.S. Code, which defines a crime punishable by less than a year—as defined in Section 924(g)—as any state offense classified by that state as a misdemeanor and punishable by two years or less. Thus, in rare circumstances it might not be clear when a person might be prohibited from possessing a firearm. Section 921(a)(20) also exempts from the prohibitions of Section 924(g) those persons who have been convicted of a felony concerning certain white-collar financial crimes. It also exempts those persons who have received a pardon for their crimes or whose criminal records have been expunged and civil rights restored.

It is patently obvious that persons incarcerated in prisons should not have access to firearms. Indeed, once a person has been convicted of a crime and incarcerated in prison, that person is stripped of many of his or her fundamental rights and not just the right to keep and bear arms. Thus, the Second Amendment cannot be used as a basis to allow inmates access to firearms.

In the context of community corrections, the issue of possession of firearms is extremely sensitive. Community corrections involves placing the offender back into the community and working with the offender to maximize his or her reintegration into the community. The issues surrounding community corrections are not limited to the offender and the corrections system but also involve the surrounding community, where the offender is to live and work.

The corrections system is necessarily and justifiably concerned that persons convicted of serious or violent crimes not be allowed access to firearms, especially in community corrections settings. Such access would pose a danger to the immediate community. Furthermore, giving such persons access to firearms might encourage them to resort to their previous ways of breaking the law. Moreover, the community would likely be alarmed if a community corrections institution, such as a halfway house located within the boundaries of that community, allowed the residents to keep and bear arms. Thus, there are very important reasons for denying persons convicted of serious or violent crimes access to firearms.

Some authorities raise the issue that the right to keep and bear arms is a fundamental right and that to deny persons convicted of crimes the right to firearms violates their constitutional rights. However, such an argument does not account for the fact that even fundamental rights can be curtailed where there is a compelling governmental interest. It can hardly be rationally argued that there is no compelling government interest in keeping firearms away from persons convicted of serious or violent crimes that constitute felonies. Even after offenders have completed their sentences, whether in a prison or in halfway houses, because of their history of committing crimes society has enacted laws to minimize the potential danger to the community by preventing such persons from accessing firearms.

Wm. C. Plouffe Jr.
Independent Scholar

See also Civil and Political Rights Affected by Conviction; Conditions of Community Corrections; Firearms and Community Corrections Personnel; Loss of Individual Rights; Offender Risks; Pardon and Restoration of Rights; Public Safety and Collaborative Prevention

Further Readings

Bone, D. "The *Heller* Promise Versus the *Heller* Reality: Will Statutes Prohibiting the Possession of Firearms by Ex-Felons Be Upheld After *Britt v. State*?" *Journal of Criminal Law and Criminology*, v.100/4 (2010).
District of Columbia v. Heller, 554 U.S. 570, 128 S.Ct. 2783 (2008).

Greenfield, Lawrence A. and Marianne W Zawitz. *Weapons Offenses and Offenders: Firearms, Crime, and Criminal Justice.* Washington, DC: U.S. Department of Justice, Office of Justice Programs, Bureau of Justice Statistics, 1995.

Halbrook, Stephen P. *Firearms Law Deskbook.* St. Paul, MN: Thomson/West, 2006.

McDonald v. City of Chicago, 561 U.S. 3025 (2010).

Loss of Welfare Benefits

There are many reentry barriers for ex-offenders returning to society after serving their time either in prison or under parole supervision. One of these barriers is the loss of welfare benefits. Federal law imposes on individuals convicted of a state or federal felony drug crime a lifetime ban on receipt of welfare benefits and benefits from similar programs. This loss impacts community corrections by limiting the resources that are available to assist these individuals with their reentry goals.

In 1996, President Bill Clinton signed the Personal Responsibility and Work Opportunity Reconciliation Act (PRWORA), also known as the Welfare Reform Act of 1996. General individual welfare programs such as Aid to Families with Dependent Children (AFDC) were eliminated, and Temporary Assistance for Needy Families (TANF) was implemented. This new version of welfare assistance attached work requirements and time limitations to the benefits of recipients. Section 115 of the Welfare Reform Act denied certain welfare benefits to individuals convicted of any felony offense involved in the possession, use, or distribution of a controlled substance as defined by the Controlled Substances Act. This meant that states were now allowed to test welfare recipients for illegal drug use and restrict their benefits. Benefits denied included (1) assistance from any state program funded under part A of Title IV of the Social Security Act and (2) benefits from the food stamp program designated in the Food Stamp Act of 1977, as well as any state program operated under the Food Stamp Act of 1977.

The Welfare Reform Act allowed states two options within the new welfare limitations. States could either (1) opt out completely, exempting any or all individuals from application of the act, or (2) restrict the period of time individuals could be denied benefits. The act also specified that the

Current federal law imposes a lifetime ban from welfare benefits and similar programs on individuals convicted of a state or federal felony drug crime. (Photos.com)

new restriction was not retroactive. Only individuals convicted after August 22, 1996, the date the act was implemented, would be affected by the new restrictions. The introduction of this act later triggered what are often called welfare-to-work programs, in which state and federal employers are urged to employ those receiving TANF benefits in order for those individuals to obtain gainful employment rather than continue receiving welfare benefits.

The effects of the Welfare Reform Act were not realized for quite some time, and some government officials were not even aware of the portion of the act that outlined restrictions for felony drug offenders. As states began to realize the limitations that elimination of welfare benefits placed on offenders attempting to reintegrate into society from prison, the number of states utilizing the act dropped. By 2002, six years after passage of the bill, 22 states had applied the lifetime ban on benefits, 10 had partial denials, 10 required drug treatment participation to receive benefits, and 9 had opted out of the ban altogether.

The loss of welfare benefits affected women and their children at a greater rate than men, because of the higher rate of drug offenses for women. Even though men are convicted of drug crimes more often, women are more likely to receive welfare benefits. Research has shown that as many as 35 percent of women were receiving welfare benefits prior to their arrests, compared with 11 percent of men.

As of 2011, 35 states had decided either to modify or to opt out of the welfare ban. New Jersey, for example, passed three new legislative bills that would affect ex-offenders' ability to receive welfare benefits. These laws allow ex-offenders to receive welfare benefits upon their release. They also require that inmates receive the equivalent of a high school education while in prison and ensure that they are given copies of personal documents (such as birth certificates) upon their release. The immediate availability of these documents allows these individuals to apply for public assistance more quickly, as many of these documents must be produced to complete the application process.

The hope in allowing ex-offenders to receive welfare benefits is that they will have a greater success rate in avoiding recidivism. Even though, in the example given for New Jersey, the extension of welfare benefits is a $6 million project, overall savings could be immense if these individuals remain out of the correctional system. New Jersey spends an annual average of $48,000 per inmate for nearly 26,000 state inmates (nearly $1.25 billion).

Additional legislation that may assist offenders in dealing with the loss of welfare benefits and meeting their reentry goals includes the Second Chance Act. This act was introduced in 2005 and has been amended and expanded several times since its inception. The Second Chance Act includes funding for alcohol and drug treatment programs, which in many states ex-offenders must complete in order to qualify for welfare benefits.

Nick Harpster
Sam Houston State University

See also Costs of Community Corrections; Female Offenders and Special Needs; Financial Penalties; Recidivism; Reentry Programs and Initiatives; Reintegration Into Communities

Further Readings

Allard, P. *Life Sentences: Denying Welfare Benefits to Women Convicted of Drug Offenses*. Washington, DC: The Sentencing Project, 2002. http://www.sentencing project.org/doc/publications/women_smy_lifesentences.pdf

Controlled Substances Act, 21 U.S.C. 802(6).

Food Stamp Act of 1977, Pub. L. No. 95-113, 91 Stat. 913-1045.

Personal Responsibility and Work Opportunity Reconciliation Act of 1996. Pub. L. No. 104-193, 110 Stat. 2105.

Petersilia, J. (2003). *When Prisoners Come Home*. New York: Oxford University Press, 2003.

Maconochie, Alexander

Alexander Maconochie (1787–1860)—prison reformer, naval officer, and "father of parole"—was born in Edinburgh, Scotland. Best known for his work in Tasmania and the Norfolk Island penal colony, he was a pioneer in penal reform, and his ideas and philosophies provide the basis for many modern Western penal systems. Throughout his career, he believed that prisoners should be treated humanely and decently and that, if given the opportunity, the majority would learn to live honest and productive lives. One of his many disciples was Walter Crofton, who, as chairman of the board of directors of the Irish prison system, implemented many of Maconochie's principles in his own system.

Maconochie joined the Royal Navy in 1803 and attained the rank of commander in 1815. During the Napoleonic Wars, he was a prisoner of war for three years (1811–1814), and his experiences during that time no doubt influenced his philosophy regarding the transportation and treatment of prisoners. After the war, in 1822, Maconochie married, and he moved to London in 1829. He joined University College, London, where he became the first professor of geography and in 1830 a founder and first secretary of the Royal Geographical Society.

Sir John Franklin, the famous Arctic explorer, was appointed lieutenant-governor of Van Diemen's Land (Tasmania) in January 1836. The English viewed this land as basically an island prison colony and operated it as such. Because of Maconochie's

background and experience, Franklin asked him to accompany him as his private secretary, and Maconochie accepted with some reluctance. Prior to his leaving London, he was asked to complete a questionnaire for the Society for the Improvement of Prison Discipline concerning the penal system in Van Diemen's Land. He arrived in the capital, Hobart, early in 1837 with a number of new ideas on how to reform convict discipline and the penal system.

In October 1837, Maconochie forwarded a report on convict discipline to the English parliament, and in 1838 he published *Thoughts on Convict Management and Other Subjects Connected With the Australian Penal Colonies*. He added a short supplement in 1839 with a new title, adding *Australiana*. It was here that he presented his ideas that criminals should be punished for their past behavior and trained for the future in government employment. This so impressed the colonial office that in May 1839 Maconochie was offered the position of superintendent of Norfolk Island. He readily accepted the position but pointed out that he did not consider Norfolk Island suitable for testing his methods.

Norfolk Island was first settled in the 14th or 15th century by East Polynesians from the Kermadec Islands north of New Zealand or from what is now known as New Zealand's North Island. Norfolk Island was named after the duchess of Norfolk by Captain James Cook, the first European to arrive there. In March 1788, Philip Gidley King led an expedition of 15 convicts and seven freemen to settle and prepare for further development. Over the next few years, an increasing number of convicts were sent to Norfolk Island, and it became nothing more than a penal colony for the most incorrigible convicts. By 1814, the island was abandoned, because it was seen as too costly and to remote to maintain. In 1824, the British government began to reconsider this, and a new penal colony was established for new inmates from Britain and the most serious felons from other parts of Australia.

In March 1840, Maconochie assumed his new position and immediately applied his own penal practices and philosophies. The existing cruel and degrading conditions were improved and sentences were served in stages, each stage providing the inmate with increasing responsibility. He also established the marks system in which inmates could earn their release or reduced time through good behavior and hard work. These "marks" could also be used to purchase goods and food. When Walter Crofton became the head of the Irish prison system in 1854, he attempted to implement Maconochie's marks system with some success.

Maconochie was replaced in 1844 by Major Childs, who immediately sought to restore the island to its previous harsh and brutal ways, and Maconochie's policies and ideas were abandoned. The second penal colony was closed, and the last convict inhabitants were sent to Tasmania in 1855. The primary reason for its closure was that transportation to Van Diemen's Land as a punishment was ended in 1853 and was replaced by prison sentences in Britain. In 1856, descendants of the HMS *Bounty* mutineers and Tahitians resettled Norfolk Island.

Maconochie returned to England in 1844 and tried to implement his reforms when he was appointed governor of the new Birmingham Borough Prison in 1849. He was dismissed in 1851 because his methods were seen as too lenient and ineffective. He retired after his dismissal and, because of poor health, never worked again in the prison system. He died in Morden, Surrey, on October 25, 1860, at the age of 73.

Charles B. Fields
Eastern Kentucky University

See also Irish Marks System; Probation and Parole: Intensive Supervision

Further Readings

Barry, John V. *Alexander Maconochie of Norfolk Island.* Melbourne: Oxford University Press, 1958.

Clay, John. *Maconochie's Experiment.* London: John Murray, 2001.

Maconochie, Alexander. *Australiana: Thoughts on Convict Management and Other Subjects Connected With the Australian Penal Colonies.* London: J. W. Parker, 1839.

Maconochie, Alexander. *Norfolk Island.* London: Statistical Society, 1845.

Maconochie, Alexander. *On Reformatory Prison Discipline.* London: C. Gilpin, 1851.

Maconochie, Alexander. *The Principles of Punishment, on Which the Mark System of Prison Discipline Is Advocated.* London: J. Ollivier, 1850.

Maconochie, Alexander. *Secondary Punishment: The Mark System.* London: J. Ollivier, 1848.

Morris, Norval. *Maconochie's Gentlemen: The Story of Norfolk Island and the Roots of Modern Prison Reform.* New York: Oxford University Press, 2002.

MANHATTAN BAIL PROJECT

The Manhattan Bail Project was undertaken in 1961 by the Vera Institute of Justice to assess whether suspects who were released on a promise to appear in court, as opposed to bail, would make their court appearances. Prior to this time, suspects who could not afford to pay monetary bail had to spend time in jail awaiting their trial. The results of the Manhattan Bail Project showed that those defendants who had family and employment ties and were released before their court appearance with a promise to return did, indeed, show up for their court appearances. The results of this study ushered in the widespread use of releasing defendants on their own recognizance.

The project sought to answer the question of whether the practice of bail was necessary to ensure that the defendant would make his or her court appearance. Bail is money or some other security given to the court to ensure that the defendant will appear at every subsequent stage of the criminal justice process. The purpose of bail is to obtain the release from custody of a person charged with a crime. If the defendant is released on bail but does not appear in court when scheduled, the bail deposit is forfeited. A defendant who fails to make bail is confined in jail until the court appearance.

One incentive of the Vera Institute of Justice to undertake this study was the recognition of discrimination inherent in the bail system: Defendants with financial resources can make bail, whereas poor defendants must stay in pretrial detention in jail.

About 50 percent of those held in local jails have been accused of crimes but not convicted, whereas others have been convicted and are serving a sentence of a year or two. Conditions in jails tend to be very harsh, and overcrowding has historically been a problem. Another factor influencing the Manhattan Bail Project was that pretrial detention cost taxpayers money, because the costs of paying for jail were passed on to them. If it could be shown that defendants who were released before their trials, based on a promise to make the appearance, would indeed show up, then the widespread practice of bail and pretrial detention could be minimized.

The Vera Institute of Justice funded the project and coordinated the efforts of its staff: law students and personnel from New York City University, the Institute of Judicial Administration of New York University, and the criminal courts. Defendants appeared in Felony Court of the Borough of Manhattan and had charges including grand larceny, forgery, and felonious assault. The Manhattan Bail Project staff gathered information about each defendant, including offense type, family ties in the city, and employment status and length. Based on this information, the defendant was given a numerical score. Defendants with higher scores had more ties and were predicted to show up for their court appearances, whereas those with lower scores were predicted to abscond. The staff met with criminal court judges in Manhattan and presented their

The Manhattan Bail Project studied the likelihood of suspects released on bail to make court appearances. The results showed that employed defendants with family ties were the most likely to return to court for their hearing. (Photos.com)

recommendation for release for each defendant, based on this information.

The study found that if the court had enough background information about the defendant, it could make a good prediction of whether the accused would return to court. If the bases for the release decision incorporated the nature of the offense, family ties, and employment record, most defendants returned to court when released on their own recognizance.

The Vera Institute of Justice stated that the group that was released based on only a promise to return to court actually had double the rate of making their court appearances, compared to those defendants who were released on bail. The findings showed strong support that releasing a person on this type of information more effectively guaranteed appearance in court than did money bail.

The policy implications of the Manhattan Bail Project have been widespread. As a result of the findings of the Manhattan Bail Project, the practice of release on own recognizance (ROR) in lieu of bail spread across the nation. ROR programs are seen in almost every major jurisdiction today. Of course, different states have restrictions on the use of ROR, and in many cases defendants charged with violent or felony offenses may not be eligible.

Two acts followed the dissemination of the results of the Manhattan Bail Project. The Bail Reform Act of 1966 was the first change in federal bail laws since 1786. This act stated that, for all noncapital cases, the defendant would be granted release if there were sufficient reason to believe that the defendant would return to court. In essence, the Bail Reform Act of 1966 established a presumption of ROR that should be overcome before money bail is required and allowed for a deposit of 10 percent bail. It also introduced the concept of conditional release. The Bail Reform Act of 1966 established the standard that release should be under the least restrictive method necessary that will ensure court appearance by the defendant.

During the 1970s, the pretrial movement was challenged by some criminal justice actors and the general public in response to crimes committed by defendants who were on pretrial release at the time of their offense. As a result, the Bail Reform Act of 1984 mandated that defendants should not be kept in pretrial detention just because they could not afford money bail, but required that community safety, as well as flight risk, be considered in the release decision.

In addition to the federal acts, a number of state jurisdictions have incorporated elements of preventive detention into their bail systems. These include (1) exclusion of certain crimes from bail eligibility (such as murder in Pennsylvania), (2) definition of bail to include appearance in court and community safety, and (3) limitations on the right to bail for those previously convicted.

Virtually all jurisdictions in the United States have pretrial release in one form or another. The basic criteria in deciding who gets released are defendants' community ties and prior criminal justice involvement. Many jurisdictions have conditional and supervised release, in addition to release on one's own recognizance.

Liz Marie Marciniak
University of Pittsburgh, Greensburg

See also Bail Reform Act of 1984; Offender Risks; Pretrial Detention

Further Readings

McDonald, Douglas Corry. *Punishment Without Walls: Community Service Sentences in New York City*. New Brunswick, NJ: Rutgers University Press, 1986.

Siegel, Larry J. and Joseph J. Senna. *Introduction to Criminal Justice*, 11th ed. Belmont, CA: Thomson Wadsworth, 2008.

Vera Institute of Justice. *Manhattan Bail Project: Official Court Transcripts, October 1961 to June 1962*. http://www.vera.org/content/new-Areas-Bail-Reform-Report-Manhattan-Bail-Reevaluation-Project-June-1966-August-1967 (Accessed January 2011).

Vera Institute of Justice. *New Areas for Bail Reform: A Report on the Manhattan Bail Reevaluation Project, June 1966–August 1967*. http://www.vera.org/content/new-Areas-Bail-Reform-Report-Manhattan-Bail-Reevaluation-Project-June-1966-August-1967 (Accessed January 2011).

Vera Institute of Justice. *A Short History of Vera's Work on the Judicial Process*. http://www.vera.org/content/short-History-Veras-Work-Judicial-Process (Accessed January 2011).

Martinson, Robert

Robert Magnus Martinson (1927–80) was a professor of sociology at the City College of New York. His name has become synonymous with the "nothing works" view of rehabilitation, and he is sometimes credited with ending the rehabilitation movement and ushering in a conservative era of just deserts. This is ironic, since Martinson almost certainly did not intend to contribute to severer punishment in the United States.

Martinson attended college at the University of California, Berkeley, where he earned his B.A. in 1949, his M.A. in 1953, and his Ph.D. in 1968. His M.A. thesis focused on the role of the Communist Party as a totalitarian organization in the Spanish Civil War, and his Ph.D. dissertation examined organizational change in the context of treatment ideology and correctional bureaucracy. Martinson supported civil rights, participating in the Freedom Rides from New Orleans to Jackson, Mississippi, where he was arrested in June 1961 for breach of the peace and incarcerated for 40 days.

In 1968, along with Douglas Lipton and Judith Wilks, Martinson was hired by the New York State Governor's Special Committee on Criminal Offenders to conduct a systematic appraisal of rehabilitation programs. Many of these programs—featuring education, vocational training, counseling, medical treatment, parole, or community supervision—had been touted as viable remedies for recidivism. Lipton, Martinson, and Wilks reviewed 231 English-language studies of rehabilitative programs undertaken between 1945 and 1967, comparing the experimental groups (which received treatment interventions) with control groups (which did not). They focused particularly on recidivism rates.

The researchers produced a 1,400-page report, concluding that rehabilitation programs did not appear to have a demonstrable effect on recidivism. However, New York State, afraid of the political consequences of the study, refused to issue their report and prohibited the researchers from releasing their findings independently. Eventually, however, the report was introduced as evidence in a court case, and the state authorized the authors to publish their findings as a book. In 1975, they published *The Effectiveness of Correctional Treatment: A Survey of Treatment Evaluation Studies*.

Their book was critical of rehabilitation and its effects on recidivism but did not reach a novel conclusion (many social scientists had been critical of rehabilitation) and did not have much impact on policy (it was a 736-page scholarly monograph). This was not true, however, of Martinson's 1974 article, "What Works? Questions and Answers About Prison Reform." Published in *The Public Interest*, Martinson's distillation of the results from the New York recidivism study were highly influential and immediately catapulted him into the national spotlight.

This was, in part, a function of an existing dissatisfaction with the state of punishment in America. Throughout the late 1960s and early 1970s, progressive reformers had criticized the government for its paternalism and for its use of coercive power to "treat" offenders, not to help these individuals but to maintain social order. Correctional officials and parole boards, it was claimed, exercised unfettered discretion over the lives of others. Conservatives joined in this criticism, though not because correctional officials were racist or class-biased in how they used their discretion but because they were seen as too lenient. Instead of coddling criminals with rehabilitation, conservatives argued, criminals should be punished. Martinson's article attracted attention by appealing to both camps and providing them with a scientific foundation for their respective ideologies.

In part, however, Martinson's article attracted attention because of its tone. Instead of couching his conclusions in the cautious language of social scientists—for example, calling for more research on rehabilitation—Martinson made sweeping conclusions. Regardless of the fact that many of the rehabilitation programs had been underfunded or understaffed, Martinson concluded that, with few exceptions, rehabilitative programs had no appreciable effects on recidivism; he also concluded that existing strategies could not overcome the tendencies of offenders to reoffend. Martinson thereby intimated not only that existing programs were inadequate to rehabilitate offenders but also that the entire endeavor was doomed. "Nothing works" soon became accepted as a mantra in policy circles.

In this way, Martinson became a public intellectual, appearing in popular publications such as *People* magazine. During an August 24, 1975, interview on the television news program *60 Minutes*, Martinson continued to denounce rehabilitation in broad, unqualified terms. Asked by journalist Mike Wallace if it was conceivable that "nothing works," Martinson replied that it certainly was and may well be the case.

Martinson certainly defended his views against the attacks of his critics, but he remained a sociologist who was committed to the study of rehabilitation. Accordingly, in 1979, he published an article in the *Hofstra Law Review*, retracting many of the claims from his "What Works?" article. He noted that, contrary to popular opinion, the U.S. recidivism rate was quite low, not high. He also noted that, contrary to his previous findings, many rehabilitation programs do have an effect on recidivism. Although he had often described treatment as ineffectual ("nothing works"), he withdrew that characterization also.

However, whereas the *Public Interest* article had made him a celebrity, the *Hofstra* article went unnoticed; it did not turn the rising punitive tide. Only academics took note of the article, and to them, it cast doubt on Martinson's credibility. The City College of New York denied him tenure. In 1980, beset by personal and professional troubles, Martinson jumped to his death from the window of his ninth-story Manhattan apartment. Curiously, although Martinson's publications are frequently cited, virtually nothing was written about his death.

James C. Oleson
University of Auckland

See also Evaluation of Programs; Recidivism; "What Works" Approach and Evidence-Based Practices

Further Readings

Abramsky, Sasha. *American Furies: Crime, Punishment, and Vengeance in the Age of Mass Imprisonment*. Boston: Beacon Press, 2007.

Martinson, Robert. "New Findings, New Views: A Note of Caution Regarding Sentencing Reform." *Hofstra Law Review*, v.7/2 (1979).

Martinson, Robert. "What Works? Questions and Answers About Prison Reform." *The Public Interest*, v.35 (Spring 1974).

MEDIATION

Over the past several decades, there has been a growing interest in the use of restorative justice practices and principles in the United States. Mediation is generally understood to fit under the umbrella of restorative justice and has been employed in corrections for many years. This strategy of restorative justice is generally defined as a dispute resolution process in which an impartial person trained in conflict resolution facilitates a dialogue or negotiation between parties in conflict. The process of mediation is an important area of discussion in community corrections, as it offers an alternative to traditional judicial proceedings for less serious criminal offenses. Criminal mediation currently exists in two forms: victim-offender mediation and community mediation. Each of these forms plays a distinct role in community corrections.

History and Overview

Criminal mediation has been used as an alternative to court proceedings since the 1970s, although other forms of mediation have been present in the United States since the early Native American tribal systems of justice. The use of mediation in the criminal setting is becoming increasingly common, as it provides for a judicial outlet for less serious criminal offenses, such as trespassing, vandalism, and minor assaults, and can be used during a number of points in the life of a criminal case. Limits on access to traditional processes of justice because of court backlogs and court costs have contributed to the increase and development of mediation programs in the United States. In addition, increased participation in mediation can be attributed to the appeal of an informal setting used to discuss the needs of the victim, the offender, and the community.

Two basic types of mediation exist in the United States. The first is government-sponsored programs that are typically classified as victim-offender mediation (VOM) programs and are operated by justice system agencies, such as police departments, courts, and correctional agencies. The second type of criminal mediation program in the United States is community-based programs, which are sponsored by nonprofit organizations. These programs receive case referrals through walk-ins, justice system agencies, and other governmental agencies. One prominent distinction between VOM and community mediation programs is that community mediation deals primarily with conflicts among acquaintances, whereas VOM typically resolves conflicts among strangers. Both forms of mediation emerged around the same time period and at similar rates; however, these two areas of mediation have since grown into independent processes.

Victim-Offender Mediation

The first form of mediation to be discussed, victim-offender mediation (VOM), is the less well known

of the two, despite the fact that there are nearly 300 VOM programs in the United States. The VOM process typically begins with offenders who admit guilt prior to the mediation session and victims who are not responsible for the offense. Thus, the primary purpose of VOM is not to resolve disputes but to allow victims the opportunity for an open dialogue with the offender. During this process, victims are encouraged to question the offender directly about the offense, as well as to express their emotions and concerns.

The majority of cases referred to VOM are misdemeanors, the most common being vandalism, minor assault, theft, and burglary cases. Although reaching an agreement is not the primary goal in resolving these cases, approximately 95 percent of VOM sessions result in an agreement, and those who participate are more likely to express satisfaction and fairness with the process than similar counterparts who go through the traditional justice process. Furthermore, researchers suggest that recidivism rates of offenders who participate in VOM are lower than those of offenders who do not participate.

Community Mediation

Like VOM programs, community mediation programs have experienced promising outcomes; however, the process and structure of community mediation differ from VOM and require further exploration.

Community mediation is typically viewed as an appropriate forum for unsolved disputes whereby both parties have some degree of responsibility or participation in the conflict. Mediators in community mediation are typically volunteers whose training in conflict resolution helps disputants reach a mutually agreeable resolution to the conflict. Agreements in community mediation often include apologies, restitution, community service, and counseling. Community mediation is an important alternative to the traditional justice process, as it provides an appropriate forum for conflicts that may not be appropriate for court proceedings. Furthermore, community mediation may be the preferred process in some situations, as court proceedings tend to polarize parties and increase conflict.

Traditionally, community mediation programs have solely addressed criminal cases; however, community mediation programs have expanded to handle civil cases, school-based disputes, divorce and custody disputes, and juvenile truancy cases. Community mediation programs are also becoming involved in intergroup dispute resolution, which focuses on gangs and other groups of youths to help prevent future violence and to resolve conflicts between and among those groups. Most community mediation programs are affiliated with the National Association for Community Mediation (NAFCM), and this association is largely responsible for giving the practice of community mediation a national presence. In 2011, NAFCM currently had a membership of more than 300 community mediation programs. This increasing visibility of community mediation bodes well for the continued use of mediation as a tool in community corrections.

The Future of Mediation

Mediation is a growing area in community corrections, as it allows disputants involved in less serious offenses an alternative to traditional criminal proceedings. Depending on the particular situation, parties in mediation typically are involved in VOM or community mediation programs, both of which focus on restoring the victim, the offender, and the community. Mediation also has been used by police departments focusing on community policing, as mediation training allows officers the skills to mediate less serious disputes that they encounter instead of relying on traditional police responses.

Unlike conventional criminal proceedings, mediation allows the victim to play an active role in the justice process without subjection to a delay in justice because of court backlog and costs. At the same time, researchers suggest that mediation does not significantly affect overall court caseloads and court costs and have found that in order for mediation to have substantial impacts, measures must be in place to promote higher numbers of case referrals and case processing. Despite these findings, advantages and disadvantages of criminal mediation still warrant further exploration in order to make a full understanding of community mediation and VOM, in comparison to traditional case processing, possible.

Beverly R. Crank
Georgia State University

See also Restorative Justice; Victim-Offender Reconciliation Programs

Further Readings

Bazemore, Gordon and Mark Umbreit. "Balanced and Restorative Justice for Juveniles: A Framework for the 21st Century." In *Juvenile Justice Bulletin*. Washington, DC: U.S. Department of Justice, Office of Juvenile Justice and Delinquency Prevention, 2001.

Bellard, Jan. "Victim Offender Mediation." http://www.voma.org/docs/bellard.pdf (Accessed January 2011).

Go, Flora. "Mediation as Practiced in Criminal Law: The Present, the Pitfalls, and the Potential." http://www.abanet.org/dispute/docs/2010_BoskeyEssay_Winner_FloraGo.pdf (Accessed January 2011).

Hedeen, Timothy. "The Evolution and Evaluation of Community Mediation: Limited Research Suggests Unlimited Progress." *Conflict Resolution Quarterly*, v.22/1–2 (2004).

McGillis, Daniel. *Community Mediation Programs: Developments and Challenges*. Washington, DC: U.S. Department of Justice, National Institute of Justice, 1997.

Umbreit, Mark S. "The Development and Impact of Victim-Offender Mediation in the United States." *Conflict Resolution Quarterly*, v.12/3 (1995).

Wright, Martin and Burt Galaway, eds. *Mediation and Criminal Justice: Victims, Offenders and Community*. Thousand Oaks, CA: Sage, 1989.

MENTAL HEALTH COURTS

Several factors over the past 40 years have led to a massive increase in the number of mentally ill individuals housed in prisons and jails, including the rise of the community mental health movement, which resulted in the deinstitutionalization of thousands of mentally ill patients from state hospitals; the early successes of Thorazine, dubbed the "wonder drug" because of its ability to control psychotic behavior; and the decline of psychiatry, prompted by public exposés, such as Ken Kesey's novel *One Flew Over the Cuckoo's Nest*, which revealed the deplorable conditions of many state psychiatric hospitals of the 1960s. As a result, in a process coined the "criminalization of the mentally ill," the criminal justice system has become the de facto mental healthcare system in the United States.

There are more persons with mental illness residing in prisons and jails today than in public psychiatric hospitals. Once incarcerated, the mentally ill offender faces higher rates of victimization, imposed isolation, and even new charges for prosecution in the system, mostly because of his or her inability to comprehend directives and respond with conforming behavior. The recognition that the traditional criminal justice response is inappropriate for the mentally ill offender led to the creation of mental health courts, which built upon the success of drug courts (a prior experiment with problem solving-courts). Mental health courts were created in the 1990s to divert qualified offenders from the criminal justice and correctional systems to the mental health system, with the ultimate goal of providing immediate alternatives to incarceration for people with mental illness. Therapeutic jurisprudence provides a framework for mental health courts, which can have both benefits and disadvantages as diversion programs.

Underlying Theory

Mental health courts encompass the principles of therapeutic jurisprudence, which advocate using the criminal justice system to address the underlying factors that may lead a person to come into contact with the law. By focusing on using the application of the law in a beneficial or therapeutic way, the theory works within the confines of the traditional goals of the criminal justice system (that is, incapacitation and deterrence) to influence the offender in a beneficial way.

The objective of diversion programs is to redirect individuals from the criminal justice and correctional systems to appropriate mental healthcare services, while considering and balancing the safety of the offender and the public. Mental health courts divert offenders through collaborative efforts between criminal justice and mental health professionals to screen and identify offenders who are mentally ill, to assist in creating and monitoring a treatment program for offenders that provides necessary psychiatric and psychological services in the least restrictive environment, and to serve as a liaison between offenders and community mental health services.

Who Is Eligible?

To be eligible for having his or her case heard before a mental health court, an offender must be diagnosed with mental illness. Existing courts focus on Axis I psychiatric diagnoses, as defined in the American

Psychiatric Association's *Diagnostic and Statistical Manual* (DSM). However, courts routinely exclude personality disorders, mental retardation (Axis II), and other medical conditions (Axis III).

The second common eligibility criterion concerns the volition of the offender. Approximately half of American mental health court programs require a "guilty" or "no contest" plea from the offender prior to the offender's entry into the program, although some of these programs offer an opportunity to expunge the plea after successful completion of the program. Other mental health courts suspend the plea until diversion is complete. The mechanism whereby the mentally ill offender is received into the program may have implications for perceived coercion and fairness and ultimately a successful outcome for the mentally ill offender. For these reasons, mental health courts admit only those offenders who are willing to accept treatment and voluntarily consent to participation in the court.

Last, the safety of the public must not be compromised. Few would disagree that offenders who pose a danger to themselves or others, mentally ill or not, should be institutionalized. For these reasons, mental health courts have focused their efforts on mentally ill offenders most often arrested for nuisance crimes (such as trespassing, shoplifting, and public urination). Unfortunately, accepting only nuisance crime cases to maintain public safety does not allow mental health courts to address the most meaningful problem offenders. The ongoing concern with diversionary programs is that, if the program does not reach its target population but rather serves only less serious offenders, it in essence widens the net of the criminal justice system. Net widening actually results in more, rather than fewer, individuals becoming involved in the system than before the diversion. However, assuming a riskier mix of cases could put citizens and public safety at risk. For this reason, the criminal offense needs to be as a result of the mental disorder.

How Does It Work?

It has often been said that there are no two mental health courts alike, but integral to the functioning of a mental health court is a multidisciplinary team approach. The team involves judges and lawyers who collaborate with caseworkers, psychiatrists, and social workers to meet the specialized needs of the offender. By including experts from the various disciplines, teams are best able to assess the needs of offenders and create an appropriate response.

The success of the mental health courts depends, in a large part, on the commitment of those involved in the criminal justice system to maintain therapeutic jurisprudence. Mental health court members utilize different "tools" from those of traditional criminal justice courts. For example, knowing that often the factors that place offenders in the criminal justice system could be addressed more effectively outside traditional criminal justice sanctions, mental health courts often focus on the treatment of the mental health disorder (as well as housing, treatment for substance abuse, and job training) rather than probation, jail, and fines.

Once the team is assembled, its members are generally responsible for determining the eligibility of the offender for inclusion. There are several points at which the potential diversion can occur, including prior to the initial court appearance, after the first appearance, after a bail hearing, and after a fitness evaluation and hearing. At any of these points, the offender may be deemed eligible for participation in a mental health court.

Advantages and Future Challenges

Mental health courts embody a streamlined approach to a complicated and growing problem, restoring humanity and dignity to the mentally ill. By placing all participants in one court and creating a single point of entry, the court has increased the continuity and accountability of the process. Research on the effectiveness of mental health courts is promising. Several studies have reported that mental health court programs are successful in reducing incarceration time and improving quality of life measures in housing, functioning, and family relationships. This means real improvement in the lives of the mentally ill and a savings of resources for the criminal justice system. If the next generation of mental health courts can begin to address theoretically important issues of homelessness and co-occurring substance abuse, responding with more comprehensive services, the effectiveness of the courts will likely increase. However, although mental health courts as a form of diversion clearly constitute a step in the right direction, these programs suffer from an absence of funds and services to support them. Hence, the challenges ahead for mental health courts are great.

There has been a massive growth of mental health courts in the United States. In 2007, it was estimated that there were 150 courts nationwide, with dozens more planned in coming years. By comparison, the United States has seen a steady decline in the provision of mental healthcare services, starting with the deinstitutionalization movement in the latter half of the 20th century. Today, adequate mental healthcare services are scarce; mental healthcare systems continue to be underfunded and overextended. As the community mental health model gains support, monies saved from closing institutions must be reinvested in community treatment. Without adequate community mental health services, the criminal justice system will likely see a further increase in mentally ill offenders, with few mental health resources to treat them. The diversion of the mentally ill offenders cannot be successful until the mental healthcare system is restructured to meet the needs of the mentally ill and those who care for them.

Cara Rabe-Hemp
Illinois State University

See also Diversion Programs; Drug Courts; Net Widening; Offenders With Mental Illness; Therapeutic Jurisprudence

Further Readings

Fisher, William et al. "Patterns and Prevalence of Arrest in a Statewide Cohort of Mental Health Care Consumers." *Psychiatric Services*, v.57/11 (November 1, 2006).

Lamb, H. Richard and Linda E. Weinberger. *Deinstitutionalization: Promise and Problems.* San Francisco: Jossey-Bass, 2001.

Loveland, David and Michael Boyle. "Intensive Case Management as a Jail Diversion Program for People With a Serious Mental Illness: A Review of the Literature." *International Journal of Offender Therapy and Comparative Criminology*, v.51/2 (2007).

Schneider, Richard D., Hy Bloom, and Mark Heerema. *Mental Health Courts: Decriminalizing the Mentally Ill.* Toronto, ON: Irwin Law, 2006.

Steadman, Henry J. et al. "Effect of Mental Health Courts on Arrests and Jail Days: Multisite Study." *Archives of General Psychiatry*, v.68/2 (2011).

MOTIVATIONAL INTERVIEWING

Motivational interviewing (MI) is an empirically supported counseling approach that facilitates a client's recognition and resolution of ambivalence about changing his or her behavior. Originally implemented in substance abuse counseling, it has been found in subsequent studies to be effective in modifying a variety of risk-related behaviors. The utilization of MI has been growing in community corrections settings for both staff-offender interactions and staff-supervisor interactions as agencies have moved toward implementation of evidence-based practices. Within community corrections, MI is applied with the underlying assumption that offender motivation is not a fixed trait and that, with the appropriate environment, rehabilitation efforts, and interaction with community supervision officers, offenders have the ability to increase their level of motivation to achieve behavioral change. Experts note that MI might be especially useful in community corrections settings, because it is empirically supported in related fields, emphasizes offender responsibility through self-motivational speech, and allows for client-officer engagement in positive behavioral change discussions, including addressing with clients how to handle resistance and other difficult situations.

The interview and counseling style of MI encourages adherence to four key principles: expressing empathy for the client's perspective, developing a distinction between the client's values and the client's behavior, diffusing client resistance, and supporting the client's self-efficacy. Under the MI model, probation officers are expected to express empathy with offenders by presenting a genuine understanding of the offender's predicament as he or she is going through the cycle of behavioral change. In their interactions, officers must practice active listening and reflect on the offender's verbalizations, while also avoiding arguments with the offender.

MI challenges how much an offender wants to change, which may provoke arguments and, in turn, increase the offender's resistance to change; consequently, it is important for probation officers to encourage offenders to talk about change, as opposed to arguing. By supporting offenders in making positive statements regarding their sense of self-efficacy, probation officers provide offenders

Under the motivational interviewing (MI) model, probation officers should use empathy with offenders and conduct themselves in a nonconfrontational manner. MI counseling and interviewing has been found effective in modifying many risk-related behaviors. (Photos.com)

with the ability to reframe their thinking patterns. Moreover, when an offender does display resistance to change throughout different stages of the change process, probation officers can address the situation by "rolling with resistance." This is accomplished by delicately challenging the offender through questions, clarifying, and elaborating upon the thought processes that underlie the behavior that is the target of change. Finally, it is important for the offender to have specific goals toward which he or she wants to work and for the officer to identify the discrepancies that exist between the present situation and how the offender's goals will be achieved.

Probation officers can use many motivational interviewing techniques when interacting with clients to promote a behavioral change. The work of W. R. Miller and S. Rollnick includes a discussion of some of the specific motivational interviewing techniques that should be used in community corrections, such as asking open-ended questions, engaging in reflective listening, expressing positive affirmations and support, summarizing what the offender has stated, eliciting self-motivational statements, elaborating on motivational topics, using extremes in examples, looking backward and forward, and exploring the offender's goals.

Studies on MI emphasize that, even with implementation of the MI technique, behavioral change takes time and offenders must progress through numerous stages before a permanent change will occur. These stages are typically identified as precontemplation, contemplation, preparation/planning, action, and maintenance. Officers who acknowledge the effectiveness and need for MI are better able to guide their clients in making the necessary attitudinal and behavioral modifications from existing antisocial behavior to prosocial behavior. To increase an offender's level of motivation toward changing a specific behavior, MI promotes client- and situation-specific strategies for the community supervision officer to implement with each client. Motivational strategies include giving advice, removing barriers, providing choice, decreasing desirability, practicing empathy, providing feedback, clarifying goals, and actively helping. In line with these strategies, probation officers should provide counsel regarding the identification of specific behaviors that require change, but they must also further assist by removing barriers for the offender and increasing service linkages to particular community-based treatment programs. The officer can also enlighten the offender by emphasizing all of the available choices and making it clear that the offender's ability to change lies within him- or herself. Moreover, MI suggests that, while change should be encouraged by the officer, it should not be insisted upon, since such insistence by the officer may cause the offender to develop a defensive stance.

In summary, the impetus behind MI is that officers should decrease the client's ambivalence, or uncertainty, toward behavioral change. So that offenders understand the scope of their present situation, they should be provided with ongoing feedback by people (such as probation officers, family, friends, and treatment providers) with perspectives that are different from their own. Once an offender receives feedback, the officer should attempt to aid the offender in aligning the feedback with the ideal values and goals he or she wishes to achieve. In doing so, the officer can help the offender more clearly distinguish a pathway to those goals. Finally, officers should actively assist offenders in meeting their goals by demonstrating a genuine interest in helping offenders achieve change. Based on the success of MI in parallel areas (such as substance abuse counseling), experts anticipate that probation officers who use the MI strategies and techniques listed above, in addition to following the key principles of motivational interviewing, will be well equipped to help their clients make the changes in their lives necessary to become productive citizens of society.

Gaylene S. Armstrong
Sam Houston State University

See also Correctional Case Managers; Effectiveness of Community Corrections; Offender Supervision

Further Readings

Bundy, C. "Changing Behaviour: Using Motivational Interviewing Techniques." *Journal of the Royal Society of Medicine*, v.97/44 (2004).

Clark, M. D., S. Walters, R. Gingerich, and M. Meltzer. "Motivational Interviewing for Probation Officers: Tipping the Balance Toward Change." *Federal Probation*, v.70/1 (2006).

Miller, W. R. and S. Rollnick. *Motivational Interviewing: Preparing People to Change Addictive Behavior*. New York: Guilford Press, 1991.

National Institute of Corrections. *A Guide for Probation and Parole: Motivating Offenders to Change*. Washington, DC: U.S. Government Printing Office, 2007.

N

NEIGHBORHOOD PROBATION

Many jurisdictions have begun to embrace a particularly new and innovative alternative sentencing program of supervising offenders in collaboration with other key agencies, resources, and organizations within the immediate community where the probationer resides. Commonly known as neighborhood probation (although also referred to as community probation, community supervision, community justice, or neighborhood-based supervision), this method places strong emphasis on public safety, accessibility, and accountability by establishing relationships with local police departments, charitable organizations, faith-based groups, probationer-friendly employers, human services and treatment providers, and other community groups.

These partnerships serve to develop a visible presence for probation agencies whereby officers can take an active role in community development and service delivery and collaborate with key players in the supervision of community service orders and in developing solutions to local problems. The aim is to improve the efficacy of probation services, enhance the quality of life for both probationers and communities, and contribute to crime reduction. Depending on location and resources, probation agencies will typically assign officers and staff to a neighborhood probation office located in the community they serve, in order to ensure visibility, accessibility, and centralization of services for both probationers and communities. Generally, offenders under neighborhood probation are those who are considered problematic to communities—such as gang members, substance abusers, and other chronic and nuisance offenders—who therefore require a combination of services, treatment, and monitoring in order to be managed effectively while completing their probation orders.

One of the first examples of neighborhood supervision may have originated from Madison, Wisconsin, where, between 1989 and 1991, there was a threefold increase in police calls for service in Broadway-Simpson, an area of more than 900 apartments with 500 children and a large number of offenders who were known to reside there, thus leading to a high number of probation violations. The problem continued despite greater policing efforts, until an experienced African American probation officer, Cheryl Knox, volunteered to take responsibility for establishing an office in the neighborhood center, where she began working both with police, to identify offenders, and with other agencies, to coordinate services in conjunction with probation supervisions. For example, she accompanied various staff members (such as healthcare, human services, and housing workers) on home visits to probationers. Over time, this helped to develop strong working relationships with key agencies and other contacts in the community, creating opportunities to educate the community about neighborhood probation strategies and providing a more positive experience for probationers.

In 1991, Project Safeway was established in Chicago, Illinois, in a neighborhood facility within an area that had a high offender population in close proximity to the center and a number of community resources. The main goals were to strengthen relationships with probationers and the community, provide full probative services, and initiate long-term and lasting change to the lives of probationers through a variety of individual, family, and neighborhood interventions. To do this, the project formed an advisory board consisting of community representatives who could help identify the needs of the community and offenders; address project concerns, implementation, and delivery; find volunteers; coordinate services; and plan activities for networking. Once implemented, Project Safeway provided a number of offender programs, including probation orientation, classes leading to the general equivalency diploma (GED), substance abuse evaluations, community service opportunities, job training and placement, parenting skills, and health education—all of which made use of local community resources.

In the mid-1990s in Maricopa County, Arizona, five neighborhood probation offices were established in Phoenix using a more inclusive approach to supervise offenders in the community. Utilizing a community-policing philosophy, probation offices improved quality of life through community development by focusing on unique needs of neighborhoods struggling with crime and involving a number of key people, such as neighborhood residents, local businesses, and probationers' families—all major players in the effort to reduce crime and provide effective supervision for probationers. A neighborhood office was established in one inner-city area in demographic transition, Coronado, which was home to more than 12,000 residents within two square miles who had annual incomes lower than $30,000 and were plagued with increasing crime rates, safety concerns, and socioeconomic deterioration. In addition to providing a range of services to probationers, officers played an imperative role in the community by involving citizens in decision making, attending weekly neighborhood association meetings, sharing knowledge and ideas with community members, and conducting surveys—all of which were intended to provide for more innovative techniques for supervising probationers while reflecting the residents' interests and aspirations for neighborhood improvement.

Last, other neighborhood probation initiatives have relied primarily on relationships with police in order to monitor and enforce probation orders, which may be linked to crime and disorder problems within the communities. For example, Operation Night Light was introduced in Boston in 1992. There, police and probation officers worked alongside each other mainly to determine whether probationers were fulfilling their conditions, such as observing curfew and keeping away from certain areas or groups. Probation officers were able to travel safely with police officers to crime-ridden areas; in turn, police offers were able to obtain information from probation officers, who usually knew the offenders well.

On a statewide level in Maryland, a similar partnership was initiated between police and probation officers through Operation Spotlight in 1995. This program later developed into the HotSpot Initiative community initiative, which specifically identified high-crime areas, developed partnerships with key public agencies, and incorporated a number of programs found to reduce crime, including neighborhood probation offices. Interestingly, in a follow up study of this initiative that compared recidivism patterns over 12 months of offenders under HotSpot supervision, matched with pre-HotSpot cases under normal probation (both groups numbering 500), no major differences were found.

While innovative and resourceful, neighborhood probation faces a number of challenges and concerns. These initiatives in some cases may require additional funding and resources in terms of staffing, services, and facilities in order to establish, operate, and maintain the neighborhood probation offices. Probation officers are then asked to perform their duties outside in a community setting, which may pose serious safety risks if they are managing potentially dangerous offenders in a nonsecure environment. Therefore, additional training in safety awareness and protection strategies is required—for example, skills for identifying safe apartments and emergency escape routes before entering potentially troublesome areas and situations.

As neighborhood demographics may change over time, probation staff will continually need to monitor communities and gather information on, for example, the number of probationers residing in a particular area and their links with the community, including crime problems. Such duties need to be completed in conjunction of other probation responsibilities, such as coordinating meetings, caseloads, and paperwork. Given these demands, neighborhood probation offices, to be successful, may need to hire reserve staff to help share responsibilities, manage caseloads, coordinate resources, and provide assistance in responding to growing community needs and delivering effective probation supervision.

Michael J. Puniskis
Middlesex University

See also Boston's Operation Night Light; Community Partnerships; Community-Based Centers; Field Visits; Offender Supervision; Probation: Early Termination; Project Safeway

Further Readings

Clear, T. R. and J. B. Cannon. "Neighborhood Probation Offices in Maricopa County, Arizona." In *What Is Community Justice? Case Studies in Restorative Justice and Community Supervision*, D. R. Karp and T. R. Clear, eds. London: Sage, 2002.

Corbett, R. P., B. L. Fitzgerald, and J. Jordan. "Boston's Operation Night Light: An Emerging Model for Police-Probation Partnerships." In *Community Corrections: Probation, Parole and Intermediate Sanctions*, J. Petersilia, ed. New York: Oxford University Press, 1998.

Drapela, L. A. and F. E. Lutze. "Innovation in Community Corrections and Probations Officers' Fear of Being Sued: Implementing Neighborhood-Based Supervision in Spokane, Washington." *Journal of Contemporary Criminal Justice*, v.25/4 (2009).

Leaf, R., A. Lurigio, and N. Martin. "Chicago's Project Safeway: Strengthening Probation's Links With the Community." In *Community Corrections: Probation, Parole and Intermediate Sanctions*, J. Petersilia, ed. New York: Oxford University Press, 1998.

Nevers, D. "Neighborhood Probation: Adapting a 'Beat Cop' Concept in Community Supervision." in *Community Corrections: Probation, Parole and Intermediate Sanctions*, J. Petersilia, ed. New York: Oxford University Press, 1998.

Piquero, N. L. "A Recidivism Analysis of Maryland's Community Probation Program." *Journal of Criminal Justice*, v.31/4 (2003).

NET WIDENING

The term *net widening* has been used to describe a particular phenomenon associated with the utilization of various alternatives to traditional sentencing, such as diversion programs, probation, parole, and community sentencing. When offenders are included in these various programs, a wider array of the population comes under the oversight of state agencies. The creation of these various programs produces a need for them to be inhabited. Many of these measures were introduced to reduce the prison population, to lower the court dockets, or to develop a more appropriate and effective offender program, but there has been an unintended effect of increasing the total number of the population under state control while the target population has not been reduced. In addition, the recidivism rate for many new programs (indeterminate sanctions, excluding probation and parole) does not show a lowering of recidivism in comparison to more traditional probation and parole programs—albeit the cost for these alternative programs is lower. Ultimately an effect is created in which the capacity to punish increases. This issue is especially pertinent for the United States, which already has the highest rate, percentage, and number of people incarcerated of all countries in the world. The rate of crime engagement and victimization in the United States, however, is very similar to those rates in other industrialized nations, with exception of homicide.

Before these various alternative sanctions, a police officer, through the use of his or her discretion, would be less inclined to send an offender through the formal criminal justice system. Now, an officer is more inclined to utilize such a formal process. Currently, various procedures have been implemented in which formal sanctioning has increased.

According to data from the *Sourcebook of Criminal Justice Statistics*, in all categories of probation, jail, prison, and parole, there is an increase of the total population under direct control of a correctional agency. In 1980, there were 1,840,400 people total in the correctional population (probation, jail, prison, and parole). In 2009, this number jumped to 7,225,800, a 293 percent increase. Those on probation in 1980 totaled 1,118,097; in 2009, this figure was 4,203,967, a 276 percent increase. Individuals on parole in 1980 were 220,438. In 2009, the figure was 819,308, a 217 percent increase. These percentages do not include various other diversion and community programs.

Also from data from the *Sourcebook of Criminal Justice Statistics*, there was an overall increase of the number held in jail and supervised outside a jail facility within a 10-year time span (1995–2005). The total for those in jail and outside jail in 1995 was 541,913. In 2005, this increased to 747,529, a 51 percent increase. This increase was echoed in a variety of programs during the same time period: Electronic monitoring saw a 68 percent increase; home detention, a 9 percent increase; day reporting, a 270 percent increase; community service, a 51 percent increase; weekender programs, a 639 percent increase; and other pretrial supervision, a 379 percent increase. The only two areas in which there has been a percentage decrease are other work programs, with a 37 percent decrease, and treatment programs, with an 81 percent decrease. (For treatment, the percentage calculated is between the years 1996 and 2005.) This was during a period of an overall crime decrease, according to the Bureau of Justice Statistics.

Many of the community-based programs are selective, including offenders who will be most likely to succeed in the program (thus, nonviolent offenders who have a history of compliance with authority are often selected as clients). Under ordinary conditions, therefore, many of these offenders would be provided only a warning by the criminal justice gatekeeper, the police officer, but officers may be more inclined to arrest and process these offenders because of the existence of these various programs. The result is that many offenders receive more restrictive sanctions than they would otherwise.

J. Michael Botts
Belmont Abbey College

See also Community Corrections and Sanctions; Community Corrections as an Add-On to Imprisonment; Community Service Order; Diversion Programs; Juvenile and Youth Offenders; Probation and Parole: Intensive Supervision; Residential Correctional Programs

Further Readings

Alarid, Leanne Fiftal and Rolando V. del Carmen. *Community-Based Corrections,* 8th ed. Belmont, CA: Thomson Wadsworth, 2011.

Blomberg, Thomas G. and Karol Lucken. *American Penology: A History of Control,* 2nd ed. New Brunswick, NJ: Transaction, 2010.

Champion, Dean John. *Probation, Parole, and Community Corrections.* Upper Saddle River, NJ: Pearson, 2008.

Kappeler, Victor E. and Gary W. Potter. *The Mythology of Crime and Criminal Justice.* Waveland, IL: Waveland Press, 2004.

Mays, G. Larry and L. Thomas Winfree Jr. *Essentials of Corrections,* 4th ed. Belmont, CA: Thomson Wadsworth, 2009.

Schmalleger, Frank and John Ortiz Smykla. *Corrections in the 21st Century,* 4th ed. Boston: McGraw-Hill, 2009.

U.S. Bureau of Justice Statistics. "Adults on Probation, in Jail or Prison, and on Parole." In *Sourcebook of Criminal Justice Statistics.* Washington, DC: U.S. Department of Justice. http://www.albany.edu/ sourcebook (Accessed February 2011).

U.S. Bureau of Justice Statistics. "Persons Under Jail Supervision." In *Sourcebook of Criminal Justice Statistics.* Washington, DC: U.S. Department of Justice. http://www.albany.edu/sourcebook/pdf/t6152005.pdf (Accessed February 2011).

U.S. Bureau of Justice Statistics. *Violent Crime Rate Unchanged During 2005 Theft Rate Declined.* Washington, DC: U.S. Department of Justice, 2005. http://bjs.ojp.usdoj.gov/content/pub/press/cv05pr.cfm (Accessed February 2011).

NIMBY Syndrome

NIMBY is an acronym that stands for "not in my backyard." It is a term applied to a social phenomenon that occurs when a significant number of people in a local social, geographic, or political group opposes some event. NIMBY, as it is generally used, has a negative connotation when it is applied against a particular group and is usually employed by those parties who are in favor of the event or development in question. When referred to as a general phenomenon, it is frequently called NIMBY syndrome. One of the earliest uses of the term *NIMBY* was in an article in the *Christian Science Monitor* in 1980.

NIMBY syndrome is a form of social or political activism that occurs when the members of a particular group oppose an event or development in their neighborhood or community. As with any new project or development in any neighborhood or community, there are always proponents and detractors. Indeed, under the American political system, opposing points of view are not only expected but encouraged. For example, the American criminal justice system involves an adversarial process that uses opposition in the search for the truth.

However, the NIMBY syndrome is triggered not by a criminal justice proceeding but from grassroots community activists who band together temporarily to oppose the installation of a project or development near where they live. The term *NIMBY syndrome* is usually not employed until the group opposing the proposed new project or development begins to seriously affect the chances of the proposed project or development's reaching reality. Opponents to such projects frequently take social, political, or legal action. Social steps may include seeking support from neighbors, circulating petitions, writing letters to the editor, or arranging protests. Political steps may include asking a local board to prohibit the proposed project or development, such as through zoning ordinances. Legal steps may include seeking a legal injunction from a court to stop the proposed project or development.

Some of the more common projects that have triggered the NIMBY syndrome include the installation of waste incinerators, landfills, airports, nuclear power plants, community mental health residences, and prisons. Each of these examples have in common the possibility (or perceived possibility) of affecting the quality of life in the neighborhood or community where the facility will be located. Waste incinerators, for example, can generate foul odors and pollute the air. Landfills have foul odors, can pollute groundwater, and are unsightly. Airports generate a large degree of traffic and noise produced by airplanes landing and taking off. Nuclear power plants present, however small, a risk of nuclear meltdown, which was highlighted in 1979 by the Three Mile Island incident in Pennsylvania (which largely contributed to the nationwide moratorium on construction of nuclear plants).

In the context of community corrections, community mental health residences, where people with psychiatric problems are placed to live, are frequently perceived as sources of social and crime problems

"Not in My Backyard" (NIMBY) Syndrome is a social phenomenon that occurs when the population has a negative reaction to the planning and execution of developments like nuclear power plants, landfills, community mental health residences, or prisons. (Photos.com)

in the area. Prisons raise the specter of escaped convicts terrorizing the neighborhood. In each of these examples, concerns over the proximity of these facilities contribute to the lowering of property values. Thus, NIMBY syndrome is arguably brought about by a local concern for both quality of life and property value.

One of the valid criticisms of the NIMBY syndrome is that the opponents to a proposed project or development frequently do not consider the countervailing benefits of the project they are opposing. For example, a prison will bring new jobs. An airport can enhance tax revenues and bring new jobs. A waste incinerator or landfill might address lacking or inadequate facilities to handle garbage and trash. A nuclear power plant might provide electricity that would otherwise cost significantly more. A community mental health residence can provide a decent home for local people with psychiatric problems who might otherwise be in prison.

In the context of the criminal justice system, one of the most significant projects or developments that encourage NIMBY syndrome is prisons. The construction of new police stations usually does not cause the local populace to rise up in protest and frequently results in just the opposite reaction. Prisons, however, do not fit the American dream of what belongs in or near a middle-class neighborhood. Moreover, the idea of a prison population being present 24 hours a day and seven days a week only increases the social phenomenon of "fear of crime," which has generated much recent research in the fields of criminology, penology, and criminal justice.

One of the subfields of criminology, penology, and criminal justice is that of community corrections. In the past few decades, there has been a significant political trend to "get tough on crime" and imprison persons convicted of committing crimes for longer prison sentences. This philosophy has, however, failed to deliver on its promise and has, rather, resulted in significantly increasing costs without a corresponding benefit to society of reducing crime. Accordingly, local, state, and federal governments have been seeking alternative methods of handling persons convicted of crimes.

In the context of community corrections and the NIMBY syndrome, three types of correctional facilities are relevant: halfway houses or community residential centers, day attendance centers, and parole offices. Halfway houses or community residential centers are residential facilities for those persons recently released from prison on parole. Day attendance centers are for those persons who are on parole or probation who must report in at regular intervals and participate in programs offered by the center to help them reintegrate into society or to develop social or economic skills to become a productive member of society. Parole offices are those places where persons who have been placed on probation must report at regular intervals. Each of these facilities has the possibility of awakening a NIMBY syndrome.

Halfway houses and community residence centers are designed to help parolees start their reintegration into society. These facilities are residential but usually allow the resident to work at an outside job. When these facilities are first being built or established, they usually cause much resistance in the neighborhoods or communities where they are to be located. The primary cause of this resistance is that the facility's residents will not be under lock and key 24 hours a day; that raises the fear of crime among neighborhood residents.

Day attendance centers are places where persons convicted of crimes must report at regular intervals and attend various programs to help them reintegrate into society. These facilities are not residential but involve the coming and going of persons who have recently been released from prison or are on parole. Their location can be determinative of any resulting NIMBY response. If located in a residential or commercial area, these facilities can result in the same fear of crime as do halfway houses or community residential centers, but they are somewhat different in that their traffic is usually higher, as there are more persons traveling to and from these programs than there are at halfway houses or community residential centers. Thus, in some instances, there can be a greater NIMBY response to a proposed day attendance center than at a halfway house or a community residential center.

Parole offices are frequently located next to or inside courthouses and, thus, usually do not raise the same NIMBY concerns as halfway houses, community residential centers, or day attendance centers. However, when such offices are to be newly established in residential or commercial areas, the NIMBY syndrome can result. This is especially true in urban commercial areas, where the ongoing traffic of people who have been convicted of crimes can result in decreasing local business traffic and hence sales.

One of the most serious problems involving the NIMBY syndrome in the context of community corrections, no matter what type of facility is involved, is the presence of sex offenders. In America, sex offenders, especially sex offenders involving juveniles, inspire intense neighborhood and community opposition. It is difficult to find neighborhoods or communities that are willing to accept a residence or center for sex offenders.

A problem that can complicate the handling of the NIMBY syndrome is the recent trend of privatization in corrections. Although the NIMBY syndrome frequently appears in opposition to government projects, it can also occur in opposition to private ventures. The difference between opposing a private project or development and opposing a public one can directly influence the potential success of a NIMBY-inspired opposition campaign.

Wm. C. Plouffe Jr.
Independent Scholar

See also Community-Based Centers; Day Reporting Centers; Group Homes; Halfway Houses and Residential Centers; Neighborhood Probation; Reducing Prison Populations; Reintegration Into Communities; Sex Offenders in the Community

Further Readings

Allen, Harry, Edward Latessa, Bruce Ponder, and Clifford Simonsen. *Corrections in America: An Introduction*, 11th ed. Upper Saddle River, NJ: Pearson/Prentice Hall, 2007.

Brion, Denis. "An Essay on LULU, NIMBY, and the Problem of Distributive Justice." *Boston College Environmental Affairs Law Review*, v.15/437 (1988).

Fischel, William. "Voting, Risk Aversion, and the NIMBY Syndrome: A Comment on Robert Nelson's Privatizing the Neighborhood." *George Mason Law Review*, v.7 (1999).

Livezey, Emilie Travel. "Hazardous Waste." *Christian Science Monitor* (November 6, 1980). http://www.csmonitor.com/1980/1106/110653.html (Accessed July 2011).

Martin, Brian. "Activism, Social and Political." In *Encyclopedia of Activism and Social Justice*, Gary

Anderson and Kathryn Herr, eds. Thousand Oaks, CA: Sage 2007.

Myers, David and Randy Martin. "Community Member Reactions to Prison Sitting: Perceptions of Prison Impact on Economic Factors." *Criminal Justice Review*, v.19/1 (Spring 2004).

Wheeler, Michael. "Negotiating NIMBYs: Learning From the Failure of the Massachusetts Siting Law." *Yale Journal on Regulation*, v.11 (Summer 1994).

OFFENDER NEEDS

More than 2 million offenders are incarcerated in American prisons and jails. These inmates have many needs, not only in prison but also after their release into the community. It is important for a successful reintegration that programs and services are tailored to the specific needs of the offender. Thus, needs assessment tools are used to classify offenders. While incarcerated, inmates have a variety of needs, including drug abuse and mental health treatment, programs that teach marketable skills, vocational programs, educational programs, life skills programs, parenting programs, and other programs, depending on the specific offender. The main purpose of the programs is to decrease recidivism and promote positive changes that will benefit the offender, his or her family, and the community.

After release, offenders need help in building a support system. They must find meaningful employment and housing. They need to reconnect positively with family members. They must locate drug counseling and mental health programs that allow them to continue treatment in the community. Research shows that returning offenders are significantly more like to abstain from crime if they have a support system, a stable job, housing, and ongoing treatment for any drug abuse and mental health disorders. Offenders who are homeless, jobless, and have lost family ties often return to criminal behavior.

Offender Needs Assessment

Since 1980, the prison population has grown by more than 100 percent, resulting in more than 2 million persons incarcerated in U.S. prisons and jails and representing the highest incarceration rate of any nation in the world. The increase in the prison population and the resulting prison overcrowding make it very difficult to meet offender needs. Offender needs are typically determined by using assessment instruments that help classify offenders and identify which programs and other services will be most helpful to them. These assessment instruments measure criminal history variables such as severity of the crime, assaultive offense history, escape history, legal issues, prior institutional violence or major disciplinary history, returns to higher custody, and identifiable criminal patterns due to substance abuse. Additionally, these instruments assess social history variables, including family relationships, educational history, vocational history, and work history.

The outcome of an offender needs assessment has implications for security and programming options. The better the programming is tailored toward the individual, the greater the chances of that individual's successful reintegration after release. The assessment also impacts the security level of the offender. As a general rule, the lower the security level of an offender, the better the treatment and programming options. This is problematic, because many high-risk offenders with drug addiction and mental health disorders have great need for treatment options that may not be available to them because of their high security level and the shortage of effective treatment in high-security prisons.

Meeting Offender Needs While Incarcerated

All offenders have basic needs, such as food, clothing, housing, and safety. Most offenders, however, also have other needs, including medical treatment and vocational and educational programming. Meeting the needs of offenders is crucial for a successful reintegration into society. Depending on the offender, the specific needs vary considerably. For instance, drug-addicted offenders have needs that are very different from those of sex offenders, and female offenders have needs that differ from those of male or juvenile offenders. Research shows that the most successful programs specifically match the services to the offender's needs and utilize a case management program that is based on the life circumstances of the offender.

There are many offenders with special needs. For instance, in 2000, the Bureau of Justice Statistics estimated that about 70 percent of jail and prison inmates have drug abuse issues. If treatment is not provided or is ineffective, these offenders will likely be rearrested within the first few months after release from prison or jail, because criminal behavior often results directly from the drug-using behaviors, such as buying drugs, selling drugs, and committing crimes to get money for drugs. In fact, recidivism rates of offenders with drug abuse issues are substantially higher than for other offenders. Research demonstrates that the cycle of drug abuse, criminal behavior, and incarceration can be stopped if effective treatment programs are provided while the offender is incarcerated as well as after release in the community. However, only about 20 percent of drug-addicted offenders receive treatment while they are incarcerated. The lack of treatment has implications for recidivism rates, crime rates, prison crowding, and budgets. In an attempt to address these problems, all states have created drug courts, which divert drug-addicted offenders into treatment programs in the community rather than sending them to jail. These drug courts have been effective in reducing recidivism rates among drug-addicted offenders.

Many drug-addicted offenders also suffer from mental health disorders. It is estimated that as many as 10 percent of inmates suffer from co-occurring disorders, that is, they have both drug abuse and mental health disorders. Offenders with co-occurring disorders are more difficult to manage with regard to treatment and programming. Additionally, co-occurring disorders can cause problems for the prison staff; offenders may be disobedient and violent, may not be able to participate in programming, may create dangerous situations because of their erratic behaviors, and thus may constitute a danger to themselves and other inmates. It is therefore imperative to provide these offenders with comprehensive treatment programs. Moreover, their co-occurring disorders make it more difficult to find a diversion program; they often do not qualify for the drug court programs. Very few programs are specifically aimed at offenders with co-occurring disorders. Still, some efforts have been made to divert these offenders into treatment programs in the community. For instance, California has created co-occurring disorder courts that operate similar to drug courts. Research suggests that these courts are effective in improving the offenders' social functioning and reducing drug abuse, both of which are crucial for a successful reintegration into society.

Additionally, between 1 and 2 percent of inmates have the human immunodeficiency virus or acquired immune deficiency syndrome (HIV/AIDS), and many have other infectious diseases, such as hepatitis. The prevalence of HIV/AIDS is significantly higher among the incarcerated population than it is in the general population. The vast majority of these HIV-positive inmates will return to the community, where they could spread the disease. Many inmates with HIV/AIDS also abuse drugs and have mental health disorders, which increase HIV risk behaviors such as risky sexual behaviors and the sharing of needles. Thus, these offenders need consistent medical treatment and education classes pertaining to their disease, both while incarcerated and after release.

Female offenders have special needs as well, because many of them have children who live with relatives or in a foster home while their mothers are in prison. After a female offender is released, her children often return to her. It is therefore important to maintain the relationship between child and mother while the woman is in prison. At the same time, this can be very difficult in the prison setting, especially if the prison is far from the community where the children live. Furthermore, these women often lack parenting skills, which should be addressed via parenting programs while they are in prison.

Pregnant females constitute another difficult inmate group. These women have unique medical needs that have to be met. It is estimated that about 5 percent of female inmates are pregnant. Their needs pose a great challenge for both prison staff and the pregnant inmates, because correctional facilities do not typically have the resources and facilities necessary to provide proper care. Additionally, a substantial number of female inmates have been sexually or otherwise physically abused, a risk factor that decreases their chances of successful reintegration. Treatment and counseling while they are incarcerated can help them overcome the obstacles they will face after release; in turn, such programs will benefit their children and the community at large.

Offender Needs After Incarceration

Nationwide, about 97 percent, or approximately 600,000 prison inmates, return to the community annually. Meeting offenders' needs after their release is crucial to promote their successful reintegration of offenders. That successful reintegration is very important, because offenders who keep going back to prison are costly for the state, for their families, and for their communities. Offenders who are incarcerated do not contribute to the economy, do not support their families (including their children), provide negative role models, and cost taxpayers monies that therefore cannot be used for education and other services needed by the citizens in the community. Considerable reintegration issues must be addressed for reentry to be successful. In reality, however, there are few effective reintegration programs, and the need for these programs far exceeds their availability.

The National Institute of Corrections (NIC) has emphasized that reintegration programs must address the following risk factors: age at first conviction, childhood abuse, number and severity of prior convictions, abuse and/or mental health issues, life skills and social skills deficiencies, behavior while incarcerated, anger management issues, and history of education, employment, family, and social failures.

Research has consistently shown that released offenders have great needs for services that assist them in finding employment and housing. Many released offenders have great difficulty finding a job that provides for their basic needs. When applying for a job, they must disclose their felony record. Employers are hesitant to hire felons, especially if they have other, equally or better qualified applicants. Offenders are often the least qualified for the job, because they typically lack computer skills and other job skills, since prisons do not have the resources to keep prisoners up to date with technology. This is a major problem, as technology is changing rapidly and increasingly all jobs require such knowledge. In an age of high unemployment when the general population is struggling with similar issues, felons have especially great difficulty in this area.

Released offenders also must find stable housing, which is equally difficult—not only because they lack money but also because they are often not eligible for public housing if they have been convicted for a drug offense. Thus, many returning prisoners move in with relatives or friends, which is not a permanent solution. Those with no family or friends to rely on may become homeless. Stable housing is therefore key to successful reintegration, because homeless offenders are substantially more likely to commit new crimes.

Conclusion

Meeting offender needs inside and outside prison is an increasingly challenging task, given the great increase in the number of offenders in prison as well as those returning to the community. Different agencies, both inside prison and in the community, must work effectively together to enhance the chances of successful reentry. If offender needs cannot be met, it is likely that recidivism rates, and as a result incarceration rates, will continue to grow, more children will grow up in single-family homes, and states will spend more money on corrections and less money on education, health services, and other services needed by the citizens in the community.

Janine Kremling
California State University, San Bernardino

See also Diversity in Community Corrections; Offender Risks; Offender Supervision; Offenders With Mental Illness; Reentry Programs and Initiatives; Reintegration Into Communities; Risk and Needs Assessment Instruments

Further Readings

Bloom, Barbara. *Effective Management of Female Inmates: Applying the Research on Gender Responsive Correctional Strategies to Local Jails.* Albuquerque,

NM: American Jail Association, 2003. http://nicic.gov/pubs/2003/018812.pdf (Accessed July 2011).

Chandler, Redonna K., Bennett W. Fletcher, and N. D. Volkow. "Treating Drug Abuse and Addiction in the Criminal Justice System: Improving Public Health and Safety." *Journal of the American Medical Association*, v.301/10 (2009).

Forcier, Michael W. *Development of an Objective Classification System: Final Report*. Washington, DC: National Institute of Corrections, 2001.

Hammett, Theodore M., Sofia Kennedy, and Sarah Kuck. *National Survey of Infectious Diseases in Correctional Facilities: HIV and Sexually Transmitted Diseases*. Washington, DC: U.S. Department of Justice, 2007. http://www.ncjrs.gov/pdffiles1/nij/grants/217736.pdf (Accessed July 2011).

Kleinpeter, Christine et al. "Providing Recovery Services for Offenders With Co-Occurring Disorders." *Journal of Dual Diagnosis*, v.3/1 (2006).

National Institute of Corrections. *Questions and Answers: Jail Inmates With Mental Illness, a Community Problem*. Washington, DC: Author, 2002. http://nicic.gov/downloads/pdf/video/jailinmate-Questions.pdf (Accessed July 2011).

National Institute of Justice. *Drug Courts: The Second Decade*. Washington, DC: Author, 2006.

Prendergast, Michael L. et al. "Amity Prison-Based Therapeutic Community: 5-Year Outcomes." *The Prison Journal*, v.84/1 (2004).

U.S. Bureau of Justice Statistics. *Special Report: Drug Use, Testing, and Treatment in Jails*. Washington, DC: U.S. Department of Justice, 2000.

U.S. Department of Justice, Federal Bureau of Prisons. *Inmates Matters*. http://www.bop.gov/inmate_programs/index.jsp (Accessed July 2011).

Warren, Jennifer. *One in 100: Behind Bars in America 2008*. Washington, DC: Pew Charitable Trusts, Pew Center of the Streets and the Public Safety Performance Project. http://www.pewcenteronthestates.org/uploadedFiles/One%20in%20100.pdf (Accessed July 2011).

Wexler, Harry K. and Bennett W. Fletcher. "National Criminal Justice Drug Abuse Treatment Studies (CJ-DATS) Overview." *Prison Journal*, v.87 (2007).

Offender Responsivity

Responsivity is one component of the Risk-Need-Responsivity (RNR) model of treatment and rehabilitation. Andrews and Bonta are widely credited with developing the Risk-Need-Responsivity model, which addresses the question of who, what, and how to treat. The Risk principle stipulates that the highest-risk offenders receive the most intense treatment. It is important to understand that the risk principle is not necessarily related to the severity of the crime, but rather to the probability that the offender might reoffend. The need principle stipulates that criminogenic needs, which are closely tied to reoffending, be targeted as treatment goals. Criminogenic needs include risk factors such as antisocial attitudes and a history of antisocial behavior. The responsivity principle addresses the means by which to maximize the effectiveness of treatment, which includes cognitive behavioral treatment that is personalized to the offender. Offender responsivity, then, takes into account the individual qualities of an offender, as well as therapeutic and programmatic factors, that impact and conceivably limit the effectiveness of treatment and, by extension, rates of recidivism.

The Risk-Need-Responsivity model has also been applied to risk assessment. In this model, risk addresses the propensity to engage in criminal conduct, need addresses the criminogenic and protective factors influencing the likelihood of criminal behavior, and responsivity addresses the receptivity of the offender to treatment designed to reduce recidivism. In the context of assessment, responsivity still pertains to the highly individualized characteristics that impact appraisal of risk and effectiveness of treatment.

Consideration of offender responsivity includes individual qualities such as intellect, learning style, motivation, criminal attitudes, personality, and culture. A balanced consideration of responsivity also takes into account the strengths and buffering factors that the offender brings to the table, such as an involved and supportive family. A particular challenge in working with offenders is a lack of motivation compounded by outright resistance to treatment, which may result in less than optimal compliance with the intervention. The most effective treatment consists of a personalized and research-based intervention.

The responsivity principle has two pieces, consisting of general and specific responsivity, both of which address the delivery of the intervention. General responsivity refers to the theoretical orientation of the program; research clearly supports cognitive-behavioral strategies. Specific responsivity refers to the interpersonal characteristics of the offender, such as anxiety, intelligence, and insight. Consideration of specific qualities allows offenders to be matched to a treatment program from which they are more likely to derive benefit and/or prepares offenders for the program in order to ensure their success.

General and specific responsivity are not as directly tied to the risk of reoffending as are criminogenic factors. For instance, procriminal attitudes and associates, which are criminogenic factors, have a direct bearing on the likelihood of future criminal behavior. In contrast, the ability to grasp what is taught in a rehabilitation program, which may pertain to intellect, learning style, or maturity, may interfere with treatment effectiveness and thereby indirectly increase risk of reoffending. In sex offender treatment programs, denial and minimization are examples of responsivity factors that are highly likely to impact the degree to which offenders are engaged in and responsive to treatment.

It is not uncommon for offenders to be placed in correctional treatment programs based on their criminal charge, which does not necessarily speak to the extent or severity of their personal involvement in the crime. For instance, if a drug-related charge is the only criterion for admission to a substance abuse treatment program, there will be no differentiation between a drug addict and a drug dealer or between a first-time user and a long-term addict. However, these distinctions have ramifications for the responsivity principle, by virtue of motivation for and receptivity to treatment.

As with any clinical intervention, therapeutic process variables influence the efficacy of the outcome, and these, too, are considered responsivity factors. For instance, the quality of the therapeutic alliance and the personal qualities of the therapist are not specific risk factors for criminal recidivism but may hinder treatment progress, thereby indirectly increasing the risk for reoffending.

Issues unique to mentally ill and female inmates have relevance to the responsivity principle. Mentally ill persons are overrepresented in jails and prisons and commonly have comorbid diagnoses, such as substance abuse. The mentally ill are likely to be referred for treatment, yet significant issues, such as mental impairment and personal distress, may interfere with the efficacy of that treatment.

Females have needs similar to those of male inmates, though studies reveal higher rates of past traumatization and substance abuse among female inmates. Therefore, it is critical that treatment programs attend to the unique treatment issues of the mentally ill and of female inmates in order to maximize treatment efficacy.

The responsivity principle applies to and incorporates issues at the management level of an organization. Agency leaders need to be dedicated to recruiting, training, and retaining skilled clinicians to implement treatment programs. Agency leaders must also be committed to providing the resources and supervision needed to operate a quality program. Training needs to address the inherent challenges in building relationships with high-risk and difficult offenders, who are often hostile, defensive, and resistant.

The effects of risk, need, and general responsivity have been shown to enhance the effectiveness of relapse prevention programs. Interestingly, treatment outcome appears not to be affected by the setting itself, such as a correctional facility versus a community program.

Treatment is most effective, with subsequent reduction in criminal recidivism, when all three elements of the Risk-Need-Responsivity model are addressed. It is critical that high-risk offenders receive priority placement in treatment programs. Criminogenic needs, including those occasioned by antisocial attitudes and substance abuse, must be the primary focus of treatment. The programs need to be effectively implemented and monitored, with adequate training for the staff.

Nancy Zarse
Chicago School of Professional Psychology

See also Offender Needs; Offender Risks

Further Readings

Andrews, D. and J. Bonta. "Rehabilitating Criminal Justice Policy and Practice." *Psychology, Public Policy and Law*, v.16/1 (2010).

Andrews, D., J. Bonta, and J. Wormith. "The Recent Past and Near Future of Risk and/or Needs Assessment." *Crime and Delinquency*, v.52/1 (2006).

Bonta, J. and D. Andrews. "Risk-Need-Responsivity Model for Offender Assessment and Rehabilitation." Public Safety Canada, 2007. http://www.publicsafety.gc.ca/res/cor/rep/risk_need_200706-Eng.aspx (Accessed July 2011).

Dowden, C., D. Antonowicz, and D. Andrews. "The Effectiveness of Relapse Prevention With Offenders: A Meta-Analysis." *International Journal of Offender Therapy and Comparative Criminology*, v.47/5 (2003).

Guidry, L. "Sex Offender–Specific Treatment: Historical Foundations, Current Challenges, and Contemporary Approaches." In *Handbook of Violence Risk Assessment*, R. Otto and K. Douglas, eds. New York: Routledge, 2010.

Heilbrun, K., K. Yasuhara, and S. Shah. "Violence Risk Assessment Tools." In *Handbook of Violence Risk Assessment*, R. Otto and K. Douglas, eds. New York: Routledge, 2010.

Lowenkamp, C. T. and E. J. Latessa. "Understanding the Risk Principle: How and Why Correctional Interventions Can Harm Low-Risk Offenders." In *Topics in Community Corrections, 2004*. Washington, DC: U.S. Department of Justice, National Institute of Corrections, 2004.

Singapore Prison Service, Strategic Research Branch. *Literature Review of the Risk Needs and Responsivity Framework*. Singapore: Author, 2010.

Stohr, M., A. Walsh, and C. Hemmens. *Corrections: A Text/Reader*. Thousand Oaks, CA: Sage, 2009.

Taxman, F., M. Thanner, and D. Weisburd. "Risk, Need and Responsivity (RNR): It *All* Depends." *Crime and Delinquency*, v.52/1 (2006).

Wong, S. and M. Olver. "Two Treatment- and Change-Oriented Risk Assessment Tools: The Violence Risk Scale and Violence Risk Scale—Sexual Offender Version." In *Handbook of Violence Risk Assessment*, R. Otto and K. Douglas, eds. New York: Routledge, 2010.

OFFENDER RISKS

The assessment of offender risk within the context of community corrections is a vast and complicated area of study. There are myriad issues to consider related to recidivism, not the least of which includes risk assessment, risk management, and community reintegration. Recently, there has been much discussion devoted to the implementation of actual risk assessment measures, particularly for use with offenders who are placed in alternative correctional programs, such as probation, parole, or work release.

Case Law Related to Offender Risk

A number of landmark cases are related to the management of offenders who potentially pose a risk (particularly of violence) to others in the community.

It is important that clinicians are aware of the relevant case law pertaining to issues of civil commitment, as it relates to the assessment of offender risk. In *Jones v. United States* (463 U.S.354, 103 S. Ct. 3043, 1983), the District of Columbia Court of Appeals ruled that an insanity acquittee may be civilly committed to a hospital for a longer period of time than the potential sentence he or she would have received if found guilty. The court reasoned that, because an insanity acquittee has not been convicted of a crime, any resulting psychiatric commitment is not considered punishment. Rather, civil commitment following a finding of not guilty by reason of insanity (NGRI) is based on the offender's mental illness and the danger he or she poses to society as a result of that illness.

In *Foucha v. Louisiana* (112 S. Ct. 1780, 1992), the Supreme Court ruled that it is unconstitutional to detain an insanity acquittee indefinitely, as this confinement violates an individual's right to due process. Terry Foucha was initially committed to a forensic hospital in Louisiana after being found NGRI on charges of aggravated battery and the illegal discharge of a firearm. At the time, Louisiana law outlined that an individual found NGRI would remain committed until a hospital review committee determined that the individual no longer was dangerous; if the person was found to present as a continued danger to the community, regardless of whether he or she were mentally ill, that individual would remain committed to the hospital. In this particular case, Foucha had remained civilly committed on the basis that he was diagnosed with antisocial personality disorder. The Supreme Court held that the state of Louisiana could not continue confinement on the basis of this diagnosis alone, and that an individual has a constitutional right to a civil commitment proceeding in order for the state to prove that he is both mentally ill and dangerous. Other case law related to civil commitment as it may pertain to criminal offenders includes *Addington v. Texas* (441 U.S. 418, 99 S. Ct. 1804, 1979), *O'Connor v. Donaldson* (422 U.S. 563, 95 S. Ct 2486, 1975), and *Jackson v. Indiana* (406 U.S. 715, 92 S. Ct. 1845, 1972).

Almost all of the pertinent case law as it relates to offenders and risk speaks to the presence of both a mental disorder and the potential for violence as it directly relates to the symptoms of a mental disorder. As a result, it is imperative for clinicians to recognize that civil commitment as it relates to dangerousness does not include those offenders for whom no mental illness (or a personality disorder only) is present.

It is also important to note that case law regarding the assessment of individuals determined to be at risk for sexually violent recidivism is somewhat different from the case law as outlined above. In slight contrast with the aforementioned legal cases, the Supreme Court in *United States v. Comstock* (560 U.S. ___, 2010) upheld as constitutional the indefinite commitment of a sexually violent person who, upon completion of his or her criminal sentence, continues to pose a danger to others by virtue of a mental abnormality *or* personality disorder.

Risk Assessment Instruments and Methods

The area of "offender risk" can generally and broadly be divided into two categories: risk for general recidivism and risk for violent recidivism. Offender risk for general and violent recidivism can be further subdivided into two associated categories, those of assessment and treatment interventions. The majority of risk assessment literature focuses on the risk for future violent behavior. While violence is an obvious area of concern, this is, broadly speaking, a relatively low-base-rate behavior within the community. It is important for clinicians to be aware of the base rates of particular behaviors within the populations they are evaluating.

According to the Risk-Need-Responsivity (RNR) model, the highest-risk offenders need to be targeted in order to implement appropriate and effective intervention strategies. Assessment methods with demonstrated predictive validity need to be employed in order to classify offenders accurately according to their level risk and to determine their treatment needs. Ultimately, the goal is to reduce recidivism in the community. Several widely used actuarial instruments have been designed to assess the risk of violence specifically within the community, such as the Violence Risk Assessment Guide (VRAG) and the Classification of Violence Risk (COVR). These types of tools use algorithms or specific cutoff scores, which numerically estimate the likelihood of future violence within a particular setting, such as the community. These tools are useful because they employ empirically derived predictor variables found to correlate with later violent behavior. The results are replicable and provide an empirically based foundation upon which to assess an offender's risk for violence. However, it is important for clinicians to note that the predictive accuracy of actuarial tools may decrease if the individual being evaluated is unlike the group upon which the tools were derived or normed. Additionally, these tools do not allow clinicians to take into account individual factors that may mediate or increase an individual's risk for future offending.

Structured professional judgment (SPJ) instruments and methods allow clinicians to use empirically derived predictor variables, as seen in actuarial tools, and allow for clinical judgment related to individually specific risk factors for a particular offender. While technically not viewed as a combination of actuarial instruments and unstructured clinical judgment, the SPJ model structures assessment using empirically derived factors, takes into account how these risk factors may be most relevant for a particular individual, and also specifies risk-reduction strategies, which is essential with regard to risk management within the community. Tools that follow an SPJ model include the Historical, Clinical, and Risk Management Scheme (HCR-20) and the Hare Psychopathy Checklist–Revised or Screening Version (PCL–R or PCL–SV). Broadly speaking, the presence of psychopathy in an offender has been demonstrated to increase that individual's risk for both general and violent recidivism. However, recent research has indicated that, when used in the field, the PCL–R may have low inter-rater reliability; some 30 percent of the differences in PCL–R scores may be attributable to differences among evaluators. It is important that clinicians are properly trained in the use of offender risk assessment tools in order to ensure reliable results.

More recently, research has demonstrated that the predictive validity of the HCR-20, which takes into account empirically derived historical risk factors (such as young age at first violent act and presence of psychopathy), clinical factors (such as impulsivity/instability), and risk management factors (such as exposure to destabilizers), is not significantly impacted by removing psychopathy (as defined by PCL score) from its list of risk factors. The authors of this study note that psychopathy or antisocial behavior of an offender continues to be an important area of inquiry with regard to any risk assessment. It is noted that, in general, many aspects of the construct of psychopathy have been found to be empirically related to risk for future offending, and as such these factors should be taken into account in any risk assessment.

The Level of Service Inventory–Revised (LSI–R) is a widely used instrument designed in part to predict and assess offender outcomes and general recidivism in community corrections, such as parole or residential programs. This inventory contains 54 items and 10 scales related to relevant areas of risk assessment. These include criminal history, education/employment, financial issues, relationships, leisure/recreation activities, companions, alcohol/drug problems, attitudes, and emotional issues. The LSI–R is designed for use by mental health professionals as well as direct care and supervision staff, such as probation officers. Offenders are then classified into a risk-level category, which includes low/moderate, moderate, medium/high, and high risk. Research regarding the LSI–R has indicated that these risk levels provide a valid indicator to predict recidivism rates for many offenders, including those residing in the community on probation.

Some researchers have expressed concern over the accuracy and inter-rater reliability related to the use of such instruments in real-world correctional settings. For example, one study, evaluating approximately 1,000 offenders who were released in the community for at least one year, found that only eight of the 54 items on the LSI–R possessed strong predictive validity with regard to recidivism. These items included any prior convictions, arrests prior to age 16, prior probation/parole violations, three or more address changes in the past year, current drug problems, past mental health treatment, and problems that had an impact on school or work. These items were also found to more distinctively identify offenders who fall into the category of "high risk" to reoffend. At least two other field studies, conducted in state correctional facilities and probation departments that have implemented the LSI–R, have yielded similar results. Another study, conducted by the same author, found that only 16 of the 54 LSI–R items produced an inter-rater agreement of 80 percent or higher, while the other items fell in the 60–70 percent range. Despite field use concerns, it is important that the assessment of offender risk upon release into the community is guided by a methodology that examines a multitude of factors, particularly those that include empirically derived static and dynamic variables.

Intervention Model Designed to Reduce Recidivism

A major issue related to the assessment of offender risk and community corrections involves offender type, as both assessment and risk management issues will differ depending on the specific population. The Risk-Need-Responsivity (RNR) model provides a format with which to assess and manage offender recidivism in an individualized and evidenced-based manner. A number of state community correctional agencies have structured intervention programs based on this model. A meta-analysis originally published in 1990 reviewed 80 studies of both adult and juvenile offenders. The authors of this study found that treatment interventions that followed the RNR model demonstrated an effect size of approximately .32, whereas treatment programs that did not follow these principles demonstrated an increase in recidivism rates. Since this time, the RNR model has been considered to be efficacious in the realm of community corrections and the reduction of offender risk for recidivism.

According to this model, intervention and treatment programs should be individually tailored and delivered to offenders based on their perceived level of risk, with the most high-risk offenders receiving the most intensive treatment services. The risk principle indicates that there will be a reduction in offender recidivism if interventions are focused on specific criminogenic needs of the high-risk offender, which are dynamic in nature. Criminogenic needs that typically serve to promote antisocial and criminal behaviors are viewed as amenable to treatment intervention. These needs have been empirically demonstrated to be associated with recidivism and thus become the major focus of community intervention programs. Major criminogenic needs include substance abuse, association with antisocial or crime-supporting networks, antisocial personality patterns, poor school or work performance, poor family relationships, and lack of prosocial recreational activities. The responsivity aspect of the RNR model suggests that the most successful interventions to reduce recidivism will use cognitive behavioral and social learning strategies, such as teaching problem-solving skills, providing reinforcement for change, and modeling desired, appropriate behaviors. Additionally, the responsivity principle dictates that interventions be designed according to the needs of the individual offender. That is, the most effective methods of treatment delivery must take into account offenders' learning styles, strengths, and personalities.

Evaluation of Risk Reduction Programs in the Community

It has been suggested that community corrections programs should focus on intervention of dynamic risk factors, empirically related with recidivism, in order to reduce reoffense rates. When reviewing the effectiveness of any treatment delivery model, it is important to consider research method and design. The nature of community correction intervention programs makes it difficult to study real-world applications and efficacy in an empirically based manner. Despite such challenges, it appears as though there is some support for the implementation of programs that adhere to the RNR model. One study, which examined jail and prison diversion programs, including intensive supervision, found that the more aspects of the RNR model on which a program focused, the greater was the reduction in recidivism rates. Specifically, the authors found that programs that targeted high-risk offenders, kept them in treatment longer than lower-risk offenders, provided a larger number of treatment referrals, and made treatment referrals based on criminogenic needs (such as substance abuse intervention, employment placements, and cognitive behavioral therapy) tended to have lower recidivism rates compared to supervision programs that did not adhere to these principles (for example, those programs that only required community service as an aspect of probation).

One area that deserves attention involves the treatment of mentally disordered offenders in the community. These may include individuals who have been found NGRI and have been subsequently returned to the community on conditional release, as well as offenders diagnosed with mental disorders who are placed on probation, parole, or work release. Research has demonstrated that significant predictors for recidivism by mentally disordered offenders are similar to those of offenders without mental illness. More specifically, variables that have been seen in violence risk literature—including juvenile delinquency, past history of violence, antisocial personality disorder, poor living arrangements, substance abuse, single marital status, and past weapons use—tend to be more predictive of both general and violent recidivism when compared to other clinical variables.

Casey Sharpe
Chicago School of Professional Psychology

See also Actuarial Risk Assessment; Felony Probation; Firearms Charges, Offenders With; Furloughs; Offender Supervision; Parole Guidelines Score; Prediction Instruments; Public Safety and Collaborative Prevention; Recidivism; Risk and Needs Assessment Instruments; Risk Assessment Instruments: Three Generations; Serious and Violent Offender Reentry Initiative; Sex Offenders in the Community; Wisconsin Risk Assessment Instrument

Further Readings

Addington v. Texas, 441 U.S. 418, 99 S. Ct. 1804 (1979).
Andrews, D. A. et al. "Does Correctional Treatment Work? A Psychologically Informed Meta-Analysis." *Criminology*, v.28 (1990).
Austin, James. "How Much Risk Can We Take? The Misuse of Risk Assessment in Corrections." *Federal Probation*, v.70/2 (2006).
Boccaccini, Marcus T., Darrell B. Turner, and Daniel C. Murrie. "Do Some Evaluators Report Consistently Higher or Lower PCL–R Scores Than Others?" *Psychology, Public Policy, and Law*, v.14/4 (2008).
Bonta, James and D. A. Andrews. *Risk-Need-Responsivity Model for Offender Assessment and Rehabilitation.* Ottawa, ON: Public Safety Canada, 2007.
Bourgon, Guy et al. "The Role of Program Design, Implementation, and Evaluation in Evidenced-Based 'Real World' Community Supervision." *Federal Probation*, v.74/1 (2010).
Byrne, James and April Pattavina. "Assessing the Role of Clinical and Actuarial Risk Assessment in an Evidence-Based Community Corrections System: Issues to Consider." *Federal Probation*, v.70/2 (2006).
Douglas, Kevin S. "Assessing Risk for Violence Using Structured Professional Judgment." *American Psychology-Law Society (APLS) Newsletter*, v.29/1 (2009).
Foucha v. Louisiana, 112 S. Ct. 1780 (1992).
Guy, Laura S., Kevin S. Douglas, and Melissa C. Hendry. "The Role of Psychopathic Personality Disorder in Violence Risk Assessments Using the HCR-20." *Journal of Personality Disorders*, v.24/5 (2010).
Heilbrun, Kirk and Lori Peters. "Community Based Treatment Programmes." In *Violence, Crime and Mentally Disordered Offenders: Concepts and Methods for Effective Treatment and Prevention*, Sheilagh Hodgins and Rudiger Muller-Isberner, eds. New York: John Wiley, 2000.
Jackson v. Indiana, 406 U.S. 715, 92 S. Ct. 1845 (1972).
Jones v. United States, 463 U.S. 354, 103 S. Ct. 3043 (1983).
Lowenkamp, Christopher T., Jennifer Pealer, Paula Smith, and Edward J. Latessa. "Adhering to the Risk and Need Principles: Does It Matter for Supervision-Based Programs?" *Federal Probation*, v.70/3 (2006).
O'Connor v. Donaldson, 422 U.S. 563, 95 S. Ct 2486 (1975).
United States v. Comstock, 560 U.S. ___ (2010).

OFFENDER SUPERVISION

Technically, offender supervision includes all forms of correctional supervision, including incarceration. Typically, however, the term refers to community supervision. Community-based supervision attempts to control the behavior of offenders while allowing them to remain in the community. The premise is to promote law-abiding behavior, either by continuing or creating prosocial roles, while monitoring for a return to criminal activities. It is a least-restrictive response to criminal behavior and saves a significant amount of money for taxpayers. Not only is society saved the tremendous cost of incarceration, but offenders are often required to pay for supervision expenses. Furthermore, the government benefits from payment of taxes on their earnings, and victims are more likely to receive restitution. However, community supervision is not warranted for chronic or violent offenders.

The concept of community corrections is not without controversy. Many believe that it is too lenient as a response to criminal conduct. However, the presumption with community-based offender supervision is that it is advantageous to both offenders and society not to disrupt prosocial activities, such as employment and social support networks (such as those with partners and children). It is also widely thought that community-based offender supervision benefits offenders by not exposing them to prison and hence the large group of criminals there who might prompt them to commit additional or more sophisticated crimes.

Probation is a judicial action in which the court mandates supervision in the community without a period of incarceration. A prison sentence is determined and then suspended during the supervision period. However, if the probationer violates the terms of supervision, the prison sentence is imposed. Public perception to the contrary, some offenders regard supervision as more onerous than prison, because of the conditions and requirements that accompany community supervision.

Parole is a form of early release, before the completion of the court-ordered prison sentence. Parole is a period of community-based supervision following positive adjustment during incarceration. Parole typically includes court-mandated conditions, such as no contact with felons and treatment for substance abuse. If the offender violates the conditions of parole or commits a new criminal offense, he or she may be returned to confinement. Failure to comply with parole conditions is known as a technical violation, which is not criminal conduct in itself but does constitute grounds for reincarceration. For parolees returning to prison, it is common for technical violations to outnumber new criminal conduct. It is important to remember that parolees have served time in prison and therefore may well be more entrenched in their criminal lifestyles. As a result, parolees are often more challenging to supervise than probationers. Parole has been abolished or severely restricted in many states, as a result of a national get-tough-on-crime movement that followed some high-profile violent acts of parolees. Instead, mandatory minimum sentences have been implemented in many jurisdictions, thereby restricting the discretion of the judge.

Supervised release is a period of supervision following incarceration. It does not reduce or replace the sentence of confinement. Supervised release mandates conditions intended both to facilitate the offender's readjustment back into society, as a law-abiding and productive member of society, and to prevent recidivism.

Relapse prevention programs and social skills training are believed by some to be more effective when delivered in the community rather than in prison. Therefore, a critical element of adequate supervision is the capacity to identify risk factors and triggers to relapse, followed by the provision of the services needed to manage the risk and prevent reoffending. Research indicates that cognitive and behavioral strategies are the best way to target self-efficacy, coping skills, and motivation, all of which are essential components of a relapse prevention model.

A pivotal, but often unacknowledged, aspect of a successful reintegration into society is employment. It is common for inmates to possess few job skills, to have a limited or nonexistent employment record, and to have a history of substance abuse. All of these factors combine to hamper their likelihood of finding a job. Without employment, which brings both a source of income and self-respect, ex-convicts are more likely to return to crime.

Halfway house placement is a temporary residential placement designed to ease the offender's return to society, with fewer restrictions than prison but more supervision than in society. A halfway house allows for greater monitoring of offenders while also granting access to supportive programming. Halfway house residents are frequently subject to random drug and alcohol testing, conditions related to work or job hunting, and treatment programs.

House arrest and electronic monitoring ensure that the offender is at home, except for time spent at a job, getting an education, or undergoing treatment. The reduced cost of house arrest and electronic monitoring makes it attractive from a fiscal point of view. However, it is important that the attractiveness of cost savings not outweigh careful consideration of the appropriateness of this program for a particular offender.

The Risk-Need-Responsivity (RNR) principle holds that services should be provided based on the highest risk of reoffending, should address the criminogenic needs that predispose the offender toward reoffending, and should be responsive to the individual learning styles and needs of the offender. This principle has relevance both to assessment of risk and to treatment. The RNR principle suggests that both supervision and treatment be responsive to risk levels, such that the higher the risk of reoffending, the higher the priority for supervision and rehabilitation.

The RNR principle has massive ramifications for effective community-based offender supervision. Probation officers often have large caseloads, regardless of the risk level of the offenders, and lack adequate resources to manage them. To assess risks and needs accurately, the probation officer must possess strong interviewing skills and an assessment tool to supplement the information provided by the court. However, it is not uncommon for probation officers to devote insufficient time to interviews or lack the requisite skills to develop an empathic relationship with the offender. A number of probation officers have not been adequately trained to administer assessment tools.

Typically, around 25 to 33 percent of inmates report the use of alcohol or drugs during their instant offense, and about 75 percent have a history of drug or alcohol use. Substance abuse treatment in prison varies in its nature and quality but is often less than ideal. Furthermore, it is all too common that community resources do not adequately meet individual treatment needs. In addition, the rate of offenders with convictions for driving under the influence of alcohol or drugs (DUI) or driving while intoxicated (DWI) has increased, as has the number of offenders with prior DWI offenses. There is a risk not only of relapse on supervision but also of assaultive behavior. Finally, secondary issues, such as coexisting mental disorders, difficulty securing and maintaining employment, and relationship problems, are common with substance abusers. As a result, substance abuse represents a significant challenge for community supervision.

Mentally ill offenders represent a unique challenge to supervision. Individuals with a major mental illness, such as schizophrenia, are at higher risk for reoffending and for violence. Furthermore, it is common that individuals with mental illness have a comorbid diagnosis, such as substance abuse, which increases their risk for recidivism and for revocation of supervision. It is important to note that most major mental illnesses can be treated and thereby effectively managed with psychotropic medication. Thus, it is critical that offenders with a major mental illness receive the proper level of monitoring in order to prevent recidivism or technical violations of supervised release, which can result in a return to prison.

Mental health courts are one way in which society is attempting to manage, rather than incarcerate, those with mental illness who come into contact with the criminal justice system. It is also helpful to differentiate the developmentally disabled from the mentally ill and to provide training to the staff members who provide supervision. It is particularly helpful to identify effective treatment programs to supplement community supervision for the mentally ill.

The demographic characteristics of female offenders reveal a higher percentage of minorities and parents, little to no medical care, a higher rate of mental disorders, and a significant history of abuse or domestic violence. Imprisoned women are far more likely to maintain contact with their children, both during and after incarceration, than are male inmates. To provide effective community supervision for females, it is critical to recognize the unique experiences and issues of this population.

Although the public demands tough sentencing in response to criminal behavior, the cost of incarceration is considerable. Studies show that probation, although problematic, is a less expensive alternative to prison. Moreover, growing research demonstrates the effectiveness of correctional treatment programs in reducing recidivism. A system that incorporates effective alternatives to incarceration, based on solid research of what works, has great promise to minimize the risk to society while maximizing the prosocial behavior of offenders.

Nancy Zarse
Chicago School of Professional Psychology

See also Offender Needs; Offender Responsivity

Further Readings

Latesa, E. and P. Smith. *Corrections in the Community,* 4th ed. Cincinnati, OH: Anderson/LexisNexis, 2007.

Lowenkamp, C. T. and E. J. Latessa. "Understanding the Risk Principle: How and Why Correctional Interventions Can Harm Low-Risk Offenders." In *Topics in Community Corrections, 2004.* Washington, DC: U.S. Department of Justice, National Institute of Corrections, 2004.

Meloy, R. *Violence Risk and Threat Assessment.* San Diego, CA: Specialized Training Services, 2000.

Quinsey, V., G. Harris, M. Rice, and C. Cormier. *Violent Offenders: Appraising and Managing Risk*, 2nd ed. Washington, DC: American Psychological Association, 2006.

Stohr, M., A. Walsh, and C. Hemmens, eds. *Corrections: A Text/Reader.* Thousand Oaks, CA: Sage, 2009.

Wagaman, G. L. "Managing and Treating Female Offenders." In *Correctional Mental Health Handbook*, T. Fagan and R. Ax, eds. Thousand Oaks, CA: Sage, 2003.

Offenders With Mental Illness

Prisoners with mental illness have long been a strain on the criminal justice system. Early American settlers generally treated mentally ill offenders the same as other offenders and subjected them to the same punishments. America's treatment of the mentally ill grew with its national consciousness, and the norm turned from presumptive institutionalization to deinstitutionalization. This change in policy was accompanied by passage of the Americans with Disabilities Act (ADA), which was enacted to ensure that the mentally ill enjoyed the same rights and societal experiences as other citizens. However, the ADA and closure of institutions led to more mentally ill individuals in society, and society did not have the necessary community resources available to help them. As a result, jails and prisons became the unfortunate default system for dealing with the mentally ill.

The rate of mentally ill prisoners has swelled in the United States. Every year, more than 2 million people with serious mental illnesses are booked into jail or prison. Estimates suggest that 14.5 percent of men and 31 percent of women entering jails have serious mental health problems. By comparison, national mental health statistics show that only 3 to 6 percent of Americans suffer from mental illness. Of all mentally ill adults, 40 percent will have some interaction with the criminal justice system, including either run-ins with law enforcement or stints in jail or prison. These numbers are even more surprising when one considers that those with mental illness commit only 10 percent of violent crimes,

More than 2 million people with serious mental illnesses are booked into the U.S. prison system annually. A 2003 study by the Human Rights Watch and the Correctional Association of New York found that nearly 25 percent of prisoners in disciplinary lockdown are mentally ill. (Photos.com)

and the vast majority of crimes committed by the mentally ill are nonviolent public-disorder offenses.

Complicating the problem of offenders with mental health issues is their common usage of alcohol and drugs. Many mentally ill individuals self-medicate with drugs and alcohol, and others turn to such substances out of despondency. Illicit drug use is a crime for which an individual may be arrested, but both alcohol and drugs often react badly with symptoms of mental illness. Some studies have shown that 60 percent of mentally ill inmates who were arrested were under the influence of alcohol or drugs, and a full third were alcoholics.

History of Mentally Ill Offenders

In North America, early colonists rarely differentiated between mentally ill and routine criminal offenders, mostly because there was no real definition or understanding of mental illness. All mentally ill were considered simply "lunatics." When such people committed crimes, they would usually be punished the same way any sane person would be punished, with whippings, banishment, branding, or even death. In rare instances, the disabled would be treated as mentally ill and would be turned over to the care of his or her family, placed in a poorhouse, or segregated in a cage from the rest of society until death.

The first American mental institution—a place meant specifically for the treatment of the mentally ill—was not opened until 1773 in Williamsburg, Virginia; the second opened in 1824. Although these hospitals had doctors on staff, no relief or treatment was offered to patients. They were merely kept segregated from the rest of society. Early 19th-century America embraced the building of several large institutions, both for criminals and for the mentally ill. While some persons placed in these institutions were indeed dangerous, others were put in these institutions simply because their families were unable or unwilling to care for them or they were homeless.

Toward the end of the 19th century, mental illness and its causes became better understood, and society became able to differentiate between mentally ill offenders and sane criminals. This led to a reconsideration of the purpose for institutions, and advances led to the belief that there could be treatment, or in some cases even rehabilitation, of the mentally ill. Institutions were the norm for mentally ill offenders through the mid-20th century. The 1950s showed great breakthroughs in utilizing antipsychotic medications such as Thorazine; the interest in psychopharmacology grew as society began to understand mental illness more fully.

The 1970s brought forth the greatest change in society's treatment of the mentally ill as institutions lost favor with the public and were shut down in droves. In 1977, President Jimmy Carter instituted the Commission on Mental Health. The commission found that the most desirable option for mentally ill persons was deinstitutionalization. Deinstitutionalization was the least restrictive alternative, as it allowed the mentally ill the greatest degree of autonomy while they continued to receive outpatient treatment and services. This change was brought about in part by fiscal conservatives who considered the cost of numerous hospitals prohibitive and who were being forced to reduce state budgets. Moreover, civil rights activists supported the closing of institutions. The public had become aware of the atrocious conditions in many of the hospitals, and activists were also shocked at the lack of due process available for the involuntarily committed. By some accounts, psychiatric inpatient beds were reduced by more than 85 percent nationwide from 1970 through 2000. In some areas, this caused a 300 percent rise in the population of mentally ill persons in jail within five years, along with huge increases in the homeless population. It was noted in 1972 that jails were filled with mentally ill who had committed minor crimes, and the phrase "criminalization of the mentally ill" was coined.

The Americans With Disabilities Act

On July 26, 1990, the Americans with Disabilities Act (ADA) was signed into law, paving the way for perhaps the most important step forward for the mentally ill since deinstitutionalization. The ADA was designed to protect the disabled (which included the mentally ill) from discrimination and to ensure that the disabled were allowed to participate as fully in society as those without disabilities. To be eligible for such protections, a mentally ill person had to demonstrate three criteria: actual presence of mental illness; denial of benefits or services by, or discrimination by, a public entity; and denial of benefits or discrimination due directly to the person's mental illness. The discrimination did not need to be intentional, merely present.

Title II of the ADA was most important for the mentally ill, as it protected them in dealings with public institutions, which were deemed to include dealings with the police and the court system. To avoid violation of the ADA, public entities such as police have to prevent discrimination by enacting "reasonable accommodations" or "reasonable modifications" in their policies and procedures. Currently, courts have limited ADA protections to mentally ill offenders' dealings with arrest, post-arrest, and pretrial involvement.

Mentally ill offenders are generally protected from arrests arising out of nonviolent actions induced by their mental illness. Up to 70 percent of crimes committed by the mentally ill are nonviolent public-disorder offenses. Of these public-disorder offenses, a significant number of arrests have occurred when uninformed police come across a mentally ill individual and mistake his or her slurring of speech and strange behavior for drug or alcohol intoxication. Some police have also mistaken a person's inability to answer simple questions as obdurate and evasive behavior. Theoretically, the ADA would significantly reduce first-responder (police) arrests of the mentally ill in such circumstances.

The mentally ill must be protected in post-arrest and pretrial situations as well. Transport of a mentally ill individual should be accommodating, and in the least restrictive way. A clearly mentally ill individual must be questioned in an appropriate manner or not at all if his or her disability is so profound as to render him or her incompetent. That said, the individual who is mentally ill but still competent must be allowed to participate in his defense, even if the attorney assigned to him or her disagrees with his or her desire to cooperate.

Perhaps most important, the ADA affects the detainment of the mentally ill before trial or during questioning. The stresses of being incarcerated can exacerbate preexisting mental conditions and cause the mentally ill to act out. Furthermore, the mentally ill are often targeted by other inmates and are more likely to be victims of violence rather than the aggressors. Jail is an especially bad fit for the mentally ill, as it has strict structural and procedural rules that many mentally ill are unable to follow. In this setting, every time the mentally ill break the rules, they are likely to be punished. These punishments lead to longer sentences, meaning that many mentally ill individuals end up spending more time in jail for the same crime than their sane counterparts.

Additionally, corrections officers may not be aware of the offender's mental health issues and come down more harshly upon him.

The answer, however, is not simply to segregate the mentally ill physically from others in jail. Many jails and prisons simply do not have the room for a separate group of offenders, and placing the mentally ill in solitary confinement would punish the offender unnecessarily. Solitary confinement has been found to increase risks of suicide and self-mutilation in mentally ill individuals. This means that jails and prisons are constantly attempting to balance the priorities of ensuring safety for corrections officers, sane inmates, and mentally ill offenders while not violating any portion of the ADA or other civil rights. This creates another layer of strain on the criminal justice system that it cannot handle.

Post-ADA Problems and New Solutions

Both the deinstitutionalization movement and the ADA were created to reintegrate the mentally ill into society and to change societal misgivings toward and poor treatment of the mentally ill. However, the anticipated benefits from these steps forward have never materialized. In fact, deinstitutionalization has not really ended; jails have become the de facto institutions for the mentally ill.

The first reason is the failure of society to provide proper training for first responders, who are usually the police—those who are most likely to first encounter the mentally ill during times of crisis. When first responders receive calls and complaints about mentally ill people acting out in the community, they often do not know how to respond appropriately. There has been little or no formal training for first responders to teach them to recognize and deal with the mentally ill.

The problem of recognizing mental illness is made even more difficult if the individual is under the influence of drugs or alcohol. The first responder might confuse the illness for simple intoxication and release the individual without much-needed services or treatment. Even worse, the police might arrest the individual on a petty offense such as loitering or public intoxication, exposing him or her to the criminal justice system. Some police, upon recognizing mental illness, might unnecessarily take the individual to a hospital for psychiatric inpatient treatment, when less restrictive outpatient services, such as drug or alcohol counseling, would suffice.

The public mischaracterization of the mentally ill as dangerous and prone to violence may also color officers' response.

Some officers, upon encountering homeless mentally ill individuals, might engage in a "mercy arrest," arresting the individual for the sole purpose of putting the person in jail so that he or she can enjoy a warm, safe bed and a hot meal. This is only a temporary solution, as the next day the individual is released with no follow-up services or care. In these circumstances, the police also act in direct contravention to the goals of the ADA, penalizing the mentally ill by putting them in jail unnecessarily, even if for a seemingly good cause. It also may have the unintended detrimental effects of exacerbating the mentally ill individual's fear of police and crowding the jails unnecessarily.

Despite these problems, there has been progress in the fight to find justice for mentally ill offenders. The advent of the mental health court—a combination of criminal court and mental health treatment planning devised to serve offenders who have mental health problems—has offered an avenue whereby the mentally ill can benefit more from long-term mental health follow-up care. These mental health courts have been very successful in keeping mentally ill offenders from the cycle of homelessness and involvement with the criminal justice system. The Mentally Ill Offender Treatment and Crime Reduction Act (MIOTCRA) was signed into law in 2004 by President George W. Bush, and promised more funding for mental health courts.

Furthermore, many officers are beginning to receive the necessary training to help them effectively identify and deal with the mentally ill. Crisis intervention teams (CITs) began in 1988 after a mentally ill individual was shot and killed by an officer. Police are taught to recognize the signs of mental illness, approach mentally ill individuals in a calm fashion, and determine what sort of follow-up services might be necessary. Officers throughout the nation have generally shown interest in receiving CIT training, and there is hope that it will lead to better understandings between police and those with mental health needs.

Erica L. Fields
Rutgers University

See also Diversity in Community Corrections; Mental Health Courts; Prison Overcrowding

Further Readings

Americans With Disabilities Act of 1990, 42 U.S.C.A. § 12191 *et seq.*

Bal, Peter and Frans Koenraadt. "Criminal Law and Mentally Ill Offenders in Comparative Perspective." *Psychology, Crime and Law,* v.6/4 (2000).

Bard, Jennifer S. "Re-Arranging Deck Chairs on the *Titanic*: Why the Incarceration of Individuals With Serious Mental Illness Violates Public Health, Ethical, and Constitutional Principles and Therefore Cannot Be Made Right by Piecemeal Changes to the Insanity Defense." *Houston Journal of Health Law and Policy,* v.5 (Spring 2005).

Beran, Nancy J. and Beverly G. Toomey. *Mentally Ill Offenders and the Criminal Justice System.* New York: Praeger, 1979.

Colb, Sherry F. "Insane Fear: The Discriminatory Category of 'Mentally Ill and Dangerous.'" *New England Journal on Criminal and Civil Commitment,* v.25/2 (Summer 1999).

Danjczek, Liesel J. "The Mentally Ill Offender Treatment and Crime Reduction Act and Its Inappropriate Non-Violent Offender Limitation." *Journal of Contemporary Health Law and Policy,* v.24 (Fall 2007).

Fischer, Jennifer. "The Americans With Disabilities Act: Correcting Discrimination of Persons With Mental Disabilities in the Arrest, Post-Arrest, and Pretrial Process." *Law and Inequality,* v.24 (Winter 2005).

James, Doris and Lauren Glaze. *Mental Health Problems of Prison and Jail Inmates.* Washington, DC: U.S. Department of Justice, Bureau of Justice Statistics, 2006.

Kansas v. Hendricks, 521 U.S. 346 (1997).

Lamb, H. Richard, Linda E. Weinberger, and Bruce H. Gross. "Mentally Ill Persons in the Criminal Justice System: Some Perspectives." *Psychiatric Quarterly,* v.75/2 (2004).

Pennsylvania Department of Corrections v. Yeskey, 524 U.S. 206 (1998).

Phillips, Daniel W. "Mentally Ill People and the Criminal Justice System." *Georgia State University Criminal Justice Review,* v.30 (2005).

Rivera, Ralph M. "The Mentally Ill Offender: A Brighter Tomorrow Through the Eyes of the Mentally Ill Offender Treatment and Crime Reduction Act of 2004." *Journal of Law and Health,* v.19/1 (2005).

Silver, Eric, Richard B. Felson, and Matthew Vaneseltine. "The Relationship Between Mental Health Problems and Violence Among Criminal Offenders." *Criminal Justice and Behavior,* v.35/4 (2008).

Pardon and Restoration of Rights

In the United States, criminal convictions lead to the loss of various rights and privileges. Specifically, many state and federal statutes place restrictions on those with a criminal record. Commonly known as collateral sanctions or discretionary disabilities, such restrictions often have an impact on convicted criminals permanently. In most instances, however, individuals can reacquire rights and privileges lost as the result of a criminal conviction if they seek out and receive clemency.

Clemency is a general term that refers to several methods whereby convicted criminal offenders can eliminate or reduce the negative impact of a criminal record. A pardon and a restoration of rights are each forms of clemency. Similarly, both a pardon and a restoration of rights reinstates to an individual, either entirely or partially, the rights and privileges of citizenship. Jurisdictionally, the mechanics of applying for and receiving a pardon or a restoration of rights vary wildly. One crucial difference between a pardon and a restoration of rights is that a citizen seeking a pardon must always initiate the pardon process. Contrarily, in some jurisdictions, a restoration of rights occurs automatically at the conclusion of an imposed sentence. Moreover, many view pardons as legal forms of forgiveness, whereby executive authorities officially excuse a convicted criminal for his or her lawlessness. Conversely, a restoration of rights is a far less meaningful declaration.

Nevertheless, in either instance, both a pardon and a restoration of rights largely restore offenders to the social status that they occupied prior to committing a criminal offense.

Pardons

In the federal criminal justice system, only the president of the United States has the power to grant a pardon. The U.S. Constitution codifies the presidential pardoning power in Article II, Section 2. It reads, "The President . . . shall have power to Grant Reprieves and Pardons for Offenses against the United States, except in Cases of Impeachment." To receive a presidential pardon for a federal criminal offense, an individual must actively apply. The U.S. Department of Justice's Office of the Pardon Attorney typically reviews all requests for a presidential pardon. The Office of the Pardon Attorney then makes a nonbinding recommendation to the president, whereupon the president can either grant or deny an individual's request for pardon.

Most states have a pardon system that mirrors that of the federal criminal justice system. In such instances, state governors retain pardoning power expressly or implicitly granted to them by their respective state's constitution. In some instances, states allow appointed regulatory or administrative agencies to grant or deny a request for pardon. In still other states, California for instance, that jurisdiction's supreme court must approve a governor's choice to grant a pardon.

Almost all jurisdictions require that applicants meet certain general prerequisites prior to receiving a pardon. For instance, in almost all states and the federal criminal justice system, a pardon application requires that an applicant describe why and how a pardon is necessary and deserved. These applications differ jurisdictionally. In some jurisdictions, applicants must pay a substantial processing fee and must complete a lengthy application document to satisfy both objective and subjective criteria. For example, in such jurisdictions, applicants must prove that their imposed sentence has officially expired and that they have taken tangible steps toward achieving full rehabilitation. Conversely, in less demanding jurisdictions, applicants must only pay a nominal fee and must only complete a brief form outlining the committed offense and the reasons for requesting a pardon. Jurisdictions also vary with respect to when a convicted criminal can apply for a pardon. For example, in the federal criminal justice system, officials recommend that an individual convicted of a federal crime wait five years from the date of the expiration of the imposed sentence before applying for a pardon. States also adhere to such waiting provisions, but the length of time an applicant must wait varies considerably.

Restoration of Rights

A restoration of rights is similar to a pardon, as it operates to restore a convicted criminal's rights and privileges lost as the result of a conviction. However, a restoration of rights is less symbolic and is often a far less burdensome process for those with a criminal record. Only state jurisdictions can grant an offender a restoration of rights; the federal criminal justice system does not have a restoration of rights process.

Among the states there are generally three jurisdictional approaches to a restoration of rights. First, in some jurisdictions, a convicted criminal will automatically receive a restoration of rights at the expiration of an imposed sentence. Second, in other jurisdictions, convicted criminals must apply for a restoration of rights. In such instances, as with the pardons process, offenders often confront waiting periods, administrative processing fees, and applications of varying length and detail. Finally, some jurisdictions couple pardons with a restoration of rights. In these states, a convicted criminal must apply for and receive a pardon prior to applying for or receiving a restoration of rights.

Muddling this national patchwork of application procedures is the efficacy and necessity of a restoration of rights. In some jurisdictions, a criminal conviction leads to the permanent loss of certain rights and privileges, even when the jurisdiction grants an offender a restoration of rights. In other jurisdictions, a restoration of rights is a superfluous exercise that is uncommon or nonexistent. For example, in Maine, convicted criminals do not lose rights and privileges as a result of a conviction. Hence, in Maine, a restoration of rights is not required to restore a convicted criminal to his or her preconviction status.

For some criminal offenders, jurisdictional overlap also confounds the process of applying for and receiving a restoration of rights. For example, some individuals convicted of a federal crime may seek a restoration of rights in their state of residence. In many states, however, to receive a pardon or a restoration of rights following a federal criminal conviction, an offender must first receive a presidential pardon. Generally in such cases, clauses contained in state constitutions prohibit state authorities from granting a federal criminal offender a pardon or a restoration of rights prior to the receipt of a presidential pardon.

James M. Binnall
University of California, Irvine

See also Civil and Political Rights Affected by Conviction; Loss of Individual Rights

Further Readings

Chiang, Melissa. "Some Kind of Process for Felon Reenfranchisement." *University of Chicago Law Review*, v.72/1331 (2005).

Kutz, Amanda L. "A Jury of One's Peers: Virginia's Restoration of Rights Process and Its Disproportionate Effect on the African American Community." *William and Mary Law Review*, v.46/2109 (2005).

Mitchell, S. David. "Undermining Individual and Collective Citizenship: The Impact of Exclusion Laws on the African-American Community." *Fordham Urban Law Journal*, v.34/833 (2007).

Parole

Parole refers both to a process of release from prison and to the community supervision of individuals who have served prison terms. In indeterminate sentencing schemes, individuals sentenced to prison are sentenced to a range of years and can be released by the paroling authority (usually a parole board) at any point after they have served the minimum sentence. This is referred to as discretionary parole. Parole also refers to the period of time an individual must serve in the community under the supervision of a parole officer after having served a sentence in prison. People on parole supervision are subject to a list of conditions with which they must comply or risk being sent back to prison. Parole release and parole supervision have both changed significantly since their origins, but they remain an important part of criminal justice systems in the United States.

Origins of Parole

The origins of parole in the United States can be traced back to the work of Alexander Maconochie on Norfolk Island in the 1840s and Sir Walter Crofton in Ireland during the 1850s. Parole was introduced in the United States by Zebulon Brockway, who was appointed superintendent of New York State's Elmira Reformatory in 1876. At Elmira, with the goals of both managing the prison population and preparing prisoners for release, Brockway implemented an indeterminate sentencing model along with parole release. Prisoners were classified based on their behavior, and after a certain period of good conduct, were released to the community while remaining under the authority of the correctional institution. For six months they were required to make monthly reports to a "guardian," and these reports were sent back to the institution. New York formally adopted all the elements of parole in 1907, and by 1942 all states and the federal government had enacted parole legislation.

For most of the 20th century, the vast majority of prisoners in the United States were released under this original model—an indeterminate sentence (such as three to eight years), discretionary release by a parole board, and post-release supervision. The premise of the system was that rehabilitation was the main goal of corrections, and so sentencing decisions should be made on a case-by-case basis. The amount of time the person actually spent in prison depended on the decision of the parole board, which made a determination as to whether an individual had been rehabilitated and was ready for release. Most people became eligible for parole after serving their minimum sentence less any time off for good behavior.

In the United States, parole differs from amnesty or commutation of sentence in that parolees are still considered to be serving their sentences and will have to return to prison if they violate the conditions of their parole. (Photos.com)

The Decline of Discretionary Parole Release

Beginning in the 1970s, indeterminate sentencing and the rehabilitative ideal came under attack from a number of fronts. Criticisms included the fact that there was little evidence that rehabilitative programming reduced recidivism. Furthermore, there was no evidence that parole supervision reduced recidivism. In addition, a system where prisoners did not know when they would be released was seen as inhumane, while the uncontrolled discretion of parole boards was criticized as racist. On the other hand, some felt that the system was too lenient and that prisoners did not serve enough time.

These attacks led to a shift in many states to a determinate, structured sentencing scheme, where broad sentence ranges were replaced with fixed sentences. In most states, legislatures increased maximum penalties or added sentence enhancements. These sentencing changes were accompanied by changes in the way people were released from prison and by moves toward the abolition of discretionary parole release by parole boards. However, just two states—Maine and Virginia—abolished parole entirely, meaning both parole release and supervision, and Virginia brought back post-release supervision just four years after abolition. More common was the replacement of discretionary parole release with mandatory release based on statutory requirements combined with some form of post-release supervision, as was done in both

California and Colorado. Other states eliminated discretionary release for certain groups; for example, in 1998, New York did away with discretionary parole release for people convicted of violent felony offenses and replaced it with court-imposed post-release supervision.

Therefore, although there has been an increase in the proportion of people who are released from prison without parole, most people leaving prison are still released conditionally to some other form of post-prison supervision. In 2008, approximately 80 percent of prison releases were conditional releases, meaning that people leaving prison are supervised and have to comply with certain conditions for a specified period after prison release, or they can be returned to prison.

Although many states no longer refer to "parole" and instead use terms such as "community supervision" and "supervised release," qualitatively there are few differences in what this means once the person has been released. For example, Oregon abolished parole in 1989 and replaced it with post-prison supervision for all new sentences, but both people on parole supervision (sentenced under the old system) and those on post-prison supervision are supervised by the same local agencies and by the same officers. In New York, people released on parole are supervised by the same officers and are subject to the same standard conditions as those released on mandatory supervised release. For this reason, for the remainder of this entry, unless otherwise specified, the term *parole supervision* is used to refer to all forms of post-release supervision.

Parole Supervision: Conditions and Revocation

Regardless of the operable release mechanism, a person on parole supervision is subject to a long list of conditions with which he or she must comply or risk being sent back to prison. In most states, there is a list of standard conditions that apply to everyone on parole. These conditions usually include reporting requirements, requirements to seek and maintain employment, prohibitions on drug and/or alcohol use, requirements to avoid police contact, and restrictions on travel and residency. While on parole, individuals are also subject to searches and seizures without the Fourth Amendment requirements of probable cause or a warrant. In addition, special

conditions may be imposed, usually related to the crime of conviction or particular risks or needs of the individual. Special conditions are imposed either by parole boards or by supervision officers (or, in the federal system, by judges). These include requirements to attend programs such as drug treatment or anger management programs, driver's license restrictions, and prohibitions on associating with particular individuals.

Violation of any of these conditions can result in parole revocation, which means that a person can be returned to prison. However, it is rare that a first violation results in revocation. Instead, most states use graduated sanctions (in some cases formal, in others informal), which can range from verbal or written warnings to requirements to attend day or evening reporting centers to short jail stays. Ultimately, however, a person may have his or her supervision revoked and go back to prison, in some cases for a fixed term, usually for at least three months, and in some cases to complete the original sentence. Whether a person will receive sentence credit for the time they spent on parole depends on the state.

Because of the liberty interest implicated by revocation, the Supreme Court has held that there are certain due process requirements for parole revocations. In *Morrissey v. Brewer*, the Court held that the minimal due process requirements for parole revocation include a preliminary hearing to determine probable cause for the alleged violations and a formal revocation hearing at which certain due process requirements must be observed, including the right to be given written notice of the claimed violations, the opportunity to be heard and to present witnesses, and the right to a hearing in front of a "neutral and detached" body. There is no automatic right to counsel at a parole revocation hearing.

Parole Supervision: From Casework to Surveillance

The nature of parole supervision has changed significantly since its inception. Initially, parole did not involve much active supervision, and people on parole were simply required to file monthly reports with the correctional institution and maintain employment. Beginning in the 1950s, supervision became more meaningful, and parole began to operate under a clinical or casework model that balanced treatment and reintegration of the individual with protection of society. The supervision and case management of parole were believed to contribute to prisoner reform by encouraging participation in rehabilitative programming and to prepare people to transition into the community. Law-enforcement strategies by officers were discouraged.

Over the past 30 years, a surveillance model dominated by risk management has become more common among supervision agencies. The number of people on parole has increased substantially over the years without a corresponding increase in resources, which in turn has led to increased caseloads. This, combined with increased punitiveness in corrections generally, has shifted the focus in many agencies from reintegration to monitoring. High caseloads have meant that there is not enough time to provide counseling or referrals, and many officers spend more time on paperwork and record keeping than dealing with clients. While employment was once seen as an indicator of success on parole, drug testing now dominates a person's interactions with his or her parole officer. Most scholars agree that parole officers today spend more time monitoring conditions than providing services. In how they carry out their jobs, parole officers look less like social workers than police officers.

However, this shift has not been comprehensive and in some cases has occurred without any corresponding change in the rehabilitative mission and ideology of the parole agencies, which, according to some scholars, has led to an unstable parole system. Most supervision agencies have multiple missions. All continue to cite public safety as their mission, but many also cite rehabilitation or reentry as a mission. Furthermore, some line-level parole officers themselves believe the casework functions that they perform are more effective than their control and surveillance functions. However, because of large caseloads and pressure from managers, who are forced to respond to punitive public sentiment, officers end up using a surveillance approach.

The Effectiveness of Parole

Given how many people on parole return to prison and the high proportion of prison admissions accounted for by parole revocations—one third of admissions nationwide—parole's effectiveness has been questioned, generally by looking at the recidivism rates of people on parole. There is no doubt

that former prisoners do contribute to crime, and it is also true that recidivism rates among people on parole are high; most released prisoners are rearrested and returned to prison. Patrick Langan and David Levin's classic study of people leaving prison in 1994 found that 30 percent were rearrested in the first six months, 44 percent within the first year, and 68 percent within three years of release. The percentage of those on parole returned to prison has remained stable (around 40 percent) since about 2000, as has the percentage of discharged parolees who are discharged successfully (around 45 percent).

However, there is little evidence that people on parole have higher recidivism rates than people released from prison without any supervision. A 2006 study found that parole supervision had very little effect on overall recidivism rates. The authors found that those released through discretionary parole, as opposed to mandatory parole or unsupervised release, were slightly less likely to be arrested; 61 percent of unconditional releases and mandatory parolees were rearrested within two years of release, compared with 54 percent of discretionary parolees. However, when criminal history and other variables are controlled for, the difference is reduced. A recent meta-analysis looking at the effectiveness of community supervision concluded that community supervision does not appear to work very well. The authors reviewed 15 studies published between 1980 and 2006 and found only a very small decrease in overall recidivism associated with community supervision—and no relationship at all between community supervision and violent recidivism.

Furthermore, the style of supervision does not seem to have much of an effect on outcomes. Success rates have not changed significantly over the years, but what the changes in supervision style have done is increase the numbers of people returned to prison for technical violations. Parole violations made up less than one fifth of prison admissions in 1980 but now constitute almost twice that amount. Moreover, there is no evidence that revoking people's parole has any effect on recidivism.

The Future of Parole: Parole Innovations and Suggestions for Reform

Parole has been the subject of criticism since its inception. High-profile crimes committed by people on parole often lead to calls for the repeal of parole.

Although the crisis of rehabilitation in the 1970s did lead to changes in parole, including the abolition of discretionary parole release in many states, parole supervision remained in virtually all states, and criticisms of parole have continued. In recent years, the high costs of supervision, high recidivism rates, the negative impact that parole supervision can have on reintegration, and the increasing costs of housing people who are revoked and returned to prison have all resulted in a variety of suggestions for reform, from both scholars and government officials.

Although some still argue that parole should be abolished entirely, more common are calls for the abolition of parole *release* or other reforms, and most of these suggestions involve retaining some form of community supervision. For example, Jeremy Travis has argued that parole release should be abolished but that it should be replaced with universal post-prison supervision with limited conditions that are tailored to the risks and needs of individuals. On the other hand, Joan Petersilia argues that discretionary parole should be brought back and cites evidence that people released through discretionary parole are more likely to complete their parole terms successfully than are those released through mandatory parole.

Petersilia and others emphasize the importance of the research on "what works" and relying on evidence-based practices, which research has shown to be effective. These practices include assessing risk and needs, targeting interventions based on risk and needs (focusing resources on moderate- and high-need individuals), relying on graduated sanctions (including the use of positive reinforcements), utilizing cognitive behavioral therapy, and measuring outcomes beyond recidivism, including drug use and employment. This approach is increasingly popular among states and shows promise. For example, as part of a systemwide strategy to reduce recidivism and cut corrections costs, Kansas set a goal of reducing parole and probation revocations by 20 percent. The initial results are positive. In part by implementing evidence-based practices, Kansas, between 2006 and 2009, reduced the number of revocations to prison by almost 25 percent.

Another approach has been to end supervision of low-risk people entirely. For example, California recently underwent a thorough study of its parole system and enacted a number of reforms, including instituting "nonrevocable" parole. This allows certain people who are at low risk to reoffend to be released from prison without any supervision or conditions, meaning that they cannot be returned to prison unless they commit a new crime. However, some have criticized this new law because people are still considered to be on parole and are subject to search and seizure provisions but are not entitled to any reentry services other than those they may have received in prison.

Christine S. Scott-Hayward
New York University

See also Conditions of Community Corrections; Continuum of Sanctions; Offender Supervision; Parole Boards and Hearings

Further Readings

Bonta, James et al. "Exploring the Black Box of Community Supervision." *Journal of Offender Rehabilitation*, v.47 (2008).
Caplan, Joel. "Parole System Anomie, Conflicting Models of Casework and Surveillance." *Federal Probation*, v.70/3 (2006).
Langan, Patrick and David Levin. *Recidivism of Prisoners Released in 1994*. Washington, DC: U.S. Department of Justice, Bureau of Justice Statistics, 2002.
Messinger, Sheldon L. et al. "The Foundations of Parole in California." *Law and Society Review*, v.19 (1985).
Morrissey v. Brewer, 408 U.S. 471 (1972).
Petersilia, Joan. *When Prisoners Come Home: Parole and Prisoner Reentry*. New York: Oxford University Press, 2003.
Simon, Jonathan. *Poor Discipline: Parole and the Social Control of the Underclass, 1890 to 1990*. Chicago: Chicago University Press, 1993.
Solomon, Amy. "Does Parole Supervision Work? Research Findings and Policy Opportunities." *Perspectives*, v.30/2 (2006).
Travis, Jeremy. *But They All Come Back: Facing the Challenges of Prisoner Reentry*. Washington, DC: Urban Institute Press, 2005.

Parole Boards and Hearings

Parole boards are governing bodies whose members are appointed officials. Their main job is to determine when an offender or inmate is eligible for release and, when that time comes, to determine if he or she is fit to return to society. Once that offender is in society, the board sets his or her conditions of parole, the conditions that must be met in order to stay in the community. If these conditions are not met, it is the board's job to revoke the offender's parole rights and sanction the offender by returning him or her to prison or some alternative program. If the conditions are met, it is the board's job to release the offender from parole when the appropriate time comes.

The decision to return an offender to the community must be based on certain criteria, including the type of crime committed, the offender's prior criminal history, and the parole prognosis. The prognosis is the determination of how well the offender will do while on parole in the community—that is, whether he or she will succeed or fail. The methods for determining whether an offender is fit for parole have changed recently; less discretion is given to parole boards and more emphasis is placed on using guidelines.

Parole boards play a significant role in community corrections, especially in regard to regulating the offender. They have control over all of the major aspects of when the offender reenters the community: the date of return, the conditions that must be followed in the community, the length of time on parole, the date of release from supervision, and the punishment if the parolee violates the conditions of parole. Although parole boards are being used less frequently—17 states and the federal government have limited their usage—all the states still use parole boards or chairs to govern the release of prisoners, and this will continue to be the trend for the foreseeable future.

The Parole Board

Parole is a method of releasing offenders from prison prior to the completion of their sentence. It is similar to probation but generally severer. Offenders eligible for parole must be granted release by a parole board.

Parole board members have two main areas of responsibility: first, general policy making, which includes interpreting parole to the public, creating good parole legislation, and formulating statutes and policies on matters related to the work of the parole board, and second, managing and making decisions regarding individual cases. The latter responsibilities can include reviewing cases, fixing eligibility dates, granting and revoking paroles, removing offenders from parole supervision, and determining the conditions of parole.

In the majority of states, members of parole boards are appointed by the governor and generally serve terms of six or fewer years. It is not unusual to have new board members appointed when a new governor takes office. This has resulted in appointments based on political affiliations rather than necessary qualifications. To avoid this, some states have adopted civil service or merit systems for parole board appointments.

Most states do not require specific qualifications or credentials to serve on parole boards. However, the American Correctional Association suggests that a prospective parole board member should have the following qualifications: He or she should not be a political official, should maintain good character, should have academic training in corrections or a related field in criminal justice or criminology, and should be able to relate to offenders and their problems. Parole boards range from three to 19 members, with the national average being seven parole board members. Being selected for a parole board is not as attractive as many other political appointments that a governor may make.

Parole Board Procedures

There are several types of parole-related hearings. In states where indeterminate sentences are used, the parole board sets the offender's parole eligibility date. In every other jurisdiction, this date is set by a legal statute or court order. After this date is set, the board has the authority to conduct additional hearings to assess an offender's progress. Parole boards are responsible for chairing hearings to determine whether an offender is ready for release. Offenders will often have multiple hearings before they are informed of when they will be released.

Parole board hearings are generally held within the state's prisons. The members of the parole board will have access to pertinent information about each offender. This file is prepared by either a parole officer or a correctional officer inside the prison. Each file contains information concerning the presentence investigation; institutional reports regarding education, training, and treatment; physical and psychological examinations; misconduct reports; and a release plan should the offender be granted parole by the board.

In most states, one to three members of the parole board will interview the offender who is available for parole. In some states, specific interviewers or examiners will interview the offender and report back to the parole board with a recommendation. The use of a hearing examiner reduces the board's workload and allows the members of the parole board more time to focus on other issues, such as policy making. Some states do not use interviews or hearings at all; they simply rely on written briefs to make their decisions. Some believe that parole board hearings or interviews have very little value. Research suggests that parole board hearings do not effectively evaluate whether or not the offender will be successful while on parole. Furthermore, parole board hearings require board members to travel great distances on a regular basis, especially in large rural states.

Parole Board Release Decisions

The criteria that a parole board uses when deciding to parole an offender include the crime committed, the amount of time the offender has served, the offender's age, his or her criminal history, his or her substance abuse history, and his or her behavior while incarcerated (such as treatment programs attended, educational programs participated in, and misconduct). Most parole boards will also consult the prosecution's office, police departments, and the media. The American Law Institute created a model penal code that lists 13 guidelines that parole boards should follow when determining if an offender should be granted release. They include such items as the offender's family status, employment history, housing situation, and physical or mental illnesses.

Another criterion that is considered when deciding to parole an offender is the victim or the victim's family. In the United States, the majority of states allow victims to participate in parole board hearings, either in person or via written correspondence. Many states usually include a victim impact statement (VIS) in the files given to parole board members undertaking a hearing. If the decision not to parole an offender occurs, this decision must be fully explained to the offender so that he or she can make the necessary improvements to be considered for release at a later date. The parole board's use of discretionary criteria has been reduced in recent years because of the increased use of parole guidelines.

Another crucial component in the decision of whether to release an offender to parole is his or her Salient Factor Score (SFS). The SFS was adopted by the U.S. Parole Commission in 1972. It marked the first time that an empirical instrument was used to aid parole boards in decision making. The SFS is composed of ratings on approximately six items: prior convictions and adjudications, prior commitments (30 or more days), age at current offense, recent amount of time offender was commitment-free, technical violations, and drug dependency. To ensure that the SFS remains current and maintains its predictive qualities, it is routinely updated or reviewed.

Generally, one of three models has been used when deciding whether to release an offender on parole. The first two were used in the past, and the third is in current use. The first is the Surveillance Model; in this model, the offender was released under supervision based on the idea that informal social controls such as family and friends could create structure for the individual and help the individual succeed. The second model, known as the Procedural Justice Model, used fairness and due process to guide the board's decisions. The third and final model, known as the Risk Prediction Model, is the model used today. This model uses risk factor scores, including type of crime and prior criminal history.

Studies have shown that the number of back-end sentences (or parole revocations) increased from 18 percent in 1980 to 34 percent in 2000. Furthermore, of those offenders entering the California prison system in 2005, 47 percent were the result of parole revocations—a full 9 percent more than the 38 percent entering the prison system because of new felony convictions.

Parole Revocation

There are two main types of parole violations: a legal violation, which usually consists of a new crime committed by the offender, and a technical violation, which is a violation of one of the conditions of parole set forth by the parole board. Revocation of parole is not automatic upon the commission of a violation. The offender's parole officer has the choice to initiate the revocation process or deal with certain technical violations in another manner. Usually, in the case of a legal violation, the revocation process begins, but the offender is not always returned to prison.

The revocation process was revamped during the 1960s and 1970s because of a few court cases ruling that parole violators are accorded some forms of due process. In 1972, the Supreme Court ruled in *Morrissey v. Brewer* that minimum due process requirements must be met. As a result, the revocation process itself involves due process for the offender, including a two-stage hearing. The first stage, a preliminary hearing, is held in front of an uninvolved person or officer (who does not have to be a judicial official), who determines if there is reasonable cause to believe that the offender violated the conditions of parole. If this occurs, the offender is then provided a notice of the hearing and a list of the charges. The second stage includes a hearing in front of the parole board or its representative (a hearing examiner, for example). During this stage, the offender has the rights to have access to the evidence against him or her, to provide witnesses on his or her behalf, to cross-examine the state's witnesses, and to receive a written statement with the board's decision.

A revocation decision does not necessarily mean a return to prison. Many states will seek alternative punishments, such as loss of time served on parole or additional parole conditions, which can include drug testing, electronic monitoring, or increased reporting. Some states are more willing to be flexible when it comes to parole revocations. This can occur for a number of different reasons, such as prison crowding, which can discourage readmissions to prisons, as well administrative pressure to make it appear that the parole failure rate is low.

However, many parole boards are quick to sentence offenders. In a study conducted in California, 69.3 percent of criminal violation cases resulted in prison sentences, 82.1 percent of technical violations resulted in prison sentences, and an astonishing 82.7 percent of absconding cases resulted in prison sentences. This may be a result of the leniency and discretion that many parole boards enjoy. In most states, parole boards need only meet the "preponderance of the evidence" standard to revoke parole, compared to the "beyond a reasonable doubt" standard to which the courts must adhere. Another reason revocations may be so high is that parole officers may often stack the evidence against an offender. For example, some parole officers may compile multiple points of evidence against one offender and submit them all at the same time.

Problems With Parole Boards' Discretionary Power

During the 1970s, the U.S. Board of Parole decided to create guidelines to make the decision-making process for parole boards less discretionary. The hope was that this more streamlined process would help make parole boards' decision-making process clearer and more objective for both offenders and society. These guidelines usually look beyond the rehabilitative model on which indeterminate sentencing is based. According to these guidelines, good behavior is expected, although it may not be rewarded. However, poor behavior within the institution may result in denial of parole.

The guidelines used by state parole boards must consider the seriousness of the current crime, the criminal history of the offender, rehabilitative programs undertaken during incarceration (such as treatment, education, and training), and parole outlook (the likelihood the offender will succeed or fail while on parole). Parole boards use a seven-point index to determine the severity of the offender's crime. The board also determines the offender's likelihood of parole success by using factors such as prior imprisonment, previous parole or probation failures, substance abuse, and unemployment.

Based on these guidelines, the U.S. Parole Commission (as the U.S. Board of Parole was renamed in 1976) developed a scale known as the Salient Factor Score. This scale uses two factors to determine the period of confinement for offenders: offense severity and parole prognosis. Fourteen states, the District of Columbia, and the federal system have implemented similar instruments. If a parole board chooses not to use these guidelines, it must justify its actions in writing.

Furthermore, in some states mandatory minimums and truth-in-sentencing guidelines were implemented in an effort to keep repeat offenders and serious and violent offenders from getting out of prison early. In these states, more serious offenders are required to serve a minimum of 85 percent of their sentences, and the use of good-time credits for this group has been eliminated.

Some believe that part-time parole boards, which are found in approximately half the states, represent one of the most significant problems in corrections, because members of these boards are able to devote only a limited amount of time and resources to their parole board duties. Business or other professional commitments make it difficult for part-time parole board members to engage fully in the critical decision-making process.

Parole Boards and Community Corrections

The role of the parole board has changed in recent years. Previously, parole was viewed as a transition from prison to the community to assist in the reintegration of offenders. However, today parole is viewed as protecting the public from released offenders. This is accomplished in three ways: first, by enforcing restrictions and controls on offenders in the community; second, by providing offenders with services that help them reenter society and follow a noncriminal lifestyle; and third, by increasing the public's perception that the programs in which offenders are participating are effective.

Some believe that this transition from reentry program to enforcement agency is the reason for the high rate of revocations among parolees. Parole boards play a vital role in offenders' release back into the community and their participation in community corrections. Ultimately, the parole board has four main roles when it comes to its influence on offenders' place in the community. First, the board must decide when the offender is available to return to the community or be released. Second, the board must determine each offender's conditions of parole; these will have a significant impact on what the offender is able to accomplish once he or she returns to the community. Third, the board must decide when the offender is officially released from supervision, that is, when the offender no longer has to follow the conditions laid down by the board; at this point the offender will be considered a free and regular civilian. Finally, the board has the authority to revoke the offender's parole. This is the most important role the board plays, because in this situation the board has the ability to remove the offender from all forms of community correction and place him or her back in prison for the rest of the offender's term.

Changing of the Guard: Reduction of Parole/Parole Boards

Over the last several years, parole has been limited in 17 states and the federal government. However, these states have maintained some form of community supervision of released offenders similar to parole. In many of these states, the abolition has occurred only in regard to the parole board's decision-making process. The idea of parole and its practice are still being implemented.

Each state has a different level of involvement for its parole boards. Currently, there are three levels: full, limited, and what is referred to as "old case" or states that have people still on parole. There are 26 states with full parole boards. In these states, the parole board has the ability or discretion to release

all inmates or offenders. In states with limited parole boards, the parole board has the discretion to release only certain types of offenders, and parole is denied to offenders who have recidivated or have been convicted of violent crimes. Currently, there are 10 states with this type of board. States labeled as "old cases" do not have parole boards with discretionary power but still are involved with those cases from the past that were granted under the former law. There are 14 states currently operating under this model. Every state, however, has some form of parole board in operation, despite the limited capacities of some of these boards.

The future of parole boards is cloudy. There are a number of issues that arise in discussions of eliminating parole boards altogether. More research needs to be done on the effectiveness of parole boards, not only in terms of recidivism among parolees but also in terms of their cost-effectiveness for taxpayers. Regardless of what happens, something similar to parole boards will be necessary to determine lengths of sentences, dates when offenders can be released, the conditions of offenders' release, when they no longer need to be supervised, and what determines when they get into trouble and need to be returned to prison. Whether such an instrument is called a probation or parole board or something else, a governing body will be necessary.

Sean M. Falconer
Washington State University

See also Parole Commission, U.S.; Parole Officers; Probation and Parole: Intensive Supervision; Revocation

Further Readings

Abadinsky, Howard. *Probation and Parole: Theory and Practice,* 11th ed. Upper Saddle River, NJ: Pearson, 2011.

Alarid, Leanne Fiftal and Rolando V. del Carmen. *Community-Based Corrections,* 8th ed. Belmont, CA: Thomson Wadsworth, 2011.

Kerbs, Jones et al. "Discretionary Decision Making by Probation and Parole Officers: The Role of Extralegal Variables as Predictors of Responses to Technical Violations." *Journal of Contemporary Criminal Justice,* v.25 (2009).

Lin, Grattet et al. "Back-End Sentencing and Reimprisonment: Individual, Organizational, and Community Predictors of Parole Sanctioning Decisions." *Criminology,* v.48/3 (2010).

McCarthy, B. R., B. J. McCarthy Jr., and M. C. Leone. *Community-Based Corrections,* 4th ed. Belmont, CA: Thomson Wadsworth, 2001.

Montgomery, Dillingham, Jr. *Probation and Parole in Practice.* Cincinnati, OH: Anderson, 1983.

PAROLE COMMISSION, U.S.

Early use of parole at the federal level can be traced back to the beginning of the 20th century. During a period of growth in the 1930s and 1940s, federal parole was administered by the U.S. Board of Parole in the U.S. Attorney General's office. Administrative reorganization—from centralization of administrative functions to decentralization—took place in the 1970s, and the board was renamed the U.S. Parole Commission (USPC) in 1976. With the onset of the "get-tough" approach to crime, the USPC was scheduled for phaseout.

History

Parole was initially established in the mid-1800s as a Progressive Era penal reform at the local and state levels. Parole at the federal level was first utilized in 1910. Each of the three existing federal penitentiaries had its own parole board, which consisted of the prison warden, the physician of the institution, and the superintendent of prisons from the Department of Justice.

The U.S. Board of Parole was established in 1930, shortly after the establishment of the Federal Bureau of Prisons (BOP), with three full-time members appointed by the U.S. attorney general. Administrative operations of the U.S. Board of Parole fell under the BOP during this period. In 1945, the administrative functions of the board were placed under the U.S. attorney general. Two additional members were added to the board in 1948 because of an increase in the federal prison population after World War II. The board was increased to eight members in 1950. These members were appointed by the president to six-year staggered terms and administrative functions were placed under the Department of Justice.

Administrative Reorganization in the 1970s

As the BOP built new prisons and housed more inmates eligible for parole, operating one central office was deemed inefficient. In 1972, the U.S. Board of Parole initiated a pilot reorganization project. This reorganization created five geographic regions, explicit parole guidelines for parole hearings, the requirement of written reasons for parole decisions, and an administrative appeal process in cases where an inmate was denied release after the parole hearing. The five geographic regions were operational by 1974, with each region having one member and five hearing examiners. In addition, the chair of the Board of Parole and two members remained in Washington, D.C., at the board's headquarters. In 1976, the Board of Parole was renamed the U.S. Parole Commission (USPC) under the Parole Commission and Reorganization Act. This act allowed for nine commissioners to be appointed by the president to six-year terms. They would include the chair, five regional commissioners, and a three-member National Appeals Board. In addition, this act incorporated many features from the pilot reorganization project, including explicit parole guidelines, written reasons for parole decisions, an administrative appeal process, and a regional structure.

The Tough-on-Crime Movement and Federal Parole

During the 1980s, the role of the USPC was changed considerably with the onset of the "tough-on-crime" movement, which resulted in stricter sentencing practices, an increase in prison populations, and a lack of support for rehabilitative programs for prison inmates and for community-based initiatives such as parole. The changing landscape of corrections and criminal justice at large during this period led to the passage of the Comprehensive Crime Control Act of 1984. This act established federal sentencing guidelines, which were influenced by the success of the USPC in creating and using parole guidelines. Rather than operating as a discretionary release decision by the members of the USPC, supervised release became a part of the sentence handed down by the court to the offender. However, it should be noted that the USPC still maintained jurisdiction over federal offenders sentenced prior to November 1, 1987, who were subject to early release consideration.

The Comprehensive Crime Control Act of 1984 called for the abolition of the USPC on November 1, 1992. However, because there were no specific stipulations for how inmates still serving time under jurisdiction of the USPC would be handled, the life of the USPC was extended on three separate occasions. The Parole Commission Phaseout Act of 1996 extended the USPC until November 1, 2002, while also reducing the number of parole commissioners. The 21st Century Department of Justice Appropriations Authorization Act of 2002 extended the USPC until November 1, 2005, and the United States Parole Commission Extension Act of 2008 extended the USPC until November 1, 2011.

Offenders Currently Under USPC Jurisdiction

The USPC has jurisdiction over several different types of offenders. The USPC is responsible for granting or denying parole for federal offenders who committed their offenses prior to November 1, 1987, for Uniform Code of Military Justice offenders, and for state probationers and parolees in the Federal Witness Protection Program. In addition to granting or denying parole for these types of offenders, the USPC is responsible for setting the conditions for their supervision, for modifying the conditions for supervision, for making early discharge from supervision decisions, for issuing warrants or summonses for parole violations, and for revoking parole. The USPC also has jurisdiction over D.C. Code offenders who committed offenses after August 4, 2000, and are sentenced to a determinate sentence of imprisonment followed by a term of supervised release. Last, the USPC is responsible for transfer-treaty cases, setting release dates for U.S. citizens serving prison terms imposed by foreign countries who are serving their sentences in the United States.

Rhonda R. Dobbs
University of Texas, Arlington
Courtney A. Waid
North Dakota State University

See also Parole Boards and Hearings; Parole Commission Phaseout Act of 1996; Parole Guidelines Score; Parole Officers; Risk and Needs Assessment Instruments; Salient Factor Score

Further Readings

Blomberg, Thomas G. and Karol Lucken. *American Penology: A History of Control,* 2nd ed. New Brunswick, NJ: Transaction, 2010.

Hoffman, Peter B. "History of the Federal Parole System." http://www.justice.gov/uspc/history.pdf (Accessed February 2010).

Rothman, David J. *Conscience and Convenience: The Asylum and Its Alternatives in Progressive America.* New York: Aldine de Gruyter, 2002.

Parole Commission Phaseout Act of 1996

The Parole Commission Phaseout Act of 1996, which was passed by Congress and signed into law by President Bill Clinton, is one of a series of laws that narrowed the scope, power, and authority of the U.S. Parole Commission. Although the 1996 act contains several key provisions, the most important extended the commission beyond the date it was supposed to have been disbanded. Despite numerous legal challenges, the commission continues to this day. The commission has the sole authority to determine, with some limitations, which federal prisoners are eligible for early release into the community, following a hearing held for that purpose, and for monitoring them for the duration of their parole.

The U.S. Parole Commission was first created in 1930 (then named the U.S. Board of Parole), and its basic duties and responsibilities remained largely unchanged for almost 54 years. The initial blow came with the Sentencing Reform Act (SRA) of 1984, which is part of the Comprehensive Crime Control Act of 1984 that President Ronald Reagan signed into law to stem rising crime rates. The SRA fundamentally altered federal parole law by removing from parole consideration any non-military individual who had committed a federal crime after November 1, 1987. Federal judges were now required to use sentencing guidelines when determining the punishment of those found guilty, including the number of years to be served in a federal prison. The SRA also sought to end the U.S. Parole Commission by requiring its termination five years later, on November 1, 1992. The Judicial Improvements Act of 1990, however, extended the commission's life by an additional five years, to November 1, 1997.

It was within this context that the Parole Commission Phaseout Act of 1996 became law. While the new law continued the earlier pattern of delaying the U.S. Parole Commission's termination date by adding another five years to its life (this time extending it to November 1, 2002), three other provisions of the Phaseout Act revealed a seriousness on the part of Congress to limit the commission's role and influence. The first two provisions reduced the members of the commission to two by December 1, 1999, and to one (the commission chair) by December 31, 2001. Under the third provision, the U.S. attorney general was required to report to Congress annually, on May 1 from 1998 until 2002, on a number of issues regarding the Parole Commission, including whether maintaining the commission would be effective, worthwhile, and practical.

Between 2002 and 2008, Congress passed four laws that delayed the date on which the commission was supposed to have come to an end. The first was the 21st Century Department of Justice Appropriations Authorization Act of 2002, which set the date at November 1, 2005; this law also questioned, but did not resolve, whether those individuals who violated District of Columbia law should remain under the jurisdiction of the U.S. Parole Commission. The next termination date was set at November 1, 2008, by the United States Parole Commission Extension and Sentencing Commission Authority Act of 2005. The Parole Commission Extension Act of 2008, in turn, further delayed the U.S. Parole Commission's final day of operation.

The Phaseout Act has been a factor in a number of rulings involving parole violation cases, especially by the federal appellate courts. For example, in *Walden v. United States Parole Commission* (1997), Darryl Walden argued that the commission did not have the authority to return him to prison; the U.S. Court of Appeals for the Eleventh Circuit, citing several laws including the SRA and the Phaseout Act, ruled against him. The plaintiff in *Robert Hutchings v. U.S. Parole Commission* (2000) similarly tried to convince the U.S. Court of Appeals for the Eighth Circuit that he did not fall under the commission's jurisdiction and that it had violated his due process rights; Hutchings lost his appeal. Jurisdiction was also among the issues struck down by the U.S. Court of Appeals for the Ninth Circuit in the case *Benny v. United States Parole Commission* (2002).

Even though the U.S. Parole Commission has been challenged in court and given numerous termination dates, it continues to this day as an important, and vital, part of the federal criminal justice system. While it no longer has jurisdiction over individuals who violated federal law after November 1, 1987, it continues to have jurisdiction with respect to offenders who committed federal crimes prior to that date. The commission also maintains parole responsibilities for all individuals found to have violated the Washington, D.C., Code or the Uniform Code of Military Justice. Other responsibilities of the Parole Commission include the jurisdiction it has in cases involving U.S. citizens convicted of crimes, and subsequently imprisoned, in foreign nations who can be returned to the United States in accordance with certain treaty conditions, as well as state criminals on probation or parole who are in the Federal Witness Protection Program.

Legislative moves to terminate the Parole Commission may soon come to an end. On February 24, 2010, Congresswoman Eleanor Holmes Norton introduced House Resolution 4685, the United States Parole Commission Authorization Act of 2010, in Congress. The bill would have granted permanent status to the commission, but it never became law.

Dula J. Espinosa
University of Houston, Clear Lake

See also Parole Boards and Hearings; Parole Commission, U.S.

Further Readings

Abadinsky, Howard. *Probation and Parole: Theory and Practice,* 11th ed. Upper Saddle River, NJ: Pearson, 2011.

Benny v. U.S. Parole Commission, July 2, 2002, No. 00–16867.

Comprehensive Crime Control Act of 1984, 98 Stat. 1976.

Judicial Improvements Act of 1990, 104 Stat. 5089.

Parole Commission Phaseout Act of 1996, 110 Stat. 3055.

Petersilia, Joan. *When Prisoners Come Home: Parole and Prisoner Reentry.* New York: Oxford University Press, 2003.

Robert Hutchings v. United States Parole Commission, February 2, 2000, No. 99–2273.

Sentencing Reform Act of 1984, 98 Stat. 1987.

21st Century Department of Justice Appropriations Authorization Act of 2002, 116 Stat. 1758.

United States Parole Commission Authorization Act of 2010 (H.R. 4685, 111th Congress).

United States Parole Commission Extension Act of 2008, 122 Stat. 3013.

United States Parole Commission Extension and Sentencing Commission Authority Act of 2005, 119 Stat. 2035.

Walden v. United States Parole Commission, June 12, 1997, No. 95–8556.

Parole Guidelines Score

Prior to national efforts to reform prison conditions and improve parole guidelines, criminal behavior was thought to have its roots in the psychosocial and environmental aspects of an offender's life. Parole was seen as a major adjunct to the rehabilitation philosophy that dominated American corrections from the 1930s through the 1960s. This rehabilitation-over-retribution ideal, known as the "medical model," assumed that criminal behaviors could be corrected. Theoretically, every offender could be dealt with on an individual basis to determine the precise causes of his or her criminal behavior. Parole was granted to those deemed to have met the then-nascent correction standards.

The national purpose of revising parole guidelines was to facilitate and improve parole boards' decision-making processes. The use of accountability-driven guidelines aids in helping to make policies more transparent. As a result, predictions about population projections can more easily and efficiently be made and revised. These forecasts can then help to educate and improve the planning of other prison-capacity management policies, including those framing reforms and legislative mandates.

Discretion and Independence

Parole board members, while independent and allowed to deliberate outside their board's guidelines and individually interpret policy, cast their votes as a unified body. As do parole policies of most other states, Texas's parole guidelines grant individual interpretations, and board members exercise their discretion to vote collectively outside the guidelines when necessary. California parole board members individually interpret guidelines yet vote as a caucus on parole issues. Similarly, Georgia's State Board of Pardons and Paroles, Michigan's Parole and Commutation Board, and the New York State Division of Parole all grant unrestricted, individual discretion to their members, whose deliberations will be finalized as well as perceived as collective decisions under their boards' signatures.

An independent parole board is as vital and as necessary as an independent judiciary. The U.S. Supreme Court ruled, in *Swarthout v. Cooke*, that a federal appeals court exceeded its power when it

The U.S. Supreme Court made a unanimous ruling that federal judges have no power to overturn state parole decisions, reversing a decision by the California Board of Parole Hearings and thus ensuring the independence of parole boards. (Environmental Protection Agency)

reversed a decision by the California Board of Parole hearings. Federal judges have no power to overturn state parole decisions, the Court said in a unanimous ruling that could affect, in the coming years, hundreds of cases in federal courts throughout the United States.

Parole Guidelines

Parole guidelines are a tool that parole boards use to "score" inmates eligible for parole consideration. Scores are computed by calculating (1) inmates' risk factors and (2) their offense severity rankings. The purpose is to make the process of parole consideration a science and not a gamble. Most notable in this endeavor are Texas and Michigan. Texas parole guidelines consider, as risk factors, prior incarcerations and prison disciplinary conduct. The parole board relies on its own ratings of 1,931 felony offenses in the penal code and translates offense severity rankings into an arithmetic value. Risk and severity factors are scored separately and then merged in a composite score ranging from 1 to 7, with 1 representing the highest-risk and highest-offense severity. Offenders in the highest-risk and highest-severity category are scored as 1, and the approval probability range is 0 percent to 5 percent. Offenders in the lowest-risk and lowest-severity category are scored as 7, with an approval probability of 76 percent to 100 percent.

In Michigan, whenever a parole eligibility report (PER) is prepared, the Michigan Parole Board reviews the report and other relevant information in the inmate's central office file and enters into the Michigan Department of Corrections' computerized database the information that is required to calculate the inmate's parole guidelines score. A printed parole guidelines score sheet is generated after each calculation and placed in the inmate's central office file. A copy of the parole guidelines score sheet is provided to the inmate.

The Parole-Scoring Process

Parole boards understand the complexities of predicting human behavior and want the futures of pre-parolees to be informed by board members' input and not solely by computerized calculations. Despite its members' active participation in various time-intensive pre-parole tasks, a parole board's final decision can come back to haunt it. Notably, Massachusetts's entire parole board resigned after a parolee shot and killed a police officer near Boston on December 26, 2010. The parole board had voted for his release on parole despite his three life sentences. In the wake of the slaying, Governor's Council member Christopher Iannella urged the local city council to reverse current policies that allowed parole board members to cast secret votes and, instead, mandate that board members publicly disclose their voting practices.

Parole boards or panels comprising certain of their members review an inmate's parole guidelines score when considering the inmate for parole. The parole board may deny parole without an interview if the inmate's parole guidelines score indicates a low probability of parole. The parole board may grant parole without an interview if the inmate's parole guidelines score indicates a high probability of parole. Exceptions are for inmates who are incarcerated for a sex offense or an offense involving the death of a victim. They must be interviewed before being considered for parole. Similarly, inmates whose parole guidelines scores indicate an average probability of parole are required to be interviewed prior to being granted or denied parole.

Limitations on Parole Boards

After conducting inmate interviews, parole boards still retain the prerogative to depart from the parole guidelines scores by denying parole to an inmate who has a high probability of parole or by granting parole to an inmate who has a low probability of parole. The departure must be for substantial and compelling reasons and must be stated in writing. Parole boards are prohibited, however, from using an inmate's gender, race, ethnicity, national origin, or religion in either the initial parole-eligibility scoring or as a basis for a departure from, or disregard of, the parole guidelines score. Thus, every offender facing the parole board can be treated strictly as an individual when a determination is made about his or her success prospects as a law-abiding parolee.

James E. Shaw
Chicago School of Professional Psychology

See also Parole Boards and Hearings; Pre-Parole Plan; Risk and Needs Assessment Instruments; Salient Factor Score

Further Readings

California Department of Corrections and Rehabilitation. *Parolee Conditions.* Sacramento, CA: Author, 2010.

Cheney, Kyle. "Council Advocates Overhaul of Paroles." *The Boston Globe* (January 20, 2011). http://articles .boston.com/2011-01-20/news/29342401_1_parole -board-parole-system-police-shooting (Accessed July 2011).

Michigan Department of Corrections. *Parole Eligibility Report.* Lansing, MI: Author, 2003.

Michigan Department of Corrections. *Parole From Past to Present.* Lansing, MI: Author, 2003.

New York State Division of Parole. *New York State Parole Handbook (Revised).* New York: Author, 2007.

Slobogin, Rai, Arti Rai, and Ralph Reisner. *Law and the Mental Health System: Civil and Criminal Aspects,* 5th ed. St. Paul, MN: Thomson/West, 2009.

Southern Center for Human Rights, Law Office. *Parole Handbook: A Guide to the Parole Consideration Process for People in Georgia Prisons.* Atlanta, GA: Author, 2007.

Swarthout v. Cooke, 562 U.S. 10-333 (2011).

Texas Board of Pardons and Paroles. *Parole Guidelines Annual Report*. Austin, TX: Author, 2009.

PAROLE OFFICERS

Parole officers are trained to supervise offenders who are on conditional release from prison before they have completed their sentences. They are an important part of the criminal justice system and work to protect individuals and the community from future harm. In facilitating the transition from prison to community, parole officers help parolees become productive citizens and reduce the harm they might cause by returning to crime, substance abuse, and other problematic behaviors. More than 5 million adults, or about 1 in 45 adults, were under community supervision in 2008.

Parolees have obeyed prison rules, performed prison jobs, utilized therapeutic and rehabilitation programs, and committed themselves to living a life free of crime after their release. The parole period provides them the opportunity to prove that they can do so successfully while under the watchful eye of parole officers, who visit their clients regularly to evaluate their progress. If parolees violate the conditions set for parole—for example, by breaking the law or associating with bad company—officers can recommend to parole boards that parole be revoked and the offender be sent back to prison.

Parole officers work for state parole departments, counties, or the U.S. Board of Parole. Some may work as administrators, department heads, and directors of special projects or units. Parole officers earn around $30,000 to $75,000 per year, depending on their position and qualifications. Positions in urban areas and in administration pay more. Most parole officers focus on adult offenders, but some officers work in the area of juvenile parole. Many work inside correctional institutions and assess prisoners' lives before and during incarceration. They help develop a release plan that will be submitted to the parole board for consideration. Included may be how prisoners' families will affect their rehabilitation, strengths and risk factors, community needs, and employment possibilities. Field officers work with parolees once they have returned to their communities to help parolees find jobs, schools, or therapy programs. By staying in touch with parolees and their families, parole officers keep tabs on offenders during their parole. Drug therapists, psychiatrists, and social workers often provide feedback to the parole officer.

Parole officers must travel and conduct fieldwork, sometimes in dangerous areas while interacting with criminal offenders. Most have to collect urine samples from their clients for drug testing. The caseloads for parole officers are often heavy; officers may handle between 20 and 100 cases at any given time. Officers spend time conducting investigations and writing reports about and recommendations on offenders for the courts, and they must meet frequent court deadlines. Prior to filing sentencing recommendations, officers review their decisions with the offenders and their families. Officers may be asked to provide testimony in court with regard to their reports and recommendations. Officers also bring the court up to date on the offender's obedience to the stipulations of their parole or probation and their progress with rehabilitation.

A set of qualifications and training standards is available for those who wish to become parole officers. States typically require parole officers to have a college degree. Officers may have an associate's or bachelor's degree depending on the position; a graduate degree is required for federal positions. Commonly held degrees are in criminal justice, social work, sociology, political science, education, or specially designed programs that meet state specifications for parole officers. All prospective parole officers must undergo background checks, which will reveal records for misdemeanor or felony charges, convictions, driving violations, gang affiliations, and credit standing, as well as personal and professional references. After qualifying for the job, candidates must pass an examination to demonstrate their skills and knowledge in the criminal justice and court system. Examinations can be administered by cities, counties, states, or the federal government, and they cover general parole and institution-specific topics. Most exams are a combination of multiple-choice questions and essay questions. Competition for parole officer positions is such that publishers such as Peterson have created study guides and study packages to enhance a student's likelihood of success. Peterson's program to increase scores on the Parole Officer Examination covers everything from reading and writing to parole supervision, narcotics law, self-defense, and interpersonal skills.

Once employed, newly hired parole officers often attend training programs. Programs may consist of workshops, seminars, field observation, fitness training, and firearms practice. Some states require parole officers to attend refresher and retraining programs periodically in order to be eligible for career advancement opportunities or to obtain certifications.

Effective parole officers are patient, work well under pressure, are emotionally stable and mature, have physical endurance, and communicate clearly in an authoritative manner. Not everyone is cut out to be a good parole officer. Good mental and physical health is a prerequisite for working as a probation officer or correctional treatment specialist. The federal government places an age cap at 37 on new officers, and most jurisdictions require prospects to be at least 21. Convicted felons are typically disqualified from these positions.

Computer-related knowledge and skills are helpful, as officers must increasingly use computers to accomplish their work. A working knowledge of laws, statutes, and policies with regard to correctional issues is essential. Because of the large number of reports a correctional treatment specialist or probation officer will produce over his or her career, candidates should possess strong writing skills. Experience in the supervision of offenders is a plus, as is knowledge of the community resources that can be utilized as offenders reintegrate into their home communities. Counseling skills, motivational interviewing, and assessment of misrepresentations of the truth are important. Parole officers should have the ability to work effectively with family members, service agencies, and community groups to ensure the offender has the resources and supports necessary to change antisocial behaviors. The parole officer must have the expertise to give courtroom testimony and to manage the offender both in and out of the legal system.

In order for parole officers to be effective in motivating offenders to exhibit more socially appropriate behavior, they must demonstrate good communication skills and interpersonal sensitivity. By listening to offenders and following up on the positive aspects of their speech and thinking, corrections professionals can help increase offenders' motivation to make positive changes in their lives that will reduce their risk of reoffending. They must have a conceptual understanding of why people change, and they must be able to transform that knowledge into positive management of the offenders in their caseloads.

The roles of empathy, resistance, discrepancy, and self-efficacy are identified and examined as elements in the dynamics that encourage change. Also important is that parole officers know how to work with deception; what types of positive and negative, formal and informal sanctions to use; and how to handle violations.

The field of parole has changed from one of surveillance to one of community support using evidence-based practices. Surveillance alone has not been found to have a big impact on recidivism, and while important, it is now combined with the use of community supports and partnerships. This was supported by the Urban Institute in a 2008 study on parole practices. The professional duality between law enforcement and social service reflects changes in the institutional environment of parole and probation. This can be observed in the relabeling of parole and police education as "peace officer state training" (POST).

The American Probation and Parole Association (APPA) is the main professional association for parole officers. APPA conducts the largest national training institute for community corrections, offering workshops, special sessions, a resource expo, and networking opportunities tailored to the needs of parole officers. Information on research, theory, and practical applications is provided across the nation several times a year on a variety of topics. Specific areas in which the APPA provides training are cognitive behavioral change, management training, motivational interviewing, occupational languages, officer safety, sexual offender management, victim issues, and strength-based practices. APPA also provides training in family support models, community supervision, distance-learning opportunities, firearm safety, elder abuse, and domestic violence. Workshops on how to handle substance abusers, community reintegration, and working with families may also be provided by educational programs for parole officers. In order for parole workers to receive credit for ongoing training, they must attend accredited programs, workshops with approved contact hours that are research based and tailored to the needs of those working in this field. Training is increasingly offered online as well as in community colleges, at conferences, and at local, state, regional, and professional meetings.

Role conflict is sometimes experienced by parole officers because of their dual obligations to (1) help the offender, (2) enforce the law, (3) demonstrate fairness, and (4) protect the community. Studies indicate that most parole officers are more inclined to exhibit clear preferences and behaviors for some roles than for others. As a result, not all probation officers act the same way, even when they have the same training. Attitudes toward authority and assistance have been found to influence parole officers' willingness to revoke an offender's parole.

The issue of taking a punitive versus rehabilitative approach must be considered. Officers with a higher punishment orientation are more likely to take formal action and recommend a return to prison, whereas officers with an assistance orientation may turn a blind eye on a behavior that breaks some aspect of the law. Giving an offender a second chance may be seen to have more long-term value to the individual and community than enforcing a law that others violate without penalty. This role conflict is a significant concern, as it can put parole officers in an uncertain professional status and create a "civil service malaise" that typically results in an officer's choosing one role or the other. Thus, officers' orientations directly influence job performance and case outcomes.

Parole officers are facing other occupational challenges. They can no longer be merely law-enforcement authorities. Despite budget increases of more than 20 percent for many agencies and major improvements in risk management, more than 75 percent of all agencies have indicated that staff increases have not kept pace with increasing caseloads. In addition to increases in staff-to-client ratios, offenders have greater supervision needs than in the past. Moreover, many parole officers feel that salaries are too low to attract qualified applicants and retain such staff. Greater community resources are needed to help parole officers become and remain successful in helping offenders. Expansions of programs and services in job readiness, general education, vocational education and employment, drug and residential programs, affordable housing and housing referral, individual and family counseling, and mental health are needed. Since the 1990s, agencies have expanded their responsibilities from primarily pre-sentence investigation and offender supervision to pretrial diversion, halfway houses, and other alternative programs and activities. This shift in job function requires additional training and retraining.

Because parole officers are assigned the responsibility of supervising convicted criminals in a community setting, the competing goals of punishment, public safety, offender rehabilitation, and deterrence all intersect. These tasks must all be accomplished within the confines of shrinking budgets, large caseloads, increasingly high-risk offenders, low occupational prestige, and considerable political and public scrutiny. These competing demands often result in especially high levels of work-related stress. Studies indicate that officers who feel educationally underprepared are likely to experience higher levels of occupational stress and are more likely to have negative manifestations of stress than those officers who feel well prepared.

Stress is also a significant factor when parole officers feel as though reform movements in the criminal justice field make it difficult to do their work. A study in Ohio found that officers were generally dissatisfied with the restrictions on their discretion resulting from reforms. Analyses revealed that organizational factors such as officers' perceptions concerning how the sanctioning policy was implemented and its intended purposes were more influential on their attitudes than were individual characteristics in shaping officers' views concerning the efficacy of the reform.

The job market for parole officers is expected to grow through 2014. Many officers and specialists are projected to retire in the near future, and others will inevitably leave the field, which, along with natural job growth, is creating many job opportunities. Mandatory sentencing guidelines, which have called for longer prison terms and fewer opportunities for parole, are being reconsidered in many states because of budgetary constraints and court decisions. If additional prisoners gain early release, more parole officers may be needed to supervise them. However, the highly stressful, heavy workloads and comparatively low pay of parole positions may dissuade applicants if they are able to find more lucrative and less stressful fields of employment.

Yvonne Vissing
Salem State University

See also Juvenile Probation Officers; Parole; Parole Boards and Hearings; Pre-Parole Plan; Probation and Parole: Intensive Supervision; Probation Officers; Probation Officers: Job Stress

Further Readings

Bonczar, T. and L. Glaze. "Probation and Parole in the United States, 2008." Bureau of Justice Statistics. December 8, 2009. http://bjs.ojp.usdoj.gov/index .cfm?ty=pbdetail&iid=1764 (Accessed July 2011).

CareerOverview.com. "Probation Officer Career, Jobs and Training Information Center." http://www.career overview.com/probation-Officer-Careers.html (Accessed July 2011).

Champion, J. *Probation, Parole and Community Corrections*. Upper Saddle, NJ: Prentice Hall, 2002.

Clark, John. "The Construction of Meaning During Training for Probation and Parole." *Justice Quarterly*, v.13/2 (June 1996).

Clear, Todd R., George F. Cole, and Michael D. Reisig. *American Corrections*, 9th ed. Belmont, CA: Thomson Wadsworth, 2010.

Fulton, B., A. Stichman, L. Travis, and E. Latessa. "Moderating Probation and Parole Officer Attitudes to Achieve Desired Outcomes." *The Prison Journal*, v.77/3 (1997). http://www.uc.edu/ccjr/Articles/Probation_ Parole_Officer_Attitudes.pdf (Accessed July 2011).

Guynes, R. *Difficult Clients, Large Caseloads Plague Probation, Parole Agencies*. Washington, DC: National Institute of Justice, 1988. http://www.ncjrs.gov/App/ abstractdb/AbstractDBDetails.aspx?id=113768 (Accessed July 2011).

Lurigio, A. "An Evaluation of a Safe Haven's Workshop for Illinois Parole Agents. Loyola University." 2009. http:// www.asafehaven.com/news/ASH%201oyola%20 Parole%20Officer%20Report%205-26-09.pdf (Accessed July 2011).

Meredity, T. and J. Prevost. "Developing Data Drive Supervision for Positive Parole Outcomes." U.S. Department of Justice. November 2009. http://www .ncjrs.gov/pdffiles1/nij/grants/228855.pdf (Accessed July 2011).

Petersen's Guide to Law Enforcement Exams. Peterson's College Search. 2011. http://www.petersons.com/college -Search/law-Enforcement-Test-Practice.aspx (Accessed July 2011).

Pitts, W. "Educational Competency as an Indicator of Occupational Stress for Probation and Parole Officers." *American Journal of Criminal Justice*, v.32/1–2 (2007). http://www.springerlink.com/content/ jn84371474476688

Raymond, F. and J. Jones. "Administration in Probation and Parole." In *Social Work in Juvenile and Criminal Justice Settings*, 3rd ed, Albert R. Roberts and David W. Springer, eds. Springfield, IL: Charles C. Thomas, 2007.

Steiner, B. L. and M. Travis Makarios. "Understanding Parole Officers' Responses to Sanctioning Reform." *Crime and Delinquency* (August 2009). http://cad .sagepub.com/content/early/2009/08/14/0011128709343 141 (Accessed July 2011).

Walters, Scott T., Melissa Alexander, and Amanda M. Vader. "The Officer Responses Questionnaire: A Procedure for Measuring Reflective Listening in Probation and Parole Settings." *Federal Probation* (September 2008). http://heinonline.org/HOL/Landing Page?collection=journals&handle=hein.journals/ fedpro72&div=27&id=&page=

Walters, Scott T., Michael D. Clark, Ray Gingerich, and Melissa L. Meltzer. *Motivating Offenders to Change: A Guide for Probation and Parole*. Washington, DC: National Institute of Corrections, 2007. http://www .ncjrs.gov/App/Publications/abstract.aspx?ID=240750 (Accessed July 2011).

Philosophy of Community Corrections

Conservative philosophers have enshrined punishment as the cornerstone of moral authority and thus the central purpose for intervention in response to crime. This philosophy of corrections generally places little credence in the capacity of most offenders to change behavior, except in response to a threat of incarceration. The liberal or progressive philosophy of corrections, by contrast, traditionally focuses on rehabilitative strategies that seek to treat the assumed underlying causes of crime. Accordingly, it is assumed that criminal justice intervention must be kept to a minimum. In a third approach, libertarians are skeptical of the motives of those seeking either to punish or to treat offenders; they are more concerned that intervention, no matter what the intent, often makes matters worse. Essential to any philosophical underpinning to community corrections, however, is the notion of treating the offender with dignity. The best effort at doing this today is through restorative justice.

Community corrections is a rubric for various activities and programs that are designed to encourage the offender's law-abiding behavior through the application of various forms of punishment and the use of treatment programs when necessary. The philosophy of community corrections is based on the notion that society is willing to take a chance on offenders who desire to stay crime-free and are willing to participate in programs intended to help them with their problems. Offenders are allowed to stay in the community as long as they comply with the conditions of probation, such as participating in drug treatment programs, maintaining employment, attending school, providing support and care for their families, and leading crime-free lives. Offenders are supervised by community corrections officers as long as they follow the prescribed plan put forward by the court. Failure to live according to these requirements can lead to imprisonment.

From the start, the purposes of community corrections were consistent with the belief that the offender benefited most from addressing concrete issues related to finding work or attending school. Community corrections personnel are drawn to this line of work because of their interest in people, their interpersonal skills, and their problem-solving abilities. The professional orientation of the community corrections officer, who is the bedrock of the profession, stems from several conditions. Community corrections personnel for the most part are required to have a college degree in the social sciences (particularly those related to social work, psychology, and other social sciences related to the field) and prior experience working with people and their problems.

Community corrections officers work in agencies with organizational structures that are far less militaristic and regimented than is generally found in law enforcement and other criminal justice fields. Community corrections personnel are encouraged to adapt to a professional culture that emphasizes a philosophy supportive of community corrections, a unique disciplinary language, a set of identified goals and objectives for the work, and a knowledge base necessary to do the job. Community corrections personnel further develop their professional orientation through the application of social science principles to their caseloads. These "clients" are met on a regular basis both in the office and in the field. During these meetings, the officer evaluates how the client is progressing in terms of education, work, family relationships, and any required treatment programs. Community corrections personnel also acquire a professional orientation by their association with the judiciary, with which they must work closely in developing the community corrections plan as the result of writing up a pre-sentence investigative report, on which the judge relies to get an accurate description the offender.

Any consideration of the field of community corrections must begin with a discussion of the basic philosophy of the community corrections officer. It is axiomatic that community corrections personnel must have some interest in their clients and what

Along with the consequences of the stigma of criminal conviction, the penalties for driving under the influence, for example, can include paying DUI fines, jail time, community service, probation, and the loss of driving privileges. (Photos.com)

their problems are if they are to do their work properly. More than ever before, however, community corrections is being asked to justify its mission by attending to concerns other than clients' reformation. Probation, for example, has had to assure various stakeholders that it is engaged in a process that encompasses not only rehabilitation but also retribution ("just deserts"), deterrence, and incapacitation. If a probation officer is asked why community corrections personnel have any interest in helping the client, today a typical response would indicate that the officer is interested in keeping the community safe through preventive treatment measures. These concerns notwithstanding, there are personnel who have a genuine concern for the life circumstances of the offender and are engaged in a process whereby the offender is granted some measure of redemption through community reintegration. This is most evident in those community corrections officers who recognize the inherent value and worth of each client.

Punishment

One of the central goals of criminal law is to impose a penalty on someone convicted of an offense. For many years, community corrections was viewed by professionals in the field as an alternative to punishment. This position has changed over the last several years, with the courts imposing on probationers various penalties that can be quite onerous.

What is central to any idea of community corrections is that the condition imposed by the court is by nature unwelcome, that it is statutorily restricted (there are limits attached to it), and that it should have some meaning for the offender despite his or her prior record. The penalty must be consistent with the law and must not be taken lightly, or it will have a limited deterrent effect. Despite the fact that many people assume probation is not a serious penalty, it does require time and consideration. Minor incidents, for example—such as an offender's forgetting that he or she is not supposed to use alcohol—can cause major difficulties if the offender finds himself or herself randomly tested after such a lapse.

The offender must also realize that the penalty can be almost anything of which the court approves. Many penalties can be imposed to serve the needs of the community, such as community service orders, fines, and restitution. Offenders may find it difficult not knowing when they are going to be released from community corrections. For the sake of justice, it is incumbent on the court to schedule annual reviews of the offender's performance.

Last, it is necessary that the punishment take into account the offender's prior record. Ignoring a record of prior offenses does not take into account the offender's failure to learn from an earlier experience. This leads to some problems, in that each penalty must be individualized for it to have any meaning. Placing the offender under such strict house arrest that attending a treatment program or complying with other conditions would be impossible renders the sentence meaningless and the whole experience farcical. To levy a set of sanctions that involve various forms of high fee payments, reparations, and fines that the offender cannot work off is also counterproductive. Placed under such constraints, some offenders may simply stop working or stop attending programs. The scheme of punishment must therefore be consistent with the offender's ability to comply with it.

Retribution

The concepts of "just deserts" and retribution are used interchangeably. Retribution requires the imposition of a punishment because it is deserved. Underlying this philosophy is the assumption that the penalty is being imposed on a rational and culpable agent. Thus the state must treat the offender, as it must treat every citizen, in a manner that respects, within reason, the autonomy, freedom, and privacy of the person. "Just deserts" is philosophically based on the principle that community corrections clients should serve neither too harsh nor too lenient a sentence, but rather should sustain only that amount of punishment that corresponds with the seriousness of the offense. Similar crimes, in theory, should receive similar penalties. This approach to corrections thus exhibits little interest in treatment requirements or assumptions about what might be the offender's future behavior. One consideration matters—the offender's prior record. Offenders with extensive prior records deserve severer punishments than offenders who have committed the same crime but have no or few prior offenses.

Changing the nature of community corrections toward a justice model was resisted by many community corrections personnel, who felt that deemphasizing the constructive nature of community corrections work and focusing instead on the irksome conditions placed on the offender essentially violates the basic professional philosophy of community corrections, which focuses on redirecting offenders' attitudes and behaviors. Coercive intrusion into the life of the offender is gained by reference only to the offense and not to some unrelated factor in the offender's life.

Deterrence

Deterrence is concerned with the broad prevention of crime. It is a utilitarian and future-oriented theory directed at the education of the general public. Prevention, whether viewed as general deterrence or specific deterrence, seeks to punish specific offenders so they do not repeat their crimes and to give members of the public a sense that they too will be punished if they break the law. Deterrence is focused on mental processes, in that it is intended to impact the inclinations of others toward crime. For many years, the general thinking was that community corrections offered little by way of general deterrence. It was thought that offenders "got off easy" if they were directed toward community corrections programs and did not go to prison.

Today, probationers are saddled with various conditions that are designed to communicate to them the community's disapproval of their actions and also to place expectations on them to repair whatever harms were inflicted. Someone placed on community corrections today has a much different experience from that of an offender just a decade ago. More than a mere stigma, community corrections can involve some very disagreeable experiences. For many offenders, community corrections involves taking the time and effort to report to a community corrections officer when required to do so. There is also the loss of privacy associated with home visits and visits at the offender's workplace, which can be embarrassing. To reemphasize individual deterrence and to reduce the state's financial obligation toward the offender, many jurisdictions have increased the financial cost of participating in community corrections. For example, offenders have been required to pay fines, restitution, reparations, treatment costs, jail fees, monitoring fees, drug testing fees, and supervision fees. When one includes the cost of an attorney, the burden of committing a simple crime such as driving while intoxicated can be considerable.

It is essential to recognize the necessity of parsimoniously assigning these obligations. Requiring high fees of a destitute probationer can lead to nothing more than a jail sentence and ultimately become counterproductive.

Incapacitation

Philosophically speaking, incapacitation requires placing reasonable limits on the offender to ensure that the offender is accountable for his or her actions. Incapacitation is intended to situate the offender in the community in such a manner that he or she is unlikely to commit another offense. This theory of punishment is related to preventive restraint, isolation, and risk control. There is also a utilitarian and forward-looking aspect to incapacitation, because it is intended to reduce crime.

Incapacitation focuses on the individual offender rather than the potential offender and seeks to impact opportunities rather than inclinations. By reducing the opportunity for crime, one increases the offender's chances for success. This is achieved with a risk assessment instrument, a device that considers the offender's criminal history and other factors associated with criminal activity. Once this is completed, the offender is subject to discussions of daily activities, unannounced home visits, random drug testing, and electronic monitoring. The ability to incapacitate

the offender is limited only by the current technology. Some community corrections departments not only monitor an offender electronically through devices attached to the leg, to indicate when he or she has left a zone of activity, but also use global positioning systems to tell community corrections personnel if the offender has entered a no-go region; in such a situation, the offender may have five minutes to remove him- or herself before being arrested.

Treatment

Another utilitarian philosophy aimed at reducing the individual's criminal inclinations in the future is treatment. The idea is to meet the needs of offenders for education, job training, counseling, drug treatment, and anything else with which they can use assistance in preventing future crime. Determining these needs is done with a risk-needs assessment instrument aimed at identifying problems to be addressed to reduce future crime. Operating in such a manner can augment the efforts of specific deterrence.

The treatment model of community corrections relied extensively on a medical model for analysis of the offender's problems. This model presumed that there was sufficient scientific knowledge to diagnose the offender's problems, that it was possible to apply the appropriate therapy, that there was sufficient monitoring of changing attitudes and behavior so as to know when the offender had shown the sought-after changes, and finally, that it was necessary to release him or her from supervision in a timely manner that acknowledged the changes, thus rewarding the offender's hard work. This model relied heavily on the assumptions that sufficient numbers of professionals were available, that they were skilled in understanding the offender's needs, that effective treatment programs existed, and that real change would take place within the individual, despite outside community pressures to do otherwise.

One critique of this model argued that the treatment model denied offenders their standing as responsible moral agents and disguised treatment as a form of coercive manipulation. The model was also challenged by critics who thought that none of the treatment programs actually worked. Sufficient efforts directed toward identifying best practices and evidence-based programs, however, have offered the research necessary to resurrect treatment as a viable philosophical component of community corrections efforts. The public in general continues to support the notion of offender rehabilitation.

Human Dignity

Individual persons do not vary in their dignity or worth just because someone has a disability, has committed a crime, or is a member of a particular racial or ethnic group or social class. An impoverished Native American has the same dignity as a Caucasian U.S. senator. Human dignity is shared equally, essentially as a form of moral egalitarianism. Under the law, everyone assumes an equal amount of responsibility and obligation; no one can act with impunity.

Various community corrections departments, along with the American Probation and Parole Association, have vision, mission, and value statements supporting the concept of human dignity. A key philosophical principle in support of community corrections is recognition of the offender's basic human dignity. In community corrections, a principal reason for treating clients with dignity is that people are seen as still having the capacity to do good. It is their human potential, not what they deserve or have done in the past, that matters.

Human dignity is the lofty moral status that every human being uniquely possesses. It is not that all humans are morally praiseworthy, but humans are, by their nature, worthy of a special level of respect fundamentally above that of nonhumans. At its core, human dignity is a concept that has a reality in the very substance of the human being. Dignity is inseparable from human nature when it is understood intuitively rather than through reason. As a result, almost everyone expects to be treated with dignity, but most people cannot explain why. Human dignity is an intrinsic part of human nature, and not contingent upon any functional capacity that varies. Evidence of this is found in our reasoning, language, conscience, and free will, which humans have the capacity to exercise and develop unless restricted by disease, coercion, or others' will.

Immanuel Kant declared that humans are denied dignity when they are treated as a means to an end rather than an end unto themselves. People are treated as a means to an end when their treatment is the result of political decisions rather than proven effective ideas. To address this issue, Kant suggested the categorical imperative as a central guide for our actions. The categorical imperative requires that one act only in accordance with that maxim through which one can at the same time will that it become a universal law. The categorical imperative is an imperative because it commands us to act in a particular way. It is categorical in that it applies to us unconditionally, especially as we possess rational wills without reference to any ends. The categorical nature of this command suggests that it is antecedent to any goals we might have set for ourselves. Our actions have moral worth if we act from our duty, as probation officers, for example, to offer whatever services that will benefit our clients. Motivation from duty is provided by our respect for whatever law it is that makes our actions a duty because we are members of the "alliance" of rational agents who are capable of guiding our own behavior on the basis of directives, principles, and laws of rationality. We cannot choose to lay aside our membership in the category of such beings. We have a duty that we cannot put off.

The categorical imperative receives so much support because of the humanity formula. This formula states that we should never act in such a way that we treat humanity, whether in ourselves or in others, as a means only but always as an end in itself. This is often seen as introducing the idea of respect for what is essential to our humanity. Hence, one's humanity is the source of the duty to develop one's talents and perfect one's humanity. We further the humanity of others when we pursue ends that allow others to pursue their humanity. Proper regard for something with absolute value or worth requires that we respect it. Respect involves valuing someone for some specific attribute that person possesses. This notion is central to offender corrections in that probation officers must see beyond clients' actions and see their humanity so as to recognize that no offender is the sum total of his or her worst deeds. Understanding this is an example of the recognition that respect does not vary within anyone.

Central to Kant's understanding of human dignity is his notion of autonomy. It is from human dignity that we derive our capacity for autonomy and mutuality. Autonomy is characterized as a sense of insight, competence, control, assessment, and achievement. Autonomy is having the independence to make our own rules and to live by them. Probationers or parolees, by virtue of being offenders, have restrictions on their autonomy. They nonetheless have to make moral choices about many of their daily actions, especially as those actions apply to the conditions of probation. The autonomous person is bound by his or her own will; thus the authority binding this will is internal and consistent with what the person has willed. Humans can make choices to act or not to act.

This autonomy is analogous to a probationer determining each day how he or she is going to comply with the conditions of probation. The probationer may decide to compromise on one restriction and not on others. The offender may be good on drug treatment and choose not to look for work. He may be restricted from drugs and alcohol but find that his probation officer will permit a little social drinking but nothing else. Community corrections personnel assess the performance of the clients over time, while getting them to go along with changes made in goals and targeted behavior. Autonomy is aided by rational thought that enables us to understand the world in which we live and how to maximize our self-interests within it.

It is from human dignity that we derive our capacity for autonomy and mutuality. Notwithstanding the requirements of community corrections, people must be free from the control of others, be able to make moral choices, and have some control over their lives. However, it is also necessary to recognize that to supervise offenders in the community effectively, it is necessary to grant offenders an opportunity to fail. Denial of this opportunity provides little chance to learn from mistakes and to develop confidence in the choices made in the future. To respect people's autonomy is to grant them at least the opportunity to make their crucial, life-affecting choices in a rational manner. This understanding also imposes restrictions on the efforts of others, who desire to suppress freedom for the benefit of particular social groups without sound justifications that can be explained and accepted by those affected. This means that any control over anyone's behavior should be based on the benefits that derive to them, in an effort to enhance their rationality and mutuality. Mutuality is a measure of the extent to which a society operates around a series of reciprocal relationships intended to benefit everyone. This is the central activity of restorative justice.

Restorative Justice

In considering the importance of treating the offender with dignity, it is appropriate to consider its application through restorative justice programs or the philosophy of reparations. Restorative justice is based on the assumption that the community must take a greater interest in the offender and some activities must be undertaken that allow the offender and the victim, through mediation and discussion, to achieve some measure of understanding. The victim wants to understand why the offense occurred and explain to the offender the impact of the crime. The offender would like to explain himself or herself and to seek some means by which he or she can gain some forgiveness and provide some measure of satisfaction to the victim. Restorative justice requires that we work to heal victims, offenders, and communities injured by crime. Victims, offenders, and communities should have the opportunity for active involvement in the justice process as early and as fully as they wish.

Behind this is the rethinking of the relative roles and responsibilities of government and community in promoting justice. Government is responsible for preserving a just order, and the community is responsible for establishing a just peace. The key values of restorative justice are amends, assistance, collaboration, empowerment, encounter, inclusion, moral education, protection, resolution, and reintegration. The restorative approach to offender rehabilitation requires a naturalistic process of maturation during a reintegrative process that is referred to as earned redemption, thus allowing offenders to make amends to those whom they have harmed in order to earn their way back into the trust of the community. To be effective, reintegrative ceremonies focus on earned redemption, which also requires rehabilitative efforts to work in close harmony with the sanctioning processes intended to promote the needs of crime victims and promote safer communities.

Edward W. Sieh
Lasell College

See also Attitudes and Myths About Punishment; Offender Needs; Offender Risks; Offender Supervision; Prediction Instruments; Probation: Early Termination; Probation and Parole: Intensive Supervision

Further Readings

Bazemore, Gordon. "Restorative Justice, Earned Redemption: Communities, Victims, and Offender Reintegration." *American Behavioral Scientist*, v.41/6 (1998).

Duff, R. A. *Punishment, Communication and Community*. New York: Oxford University Press, 2001.

Kant, Immanuel. *Groundwork for the Metaphysics of Morals*. New Haven, CT: Yale University Press, 2002.

Kant, Immanuel. *The Metaphysics of Morals*, Mary Gregor, trans. New York: Cambridge University Press, 1996.

Kateb, George. *Human Dignity*. Cambridge, MA: Belknap Press, 2011.

Sieh, Edward. *Community Corrections and Human Dignity*. Sudbury, MA: Jones and Bartlett, 2005.

POLITICAL DETERMINANTS OF CORRECTIONS POLICY

Ideology and budgets are prominent at each step of the public policy process. This process involves problem identification, formulation, and evaluation. Tough choices must be made to address crime and to create correctional options, including incarceration/incapacitation in prison (or jail) and community alternatives. Conflicts between conservative and liberal ideologies and the reality of scarce funding are contributing to the evolution of corrections policy. Nonetheless, the promulgation of correctional policies precedes few ideological compromises. Examples include the crime and corrections laws in the United States based on the Model Penal Code published by the American Law Institute in 1962. States have made subsequent changes to crime categories, and there are explicit divergences from the Model Penal Code for punishments that are aligned to contemporary jurisdictional practice. Community sanction alternatives for offenders have become an integral part of the criminal justice system as police, prosecutors, and adult and juvenile corrections personnel use laws to place nonviolent and less serious offenders under community supervision.

A prominent theme that influences corrections policy is interest in reintegrating offenders into the community. Interdisciplinary concerns of offender reentry converge in crime and corrections policy areas as traditionalists in fields of criminology, sociology, and psychology and scholars in public affairs, administration, and law try to understand policy making. In the United States, corrections policy is a product of the political process. The 21st-century movement to place offenders in community programs, such as work release and therapeutic housing programs, rather than "warehousing" them in prisons (or jails), is primarily for economic reasons; support is waning for "overreliance" on incarceration. Ideally, the policy process would have what it needs to make "commonsense" crime and corrections policies. Although some believe the political determinants of corrections policy are limited to politicians in the legislative process, an expanded view of corrections policy examines the public policy process and effects of ideology, law, and actors.

The Corrections Public Policy Process

Generally, laws or policies are the product of the legislative process. Best described by John W. Kingdon, this process involves problem identification as well as policy formulation, implementation, and evaluation of correctional programs offered as solutions to crime. Understanding the relationship between the policy process and corrections performance helps scholars interested in solutions to crime problems. In the United States, the criminal justice system comprises police, prosecution (courts and attorneys), and corrections. People who enforce the law find that their jobs are influenced by policies or political factors. For example, politicians may support crime and corrections legislation and allocate resources to create programs in response to judicial decisions that deviate from corrections practice and law. There are a host of criminal problems that require corrections policies that involve Congress and state and local legislative systems. These policy-making entities will make laws that have an enduring effect on crime and corrections.

Since the mid-1990s, many, if not most, criminologists and policy scholars have striven to understand the corrections policy process to make effective and efficient policies for offenders released back into the community. The political process is quite intense, and politicians use their discretion to make laws. For example, the legislative branch uses information to identify crime problems, propose policy solutions, and set the political agenda to hear the proposed policy. The Omnibus Crime and Safe Streets Act of 1968 is an example of a law that allocated federal funds for criminal justice (including corrections) services to the state and local governments by creating the Law Enforcement Assistance Administration (LEAA).

Although the legislature plays a critical role in the correctional policy process, the judicial and executive branches of government are also involved. The judicial branch engages in activities that are quasi-legislative and use the standard of *stare decisis* (precedent case decisions) to make corrections policy comply with or overrule prior correctional law. Examples include the role of the Supreme Court in the legendary 1966 *Miranda* decision, which requires law enforcement to inform the accused of his or her right to remain silent when arrested, and in decisions that give juveniles due process rights in an adjudicatory hearing. The Supreme Court's decision in *Graham v. Florida* (2010) will affect all courts and departments of corrections nationwide because of restrictions on giving the sentence of life without the possibility of parole to juvenile offenders.

The executive branch will implement the law as made by the legislature and interpreted by the Court, in accordance with the Administrative Procedure Act (APA). The APA requires that new corrections policies receive public input through "notice and comment" and that public bureaucracies (or agencies) write rules for planning how offenders will access correctional services. The bureaucracies employ the civil servants, such as probation and parole officers, who work for state and local departments of corrections. Examples are the U.S. Federal Bureau of Prisons, which uses the rule-making process to make regulations governing the management and operations of prisons and enforcement and compliance with prison rules. Data and information from the Bureau of Justice Statistics show that there are about 100 federal prisons and hundreds of state-operated correctional facilities that employ thousands of civil servants to provide services such as custody, food, medical treatment, education, and counseling to offenders. In 2008, there were about 2 million prisoners and nearly 6 million offenders under correctional supervision, and 84 percent were supervised by probation officers and parole agents in accordance with rules outlined in corrections policy. Although

the legislative, judicial, and executive branches play a major role in the corrections policy-making process, they are by no means the only actors. Moreover, the interaction between and among these entities does not necessarily mean the creation of effective policy. The policy process of identification, implementation, and evaluation and the resulting corrections policies are determined by ideology.

Political Goals and Ideology Influence Policy

The fear of crime and the development of criminal laws are politicized. A political determinant of crime and corrections policy means the approach taken by governments to control crime and provide community (public) safety. The Constitution does not impose a national (federal) authority to create sanctions for crimes that occur at the local level. Instead, the Founders shared the idea that states, as self-governing bodies, should retain responsibility for developing criminal justice policies to address crimes in their jurisdictions. The Eighteenth Amendment (which prohibited manufacture and sale of alcohol until its repeal in 1933) and the subsequent era of Prohibition had a profound effect on the fight against organized crime. Conservative ideology surfaced as urban violence soared.

There are complaints that the Federal Bureau of Investigation (FBI) may exceed its authority in wiretapping. Federal and state law-enforcement agencies must work together to address crime and corrections. Statistics show that state and local justice services (police, courts, and corrections) cost nearly $180 billion, which is twice the cost of federal expenditures on justice services. In the 1960s, conservatives continued to argue for "law and order," fearing the rise in crime rates and tired of court protections of the rights of the accused. The liberals opposed crime control and law-enforcement practices in violation of civil rights and liberties. The Omnibus Crime Control and Safe Streets Act of 1968 (42 U.S.C. 3789) is one example of the conflict between conservative and liberal ideology; President Johnson was urged to sign into law criminal justice policy that epitomized the law-and-order position.

Liberals generally support policies that make neighborhoods safe and that emphasize rights and treatment as part of the rehabilitative ideal. Partnerships with the community create a new role for corrections and citizen groups. Some believe that the community approach offers a path out of the criminal life for offenders. The discourse among criminologists, sociologists, and public policy experts is that social and biological factors can influence the crime choice, and central to offender reform is not incarceration and punishment but treatment and community sanctions for offenders who commit petty theft and may use drugs but are nonviolent. The tough-on-crime view was embraced in the 1970s as support for the "causes and cures" approach to crime and rehabilitation began to wane. As youth crime figures rose and there was a significant change in drug offense statistics, public sentiment swung toward conservative ideology and its tough-on-crime stance. Policies were generated in response to such ideology and media attention to crime. Some believe that the election of Republican president Richard Nixon was largely attributable to the conservative drive toward a tough-on-crime criminal justice policy.

Symbolic and Substantive Politics

The tough-on-crime movement, spurred by conservatism, characterized the 1980s and 1990s and served as the framework for the promulgation of criminal justice policies. Although there is a dearth of research in the criminal justice literature about the effect of political factors, both symbolic and substantive, on this movement, there is information about the explosion of crime policies propagated by Congress and state legislatures in the two decades that followed the 1970s. The U.S. Department of Justice worked with Congress to pass a comprehensive federal crime code, and state legislatures moved rapidly to stem the uptick in crime by revising criminal justice policies. In the 1990s, American corrections locked up about 1.5 million offenders in prisons (or jails) and supervised some 5 million felons on probation or parole. There was substantive use of political ideology and clout to make measurable reductions in crime, although some consider this a symbolic (empty words) approach to justice policy making by politicians to control crime and make communities safer.

In 1994, President Bill Clinton appealed to conservatives with a tough-on-crime agenda to fund 100,000 more police officers on the streets and encouraged liberals in Congress to promulgate laws that created the Community Oriented Policing

Services (COPS) office, emphasizing a policing style that works with the citizens of minority communities. Some say that Clinton's statements reflected a substantive approach to crime problems; others believe that inadequate funding for the COPS program reflected its simply symbolic approach to criminal justice policy, a political means of addressing the public's fear of crime. National politics and policy trends do sway state legislatures' decisions to be the toughest on crime. Federal crime policies such as the Violent Crime Control and Law Enforcement Act of 1994 created programs and allocated funds to corrections for reduction of gang crimes and domestic violence and removed "habitual offenders" from the street. Laws to protect children from crimes around schools are widely noted. Similar policies are packaged and passed by state legislatures to curb violence at home, in schools, and on the streets. Community alternatives also require resources in the form of federal block grants and formula grants, which may be embraced by both conservatives and liberals.

Policy Actors and Corrections Policy

The question of who is involved in the corrections policy-making process is of interest, as a variety of issues spark discourse about the overreliance on incarceration. Some believe the tough-on-crime model of crime control overrelies on imprisonment and presents impediments to rehabilitation. Others argue that sentencing schemes are problematic and corrections policy must create a comprehensive sentencing model that is effective at both punishment and rehabilitation of the offender. The "some" and "others" are called policy actors and include the media, public opinion, and special interest groups. Examples of goals include police focus on deterrence, prosecution emphasis on retributive justice, and corrections pursuit of punishment, rehabilitation, and restoration. The actors use lobbying strategies to share their policy ideas with politicians, staff, and bureaucrats.

Since the 1970s, sentencing reform has been a major goal with enormous impact on corrections policy. Prior to the 1970s, indeterminate sentencing laws (ISLs) guided sentencing practices, and judges had wide latitude to impose minimum and maximum terms of confinement on offenders. The explosion of media attention to such issues since the 1980s and the public outcry for sentencing schemes that achieved justice, fairness, and equity came, in large part, from public actors such as minorities, special interest groups representing prisoners, liberal ideologues, and justice scholars. The trend toward determinacy was the result of discussions that sentencing should be more predictable and consistent.

Just as the Model Penal Code underwent changes in accordance with state corrections' priorities of humane treatment and accountability, so was sentencing reform the theme of the 1980s. In 1984, the U.S. Sentencing Commission was created to review sentencing guidelines and make recommendations about presumptive and mandatory determinate sentencing policies. Politicians, bureaucrats, and special interest groups were involved in the demise of ISLs. The determinate sentencing laws (DSLs) impose mandatory minimum sentences that correlate with guidelines. These guidelines have resulted in the constraint of judicial discretion and the reduction in the possibility of parole for offenders. DSLs have been implemented by the Federal Bureau of Prisons and nationwide by departments of corrections. The role of policy actors has an enormous effect on the direction of sentencing policy reform and the field of corrections. In the end, "some" and "others" question the effectiveness of DSL policies as the costs of corrections administration continue to soar and offender recidivism rates are as high as 70 percent. A new ethos is to use research and evaluation studies as a rational approach to the promulgation of corrections policies.

Rational Approach to Corrections Policy

The practical view of academics is to learn about "what works" and then identify, prioritize, formulate, implement, and evaluate the corrections policy useful to planning for the successful preparation and release of offenders back into the community. The argument for "what works" is espoused by Paul Gendreau and colleagues, and integrating "common sense" into the crime and corrections policy process represents a new ethos. To some, this view is too theoretical and difficult to achieve, considering the sacrosanctity of ideology and the politicization of corrections issues. Literature is replete with examples of corrections failures. Prevention policies and programs are costly. Examples of arguments for rational policies include expansion of treatment services for drug offenders, placement in therapeutic and secure community facilities, and cost-efficient

community alternatives for nonviolent (such as petty theft) offenders.

Aspects of rehabilitation and restoration have appeal for supporters of community alternatives to incarceration. Community treatments compared to prison may save state departments of corrections about $24,000 per prison bed. The goal is to shrink budgets and make use of community sanctions to allow offenders to keep their jobs and support their families. In the mid-1990s and 2000s, there was a nationwide decline in violent crimes. Moreover, the criminal composition of most state prisons and jails became swollen with disproportionate numbers of drug and nonviolent offenders, for which corrections policy has not provided a rational alternative. A democratic society must invite all to exchange ideas to improve future crime policies. The political view is that tough-on-crime policies satisfy constituents, but the practical view of academics is to learn from "what works" and make sensible policy decisions.

Conclusion

Correctional facilities are overcrowded and costly, and they fail to reform offenders. The goals of corrections that embrace offender rehabilitation and restoration to the community are hard to attain within the current correctional structure. Policy makers who seek to use evidence about "what works" to support offender reentry objectives are concerned with the destabilization of families and neighborhoods when offenders are returned unprepared to reintegrate. Modern state and local correctional facilities confront policies about DNA testing, medical care, and various forms of privatization—prison industries that put offenders to work in private companies and incarceration in privately operated prisons such as those of The GEO Group Inc. These policies influence how departments of corrections fulfill their mission and goals.

Crime and corrections issues are no longer restricted to the field of criminal justice. Scholars of law and public affairs are equally concerned about policies that affect the management and operations of prisons and jails. The interdisciplinary approach to planning for offender reentry success can satisfy broader interests. Sentencing laws are central to punishment, rehabilitation, and restoration. Sentencing schemes are vital to offender reentry. Community corrections regulations in states such as Minnesota,

Oregon, and Washington indicate a movement away from overreliance on imprisonment and the use of community sanctions. Many, if not most, do not support elimination of incarceration altogether; they acknowledge that strict adherence to incapacitation is costly. The challenge is to reform sentencing policies and create a sentencing model that embraces 21st-century pragmatism and ideological compromise to make corrections policies that tackle the problems of, and improve the rates of success for, offender reentry.

Kimberley Garth-James
California State University, Sonoma

See also Community Corrections and Sanctions; Sentencing Guidelines

Further Readings

Garth-James, K. "A Public Administration Perspective of Penal Institutions." In *Eleuthera: Improve Corrections Performance and Save Our Communities*. Salt Lake City, UT: American University and College Press, 2011.

Gendreau, P., C. Goggin, F. Cullen, and M. Paparozzi. "The Common-Sense Revolution and Correctional Policy." In *Offender Rehabilitation and Treatment: Effective Programmes and Policies to Reduce Re-Offending*, James McGuire, ed. Chichester, UK: Wiley, 2002.

Graham v. Florida, 560 U.S. ___ (2010).

Kingdon, John W. *Agendas, Alternatives and Public Policies*. New York: Addison-Wesley, 1995.

Marion, Nancy E. and Willard M. Oliver. *The Public Policy of Crime and Criminal Justice*. Upper Saddle River, NJ: Pearson Prentice Hall, 2006.

U.S. Bureau of Justice Statistics. *Corrections Facts*. http://bjs.ojp.usdoj.gov (Accessed July 2011).

PREDICTION INSTRUMENTS

Prediction involves making an educated guess about the outcome of an event before it happens. Depending on how they are derived, predictions can be quite accurate. In the criminal justice field, prediction is increasingly being used to decide who to release after arrest or from prison, which offenders to refer for program participation (for community-based programs), how to allocate offenders to supervision caseloads, and where to deploy police.

Well-crafted prediction instruments improve decision accuracy, and the value and utility of any prediction instrument increases as its accuracy increases.

Risk Factors

Prediction instruments used to determine the likelihood of an offender recidivating rely on two types of information or risk factors, static and dynamic. Static factors, such as criminal history, age, and family history, cannot be changed. Research consistently finds that the numbers of prior incarcerations and prior offenses, as well as certain types of nonviolent crimes, are strongly associated with (that is, they predict) the likelihood of committing future crime. As a result, most prediction instruments rely heavily on static risk factors.

Dynamic factors, although used less often in prediction instruments, are usually the targets of offender programming because they are malleable and, as such, can be changed. They include personal beliefs and attitudes, associating with others who share these beliefs and attitudes, educational level, and employment.

Prediction Methods

Predictions are only as accurate as the information on which they are based. Clinical and actuarial methods are used to gather information for predicting offender behavior. Clinical methods involve gathering information through an interview consisting of both open- and closed-ended questions with the person being assessed. The prediction is based on the interviewer's interpretation and professional judgment of the answers given, visual and verbal cues, and overall impressions of the person interviewed. Clinically based predictions are influenced by the offender's personality as well as the facts of the situation. Furthermore, accurate prediction is highly dependent on the interviewing skills of the assessor.

Actuarial methods, which have a much higher level of accuracy, may include an interview but are much more structured; specific questions and answer choices are derived from a statistical analysis of the relationships between each answer and the likelihood of the outcome being predicted. Actuarial methods shift from decision making based on professional judgment (clinical method) to decisions based on statistical relationships.

Where the information-collection process includes offender interviews, inconsistent results may occur as a consequence of poor inter-rater reliability, defined as differences in how interviews are conducted from one interviewer to the next. Problems with inter-rater reliability are more likely and a greater concern where clinical methods are employed. Interviewer training and monitoring are crucial.

Generations of Prediction Instruments

Researchers have described three generations of prediction instruments in criminal justice. The first generation involved the review of whatever information was available on the offender and then making a professional judgment. These instruments were generally informal, included a clinical interview, and were influenced by the personal opinions of the assessor. Second-generation instruments moved to structured, empirically based questions predetermined through a prior statistical analysis to be associated with the outcome. Each answer carried a numerical weight toward the final prediction score. Although much improved, these predictions were based on historical information (static factors), which limited their utility in making decisions about treatment or programming. Third-generation instruments continue to use weighted, statistically derived factors. However, in order to assess or predict current risk accurately at the time of the prediction, they use a combination of static and dynamic factors.

Although offender attributes are similar from one jurisdiction to the next, they often vary at least to a small degree in the amount of influence each factor contributes to the prediction. For this reason, all prediction instruments, whether newly created or purchased, should first be tested or normed on any new population. This is accomplished by applying the prediction instrument to a set of offenders with known outcomes.

Prediction Accuracy

The accuracy of any prediction instrument is measured across groups of people and not by individuals in the group. As noted above, unless the tool is 100 percent accurate, the prediction will be inaccurate for some individuals in the group (that is, it will yield false positives and false negatives). If an instrument predicts with 70 percent accuracy, the combination of accurate predictions and inaccurate predictions across the entire group will result in an overall outcome for the group in the predicted range.

Consideration must be given to addressing the implications of false positive and false negative predictions. A false positive wrongly predicts that the event will occur, which could affect an offender's liberty if used for release-from-confinement decisions or if it results in added supervision requirements if released to community supervision. A false negative, which wrongly predicts the event will not occur, may result in a dangerous person being released without proper supervision. Although the goal is to eliminate both types of errors, the result is more often a trade-off where a decrease in one type of error results in a corresponding increase in the other.

A final consideration is the cutoff, the score at which action is taken against an offender. For all prediction instruments, rather than scores of risk/no risk, prediction scores increase incrementally across the group from low risk to high risk. Officials must decide what prediction score will trigger action. Often the resources available to manage the number of people on each side of the cutoff determine where the cutoff will be set. Prediction error and cutoff decisions in criminal justice are significant, especially if the prediction is about violence. For this reason, officials must clearly understand what each instrument is predicting and test and tailor each instrument to the specific application.

John Prevost
Lisa R. Muftić
Georgia State University

See also Actuarial Risk Assessment; COMPASS Program; Level of Service Inventory; Risk and Needs Assessment Instruments; Salient Factor Score

Further Readings

Andrews, D. A., James Bonta, and Stephen Wormith. "The Recent Past and Near Future of Risk and/or Need Assessment." *Crime and Delinquency*, v.52/1 (2006).

Bonta, James. "Offender Risk Assessment: Guidelines for Selection and Use." *Criminal Justice and Behavior*, v.29/4 (2002).

Gendreau, Paul, Tracy Little, and Claire Goggin. "A Meta-Analysis of the Predictors of Adult Offender Recidivism: What Works!" *Criminology*, v.34/4 (1996).

Gottfredson, Don. "Prediction and Classification in Criminal Justice Decision Making." *Crime and Justice*, v.9 (1987).

Smykla, John. "Critique Concerning Prediction in Probation and Parole: Some Alternative Suggestions." *International Journal of Offender Therapy and Comparative Criminology*, v.30/2 (1986).

PREDISPOSITIONAL REPORTS FOR JUVENILES

The predispositional report (PDR) for juveniles is the result of an investigative process conducted by an officer of the juvenile courts after the juvenile has been adjudicated delinquent (or, in adult court, convicted) but before the disposition (sentence) has been imposed. In this respect, the PDR is exactly parallel to the pre-sentence investigation (PSI) report process found in adult courts. Thus, the PDR is vitally important, as it may largely determine the final disposition that will be affixed by the judge. The court official who conducts this investigation may be a juvenile probation officer or an intake officer and frequently performs all functions interchangeably in the court, depending on need. Indeed, in some courts there is no real differentiation between the roles of intake and probation officers. What often transpires, especially in large cities as well as in offices that provide adult probation services, is that officers who are particularly good at writing write reports; officers who are good at revocations and enforcement more often perform those functions. This is called "functional specialization." Some highly specialized offices may arrive at their reports using a collective or team-based process. Variously called a juvenile treatment screening team, evaluation team, or youth placement committee, such a team may include the probation officer, psychologists, police officers, educators, social workers, a public defender, and a prosecutor, as well as the offender and his or her parents. If appropriate, a guardian ad litem (legal guardian) or substance abuse expert may serve on a specific dispositional team. Such teams collectively, or the probation officer singly, may prepare a risk assessment, which will list and evaluate factors concerning the delinquent's dangerousness to the community and his or her problems in general. The risk assessment will be incorporated into the PDR.

The delinquent may be subject to various physical and psychological examinations after intake or following adjudication. These analyses may reveal physical or mental illnesses or various learning disabilities (LDs). Various forms of undiagnosed LDs are common among juvenile offenders. These problems often impact their academic performance and lead them eventually into disruptive and deviant behavior in and around school. Additionally, alcohol and substance abuse issues may be revealed. The outcome of these results, reported on the PDR, can help the judge arrive at a disposition that will help the delinquent resolve these issues, as well as provide security to the community at large.

The report itself will feature a lengthy exposition of the background facts concerning the instant offense. The severity of the offense is an important factor, but the context in which the offense occurred must be also considered. The question of collective behavior must be addressed: For example, was the delinquent act a product of group dynamics? The characteristics of the victim—such as age, gender, an involved teacher—are important. The involvement of a weapon, such as a knife or firearm, or membership in a gang will merit special mention and may constitute aggravating factors in the final disposition, as may the advanced age of the victim. At this juncture, the attitude of the delinquent toward the offense is important; for example, is he or she remorseful and interested in a constructive outcome?

Probation officers or caseworkers prepare predispositional reports to assess the needs of juveniles living in a violent or unsafe family situation, which will include recommendations for the care, treatment, rehabilitation, or placement of the child in a group home or halfway house. (Photos.com)

Other sections of the PDR involve a structured interview with the delinquent and his or her parents, ideally in the course of a home study. Family involvement in the community, religious commitment, substance abuse, mental health, and employment status and history will be examined. A dysfunctional or violent family situation may lead to the juvenile's placement in a residential facility, such as a therapeutically oriented halfway house. Alternately, parents or guardians may be enjoined to take an effective parenting class in order that they might gain more insights into disciplinary approaches and ultimately be able to control the child. Occasionally parents will actively encourage the court to take a strong hand to get the child's attention, even to the extent of advocating institutionalization. A negative or sardonic attitude manifested by the parents toward the court, the writer of the PDR, or the proceedings will definitely be unfavorably mentioned in the report itself. Finally, parents who do not get the child properly prepared for court, in terms of completing any assigned pre-hearing interventions, will maximize the severity of the dispositional outcome that the court assigns.

Additionally, the court officer obtains a school report. This should involve interviews with teachers, principals, and guidance counselors, if practical. This is a critical part of the report. If a youth has poor grades, a poor school attitude, and low educational aspirations, the courts will often attempt to address these in some fashion. Frequently judges mandate that juveniles who receive probation must attend school and must graduate, if they are to be continued on probation and not be placed in a juvenile facility. If other private or social service agencies have worked with the delinquent, they are contacted, and their information, if not confidential, is included in the report.

Perhaps the most critical part of the report involves the juvenile's prior delinquent history and his or her record with the court. The report may contain statements from victims, if relevant. Youths who have prior records can expect to receive harsher dispositions than first-time offenders. The report concludes with the court officer's recommendations for treatment or incarceration. It may follow highly structured guidelines dictated by state mandate or may reflect municipal expectations. More often, the recommendations are a result of the report writer's interaction and experience with the judge handling that disposition. That is, as an insider who works with the judge

on a daily basis, the court officer knows what the judge wants to see in the way of recommendations. Also, the officer and judge generally know what treatment and custodial options are available; such information is accessible through Websites run by the state youth or juvenile authority. Sometimes the officer may make a formal or informal phone call or send an e-mail to a facility or private agency to ascertain availability of a treatment or custodial option before presenting recommendations to the judge. The judge, unfortunately, may make a treatment or custodial decision based on what is available and not based on what is in the child's best interest.

Francis Frederick Hawley
Western Carolina University

See also Juvenile and Youth Offenders; Juvenile Probation Officers; Pre-Sentence Investigation Reports; Teen Courts

Further Readings

Martin, Gus. *Juvenile Justice: Process and Systems.* Thousand Oaks, CA: Sage, 2005.

Mays, G. L. and L. Winfree. *Juvenile Justice.* Boston: McGraw-Hill, 2000.

Sanborn, J. and A. Salerno. *The Juvenile Justice System: Law and Process.* Los Angeles: Roxbury, 2005.

Pre-Parole Plan

Although the purposes of pre-parole and parole are different, the distinction is less mutually exclusive than it might appear. Pre-parole is intended to reduce prison overcrowding; parole is designed to help reintegrate the inmate into society. Parole can also reduce prison overcrowding. Prisons may operate two programs for the conditional release of inmates before the expiration of their sentences. The first program is formal parole; the second, a pre-parole conditional supervision program.

Generally, pre-parole is intended for use whenever the population of the prison system exceeds 95 percent of its capacity. To be considered eligible, an inmate could be placed in pre-parole after serving 15 percent of his or her sentence; thereafter, the inmate is eligible for parole when one third of the sentence has elapsed. Parole boards operating with this policy assume an active role in the placement of both parolees and pre-parolees. The boards themselves determine who can participate in the program. State governors, based on their boards' recommendations, ultimately decide whether an inmate is to be paroled. Neither parole nor pre-parole is an end in itself; they are merely routes, with conditions, in the journey toward freedom. Pre-employment training and employment following release are anchors required and used by boards for evaluating rehabilitation, stability, and success on parole. Inmates who violate the behavioral conditions framing both programs can be immediately reincarcerated for cause.

Prisoners' Rights Under Law: Early Release

Two cases decided in the late 1990s pertained to prisons releasing inmates early (pre-parole) to relieve overcrowding; subsequently, however, the prisons revoked their pre-parolees' release statuses. In 1983, the Florida state legislature enacted a series of laws authorizing the awarding of early release credits to prison inmates when the state prison population exceeded predetermined levels. In 1986, Kenneth Lynce received a 22-year prison sentence on a charge of attempted murder. In 1992, he was released based on the determination that he had accumulated five different types of early release credits totaling 5,668 days, including 1,860 days of "provisional credits" awarded as a result of prison overcrowding. Shortly thereafter, the state attorney general issued an opinion interpreting a 1992 statute as having retroactively canceled all provisional credits awarded to inmates convicted of murder and attempted murder. Lynce was rearrested and returned to custody. He filed a habeas corpus petition alleging that the retroactive cancellation of provisional credits violated the *ex post facto* ("from a thing done afterward") clause of the Constitution. The Supreme Court agreed with him, in *Lynce v. Mathis* (519 U.S. 433, 1997).

The second case concerned Oklahoma's Pre-Parole Conditional Supervision Program, which took effect whenever the state's prisons became overcrowded; this program could authorize the conditional release of prisoners before their sentences expired. An inmate was eligible for pre-parole after serving only 15 percent of a sentence and was eligible for parole after one third of the sentence had elapsed. Inmate Ernest Harper was released under the pre-parole program. After he spent five apparently uneventful (law-abiding) months outside prison, the governor of Oklahoma revoked his pre-parole and returned him to prison on less than five hours' notice. Harper claimed that his reincarceration deprived him of liberty without due process, in violation of the Fourteenth Amendment. The corrections department argued that a hearing was not necessary to transfer a prisoner from a low-security prison to a higher-security one and that was what they had done. The Tenth Circuit Court of Appeals, however, held that the pre-parole program was sufficiently like formal parole, and a program participant was entitled to procedural protections. In *Leroy L. Young v. Ernest Eugene Harper* (65 LW 4197, 1997), the Supreme Court upheld the decision of the Tenth Circuit Court. It ruled that Oklahoma had violated Harper's due process rights by revoking his pre-parole without a hearing to set forth the allegations that he had not met the conditions of the program.

One State Improves Process, Another Harbors "State Secrets" View

Pre-parole and conditional supervision policies and procedures continue to evolve. More important, efforts to make protocols effective yet humane are ongoing. Nationally, there is more uniformity than there is uniqueness. Two cases, though, significantly illustrate (relative to each other) their oppositional extremes in attitudes and actions. In Texas, prior to 1984, both parole and executive clemency acts required the affirmative action of the Board of Pardons and Paroles and the governor before relief could be given. The Texas Constitution was then amended to remove the governor from the parole process and make the Board of Pardons and Paroles the final parole authority for the state. The Texas Board of Pardons and Paroles used Salient and Significant Factor Score sheets when making pre-parole decisions. The Salient Factor Score sought to classify pre-parole candidates according to their risk for succeeding or failing under parole supervision. The Significant Factor Score reflected the seriousness of the offense committed. If parole was denied, an offender was "set off," or postponed, and the case was reviewed within one year. If the offender was given a "serve-all," he or she would remain in prison until released to mandatory supervision or until discharged following completion of all of his or her sentence in prison.

The second case concerns the state of Georgia, where prison inmates do not have a legal right to parole. This may be less surprising when one considers that Georgia's rather ignoble origin, in 1733, was as America's penal colony. Today, the state's inmates merely retain the right to be considered for, but not guaranteed, parole. Inmates cannot appear before the parole board. The members of the parole board review each parole file individually. As inmates do not have a legal right to meet or speak with members of the parole board, the board does not interview parole candidates. Surprisingly, in an operational policy that belies its democratic-sounding name—the Georgia State Board of Pardons and Paroles—the board does *not* meet as a group to make parole decisions. The board does not have to explain its decisions. Every inmate considered for parole has a parole file. Georgia law classifies these files as a "state secret." The parole files are sealed. Thus Georgia prison inmates do not have a legal right to access or see their parole file.

To Be or Not to Be . . . Paroled

The parole board ("parole commission" in some states) is the state's legal body with the vested power to grant or deny the parole application of any inmate desiring, and also eligible for, parole consideration. The board's task is to apply the guidelines governing parole release and make a formal finding, to the governor of the state, of good cause for either granting or denying parole. The board is autonomous and its independence is virtually impenetrable.

Parole eligibility dates are fixed points in time that mark when an inmate is eligible for release on parole. This date is the earliest date on which an inmate convicted of a felony is eligible for parole. This date can be likened to the crossing of the Rubicon. The date's activation is strictly contingent on the good behavior of the inmate prior to its long-awaited arrival. Prisoners cannot claim an absolute right to be released on parole, simply because they have served their time. Hence, parole boards are particularly interested in seeing a rehabilitation profile showing psychological and emotional development, pre-employment training and substantial job-readiness skills, prosocial improvement and tolerance, and a connection to community treatment and support agencies.

Without these urgent requirements, there would likely be little or no attenuation in the post-95

percent overcapacity census. Fraught as it is with health, welfare, and safety ramifications, this statistic is a burden for parole boards and legislatures. It is at once an enlightening and embarrassing bellwether of the kind and quality of community correction efforts. However, reincarceration is viewed as failure whose backwash touches multiple interests. Neither the administrators pressured to reduce prison overcrowding nor the parole board nor the parolee take pleasure in this reversal of fortunes. Therefore, treatment options that promise long-term placement are deemed preferable.

James E. Shaw
Chicago School of Professional Psychology

See also Case Management; Parole Guidelines Score; Prison Overcrowding; Reducing Prison Populations

Further Readings

Florida State Legislature Senate. "Early Release Credits." Senate Bill 644, 1983.

Heirens v. Mizell, 729 F.2d 449 (7th Cir. Ill. 1984).

Horton v. Parole Eligibility Review Board, 2000 Tenn. App. LEXIS 701 (Tenn. Ct. App. October 20, 2000).

In Re Troglin, 51 Cal. App. 3d 434 (Cal. App. 1st Dist. 1975).

Laivinieks v. True, 1994 U.S. Dist. LEXIS 2574 (N.D. Ill. March 3, 1994).

Leroy L. Young v. Ernest Eugene Harper, 520 U.S. 143 117 (1997).

Lynce v. Mathis, 519 U.S. 433 (1997).

Moore v. Holt, 16 Fed. Appx. 902 (10th Cir. Colo. 2001).

Oklahoma Pardon and Parole Board. "Pre-Parole Conditional Supervision Program." http://www.ppb .state.ok.us (Accessed February 2011).

Parker v. Corrothers, 750 F.2d 653 (8th Cir. Ark. 1984).

Priore v. Nelson, 626 F.2d 211 (2d Cir. Conn. 1980).

Schuemann v. Colorado State Board of Adult Parole, 624 F.2d 172 (10th Cir. Colo. 1980).

Silmon v. Travis, 95 N.Y. 2d 470 (N.Y. 2000).

Texas Constitution. http://www.statutes.legis.state.tx.us (Accessed February 2011).

Walker v. New York State Div. of Parole, 203 A.D. 2d 757 (N.Y. App. Div. 3d Dep't 1994).

PRE-SENTENCE INVESTIGATION REPORTS

The pre-sentence investigation report, commonly called the PSI report or just PSI, is a document prepared to assist judges in making decisions involving sentences in criminal cases in federal, state, and local jurisdictions. The report, normally prepared by probation officers, gives detailed information not only to the courts but also to others in the criminal justice system who work with offenders.

The first PSI report was probably prepared around 1841 by John Augustus, considered the father of probation in America, and although the informal document used at that time probably bears little resemblance to the formal ones of today, it marked the beginning of the current report. Presentence investigation reports continued to be fairly informal documents that were prepared by various court staff until a standardized federal version was adopted in 1943. The PSI reports prepared in state and local jurisdictions are quite varied in style and content, according to the specific needs of the jurisdiction and the desires of the judges. The report can be in long or short format: the long version is normally reserved for offenders facing felony convictions, and the shorter version is more often used for misdemeanor offenses.

The PSI is normally prepared by personnel from the jurisdiction's probation office because the probation officer is considered to be an impartial observer, unlike the defense attorney, whose job it is to represent the offender, and the state attorney, whose function is to prosecute the defendant. Although PSI preparation is normally a duty performed by government probation officers, some private probation officers and firms now provide this function; this is a result of the general trend to privatize services that were previously reserved for governmental agents.

The PSI contains several types of data: current defendant data; circumstances of the offense (including aggravating or mitigating circumstances); current victim information; and type, amount, and recipient of restitution. The defendant's personal information often includes employment situation and history, educational level, social history, environmental and social support, substance abuse history, military history, current and past financial situation, codefendant information, and any other pertinent data about the accused that could be valuable in helping the judge arrive at an appropriate sentence. In many cases, the probation officer makes a recommendation to the judge regarding the type of sentencing, and often the probation officer confers with the prosecutor, and sometimes the defendant's attorney, prior to sentencing.

The pre-sentence investigation report is a document detailing the background and character of the person being sentenced and may contain information on prior convictions, the defendant's work, marital, financial, and/or medical history, and recommendations to assist the judge in deciding a sentence involving criminal cases in federal, state, and local jurisdictions. (Photos.com)

Earlier forms of the PSI, called offender-based reports, focused primarily on specific offender information such as criminal background, social history, details of the offense, family background, educational attainment, health, financial status, and rehabilitative potential. Later, because of sentencing guidelines that reflected a change to a more punitive ideology and determinate sentencing patterns, PSIs were shortened and modified to emphasize the offender's prior criminal history and other information that could assist judges in determining offender culpability; these have been termed offense-based reports.

Often the victim, if there is one, is contacted regarding victim information, particularly if restitution might be ordered by the court, and often a victim's impact statement is included in the report or appended to it. Arrest and investigation documents are often obtained from the appropriate jurisdiction. The arresting or investigating officials are sometimes contacted as well for details of the case, especially if arrest and incident reports are incomplete or ambiguous concerning certain details. An in-depth records check of the offender's past criminal history is normally performed by the probation officer.

The PSI is confidential and meant to be viewed only by people directly involved in the defendant's case. It is primarily for the sentencing judge, although the prosecutor and sometimes the defense attorney or defendant may view it if allowed by the court. In federal cases, all of the parties have access to the PSI, but in state and local jurisdictions the amount of access varies.

Federal PSI reports have five functions that normally are applicable to PSIs prepared in most state and local jurisdictions. First, the document is used primarily as a tool to assist judges in meting out an appropriate sentence for an offender. Second, the document provides probation staff with a detailed summary of probationer risks and needs, which in turn assists them in determining appropriate levels and types of supervision (such as field, home, office, and phone contacts) at appropriate intervals and assists in determining the appropriate adjunctive services (such as substance abuse treatment, mental health treatment, and vocational training) that will help the offender successfully complete the probated sentence. In addition, the process of PSI preparation establishes the relationship between the offender and the probation office staff. A third function of the PSI is to assist prisons and jails in determining an inmate's or detainee's potential as a candidate for parole or other form of early release. A fourth function is to provide to institutional and community corrections facilities information that can assist in the provision of placement into specific programs (such as programs that specialize in physical or mental disabilities, addictions, or elderly inmates). The last function of the PSI report is to give social science researchers, normally criminologists and sociologists, access to offender information that can be used to understand the offender's criminal behavior, sentencing patterns, correctional program evaluation, and potential challenges; such understanding promotes proposed solutions to correctional policy.

Although the exact impact of PSI reports on offender sentencing is unknown, it is probably significant. Judges' continued insistence on receiving the documents over such a long period of time in federal, state, and local jurisdictions indicates the extent and desirability of their use at the sentencing stage. The fact that PSIs are used as a foundational document for offender supervision, both in institutional and community corrections, illustrates the documents' importance to the criminal justice system. Currently, many states now use a post-sentence investigation report when an inmate is placed in a correctional system; this report is in many ways similar to the pre-sentence report but is used throughout the offender's incarceration.

Leonard A. Steverson
South Georgia College

See also Augustus, John; Investigative Reports; Probation Officers; Victim Impact Statements

Further Readings

Abadinsky, Howard. *Probation and Parole: Theory and Practice,* 11th ed. Upper Saddle River, NJ: Pearson, 2011.

Center on Juvenile and Criminal Justice. "History of Pre-Sentence Investigation." http://www.cjcj.org/files/the_history.pdf (Accessed June 2011).

Champion, Dean J. *Corrections in the United States: A Contemporary Perspective,* 3rd ed. Upper Saddle River, NJ: Prentice Hall, 2001.

Clear, Todd R., Val B. Clear, and William D. Burrell. *Offender Assessment and Evaluation: The Presentence Investigation Report.* Cincinnati, OH: Anderson, 1989.

PRESIDENT'S TASK FORCE ON CORRECTIONS

Lyndon B. Johnson formed the President's Commission on Law Enforcement and Administration of Justice on July 23, 1965, instructing it to report in two years on how to prevent juvenile delinquency and adult criminality and how to perform better policing and justice agency management. The Task Force on Corrections included five commissioners, an associate director, six full-time staffers, and dozens of consultants and advisers. The commission's associate director for corrections was Professor Elmer K. Nelson; consultants included Sanford Bates, Daniel Glaser, Richard F. McGec, Walter Reckless, Ted Rubin, and Leslie T. Wilkins; and advisers included George Beto, Abraham Goldstein, and Don M. Gottfredson. The commission's general report, *The Challenge of Crime in a Free Society,* was issued in February 1967 with major findings and recommendations; chapter 6 was devoted to corrections. As commission chairman, Attorney General Nicholas deBelleville Katzenbach wrote in the foreword to the *Task Force Report: Corrections* that it contains "the research and analysis of the staff and consultants to the Commission which underlie those findings and recommendations, and . . . elaborates on them." The Task Force on Corrections' report was generally endorsed by the panel of five commissioners.

The Task Force on Corrections needed data but had none. The commission turned to the National Council on Crime and Delinquency (NCCD), which gathered data from all 50 states, Puerto Rico, and a representative 250-county sample that included half the U.S. population. This quick and tremendous effort was accomplished by September 1, 1966, when consultant and NCCD director Milton G. Rector submitted to the commission a 280-page survey, *Correction in the United States*. Appendix A of the *Task Force Report: Corrections* is a data summary of the survey, taking up 98 of the report's 222 pages; its last section, "Correctional Standards," is copied verbatim from the NCCD survey's appendix. These standards guided the first data collection effort since 1939, leading to the survey's following observation: "Correction seems to have been less dependent on organized facts than any other American enterprise interested in continued growth and support."

A reading of the general report or the task force report reveals the guiding philosophy of rehabilitation of the offender, with the goal of reintegration into the community. The incapacitation philosophy of community protection by incarcerating the offender in jail or prison is recognized, but the decrepit state of the nation's institutions is decried as the remnants of the "penitence" era of solitary cells. The correctional institution's architectural and operational foci on supervision and control run counter to the requirements of personal responsibility needed for the inmate's rehabilitation into a productive citizen. A state's licensing and bonding requirements may nullify the released offender's opportunity to pursue a trade or gain employment in the community, and employment counselors are rarely available.

Prison inmates who are released because of "good-time credit" are technically not paroled, but the commission recommended that each state "should provide that offenders who are not paroled receive adequate supervision after release unless it is determined to be unnecessary in a specific case." Modern federal practice follows this, having abolished parole but using supervised release.

The Task Force on Corrections repeatedly noted the large caseloads and lack of consistent educational requirements or continued training for probation and parole officers, supervisors, and administrators. The commission recommended an "average ratio of 35 offenders per" probation or parole officer, making "use of volunteers and subprofessional aides in demonstration projects and regular programs."

Community resources need to be mobilized to provide help for offenders "to turn away from criminality." The commission recommended that community corrections personnel "develop new methods and skills to aid in reintegrating offenders through active intervention on their behalf with community institutions," such as schools and employers. Following the vocational rehabilitation model used to aid persons with disabilities, the commission recommended that community corrections agencies receive "substantial service-purchase funds . . . for use in meeting imperative needs of individual offenders that cannot otherwise be met."

The Task Force on Corrections criticized a "one-size-fits-all" mentality, and the commission recommended caseloads that "vary in size and in type and intensity of treatment. Classification of offenders should be made according to their needs and problems." This approved ongoing experiments with intensive supervision probation (ISP) and treatment for special offender groups (such as alcoholics, drug addicts, and females). Another recommendation was to provide intensive community treatment programs "as an alternative to institutionalization for both juvenile and adult offenders." The Task Force on Corrections stressed reintegration of offenders through study release to attend school or work release to be employed during the day and return to the institution otherwise. The commission recommended that partial or "graduated release and furlough programs should be expanded . . . and coordinated with community treatment services."

In the corrections survey, one third of the counties had no probation agency for misdemeanor offenders. Therefore, the commission recommended that "parole and probation services should be available in all jurisdictions for felons, juveniles, and those adult misdemeanants who need or can profit from community treatment." To accomplish this, they recommended integrating local jails into state corrections and instituting rehabilitative programs.

The commission recommended professionalizing and depoliticizing state parole boards. It recommended that members "should be appointed solely on the basis of competence and should receive training and orientation in their task. They should be required to serve full time and should be compensated accordingly." The *Task Force Report* recommended a salary similar to that of a general jurisdiction trial judge.

"Juvenile Delinquency and Youth Crime" is chapter 3 of *The Challenge of Crime in a Free Society*. The commission found that juvenile probation, if available at all, involved high caseloads and minimal contacts by phone or visit. As an alternative to juvenile court, the commission recommended that the police, schools, parents, and juvenile court refer both delinquent and nondelinquent juveniles to "neighborhood youth-serving agencies—Youth Services Bureaus," to be sited in nearby community centers. The bureaus would work individually "with troublemaking youths." Communities should apply for federal grants to establish such bureaus if they did not exist.

The *Task Force Report* did make an impact in recommending better offender classification and more resources for corrections. It did not, however, foresee the rise of private prisons or intermediate sanctions such as electronic monitoring and house arrest. The commission did not forecast that prison overcrowding in the 1980s and beyond would place correctional administrators in a crisis management mode, leading to extensive litigation and leaving little time and few resources for rehabilitation or community reintegration programs.

Nigel J. Cohen
Independent Scholar

See also Caseload and Workload Standards; Furloughs; Reintegration Into Communities; Specialized Caseload Models; Work/Study Release Programs

Further Readings

National Council on Crime and Delinquency. *Correction in the United States*. New York: Author, 1967.

President's Commission on Law Enforcement and Administration of Justice. *The Challenge of Crime in a Free Society*. Washington, DC: U.S. Government Printing Office, 1967.

President's Commission on Law Enforcement and Administration of Justice. *Task Force Report: Corrections*. Washington, DC: U.S. Government Printing Office, 1967.

Stojkovic, Stan. "The President's Crime Commission Recommendations for Corrections." In *The 1967 President's Crime Commission Report: Its Impact 25 Years Later*, John A. Conley, ed. Cincinnati, OH: Anderson, 1994.

U.S. Department of Justice. *The Challenge of Crime in a Free Society: Looking Back Looking Forward*. Washington, DC: U.S. Department of Justice, Office of Justice Programs, 1997.

PRETRIAL DETENTION

The Eighth Amendment to the U.S. Constitution prohibits excessive bail for individuals charged with a crime. The intent of this amendment has been a controversial subject in the legal community, as some commentators believe that the Eighth Amendment provides a clear constitutional right to bail, a position that they claim is further supported by the language found in the Federal Rules of Criminal Procedure. This interpretation was supported by the U.S. Supreme Court in the landmark decision in *Stack v. Boyle* (342 U.S. 1, 1951). The Court ruled that bail provides the accused with the right to freedom from pretrial detention, or freedom from incarceration prior to conviction. The Court explained that pretrial detention is tantamount to punishment and also prevents defendants from participating fully in their own defense.

However, the issue of whether bail is a constitutional requirement would surface again in the courts. After the *Stack* decision, commentators noted that while individuals could not legally be denied bail, the courts could practice de facto preventive detention, whereby the courts set monetary bail requirements that defendants cannot pay and therefore they are forced into pretrial detention. Researchers, who found that cash bail was being used to detain the poor, argued for bail reform in the 1960s and spurred the first Bail Reform Movement of 1966. This movement focused on the increased use of the nonfinancial release alternative known as release on own recognizance (ROR). ROR occurs when the court releases a defendant upon the defendant's word that he or she will return for all future court appearances. The increased use of ROR and conditions of nonfinancial release fostered the development of pretrial agencies nationwide. These agencies, now a common feature of the criminal justice system, assist the court with pretrial release

Pretrial detention refers to the length of time that an individual can be held and questioned by police prior to being charged with an offense. The U.S. Supreme Court ruled that bail provides the accused with the right to freedom from pretrial detention, stating that is was tantamount to punishment and prevents defendants from full participation in their defense. (Wikimedia)

decisions and supervise offenders who receive some type of conditional release.

While bail reformers were pleased, this reform did not last for long. The rehabilitative model of justice guided our system until the late 1970s. However, this model was attacked on several different fronts in the early 1980s for being "soft on crime" and for contributing to rising crime rates. The economic and political climate gave rise to a new regime of "tough-on-crime" legislation, which included harsh mandatory drug penalties, three-strikes laws, and much stricter sex offender policies. The change in philosophy extended to pretrial operations as well, which became apparent when the Bail Reform Act of 1984 was passed, allowing for the pretrial detention of "potentially dangerous" offenders. This new act expanded the original goal of bail. Specifically, Section 3142(b) explains that a defendant should not be released pretrial if the release would endanger the safety of a specific individual or the community at large.

The mandate of the Federal Reform Act of 1984 was clarified and strengthened shortly after in the Court's decision in *United States v. Salerno* (481 U.S. 739, 1987). The issue of the preventive detention of juveniles had already been addressed in *Schall v. Martin* (467 U.S. 253, 1984). The Court in *Schall* found constitutional the portion of a statute authorizing pretrial detention for juveniles who posed a risk of committing further crimes if released prior to trial. However, the *Salerno* case brought the issue

of pretrial detention to the forefront of the adult courts. Anthony Salerno and Vincent Cafaro, both Genovese family crime bosses, were arrested in connection with several charges under the Racketeer Influenced and Corrupt Organizations (RICO) Act and were denied bail because their release might have endangered the community. The appellate court found this decision unconstitutional; however, the U.S. Supreme Court overturned the appellate court's decision, finding the preventive detention of these defendants constitutional. The *Salerno* court therefore upheld the constitutionality of the Bail Reform Act of 1984, and to date 44 states and the District of Columbia have implemented bail legislation similar to that of the federal system.

Both *Schall* and *Salerno* brought to light the controversial issue of predictions of dangerousness. While mental health specialists are often relied upon to predict future dangerousness, judges must also make these decisions when considering whether to order pretrial detention. A lot of research has been conducted about predictions of dangerousness, and while the research is mixed, some very well-known studies have shown that mental health specialists do no better than chance when it comes to these predictions. These predictions become even more problematic for judges, who do not specialize in mental health issues and who must usually make these decisions quickly and with very little information. Some commentators argue that judges are not qualified to make these decisions. Nevertheless, they have been required to do so since the passage of the Bail Reform Act of 1984. More commonly though, without ordering pretrial detention, judges make decisions every day that can result in pretrial detention.

Judges are prohibited from the practice of de facto pretrial detention, which essentially occurs when the court intentionally orders financial bail requirements that defendants cannot meet for purposes of detaining certain defendants—that is, potentially dangerous offenders. While this practice is not allowed, it can still be argued that requiring any amount of cash bail from most defendants will result in pretrial detention. Most offenders are represented by public defenders because they are indigent and they cannot afford to pay legal fees. In the United States, approximately 62 percent of the 767,000 inmates held in jails per year are being detained prior to trial.

Although some commentators have noted that the pretrial detention of criminal offenders is better for the community, pretrial detention can have disastrous effects on individuals, family members, and the community. Pretrial detention, even if brief, is tantamount to a term of incarceration. May experts on the topic indicate that pretrial detention is connected to lower employment rates, broken familial bonds, psychological and medical problems, and higher recidivism rates. In addition, pretrial detention can have a negative effect on the entire course of a case. A solid body of research indicates that defendants who are detained pretrial are more likely to be convicted, more likely to receive a term of incarceration, and more likely to receive longer sentences when they receive a term of imprisonment. The potential consequences of pretrial detention indicate the need for ongoing legal discussion and evaluations of this practice.

Meghan Sacks
Fairleigh Dickinson University

See also Bail Reform Act of 1984; Manhattan Bail Project; Pretrial Supervision

Further Readings

Bail Reform Act of 1984, 18 U.S.C. 3142.

Fagan, Jeffrey and Martin Guggenheim. "Preventive Detention and the Judicial Prediction of Dangerousness for Juveniles: A Natural Experiment." *Journal of Criminal Law and Criminology*, v.86 (1996).

Goldkamp, John. "Danger and Detention: A Second Generation of Bail Reform." *Journal of Criminal Law and Criminology*, v.76 (1985).

Goldkamp, John. *Two Classes of Accused: A Study of Bail and Detention in American Justice*. Cambridge, MA: Ballinger, 1979.

Schall v. Martin, 467 U.S. 253 (1984).

Stack v. Boyle, 342 U.S. 1 (1951).

United States v. Salerno, 481 U.S. 739 (1987).

PRETRIAL SUPERVISION

Following arrest on a criminal charge, a suspect may be released from jail dependent upon two factors. First, the defendant must be a low risk of flight. In other words, the court needs to be assured that the defendant will appear at all future court proceedings. Some factors that increase the likelihood of a defendant's return to court are forfeiture of passport, strong ties to the community, no current warrants on other criminal matters, and no previous history of failure to appear for court proceedings. Second, the defendant must be a low risk of harm to him- or herself and others in the community. If the accused is suicidal, then pretrial release may not be the best option at that time. If the defendant has a high likelihood of violence, a history of absconding while under court supervision, or unsuccessful behavior while previously on court supervision, others in the community may be at risk. The defendant's past behavior is a strong indicator of the defendant's ability or inability to follow the conditions of pretrial release while awaiting trial.

How does a judge determine who is suitable for pretrial release and who should be detained pending trial? In the federal system, a pretrial services officer or probation officer interviews the suspect regarding past criminal history, substance abuse, family ties, the amount of time he or she has lived in the area, mental and physical health, and finances. Since the defendant is presumed innocent at this stage, the interviewing officer cannot ask questions about the current offense; however, the seriousness and the penalty associated with the crime are taken into consideration. The interviewing officer then attempts to verify as much of the information as possible that was received from the defendant. This is done through criminal records checks, interviews with law-enforcement officers, and conversations with family members, employers, and others who are well acquainted with the defendant. After gathering and verifying as much information as possible, usually in a very short time frame, the pretrial officer prepares a report for the judge summarizing the strengths and weaknesses of the defendant. The pretrial officer also makes a recommendation as to the suitability of the defendant for release. Finally, if the pretrial officer recommends pretrial release for the defendant, the officer will recommend conditions to ensure the safety of the victim or victims, community, and defendant.

A defendant who is released from custody pending trial may be required to post bail, be under the guidance of a third party custodian, and/or follow specific conditions that will then be verified by a pretrial officer. The conditions for release from custody pending trial can take many forms, such as a cash deposit, percentage bail, unsecured bail, signature bail, and release on own recognizance (ROR). Indigent defendants, if released, are typically released on their own recognizance or released on a signature bond. If an indigent defendant is unable to post bail, he or she may require the services of a bail bondsperson.

Studies suggest that not all types of defendants receive the same consideration for pretrial release. Females and younger defendants are most likely to be released from jail pending trial. With regard to race, it has been said that Hispanics face a triple burden at the pretrial release stage. That is, they are the group most likely to be required to pay bail to gain release, the group that receives the highest bail amounts, and the group least able to pay. This is particularly disturbing, as one who is denied bail tends not to fare as well in the pending criminal case as do counterparts who were released on pretrial supervision. When comparing detained defendants to those released on pretrial supervision, researchers have found that the detainees are more likely to be convicted of the charged offenses and to receive harsher punishments. Therefore, being granted pretrial release not only is a convenience and a comfort for the accused but also may be a factor in the disposition of the case.

Typically, a defendant released from custody pending trial will be placed on pretrial supervision. Supervision efforts are similar to those carried out on probationers. The major difference between pretrial supervision and probation supervision is that the pretrial supervisee has not been convicted and is presumed innocent. During the pretrial investigation, the interviewing officer assesses the defendant's history and current situation. Issues such as chemical dependency, unemployment or underemployment, lack of suitable housing, and association with codefendants or others involved in the case are taken into consideration. In order to enforce the conditions imposed by the court, the supervising pretrial services officer will conduct both announced and unannounced visits to the defendant's residence. An unannounced visit can paint a much more accurate picture of the defendant's lifestyle and habits than a scheduled visit in the pretrial office. During contacts with the defendant, the supervising officer may implement testing to determine if alcohol or drugs are being used.

Furthermore, it is the duty of the supervising pretrial officer to ensure the safety of any victim or witness in the case. Defendants are restricted from approaching the victim or witness in person, by telephone, by letter, or by e-mail, or through a third party. Contact of the victim or witness by the defendant can result in revictimization, intimidation,

or harassment. Specifically, a defendant may try to coerce a victim or witness into recanting statements made to law-enforcement officers, thus possibly damaging the prosecution's case and resulting in a dismissal of the defendant's charge. Furthermore, a defendant may be restricted from contact with potential victims. For example, a defendant accused of child molestation would likely be prohibited from residing with or having contact with children.

If a defendant cannot return to his or her previous residence, the pretrial officer may move him or her to a more suitable home. If the defendant's behavior cannot be adequately supervised or if he or she requires intensive programming, the pretrial officer can place the defendant in an inpatient treatment facility or a residential community corrections facility for part or the duration of the pretrial release period.

Once the defendant pleads guilty or is found guilty of the pending charge, he or she no longer is presumed innocent. At this time, the judge reevaluates whether the defendant can be continued on pretrial supervision pending sentencing. Because the sentencing hearing may not take place until several weeks or even a few months after the conviction, discontinuation of pretrial release can result in a significant amount of time spent in the local jail. Adjustment to pretrial supervision conditions prior to conviction is often the key factor in determining whether a defendant may remain in the community pending sentencing. Violations of conditions are brought to the attention of the court. More serious violations, such as the breaking of laws, are immediately reported to the court, at which time the defendant's bond may be revoked. Less serious violations, such as failure to keep an appointment with the supervising pretrial services officer, are usually handled at the discretion of the pretrial services office. Minor infractions are reported to the court either in the pre-sentence investigation report or verbally at the sentencing hearing.

Brenda Donelan
Northern State University

See also Bail Reform Act of 1984; Discretionary Release; Pretrial Detention

Further Readings

Demuth, Stephen. "Racial and Ethnic Differences in Pretrial Release Decisions and Outcomes: A Comparison of

Hispanic, Black, and White Felony Arrestees." *Criminology*, v.41/3 (2003).

Demuth, Stephen and Darrell Steffensmeier. "The Impact of Gender and Race-Ethnicity in the Pretrial Release Process." *Social Problems*, v.51/2 (2004).

Freiburger, Tina L. and Carly M. Hilinski. "The Impact of Race, Gender, and Age on the Pretrial Decision." *Criminal Justice Review*, v.5/3 (2010).

Goldkamp, John S. and Michael D. White. "Restoring Accountability in Pretrial Release: The Philadelphia Pretrial Release Supervision Experiments." *Journal of Experimental Criminology*, v.2/2 (2006).

Henning, Kris and Lynette Feder. "Criminal Prosecution of Domestic Violence Offenses: An Investigation of Factors Predictive of Court Outcomes." *Criminal Justice and Behavior*, v.32/6 (2005).

Prison Overcrowding

Prison overcrowding is a problem that has long been recognized, but during the past 20 years the overcrowding problem has greatly increased because all states and the federal government have been inundated with growing numbers of offenders sentenced to long prison terms. Currently, prisons in 30 states and the federal government operate above their capacity, meaning that they have more inmates than the prison was designed to accommodate. The main reason for the overcrowding is the great increase in the prison population since the mid-1970s, due largely to "tough-on-crime" policies, such as the three-strikes laws and mandatory sentences, as well as the "war on drugs," which arose in that period.

In 2005, approximately 2.1 million Americans were incarcerated in state and federal prisons, according to the American Legislative Exchange Council. This equals an imprisonment rate of one inmate for every 100 adults in the United States, generating a yearly bill of $60 billion, according to the Bureau of Justice Statistics. Overcrowded prisons cause serious problems for inmates and for the prison management, such as violence and stress, safety issues, prisoner rights issues, programming issues, reentry issues, and issues pertaining to the proper functioning of the facility itself. The responses to the overcrowding issues vary by state and include reducing the prison population, building more prisons, outsourcing inmates to private prisons, and diverting offenders away from prison to drug courts.

The Extent of the Problem

Overcrowding of prisons for male and female inmates has been a serious problem for state and federal facilities for more than two decades. Prisons have been plagued by overcrowding for the past three decades. Since the 1980s, however, the overcrowding problem has greatly increased, and currently 30 states and the federal prisons operate above capacity. Specifically, the federal prisons have about 34 percent more inmates than they were designed to hold. The overcrowding in state prisons is even higher. State prisons operate at an average capacity of 107 percent over capacity, meaning that they have on average twice as many inmates as they were built to accommodate.

As a result of prison overcrowding, thousands of prisoners are held in local jails until space becomes available in prisons. This practice has led to a greater population in jails, and thus jails also suffer from overcrowding. The state with the highest prison population and the greatest overcrowding problems is California, which operates at about 200 percent over capacity statewide and up to 300 percent in some prisons. This overcrowding problem has been recognized by the courts. Several states, including California, operate under court order to reduce their inmate population and alleviate the overcrowding problems. Additionally, several states, including Michigan, Maryland, and California, have declared a state of emergency because of overcrowding.

The Causes of Overcrowding

There are multiple reasons for the rising incarceration rate and the increase in prison overcrowding. During the early 1980s, legislatures, law enforcement, and the judiciary implemented several tough-on-crime policies. These policies were a reaction to the increasing crime rates in the 1960s and 1970s. During the early 1980s, the crime rate reached an all-time high, and citizens demanded a solution to the growing crime problem. The tough-on-crime approach became very popular, and several new sentencing laws were implemented. The sentencing reforms included mandatory sentencing, determinate sentencing, and truth-in-sentencing laws. At the same time, new laws were implemented that were intended to fight the increasing drug problem. Mandatory sentencing and the drug laws are generally cited as the most salient factors in the growth of the incarceration rate and prison overcrowding, because they lead to a greater number of offenders receiving prison sentences and a substantial increase in the length of the prison sentences.

Mandatory sentencing requires judges to impose a predetermined sentence for certain offenses, as a result removing discretion from the judges. These sentences were determined by the legislature and target violent offenders, drug offenders, repeat offenders, and offenders who use weapons. There are, however, also mandatory sentences for nonviolent crimes. These mandatory sentences vary by state and for the federal government. For instance, in Florida the mandatory minimum sentence for robbery is 10 years; if a weapon is discharged, the minimum increases to 20 years; and if someone is injured or killed, the sentence is 25 years to life. Judges must impose at least the minimum sentence.

Similarly, the war on drugs also increased the sentence length because of the implementation of harsher punishments, especially incarceration. More than 500,000 offenders are incarcerated each year for drug offenses. In fact, about 21 percent of state inmates and 55 percent of federal inmates are incarcerated for drug offenses. Not only are more drug offenses punishable by imprisonment, but the sentences have also significantly increased. Thus, prison overcrowding continues to grow.

The implementation of mandatory sentences and drug laws has led to an increase in the incarceration rate, from 330,000 in 1980 to about 2.1 million in 2005, and as a result mandatory sentences have had a substantial impact on prison overcrowding. Research has estimated that the expansion of drug offenses alone has led to a total growth of the inmate population by 27 percent.

Negative Effects of Overcrowding

Prison overcrowding has negative effects for inmates, staff, and the community at large. The main problems caused by overcrowding are risks of health and safety for inmates, staff, and the public; increases in harm to people; riots and unrest; lack of programming; lack of treatment and rehabilitation programs; and higher recidivism rates. Overcrowding also causes problems for the operation of the facility itself, because of an overload of the sewer and wastewater system, which can cause groundwater contamination and environmental pollution.

First, many researchers argue that overcrowded prisons are in violation of prisoners' basic rights, including the right to be safe from bodily harm. Research suggests that the lack of safety can lead to an increase of violence and higher suicide rates. According to a 2010 study by Meredith Huey Dye, suicide rates in prisons that were overcrowded were significantly higher, as compared to prisons that were not filled over capacity. The more a prison is overcrowded, the more difficult it is for inmates to avoid interaction with other inmates. They experience a constant threat to their safety, which increases the possibility that an inmate will overreact to a perceived threat and seriously injure or even kill another inmate. This argument is not supported by all studies; a substantial amount of research also suggests that prison overcrowding does not necessarily increase inmate misconduct and violence. According to Travis W. Franklin, Courtney A. Franklin, and Travis C. Pratt, other factors, such as managerial skills, appear to be more salient in predicting misconduct and violence. Data, however, demonstrate that overcrowded prisons are plagued by inmate riots endangering the lives of inmates and the prison staff. Research also demonstrates that idleness is a strong predictor of violence and disorder. Overcrowded prisons lack programming options, which results in inmates' inactivity and idleness. According to the Commission on Safety and Abuse in America's prisons, prisons that have highly structured programs for inmates experience less misconduct and unrest among the prisoners and staff.

Second, prisoners have the right to medical treatment, both short- and long-term. This treatment must be adequate and appropriate. Prisons that operate over capacity may not be able to provide such treatment, and as a result prisoners may die or suffer adverse health consequences. In *Plata v. Schwarzenegger*, the U.S. District Court for the Northern District of California stated that in California one prisoner dies every six or seven days because of the lack of medical treatment. The court concluded that the overcrowding in California's prisons constitutes cruel and unusual punishment because basic needs cannot be met. The court ordered that California reduce its current rate of overcrowding from 200 percent statewide to 137.5 percent, which equals between 38,000 and 46,000 inmates. California appealed the case to the U.S. Supreme Court in 2011. At that time, the Supreme Court postponed the case until hearing the information on its merits (*Brown v. Plata*). The overall bad health of the inmates is also problematic for the community at large, because 95 percent of all prisoners return to the community, along with their diseases. In 2006, the Commission on Safety and Abuse in America's Prisons estimated that each year about 1.5 million prisoners return to the community with a contagious disease that may spread to other individuals, putting lives at risk and increasing healthcare costs.

Third, much research has examined the impact of overcrowding on inmates' mental health. Several studies have demonstrated that overcrowding in prisons increases the "pains of imprisonment" and the experienced deprivation for prisoners. Inmates suffer from a lack of access to basic goods and services, such as washroom access, hygiene, and medical supplies, because resources are limited and the more prisoners compete for these resources the more the resources have to be stretched. Crowding also increases the competition for recreational resources, such as the access to the library, television, and commissary. Being denied access to these resources can lead to frustration and aggression, which may increase violence. Additionally, in overcrowded prisons it is not always possible to house the violent offenders in an area separate from the nonviolent offenders; the results can include rape, beating, and death. Inmates experience more stress because of the constant noise, lack of privacy, and inability to avoid interaction and confrontation with other inmates. Living under such conditions has been argued to be cruel and unusual; a 1984 study by Verne C. Cox, Paul B. Paulus, and Garvin McCain demonstrated that this stress may result in higher suicide rates and violence.

Finally, overcrowded prisons have negative consequences for the community at large, because inmates who serve time in overcrowded prisons have higher recidivism rates than inmates in prisons that are not overcrowded. There are several reasons for this relationship between overcrowding and recidivism. Inmates in overcrowded prisons have less access to treatment and rehabilitation programs for drug abuse and mental health issues. Approximately 70 percent of prison inmates have drug abuse issues. Many inmates with drug abuse issues also suffer from a mental illness. Roger Peters and colleagues estimated that approximately 50 percent of prisoners suffer from co-occurring disorders. Most prisons do not have the staff and resources to address these severe mental illnesses or drug addictions adequately. When these issues are not treated effectively, they will likely prompt the offender to relapse into criminal behavior after release. Inmates in overcrowded prisons also lack access to vocational and educational programming. Researchers estimate that about 70 percent of prisoners do not have a high school diploma and about 19 percent are illiterate. This lack of education and work skills is problematic, because after release these individuals are unable to find employment and housing. Jordan Baker and colleagues have noted that, in order to meet their basic needs, they often return to criminal behaviors.

Solutions to Prison Overcrowding

Solutions to the problem of prison overcrowding focus on limiting the number of new prison inmates, releasing prisoners early, building new prisons, outsourcing prisoners to private facilities, or restructuring the current prison system and focusing on rehabilitation and reentry programs in an effort to reduce the recidivism rate.

Many states—including Colorado, Connecticut, Delaware, Illinois, Indiana, Maine, Michigan, North Dakota, New York, and Texas—have started to reverse criminal justice policies that led to increases in incarceration rates and significant increases in the costs of incarcerating inmates. Mandatory sentencing and three-strikes laws, enacted in the 1980s and 1990s, appear to have had the largest impact on the growth in the prison population and the overcrowding. Daniel F. Wilhelm and Nicholas R. Turner noted in 2002 that the reversal of these policies led to a decrease in the growth of the prison population and overcrowding.

Some states have declared a state of emergency and have implemented new procedures that allow them to release inmates early. For instance, Michigan declared a state of emergency in 1981 and implemented the Prison Overcrowding Emergency Powers Act. This act allowed the prisons to decrease the sentences of inmates who were serving minimum sentences by 90-day increments. Additionally, inmates could be released on parole via order by the governor. Jordan Baker and his colleagues note that, as a result of these measures, Michigan significantly reduced its overcrowding problem.

In order to alleviate overcrowding, almost all states and the federal government have built more prisons. Since 2000, 34 states and the federal government have built or expanded more than 110 correctional facilities in order to house more prisoners.

Sheilla O'Rourke noted that the state with the largest number of new or expanded prisons is Texas, with 22 facilities.

Another solution to prison overcrowding of state and federal facilities is the privatization of prisons and the movement of prisoners into these private prisons. In fact, 27 states and the federal government use private prisons to alleviate their overcrowding problems. Altogether, 264 private prisons house more than 99,000 inmates. The number of privately owned correctional facilities has increased by 60 percent since 2000 and has generated billions of dollars in profit. Critics state that incarceration has become one of the most profitable businesses in the United States. Corrections Corporation of America, the largest private prison corporation, made a profit of $419.4 million for each quarter in 2010, generating more than $1 billion.

Finally, all 50 states, the District of Columbia, Northern Mariana Islands, Puerto Rico, and Indian Country have made some effort to reduce overcrowding problems by diverting nonviolent drug offenders to drug courts. To date, there are 2,038 active drug courts. Research suggests that drug courts are effective in reducing the recidivism rate and, as a result, prison overcrowding. For instance, a 2006 study of California drug courts by the Administrative Office of the Courts demonstrates that the recidivism rate of graduates is 17 percent, as compared to 41 percent of offenders who did not participate in the drug court program.

Janine Kremling
California State University, San Bernardino

See also Determinate Sentencing; Recidivism; Reducing Prison Populations

Further Readings

Administrative Office of the Courts, Center for Families, Children, and the Courts. "California Drug Court Cost Analysis Study." 2006. http://www.courts.ca.gov/documents/cost_study_research_summary.pdf (Accessed July 2011).

American Legislative Exchange Council. "The State Factor: A Plan to Reduce Prison Overcrowding and Violent Crime." 2007. http://www.americanbailcoalition.com/documents/ALEC_State_Factor_Prison_Overcrowding.pdf (Accessed January 2011).

Baker, Jordan, et al. *A Solution to Prison Overcrowding and Recidivism: Global Positioning System Location of Parolees and Probationers.* Thesis. University of Maryland, 2002.

Brown v. Plata, 131 S.Ct. 1910, U.S. Cal., 2011, May 23, 2011.

Coleman v. Schwarzenegger (2009), Docket No. 2:90-Cv-00520-LKK-JFM (N.D. Cal).

Commission on Safety and Abuse in America's Prisons. "Diverse Commission Reaches Consensus." New York: Author, 2006. http://www.prisoncommission.org/report.asp (Accessed January 2011).

Cox, Verne C., Paul B. Paulus, and Garvin McCain. "Prison Crowding Research: The Relevance of Prison Housing Standards and a General Approach Regarding Crowding Phenomena." *American Psychologist*, v.39 (1984).

Franklin, Travis W., Courtney A. Franklin, and Travis C. Pratt. "Examining the Empirical Relationship Between Prison Overcrowding and Inmate Misconduct: A Meta-Analysis of Conflicting Research Results." *Journal of Criminal Justice*, v.34 (2006).

Haney, Craig. *Reforming Punishment: Psychological Limitations to the Pains of Imprisonment.* Washington, DC: American Psychological Association, 2006.

Huey Dye, Meredith. "Deprivation, Importation, and Prison Suicide: Combined Effects of Institutional Conditions and Inmate Composition." *Journal of Criminal Justice*, v.38 (2010).

O'Rourke, Sheilla Vennel. *New and Expanded Federal and State Prisons Since 2010.* http://www.prisonersofthecensus.org/50states/newprisons.html (Accessed July 2011).

Peters, Roger, Paul E. Grenbaum, John F. Edens, Chris R. Carter, and Madeline M. Ortiz. "Prevalence of DSM-IV Substance Abuse and Dependence Disorders Among Prison Inmates." *American Journal of Drug and Alcohol Abuse*, v.24/4 (1998).

Pew Center on the States. "Prison Count 2010: State Population Declines for the First Time in 38 Years." http://www.pewcenteronthestates.org/uploadedFiles/Prison_Count_2010.pdf (Accessed July 2011).

Plata v. Schwarzenegger, 560 F. 3rd 967 (2009).

U.S. Bureau of Justice Statistics. "Prisoners in 2009." http://bjs.ojp.usdoj.gov/content/pub/pdf/p09.pdf (Accessed January 2011).

Wilhelm, Daniel F. and Nicholas R. Turner. *Is the Budget Crisis Changing the Way We Look at Sentencing and Incarceration?* New York: Vera Institute of Justice, 2002.

PRISONER'S FAMILY AND REENTRY

For prisoners returning to the community, families often represent both an invaluable reentry asset and a potential source of tremendous detrimental pressure. Returning prisoners commonly rely on family to overcome initial reentry obstacles. For instance, prisoners' families routinely provide their newly released loved ones housing, a job, and financial support. However, while many families are assuredly elated when one of their members returns from a period of incarceration, there are also several struggles that plague the reconnected familial unit. Many former prisoners often return to live with family members who have had to endure significant financial and emotional strains during the returning prisoner's incarceration. In addition, former prisoners are typically in financial disarray upon release, prompting them to perhaps unrealistically expect family members to fund a lengthy period of readjustment. Finally, most former prisoners are subject to the rules and regulations of supervised release. Such restrictions are usually burdensome, leading some families to question their decision to house a family member just home from jail or prison.

Family Support

Currently, U.S. prisons and jails house almost 2 million Americans, many of whom will eventually return to the community. For example, in 2002, more than 600,000 prisoners reentered society after a term of incarceration. In *But They All Come Back: Facing the Challenges of Prisoner Reentry*, reentry scholar Jeremy Travis notes that prisoners' families are perhaps the most significant factor in successful reintegration and that returning prisoners are well aware of the importance of family support. Studies have shown that most prisoners are exceedingly optimistic about reestablishing family ties upon their release from prison. Moreover, research demonstrates that, prior to release, many prisoners actively plan to rely on family for housing, employment, and financial support. Research also shows that, in many instances, prisoners' families do ultimately provide this expected support.

In *When Prisoners Come Home: Parole and Prisoner Reentry*, prominent reentry scholar Joan Petersilia cites research focused on returning prisoners' first 30 days of freedom. The research found that a majority of returning prisoners live with family upon release. Researchers conducting the study also discovered that, in most instances, families aid returning prisoners by providing assistance with immediate financial responsibilities, employment searches, and efforts to abstain from alcohol and drugs. Although empirical data on the success of

returning prisoners who receive familial support are sparse, the research that does exist seems to suggest that prisoners who rejoin the family unit make a smoother transition from prison to free society. For instance, Petersilia points to research indicating that incarcerated men who maintain strong family ties and who assume family roles upon release enjoy greater measures of reentry success than their counterparts. Travis also cites empirical data showing a strong correlation between the strength of the family unit and the eventual success of a returning prisoner. As a result, many jurisdictions now pursue policies aimed at enhancing the family structures that serve as support networks for returning prisoners.

Family Strain

While they often help facilitate successful reentry, families can also represent a source of great strain for returning prisoners. Incarceration can cause tremendous tensions within a family—tensions directly resulting from economic and emotional sacrifices that accompany a period of imprisonment. Families often expect immediate household contributions from returning prisoners, yet returning prisoners can face significant barriers to finding work. Moreover, a period of incarceration spawns lasting psychological effects, some of which can make meaningful reintegration into a family difficult if not impossible. In addition, almost all returning prisoners must cope with the regulations of parole or probation. These regulations uniformly impact those with whom returning prisoners reside, creating yet another level of tension with which reunited families must contend.

Financial Difficulties

During the offender's incarceration, his or her family must meet recurring expenses and must survive without contribution from the incarcerated family member. Additionally, prisoners often place separate financial burdens on family members during the incarceration period. For example, for many prisoners, phone calls and visits are their only form of contact with loved ones. Collect phone calls from prisoners are expensive, routinely costing prisoners' families six to seven times the normal collect call rate. Also, most prisons are not located close to metropolitan areas, and family members' travel to and from the prison to visit the offender requires substantial monetary output. Such expenses can create resentment that surfaces upon a prisoner's return.

Families often assume that, following their release, returning prisoners will very soon, if not immediately, contribute to the family financially. However, occupational barriers usually plague a returning prisoner's job search. In the United States, most states permit employers to inquire about criminal histories and to use such data when screening potential employees. Hence, returning prisoners frequently find that obtaining employment and assisting their families financially are difficult and frustrating tasks. These reentry obstacles can delay the offender's successful reintegration not only by limiting job opportunities but also by causing family support to erode.

Emotional Difficulties

Psychologists have discovered that incarceration has lasting effects on those subjected to confinement in prisons and jails. For example, psychologist Craig Haney found that during a period of incarceration, prisoners develop psychological coping mechanisms to manage their experience of institutionalization. For example, some prisoners become dependent on institutional structure and rigidity. Many prisoners also become fearful of trust, often seeking to distance themselves psychologically from others. Such social isolation, Haney contends, serves as a survival mechanism for those forced to live in an environment where violence and manipulation occur regularly.

These adaptations, while useful in prison, make family reintegration exceedingly difficult. Returning prisoners may find that they are unable to organize or make independent decisions. They may also feel a need to withdraw from familial relationships, making family interdependency impossible. Such situations strain families with a member who has served time and can prove fatal to the readjustment efforts of a returning prisoner.

Legal Difficulties

In most jurisdictions, a period of supervision follows one's release from prison. Such supervision takes the form of either probation or parole. Generally, probation is a term of supervision imposed in lieu of incarceration. Nevertheless, in many jurisdictions, courts often sentence offenders to a period of proba-

tion to follow a term of imprisonment. Parole is a term of supervision during which an offender serves the remainder of an imposed prison sentence outside prison.

Although different, probation and parole are similar in that each involves federal or state agents responsible for supervising former prisoners and ensuring that each complies with the multitude of rules and regulations common to supervised release. For example, probationers and parolees normally cannot travel more than certain designated distances from their residence, cannot associate with known criminals or gang members, cannot consume alcohol or use illegal drugs, cannot change residences without notifying supervising authorities, and must, in writing, submit to warrantless searches of their home or person. Because most probationers and parolees reside with family members upon release, such rules have an impact on the lives of family members as well and often create tension within households.

James M. Binnall
University of California, Irvine

See also Civil and Political Rights Affected by Conviction; Reentry Programs and Initiatives; Reintegration Into Communities

Further Readings

Haney, Craig. "The Psychological Impact of Incarceration: Implications for Post-Prison Adjustment." In *From Prison to Home: The Effect of Incarceration on Children, Families, and Communities.* Washington, DC: U.S. Department of Health and Human Services, 2001. http://aspe.hhs.gov/hsp/prison2home02/Haney.htm (Accessed July 2011).
Petersilia, Joan. *When Prisoners Come Home: Parole and Prisoner Reentry.* Oxford: Oxford University Press, 2003.
Travis, Jeremy. *But They All Come Back: Facing the Challenges of Prisoner Reentry.* Washington, DC: The Urban Institute Press, 2005.

PROBATION

Probation is a correctional sentence that allows an offender sentenced in criminal court to remain in the community provided that he or she agrees to abide by certain conditions imposed by the sentencing court. In order to ensure that these conditions are being followed, a probation officer supervises the offender and reports back to the court. Probation can be considered a second chance, in that a person who violates the law, especially if it is a minor offense or a first-time offense, can learn from his or her mistake while remaining in the community. Probation is also increasingly being used for repeat offenders and those convicted of felonies.

History and Mission

John Augustus is known as the father of probation. In 1841, Augustus began bailing men out of jail in Boston, Massachusetts. He bailed out those who were first-time offenders and who expressed a willingness to reform. By 1842, Augustus expanded his informal probation efforts to women and children. Augustus assisted his charges in abstaining from alcohol, finding homes, securing employment, and dealing with family strife. He was not paid for his services, but did receive donations from local businesses and individuals who believed in his efforts. Enactment of the first probation law in the United

The probation officer is charged with enforcing the conditions imposed by the court. Probation officers need a broad knowledge of the criminal justice system and an understanding of the distribution of responsibilities among courts, the parole authority, corrections facilities, social services, and the prosecutor. (Photos.com)

States took place in Massachusetts in 1878. This law provided for paid probation officers to supervise both adults and juveniles. It was deemed a success, and similar programs began to develop throughout the United States.

President Calvin Coolidge signed the Probation Act of 1925, which established probation as an actual sentence in the federal court system. Prior to the signing of this act, federal courts used suspension of sentences as a conditional means of lessening punishment. In 1916, the Supreme Court held that federal courts did not have the power to suspend sentences indefinitely. The Probation Act of 1925 allowed courts to place offenders on probation for a term and under the conditions the court thought would best suit the offender and his or her needs.

By 1956, all forty-eight states had paid probation departments for adults and juveniles, and today probation is the primary sanction for criminal offenders in the United States. As of 2008, there were more than 4 million adults on probation. About half of all people are placed on probation for misdemeanor offenses; the other half are serving a term of probation because of felony convictions.

The mission of probation is to carry out what is known as the trinity. The trinity involves protecting the public, carrying out the orders of the court, and providing rehabilitation and treatment. Protection of the public is accomplished through activities such as random home visits, drug tests, notification to victims, and verification of sex offender registration. The supervising probation officer carries out the orders of the court by ensuring the offender pays his or her restitution, fines, and fees. In addition, it is the duty of the probation officer to enforce all other conditions imposed by the court. This will include all of the mandatory and standard conditions of supervision as well as the conditions specific to a particular offender. Finally, the supervising probation officer is charged with providing treatment and rehabilitation for offenders. This may entail chemical dependency treatment, mental health services, furtherance of education, vocational training, and financial assistance, depending on a specific offender's issues and needs.

Managing Probation

Probation is divided into two separate areas; the pre-sentence investigation and supervision of offenders. Some probation officers are assigned to perform only one of these tasks, whereas other officers, particularly those in smaller offices, carry out both duties. Offices in which the pre-sentence and supervision duties are carried out by different groups of probation officers are called "bifurcated" offices. Pros and cons exist with both the bifurcated and combined approaches. The bifurcation of supervision and pre-sentence writing allows probation officers to specialize in one of the areas. Unfortunately, specializing in one area can mean the officer is not as knowledgeable in the other area. In a combined office, the same probation officer may prepare the pre-sentence report and then supervise the offender. This allows the officer to have a more in-depth understanding of the offender at the beginning of the supervision process. On the other hand, an officer who both writes pre-sentence reports and supervises offenders may experience some degree of information overload, since this officer "wears many hats" in the completion of his or her duties.

The pre-sentence investigation is conducted after the entry of a guilty plea by a defendant or after a finding of guilty by a jury or judge. At this time, the judge requests a pre-sentence report prior to sentencing. The purpose of the pre-sentence report is to provide the court with a detailed picture, past and present, of the offender. The pre-sentence report covers the current offense, past adult criminal offenses and juvenile court matters, current and past living situations, family connections, mental and physical health, chemical dependency, financial situation, and employment. After reading the pre-sentence report and recommendation from the probation officer, the judge is able to make an assessment of the offender and the current offense and then sentence him or her accordingly.

Supervision of offenders begins following imposition of a probation sentence by the court. At the end of 2009, more than 4.2 million individuals were on probation supervision in the United States. The probation officer is charged with the duties of monitoring and assisting the offender. The first step in the supervision process is to review the conditions of probation with the offender to ensure that the offender is fully aware of what he or she can and cannot do while under supervision. The standard conditions of supervision require probationers to do things such as regularly work or attend school; submit to warrantless searches of their person, home, vehicle, and belongings; meet regularly with the probation officer; seek permission to travel outside the judicial jurisdiction; submit monthly reports to the probation office; and avoid associating with others who have a criminal record or engage in illegal activities. Some probation offices also require offenders to pay fees for the supervision of probation.

Special conditions of probation are specific to the offender's issues and needs. Special conditions require offenders to do things such as attend chemical dependency and mental health treatment; submit to alcohol and drug testing; pay restitution and fines; register as a sex offender; avoid all contact with the victims of the offense; complete community service work; and disclose all purchases over a particular dollar amount (such as $500) to the probation officer. Probation officers act as a referral agent for chemical dependency and mental health treatment, financial counseling, education, and vocational training. These services are not provided on site by probation officers, but the officers have close connections with agencies that do specialize in these particular areas.

Probation officers typically have a large number of people on their caseloads. Not every offender needs the same amount of supervision or assistance. As a means of determining which people need the most supervision, probation departments classify the offenders on their caseloads. The highest level is intensive supervision; it is used for the highest-risk offenders or those who are one step away from going to prison because they cannot follow their conditions or because of the seriousness of the offense. Certain types of offenders pose a challenge to the supervising probation officer and are at a high risk of failing on probation. Offenders with a history of violence and those with mental health issues need the most services and require a large portion of the supervising officer's time and resources. Probation officers may specialize in intensive caseloads, such as mental health, drugs, or sex offenses, thus having fewer probationers than the average officer. Intensive probation supervision involves multiple contacts each week in person and by telephone. Furthermore, the probationer may be confined to his or her home, restricted to a curfew, or monitored through electronic surveillance. Frequent testing for the use of alcohol and drugs is also implemented.

The lowest level of probation supervision is administrative. A probationer on the administrative caseload has demonstrated over time that he or she can follow the conditions of supervision without much trouble. This type of probationer tends to have fewer issues in the areas of chemical dependency, mental health, and financial hardships. Offenders who are moved to the administrative caseload typically do not need to have regular meetings with the probation officer. They are required to submit a monthly report and follow all conditions of supervision. After the offender has been on the administrative caseload for a period of time and has had no violations or new issues, they may be discharged early from their term of probation.

Most probationers fall somewhere between the intensive and administrative levels of supervision. These offenders may meet with the probation officer from once per week to once every two or three months, depending on their individual risk levels and needs. In meeting with their probationers, officers need to see offenders in a variety of settings and under different circumstances. A scheduled office visit is acceptable on occasion, but it really does not provide the officer with an accurate assessment of the offender. An offender who is told to report to his or her probation office on a particular day is most likely going to be on best behavior and will have rehearsed some answers to anticipated questions. Random visits at home, school, and work can give the supervising officer a much clearer picture of the offender and his or her surroundings. During an office visit an offender may tell the officer that he or she has not been consuming alcohol; on a random visit to the home, the officer might, however, observe empty beer cans in the trash can. In addition, the officer can conduct a warrantless search of the home to determine if any contraband is in the residence. Furthermore, the officer can meet family members or others in the home, which can verify or refute information the offender provided. A random visit to the offender's place of employment can serve as verification that the offender is indeed working and can also offer an opportunity to meet and talk with the offender's supervisor or employer. Random visits at home and work, therefore, reveal much more about an offender and his or her lifestyle than scheduled office visits.

A probationer can violate probation in two different ways. First is a violation of law. This is something that would be considered a crime, no matter who committed the act. Second is a technical violation. A technical violation is not against the law but rather violates the offender's conditions of probation. For example, the offender may fail to submit monthly reports, may consume alcoholic beverages, or may travel outside the jurisdiction without permission. The sanctions for violations of law and technical violations depend on the nature and circumstances of the violation, the number of previous violations, and the efforts already expended by the probation office to aid the probationer. A violation of law is typically reported to the court, along with the probation officer's recommendation for sanctions.

Violations of law and technical violations can be handled in three different ways. First, if the violation is minor and it is a first offense, the probation officer might issue a verbal reprimand followed by a letter detailing why the probationer's actions were wrong, the behavioral changes expected, and the consequences of noncompliance. Second, the offender can be summoned to the probation office for a compliance conference if the violation is more serious or repeated. A compliance conference is a formal meeting between the supervising probation officer, the probation officer's immediate supervisor, and the offender. During this conference, the consequences of further violations are discussed at length and a plan for compliance is set forth. Finally, if the offender has committed a felony offense or has repeated technical violations, the probation officer can petition the sentencing court for revocation of the offender's probation. At a court hearing, the judge determines if the offender has in fact violated probation and if the term of probation should be reinstated, if the term of probation should be lengthened or additional conditions added, or if probation should be revoked and the offender sent to prison.

Advantages and Disadvantages to Probation

Probation is viewed as an attractive alternative to prison, in part because of cost. The average cost to imprison one person for one year is $30,000, whereas the cost to supervise one person on standard probation is around $4 per day, or $1,460 per year. When an offender is imprisoned, all of his or her basic needs must be tended to at the expense of the prison, which is paid for primarily by tax dollars. Food, clothing, medical care, treatment programs, staff salaries, and prison maintenance all add to the overall cost of confining an offender. When this same offender is sentenced to probation, he or she will most likely be paying for food, rent, medical care, education, transportation, care for his or her family, and other necessities. In addition, an offender on probation can typically maintain community ties that would be broken or severely damaged if he or she were incarcerated. The offender can usually live in a residence with family members, maintain employment, and be a contributing member of society. Under probation, offenders avoid the stigma of being ex-convicts and the psychologically damaging effects of incarceration.

There are also disadvantages to probation. The main concern is protection of the community. A probation officer cannot physically supervise every offender 24 hours a day. If an offender is tempted or determined to reoffend, then he or she will find a way to carry out those actions. Another concern voiced by critics is that probation is granted to too many felony offenders. They believe probation should be allowed for misdemeanor cases and only for very few felonies.

Effectiveness of Probation

Is probation effective? One measure of effectiveness is the level of recidivism by offenders placed on probation. Recidivism can be measured by technical violations of probation conditions, arrests and convictions for new offenses, and revocation of the probation sentence. The rate of recidivism varies by type of offender, classification level, supervision efforts of probation officers, and size of the officer's caseload. Offenders on intensive supervision have a higher rate of recidivism because of the seriousness of the offense, the increased supervision efforts by the probation officer, and the increased resistance to following the rules. First-time offenders and those on probation for misdemeanor offenses tend to have lower recidivism rates.

Another measure of effectiveness is whether probationers successfully complete their programs. If the offender completes mental health counseling, parenting classes, chemical dependency treatment,

educational classes, or any other rehabilitative program, then the probation is considered a success. The effectiveness of probation is also measured by the level to which offenders use the programs in their daily lives. For example, implementation of programming would be considered successful if a man attended mental health counseling for his anger issues and is now dealing with his family and coworkers in healthy and appropriate ways. Sometimes a reduction in antisocial behavior can also be seen as a measure of effectiveness in the criminal justice system. A woman who consumed alcohol to excess on a daily basis before being placed on probation could be considered a successful probationer if, after chemical dependency treatment, she relapsed only once in a six-month period. Success, as this second example illustrates, is not always measured by complete absence of antisocial behavior.

Are the goals of probation being met? Studies generally support the use of probation as a sanction, finding that it is not only more cost-effective than prison but also can offer rehabilitative benefits to a greater degree than found in prisons. Probation officers can require offenders to attend counseling or treatment that is fitted to their needs, rather than just the one-size-fits-all treatment programs that are found in many prisons. Moreover, probation is not just a "get out of jail free" card, in that it is punitive. Offenders are required to abide by conditions; if they fail to do so, revocation and a prison sentence are likely outcomes. Quality supervision efforts by the probation officer can provide the community with a feeling of safety from the offenders living in the neighborhood. However, one high-profile case of an offender on probation who commits a new violent crime is likely to tarnish the reputation of the probation office, call into question the effectiveness of probation as a punitive measure, and make the community feel unsafe. Evidence-based practices at the federal level provide information on which aspects of probation are producing desired outcomes and which ones are not. This allows for ongoing evaluation of probation practices, such as home visits and chemical dependency treatment.

Brenda Donelan
Northern State University

See also Case Management; Offender Risks; Offender Supervision; Pre-Sentence Investigation Reports

Further Readings

Alarid, Leanne F. and Philip L. Reichel. *Corrections: A Contemporary Introduction.* Boston: Allyn and Bacon, 2008.

Alexander, Melissa and Scott VanBenschoten. "The Evolution of Supervision in the Federal Probation System." *The Journal of Offender Rehabilitation,* v.47/3 (2008).

Baber, Laura. "Results-Based Framework for Post-Conviction Supervision Recidivism Analysis." *Federal Probation,* v.74/3 (2010).

Siegel, Larry and Clemens Bartollas. *Corrections Today.* Belmont, CA: Thomson Wadsworth, 2011.

U.S. Bureau of Justice Statistics. "Community Corrections: Probation and Parole." http://www.bjs.ojp.usdoj.gov/index.cfm?ty=tp&tid=15 (Accessed June 2011).

PROBATION: ADMINISTRATION MODELS

Probation officers are responsible for a variety of important offender supervision and case management functions, including visiting and interviewing clients, making referrals, maintaining rapport with court personnel and social service agencies, monitoring probationers' progress, enforcing terms of probation, and writing reports. There are several models of probation administration that place varying levels of emphasis on these important functions. The most salient models that are used in jurisdictions throughout the United States include the resource broker/advocate model, the law-enforcement/control model, the caseworker model, and the mixed model.

Resource Broker/Advocate Model

According to I. J. Silverman and Howard Abadinsky, most community corrections agencies' probation officers serve as brokers or advocates for probationers. Under the broker model, the probation officer does not counsel, advise, or treat the client, as a social worker would, but instead acts as a referral agent who links the probationer to appropriate services within the community that are provided by both public and private agencies. As a broker, the probation officer is responsible for assessing and determining the needs of the probationer, locating an agency that can provide the appropriate services,

referring the probationer to the identified agency, and following up with the referral agencies to make sure that the probationer is receiving the required services and is making satisfactory progress.

Silverman and Abadinsky also note that probation officers who follow the brokerage approach are concerned primarily with assessing the probationer's needs, connecting him or her with community-based services, and monitoring his or her progress. If the probationer has difficulty attaining the required services, the probation officer serves as an advocate who assists the client in securing the services. Limited emphasis is placed on the quality of the relationships that probation officers develop with probationers, and greater emphasis is placed on the quality of relationships that the probation officer develops with professionals and staff from social service agencies within the community that provide services to their clients. Accordingly, the probation officer has limited concern for understanding the probationer's behavior or attempting to change his or her behavior with advice or counseling. In fact, the broker model views counseling and therapy as inappropriate and beyond the scope of the probation officer's duties.

Law-Enforcement/Control Model

According to Silverman and Abadinsky, probation officers who follow the control model also broker services but supervise clients in a much more aggressive manner than probation officers who follow the broker/advocate model. Under the control model, probationers are closely monitored through a variety of surveillance activities, ranging from random drug screens to unannounced home and employment visitations. Probationers who violate the terms of their probation may be sanctioned by the probation officer or referred back to the court for review, and probationers who violate the law are reported to law enforcement. Under this model, it is standard practice for probation officers to have close working relationships with court personnel and law-enforcement agencies. The control model is becoming increasingly popular, because many states are placing greater emphasis on retribution and risk-control strategies.

The law-enforcement model is a control model that grants arrest powers to probation officers. Several states follow the law-enforcement model and grant probation officers the authority to serve subpoenas, conduct searches and seizures, and make arrests; in some states, officers are allowed to carry firearms. According to J. Jones and C. Robinson, in 1986 the Oklahoma Department of Corrections conducted a survey of all 50 states and found that 48 percent of the surveyed probation and parole agencies allowed officers to carry firearms, whereas only 24 percent of the agencies reported having officers that carry firearms on a routine basis. According to Silverman, many jurisdictions that give probation officers law-enforcement responsibilities discourage officers from carrying firearms on duty; however, as more states move toward the control model, the carrying of firearms to increase probation officer safety has become an increasingly common practice.

Caseworker/Case Management Model

According to Silverman and Abadinsky, the caseworker approach places emphasis on developing strong one-to-one relationships with probationers and providing counseling and treatment services with the intention of understanding and correcting the offender's behavior. One-on-one counseling is an important component of the caseworker model because it builds the level of trust that clients have with probation officers, which may positively influence their behavior. This practice dates back to the works of John Augustus and the positive influences he had on offenders that he mentored. Many principles of the caseworker model date back to the traditional medical model, which continues to influence the practices of many probation agencies today. For instance, many probation agencies continue to include the rehabilitation of offenders as one of the primary objectives in their mission statements.

The strength of the caseworker model is that it requires the probation officer to go beyond the traditional tasks of the "service broker" model to meet the needs of high-risk clients. The caseworker/case management model is particularly beneficial when the probation agency wants to focus on behavioral change. R. Enos and S. Southern identified six classes of offenders who are best suited for case management: juvenile delinquents, substance abusers, offenders diagnosed with specific personality disorders, offenders with impulse control disorders, sex offenders, and offenders with other types of metal or social disorders.

Some scholars and practitioners question the appropriateness of the caseworker model because most probation officers' highest level of education is a bachelor's degree, and they do not have the training or professional background to develop therapeutic relationships with their clients or serve as agents of behavioral change in offenders. One researcher has argued that, because probation officers lack professional training in counseling, encouraging them to become caseworkers may actually do more harm than good; the development of a caseworker model without proper training for probation officers can provide a disservice to probationers because they are then at risk of being counseled by untrained and unlicensed professionals. Critics of the caseworker model argue that, even if probation officers are provided with proper training in counseling and therapy, the caseworker model will continue to be infeasible in the probation and parole setting, because most probation officers have caseloads that average between 80 and 100 cases. Given the prevalence of high caseloads, most probation officers are too busy to dedicate one-to-one counseling time with their clients.

Mixed Model

According to Silverman and Abadinsky, many community corrections agencies have adopted a mixed model that incorporates principles from each of the three predominant probation administration models. Under the mixed model, the probation officer provides brokerage and advocacy services, monitors progress, enforces terms of probation, and engages some higher-risk clients throughout the entire treatment process. Whether an agency or individual parole officer decides to follow a mixed model depends on a variety of factors, including the level of risk that the client poses to the community, specific needs of individual clients, agency policy, and the individual officers' preferred management style. It is important to acknowledge that in many jurisdictions probation officers are given a wide degree of discretion to determine which clients they should engage the most throughout the treatment process. According to the American Probation and Parole Association, the national average caseload is 106 cases per officer. Given the reality of growing caseloads, probation officers have limited time to dedicate to offenders who are in the greatest need of behavioral change.

Blake M. Randol
Washington State University

See also Caseload and Workload Standards; Community Corrections as an Alternative to Imprisonment; Probation: Early Termination; Probation Officers

Further Readings

Abadinsky, Howard. *Probation and Parole: Theory and Practice,* 11th ed. Upper Saddle River, NJ: Pearson, 2011.

American Probation and Parole Administration. "Facts from the Field." 2011. http://www.appa-net.org/eweb/DynamicPage.aspx?WebCode=VB_Facts (Accessed July 2011).

Bemus, B., G. Arling, and P. Quigley. *Workload Measures for Probation and Parole.* Washington, DC: National Institute of Corrections, U.S. Department of Justice, Office of Justice Programs, 1983.

Carlson, Eric W. and Evalyn C. Parks. *Critical Issues in Adult Probation: Issues in Probation Management.* Washington, DC: U.S. Government Printing Office, 1979.

Enos, R. and S. Southern. *Correctional Case Management.* Washington, DC: U.S. Department of Justice, Office of Justice Programs, 1995.

Jones, J. and C. Robinson. "Keeping the Piece: Probation and Parole Officers' Right to Bear Arms." *Corrections Today,* v.51/1 (February 1989).

Silverman, I. J. *Correction: A Comprehensive View,* 2nd ed. Belmont, CA: Thomson Wadsworth, 2001.

PROBATION: EARLY TERMINATION

Probation is the most common form of criminal justice supervision in the United States. In 2011, there were more than 4.2 million adult offenders on probation—nearly three times as many as there were housed in state and federal prisons. As a result, heightened pressures have been placed on the field of probation to meet demands of both public safety and cost-effectiveness, in addition to alleviating the burden imposed on prisons and jails by scarce resources. In response to overwhelming caseloads and pressures to shift the paradigm of community corrections away from purely punishment-based policies, some probation departments have implemented a policy rewarding low-risk offenders who exhibit good behavior with early termination of their probation by the courts. Early termination of probation provides incentives for offenders to engage in prosocial endeavors. In addition, early termination

allows a more effective and efficient allocation of scarce resources. By rewarding compliant probationers with early release, the probation system can reallocate resources to those who pose the greatest threat to public safety.

High Caseloads and Probationer Risk

Probation has expanded rapidly and has been viewed as a cost-effective alternative to incarceration. Approximately 60 percent of adults convicted of a felony in a given year receive a sentence of probation, resulting in caseload estimates ranging between 100 and 130 probationers per officer. Concerns over public safety have been raised because of the sheer volume of offenders serving their sentences in the community and the workload manageability of probation officers. Inadequate funding and high revocation rates have forced corrections policy makers to search for solutions based on principles of risk. One solution has been the implementation of early probation termination policies.

Low-risk offenders are classified as such because they are viewed as posing little threat to the community and are not expected to reoffend. Considering excessive caseloads and strapped budgets, an important question to be considered is whether providing cursory oversight to these individuals constitutes an effective use of limited resources. According to the risk principle, the lengthiest and most intensive correctional treatment programs should target those offenders who are considered to pose the greatest likelihood of reoffending. Empirically established predictors of recidivism suggest that high-risk offenders have poor self-management, low self-control, a history of prior offending, antisocial peer associations, and weak ties to prosocial networks. Based on these criteria, compliant, low-risk offenders may be granted early termination of their probation by a judge. When these offenders are allowed to apply for early termination of probation, caseloads can be lessened, resources can be allocated more effectively, and offenders can be given incentives to comply with their programming. Shorter probation terms are less likely to disrupt the prosocial networks characteristic of low-risk offenders, and probationers are less likely to incur technical violations. Such violations may lead to probation revocation and incarceration—a costly and unintentional outcome for low-risk offenders.

Incentive-Based vs. Punishment-Based Programming

Early termination of probation is one of the policies to emerge from the growing dissatisfaction with strictly punishment-based correctional programming. Extant literature on evidence-based interventions reveals that attempts to use predominantly punishment-based or cost-based programs are not effective in reducing recidivism. These efforts are directed toward intensely monitoring probationers and threatening them with the use of swift punishment if they do not comply with the terms of their probation. These cost-oriented programs operate within a correctional paradigm that is dominated by a rational choice ideology. Accordingly, crime is considered a deliberate decision that individuals make after considering the costs and benefits associated with doing so. Offending, then, is assumed to be preventable by increasing the costs of crime through the imposition of severe sanctions. This principle can be dangerous, because it may generate defiance among probationers and also because it is difficult to prove this false. If recidivism is not prevented, claims can be made that the costs of offending merely were not high enough. Since these cost-oriented approaches to probation are largely ineffective, researchers and practitioners have begun to focus on incentive- or reward-based strategies, such as early termination.

While still operating within a rational choice framework, incentive-based interventions are an improvement upon cost-oriented models. Researchers emphasize that strategies to ensure compliance may be more effective when they highlight rewards rather than punishments. Social learning principles suggest that people respond better to a higher ratio of positive reinforcements and that they are more likely to comply when a positive outcome is expected. Early termination may be an effective way to use discretion to reward good progress among probationers. Even though punishment-based strategies largely dominate correctional interventions, early termination of probation represents a promising strategy for yielding lower reconviction rates.

On average, the reported daily costs of incarceration are 22 times greater than the daily costs of community supervision. In light of these costs, states are taking a closer look at cost-saving strategies, especially for less serious offenders, who can be managed safely in the community. The goal is to identify evidence-based practices that will improve the probationer's compliance and achievements while on probation, reduce a probationer's time on probation, reduce the likelihood that probationers will be revoked to prison for technical violations, and decrease the subsequent recidivism rate of probationers. Utilizing rewards, along with risk- and evidence-based programming in community corrections, can generate much-needed savings. Such savings can be allocated to better supervise high-risk probationer, to provide services within high-risk communities, and to implement early intervention programs.

Marie L. Griffin
Jillian J. Turanovic
Arizona State University

See also Conditions of Community Corrections; Offender Risks; "What Works" Approach and Evidence-Based Practices

Further Readings

Andrews, D. A., James Bonta, and Stephen J. Wormith. "The Recent Past and Near Future of Risk and/or Need Assessment." *Crime and Delinquency*, v.52 (2006).

Shelley, N. "Early Termination of Probation." *Probation Journal*, v.40/3 (1993).

U.S. Bureau of Justice Statistics. *Probation and Parole in the United States, 2009*. Washington, DC: U.S. Department of Justice, 2010.

Probation: Organization of Services

Probation services are provided under various models in different jurisdictions throughout the United States. Some states have centralized probation functions under the aegis of a state correctional authority, while other states maintain a more localized structure in which the services are administered under the aegis of municipal or county courts. Juvenile probation services usually reflect a highly localized orientation and generally attempt to provide various treatment modalities and other services utilizing nearby facilities and public and private agencies with which probation officers and judges are familiar. This reflects both a concern with political and economic realities and an interest in keeping a close level of supervision on delinquents in their care.

State-Level Administration

State-level administration is the dominant model for provision of probation services in the United States, with 30 states adhering to the general principle of centralization. In 25 states, probation services are exclusively provided by the centralized state agency. In most of the remaining states, at least some probation services may be contracted out to private services or local public/private agencies. Seventeen states have a mixed state/local structure under the primary aegis of the state.

State systems are less prone to be influenced by local political factors and parochial prejudices. Thus, they are mainly free from undue influence wielded by powerful interest groups and mercantile interests. Moreover, goals and objectives that are consonant with current approved practices are more likely to be promulgated by state-level agencies. This being the case, they are able to impose rigorous and uniform statewide standards for officer training and offender supervision. They are able to attract more qualified and professional educated personnel than local-oriented agencies. Finally, economies of scale assure that better uses of scarce resources can be achieved by state agencies. Simply put, they are more cost-effective and efficient than locally administered agencies.

In general, state agencies, generally part of an overarching state correctional department, may be more prone to rely on institutional rather than community-based dispositions. In any event, they are criticized as less responsive to local communities. It has been suggested that entities furnishing probation services should be deconsolidated from the control of institutionally oriented state correctional departments and henceforth should focus on a more specific mission: providing probation, parole, and aftercare. This view advocates the notion that special free-standing probation and parole departments, perhaps called "state departments of community corrections" should be established.

Local Administration

Larger cities and municipalities often have probation services provided under local authority. Some states have county probation departments in certain areas and a centralized state authority over the majority of counties. Often misdemeanant supervisory services are provided at the local level while felons are supervised at the state level. In some states, this situation may reflect a history of political bargaining for control of patronage positions, although the positions currently are under a civil service bureaucracy.

County-level agencies have difficulty attracting a pool of sufficiently qualified recruits and lack resources for staff development. Local agencies seldom have sufficient budgets to provide up-to-date preservice or on-the-job training. Hiring may be heavily influenced by political factors. Research is seldom conducted at this level, and professional practice is often behind the times. Provision of probationary services may be rudimentary and unduly influenced by local political factors.

Local administration of probation services does have the advantage of being able to consider area cultural, political, and economic realities when dealing with clientele. For example, finding a slot in a local drug treatment center for an addicted offender may prove easier for a locally oriented probation officer with a "folksy" approach and the backing of a local judge. Locally oriented probation officers may be in closer touch with the "street" milieu in which their clientele operates and thus may be more responsive than agents operating from a large, centralized bureaucracy. Moreover, local communities, law-enforcement agencies, educators, and employers may be much more responsive to working with a local person than with someone from a large state organization based in a remote state capital. It is thought that local agencies favor a more community corrections–oriented approach over a more institutionally focused disposition.

Provision of Juvenile Probation Services

There is tremendous variation in the provision of juvenile probation services from state to state. This reflects the fact that the various juvenile probation departments are largely creatures of the juvenile courts, which also have a wide variety of structures. In general, juvenile courts may be separate courts, part of the local trial court system, or part of the family court system. Thus, juvenile probation services may be provided by any or all of these agencies. Few states have their own discrete juvenile courts operating on a statewide basis; most states, therefore, use the final two models, although juveniles are most commonly dealt with by a variation of the local trial court system. Since more than one third of juvenile delinquency cases handled by the juvenile court are probated (as much as 60 percent in some courts), the provision of services is a critical role of the juvenile court and a core function of juvenile probation officers.

Probation officers are usually hired by and operate under the titular supervision of a juvenile court judge and are generally county employees with benefits common to other county employees. The provision of juvenile probation services thus often resembles the local administrative model of adult probationary services, with all the strengths and limitations of that particular type of agency. As such, the provision of probation services often reflects the preferences, training, orientation, and personality of the judge under whose span of control juvenile probations officers serve. Judges who favor treatment and counseling hire officers with backgrounds geared toward those approaches; judges who favor enforcement will hire officers who demonstrate abilities in apprehending and revoking the probation of violators. In any event, locally run juvenile courts and the services they typically utilize usually reflect the treatment preferences and jurisprudential philosophies of the constellation of judges who serve on the local juvenile bench.

Francis Frederick Hawley
Western Carolina University

See also Juvenile and Youth Offenders; Probation Officers; Probation Officers: Job Stress

Further Readings

Abadinsky, Howard. *Probation and Parole: Theory and Practice,* 11th ed. Upper Saddle River, NJ: Pearson, 2011.

Clear, Todd R., George F. Cole, and Michael D. Reisig. *American Corrections,* 9th ed. Belmont, CA: Thomson Wadsworth, 2010.

Cromwell, Paul et al. *Community-Based Corrections.* Belmont, CA: Thomson Wadsworth, 2002.

Petersilia, J. "Probation in the United States." *Crime and Justice,* v.22 (1997).

PROBATION: PRIVATE

The emergence of private probation in the United States correlates with the explosive increase in incarceration in the last few decades. The United States currently incarcerates more than 2 million people, which is more than any other country in the world, both in absolute numbers and in proportion to its population. Overcrowded prisons have turned to both private prisons and community corrections to relieve their belabored institutions. As a result, more than 5 million people are currently serving probation or parole in the United States. Overworked probation officers have difficulty monitoring and managing so many charges, many of whom were sentenced to community corrections simply because of overcrowding. As a result, probation, too, has turned to the private sector to relieve its increasingly burdensome caseload. Hence, private probation has emerged as a method of allowing private agencies and not-for-profit programs to supervise and monitor probationers.

John Augustus

In 1841, John Augustus, a Boston cobbler, convinced a judge to give him custody of a convicted drunkard, who otherwise would have been imprisoned. The judge agreed, as long as a fine was paid. The offender was to return in three weeks for an evaluation of his progress. Augustus found the drunkard a job, and, after three weeks, the two returned to court. The judge was surprised to see the man sober and respectable. Impressed, the judge allowed Augustus to continue taking offenders into his custody. Over many years, Augustus took in more than one thousand offenders, the vast majority of whom never returned to court. Thus did the United States find its first probation officer. Augustus's method would later be adopted formally by Massachusetts, and probation soon became a standard alternative to incarceration across the United States.

Thus, American probation began in the private sector. Crucially, however, Augustus offered volunteer service. Much of the contemporary private probation landscape is, in contrast, a profitable community corrections industry.

Recent History

In 1975, Florida became the first state to institute private probation, allowing the Salvation Army and other approved groups to supervise low-level offenders. About 10 states now contract probation to private companies. Private probation can take the form of a for-profit private probation agency or a nonprofit community-based private treatment provider. Private probation agencies usually model their practices after the bail bond system. Probationers would post a bond as insurance for their good behavior. Meeting probation conditions, such as attending court on a certain date, means that the probationer regains the bond. Failure to meet probation conditions means the probationer loses the bond. Most private probation agencies tend to specialize in certain kinds of offenses in an attempt to reduce their overall caseload.

Advocates of private probation point out the need to overcome the shortcomings of the state and federal probation systems. Case overload means, on one hand, that violations of probation conditions are often overlooked, or, on the other hand, that social factors leading to minor violations are left unaddressed and probationers are sent back to prison unnecessarily. Proponents of privatization argue that by requiring probationers to post a bond in guarantee of good behavior, probationers have an incentive to comply with the terms of probation, while incurring no cost to taxpayers. Moreover, the specialization of private probation agencies means that the services provided can be more attuned to probationers' needs and may often be of superior quality to comparable public services. Specialized private probation agencies can also maintain a lower caseload than the more generalized public model. Finally, advocates point out that private probation is not always for profit and is often in the hands of community organizations whose primary motivation is not profit but social good. Such organizations may be more likely than the state to meet a community's needs.

Two main areas of criticism of private probation persist. First, private probation is less subject to oversight and regulation than public probation. One arena in which this becomes clear is that of formal credentials. Private probation agencies generally require less certification, licensure, education, training, and employment recommendations than that required of probation officers in the employ of the state. Moreover, while a heavy caseload is burdensome to the state, for a private agency heavy caseloads may actually be profitable, even as services for individual clients deteriorate. States rarely employ minimum standards for private probation agencies. Therefore, agencies have less incentive to report violations and less oversight requiring them to do so, raising serious public safety issues both for their clients and for the larger community.

Second, the financial interests of private probation companies may lead to a deterioration of services or to corruption, both of which would disrupt the needs of offenders and communities. For instance, a member of the Georgia Board of Pardons and Paroles was convicted on public corruption charges for accepting a bribe from a private probation agency. States generally forbid governmental officials from maintaining interests in private probation agencies, and some require that agencies post a surety bond to be allowed to supervise probationers. Nonetheless, fears of conflict of interest persist, especially in cases in which agencies also provide other services, such as mental health or housing services. These agencies often require clients to use their ancillary services, lest the probationers face a probation violation.

Ellen Dwyer
Indiana University, Bloomington

See also Felony Probation; Juvenile Probation Officers; Neighborhood Probation; Probation; Probation: Administration Models; Probation: Early Termination; Probation: Organization of Services; Probation and Judicial Reprieve; Probation and Parole: Intensive Supervision; Probation and Parole Fees; Probation Mentor Home Program; Probation Officers; Probation Officers: Job Stress; Shock Probation

Further Readings

Alarid, L. F. and C. S. Schloss. "Attorney Views on the Use of Private Agencies for Probation Supervision and Treatment." *International Journal of Offender Therapy and Comparative Criminology*, v.53/3 (2009).

American Probation and Parole Association. "Proposed Position Statement on Privatization." 2001. http://www .appa-Net.org/about%20appa/privatiz_1.htm (Accessed July 2011).

Ascher, K. *The Politics of Privatization: Contracting-Out Public Services.* New York: St. Martin's Press, 1987.

Curran, D. J. "Destructuring, Privatization, and the Promise of Juvenile Diversion: Compromising Community-Based Corrections." *Crime and Delinquency*, v.34/4 (1988).

Demone, H. W. and M. Gibelman. "Privatizing the Treatment of Criminal Offenders." *Journal of Offender Counseling Service and Rehabilitation*, v.15 (1990).

Durham, A. "Rehabilitation and Correctional Privatization: Observations on the 19th Century Experience and Implications for Modern Corrections." *Federal Probation*, v.53 (1989).

PROBATION AND JUDICIAL REPRIEVE

Contemporary probation practice developed from earlier models, such as judicial reprieve. Looking for alternatives to required severe sentences, courts in the 19th century found ways to give certain offenders a second chance, which began a long period of individualized, offender-based correctional practice. Through the religious and humanitarian efforts of people like John Augustus, legislatures took note and began enacting laws authorizing probation officers. A number of probation laws existed by 1900, and they expanded through the next century.

While formal criminal procedure developed slowly in England from 1215 on, penalties for most crimes remained severe until the modern era. Because of the routine application of severe punishments and the cruel conditions in prisons, by the 1700s judges began to look for ways to prevent harsh punishments for some offenders. For centuries, some criminals had been given "release on recognizance," meaning that they became indebted to the state for a financial sum, often requiring sureties, but that the debt later would be forgiven if they committed no more crime. Another method, "judicial reprieve," arose, which allowed the judge to postpone the imposition or execution of an offender's sentence temporarily in order for the offender to petition the Crown for a pardon. Judges did so for a variety of reasons, including when the indictment was weak, the evidence suspicious, or the crime was slight and the criminal sympathetic. Judges opted for this leniency because, under the common law at the time, criminals were not granted new trials or appeals. Eventually, judicial reprieve was permitted in order to deport persons sentenced to death to British penal colonies.

By the 1800s, judicial reprieve became widespread in England, and judges in the United States began similar use of the practice, known as "suspended sentences," to prevent outcomes that would otherwise end in a miscarriage of justice. The legal permissibility of such raw judicial power would be called into question later, but all of these practices foreshadowed the rising correctional shift toward individualized justice that would take hold for the next 100 years.

The movement toward humanizing punishment through such penal innovations appeared almost simultaneously in the mid-1800s in England and the United States, taking further form with the work of Matthew Davenport Hill and John Augustus. Hill was a British barrister and activist who was appointed recorder (judge). Having seen nominal jail time given to juveniles who would be supervised afterward, Hill decided to do the same thing in his court, except to give suspended sentences instead of nominal jail time. However, in the United States it is Augustus who is seen as the father of modern probation, with his influence on probation policy in Massachusetts, which eventually spread legally throughout the country.

Born in Massachusetts and a shoemaker by trade, Augustus frequented the courts because of his desire to help reform those struggling to obey the law, especially drunkards. Augustus believed that if such persons could have their sentences temporarily suspended, with his assistance they could reform themselves and thereafter convince the judge that their sentences should be suspended permanently. Thus, he began "bailing" offenders—that is, posting the recognizance bond for certain offenders he believed could be reformed. After three weeks, Augustus brought the persons back to court to report on their progress, to the general approval of judges. He sometimes referred to this as "probation," although in the sense of a period of trial as opposed to the legal term it later grew to be.

Augustus so influenced the correctional landscape in Massachusetts that in 1878 the state became the first in the nation to pass related legislation. It permitted the mayor of Boston to appoint one paid probation officer. All previous probation work had been voluntary. The statute permitted probation for any offender, given that he or she could be reasonably expected to reform without punishment. Thus, it applied to both juveniles and adults, and potentially any offense. The rest of Massachusetts's municipalities were granted the same ability in 1880, although few of them implemented it. Ten years later, a statewide framework was enacted, with the courts rather than police overseeing the probation officer.

Several other states soon created laws regarding probation or parole, with the terms sometimes mistakenly used for the same idea. Also, Massachusetts had simply authorized the use of probation officers, with the courts granting probation seemingly without explicit statutory authority. However, Missouri passed a law in 1897 that actually authorized the courts to give probation as a form of sentence. Vermont, Minnesota, Rhode Island, New Jersey, and Illinois, with its famous first separate juvenile court system, then followed suit. While Minnesota and Illinois authorized probation for juveniles alone, Vermont and Rhode Island experimented with different methods of administration, that is, county versus state, respectively.

The advent of the juvenile court system spurred a rise in the use of probation. By 1925, all states authorized probation at least for juveniles, although many localities went without it since most legislation did not provide funding. It took until the 1950s and 1960s for all states to permit probation for adults.

In 1916, the U.S. Supreme Court resolved the question of whether judges had the power to suspend sentences and grant probation without statutory authority. In *Ex Parte United States*, also known as the *Killits* decision, the Court answered this in the negative. Consequently, in 1925, Congress provided an authorizing statute with the Federal Probation Act, and many states did likewise.

Correctional, as well as legal, shifts also occurred. With Augustus, an offender's sins could be reformed through religious discipline and hard work. However, with the rise of Progressivism and social sciences such as psychology, probation officers in the 20th century began to focus less on religious and moral support and more on social problem solving.

W. Jesse Weins
Dakota Wesleyan University

See also Augustus, John; Probation: Early Termination; Recognizance

Further Readings

Abadinsky, Howard. *Probation and Parole: Theory and Practice,* 11th ed. Upper Saddle River, NJ: Pearson, 2011.

Chute, Charles Lionel and Marjorie Bell. *Crime, Courts, and Probation*. New York: Macmillan, 1956.

Dressler, David. *Practice and Theory of Probation and Parole*. New York: Columbia University Press, 1951.

Mair, George. *A Short History of Probation*. Cullompton, UK: Willan, 2008.

PROBATION AND PAROLE: INTENSIVE SUPERVISION

Intensive probation or parole supervision is an intermediate sanction designed to provide close scrutiny of convicted offenders whose offenses have been declared too serious for regular probation or parole while they are supervised in the community. Intensive supervision probation/parole can be divided into three categories: prison diversion, enhanced probation, and enhanced parole. The goal of prison diversion is to limit the number of offenders who enter prison. Enhanced probation and enhanced parole allow for specially selected offenders who have been deemed too serious for regular probation or parole and require closer supervision.

Intensive supervision probation (ISP) refers to an alternative sentence program for offenders who have been convicted of a felony. Instead of being sent to prison, the convicted offender is placed on a suspended sentence and is supervised in the community. Intensive supervision parole (also called ISP) is designed for offenders who have served part of their sentence in prison but are then given early release to serve the remainder of their sentence in the community. While under ISP, both types of offenders are closely monitored by an intensive supervision probation/parole officer. The offender is often referred to as a client while under ISP supervision.

History of ISP Programs

California initially introduced an intensive supervision program in 1950 as a form of parole. Other states, such as New Jersey and Kentucky, began their own intensive supervision programs in the 1960s. Originally, the focus of these programs was to improve the effectiveness of probation and parole, with rehabilitation being the main goal. It was believed that if the right ratio of clients to supervising officers could be achieved, then real change would occur among these offenders. As more states passed community corrections acts in the 1970s and 1980s, more intensive supervision programs began to appear. It soon became apparent that certain higher-risk offenders could benefit from these programs, which would allow them to obtain treatment services within their communities while diverting them from crowded and expensive prisons.

As more high-risk offenders began to be placed in intensive supervision programs, the main goal of the programs shifted from rehabilitation to retribution or punishment. Georgia is believed to be the first state to implement a statewide intensive supervision probation program, in 1974. By 1995, 46 states had implemented similar programs, and today all states have some form of ISP program.

Components of ISP Programs

Although there is no single generic form of ISP, most programs insist that their clients adhere to the following requirements: have multiple weekly contacts with the ISP officer, submit to random drug and alcohol testing, follow the general and specific conditions of probation/parole, participate in relevant treatment programs, be gainfully employed, make restitution payments, abide by a curfew, and perhaps do community service. Sometimes, clients may be placed on home confinement or electronic monitoring while they are on ISP supervision.

When clients are initially placed on ISP, they are expected to have at least five face-to-face contacts with the ISP officer per week. These visits may take place at the officer's office, the client's home, or the client's place of work. The ISP officer works closely with a surveillance officer to make sure his or her clients are abiding by their curfews, that random alcohol and drug testing is occurring, that clients are attending treatment programs, and that clients are showing up for work. Additionally, an ISP officer will work in conjunction with local law-enforcement agencies to conduct weekly checks of local arrest records. ISP officers carry smaller caseloads than regular probation or parole officers to allow them to perform frequent and intensive supervision of their clients. An average caseload for an ISP officer is around 28 cases per officer, versus a regular probation/parole officer, who may carry caseloads of anywhere from 60 to more than 300 cases. Caseloads may consist of either juvenile or adult offenders.

Results of ISP Supervision

Even though one of the goals of ISP programs was to reduce prison overcrowding, ISP has not alleviated prison overcrowding. Another goal of ISP programs was to reduce recidivism rates. However, most studies have found no significant difference of recidivism rates between ISP offenders and comparable offenders who did not receive ISP supervision. Intensive supervision programs are less expensive than prison, but they do not save as much money as originally thought, partly because of the phenomenon known as net widening. Net widening is the overlapping of criminal sanctions. Offenders who would not have been sent to prison are now added to ISP supervision simply because the program exists. However, ISP does appear to be more effective than regular probation or parole in meeting offenders' needs, and there does appear to be a correlation between participating in treatment and employment programs and having lower recidivism rates. One of the more important functions that ISP programs fulfill is to provide an alternative to prison. ISP is an intermediate punishment that is stricter than regular probation or parole but not as severe as prison.

The Future of ISP Supervision Programs

ISP remains a viable alternative option for offenders who are high-risk, have extensive treatment needs, and are not suitable for regular probation or parole supervision, but who are still not serious enough to require incarceration. As more and more high-risk offenders are placed in ISP programs, more technical violations should be expected because of the extra surveillance. However, when treatment and employment programs are added to surveillance, recidivism rates do decrease, indicating that these programs can fulfill their goals of diverting offenders from prison, thus saving the taxpayers money, while at the same time actually rehabilitating certain offenders, which helps to reduce recidivism rates.

Phyllis E. Berry
Washburn University

See also Community Corrections and Sanctions; Community Corrections as an Alternative to Imprisonment

Further Readings

Bennett, Lawrence A. "Practice in Search of a Theory: The Case of Intensive Supervision—an Extension of an Old Practice." *American Journal of Criminal Justice*, v.12 (1988).

Bulton, B., E. Latessa, A. Stichman, and L. F. Travis. "The State of ISP: Research and Policy Implications." *Federal Probation*, v.61/4 (1997).

Byrne, James. "The Future of Intensive Probation Supervision." *Crime and Delinquency*, v.36/1 (1990).

Byrne, James, Arthur Lurigio, and Christopher Baird. "The Effectiveness of the New Intensive Supervision Programs." *Research in Corrections*, v.2/2 (1989).

Fulton, B., P. Gendreau, and M. Paparozzi. "APPA's (American Probation and Parole Association) Prototypical Intensive Supervision Program: ISP (Intensive Supervision Program) as It Was Meant to Be." *Perspectives*, v.19/2 (1995).

Lipchitz, J. W. "Back to the Future: An Historical View of Intensive Probation Supervision." *Federal Probation*, v.50/2 (1986).

Petersilia, Joan. "A Decade of Experimenting With Intermediate Sanctions: What Have We Learned?" *Corrections Management Quarterly*, v.3/4 (1999).

Petersilia, Joan. *Expanding Options for Criminal Sentencing.* Santa Monica, CA: Rand, 1987.

Petersilia, Joan. *Reforming Probation and Parole in the 21st Century.* Lanham, MD: American Correctional Association, 2002.

Petersilia, Joan and Susan Turner. "Comparing Intensive and Regular Supervision for High Risk Probationers: Early Results From an Experiment in California." *Crime and Delinquency,* v.36/1 (1990).

Petersilia, Joan and Susan Turner. "Intensive Probation and Parole." In *Crime and Justice: An Annual Review of Research,* Michael Tonry, ed. Chicago: University of Chicago Press, 1993.

PROBATION AND PAROLE FEES

The rise of probation and parole rates in the United States has had the effect of belaboring state criminal justice institutions. Already steward to the largest incarcerated population in world history, the United States also manages more than 5 million individuals on probation or parole. Costs of probation and parole services have skyrocketed. To cope, many states have turned to assigning fees to probationers and parolees for the services that they receive.

Development

States in significant numbers began to turn to charging probation and parole fees in the 1990s. The establishment and expansion of these fees has corresponded to a period of great pressure on correctional systems to maintain programs and services. Community corrections officers have found themselves managing more and more offenders. In addition, many American taxpayers are embracing a "pay your own way" mentality. From this perspective, the cost of punishment should be borne by the offender.

The method of setting and imposing fees varies with jurisdiction. Some programs use a day fee, some use a weekly fee, and some use other intervals, whereby a probationer or parolee makes regular flat-rate payments to an office of community corrections. Others charge by service, sometimes only for specific services and at other times for the whole range. These fees are generally chosen from within a range set by the legislature and often are set as a proportion of the probationer's or parolee's net income.

Alternatively, they may be set to be commensurate to the offense involved. Under such a system, a person convicted of a felony pays more than one convicted of a misdemeanor.

Arguments Pro and Con

Proponents of instituting fees for probation and parole argue that fees are an easy way for states to regain revenue spent on correctional programs and services. The average cost of incarceration in the United States is about $23,000 per offender annually (some estimates are even higher), and the average cost of community corrections, between $1,250 and $2,750 per offender annually. By requiring probationers and parolees to pay a fee for services, states can reimburse themselves for services and may thus be able to provide more services or services of better quality and effectiveness.

Community corrections fees may also be easier to obtain than fees for serving prison time. While probationers and parolees may be deterred from not paying by threat of a technical violation of their community corrections conditions, prisoners who fail to pay their fees can be threatened only with further imprisonment, which is less successful as a deterrent. Moreover, states may be encouraged to increase rates of community corrections and, by extension, decrease rates of incarceration. Probation or parole may become more appealing alternatives than incarceration if states can be incentivized to use them as a way of gaining revenue, especially since revenue from prisoner fees is so much harder to obtain.

For some critics of the practice, this is less of a benefit than a drawback. While some see increased reliance on community corrections as positive, others see it as negative, insofar as some offenders who would otherwise have been incarcerated may be released on probation simply as a cost-reducing mechanism, rather than on the merits of that individual's ability to restore himself or herself through community corrections. There is also some worry that probation and parole fees will compete with other forms of revenue charges for offenders: those related to restitution and fines. Restitution for victims, critics argue, is more important to maintain, and the need to pay fees for probation and parole services may divert money away from victims and toward the state. In addition, in some cases fees turn probation officers into reluctant debt collectors, thus limiting their ability to supervise and help offenders.

Opponents of instituting fees for probation and parole also argue that fees create a barrier to offender reentry into society. Most of these charges have no relationship to the traditional penal goals of punishment, deterrence, and rehabilitation. They are intended to raise money for states' general funds but often fail to do so, because so many probationers and parolees are too poor to afford the fees. The fees become uncollectable, and the probationers and parolees accumulate debts that seem to be arbitrary. These debts add to the challenging stigma of conviction, and offenders striving to restore themselves to their communities have difficulty establishing a state of economic stability while trying to pay them off. To the extent that this instability contributes to recidivism, the imposition of probation and parole fees upon the indigent may actually lead to increased incarceration and subsequent expenses.

For these and other reasons, some states have abolished probation and parole fees. Others have created categorical exemptions, which recognize that many charges of community corrections are unable to pay their fees, or have replaced fees with community service requirements.

Ronak Shah
Ellen Dwyer
Indiana University, Bloomington

See also Financial Penalties; Probation: Administration Models; Restitution

Further Readings

Diller, Rebekah et al. "Maryland's Parole Supervision Fee: A Barrier to Reentry." 2009. http://brennan.3cdn.net/fbee4fbc0086ec8804_4tm6bp6oa.pdf (Accessed July 2011).

Olson, D. E. and G. F. Ramker. "Crime Does Not Pay, but Criminals May: Factors Influencing the Imposition and Collection of Probation Fees." *The Justice System Journal*, v.22/1 (2001).

Ring, C. R. "Probation Supervision Fees: Shifting Costs to the Offender." *Federal Probation*, v.53/2 (June 1989).

Ruback, R. B. "The Imposition of Economic Sanctions in Philadelphia: Costs, Fines, and Restitution." *Federal Probation*, v.68/1 (2004).

Wheeler, G. R. et al. "The Effects of Probation Service Fees on Case Management Strategy and Sanctions." *Journal of Criminal Justice*, v.17/1 (1989).

Probation Mentor Home Program

The Probation Mentor Home Program was established in Allen County, Indiana, in 1990 to provide temporary foster care to juvenile delinquents between the ages of 10 and 17. The purpose of the program was to establish a supportive collaboration among temporary mentor parents, natural parents, the school system, and the Juvenile Probation Department in order to treat at-risk juveniles in the community rather than send them to secure institutions. The program was designed for the logical reason of easing budget constraints, but it also was intended to prevent youths from being exposed to the detrimental prisonlike conditions of state facilities for juvenile delinquents. Funded by the Indiana Criminal Justice Planning Agency, it was created and executed by a county advisory committee and became the first program of its kind to integrate foster care with a rehabilitative philosophy. The Probation Mentor Home Program was thus an innovative development in community corrections, foundational in the advancement of alternatives to incarceration for delinquent youths.

Research conducted in the 1970s demonstrated that the vast majority of youths could be effectively managed outside institutional confinement. Addressing these findings, a few states adopted alternatives-to-incarceration programs for youths, which provided models for the Probation Mentor Home Program. The Massachusetts Department of Youth Services developed structured community-based programs such as foster care and group home placements for low-level youth offenders, as well as secure programs for violent and repeat youth offenders, in response to reports of abuse and insufficient treatment programs in juvenile facilities. Evaluation studies indicated that recidivism rates for youths released from alternative programs were some of the lowest in the country, far lower than those for youths released from juvenile facilities in Massachusetts. Additionally, the alternative programs proved much more cost-efficient than placement in secure juvenile facilities. In the 1980s, St. Louis implemented a similar alternative model for juveniles that was able to reduce costs and lower the recidivism rates of adjudicated youths. The costs of St. Louis's foster care program were drastically

Adolescents considered for the Probation Mentor Home Program as an alternative to being sent to secure institutions included youth who were institutionalized and those with potential delinquency problems. (Photos.com)

lower than its institutional costs, and a majority of juveniles who completed the program were able to return home without further legal intervention. The success of these programs, coupled with Allen County's ongoing financial burdens in the 1980s, led the Juvenile Probation Department in Fort Wayne, Indiana, to take steps to develop its own alternative-to-incarceration program to impede the process of housing juveniles in expensive secure state facilities.

In January 1989, the advisory committee, which consisted of probation department officials and representatives from the mayor's office, county auditor's office, school system, commissioner's office, foster parent's association, social services agencies, an insurance corporation, and law firms, as well as the county council and a professor, convened to begin the design of the program. The advisory committee formed seven subcommittees to oversee and address potential challenges. During this phase, the policies and procedures of the program were developed and clearly stated in a manual published by the county. No legal barriers under Indiana state law prohibited the development of foster programs

used to house delinquent youths. In January 1990, the program was introduced to the public. Six goals were identified: to avoid the practice of institutionalization through the use of community resources; to create an environment in which the juvenile has a focused treatment plan supported by the natural family, mentor family, and probation department; to integrate the natural family into the process of addressing behavioral concerns; to return the juvenile to his or her natural home after one semester of school; to reduce juvenile recidivism; and last, to reallocate resources from institutional placement to community supervision. In order for a juvenile to be deemed eligible to participate in the program, he or she had to be enrolled in an educational program or be employed at least part-time and be found in need of a residence outside the natural home that would be conducive to the mission of the program.

The responsibilities were divided equally among all program participants. Youths were given an active role in the development of their program objectives in order to instill within them a sense of control over the process. The natural families of the youths were to be involved throughout the process by maintaining contact with their children, participating in program activities, and ensuring that the children could return to a positive home environment at the conclusion of the program. In addition to providing a secure environment for the child, each mentor family was tasked with improving the child's social functioning, maintaining records, and tracking the juvenile's progression over the six-month span. The Juvenile Probation Department was in charge of referring juveniles to mentor homes, training mentor families, and implementing the program, as well as ensuring the credibility of the program among collaborating officials. Last, the "mentor home coordinator" and the "mentor home probation officer" served as accessible resources for mentor families and advocated for the child.

Despite significant planning efforts in the identification, referral, recruitment, and selection of juveniles as well as in the training procedures for mentor families, the program experienced delays in its implementation and operation. The Probation Mentor Home Program was designed to have the first juvenile placed by January 1990 and 25 juveniles placed in mentor homes by the third year of implementation. Instead, the first placement did not occur until June 1990. No formal evaluations of the program have been published, and Allen County Juvenile Probation has since discontinued this program. However, mentoring has remained an integral component of alternatives-to-incarceration programs for youths nationwide.

Lisa Marie Vasquez
John Jay College of Criminal Justice,
City University of New York
Douglas N. Evans
Indiana University, Bloomington

See also Community Corrections as an Alternative to Imprisonment; Costs of Community Corrections; Juvenile and Youth Offenders; Juvenile Probation Officers; Residential Programs for Juveniles

Further Readings

Abadinsky, Howard. *Probation and Parole: Theory and Practice*, 11th ed. Upper Saddle River, NJ: Pearson, 2011.

Galaway, Burt, Richard W. Nutter, Joe Hudson, and Malcolm Hill. "Specialist Foster Family Care for Delinquent Youth." *Federal Probation*, v.59/19 (1995).

Heard, Chinita. "The Preliminary Development of the Probation Mentor Home Program: A Community-Based Model." *Federal Probation*, v.54/4 (1990).

PROBATION OFFICERS

Probation is a conditional release that a guilty party receives from the court in lieu of incarceration. The probationer is supervised by a probation officer who represents the state or federal government. This is distinguished from parole, which is a conditional release from prison and requires that the parolee meet certain conditions and meet with a parole officer. Probation officers serve many functions and provide a wide variety of additional services, most of which are unknown to the public. In some states, the same agency, usually under the rubric "community corrections," handles both probation and parole, and officers may serve either function. Probation services are handled on the state executive level 75 percent of the time and on the judicial level the other 25 percent of the time. The roles of both juvenile and adult probation officers are very complex. The supervision of adults and the supervision of juveniles differ in many respects, and the former will be the focus of this description.

Duties of a Probation Officer

The probation officer has an extremely influential role in the criminal justice process. Once a defendant has been convicted, the judge instructs the probation officer (PO) to write a pre-sentence investigation (PSI) report. Writing the PSI may be very time-consuming and must be very exact, for it contains a full background report on the offender, his or her crime, his or her attitude toward the crime, and, most important, suggestions for treatment and accompanying recommendations for the sentence. In the process of writing the PSI, the PO considers what the judge is likely to accept, the availability of facilities, and the needs of the offender. The judge will accept the PSI recommendations between 66 and 95 percent of the time, as the PO is a part of the courtroom work group that interacts with the judge on a continuing basis. In some ways, therefore, it can be said that the PO has a quasi-judicial function.

In addition to the PO, a criminal justice officer supervises the progress of the probationer in the community. In that context, he or she will visit the offender's home, place of employment, and school and keep track of his or her associates. Because of huge caseloads, however, this approach is not practical with all probationers, and most probationers report to the PO in his or her office on a monthly basis. Some low-risk probationers may be required only to call the PO at stated intervals. Notwithstanding, probationers are always subject to search and regular and random drug testing. POs do not need warrants to search a probationer's room or quarters, and intensive probation units do this regularly. POs are more involved with offenders than any other person or agency in the criminal justice process.

POs are charged with ensuring that probationers meet required conditions of their conditional release. This means that the probationer must stay employed, keep the PO informed of his or her current address, and not leave the jurisdiction without permission. The probationer may have to pay fines and restitution; commonly, the probationer will need to fulfill some sort of community service requirement. Additionally, if special problems are indicated, he or she may have to finish high school (or obtain a general equivalency diploma, or GED) or attend substance abuse counseling or anger management classes. All these conditions must be supervised by the PO. Failing to fulfill these conditions or absconding could result in a revocation

An exacting and time-consuming duty of a probation officer's role involves creating pre-sentence investigation (PSI) reports, which must detail not only the offending crime and a full background report of the criminal but suggestions for rehabilitative treatment and recommendations for sentencing. (Photos.com)

hearing. However, revoking a probationer for minor technical violations has a dramatic effect on prison populations and is generally discouraged in most agencies. Probation caseloads are so large—usually more than 115 probationers to one agent as opposed to the ideal ratio of 30:1—that agents scarcely have time or inclination to invoke minor rules and regulations. Revocation hearings are held in court, and the PO must be prepared to defend a recommendation to revoke probation, because that recommendation may send the probationer to prison to finish serving his or her sentence.

Intensive Probation

For selected felons who are judged as a low risk to the community, intensive probation, a popular variation on traditional probation, may be imposed as a condition of probation. This is to divert offenders from prison, but one suspects (since it is substantially cheaper than incarceration) that economics plays the decisive role in creating such regimes. Programs of this type generally entail the use of specially trained officers with low caseloads of 40 or fewer. The officer sets specific objectives for the probationer, sees that those objectives are attained, and meets with the probationer as often as five times per week. Probationers are usually assigned to community service obligations as well as being required to stay gainfully employed. A mandatory curfew is

imposed, as are both regular and unannounced tests for substance abuse. Those probationers who do not follow conditions of probation or who reoffend are quickly back in court for revocation hearings.

Intensive supervision may produce seemingly paradoxical effects in terms of recidivism. Since rates of recidivism vary little between intensive supervision probation (ISP) probationers and non-ISP probationers, one might assume that ISP does not really work. However, perhaps it works all too well, in that the PO is more likely to catch the probationer in a minor technical violation because of the higher level of overall supervision. Furthermore, ISP-oriented officers are probably more likely to revoke probationers on technical grounds than would a PO not in the program.

Becoming a Probation Officer

Officers are usually selected through merit-based civil service–type examinations. Those who pass the test are ranked on order of performance. Education plays an important part in the process; in most states, officers need a bachelor's degree in social work, criminal justice, or psychology. Many supervisors prefer to hire those with a master's degree, and an advanced degree is a necessity for advancement. Political considerations sometimes play a part in hiring decisions, and having served an internship or worked as a volunteer in the agency can be a critical advantage. Other departments simply appoint officers, a practice that is obviously subject to political manipulation. In general, counseling or criminal justice agency experience is considered desirable and can sometimes substitute for educational requirements.

Once selected, the officer typically undergoes various weeks of training. Skills in report writing, investigation, interviewing, revocation and arrest procedures, communications, diversity sensitivity, and first-aid techniques are typically taught. Firearms training and certification are increasingly important, as POs today are typically armed. Moreover, armed officers no longer use the snub-nosed but low-powered .38 of yesteryear; they are more often armed with 9-millimeter police-issue sidearms. Some officers who are involved in revocation units may have to be certified to use automatic weapons and shotguns. In service, training is ongoing and may involve 40 hours in residence at a state criminal justice training facility.

Probation jobs are considered highly desirable by criminal justice majors and criminology educators, for several reasons. The job is not as physically dangerous as police work, much of the work is clerical, and the clientele are generally cooperative. Another advantage is that coworkers are well educated, some with higher degrees, and within the agency there is generally enthusiasm for the mission. Probation officers also are able to interact with court personnel and become part of the courtroom work group, an elite group within the criminal justice process.

Francis Frederick Hawley
Western Carolina University

See also Juvenile Probation Officers; Probation Officers: Job Stress

Further Readings

Abadinsky, Howard. *Probation and Parole: Theory and Practice*, 11th ed. Upper Saddle River, NJ: Pearson, 2011.

Clear, Todd R., George F. Cole, and Michael D. Reisig. *American Corrections*, 9th ed. Belmont, CA: Thomson Wadsworth, 2010.

Petersilia, J. "Probation in the United States." *Crime and Justice*, v.22 (1997).

Probation Officers: Job Stress

Probation officers supervise convicted criminals in the community. It is their duty to enforce the conditions set by the sentencing court, to protect people in the community from the convicted offenders, and to assist the offenders with treatment and rehabilitation. Successfully fulfilling all of these roles can lead to a great deal of stress for probation officers. Stressors range from the duties of the work itself to finding a balance between work and home life.

Probation officers report one of their main sources of frustration and stress as an overwhelming caseload. It is common for probation officers to supervise between 50 and 100 or more offenders at one time. The offenders' crimes range from nonviolent misdemeanor offenses, such as driving under the influence of alcohol (DUI), to violent felony offenses, such as aggravated sexual abuse of a child. Frequently, probation officers complain of being overworked or feeling as though they cannot provide adequate supervision and assistance to each offender because of the lack of time. The probation officer's attention is typically directed to those offenders with the most serious problems at any particular time. Offenders who are not in immediate need of corrective action are frequently neglected because of the officer's time constraints. Officers also worry about the possibility that an offender might hurt or kill someone while on supervision. This is a huge burden to carry, and it can cause a great deal of stress in the life of a probation officer.

An overload of paperwork accompanied by looming deadlines is another cause of stress for probation officers. Every contact, interaction, and attempt for each individual case must be documented in order to demonstrate that the probation officer is fulfilling the duties of his or her job. In addition, this documentation may serve as a basis for a petition to revoke probation or a petition for early release from supervision. Thus, ongoing documentation of contacts made with the offender and collateral contacts is of utmost importance.

Policies and procedures in the probation office are continuously changing. Furthermore, federal, state, and local laws change on a yearly basis. It can be challenging and stressful for an officer to remain current on the laws, regulations, and policies that determine how they must carry out their work.

Institutional corrections and community corrections are both male-dominated. Terry Wells and colleagues found that female probation officers at the state level tend to experience more stress than do their male colleagues. This heightened stress may be due, in part, to sexual harassment and gender discrimination at work. Other factors increasing the level of stress for both male and female probation officers are lower levels of formal education, a lower degree of work experience, and low involvement in the decision making of the agency.

A stressor for probation officers who deal primarily or exclusively with juveniles is often the irresponsibility of the adolescents' parents. All too frequently, parents do not hold their children accountable for violating probation. In the most extreme cases, parents themselves are very poor role models in that they show little regard for the law. At times a juvenile probation officer may feel as though the person he or she is responsible for is the adult in the life of the adolescent offender.

The effects of stress can take many forms. Probation officers may take sick leave when in reality they are not ill. Many people in the helping professions call this a "mental health day" and see it as vital to helping them manage the pressures of their work and avoid burnout. Compassion fatigue, a form of burnout, occurs when a probation officer becomes hardened to the specific circumstances of individuals. The officers feel as though they have seen and heard every imaginable horror story and, as a means of self-protection, begin to detach themselves emotionally from the people whom they have been hired to help. Headaches, stomachaches, backaches, and other somatic complaints are also common. Some of these ailments are real and some are imagined. Regardless of whether they are real, however, the fact remains that many emerge as a result of the stressors of the occupation.

As a means of reducing or coping with stress, probation officers may abuse alcohol or drugs or engage in compulsive gambling, shopping, or over-eating. All of these behaviors have negative long-term consequences; however, those who engage in them receive some temporary relief, which may be enough to keep them repeating the behavior.

Probation officers can engage in a number of healthy stress-reduction activities, both at work and at home. One of the main stress relievers is exercise. Going for a run or an hour of exercise at the gym on a regular basis can alleviate stress, boost endorphins, and help to put things in perspective. Officers also report spending quality time with their significant others, families, and friends as a way to release pressure. This can be especially beneficial when the time spent with others involves some form of physical activity. Playing with children or pets can have a calming effect and allow probation officers to distance themselves from work. Spending time with people who are not constantly demanding help and attention can have an uplifting effect on the officers' mood and outlook on life.

Talking to family and friends about the pressures of work can also help alleviate the pressures of this type of employment. Another way to reduce stress is to talk to other probation officers about the pressures of work. Hearing how other probation officers deal with similar issues, both personally and professionally, can serve as a valuable bonding tool and provide a catharsis for all parties involved. If talking to family, friends, and coworkers does not provide enough relief from the pressures of work, the probation officer may wish to engage the services of a professional therapist. A good therapist can help the officer with relaxation techniques as well as methods to reduce or cope with stress at work and at home. Finally, organizing and prioritizing work duties can be very beneficial when looking to reduce stress. Keeping a schedule, limiting distractions, and focusing on the most important tasks first all serve to limit frustration.

Probation officers deal with an inordinate amount of stress on a regular basis as a part of their work duties. An officer who can effectively handle his or her stress will not only be a more effective probation officer but also a happier and healthier person.

Brenda Donelan
Northern State University

See also Caseload and Workload Standards; Field Visits; Juvenile Probation Officers; Probation Officers

Further Readings

Lee, Won-Jae et al. "The Effect of Participatory Management on Internal Stress, Overall Job Satisfaction, and Turnover Rate Among Federal Probation Officers." *Federal Probation*, v.73/1 (2009).

Patterson, Bernie L. "Job Experience and Perceived Job Stress Among Police, Correctional, and Probation/Parole Officers." *Criminal Justice and Behavior*, v.19/3 (1992).

Pitts, Wayne J. "Educational Competency as an Indicator of Occupational Stress for Probation and Parole Officers." *American Journal of Criminal Justice*, v.32/1 (2007).

Slate, Risdon N. et al. "Opening the Manager's Door: State Probation Officer Stress and Perceptions of Participation in Workplace Decision Making." *Crime and Delinquency*, v.49/4 (2003).

Wells, Terry et al. "Gender Matters: Differences in State Probation Officer Stress." *Journal of Contemporary Criminal Justice*, v.22/1 (2006).

Project Safeway

Project Safeway began in Chicago, Illinois, in the early 1990s and was created through a partnership between the Cook County Adult Probation Department (CCAPD), Treatment Alternatives to Street Crime (TASC), and The Safer Foundation. The program rested on the notion that probation is inherently community-based and should therefore be decentralized to create stronger links among community members, nonprofit agencies, community organizations, and probation. According to N. L. Martin and A. J. Lurigio, one of the main strategies of Project Safeway was to make probation convenient by establishing one-stop community-based reporting centers and building a network of relationships to assist probationers as they began restoring their lives. The program also reduced institutional overcrowding by targeting some drug offenders who were sentenced to periodic incarceration or work release programs. These offenders were released from jail and sentenced to home confinement and probation, according to J. Robinson and Lurigio.

Funding for Project Safeway was procured through a grant from the Chicago Public Housing Authority and federal funding related to the Weed and Seed program. The initial grant was $88,368. Weed and Seed is a federal initiative of the U.S. Department of Justice. The mission of Weed and Seed is to "weed out" violent criminals, drug offenders, and gangs in disorganized neighborhoods while also "seeding" these areas with the necessary resources for economic viability and community efficacy. Project Safeway touched on the "weed" mandate of this philosophical movement through the close community contacts established by probation officers housed in community reporting centers. These relationships provided probation officers with critical information about the adjustment of probationers, information not normally available through mandatory monthly reporting at an office location far from the probationer's community. By developing more intimate relationships with community members and local agencies, probation officers were better able to provide the surveillance needed to "weed out" noncompliant probationers. The primary programmatic focus of Project Safeway, however, was to "seed" these selected communities with services that would then be easily accessible to probationers most in need of them.

Lurigio and Martin note that the community model of community corrections provided the theoretical underpinnings for the development of Project Safeway. This approach, according to P. Wack, embraces the idea that the "community must be given the opportunity to be equal partners in the justice system. Likewise, the community must recognize not only its right to safe streets and homes but also its responsibility for creating them." Developed during a time when community sentiment throughout the United States demanded more punitive sentencing of offenders, Project Safeway resisted the "get tough" approach to criminal justice, instead focusing on the integral role of the community in treating offenders. Community-based reporting sites facilitated connections and familiarity among probation officers, community members, agencies, churches, schools, and businesses. These relationships allowed officers to develop and coordinate community services integral to the successful rehabilitation of offenders.

According to Leanne Fiftal Alarid and Rolando V. del Carmen, probation is the most widely used sanction in the United States. During the 1990s, as reported by the *Chicago Sun-Times*, Cook County supervised approximately 35,000 probationers each year. While Chicago comprises approximately 78 identifiable communities, the traditional provision of probation services in Cook County had required probationers to report to the main office, located at 26th Street and California on the South Side of Chicago. In addition to holding the philosophical assumption that probation should be community-based, Project Safeway addressed very practical considerations. The geographic breadth of Chicago in addition to extended periods of inclement weather and the cost of public transportation made reporting a considerable challenge for a significant number of probationers. Project Safeway was organized into three decentralized centers in various Chicago neighborhoods: the Ida B. Wells public housing complex on the South Side, the Near North Side, and the West Side community of Lawndale. Each community in which Project Safeway operated was characterized by a disproportionate percentage of probationers relative to other Chicago communities. The decentralization of these offices allowed probationers easier access to their probation officers, thus facilitating more personal and familiar relationships between clients and providers. The convenience of a neighborhood setting helped probationers feel more comfortable and placed them near other community services that provided counseling for drug and alcohol issues.

Project Safeway offered multiple services for probationers but focused on drug and alcohol evaluation, treatment, and referrals and employment counseling. While the neighborhood centers enhanced the surveillance component of supervising the offenders with convenient drug testing, educational and vocational support services also contributed to the program's rehabilitative focus. A mandatory healthcare fair provided education particularly relevant for probationers with a history of drug dependence. Topics included the transmission of the human immunodeficiency virus (HIV), hepatitis C, and sexually transmitted diseases. Participants also received blood pressure and cholesterol screenings. Project Safeway's job fair provided networking and employment opportunities that probationers might not have received otherwise, given their criminal histories. To help probationers become more marketable, Project Safeway offered classes outlining strategies for job hunting and interviewing, as well as resume courses and courses for the general equivalency diploma (GED).

Families can be profoundly impacted by both parental drug use and contact with the criminal justice system, and Project Safeway offered services to them as well. Mental health and health education services were provided. Annually, Project Safeway invited public health providers to talk about the importance of mental health and its place in the daily lives of probationers and their loved ones. Project Safeway offered after-school programs featuring tutoring and counseling sessions for children of probationers to keep them off the streets. As a part of its annual Back to School Jamboree, Project Safeway provided school supplies to the children of probationers. Also on hand at the Jamboree were healthcare providers, who administered immunizations to children who had not yet received them.

The Cook County Adult Probation Department conducted research comparing the effectiveness of probationers receiving services through Project Safeway reporting centers, in comparison to a control group of probationers in the same catchment areas but receiving traditional probation supervision at the main reporting center. According to Lurigio and Martin, the study found that there were fewer nonreporting violations because of the ease of access and services that were provided by Project Safeway.

Project Safeway was discontinued in the late 1990s because of funding constraints.

Tana M. McCoy
Miranda Young
Roosevelt University

See also Community-Based Centers; Cook County Juvenile Court; Neighborhood Probation

Further Readings

Alarid, Leanne Fiftal and Rolando V. del Carmen. *Community-Based Corrections*, 8th ed. Belmont, CA: Thomson Wadsworth, 2011.

Chicago Sun-Times. "City in Brief Section." (August 18, 1996).

Chicago Sun-Times. "Health Class Required for Probation." (May 22, 1993).

Leaf, R., A. J. Lurigio, and N. L. Martin. "Project Safeway: Strengthening Probation's Linkages With the Larger Community." In *Community Corrections: Probation, Parole, and Intermediate Sanctions*, Joan Petersilia, ed. New York: Oxford University Press, 1998.

Lurigio, A. J. and N. L. Martin. "Making 'Community' the Operative Word in Community Corrections." *Corrections Today*, v.59/4 (1997).

Martin, N. L. and A. J. Lurigio. "Project Safeway." In *Restoring Hope Through Community Partnerships: A Handbook for Community Corrections*, B. A. Fulton, ed. Lexington, KY: American Probation and Parole Association, 1996.

Robinson, J. and A. J. Lurigio. "Responding to Overcrowding and Offender Drug Use: How About a Community Corrections Approach?" *Perspectives*, v.4/4 (1990).

Wack, P. "Forging Community Partnerships." *Perspectives* (Winter 1995).

PUBLIC OPINION OF COMMUNITY CORRECTIONS

Public opinion is an important consideration for legislators and agency officials when drafting and implementing policies and practices. The "get tough" movement in criminal justice corresponded with a shift in public attitudes during which retributive sentiments increased and support for rehabilitation faded. Support for modern community correctional initiatives exists but varies based on a number of factors. Most people are not supportive of community sanctions for violent criminals yet are highly supportive of community sanctions for nonviolent property offenders. People also consider the extent of property damage and an offender's criminal past when judging the appropriateness of community sanctions. Greater financial loss and longer criminal records reduce support.

The public views community corrections as alleviating part of the burden and costs associated with incarceration. Community sanctions also offer a blend of punishment and rehabilitation that people find appealing. Today, a major public concerns is the large number of people coming out of prison and returning to society. While the public generally supports efforts to help ex-prisoners in the community, this support has limits. Support diminishes substantially when competition develops between securing resources for reentry programs and securing resources for other social initiatives. In addition, people are much less likely to favor reentry programs when program sites are located near their own residences.

Historical Context

Correctional practices in communities date back to some of the earliest civilizations. Crucifixion and throwing criminals into the Coliseum in Rome were early forms of community punishment. In medieval and early modern Europe, a host of corporal-style punishments could be inflicted on criminals. Whippings, hangings, mutilation, the pillory and stocks, and the ducking stool were common and were brought to America with the colonists. While public opinion studies did not develop on corrections until recently, historians report strong favorable reactions to the use of public punishments. Coliseum audiences cheered as they watched "justice" being administered, and crowds would flock to public executions in the Middle Ages to watch their favorite executioners.

As Western societies progressed and the Enlightenment dawned in Europe and America, the allure of public punishment began to fade. Greater sympathy was directed at those receiving punishment and subjected to public humiliation, and suspicions heightened as to whether government authority was being misdirected and abused. In America, Pennsylvania Quakers were instrumental in limiting the use of public punishment as they pushed for the increased use of humane forms of incarceration coupled with hard labor. By the late 1800s, imprisonment, not the various types of public punishment, would become the prominent sanction for serious criminal offenders.

The prison today is viewed as almost inextricably linked to punishment for the worst criminals in society. Since the penitentiary model took root in the 1800s, the American public seemingly has been highly receptive to its use. The United States was in fact the country where the first prison boom occurred. However, while the prison holds an immutable place in the collective American psyche, dissatisfaction with

its impact on recidivism and realizations of its limitations as a humane alternative to corporal punishment have surfaced with varying intensity over time. The imperfections of the prison spurred a new age of community corrections, which bears little resemblance to its corporal predecessors. In the mid-1800s, probation and parole appeared and were slowly integrated into American justice. Since the 1990s, community corrections has become multidimensional. No longer is community corrections simply probation and parole. It now covers boot camps, halfway houses, intensive supervised probation (ISP), and house arrest with electronic monitoring, along with a wide variety of community treatment programs.

Offense Severity and Support for Community Corrections

People indicate limited support for community sanctions when they are applied to serious violent offenders, such as murderers and rapists. Public safety concerns undoubtedly underlie suspicion of community corrections for violent criminals, as imprisonment offers much greater protection of the general public from physical harm. The extent of harm is important in how crimes involving violence are evaluated. Michael G. Turner and colleagues surveyed residents from the Cincinnati, Ohio, area in 1995 about their preferred sentences for robbers, based on whether physical injury occurred during the robbery. When a robbery transpired with no injury, 24 percent of respondents preferred prison, the remainder advocating some type of community sanction. When injury was inflicted by the robbery, 36 percent of respondents preferred prison over alternative sanctions.

People are quite supportive of community options when applied to nonviolent offenders. A survey of North Carolinians in 1995 by John Doble Research Associates identified an overwhelming proportion of residents who supported the greater use of sentencing alternatives for nonviolent criminals. Specifically, 98 percent favored the greater use of restitution, 97 percent community service and boot camps, 89 percent strict probation, 88 percent treatment and day reporting centers, and 80 percent house arrest. Certain drug offenses received little support. Only about one third of North Carolinians favored alternatives when a man sold $2,000 worth of heroin to undercover cops as a first offense and when a man had a drug addiction and sold $20 of cocaine to officers as a second offense. While drug offenses are technically labeled as nonviolent in official reports, people often associate drug crimes with the violence and personal destruction that may accompany drug distribution.

The severity of the financial loss in property offenses also contributes to feelings about community sanctions. A survey of citizens in New York State by Michael Brown and Preston Elrod published in 1995 found that a majority supported electronic house arrest for those who steal or commit property damage of less than $1,000. In contrast, only about 20 percent support this sanction when the value or damage exceeds $1,000. While the North Carolinians were largely receptive to community corrections for property offenders, only 49 percent were supportive when the value of embezzlement reached $200,000, even as a first offense.

A problem in assessing support for community sanctions is the fact that many people have little knowledge about existing community options. A 1991 study in Delaware by John Doble and associates found that people's reactions to alternatives for punishment grow more positive as they learn about the alternatives. In this study, Delawareans completed questionnaires containing 23 hypothetical scenarios covering a range of offenses (both violent and nonviolent). Participants were asked whether the offender in each scenario should receive prison or probation. After completing this questionnaire, the participants watched a 22-minute film that covered the extent of prison overcrowding and documented alternative sanctions, including ISP, restitution, boot camp, community service, and house arrest. The study participants next discussed the video with a "neutral moderator" for approximately 90 minutes. Participants were then asked to fill out a second questionnaire that revisited the same offender scenarios; on this questionnaire, they could again choose between probation and prison, as well as the five alternative sanctions. On the first test, the sample wanted to incarcerate 17 of the 23 offenders; but only five of the offenders were to be imprisoned during the second test. Violent offenders and chronic drug dealers still received prison terms.

Who Supports Community Sanctions?

People are supportive of community alternatives for a number of reasons. One of the most notable is that the public appreciates the burdens imposed on the criminal justice system and views community sanctions as a means for alleviating organizational strain. A survey of Vermont residents in 1999 by Judith Greene and John Doble found that community-based reparative boards were viewed as a mechanism for reducing prison overcrowding and easing the burden on criminal court processing. Prison crowding and heavy court caseloads are stark realities in modern American justice, and the public sees community options as providing a pressure valve to release tension in an overstressed system. Similarly, potential cost savings drive support for community sanctions. Sending a person to prison costs about $25,000 a year. The expenses involved in placing an offender in a community setting typically are not nearly as high.

Community sanctions appeal by offering a combination of punitive and rehabilitative features. House arrest, for example, restricts freedom and mobility, which serves to incapacitate and punish. At the same time, offenders on house arrest can still participate in treatment programs and rehabilitative services. Elrod and Brown observed that New Yorkers who supported house arrest viewed this dual function as an asset. New York residents who supported house arrest for minor offenders felt that increasing the prison population would fail to reduce crime, and those supporting house arrest for serious offenders believed that imprisonment actually increased recidivism. As a result, support for house arrest was partially fueled by the expectation that sending offenders to prison did no good or made the situation worse.

The capability of community options to fit the needs and circumstances of offenders more precisely also factors into support. Delawareans appreciated the flexibility afforded to judges through community alternatives. In the North Carolina survey, preferred alternatives varied with the type of offense committed. Treatment centers were preferred in cases involving most alcohol and drug crimes. Driving with a suspended license one year after a drunk driving conviction warranted community service. A more punitive measure, such as boot camp, was preferred for more serious crimes, including burglary and statutory rape.

One issue that detracts from support is the leniency associated with community corrections. Julian Roberts's 2002 review of international reports on opinion toward community sanctions concluded that people across the world were concerned about the perceived lack of severity in punishment. This sentiment was expressed in a survey about boot camps published in 1990 by Phillip Reichel and

Angela Gauthier. The aspect of boot camps identified as most troubling to the respondents was that offenders would avoid the standard term of imprisonment normally given for many types of crimes.

Probation and Parole: The Cornerstones of Community Corrections

Although a variety of community sanctions now exists, most are administered under the guidance of probation and parole departments. More than 4 million Americans are on probation and approximately 800,000 are on parole. The 1996 National Opinion Survey on Crime and Justice, reported by Timothy Flanagan, identified that only 26 percent of Americans had substantial confidence in their local probation offices. Approval of probation and parole, however, varies by location. State comparisons conducted by Greene and Doble show that Vermont and New Hampshire residents in the late 1990s had similar feelings about probation and parole. Thirty-seven percent of Vermont citizens and 40 percent of New Hampshire residents felt their probation and parole departments were doing good or excellent work. In contrast, only 8 percent of Pennsylvanians had such positive feelings toward probation and parole.

The variation in perceptions of parole and probation could be linked to the specific approaches taken by offices in different states. The 1996 national opinion survey showed that a slight majority of Americans believed that community corrections programs are evidence of a lenient criminal justice system. On the other hand, a majority were positive about the use of community supervision when it involved making probationers work to repay victims and perform community service.

Although leniency is a concern for people, a poll in Massachusetts by Cheryl Roberts and her colleagues in 2005 indicates some tolerance for parole offenders. For example, 64 percent of Massachusetts residents felt that a parolee who misses an appointment with the parole supervisor but has a legitimate family-related excuse should receive a warning, 24 percent felt the supervisor should supervise the parolee more closely, and only 2 percent stated the parolee should go back to prison. Advocacy for leniency, however, had strict limits. Only 16 percent favored a warning, and 43 percent advocated closer parole supervision when a missed appointment was not justified with an appropriate excuse. Only 5 percent elected to give a warning when a parolee

was caught stealing $100 of merchandise, and 38 percent favored returning this parolee to prison.

Calls to toughen probation and parole led to the creation of intensive supervision programs, which focus more resources and attention on the highest-risk cases. As with other community-based initiatives, support for these intensive programs depends on the type of crime involved. A 1992 article by Jeffrey Senese featuring a sample of northern Indiana residents found that 84 percent of people were supportive of intensive probation for minor thefts and 53 percent for major thefts. Support dropped to 47 percent and 41 percent for drug use and DUIs, respectively. Only 6 percent supported intensive probation for murder, 8 percent for rape, and 12 percent for assault. These latter figures reinforce the thesis that, regardless of the intensity of community supervision, punishment for some criminals just does not fit perceptually within a community framework.

Support for Prisoners Who Come Home

A growing phenomenon affecting community corrections is the high volume of offenders who are leaving prison and returning to society each year. Although offenders have been released from prisons in America for centuries, the magnitude of the problem has risen to unprecedented levels because of massive increases in prison populations during the past few decades. Communities are being forced to handle an overload of ex-prisoners even as economic conditions have worsened to the lowest point since the Great Depression.

Community residents are clearly concerned about the increasing number of returning ex-prisoners. Barry Krisberg and Susan Marchionna report from a national Zogby poll conducted in 2006 that 57 percent of Americans were fearful about the large volume of people being released from prison. To address the problem, 70 percent favored reentry services for offenders both inside prison and following release. Overwhelmingly the respondents felt that a variety of services were important for successful post-prison adjustment. A majority cited job training, drug treatment, mental health services, family support, mentoring, and housing as "very important" to a successful reintegration back into society. The Second Chance Act, federal legislation that provided funding to assist offenders reentering society, was also supported by 79 percent of Americans, with 40 percent offering strong support.

Although a significant proportion of Americans have advocated general support for reentry, a closer examination of reentry in Missouri by Brett Garland and his colleagues challenges the depth of this support. While 4 out of 5 Missourians in 2008 felt that helping ex-prisoners readjust to society was a good idea, less than 1 out of 5 thought taxes should be raised to improve services for recently released ex-prisoners. Similarly, while a slight majority favored transitional housing for ex-prisoners in their towns, only 18 percent supported this if the housing unit was located in their neighborhood. This illustrates the presence of the "not in my backyard" (NIMBY) syndrome in shaping attitudes toward offenders in the community.

Conflicting values appeared when focus groups in Philadelphia were asked by John Immerwahr and Jean Johnson in 2002 about support for prisoner reentry. Philadelphians wrestled internally by weighing the desire to help and the conviction that certain offenders could experience constructive change against the need to punish and reduce public safety risks. Interestingly, the focus group participants were asked to divide a fictional dollar representing state revenue. When comparing how much should go to prisoner reentry services versus prison costs, the participants overwhelming supported funding reentry. On the other hand, when asked to divide money between reentry and childcare for low-income residents, the vast majority of the money went to childcare. What this indicates is that support for reentry is not a high priority when compared with all the other needs facing state government.

Brett Garland
Missouri State University

See also Attitudes and Myths About Punishment; Boot Camps; Furloughs; Goals and Objectives of Community Corrections; History of Community Corrections; NIMBY Syndrome; Offender Risks; Prediction Instruments; Public Safety and Collaborative Prevention; Recidivism; Risk and Needs Assessment Instruments; Risk Assessment Instruments: Three Generations; Sex Offenders in the Community; Three Strikes and You're Out

Further Readings

Brown, Michael P. and Preston Elrod. "Electronic House Arrest: An Examination of Citizen Attitudes." *Crime and Delinquency*, v.41/3 (1995).

Cullen, Francis T. et al. "Public Opinion About Punishment and Corrections." *Crime and Justice*, v.27 (2000).

Doble, John et al. *Punishing Criminals: The People of Delaware Consider the Options*. New York: The Edna McConnell Clark Foundation, 1991.

Elrod, Preston and Michael P. Brown. "Predicting Public Support for Electronic House Arrest: Results From a New York County Survey." *American Behavioral Scientist*, v.39/4 (1996).

Flanagan, Timothy J. "Community Corrections in the Public Mind." *Federal Probation*, v.60/3 (1996).

Garland, Brett et al. "To What Extent Does the Public Support Prisoner Reentry?" Paper presented at the Annual Meeting of the American Society of Criminology in Washington, DC, 2010.

Giguere, Rachelle and Lauren Dundes. "Help Wanted: A Survey of Employer Concerns About Hiring Ex-Convicts." *Criminal Justice Policy Review*, v.13/4 (2002).

Greene, Judith and John Doble. *Attitudes Toward Crime and Punishment in Vermont: Public Opinion About an Experiment With Restorative Justice*. Washington, DC: National Institute of Justice, 2000.

Hirschfield, Paul J. and Alex R. Piquero. "Normalization and Legitimization: Modeling Stigmatization Attitudes Toward Ex-Offenders." *Criminology*, v.48/1 (2010).

Immerwahr, John and Jean Johnson. *The Revolving Door: Exploring Public Attitudes Toward Prison Reentry*. Washington, DC: Urban Institute, 2002.

John Doble Research Associates. *Crime and Corrections: The Views of the People of North Carolina*. Englewood Cliffs, NJ: John Doble Research Associates, 1995.

Krisberg, Barry and Susan Marchionna. *Attitudes of U.S. Voters Toward Prisoner Rehabilitation and Reentry Policies*. Oakland, CA: National Council on Crime and Delinquency, 2006.

Peter D. Hart Research Associates, Inc. *Changing Public Attitudes Toward the Criminal Justice System: Summary of Findings*. 2002. http://www.soros.org/initiatives/usprograms/focus/justice/articles_publications/puBlications/hartpoll_20020201/Hart-Poll.pdf (Accessed February 2011).

Reichel, Philip L. and Angela Kailey Gauthier. "Boot Camp Corrections: A Public Reaction." In *Issues in Justice: Exploring Policy Issues in the Criminal Justice System*, Roslyn Muraskin, ed. Bristol, IN: Wyndham Hall Press, 1990.

Roberts, Cheryl A. et al. *Rethinking Justice in Massachusetts: Public Attitudes Toward Crime and Punishment*. Boston: The Boston Foundation, 2005.

Roberts, Julian V. "Public Opinion and the Nature of Community Penalties: International Findings." In *Changing Attitudes to Punishment: Public Opinion, Crime and Justice*, Julian V. Roberts and Mike Hough, eds. Portland, OR: Willan, 2002.

Roberts, Julian V. and Loretta J. Stalans. *Public Opinion, Crime, and Criminal Justice*. Boulder, CO: Westview Press, 1997.

Roberts, Julian V. et al. *Penal Populism and Public Opinion: Lessons From Five Countries*. New York: Oxford University Press, 2003.

Senese, Jeffrey D. "Intensive Supervision Probation and Public Opinion: Perceptions of Community Correctional Policy and Practice." *American Journal of Criminal Justice*, v.16/2 (1992).

Turner, Michael G. et al. "Public Tolerance for Community-Based Sanctions." *Prison Journal*, v.77/1 (1997).

PUBLIC SAFETY AND COLLABORATIVE PREVENTION

The release of offenders from American prisons and jails has become a major concern to policy makers, criminal justice scholars, and stakeholder groups representing the community. Data from the Bureau of Justice Statistics show that, per annum, about 600,000 offenders return to the community and face challenges related to healthcare, literacy, and employment. These challenges impede offenders' successful reintegration into the families and neighborhoods to which they are returned.

The theme of 21st-century departments of corrections is the use of community alternatives to incarceration and incapacitation as one way to maintain public safety, reduce recidivism, and mitigate the challenges offenders face when they reenter the community. Statistical data reveal that offenders returned to the community under correctional supervision will violate parole or probation and return to jail or prison within 12 months of release. Many scholars believe that overreliance on incarceration in prison or jail, coupled with high recidivism rates and poor reentry results, necessitates a new approach to both methods of incarceration and offender reentry into the community. The current system is not a benefit to offenders, and guardians of community restoration and public safety argue for community collaboration to reform offender incarceration and reentry policies.

Public Safety

Aspects of researcher Francis T. Cullen's "rehabilitative ideal" place emphasis on public safety. Public safety means protection from and reduction in community fear and violence. Crime-reporting agencies report downward trends in violent crimes, and data from departments of corrections show an overall reduction in violence in correctional facilities. Crime polls by the Pew Trusts and the National Crime Victimization Survey indicate that the *public fear* of crime is omnipresent but incongruous with the national crime statistics.

Why the public fear? The crime lens, or public perception of crime in the community, is influenced by a variety of factors, including the media and public opinion. Some believe that media reports focused on infamous crimes and criminals, such as John Dillinger, the mass murders of Charles Manson, or Amber alerts, focus the crime lens on the notion that offenders do violence when released back to their communities. The public view is that rampant crime is committed by offenders once they are returned to the neighborhoods. Even the rare escapes from prison and jails, which receive an inordinate amount of media attention, can reinforce the public perception that violent offenders are loose in the community and jeopardize public safety.

Consequently, it can be argued that the public perception that violent crime is rampant in society is irrational. Nationwide, departments of corrections house more than 2 million offenders in prisons and jails, and nearly 6 million are under correctional supervision in community therapeutic programs, electronically monitored, sentenced to house arrest, in halfway houses, or committed to work/study release programs and on intensive supervision parole/probation. It is certain that public safety is a priority of corrections, and collaborative partnerships may be a strategy to ensure the protection of the public when offenders are under correctional supervision in the community.

Collaborative Partnerships and Corrections

Offenders' reintegration into the community from which they came must include community involvement. In 2000, federal, state, and local governments, community-based organizations, victims' groups, inmate rights advocates, crime and justice scholars, policy researchers, and the general public engaged in a discourse concerning offender reentry. Discussions centered on identification of factors for successful community reentry to maintain the public safety in geographic areas where offenders are released. Groups such as the Urban Institute, the Annie E. Casey Foundation, the National Governors Association, and the Council of State Governments, as well as representatives of law enforcement and corrections, developed a model for reentry that includes analysis of neighborhoods and how to maintain well-being through community partnerships with local entities. Departments of corrections are increasingly forming partnerships with school districts, for example, to create dropout intervention and prevention programs to address juvenile delinquency and work with police organizations to create police athletic leagues (PALs) that facilitate community restoration and protection.

In the mid-2000s, states including Pennsylvania, Rhode Island, Georgia, Idaho, Massachusetts, Michigan, New Jersey, and Virginia, along with the city of Winston-Salem, North Carolina, began community partnerships with community-based organizations to address offenders' needs while in the community. Research reveals that there is an uptick in partnerships between probation and community organizations in furtherance of the goals of successful reentry of offenders. These partnerships institute and support programs such as community therapeutic centers for drug offenders and subscribe to the notion that probation should take the lead in organizing community partners to ensure that the needs of offenders under correctional supervision are met. Whatever the structure of the partnerships between the departments of corrections and community collaborators, it is essential to make partnerships work and use information from research about "what works."

"What works" research is the evidence for programs that can lead to offenders' success once back in the community and ways of forming lasting partnerships. Cost-efficiency is also necessary to sustain good prevention programs and practices; data collection and evaluation studies are also important. Reentry programs must monitor the results and provide feedback before additional resources can be allocated. Public fear is lessened and offenders' frustration and likelihood to commit violence are reduced through good community partnerships.

Offenders become frustrated when they are returned to their neighborhoods without the skills necessary to meet family and community expectations, such as gainful employment. The link between public safety and community collaboration must be made clear in order to refocus the public crime lens away from fear and toward successful offender reintegration once the offender is released from incarceration and returned to the community.

Kimberley Garth-James
California State University, Sonoma

See also Community Corrections and Sanctions; Community Corrections as an Add-On to Imprisonment; Community Corrections as an Alternative to Imprisonment; Work/Study Release Programs

Further Readings

Baer, Demelza et al. *Understanding the Challenges of Prisoner Reentry: Research Findings From the Urban Institute's Prisoner Reentry Portfolio Justice.* Washington, DC: Urban Institute, 2006.

Cullen, Francis T. "The Twelve People Who Saved Rehabilitation: How the Science of Criminology Made a Difference." *Criminology*, v.43 (2005).

Sieh, W. E. "CHP 10 Public Safety and Collaborative." In *Community Corrections and Human Dignity Prevention.* Sudbury, MA: Jones and Bartlett, 2006.

U.S. Department of Justice. *Corrections Facts.* Washington, DC: Bureau of Justice Statistics, 2010.

PUBLIC SHAMING AS PUNISHMENT

Although criminologists have made a compelling case that incarceration degrades offenders, hardens their antisocial tendencies, and is extraordinarily expensive, imprisonment rates remain high in the United States. Since the 1960s, there has been growing recognition that it makes sense to divert nonviolent and infrequent offenders to probation supervision, halfway houses, work release programs, and other community corrections programs that keep offenders out of prison and as close as possible to their families and job opportunities. As of December 31, 2009, approximately 70 percent of the men and women under correctional supervision were under community supervision, and approximately 30 percent were housed in local jails and state or federal prisons.

It strikes many as paradoxical that the increase in community-based programs that offer an alternative to imprisonment has been accompanied by what seems to be a growing judicial willingness to impose "shaming" or "scarlet letter" punishments on offenders. Convicted offenders have been forced to place bumper stickers on their cars, post signs in their yards, carry signs, or wear T-shirts proclaiming their guilt. Sometimes these punishments are imposed in addition to a jail or prison term, but often they are meted out as an alternative to imprisonment, usually as a condition of probation. This practice raises the following question: When a shaming punishment accompanies a community-based sentence, does it add to the deterrent or rehabilitative effects of the punishment, or does it undermine these laudable goals of punishment by humiliating and stigmatizing the offender?

Shaming Punishments in Early America

The early settlers in North America brought with them a firm belief in the effectiveness of shaming punishments, painful corporal punishments, or a combination of both. More than a dozen offenses, including murder, treason, robbery, and rape, were punishable by death. Corporal punishments that were meant to inflict both public humiliation and intense pain were routinely meted out to vagrants, beggars, petty thieves, Sabbath breakers, and other minor offenders. The whipping post, the branding iron, and the pillory were prominently displayed and frequently employed in the town squares of 17th- and 18th-century America. Political and religious leaders found the pillory (a set of wooden frames with holes for the head, hands, and sometimes the feet) to be an especially versatile device for inflicting a large dose of shame and a requisite measure of pain. The spectacle of a miscreant helpless in its grasp, his head protruding through its beams and his hands through two holes, was thought to educate the public as to the consequences of sinful behavior and to send a deterrent message to both the humiliated lawbreaker and others who might be tempted to stray from the strict tenets of colonial moral standards. Culprits could expect to be pelted with ridicule and insults as well as with sticks and stones.

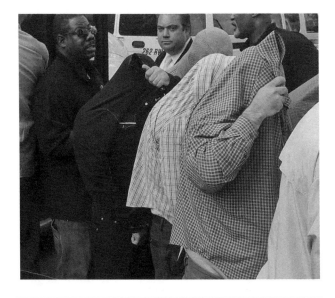

Perpetrators in high-profile criminal cases often conceal their faces from the news media while being booked and processed, a practice that has become known as a "perp walk." Once convicted, there is a trend toward subjecting offenders to a degree of public humiliation as part of their punishment. (Wikimedia)

The more serious misdemeanants were sometimes nailed through their ears to the pillory, branded, and shaved bald.

Branding, either as one part of a public degradation ritual or as a stand-alone punishment, became popular in all of the American colonies. The laws of colonial New Jersey, for example, stipulated that first-offense burglars were to be punished with a T (for "thief") burned into a hand. A second offense called for an R (for "rogue") to be burned into the forehead. A 1662 Maryland law decreed that a person twice convicted of hog stealing was to have an H burned into a shoulder. This law, however, was widely viewed as too lenient and was amended in 1666 to apply to first-offense hog stealers, who were to receive the brand on the forehead. *The Scarlet Letter*, Nathaniel Hawthorne's 1850 novel of punishment in 17th-century Massachusetts, accurately depicted the Puritan practice of forcing adulterous wives to attach an *A*, cut from scarlet cloth, to their upper garments. Others who offended Puritan notions of morality were similarly adorned; blasphemers wore a *B*, paupers a *P*, and drunkards a *D*.

The 1791 ratification of the Bill of Rights, including the Eighth Amendment's prohibition of "cruel and unusual punishments," signaled that America had entered a new era of enlightenment that would lead to doubts about the appropriateness and effectiveness of 16th- and 17th-century methods of punishment. Moreover, changing demographic patterns led to a decline in the use of shaming punishments. As populations increased, people became less closely acquainted with one another. A growing number of people migrated to larger cities characterized by increased anonymity, a greater appreciation of the value of privacy, and a decreasing dependence on close community relationships. These changes undermined the social cohesiveness that enabled shaming punishments and diluted the psychological pain of public punishment. Belief in the deterrent effectiveness of public humiliation crumbled, and shaming punishments all but disappeared for two centuries.

Today's "Scarlet Letter" Punishments

The demise of early American shaming punishments coincided with the development of the penitentiary in the early 19th century. Although questions of the desirability and efficacy of imprisonment inspired vigorous debate, incarceration emerged as the prevailing method of punishing criminals in the years following the Civil War. Today, with some 2.3 million people in prisons and jails and 4.2 million probationers (and 820,000 parolees) under community supervision, prison and probation clearly rank as the dominant societal responses to serious crime.

Two seemingly contradictory trends have developed since the 1980s—increasing pressure to expand alternatives to imprisonment and continuing public insistence that criminal courts must "get tougher" on criminals. Perhaps the most controversial result of these competing impulses is the return of punishments that bear an obvious resemblance to the scarlet-letter punishments of colonial America. To show that they too are exasperated with overly lenient sentences, judges have increasingly resorted to shaming sentences. Sometimes these sentences are stand-alone punishments, but they are imposed as a condition of probation in the majority of cases.

Today, most people convicted of a violent or serious property crime can expect to be sentenced to prison, probation, a work or school release program, community service, fines, victim restitution, or some combination thereof. However, there is a clear trend toward subjecting offenders to some degree of public humiliation as part of their punishment. This has become increasingly acceptable among state and federal trial judges. Since the 1990s, hundreds of shaming punishments have been imposed, many of which have received increased publicity through coverage in print and broadcast media. Stories of bizarre or unusual punishments, of course, are also ubiquitous on the Internet, as any devotee of YouTube knows all too well. In most of these cases, a judge has incorporated a shaming punishment into individualized probation conditions that are chosen to "fit the crime."

Today's shaming punishments often force offenders to carry or wear signs or T-shirts proclaiming their guilt. Convicted shoplifters, for example, have been compelled to stand in front of store entrances attired in a T-shirt reading "I am a thief" or "I got caught stealing." Sometimes the offender must walk on busy sidewalks wearing a sandwich board saying, for example, "I got caught with cocaine" or "I am on felony probation for burglary."

Another common form of shaming punishment is to make offenders place a sign on their property. Sex offenders, for example, have been required to post signs on their home reading "Dangerous sex offender—No children allowed," and people convicted of assault have been ordered to place signs in their yard declaring, "Warning—A violent felon lives here." Drivers convicted of driving while under the influence (DUI) have been forced to affix phosphorescent bumper stickers to their cars that proclaim "I am a drunk driver" or "Convicted of DWI."

Other varieties of shaming punishments include posting offenders' pictures in newspapers or on billboards, television, or the Internet. Some judges have required offenders to confess their crimes in church or to deliver court-approved "shaming speeches" or "apology speeches" on the steps of courthouses.

Arguments in Favor of Shaming Punishments

Defenders of shaming punishments often begin by distinguishing shaming punishments from sex offender registration laws, commonly known as Megan's laws. These laws require certain sex offenders to register with and provide personal information to state or local law-enforcement authorities either as a condition of probation or upon release from confinement into the community.

The information typically includes the offender's name, age, gender, address, occupation, and picture, and this information is then made available to the public. All 50 states enforce a version of this kind of law, and most post the information on the Internet. These laws have been challenged on constitutional grounds, but in two decisions announced in 2003, *Smith v. Doe* and *Connecticut Department of Public Safety v. Doe*, the U.S. Supreme Court upheld the Megan's laws of Alaska and Connecticut as nothing more than the dissemination of accurate information about criminal records that are already in the public domain. The Court concluded that the primary purpose of such laws is to alert the public to the risk of sex offenders in their neighborhoods and that these are civil laws that may prove embarrassing to sex offenders but do not harm offenders in a serious enough manner to amount to "punishment" in the legal or constitutional sense.

Those who advocate contemporary shaming punishments that do not include the publication of sex-offender lists contend that these punishments can save money while advancing perfectly proper goals of punishment. In an influential 1996 law review article, legal theorist Dan Kahan stressed the flexibility such punishments offer judges who wish to fit the punishment to the crime. Imprisonment, he asserted, is not only expensive but also too harsh and degrading, especially when imposed on nonviolent offenders. On the other hand, the conventional alternatives to imprisonment—probation, fines, and community service—are sometimes inadequate and ineffective in fulfilling the goals of retribution, deterrence, and rehabilitation. Lenient sentences may fail to convey the seriousness of the crimes to some offenders while concomitantly having little or no deterrent or rehabilitative value. Arguably, a criminal punishment is more likely to be effective when it has an appropriate "expressive effect." Wearing a sign in public or making a public apology imposes only a minor limitation on an offender's freedom, but it creates an unpleasant emotional experience that fulfills the goal of retribution and is likely to deter the offender (and others) from similarly offensive behavior. Whereas conventional probation and other community-based correctional programs send a morally ambiguous message both to the offender and to the community, a carefully constructed shaming punishment can speak considerably more clearly to the offender and to the community as to what kinds of behavior are socially unacceptable. Moreover, when a shaming punishment is of short duration and is proportionate to the offense, it offers the offender a chance for contrition and an opportunity to make the case that his or her punishment is complete and that he or she is now deserving of a second chance.

Kahan's endorsement of the idea that a shaming punishment can be devised as a middle-range punishment—neither too harsh nor too lenient—that sends a clear message to everyone involved has been seconded by the well-known criminologist John Braithwaite. In his classic 1989 book *Crime, Shame and Reintegration*, Braithwaite asserts that a shaming punishment can either prevent crime or cause crime. A society's best course, he argues, is not to shield offenders from any sense of shame or blame but to shame offenders judiciously and in a cultural context offering the offender both respect and a pathway to redemption. Braithwaite makes an important distinction between "stigmatizing shaming" and "reintegrative shaming." The first type of shaming will usually fail, because it conveys nothing but disgust, hatred, and public scorn for an offender. It thus has a strong tendency to label the offender, not simply his or her wrongdoing, as evil. As a result, the offender sees him- or herself, and the community identifies the offender, as a "criminal," an outcast not morally worthy of forgiveness and social support. By contrast, reintegrative shaming labels only the offender's criminal behavior as evil, while preserving the identity of the offender as essentially good and worthy of new opportunities to demonstrate goodness. Braithwaite stresses that a reintegrative-shaming punishment need not be weak or lack a punitive "bite." It differs from a stigmatizing punishment not so much in severity as in its duration and significance. The punishment is finite rather than endless. It ends with apology and repentance and is rewarded by forgiveness and opportunities to reconcile with the community. So-called restorative justice programs, such as carefully supervised meetings between offenders and victims in which both parties discuss the impact of the offender's actions and possible ways to "make things right," generally are considered as realistic examples of programs that can facilitate an offender's reintegration into a free society.

Arguments Against Shaming Punishments

Opponents of shaming punishments often express disagreement with the Supreme Court's 2003 decisions that distinguished sex offender registration laws from shaming punishments. In fact, three justices disputed this distinction in dissenting opinions in *Smith v. Doe*. Justices Stephen Breyer, Ruth Bader Ginsburg, and John Paul Stevens took the position that legislative labeling of these laws as "civil" could not hide the fact that they actually are criminal laws that are punitive in intent and severely stigmatizing in effect. Megan's laws thus should be understood as inflicting a criminal punishment on offenders and should be open to constitutional challenges. All three justices agreed that these laws closely resembled the scarlet-letter shaming punishments of colonial America. Justice Ginsburg added that offenders were subjected to profound humiliation and ostracism that made it all but impossible to live normally in the community.

According to those who oppose shaming punishments, sex offender registration laws are flawed in the same ways as are other shaming punishments: They offer a simplistic solution to the complex problem of crime, play to the most punitive instincts of the public, and fail to achieve any of the legitimate goals of retribution, deterrence, or rehabilitation. In a noteworthy 2001 article in the *Vanderbilt Law Review*, Dan Markel made the case that shaming punishments fulfill the goal of vengeance but not the very different goal of retribution. Retributive theory demands that legal punishments be proportionate to the offense and dispensed by agents of the state who are acting under but constrained by the law. Unlike the members of a vigilante mob, state officials authorized to punish convicted criminals are not expected to exhibit inappropriate rage or take great pleasure in seeing the offender suffer. Properly understood, retributive justice seeks to treat offenders with dignity by recognizing them as competent human beings who have erred but are capable of making better moral choices in the future. Retribution is meant to end the process of crime and punishment. Markel contends, however, that shaming punishments achieve none of these goals. These punishments rely to a great extent upon the public at large—the "crowd"—to express disgust and inflict humiliation on offenders. History is replete with examples of crowds that clearly took great pleasure in pelting those identified as deviants with insults, mockery, and all too often, fruit, stones, or bricks. Judges who impose shaming punishments thus are undermining the retributive principle that the state

and only the state is authorized to punish lawbreakers. Sometimes judges who sentence an offender to play the lead role in his own shaming ritual will post a police officer nearby to protect the offender from violence. This shows that judges do realize that they are making the crowd an instrument of the state and that the dominant purpose of their sentence is the public humiliation of the offender. This arguably is a classic example of revenge, the result of which is likely to prolong the process of crime and punishment and strip the offender of what remains of his or her dignity as a human being.

Critics of shaming punishments are also skeptical that shame can be an effective deterrent. Shaming punishments are imposed by only a few judges and rarely on a regular basis. They differ according to the nature of the crime, the offender, the community, and judges' notions of justice. Consequently, there have been no systematic empirical studies of the deterrent or rehabilitative efficacy of shaming punishments. The common wisdom that public degradation ceremonies will surely deter both offenders and onlookers from criminal behavior is, according to many criminologists, simply wrong. Indeed, shaming punishments may very well push the offender into more and more serious criminal behavior. A punishment that by its very nature stigmatizes and labels an offender as "criminal" creates a classic self-fulfilling prophecy that leads the offender and others to identify him as a criminal. After the public humiliation and media coverage of the offender's punishment spectacle, jobs and other opportunities to return to the community are not nearly as likely to be available to the shamed offender as they are for an offender sentenced to routine probation. A sense of humiliation and worthlessness, combined with an absence of noncriminal employment options, is a recipe for more, not less, crime.

The alleged rehabilitative benefits of shaming punishments also have been disputed. Many criminologists acknowledge the strength and logic of Braithwaite's arguments in favor of reintegrative shaming. However, in the absence of systematic, empirical studies of contemporary shaming punishments, there is no evidence that any sequence of punishments that includes a large element of public humiliation has any rehabilitative value. Some critics have asked why we would demand both shame and reintegration for offenders. The benefits of shame are illusory and unproven, they argue. However, correctional programs that place the emphasis squarely on reintegration have demonstrated considerable success. Victim-offender mediation programs and other restorative justice programs that do not rely on a shaming punishment have been shown to be effective alternatives to incarceration. Evaluations of these programs have found high levels of satisfaction among both offenders and victims, and several studies indicate that restorative justice is consistent with the goal of holding offenders accountable for their behavior and has lessened recidivism rates.

Emerging Legal Questions

The debate over the wisdom, fairness, and effectiveness of public shaming as a method of punishing criminals will not be resolved anytime soon. Even if large-scale, methodologically sound empirical studies of the impact of shaming punishments on crime rates were available, they would not resolve the issue. At heart, the question of whether a democratic society should include public shaming in its arsenal of criminal punishments is a normative question that must be answered by the people and their elected representatives one case at a time and one jurisdiction at a time. America's courts will certainly play a significant role in many cases. It is the courts, after all, that began the latest round of scarlet-letter punishments in the 1980s and 1990s. Now there is a sense that the judges who have been experimenting with creative penalties that are meant to convey a message of shame may have had unrealistic expectations and might have been better off sticking with incarceration, probation, work and restitution programs, and other traditional, well-established punishments. It is hard to believe, for example, that the pathologies that lead to domestic violence can be easily checked by forcing the abuser to apologize publicly or that a chronic alcoholic with multiple DWI arrests will suddenly see the light by affixing a "Caution: Convicted Drunk Driver" sticker to his car bumper.

Because questions surrounding the moral appropriateness and practical utility of shaming punishments are complex, it is not surprising that federal and state courts have not even come close to a consensus on the constitutionality of the varieties of shaming punishments. The U.S. Supreme Court has not yet agreed to hear a case specifically raising the issue of the constitutionality of shaming punishments other than the aforementioned cases involving

sex offender registration laws, which, according to the majority, did not impose a criminal punishment and thus were constitutionally sound. So far, the leading decision on the constitutionality of what undeniably was a shaming punishment is *United States v. Gementera*, a 2004 ruling by the U.S. Court of Appeals for the Ninth Circuit. A federal trial judge sentenced a man convicted of pilfering letters from mailboxes to two months of imprisonment and three years of supervised release, one of the conditions of which was wearing or carrying a large, two-sided sign stating "I stole mail; this is my punishment" in front of a post office for eight hours. On appeal, the *Gementera* court held that the sign-carrying punishment was reasonably related to the goal of rehabilitation, as required by federal sentencing law, and that it would stretch credulity to suggest that eight hours carrying a signboard amounted to a constitutionally cruel and unusual punishment. It is noteworthy, however, that one judge dissented on the grounds that the punishment was an anachronism with no rehabilitative value and had no place in a federal courtroom.

Although most of the federal and state courts that have reviewed shaming sentences have rejected claims of unconstitutionality, there have been noteworthy differences of opinion. For example, in *People v. Letterlough*, the New York Court of Appeals in 1995 struck down a condition of probation that required a motorist convicted of drunk driving to affix to his car's bumper a sticker reading "Convicted DWI." The New York court characterized the bumper sticker as a "scarlet letter" with no rehabilitative value and concluded that the trial judge should not have imposed a condition of probation that was not expressly authorized by statute. Yet, in *Goldschmitt v. State*, a virtually identical case, a Florida appellate court in 1986 found no statutory or constitutional problems with this kind of condition of probation. In this case, a motorist convicted of driving under the influence of alcohol was ordered to attach a sticker stating "Convicted DUI-restricted license" to his automobile's bumpers. The probationer appealed on both statutory and constitutional grounds, but the Florida court rejected his arguments. The court noted that the Florida probation statute contains a catchall provision permitting Florida judges to add conditions deemed appropriate to the offender's crime and concluded that the bumper-sticker requirement was well within the trial judge's discretion. The probationer's Eighth Amendment claim was also denied. The court conceded that the punishment was reminiscent of colonial times but held that it fell far short of the kinds of painful and oppressive punishments banned by the cruel and unusual punishment clause.

These conflicting opinions are indicative of the divergence of opinion that exists among courts, legislatures, elected officials, and the general public on the issues surrounding contemporary shaming punishments. Whether public shaming is an appropriate and effective punishment that will deter crime and rehabilitate offenders or a punishment that is ineffective at best and counterproductive at worst is a question that will remain controversial for many years to come.

Kenneth C. Haas
University of Delaware

See also Public Safety and Collaborative Prevention; Punishment; Violent Offender Reconciliation Programs; "What Works" Approach and Evidence-Based Practices

Further Readings

Braithwaite, John. *Crime, Shame and Reintegration.* Cambridge: Cambridge University Press, 1989.

Braudway, Bonnie Mangum. "Scarlet Letter Punishments for Juveniles: Rehabilitation Through Humiliation?" *Campbell Law Review,* v.27/1 (2004).

Connecticut Department of Public Safety v. Doe, 538 U.S. 84 (2003).

Deford, William. "The Dilemma of Expressive Punishment." *University of Colorado Law Review,* v.76/3 (2005).

Flanders, Chad. "Shame and the Meanings of Punishment." *Cleveland State Law Review,* v.54/4 (2006).

Garvey, Stephen P. "Can Shaming Punishments Educate?" *University of Chicago Law Review,* v.65/3 (1998).

Goldschmitt v. State, 490 So. 2d 123 (Fla. Dist. Ct. App. 1986).

Huschka, Ryan J. "Sorry for the Jackass Sentence: A Critical Analysis of the Constitutionality of Contemporary Shaming Punishments." *University of Kansas Law Review,* v.54/3 (April 2006).

Kahan, Dan M. "What Do Alternative Sanctions Mean?" *University of Chicago Law Review,* v.63/2 (1996).

Logan, Wayne A. *Knowledge as Power: Criminal Registration and Community Notification Laws in America.* Stanford, CA: Stanford University Press, 2009.

Markel, Dan. "Are Shaming Punishments Beautifully Retributive? Retributivism and the Implications for the Alternative Sanctions Debate." *Vanderbilt Law Review,* v.54/6 (2001).

McAlinden, Anne-Marie. *The Shaming of Sexual Offenders: Risk, Retribution and Reintegration.* Portland, OR: Hart, 2007.

Nussbaum, Martha C. *Hiding From Humanity: Disgust, Shame, and the Law.* Princeton, NJ: Princeton University Press, 2004.

People v. Letterlough, 655 N.E. 2d 146 (N.Y. 1995).

Smith v. Doe, 538 U.S. 84 (2003).

United States v. Gementera, 379 F. 3d 596 (9th Cir. 2004).

PUNISHMENT

Punishment can be defined as a penalty imposed under the authority of law, inflicted on a person by other persons, for the commission of a crime. This definition of punishment, however, raises a host of attendant legal and moral questions. First, can the imposition of state punishment be morally justified? Second, under what specific circumstances is it warranted? Third, what kinds of punishment should be imposed and how much of it? Philosophers have debated these questions for centuries, and as the United States grapples with serious problems of prison overcrowding and mass incarceration, punishment looms as a—controversial—public policy issue of great urgency. Changing social attitudes and rapidly evolving legal practices mean that many questions about punishment remain unanswered, despite the serious financial and social consequences of those answers.

Consensus Definition of Punishment

The term *punishment* is used in a variety of contexts. People reference the state's "punishment" of criminals, but they also reference the "punishment" of children by parents and teachers. The term is also used to denote severe handling or treatment, such as that endured by boxers and soldiers. Even extreme heat or cold can be described as "punishing." Within the context of criminal justice, however, the term is used to signify a particular sort of state behavior. Most commentators have agreed that punishment is both aversive and state-sanctioned. Thomas Hobbes described it as an evil imposed by public authority; Cesare Beccaria noted that punishment is not an act of violence of one individual against another but is inherently public, necessary, proportionate to the crime, and imposed under law. In his "Prolegomenon to the Principles of Punishment," H. L. A. Hart outlined a jurisprudential definition of punishment by identifying five characteristics: (1) It must involve pain or other consequences normally considered unpleasant; (2) it must be for an offense against legal rules; (3) it must be of an actual or supposed offender for his offense; (4) it must be intentionally administered by human beings other than the offender; and (5) it must be imposed and administered by an authority constituted by a legal system against which the offense is committed.

Many scholars also agree that stigma is another essential aspect of punishment. While a hospital patient may be quarantined for the same duration as the prisoner who serves a criminal sentence, there is condemnation inherent in the detention of the criminal.

The Moral Justification of Punishment

Although a handful of scholars have argued for the wholesale abolition of punishment, most systems of law incorporate mechanisms of its administration. What most philosophers, jurists, and legislators have debated is not *whether* punishment is justifiable, but *on what basis* it is justified. Two fundamentally different, and often conflicting, rationales have been advanced: consequentialist theories (that is, utilitarian bases of punishment) and nonconsequentialist theories (that is, retributivist bases of punishment). Consequentialist theories are prospective and instrumentalist, whereas nonconsequentialist theories are retrospective and intrinsicalist.

Consequentialist Theories of Punishment

Consequentialist theories of punishment focus on future crimes. As far as consequentialists are concerned, a crime, once committed, is finished. While steps can be taken to ameliorate its effects, the crime itself cannot be undone. Thus, the proper aim of punishment is the reduction of future crimes. In the *Protagoras*, Plato argued that when punishing, authorities do not punish a man for past wrongs unless they are wreaking blind vengeance. Instead, he argued, rational men inflict punishment to prevent

future offending. Cesare Beccaria shared this view. In *On Crimes and Punishments*, Beccaria argued that the end of punishment is to prevent the criminal from inflicting additional harm and to prevent others from committing like offenses. Perhaps the best known of the consequentialist theorists, however, was Jeremy Bentham, who in *The Principles of Morals and Legislation* devised an elaborate hedonic calculus of pleasure and pain. Bentham aspired to create a system of laws that maximized the greatest good for the greatest number of people. Crimes were evils that caused suffering to their victims and rational laws were a mechanism to minimize them. However, Bentham also cautioned that punishment is also a pain, and he urged legislators to weigh the benefits of reduced crime rates against the costs of increased punishment. It is possible, he warned, to overpunish and to create unnecessary suffering in the world. Excess or useless punishment is an evil to be avoided.

While Bentham's hedonic calculus may prove too cumbersome for practical application, the relation of punishment to measurable outcomes (such as levels of pleasure and pain, crime rates, or recidivism) can help to gauge whether a particular punishment achieves its measurable social end. Policy initiatives, in this sense, are falsifiable. For example, lawmakers can know whether three-strikes penalties empirically reduce rates of violent crime.

Of course, while the consequentialist approach is philosophically attractive in many ways, it does raise its own set of difficult questions. For example, if the general justifying aim of punishment is the reduction of *future* crime, why is the imposition of punishment conditioned upon a *past* violation of the criminal law? Could punishment be imposed with no crime to trigger it? Should, for example, an innocent man be executed if his death will produce the greatest amount of pleasure for the greatest number of people? Some utilitarians ("rule utilitarians") avoid the problem by asserting that it is not an individual act that should be assessed in terms of social utility, but the system of rules that would produce the greatest net good. Other utilitarians ("act utilitarians"), however, do not have recourse to this argument. Instead, they might suggest that the punishment of innocent parties would lead to widespread skepticism about the legitimacy of the punishing authority (thereby making the punishment of the innocent a nonoptimal social action), while others might suggest that the innocent defendant *should* be executed and that doing so offends moral intuitions only because people do not often confront such unusual circumstances.

Consequentialists typically justify punishment by identifying specific means of reducing or ameliorating crime. Most commonly, they suggest that future crime can be reduced through deterrence (in both its specific and its general forms), incapacitation, and rehabilitation, although consequentialists also describe the utilitarian values of norm reinforcement, vengeance, restitution, and restoration.

Specific Deterrence

Most consequentialists believe that humans, as rational actors, choose behaviors that maximize pleasure and minimize pain. To induce people to forgo the pleasures of crime (such as the taking of goods or services without payment, the euphoria of illegal drugs, and the killing of people who make us angry), the state must credibly enforce the penalties attached to crimes. One way that people can know the state will enforce its threats is if it imposes punishment. If an offender commits a crime and is punished for it, that offender will be less likely to reoffend. In this way, the theory of specific deterrence closely resembles the psychological theory of operant conditioning, in which the introduction of rewarding stimuli or the withdrawal of aversive stimuli increases the frequency of a behavior, or vice versa.

Psychologists of learning would recognize many of the principles of punishment advocated by early penologists. For example, Beccaria's suggestion that punishment should follow the crime without delay is supported by research showing that immediate feedback is more effective than less immediate feedback. His claim that the certainty of punishment, not its severity, leads to lawfulness is supported by research showing that consistent reinforcement and punishment lead to faster learning. His suggestion that penalties should be proportional to crimes is supported by research showing that costs and benefits are weighed against each other in choosing behavior. Criminologists have reported strong support for a deterrent effect.

General Deterrence

Of course, as suggested by social learning psychologists, people learn from the rewards and punishments visited upon them not only directly but also vicariously. Thus, punishment imposed upon an offender may deter future crime not just for him but also for others. It has been argued that it is not justice to punish one man in order to influence the behavior of others. Georg Hegel claimed that justifying punishment in this way was like raising a stick at a dog, treating people as animals instead of with the dignity they should be afforded. Criminologists have found empirical support for general deterrence. In some cases, however, specific findings can be very contentious. For example, Isaac Erlich's 1975 study, concluding that each execution carried out deterred approximately eight murders, has been the object of fierce criticism.

Incapacitation

The theory behind incapacitation is simple: Punishment can make it difficult (or impossible) for an offender to commit further crimes. Offenders can be incapacitated by spatially removing them from society (such as imprisonment or banishment) or by physically eliminating the capacity to offend (such as cutting off the hand of a thief or chemically castrating sex offenders). Some forms of punishment are more incapacitating than others: The death penalty is the ultimate incapacitant, whereas the incapacitative effects of incarceration are less certain (prisoners can escape or commit crimes against fellow inmates or corrections staff) and those associated with financial penalties and community supervision are less certain still.

Selective incapacitation is the practice of severely punishing persistent and dangerous offenders, incarcerating a modest number of people to achieve dramatic reductions in crime rates. Because criminologists have sometimes reported that a handful of chronic offenders are responsible for a disproportionate amount of crime (6 percent of the population may be responsible for 52 percent of reported crime), Peter Greenwood proposed an approach whereby chronic offenders could be identified and sentenced to extended terms of incarceration. The promise of reducing crime at minimal financial and social cost was attractive to many policy makers, but limitations and high error rates in the prediction of risk led others to challenge this approach. Today, most selective incapacitation operates in a more rudimentary way, such as the enhancement of sentences for repeat offenders under sentencing guidelines and three-strikes regimes.

Rehabilitation

In 1876, Cesare Lombroso wrote *Criminal Man*, in which he suggested that criminals are throwbacks to an earlier stage of evolution and that crime is the product of an attenuated form of epilepsy. The concept of rehabilitation is rooted in Lombroso's model of crime-as-disease. If people commit crimes because of inherent defects, one straightforward way to reduce future crime is to simply correct the defect, regardless of whether the defect is physical (such as a chemical imbalance), psychological (such as criminal thinking patterns), or social (such as association with criminal peers). During the 1960s and 1970s, many experts believed that crime was a social problem that could be diagnosed, treated, and cured. In 1974, however, catalyzed by Robert Martinson's pessimistic article "What Works?" existing dissatisfaction about the state of U.S. punishment fomented a wholesale rejection of rehabilitation as a legitimate basis of punishment. Only in recent years has genuine interest in rehabilitation reemerged within mainstream policy circles.

Norm Reinforcement

Although norm reinforcement is not one of the cornerstone foundations of punishment, it is another important consequentialist basis for punishment. Imposing punishment can build solidarity among members of society, permitting people to internalize the sense that crime will not be tolerated. If crimes appear to go unpunished, it may seem unfair to law-abiding citizens. They may be tempted to violate the laws as well, and to enjoy the advantages of crime. However, if transgressors are punished for their violations, law-abiding citizens may be more likely to view their acquiescence to the law as just and fair.

Vengeance

Vengeance is another consequentialist basis for punishment. When criminals steal from or injure victims, those victims, their families and friends, and members of their communities may feel resentful and angry. The imposition of punishment may prove cathartic for them (increasing their pleasure or eliminating their pain, under the hedonic calculus) and may discourage vigilantism and private acts of revenge. Vengeance is not synonymous with retribution (described below) and is not premised upon a theory of intrinsic moral rights; rather, it is based on the view that the punishment of the criminal may bring relief to the victim and the public, enhancing respect for the law and discouraging vigilantism.

Restitution and Restoration

Restitution, or the making whole of crime victims, is yet another consequentialist basis for punishment. When criminals commit offenses, their victims are harmed (financially, physically, emotionally, and/or socially). Punishments that include restitution may help to ameliorate those harms by requiring the criminal to compensate the victim (usually financially). In addition to repaying victims for their losses, restitution may foster respect for the law (since the victim is acknowledged as relevant to the imposition of punishment, which often seems more equitable than excluding victims from the process).

A popular idea in recent years, restoration consists of requiring offenders to perform compensatory service for the victim and/or the community, and it often incorporates processes through which the offender is reconciled with victims and the broader community. Restorative justice can help to make victims whole, but it can also help to knit neighborhoods together. If offenders are contrite and demonstrate genuine repentance, the community may be willing to forgive and welcome them back. In this way, restoration encompasses many of the qualities associated with norm reinforcement, vengeance, and restitution.

Nonconsequentialist Theories of Punishment

Instead of justifying punishment through the advantageous effects it produces for society, the nonconsequentialist justifies punishment because it is deserved; instead of attempting to reduce prospective crimes, the nonconsequentialist adopts a retrospective view and punishes the criminal for the crime that has been committed.

In effect, the nonconsequentialist justification of punishment (sometimes called retributivism or "just deserts") argues that criminals should be punished because they deserve it. Herbert Morris articulated this view of fairness theory in 1968.

He suggested that the criminal has taken advantage of society and stands in breach of the social contract, but the imposition of punishment on the criminal annuls the unfair advantage and levels the playing field. Using an elegant logical twist, Georg Hegel explains this view by suggesting that when the criminal violates the law, his crime is the negation of the right of society. Punishment is the negation of this negation, and thus an affirmation of right, solicited and brought upon the criminal by himself. This notion of inflicting harm to redress an unfair advantage is central to nonconsequentialist theories of punishment and underlies the very ancient doctrine of *lex talionis*, the principle that the punishment should be identical to the offense ("an eye for an eye"). *Lex talionis* featured prominently in the Code of Hammurabi (law number 196 states, "If a man puts out the eye of an equal, his eye shall be put out") and ancient Roman and Islamic law (similar assertions are made in Leviticus 24:19–21 and Qur'an 5:45).

There are two varieties of retributivism: Negative retributivism requires that only the guilty may be punished, and then only to the extent they deserve, but it does not require that punishments must be imposed; positive retributivism, on the other hand, requires that guilty must be punished, to the full extent of their desert. The view of positive retributivism has been forcefully articulated by Immanuel Kant, who argued that even if an island society was about to disband, the last murderers lying in its prisons should be put to death. Society not only has a right to punish them; it has a duty to do so. Otherwise, Kant claims, the islanders who refuse to execute the killers are complicit in their crimes.

Unlike the utilitarian, who is concerned with maximizing the good for the greatest number of people, the retributivist might insist upon the imposition of an appropriate punishment even if it produced undesirable social consequences: more crime, less happiness, and diminished overall social welfare. This view is expressed in the Latin maxim, *Fiat justitia ruat caelum* (May justice be done though the heavens fall).

The nonconsequentialist approach to crime is certainly attractive in some philosophical ways. By punishing past crimes, it avoids the utilitarian conundrum of relying upon antecedent crimes to influence subsequent conduct. By asserting that only the guilty may be punished to the extent they deserve, it avoids the punishment-of-the-innocent problem. The idea that people should be punished because they are morally blameworthy may be intuitively appealing. However, nonconsequentialists must face their own questions. First, there is the problem of free will. If crime is a product of causes that we do not choose, it is difficult to understand how the criminal can be punished as a morally blameworthy actor. It may be the case that, as Herbert Packer has written, the law treats people as autonomous not because they are, but because it is useful to proceed as if they were. A second problem for retributivists is this: Even if one accepts fairness theory (punishment redresses unfair advantage), it is unclear why punishment should consist of hard treatment (such as physical pain, imprisonment, or execution). Third, why is punishment a matter for the state? Presumably, when a criminal assumes an unfair advantage by committing a crime, it is the victim—not the government—who should see the balance restored. Fourth, while the utilitarian can measure the outcomes of punishment (such as crime rates) to know if punishment is achieving its intended social ends, it is not clear how the retributivist can know how much punishment to impose. Andrew von Hirsch has studied this problem at length and has suggested that the principle of proportionality can provide meaningful guidance. If crimes of like gravity are punished by penalties of like severity, parity can be maintained. If crimes can be rank-ordered in their seriousness (for example, murder is more serious than armed robbery, which is more serious than burglary), a schedule of retributive penalties can be devised. This approach, however, does not answer fundamental questions about where the top and bottom of the penalty range should be.

Other Theories of Punishment

Consequentialist and nonconsequentialist theories of punishment frequently conflict. For example, the very risk factors that make a criminal dangerous (such as poverty, drug addiction, and a hot temper) are often factors that make the criminal seem less blameworthy. However, neither consequentialist nor nonconsequentialist theories seem wholly satisfying, and for this reason many scholars have suggested hybrid theories of punishment. Norval Morris's concept of limiting retributivism is one well-known example. Under Morris's theory, retributivist concepts set upper (and occasionally lower) limits on sentencing severity. Within these outer limits, however, utilitarian principles (such as deterrence, incapacitation, rehabilitation, uniformity in sentencing, and imposing the least severe sentence that will achieve the goals of punishment) provide the necessary fine-tuning of the sentence imposed. Joel Feinberg's expressive theory of punishment is neither entirely consequentialist nor nonconsequentialist. Rather, it suggests that punishments communicate moral opprobrium to offenders, relating social attitudes about criminal behavior. Other theorists have posited variations on Feinberg's theory, justifying punishment in terms of its communicative and educational function.

Modes of Punishment

Legal punishment is as old as the law, but it has changed dramatically over time. For most of human history, punishment was corporal in nature. Serious crimes were punished by execution (such as hanging, crucifixion, and drawing-and-quartering), and less serious crimes were punished with nonlethal physical penalties (such as amputation, whipping, and the use of devices like ducking stools and pillories). Prisons existed, but they served principally as places of detention for those who could not post bail or pay their fines. Historically, it was said that *carcer enim ad continendos homines non ad puniendos haberi debet* (prisons exist only in order to keep men, not to punish them).

Between about 1750 and 1850, however, punishment underwent a remarkable transformation in Western societies. Prompted by humanitarian reformers in England and America, the prison was changed from where criminals awaited punishment to the manner of their punishment. In *Discipline and Punish*, Michel Foucault traces this evolution from a system of corporal punishments to one of carceral punishments, using the prison as a metaphor for society at large (which also relies on order, discipline, and "docile bodies" to maintain existing economic and political systems).

However, the shift from corporal to carceral punishments was not the only rapid transformation in the history of punishment. During the 1980s, another sudden shift radically affected public attitudes. When Robert Martinson published an article dismissing rehabilitation programs as ineffective, underlying dissatisfaction with the state of U.S. crime and punishment coalesced into a unified attack on correctional treatment from both conservatives and progressives, and within a year or two, the justice system was dominated by the retributivist view of just deserts. Determinate sentencing replaced indeterminate systems of parole, sentence lengths increased, and prison populations soared. The U.S. imprisonment rate, which had steadily averaged about 109 persons per 100,000 between 1925 and 1980, began to grow exponentially in the 1980s, rising from a level of 139 per 100,000 citizens in 1980 to a level of 504 per 100,000 in 2008. The Pew Center on the States has reported that when populations from jails, probation, and parole are included, the number of people under U.S. correctional control increases to more than 7.3 million (or 1 in 31 people).

Understanding the implications of mass incarceration on this scale is but one of the challenges that scholars of punishment face. Given that most of the 2.3 million people in jail and prison will eventually come out, and given that recidivism rates in many jurisdictions exceed 50 percent within a three-year period after release from prison, experts are also struggling to understand how to facilitate reentry into communities in order to break the cycle of returning to prison. Understanding the ongoing evolution of the death penalty is another challenge. The United States is unique among Western democracies in its continuing reliance upon capital punishment, but since the death penalty was reintroduced after a four-year period of de facto abolition in 1976, its scope has been limited by a number of Supreme Court decisions. Death may not be imposed on insane persons, juveniles, or the mentally retarded, and as a general matter, death may not be imposed in nonhomicide cases. Social attitudes about capital punishment continue to change, as do attitudes about punishment generally, reflecting Winston Churchill's remark to the House of Commons that one of the most unfailing tests of civilization is the mood and temper of the public in regard to the treatment of crime and criminals.

James C. Oleson
University of Auckland

See also Attitudes and Myths About Punishment; Continuum of Sanctions; Prison Overcrowding; Public Shaming as Punishment; Punishment Units; Restitution

Further Readings

Beccaria, Cesare. *On Crimes and Punishments*, Henry Paolucci, trans. Englewood Cliffs, NJ: Prentice Hall, 1963.

Bentham, Jeremy. *The Principles of Morals and Legislation.* New York: Hafner Press, 1948.

Ehrlich, Isaac. "The Deterrent Effect of Capital Punishment: A Question of Life and Death." *American Economic Review,* v.65 (1975).

Feinberg, Joel. "The Expressive Theory of Punishment." *The Monist,* v.49 (July 1965).

Foucault, Michel. *Discipline and Punish,* Alan Sheridan, trans. New York: Pantheon Books, 1977.

Greenwood, Peter W. *Selective Incapacitation.* Santa Monica, CA: Rand, 1982.

Hart, H. L. A. "Prolegomenon to the Principles of Punishment." In *Punishment and Responsibility: Essays in the Philosophy of Law.* New York: Oxford University Press, 1968.

Kant, Immanuel. *The Philosophy of Law,* W. Hastie, trans. Edinburgh, UK: T. and T. Clark, 1887.

Lombroso, Cesare. *Criminal Man,* Nicole Rafter, ed. Durham, NC: Duke University Press, 2006.

Martinson, Robert. "What Works? Questions and Answers About Prison Reform." *The Public Interest,* v.35 (Spring 1974).

Morris, Herbert. "Persons and Punishment." *The Monist,* v.52 (October 1968).

Morris, Norval. *The Future of Imprisonment.* Chicago: University of Chicago Press, 1974.

Murphy, Jeffrie G. *Punishment and Rehabilitation,* 2nd ed. Belmont, CA: Thomson Wadsworth, 1985.

Packer, Herbert L. *The Limits of the Criminal Sanction.* Stanford, CA: Stanford University Press, 1968.

Pew Center on the States. *One in 31: The Long Reach of American Corrections.* Washington, DC: Pew Charitable Trusts, 2009.

Robinson, Paul H. *Distributive Principles of Criminal Law: Who Should Be Punished, How Much?* New York: Oxford University Press, 2008.

Tyler, Tom. *Why People Obey the Law.* New Haven, CT: Yale University Press, 1990.

von Hirsch, Andrew. *Censure and Sanctions.* New York: Oxford University Press, 1993.

Zimring, Franklin E. and Gordon Hawkins. *Incapacitation: Penal Confinement and the Restraint of Crime.* New York: Oxford University Press, 1995.

PUNISHMENT UNITS

Interest in the concept of punishment units is linked to a desire to quantify the amount of punishment represented by various criminal penalties. The aim is to enable a standardized measurement of severity across different types of sanctions. As various types of community correctional programs and penalties have been adopted, policy makers have sought a simple means of ranking and comparing them in terms of their punishment value. Thus, the concept refers to a currency to be used in meting out various types and amounts of punishment or in scaling the amount of punitiveness embodied in differing types of sentences. By providing guidance as to how much of a particular type of sanction can be considered equivalent to a certain dosage of another one, punishment units facilitate substitution of different types of punishments for one another in order to satisfy varying sentencing aims without resulting in undue disparity in the treatment of similar cases.

Rationale

Although underlying purposes of sentences may vary, a guiding principle of American jurisprudence is that there should be proportionality between the seriousness of the crime and the severity of the penalty imposed. The importance of relating the weight of the punishment to the gravity of the criminal act means that a practical approach is needed for comparing the relative bite of different criminal sanctions. The value of having a simple method for doing so suggests the desirability of establishing a scale of punishment units.

The need for some way of gauging how much of a given penalty is equivalent to a certain quantity of another became increasingly apparent as the range of available nonprison penalties and intermediate sanctions expanded. The idea of punishment units arose as a means of facilitating the principled integration of multiple and varied noncustodial penalties into a comprehensive sanctioning system. The purpose is to allow judges and other decision makers to employ a variety of punishments within a reasoned and structured framework.

Early sentencing guidelines typically focused on which categories of offenders presumptively would receive sentences to incarceration and which would be placed on probation, providing no guidance as to the types of conditions to be imposed on offenders receiving nonprison sentences. As more and more sites began to add intermediate punishments to their armamentaria of sanctions, the need to have a means of assessing the relative weight or punishment power of these nontraditional penalties became clear. Subsequently, a number of jurisdictions undertook efforts to rank penalties in terms of dimensions such as how onerous or intrusive they were and to arrange them on a continuum of sanctions. The quest for scoring systems and scales that provide a simple way of comparing the relative degree of punitiveness in an array of criminal penalties has continued, and this demand could be satisfied by an agreed-upon set of punishment units.

Devising a System That Incorporates Punishment Units

In theory, designing a system for use of punishment units is fairly straightforward. It requires identifying the full range of criminal sanctions available in a particular jurisdiction and deciding what quantity of each is equivalent to a specific amount of the others. For example, it would be necessary to decide how many hours of community service or days of house arrest would be counted as equal in weight to a $500 fine or a three-month stay in a halfway house.

The reality of developing and implementing a system that incorporates punishment units is more complex. One issue concerns whose judgments are to be used in scaling the relative degree of discomfort or deprivation from various penalties—whether those of legislators, judges, researchers, practitioners, members of the general public, or offenders themselves. Another issue concerns whether exchange rates should include efforts to match various terms of incarceration with nonincarcerative options and, if so, where other penalties cease to be interchangeable with prison terms.

A significant difficulty in agreeing on a sentencing scheme that incorporates punishment units is the fact that criminal penalties vary on many dimensions, such as the degree to which they require affirmative effort on the part of the offender, restrict movement and choice, result in shame, or inflict financial hardship. Thus, arriving at a commonly accepted means of measuring the relative weight of sanctions is no simple matter. Nonetheless, punishment units are a useful tool for developing a punishment severity scale, and several impressive efforts have been made to capture the various aspects of different sanctions in a unitary measure.

Kay Harris
Temple University

See also Attitudes of Offenders Toward Community Corrections; Continuum of Sanctions; Philosophy of Community Corrections; Sentencing Guidelines

Further Readings

Morris, Norval and Michael Tonry. *Between Prison and Probation: Intermediate Punishments in a Rational Sentencing System.* New York: Oxford University Press, 1990.

Robinson, Paul H. "Desert, Crime Control, Disparity, and Units of Punishment." In *Penal Theory and Practice: Tradition and Innovation in Criminal Justice*, Anthony Duff et al., eds. Manchester: Manchester University Press, 1994.

Schiff, Mara F. "Gauging the Intensity of Criminal Sanctions: Developing the Criminal Punishment Severity Scale (CPSS)." *Criminal Justice Review*, v.22/2 (1997).

von Hirsch, Andrew. "Scaling Intermediate Punishments: A Comparison of Two Models." In *Smart Sentencing: The Emergence of Intermediate Sanctions*, James M. Byrne et al., eds. Newbury Park, CA: Sage, 1992.

RECIDIVISM

The concept of recidivism is central to understanding the criminal process, the operation of the criminal justice system, and evaluative research on correctional effectiveness. Generally, the concept of recidivism refers to criminal reoffending, but it is often unclear whether it applies to committing the same crime or a new crime. The confusion is not remedied by consulting various dictionaries. One online dictionary Dictionary.com informs us that the word means "repeated or habitual relapse," but other sources, such as the *Merriam-Webster's* online dictionary, defines the word as "a tendency to relapse into a previous condition or mode of behavior," a definition similar to that found in another online dictionary, TheFreeDicionary.com, which defines recidivism as "a tendency to recidivate." Surely the term *tendency* has limited scientific use in this context, and its meaning is vague at best.

The word *recidivism* can refer to a variety of habitual behaviors, such as the consumption of alcohol or drugs and repeated antisocial conduct, including crime. What becomes murky is whether an alcoholic who starts using opiates is a recidivist or whether someone who commits a burglary and then a robbery is a recidivist. Perhaps it does not matter, because in either case the individual has not stopped using drugs or committing crime. However, a clear definition would be helpful.

This much is clear: Recidivism refers to committing a crime again; beyond this uninformative notion are matters of both measurement and meaning. Let us start with meaning. A criminology textbook from about 50 years ago, by Richard R. Korn and Lloyd W. McCorkle, states the following:

> Most criminals are recidivists. One of the first things the police do after apprehending a suspect is to investigate his legal biography. Between 50 and 60 percent of all persons in prisons and reformatories have been imprisoned before. A larger percentage has previously been arrested.

The calculation of recidivism rates has been a mainstay of criminologists for decades. It would be a mistake, however, to think that we know what those figures mean. Some think they mean that people who return to crime are "failures" of some correctional program or are criminals who have not been caught and "corrected." Such conclusions, however, are undoubtedly incorrect.

We know that recidivism rates are higher from maximum security prisons than from medium, minimum, or camp prisons. According to Michael D. Maltz, recidivism rates of inmates are also higher than those of probationers. This makes sense, because higher-risk offenders are sent to prison, whereas lower-risk offenders are assigned to supervised release in the community.

Many studies have considered this issue. Some of them have been from government agencies, some from private sources. According to a study by Patrick A. Langan and David J. Levin for the U.S. Bureau of Justice Statistics published in 2002, 67 percent of inmates released from state prisons committed at least one additional serious crime within three years of release. There were, to be sure, substantial differences in recidivism among inmates. Car thieves, burglars, and larcenists had the highest recidivism rates (about 70 percent), while rapists (2.5 percent) and murderers (1.2 percent) had the lowest rates. Other studies of either state or federal prisons, such as one by Daniel Glaser in 1964, have reported slightly different figures, and it is not the intent of this article to review all pertinent studies to ascertain the "real" recidivism rates. For the sake of argument, however, it can be agreed that at least half of inmates released from prison have a good chance of being considered recidivists.

Such figures must be interpreted in the context of the extremely high expectations about the effectiveness of correctional programs. To some, rehabilitation and the other goals of corrections are achieved only if a former correctional client never commits another crime. However, surely such an expectation is too stringent a criterion of effectiveness. Imagine if that standard were applied to hospitals. To expect of hospitals that their patients, once cured or healed, would never get sick again, see a doctor, or need to be rehospitalized is also too stringent an expectation.

Perhaps probation, prison, and parole should be thought about the same way. Relatively few offenders returning to the community never commit crimes again, particularly after release from prison. These are individuals for whom criminality is a deep behavior pattern who are released to the same environment from which they came in the first place. Many will go back to street gangs. Others will struggle with their freedom because they have had little practice being "straight."

Perhaps a former correctional client who is committing fewer crimes should be considered a success. Perhaps the former client who is committing the same number of crimes but crimes that are less serious than before, causing much less damage to the community, should be considered at least a partial success. Perhaps the former client who is committing the same kinds of crimes as before, but is doing so over a longer period of time, could also be considered a success. The concept of recidivism masks these important distinctions.

Measurement issues must also be addressed. There is no agreed-upon measure of recidivism. Conceptually, recidivism means committing another crime, either a repeat of the original offense or a new crime. Since there is no obvious way to measure this reliably, researchers have opted to use one of three measures: rearrest, reconviction, and

reinstitutionalization. Depending on which measure is used, different estimates of recidivism will be reported. The rate will be higher with rearrest, intermediate with reconviction, and lowest with reinstitutionalization.

If we consider the parallel issues with ex-patients from a hospital, we would use whether the person contacted a physician (comparable to rearrest), whether the person was treated as an outpatient (reconvicted), and whether the person was readmitted to a hospital (reinstitutionalized). More former patients will contact their physician again than will those who receive outpatient treatment, and the fewest will be readmitted to the hospital. However, does it make sense to evaluate hospitals in this manner? Do such measures really provide us with evidence on the effectiveness of hospitals or physician visits? These, and similar questions, could be asked about the comparable measures of probation, prison, and parole effectiveness.

Probationers can go along different career paths. There are those who start their period of probation with substantial motivation to avoid crime. Some, however, experience setbacks at home or at work. The probation officer might recommend marriage counseling but cannot guarantee that the probationer and his wife will attend. The probation officer might arrange to increase the probationer's work skills but cannot control the probationer's quick temper, which alienates the boss and renders the probationer's skills useless. In other words, there are many reasons that a probationer might recidivate that have nothing to do with the probation experience itself. Clearly, recidivism may be an important concept, but its relation to the effectiveness of correctional programs is tenuous.

Robert F. Meier
University of Nebraska, Omaha

See also Actuarial Risk Assessment; Crime Control Model of Corrections; Crime Victims' Concerns; Effectiveness of Community Corrections; Evaluation of Programs; Goals and Objectives of Community Corrections; Hare Psychopathy Checklist; Long-Term Offender Designation; Offender Risks; Parole Boards and Hearings; Prediction Instruments; Risk and Needs Assessment Instruments; Risk Assessment Instruments: Three Generations

Further Readings

Glaser, Daniel. *The Effectiveness of a Prison and Parole System*. Indianapolis, IN: Bobbs-Merrill, 1964.

Korn, Richard R. and Lloyd W. McCorkle. *Criminology and Penology*. New York: Holt, Rinehart and Winston, 1959.

Langan, Patrick A. and David J. Levin. "Recidivism of Prisoners Released in 1994." Washington, DC: U.S. Bureau of Justice Statistics, 2002.

Maltz, Michael D. *Recidivism*. Orlando, FL: Academic Press, 1984. http://www.uic.edu/depts/lib/forr/pdf/crimjust/recidivism.pdf (Accessed July 2011).

RECOGNIZANCE

While pretrial detention serves to ensure a defendant's court appearance, it raises ethical and legal questions about the appropriateness of punishing people who have not yet been convicted and are thus innocent until proven guilty. Pretrial detention can also have other negative consequences, including increased chances of a conviction and imposition of harsher sentences. It is unclear exactly which aspects of pretrial incarceration are associated with these consequences. Some have posited that pretrial incarceration increases the chance of conviction by limiting defendants' ability to prepare their defense. The time spent in jail while awaiting trial might also pressure defendants to plead guilty in exchange for a quick release and a community-based sanction. Judges presiding over bench trials for inmates who have been subject to pretrial detention might also find it easy simply to sentence an inmate to time served.

The Manhattan Bail Project of 1961 highlighted the potential benefits of releasing defendants on their own recognizance (ROR). ROR involves defendants signing a written contract promising to appear in court. In exchange for that promise, defendants are released from custody without having to post bond. Between 1990 and 2004, 23 percent of releases for pretrial inmates charged with felonies in the 75 largest counties in the United States involved ROR, but such nonfinancial release is a much more common option for defendants charged with misdemeanors. ROR provides an opportunity for inmates to maintain family ties and jobs as well as participate in the preparation of their defense while awaiting the court date.

The use of bail to secure an offender's return to court for trial began in medieval England. Poor sanitary conditions and the spread of diseases in the jail, combined with delayed court proceedings, prompted the search for ways to free defendants while ensuring that they would return to court. The decision concerning who would be released on bail was largely left to the sheriff. Those posting bail were faced with the threat of losing money if the defendant failed to appear for the assigned court date. Bail is an aspect of the British pretrial system that was adopted by the United States following the revolution. The U.S. Constitution is vague on the issue of bail. The only mention of bail in the constitution is the Eighth Amendment's statement outlawing "excessive bail." The federal government, however, did mandate, in the Judiciary Act of 1789, that bail was required for all arrestees with the exception of those charged with a crime that could result in the death penalty. The first large study of bail in the United States was conducted by Arthur Lawton Beeley in Chicago in 1927. Beeley found that bail was frequently set in excess of what defendants could afford, and ROR was granted to only 5 percent of defendants in Cook County.

The circumstances under which bail should be granted were clarified by the U.S. Supreme Court in *Stack v. Boyle* (342 U.S. 1, 1951). In the *Stack* ruling, the court held that the purpose of bail is to ensure the defendants' presence in court and to protect defendants from being punished prior to conviction. Furthermore, the Court ruled that bail set in excess of what would be reasonable to ensure the defendants' appearance is in violation of the Eighth Amendment. In his study of bail practices in Philadelphia during the early 1950s, Caleb Foote found judges who were willing to admit that they sometimes purposefully set bail that was too high for offenders to pay for several reasons, including wanting to make an example out of a defendant, attempting to protect a woman from an abusive husband or boyfriend, punishing a defendant who was most likely going to be acquitted or have the charges dismissed, or to trying to reduce crime in the city.

The Vera Foundation, now known as the Vera Institute of Justice, embarked on the Manhattan Bail Project in 1961. Vera researchers concluded that pretrial detention had a negative impact on defendants and influenced the outcome of their cases. Staff from the Vera Foundation worked with students from New York University Law School to interview criminal defendants and ascertain their flight risk. The results indicated that defendants with ties to the community had a high likelihood of returning to court regardless of whether they were required to post bond. This landmark study prompted other cities and states and, eventually, the federal government to encourage courts to order "release on own recognizance" whenever possible. The Bail Reform Act of 1966 was an attempt to make ROR the first option for pretrial release, with bail or restrictions on defendants' freedom to be used only when necessary.

The 1984 Bail Reform Act set a more punitive tone and presented four factors that should be considered in determining pretrial release: the nature and circumstances of the charges; the weight of the evidence; personal characteristics of the defendant (including but not limited to ties to the community, criminal history, financial resources, history of previous court appearances, and probation or parole status); and potential danger to individuals or the community posed by the defendant's release. Three years later, in *United States v. Salerno* (481 U.S. 739, 1987), the Supreme Court upheld the 1984 act, ruling that pretrial detention is legally permissible in order to prevent danger.

The New York Criminal Justice Agency (CJA) makes pretrial ROR recommendations for defendants arrested in New York City who are facing trial in the lower court. These defendants tend to be held for relatively minor crimes, so ROR is a possibility for many of the defendants who are considered. The CJA recently updated its guidelines so staff members can include ties to the community, previous failures to appear in court, and the presence of open cases against the defendant as factors in their decision-making process. Previously, their recommendations were based solely on ties to the community. The new recommendation criteria resulted in an increase in the use of ROR but no increase in instances of failure to appear.

Research on the use of guidelines for ROR revealed that the presence of guidelines serve to increase the use of ROR when compared to decisions that were made without guidelines. Additionally, ROR decisions that were made with the assistance of guidelines tend to produce fewer instances of defendants failing to appear for later court dates.

Christine Tartaro
Richard Stockton College of New Jersey

See also Bail Reform Act of 1984; Manhattan Bail
    Project; Pretrial Detention

Further Readings

Adair, David. N., Jr. *The Bail Reform Act of 1984.* Washington, DC: Federal Judicial Center, 2006.

Beeley, Arthur. *The Bail System in Chicago.* Chicago: University of Chicago Press, 1927.

Cohen, Thomas. H. and Brian A. Reaves. *Pretrial Release of Felony Defendants in State Courts.* Washington, DC: U.S. Department of Justice, Bureau of Justice Statistics, 2007.

Foote, Caleb. "Compelling Appearance in Court: Administration of Bail in Philadelphia." *University of Pennsylvania Law Review,* v.102 (1954).

Freed, Daniel J. and Patricia M. Wald. *Bail in the United States: 1964.* New York: Vera Foundation, 1964.

Goldcamp, John S. and Michael R. Gottfredson. *Policy Guidelines for Bail.* Philadelphia: Temple University Press, 1985.

Petee, Thomas. A. "Recommended for Release on Recognizance: Factors Affecting Pretrial Release Recommendations." *The Journal of Social Psychology,* v.13/4 (2001).

Phillips, Mary. T. *Bail, Detention, and Nonfelony Case Outcomes.* New York: New York City Criminal Justice Agency, 2007.

Siddiqi, Qudsia. *An Evaluation of the New Pretrial Release Recommendation System in New York City: Phase I of the Post-Implementation Research.* New York: New York Criminal Justice Agency, 2004.

Siddiqi, Qudsia. *An Evaluation of the New Pretrial Release Recommendation System in New York City: Phase II of the Post-Implementation Research.* New York: New York Criminal Justice Agency, 2005.

Stack v. Boyle, 342 U.S. 1 (1951).

United States v. Salerno, 481 U.S. 739 (1987).

Vera Institute of Justice. *New Areas for Bail Reform.* New York: Author, 1968.

REDUCING PRISON POPULATIONS

The challenge of reducing prison populations has only recently become an issue in the realm of criminal justice. The issue has become prominent largely because of the financial crises that many states have encountered, in part because of the immense costs associated with incarcerating the increasing numbers of newly sentenced offenders. The funding available for education, healthcare, and other programs has been eroded by the costs incurred by housing inmates in correctional facilities. In fiscal year 2008, states spent more than $52 billion on corrections. One of the solutions most often mentioned in discussing how to reduce prison populations, and in turn the financial cost of institutionalization, is the utilization of community corrections. Many components of community corrections can assist in reducing prison populations.

Reasons for the Increase in the Prison Population

There was a steady increase in the incarceration rate beginning around 1972, with a steep increase beginning in the 1980s along with the advent of crack cocaine. The current incarceration rate has stopped increasing and has remained steady for the last several years. In 1970, the incarceration rate was 96 per 100,000 population; by the end of 1986, the incarceration rate had doubled, to 227 per 100,000 population; and as of 2006, the incarceration rate had reached nearly 500 per 100,000 population. The most common factor associated with the massive proliferation in the prison population is not an increase in crime but changes in sentencing policy.

During the 1980s, the "war on drugs" and the "tough-on-crime" stance in the United States led to an increase in felony convictions, as well as longer sentences for those convictions. A main reason for the increase in the prison population in general, and of incarcerated minorities specifically, is the increase in arrests and penalties for drug offenders. The number of state inmates incarcerated for drug offenses from 1980 to 1995 increased from 45,000 to nearly half a million, an escalation in the prison population of more than 1,000 percent.

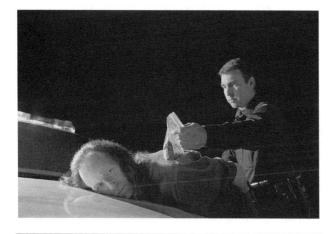

Incarceration of drug offenders is the main cause for the striking increase in the U.S. prison population—the United States has the highest incarceration rate worldwide. The *Baltimore Sun* reported that 70 percent of Maryland inmates in 2004 had been jailed for drug offenses. (Photos.com)

Another factor often associated with the increase in the prison population is the increased level of surveillance of individuals on probation and parole, which leads to an increase of technical violations that in turn result in imprisonment. The more frequent use of electronic monitoring and global positioning system (GPS) technology in the tracking of offenders has greatly increased the ability to detect individuals violating some condition of their probation or parole requirements.

Often, when offenders violate the conditions of their probation or parole, they are returned to prison even without the commission of a new crime. The incorporation of mandatory sentencing, such as "three-strikes" laws, also limits the discretion of judges; forcing them to send many people to prison when utilizing community-based sanctions would be a positive option. Mandatory sentencing guidelines also often compel judges to impose lengthier sentences that may be appropriate for the circumstances. Along these same lines is the propensity of some parole boards not to grant parole for all of those who are eligible. Sometimes in response to public scrutiny and in order to show constituents that they are not soft on crime, parole boards are reluctant to parole some individuals for fear that they might commit a new crime.

Options for Reducing the Prison Population

There is some belief that an increase in treatment and rehabilitation programs within prison can help to reduce the prison population. This option can be mostly eliminated, however, because it is well known that the increase of the prison population did not occur because of lack of treatment programs. The fact that the changes in legislation and sentencing led to this increase makes some researchers wary to believe that treatment in correctional facilities will create a reduction in the prison population. Treatment programs can help reduce recidivism in some circumstances, but the level of overcrowding based on recidivism is not even countered by the effects of in-house treatment.

Based on the fact that many of those currently incarcerated have been sentenced according to the stricter sentencing policies, the obvious and most common option for reducing the prison population is to reduce the severity of sentences and return to sentencing policies that were dominant prior to the 1970s and 1980s, when the increase began. Research has shown that that there is a certain point at which incarceration is counterproductive. When the number of incarcerated offenders reaches that high level, the stability of the community, family, and society as a whole is disrupted to a point where crime rates increase rather than decrease.

The number of crimes that ultimately end in incarceration is high. Many people contend that countless currently incarcerated individuals could have made their reparations in the community rather than being confined. Low-level and nonviolent criminals can be diverted into community correction institutions rather than being locked up with more serious, violent criminals. Decriminalizing "victimless" crimes, such as drug use and abuse, would dramatically reduce the prison population. Only about 15 percent of the crimes for which people are arrested are violent or serious property crimes. Even if certain individuals need some level of supervision, that supervision can often be successfully implemented through community corrections.

Two categories of individuals who are often seen as not needing to be incarcerated are those with mental illnesses and those who have drug or alcohol addictions. Much has been published about the unfortunate overrepresentation of the mentally ill in prisons. This is a population that would benefit much more from community intervention and treatment than from being locked up in a correctional facility where staff members are not properly trained to handle such cases and the medical programs necessary for these individuals are lacking. One option that helps in the reduction of the prison population is the use of mental health courts as a diversion process to get the mentally ill the help they need in community centers. Getting these individuals proper care in the community, with medications, treatment programs, and housing, would concomitantly reduce the prison population, enhance the chances for these individuals' success within the community, and ultimately reducing recidivism. For example, the use of halfway houses and residential treatment centers may allow these individuals to continue to work on establishing and maintaining a sustainable lifestyle, including employment, while receiving treatment.

The use of specialty courts to assist in the reduction of the prison population has grown tremendously since 1989, when the first drug court was established in Miami-Dade County, Florida. There are now more than 2,000 drug courts and more than 1,000 other specialty courts, including family courts, DWI courts, reentry courts, and domestic violence courts. The purpose of these specialty courts is to divert those persons with underlying issues that have brought them into contact with the criminal justice system into community support programs rather than sending them to prison, where it is unlikely that they will receive this type of individualized care. Many specialty courts are now activated post-conviction rather than pretrial, but they can still aid in the reduction of the prison population.

The use of specialty courts is also popular because they provide a cost savings. Research has shown that specialty court programs are at least as cost-effective as incarceration, but with the advantage that they can increase the health of those who get treatment and thereby reduce recidivism.

Nick Harpster
Sam Houston State University

See also Community Corrections as an Alternative to Imprisonment; Day Reporting Centers; Determinate Sentencing; Discretionary Release; Diversion Programs; Electronic Monitoring; Flat Time; Front-End and Back-End Programming; GPS Tracking; Halfway Houses and Residential Centers; Mental Health Courts; Political Determinants of Corrections Policy; Prison Overcrowding; Probation and Parole: Intensive Supervision; Revocation; Three Strikes and You're Out

Further Readings

Austin, J. et al. *Unlocking America: Why and How to Reduce America's Prison Population*. Washington, DC: JFA Institute, 2007.

Blom-Cooper, Louis Jacques. *The Penalty of Imprisonment: Why 60 Per Cent of the Prison Population Should Not Be There*. New York: Continuum, 2008.

Blumstein, A. "Prison Populations: A System Out of Control?" *Crime and Justice*, v.10 (1988).

Feest, Johannes. *Reducing the Prison Population: Lessons From the West German Experience?* London: National Association for the Care and Resettlement of Offenders, 1988.

Golaszewski, Paul, Anthony Simbol, and Mac Taylor. *The 2010–11 Budget: Assessing the Prison Population Reduction Proposal*. Sacramento, CA: Legislative Analyst's Office, 2010.

Pollack, Harold, Peter Reuter, and Eric L. Sevigny. *If Drug Treatment Works So Well, Why Are So Many Drug Users in Prison?* Cambridge, MA: National Bureau of Economic Research, 2011.

REENTRY COURTS

Beginning in the late 1990s, criminal justice agencies, politicians, and the general public began to express growing concern about high rates of ex-offender recidivism. While probation and parole agencies have commonly provided supervision and even some social services to individuals recently released from correctional facilities, high recidivism rates began to shed light on the need for new approaches. In the past decade, a renewed interest in prisoner reentry has resulted in a variety of changes to correctional programming, post-release supervision strategies, and the availability of community-based programs. Reentry courts constitute only one of many programs intended to assist former inmates as they transition back into the community. Generally, reentry courts are designed to offer formerly incarcerated individuals social services and support while also providing additional supervision in the post-release period.

Reentry courts are a type of specialized court. Specialized courts, such as drug courts, domestic violence courts, and gun courts, were created to reduce burgeoning caseloads by diverting some offenders from the traditional court system and to experiment with new strategies for certain types of offenders. Although reentry courts were created to supplement the traditional justice system, they do differ from other specialized courts. Most specialized courts enroll participants before they have been adjudicated; conversely, reentry courts enroll participants after they have been adjudicated and served prison sentences.

The guidelines for enrolling recently released individuals in reentry courts vary widely. Reentry court programs often target particular individuals, such as those who are under parole supervision, those who have been classified as at high risk for reoffending, or those who previously committed certain types of offenses. Reentry court participation may be voluntary and associated with some type of incentive, or it may be a requirement of release from prison. All reentry courts have a geographic focus, targeting individuals who are returning to a specific geographic area, such as a neighborhood, city, or county.

Although the program structure varies greatly among different reentry courts, participants are generally required to attend reentry court sessions that may be scheduled on a biweekly to bimonthly basis (some programs employ a phasing-out strategy in which participants are required to attend less often as they demonstrate success). Typically, all court participants are present during each session, and a reentry court judge asks each participant to report any successes and obstacles related to his or her reentry. Participants are praised for successes by the judge and other court officials involved in the proceedings. When a participant specifies a particular challenge—perhaps related to housing, employment, or substance abuse—the reentry court judge or other court officials often refer the individual to a particular social service provider. If a participant declines to identify an ongoing problem during court, the reentry court judge likely already knows about the issue as a result of discussions with parole officers or other case management staff involved in the reentry court. As in the drug court model, there are both punishments for noncompliance and rewards for progress. This stands in contrast to traditional forms of post-incarceration release supervision, which relies primarily on punishment for noncompliance.

The Office of Justice Programs (OJP) launched one of the first large-scale reentry court projects in early 2000, titled the Reentry Court Initiative (RCI). OJP provided assistance to nine sites to create reentry courts. Although there were significant program differences between sites, RCI did stipulate six core elements, including assessment and planning by a reentry court work group, active oversight, management of support services, accountability to community, graduated and parsimonious sanctions, and rewards for success. Since the development of the RCI sites, a number of county jurisdictions and more than 35 federal jurisdictions have also developed reentry courts.

Research on the effectiveness of reentry courts in reducing recidivism is relatively minimal, and the studies that exist offer mixed results. Most of the RCI sites have undergone basic process evaluations. As Christine Lindquist and colleagues discovered in their research on RCI sites, stakeholders generally believed that participation in reentry court positively influenced reentry as a result of increasing supervision, reconnecting participants with family members, and providing access to social services. The Harlem Parole Reentry Court has completed the most extensive outcome evaluation. Although an initial evaluation conducted by Donald J. Farole failed to find significant differences in reincarceration rates between a comparison group and reentry court participants during the first year following release, a more methodologically rigorous study conducted by Zachary Hamilton uncovered more positive results. This study revealed that, compared to a matched comparison group, participants were less likely to be reconvicted of a new offense at three years following release.

Despite the fact that research demonstrating the effectiveness of reentry courts is still developing, many jurisdictions believe that they offer an exciting alternative to traditional approaches to ex-offender reentry. By emphasizing a balance between supervision and the availability of social services and support, reentry courts offer a promising strategy for improving public safety.

Caitlin J. Taylor
Temple University

See also Drug Courts; Mental Health Courts; Reentry Programs and Initiatives; Reintegration Into Communities

Further Readings

Farole, Donald J. "The Harlem Parole Reentry Court Evaluation: Implementation and Preliminary Impacts." http://www.courtinnovation.org/_uploads/documents/harlemreentryeval.pdf (Accessed February 2011).

Hamilton, Zachary. "Do Reentry Courts Reduce Recidivism? Results From the Harlem Parole Reentry Court." http://www.courtinnovation.org/_uploads/documents/Reentry_Evaluation.pdf (Accessed February 2011).

Lindquist, Christine, Jennifer Hardison, and Pamela K. Lattimore. "Reentry Court Process Evaluation (Phase 1)." http://www.ncjrs.gov/pdffiles1/nij/grants/202472.pdf (Accessed February 2011).

REENTRY PROGRAMS AND INITIATIVES

In response to budgetary concerns, overcrowded prison systems, and growing recidivism rates, a number of jurisdictions have begun to rethink their approach to offender reentry. Generally, reentry is the process a criminal offender undertakes when he or she leaves prison and returns to the community. Traditionally, the U.S. criminal justice system has employed somewhat reactionary reentry policies.

In response to growing concerns about citizen safety and fluctuating crime rates, the United States customarily responded with longer prison sentences and more stringent supervised release guidelines. Yet, in recent years, many jurisdictions have turned away from these established corrections practices. Instead, many jurisdictions now take a more active approach to offender reentry and reintegration. Specifically, most jurisdictions now view offender reentry as a holistic, continuous concept that begins on an offender's day of sentencing and continues until an offender successfully becomes a contributing member of society. Common to such programs or initiatives are elements that combine resources and promote cooperation among and between correctional and community agencies. Supporters of these modern transition initiatives argue that by altering the conceptualization of reentry, jurisdictions can better protect communities by ensuring that offenders achieve post-release success. Conversely, critics of such programs contend that by aiding offenders, jurisdictions pamper those who deviated from the law while ignoring crime victims.

Each year, U.S. prisons and jails release approximately 650,000 prisoners. In addition, roughly 9 million Americans have contact with local jails yearly. For those citizens who endure a period of confinement, reintegration into the community can prove challenging. Formal and informal restrictions impact an offender's life in myriad ways. For instance, almost all offenders face obstacles relating to basic life needs, such as housing and employment. Research on reentry has shown that, to overcome such obstacles, offenders require concerted and systematic assistance. Nevertheless, in the United States, most criminal justice agencies (such as law-enforcement departments, courts, prison systems, and parole and probation organizations) exist as separate agencies, largely divorced from one another. Commentators specializing in reentry suggest that such a system is inefficient, citing as support for this proposition the prospect that about two thirds of all those leaving jails and prisons each year will ultimately return. They further note that these increased recidivism rates promote jail and prison overcrowding while putting tremendous financial strain on jurisdictional budgets. In response, some jurisdictions have altered their approach to reentry, implementing more comprehensive programs aimed at better serving offenders in their quest to reenter society successfully after a period of incarceration.

These modern reentry programs and initiatives seek to use existing resources in new ways to better address the problems of reentry. For example, such initiatives call on evidence-based research, which has become increasingly popular, that uses scientific evaluation as a method for appraising program effectiveness. Armed with this information, jurisdictions can then alter their approach to reentry using only existing resources. This approach reduces costs while perhaps increasing success. The method whereby these new initiatives alter resource allocation starts by reevaluating the goals and missions of those involved in the reentry process. For instance, instead of solely monitoring offenders, transition initiatives ask supervisory agencies to work with offenders to alter their behaviors. In addition, modern transition initiatives encourage cooperation between agencies that were customarily separate. Hence, under these new programs, agencies do not shuffle offenders from one criminal justice organization to the next. Instead, organizations like courts, prisons, and community supervision departments share information about a given offender, even customizing an offender's reentry plan. Moreover, these modern reentry initiatives seek to involve community organizations unaffiliated with the criminal justice system. Such programs have redefined reentry, classifying the concept as a large-scale community problem rather than a specified corrections problem. Finally, when appraising reentry or transition initiatives, administrators look, once again, to scientific assessments. Those charged with measuring the effectiveness of modern transition programs evaluate such programs using objective, quantifiable data.

Mechanically, modern reentry initiatives are far more proactive than those of the past. In such programs, administrators carefully monitor offenders, evaluating and reevaluating offenders' reentry needs at critical stages throughout the criminal justice process. For example, in most modern reentry programs, personnel assess offenders' reintegration requirements in pre-sentence reports, at prison intake, at monthly or bimonthly prison reviews, and upon release. These efforts allow reentry coordinators to design reentry plans that fit individual offenders. Moreover, upon release, such plans call for the assistance of community organizations invested in offenders' successful reentry. In this way, reentry becomes an ongoing process completed only when an offender becomes a contributing member of society. Hence, modern transition programs differ from traditional models in that they treat reentry as a progressive course rather than an isolated event.

Opponents of modernizing reentry programs in the United States routinely object to a perceived increase in the services provided to offenders. Critics argue that the victims of crime do not enjoy such tailored attention when attempting to deal with the aftereffects of a criminal encounter. According to this view, coddling offenders detracts from deterrence goals. In addition, those opposed to retooled reentry initiatives suggest that a focus on assisting offenders with their transition from incarceration to society jeopardizes public safety by misusing precious resources. They assert that such initiatives can be costly and can undercut the incapacitation goals of the criminal justice system. In short, many claim that modern reentry initiatives work against the established normative goals of the U.S. criminal justice system.

In response to such criticisms, proponents of modern transition initiatives note that such programs merely reallocate existing resources, creating minimal new costs. They also point out that modern criminological research drives such reallocation. Furthermore, advocates of innovative reentry policies argue that an offender's successful reintegration protects society to a greater extent than do the failed strategies of the past.

James M. Binnall
University of California, Irvine

See also Community Partnerships; Recidivism; Residential Correctional Programs; Risk and Needs Assessment Instruments

Further Readings

Engel, Len. "Toward an Evidence-Based System of Offender Reentry." 2008. http://cjinstitute.org/files/Successful%20 Community%20Transition_5%205%2008.pdf.

National Institute of Corrections. "Transition From Prison to Community Initiative (TPCI)." 2007. http://nicic.gov/Library/020285.

Taxman, Faye S., Douglas Young, and James S. Byrne. "Transforming Offender Reentry Into Public

Safety: Lessons From OJP's Reentry Partnership Initiative." *Justice and Research and Policy*, v.5/2 (2003).

Urban Institute. *The Transition From Jail to Community Initiative*. Washington, DC: Author, 2007. http://www.urban.org/projects/tjc/index.cfm (Accessed July 2011).

REINTEGRATION INTO COMMUNITIES

Prisoners returning to communities face numerous obstacles to reintegration. These obstacles can derail a returning prisoner's efforts to readjust and become a full, contributing member of society. One class of reintegration obstacles comprises legal mandates impacting criminal offenders. A second class of reintegration obstacles encompasses those psychological difficulties faced by former offenders who have spent a period of time incarcerated.

Generally, legal barriers to reintegration divide into two types: collateral sanctions and discretionary disqualifications. Collateral sanctions are statutes and regulations that automatically limit or eliminate the rights or privileges of most returning prisoners. Discretionary disqualifications are typically legal mandates that authorize third parties, for example employers, to use the existence of a criminal record as a determining factor when assessing a returning prisoner's eligibility for certain rights, benefits, or privileges. Although often severe, psychological barriers to reintegration are far less visible than reintegration barriers erected in law. Many returning prisoners struggle to assimilate outside prison because of these issues, which can remain hidden but stem directly or indirectly from the prison experience.

Theoretically, returning prisoners can overcome most reintegration barriers. Nevertheless, many returning prisoners find that certain aspects of reentry pose formidable challenges, requiring extensive commitment and substantial assistance.

Legal Barriers

Collateral sanctions and discretionary disqualifications often work in concert to create the two most significant challenges that returning prisoners face upon release: finding suitable housing and finding gainful employment. Research suggests that a returning prisoner's reentry success is largely dependent on his or her ability to secure a residence and a job. However, legal barriers make locating housing and employment difficult for most returning prisoners by limiting their already scant housing and work options.

Of the nearly two million Americans in U.S. jails and prisons, most struggled financially prior to their incarceration. Research indicates that a majority of the U.S. prison population lived at or below the poverty level prior to their imprisonment. In addition, research also shows that, upon release, virtually all prisoners return to the impoverished areas in which they spent time prior to confinement. In this way, economic factors significantly limit a returning prisoner's housing options, forcing him or her to rely on family or to seek out public assistance in attempting to find proper living quarters.

For most returning prisoners, however, federal and state legal mandates eliminate the ability to secure public assistance or public housing. Furthermore, such legislation also discourages family members who live in public housing from cohabitating with returning prisoners. For example, in the 1990s, Congress passed several measures, including the Housing Opportunity Program Extension Act of 1996 and the Quality Housing and Work Responsibility Act of 1998. Together, these statutes authorize public housing authorities to deny convicted felons federally funded housing on the basis of a criminal conviction. Moreover, these statutes

As the majority of the U.S. prison population lives at or below the poverty level before imprisonment, research shows that nearly all prisoners return to the same impoverished areas upon release, limiting housing options, job prospects, and the possibility of a successful reentry into society. (Photos.com)

helped to establish a "one strike and you're out" eviction policy for public housing, which permits public housing authorities to evict a tenant when that tenant, a member of the tenant's household, or a person under the tenant's control engages in any criminal activity on or off the public housing premise. Not surprisingly, this policy makes many families reluctant to share living quarters with returning prisoners who perhaps, in the past, struggled with drug addiction or violent behavior. Thus, economic factors, collateral sanctions, and discretionary disqualifications hinder a returning prisoner's quest for housing. As a result, in many major metropolitan areas in the United States, homelessness plagues the returning prisoner population.

Apart from housing, employment stands as a returning prisoner's greatest challenge. In most states, statutes automatically disqualify certain returning prisoners from a number of occupations. Ironically, such statutes often bar returning prisoners from jobs for which they trained while incarcerated. In *When Prisoners Come Home: Parole and Prisoner Reentry*, Joan Petersilia notes that in New York, barber training programs are exceedingly popular in prison. However, as Petersilia points out, New York does not typically license barbers with a criminal history. Many other states also restrict the number of occupations available to returning prisoners. For example, many states preclude those with a criminal record from working in the medical field, the legal profession, or the education system.

Along with the automatic barriers to employment posed by collateral sanctions, returning prisoners must also contend with discretionary disqualifications that allow potential employers to deny a position to those with a criminal record. In most states, legislation allows employers to inquire about an applicant's history of arrest and conviction. An employer can deny a returning prisoner employment if the employer can show that a business justification or a business necessity spawned the rejection. Given the malleable quality of these legal standards and the rarity with which they face a challenge, a criminal record often operates as a categorical preclusion to employment.

Psychological Barriers

Returning prisoners often face certain psychological issues that make social readjustment difficult or nearly impossible. Most returning prisoners carry with them the effects of a term of incarceration. Psychologist Craig Haney discovered that many prisoners institutionalize or adapt to incarceration. These adaptations, Haney notes, make certain tasks difficult upon release. For example, Haney contends, prisoners generally become dependent on the rigid prison schedules. He also points out that the violence and manipulation common in prison spawn within many inmates a psychological distancing that leads to a disappearance of trust and social interdependence. Moreover, Haney's research suggests that many returning prisoners suffer from post-traumatic stress disorder and feelings of low self-worth.

These psychological effects of incarceration present significant challenges for returning prisoners attempting to reintegrate into society. Families and authorities expect returning prisoners to work, to reestablish healthy relationships, and to remain law-abiding. For many returning prisoners, however, coping with the prison experience makes reentry a daunting task. Social situations and unstructured time periods typically enjoyed by free citizens are unsettling for those who have spent time in prison. Moreover, seldom do returning prisoners seek out or receive the necessary treatment for such maladies. Hence, on most occasions, returning prisoners must deal with the effects of incarceration alone, at the same time that they are trying to rebuild their post-release lives.

James M. Binnall
University of California, Irvine

See also Attitudes of Offenders Toward Community Corrections; Civil and Political Rights Affected by Conviction; Loss of Individual Rights; Pardon and Restoration of Rights

Further Readings

Haney, Craig. "The Psychological Impact of Incarceration: Implications for Post-Prison Adjustment." Paper presented at the From Prison to Home conference, January 30–31, 2002.

Haney, Craig. *Reforming Punishment: Psychological Limitations to the Pains of Imprisonment*. Washington, DC: American Psychological Association, 2006.

Mauer, Marc and Meda Chesney-Lind. *Invisible Punishment: The Collateral Consequences of Mass Imprisonment*. New York: New Press, 2002.

Petersilia, Joan. *When Prisoners Come Home: Parole and Prisoner Reentry*. Oxford: Oxford University Press, 2003.

REPARATION BOARDS

Innovative initiatives in community corrections have aimed at involving more lay counselors in managing offenders and delivering justice. One method for accomplishing this is the reparation board. Reparation boards allow citizens to serve as members of a body designed specifically to provide assistance on cases involving offenders convicted of minor or nonviolent offenses, with a view to providing a more meaningful and restorative experience to the parties involved.

To emphasize the constructive approach underpinning this practice, reparation boards are commonly referred to as neighborhood accountability boards (NABs), community accountability boards (CABs), community restorative boards, and community diversion boards. Similar bodies include juvenile community accountability boards, reparative probation community boards, and reparative boards (although the terms used in these names may undermine their positive nature, given the negative connotations associated with *juvenile*, *reparative*, and *probation*). Although an effective and inexpensive alternative for greatly reducing costly reliance on public resources, these boards have been implemented in only a handful of states, such as Arizona, Colorado, Florida, New York, Louisiana, Missouri, Washington, Nebraska, and California. The community orientation of these boards encourages and facilitates both citizen ownership and leadership in the community by providing laypersons with opportunities to play an active role in the management, supervision, mentorship, and reintegration of offenders.

Reparation boards are usually composed of three to five members specially trained to hold face-to-face meetings with offenders who are serving a judicially imposed sentence with a condition to appear before a reparation board or who have been referred to the board by the police, rather than arrested. As representatives from their respective communities, usually where the offender also resides, the board members have a stake in the offender's positive outcome and therefore are motivated to clarify, communicate, and enforce norms and standards of acceptable behavior. They provide an opportunity for all parties—the offender, the victim or victims, family members, and community volunteers—to come together following

conviction to review the nature of the offense and its effects on others and on the community as a whole. These meetings are held in a safe and constructive manner; their aim is to hold the offender accountable, make reparation for the offense, reconcile conflicting parties, aid in victim healing, and individually empower, educate, and reintegrate offenders. Victims and other affected parties are invited and encouraged to participate, either by speaking before the board or by submitting a written statement, which is then shared with the board and the offender. In some places, boards may work closely with various victims' services and advocacy groups in order to encourage participation and representation of victims.

In order to avoid the formality and intimidation often associated with courtrooms, these boards are usually held in a public facility such as a conference room in a library, town hall, or community center. Meetings average 45 minutes in length and are chaired by one member of the board, who is also usually responsible for managing staff and resources along with other administrative duties, such as scheduling and paperwork. After the meeting, board members will convene privately to review the case and collectively propose sanctions aimed to address victim restitution and community reparation, which may include apologies, compensation, and community service. These are negotiated with the offender, along with a time plan, in what is commonly

Community reparation boards monitor contract compliance, determine whether offenders and victims have worked out acceptable restitution agreements, and review the effects of the crime on the community. These boards have a high stake in the outcome because they are comprised of members of the offender's community. (Photos.com)

referred to as the accountability (or sanction) agreement (or contract). The board also seeks to identify strategies to reduce the likelihood of future offending behavior—for example, by identifying counseling, employment, and educational opportunities. Depending on the frequency of the offender's meetings with the board, monthly or quarterly reports are prepared and submitted to the court that contain information on compliance of the offender, progress toward completion of proposed sanctions, and recommendations if necessary. Those failing to comply with reparation contracts are considered in violation of their probation and are returned to the court, which may impose more serious penalties. The board continues to stay regularly involved with the offender, through such methods as mid-term review meetings, to monitor the order until all requirements have been successfully completed.

In the United States, early forms of reparation boards have been in existence since the 1920s. However, one notable example has been the center of research—the Vermont reparative probation program, which was established statewide through legislation in 1996 by the Vermont Department of Corrections in conjunction with the Bureau of Justice Assistance. By 2000, this program had processed more than 5,000 cases through 49 separate boards statewide with nearly 300 volunteers (more, if counting various assistants and coordinators) contributing more than 23,000 hours. Of 1,902 cases handled in 2000 alone, nearly three quarters of offenders successfully completed program requirements, with only a third recidivating within the following year. Many of these cases were for minor offenses, such as property crimes, vehicle offenses (such as driving recklessly and while intoxicated), and alcohol charges (such as underage drinking or providing alcohol to minors). To determine the efficacy of the Vermont reparative probation program and experiences of volunteers, offenders, and victimized individuals, many studies have been conducted. For example, David Karp and colleagues conducted evaluations of the Vermont reparative boards and found them to be effective in restoring offenders, victims, and communities. The only troublesome finding involved the lack of victim participation, although victims reported that they were generally satisfied with the program. A 2004 study by Karp, G. Bazemore, and J. D. Chesire, which investigated volunteer

experiences in the Vermont reparative probation program, found that the program was an effective alternative for offenders, had good knowledge of the principles behind restorative justice, and was representative of the community.

While a creative measure in community corrections, reparation boards are faced with a number of challenges and criticisms. As a community-driven initiative, reparation boards rely solely on volunteers, who need to be representative of the community, supportive of the program, knowledgeable of the principles of restorative justice, capable of working with others effectively and contributing to group decision making, and able to engage positively with offenders, victims, and the community. The chairs of these boards are also responsible for providing and coordinating adequate resources, such as facilities, staffing, logistics, administration, and training, all of which require time and money. Meetings with offenders need to be planned swiftly following the offense, which may be difficult given the volunteers' other commitments (such as work schedules and family activities), and held in a manner all members can easily understand. Boards also have to communicate with other organizations and agencies, including police, probation officers, victim services, and advocacy groups, in order to gather information and encourage greater victim participation and representation. Finally, reparation boards need to be marketed as effective alternatives to judges, prosecutors, defense attorneys—even to offenders and victims, who may be unaware of their existence or otherwise consider these boards as inappropriate alternatives to "true" justice, given their relative informality.

This use of reparation boards has been an inventive step in community-based corrections and will continue to improve over time as additional programs are implemented and evaluated.

Michael J. Puniskis
Middlesex University

See also Diversion Programs; Juvenile and Youth
    Offenders; Volunteers and Community Corrections

Further Readings

Boyes-Watson, C. "The Value of Citizen Participation in Restorative/Community Justice: Lessons From Vermont." *Criminology and Public Policy*, v.3/4 (2004).

Karp, D. R. "Harm and Repair: Observing Restorative Justice in Vermont." *Justice Quarterly*, v.18/4 (2001).

Karp, D. R. "The Offender/Community Encounter: Stakeholder Involvement in the Vermont Reparative Boards." In *What Is Community Justice? Case Studies in Restorative Justice and Community Supervision*, D. R. Karp and T. R. Clear, eds. London: Sage, 2002.

Karp, D. R., G. Bazemore, and J. D. Chesire. "The Role and Attitudes of Restorative Board Members: A Case Study of Volunteers in Community Justice." *Crime and Delinquency*, v.50/4 (2004).

Karp, D. R. and K. M. Drakulich. "Minor Crime in a Quaint Setting: Practices, Outcomes and Limits of Vermont Reparative Probation Boards." *Criminology and Public Policy*, v.3/4 (2006).

Karp, D. R. and L. Walther. "Community Reparative Boards in Vermont." In *Restorative Community Justice: Repairing Harm and Transforming Communities*, G. Bazemore and M. Schiff, eds. Cincinnati, OH: Anderson, 2001.

Sinkinson, H. D. and J. J. Brokerick. "A Case Study of Restorative Justice: The Vermont Reparative Probation Program." In *Restorative Justice for Juveniles: Potentialities, Risks and Problems for Research*, L. Walgrave, ed. Belgium: Leuven University Press, 1999.

RESIDENTIAL CORRECTIONAL PROGRAMS

Residential community corrections facilities are a type of community-based corrections program. Community-based corrections in general, such as probation and parole, were developed to offer a less restrictive alternative to jail or prison for people who have been convicted of an offense. Offenders are required to serve the sanctions imposed by the courts while living in the community. Most community-based corrections programs, whether residential or nonresidential, include some social services for offenders in an effort to fully reintegrate them back into society.

In nonresidential community corrections programs such as probation, parole, and day reporting centers, offenders can live at home while participating in them. However, if ordered by a court to a residential community-based corrections program, an offender or parolee is required to live in the community residential facility (not at home), typically for three to six months and sometimes longer. Residential community corrections programs are

varied and include halfway houses, residential drug and alcohol treatment facilities, post-prison reentry programs, specialized residential programs that allow female offenders to live with their children, and group homes for young offenders. Residential community corrections programs also include the more restrictive home confinement (house arrest) and correctional boot camps (primarily for young offenders). The vast majority of residential community corrections facilities are privately owned or run by nonprofit organizations; less than 10 percent are operated by departments of corrections.

Residential community corrections facilities are highly structured programs aimed at behavior modification that offer services such as drug and alcohol treatment, employment education, group counseling, and interpersonal skills classes. They allow residents to hold outside jobs or attend school. They are unique in that, in addition to providing housing and intensive treatment and programming 24 hours per day, many seek to replicate a family atmosphere or family model. Residential community corrections programs are cost-effective and have better reported success rates than do prison, probation, or parole (as measured by lower rates of reoffending upon graduation), largely because they offer more treatment services. They tend to practice closer supervision and surveillance of offenders, in comparison to most nonresidential community corrections programs.

Halfway Houses

Halfway houses, the earliest type of residential community-based correctional facility, were started by the Quakers in the mid-1800s to house people released from prison. Halfway houses did not provide treatment services at the time, only food and shelter, and they were privately owned. Not until the 1960s did the government fund federal halfway houses, but most were nongovernmental and remain so today. In 1989, the International Association of Residential and Community Alternatives was composed of 250 private and nongovernmental agencies operating 1,500 programs worldwide.

Halfway houses today, also called residential community corrections facilities (RCCFs) or community-based correctional facilities (CBCFs), house various types of offenders. Offenders are court-mandated to them as a diversion from (that is, an alternative to) prison. These offenders might be considered still "halfway in" prison. These programs offer more structure and control than regular probation. RCCFs also include reentry programs for people leaving prison. For offenders already on parole or those who anticipate getting parole within one or two years, RCCFs ease the transition from incarceration to life back in the community; such offenders can be seen as "halfway out" of prison. With the passage of the federal Second Chance Act in 2008, community-based reentry programs have proliferated in an effort to reduce recidivism and prison overcrowding.

There is no uniform model of a halfway house or RCCF; each is unique in structure, treatment programs offered, and type of client accepted. However, these programs have some common components. Most residents in halfway houses are low-risk offenders, such as drug and alcohol offenders, rather than violent or sex offenders. Residents must live in the facility (not at home); must be employed, must be seeking employment, or be enrolled in school; and may leave the facility for work only with approval (a pass for a specified duration and purpose). These programs also have a levels system, that is, a behavior modification system in which residents or "clients" earn increased freedom and more privileges based on good behavior and time spent in the program. Failure to abide by the rules results in sanctions that may range from loss of privileges to expulsion. Failure to complete the program can result in a resident's return to court or prison.

Group Homes

Group homes are a particular type of halfway house or RCCF for youths. These programs became popular in the 1970s and 1980s and are mostly minimum-security residences for young offenders. They are behavioral residential treatment programs in that they seek to change negative behavior and rehabilitate offenders, preparing them to reenter the community upon graduating.

There are different types of group homes. A "teaching family home," for example, is a family-style group home with supervising adults that uses behaviorism and a levels system with a small group of juveniles, typically six to eight. The teaching family model is a widely replicated and successful model of care developed in the 1960s at the University of Kansas. The goal is to provide

humane, individualized services and reinforce prosocial skills. Additionally, a behavior modification facility is a residential treatment institution that provides education and treatment to adolescents who display violent, antisocial behavior with the goal of changing that behavior. Most are nongovernmental, although some are operated within correctional systems. Therapeutic boarding schools, based on a therapeutic community model, offer educational programs with substance abuse treatment within a family atmosphere and with the goal of promoting prosocial skills and drug and alcohol treatment.

Residential Drug and Alcohol Treatment

Most of these programs share features with other kinds of RCCFs. Drug and alcohol offenders are typically probated by a court to a drug treatment program as a diversion from prison (otherwise, they would serve time in prison) or as a condition of parole (that is, release from prison). Some substance abuse treatment programs are based on the therapeutic community model. Therapeutic communities (TCs) are residential drug treatment programs that use behavioral and cognitive approaches, seeking to change behavior and thinking patterns.

State corrections departments contract with TCs to take drug and alcohol offenders for treatment as an alternative to incarceration. TCs also receive contracts to operate inside jails and prisons. Like other types of residential drug and alcohol treatment programs, TCs typically house nonviolent, lower-risk offenders and are minimum-security facilities; the door is unlocked, but residents must earn privileges to leave for limited outings.

TCs place special emphasis on the "community"—that is, the residential community of treatment clients—and the structure and support of the community and TC "family" are viewed as the source of recovery. The facilities themselves often resemble a house (some are large Victorian homes or other large residences). TCs use focused peer pressure from fellow residents living in the TC aimed at behavior modification both generally and specifically to address substance abuse. Professional input, such as psychotherapy, is deemphasized in favor of the group process. Staff who manage the program are typically former substance abusers and serve as role models for the residents. The daily schedule is highly structured and incorporates a levels system;

sanctions for noncompliance with the program, such as breaking rules or leaving without a pass, are graduated depending on the infraction and can include return to court or prison. Clients hold jobs within the "house," such as cooking, cleaning, and program administration; they follow a highly structured daily schedule of chores, individual and group meetings, and classes on topics including substance abuse, interpersonal communication, parenting, and anger management. They can also work outside the facility in regular paid jobs, take academic classes, visit their children and families, and attend Alcoholics Anonymous or Narcotics Anonymous meetings, once they have advanced to a higher level.

TCs began as grassroots self-help organizations, much as Alcoholics Anonymous did, in the 1950s. The first TC program, started by Charles E. Dederich, an Alcoholics Anonymous graduate, operated out of an old beach house in southern California. The program, which was voluntary, used highly confrontational encounter groups with drug users in the program. Known as Synanon, it proved to be a successful and novel response to drug addiction, including heroin addiction, which was thought to be incurable; heroin users were commonly incarcerated for long terms.

Practices that have contributed the TC's success in treating substance abusers, according to TC expert Lewis Yablonsky, include involvement in the TC community, achievable goals, offering new social roles and status to clients to promote social growth, social control of substance-abusing behavior, and the teaching of empathy and fostering of self-identity. Today, TCs are found in many countries, and a World Federation of Therapeutic Communities has been founded.

Residential Intermediate Sanctions

Intermediate sanctions are a more restrictive, punitive kind of community corrections that exist alongside other types of community corrections programs. They are used for offenders who are thought to require closer supervision than regular probationers or parolees but for whom incarceration is deemed unnecessary. Such programs can be either residential or nonresidential. Intermediate sanctions were created in the 1980s because of a perception by elected officials and sectors of the public that earlier community corrections programs—such as regular probation and parole, halfway houses, and community service—were ineffective. During this time, a national "get tough on crime" movement arose in which some politicians and members of the public demanded harsher sanctions for serious and low-level offenders; tougher crime and drug laws, many of which required mandatory prison terms, resulted and precipitated a sharp rise in the prison population and consequent overcrowding.

Intermediate sanctions adhere to intensive monitoring and surveillance of offenders. They include intensive supervision programs, day reporting centers, electronic monitoring, home confinement, and correctional boot camps. Intensive supervision probation or parole (ISP) is a more restrictive form of probation or parole whereby offenders are closely monitored and must abide by more conditions than regular probationers or parolees. This can include other intermediate sanctions, such as electronic monitoring, restitution (monetary payment to crime victims), daily reporting to a center, or home confinement (confinement in one's own home). Day reporting centers allow offenders to live in their own homes, but they must report to a center, sometimes daily, and participate in structured activities such as counseling and drug treatment. Under electronic monitoring, offenders are continually tracked by the local police department, and their movements are confined outside their private residences; some offenders, for example, may go to and from their jobs only.

Various intermediate sanctions are commonly used in combination. The two community-based intermediate sanctions that are residential are home confinement and boot camps. Home confinement (also called house arrest) places offenders under a full curfew; offenders are ordered to remain totally confined to their private residences for a given period of usually months. House arrest is commonly accompanied by electronic monitoring, whereby the offender wears a device that sends signals to a monitoring authority should he or she exceed the confines of the residence. Correctional boot camps are residential programs that follow a military model.

Correctional Boot Camps

Boot camps first began in 1983 in Georgia. They follow a military model of behavior modification that seeks to break down and rebuild a person's character with the aim of instilling respect for authority, self-discipline, and a work ethic. Generally, those admitted to boot camps are young, first-time, nonviolent offenders whose parents place them or who are sentenced to these facilities instead of probation or a prison sentence. The programs include a strict daily routine that begins at approximately 5:00 A.M. and includes intensive physical exercise, drills, and hard labor. Most boot camps also provide some form of drug and alcohol education and vocational training, counseling, or some academic education.

Offenders who fail to complete a program must serve their original prison term. Following boot camp, offenders are placed on intensive supervision probation or regular probation. Boot camps were banned in Florida in 2006 after a 14-year-old male resident, Martin Lee Anderson, died as a result of abuse by drill instructors at the facility.

Outcomes of Residential Correctional Programs

With regard to residential community-based correctional programs for youths, boot camps have a poor record of success as measured by reductions in recidivism (reoffending). Overall, studies have found, boot camps do not reduce recidivism; only those that offer good treatment services and have longer sessions with more post-release supervision have been found to have some effect.

Residential community correctional programs for youths that have the most positive effects on reducing recidivism follow the teaching family model (community-based, family-style group homes). In some studies, residential community correctional facilities were found to be especially effective for offenders who were considered to be at high risk for reoffending and for serious delinquents.

With regard to home confinement, some researchers predict that house arrest will be used for mostly low-risk offenders and will play only a small role in offering an alternative to incarceration. A widely expressed concern about intermediate sanctions such as boot camps and house arrest is their tendency to create what is called "net widening": the sentencing of offenders to harsher and more restrictive punishments than their offenses warrant. Putting an offender under house arrest who otherwise would have received only probation is an example of net widening. The net-widening effect also results in higher costs, because intensively

supervised probation with more rules increases the chance that offenders will violate these rules and return to prison.

Overall, studies show that residential community correctional facilities are cost-effective compared to incarceration and that adults and juveniles who complete these programs perform better than those on probation or parole. The better outcomes are attributed to the provision of treatment services in these programs. Reentry programs for offenders leaving prison, because they offer a transition into the community and into employment, have also been found to be effective in reducing recidivism (according to some estimates, by 15–20 percent). By extension, they also reduce prison overcrowding. Residential drug and alcohol treatment programs, especially therapeutic communities, also succeed in reducing rates of drug reoffending. In addition, they connect former substance abusers with resources and an ongoing support network in the community.

Julie A. Beck
California State University, East Bay

See also Group Homes; Halfway Houses and Residential Centers; Net Widening; Therapeutic Communities

Further Readings

Clear, Todd and Harry R. Dammer. *The Offender in the Community*. Belmont, CA: Thomson Wadsworth, 2000.

Katel, Peter. "Prisoner Reentry: Can Aid to Ex-Inmates Significantly Reduce Recidivism?" *CQ Researcher*, v.19/42 (2009).

Tonry, Michael and Kate Hamilton, eds. *Intermediate Sanctions in Overcrowded Times*. Boston: Northeastern University Press, 1995.

Yablonsky, Lewis. *The Therapeutic Community: A Successful Approach for Treating Substance Abusers*. New York: Gardner Press, 1989.

RESIDENTIAL PROGRAMS FOR JUVENILES

The juvenile justice system in the United States continues to face the challenge of punishment and accountability of youths who commit crimes, while recognizing the need to operate systems that are designed to change delinquent behaviors. Juvenile residential programs vary throughout the United

States, in terms of operational practices, size, facility locations, behavior modification techniques, length of stay, treatment philosophies, use of restraints, and how they measure outcomes. Despite the differences among residential programs across the United States, one common theme is that state systems hold fast to a rehabilitative mission.

Despite the stated mission of rehabilitation, however, the majority of state systems struggle to achieve positive outcomes with youthful offenders. Across the United States, residential programs for juvenile offenders have not shown a significant amount of success and, in many cases participation in a residential program results in an adverse impact on the youth. Programs focusing on discipline and punitive consequences have shown no success in changing the behaviors of young offenders. Typically, these programs instead contribute to further delinquent behaviors, have high recidivism rates, and are plagued by a high incidence of violence.

Successful residential programs for youths have a therapeutic foundation for achieving behavioral change. The components of such therapeutic programs can be identified and implemented so as to change behaviors and thus reduce recidivism rates. A therapeutic program for juvenile offenders consists of the following components: small and nonprison-like facilities, family engagement, facilities close to the youth's home, safety through supervision and relationships, skill building, and integrated aftercare services.

Small and Nonprison-Like Facilities

Juvenile state facilities across the United States are filled with hundreds of youths, with many of those facilities housing 200 or more. Large facilities create the challenges of maintaining safety, meeting the needs of young offenders, engaging families, and implementing treatment modules. Smaller facilities offer the opportunity to work with youths in small groups. Working with a small number of youths contributes to something very critical to the change process. Small groups create an opportunity to build relationships between youth and staff. Relationships are critical to the change process, and since behavioral change is the goal, smaller facilities create greater opportunities for this to occur. Building relationships also creates a safer environment. When the environment is safe, both emotionally and physically, programs have greater potential to achieve

change. Small facilities provide the opportunity for staff to get to know the history and experiences of the youths within the facility. Knowing the personal life stories of these young people creates a foundation on which to build relationships. Once relationships are established, the staff is then able to guide youths through the change process.

The environment must support the mission of the agency. If change and growth are the goal of juvenile programs, then the environment must be one that is conducive to therapeutic growth. The environment of residential facilities is not conducive to therapeutic growth; the environment has cells, hard furniture, plain white walls, no carpeting, and no personalized space for youths. It is challenging to build relationships in a stale environment that resembles an adult prison. Therapists deliberately soften the environments in which they engage clients. A softer environment helps a youth relax and become comfortable enough to share significant personal issues. The juvenile residential facility must accomplish the same thing. The environment should consist of carpeted floors, comfortable couches and chairs, colorful walls, ideally youth artwork throughout the living space, and an open living space that promotes safety through supervision and engagement.

Family Involvement

The majority of youths placed in residential programs will, at some point, return to their families and

U.S. residential programs for juvenile offenders have not shown much success and are considered a place of last resort for youths who are not suitable for placement in other programs. (Photos.com)

communities. Youths who are treated in small facilities that are therapeutic and nonprison-like have a greater opportunity of success in reintegrating with family. During the therapeutic process, engagement with both the youth and the family is critical to the overall success of youthful offenders. Many juvenile systems indicate that they begin this reentry process as soon as the youth enters custody. This may be the intent, but often the facility and the family are not in close proximity, and as a result the family is not involved in the residential program; clearly in such cases neither family nor community reentry will be successful. Reaching out to families immediately and connecting families to the residential program must be a priority if the program is to succeed. Families should be treated as partners in the program; families must be supported and assisted, because eventually the youth will return to the family system.

One of the chief ways of ensuring successful family participation is to locate the programs within reach of the family. Programs have a challenging time when working with youths placed far from their homes, disconnected by distance from their families and unfamiliar with community cultures and resources. Throughout the United States, however, this is the norm; juvenile residential facilities are located far from the families' communities. To increase potential program success, youths must remain close to their communities and hence close to their families. When youths are placed close to their communities, family involvement increases significantly, along with the ability to locate and connect a youth to community-based resources. Families and community resources are critical to the overall success a youth will have when reentry occurs.

Safety Through Supervision and Relationships

Residential juvenile programs throughout the United States rely on external controls, rigid rules, and positional power to maintain safety within facilities. Within a change-oriented therapeutic model, safety is achieved through supervision and by establishing relationships with youths. Supervision is not limited to watching youths but also focuses on how staff members engage and interact with youths. Simply maintaining staff presence in the room is not supervision. Staff members must be engaged with their young charges and must become aware of the various dynamics that affect them in the residential setting. For example, for any task with which a youth is involved, a staff member must be involved with as well. Seeing staff engaged and involved throughout the day helps youths to feel safe. When they know that staff are aware of all that is happening, they will feel safe enough to let down their guard and begin to invest in the change process. This engagement is the key to building the relationships necessary for positive change to occur.

Safety through supervision also means that youths must constantly be with staff. Youths should not be allowed to walk around the facility unsupervised. Many facilities allow this to occur because the facility is secure and doors are locked. The assumption is that youths are safe while unsupervised; staff members are relying on the structure of the facility for the safety of youths and staff. Through active supervision and engagement by staff, safety will be promoted and maintained. Through this engagement, staff are better equipped to build relationships with youths. Youths who have healthy relationships with staff members are more likely to invest in the program and respond to staff instructions. Youths will follow the lead of staff not because of their positional power but because they will believe that the staff want the best for them. When youths know the staff are aware of the dynamics of the facility and when staff have healthy relationships with youths, safety is achieved.

Skill Building

Residential programs for juveniles must be designed to provide services, opportunities, and supports for youths. A positive youth development approach will allow youths to grow and change. With this approach, youths will develop the necessary competencies to enhance their self-perceptions socially, academically, cognitively, and vocationally. Youths will also develop the confidence to improve their overall sense of self-worth, self-efficacy, and positive identity. Such attitudes are essential to their belief in a positive future (hope).

The program should help youths to build positive connections as well. Youths need positive bonds to people and institutions, to their peers, family, schools, and community, with relationships serving as the key factor. Youths will develop character in a program that is grounded in positive youth development. Youths will learn respect for societal and cultural rules; develop a standard for correct behaviors; increase their sense of right and wrong; and enhance their spirituality and integrity. Youths will also go through a process in which they develop a sense of caring and compassion—sympathy and empathy for others that is essential if they are to grow and change.

For this process to occur, residential programs should utilize unit-based team approaches in small group settings. This approach allows youths to engage with a consistent team of staff members who work with them on a daily basis, and this team should answer to one leader. The team approach again facilitates the building of relationships; the team will know the youth, and the youth will know the team. Traditional programs operate in a way that forces youths to navigate their way through the program, finding their own way.

Residential programs often attempt to meet the needs of youths through the use of several different departments. Youths have to work with social services, engage with mental health workers and caseworkers, attend school, and, most consistently, work with front-line staff. To develop a more positive approach, each youth should have a connection to one team, and this multidisciplinary team should be able to meet the needs of the youth in their group. With this approach, the youth does not have to navigate his or her way through a system to get needs met. The team will work together on their unit, providing services, opportunities, and supports for the youths under their supervision.

Aftercare

Youths residing in residential facilities will eventually return home to their communities. To make this transition as seamless as possible, reentry planning should be started as soon as a youth arrives. The youth within a residential program should have the same service coordinator or caseworker from commitment to discharge from the system. A single case manager working with this youth and his or her family, from adjudication to discharge, allows for relationships and connections to be established, which is critical to the change process. The case manager should be involved while the youth is in the facility as well. The case manager should attend team meetings, planning sessions, family meetings, and any other meetings or events in which the youth is involved. The case manager and facility team should work in conjunction to create treatment plans, to set goals, and to develop release plans. While the youth is residing within the residential program, the caseworker should be constantly engaging the family, assessing the family, and linking the family to community-based resources.

Case management services should intensify once a youth is released from the program. Upon release, the caseworker should meet with the youth and his or her families weekly, to assist in the transition to home. The caseworker should be making constant assessments of the youth's progress and adjust supervision according to that progress and the youth's behavior. Because caseworkers must intensely supervise youths, caseloads should be kept to fewer than 20 cases per caseworker. This enables the case manager to work intensely and to be able to build relationship with youths and their families.

Pili J. Robinson
Independent Scholar

See also Juvenile Aftercare; Juvenile and Youth Offenders

Further Readings

Inderbitzin, M. "A Look From the Inside: Balancing Custody and Treatment in a Juvenile Maximum-Security Facility." *International Journal of Offender Therapy and Comparative Criminology*, v.51/3 (2007).

Scott, E. S. and L. Steinberg. *Rethinking Juvenile Justice*. Cambridge, MA: Harvard University Press, 2008.

Soler, Mark, Dana Shoenberg, and Marc Schindler. "Juvenile Justice: Lessons for a New Era." *Georgetown Journal on Poverty Law and Policy*, v.16 (2009).

RESTITUTION

Whenever a person has been brought before a court of competent jurisdiction to answer to a criminal charge and has been convicted, the court will usually impose some form of sentence as punishment, such as a fine or a term in prison. However, there are a number of other options available to criminal courts when passing sentence upon a person convicted of a crime. Restitution is one of the possible punishments or remedies that may be imposed or granted by a court at the conclusion of a criminal trial.

Black's Law Dictionary defines restitution as a restoration of or for any loss, damage, or injury by a person who has suffered such a loss, damage, or injury as a result of an action or omission by another person. Essentially, restitution is intended to make a victim whole and place the victim in as good a position as he or she would have occupied without the act or omission by the other person.

Restitution is a commonly used remedy in civil law, especially in contract law and tort law. Concerning contracts, if one party breaks a contract, causing losses to the second party to the contract, then the first party is liable to the second party for any losses incurred because of the breach of the contract. Tort law is often called the "law of civil wrongs," as opposed to criminal wrongs. If a person commits a tort against another person, such as vandalism to the second person's property, then the second person is entitled to restitution from the first person to compensate for the damage done to the second person's property.

The principle of restitution is also used in criminal law. Many states in the United States have laws that provide for the payment of restitution for losses, damages, or injuries suffered by a victim during the commission of a crime. In this situation, restitution would be a remedy that is in addition to any fine or term of imprisonment imposed by the court for the crime. Thus, a person convicted of the crime would be required to compensate the victim for the losses, damages, or injury.

An example might be a case in which one person assaulted another person and broke the victim's jaw. If the person who committed the assault was brought to court and convicted of the crime of assault, under the principle of restitution the person who committed the assault would also be required to pay the victim's medical bills in addition to any fine or term of imprisonment imposed by the court. However, restitution does not apply only to personal injuries. It can also apply to damage to property. An example would be a case in which one person vandalized his neighbor's house with spray paint. If the person who committed the vandalism is convicted, then he would be required to pay the victim for the damage to the house as well as serve any time or pay any fees imposed by the court.

However, if the person who was suspected of committing a crime was found not guilty of the crime in a criminal trial, then the victim would not be eligible to obtain restitution from a criminal court. This does not mean that the victim would be without any additional remedy. The victim could sue the suspect in civil court for a violation of tort law. For example, even though the person who committed the assault was found not guilty in criminal court, the victim could sue in civil court for the tort of assault. Moreover, the victim of the vandalism could sue the suspect in civil court for damage to his property if the suspect was found not guilty in criminal court.

In both civil and criminal law, there must be some form of causation between the act or omission by the suspect and the loss, damage, or injury suffered by the victim. If there is no causation between the two, then the victim cannot recover restitution in either civil or criminal cases.

There are some advantages to obtaining restitution in both criminal and civil courts. In criminal court, the advantage is that the person convicted of the crime and ordered to pay restitution must do so; otherwise, he or she will be subject to additional punishments by the court, such as time in jail if he or she is on probation. Also, in criminal court, the

Restitution is a mandatory court order that a defendant pay a victim for the losses incurred as a direct result of a crime committed against another person, such as vandalism to the property. A defendant who is imprisoned will generally not be required to perform restitution payments until his or her release. (Photos.com)

victim does not have any court filing fees and does not need to hire an attorney to obtain the restitution. In civil court, the advantage is that the standard of proof is much less. Whereas in criminal court, one must prove beyond a reasonable doubt that a suspect is guilty, in civil court the standard of proof is usually only the preponderance of the evidence, which means that the victim only has to prove that it was more likely than not that the suspect caused the loss, damage, or injury.

In the context of community corrections, restitution is an extremely important component of the criminal justice process. Under the rubric of community corrections, the basic purpose of corrections is to attempt to reintegrate the offender back into the community and not just to impose punishment. The theory is that payment of restitution by the offender will foster in the offender a sense of responsibility to the community, as the offender will have restored the losses, damages, and injuries he or she has caused, both to the victim and to the community. Also, the payment of restitution to the victim and the community will, theoretically, make the victim and the community more receptive to accepting the offender back into society.

Wm. C. Plouffe Jr.
Independent Scholar

See also Attitudes and Myths About Punishment; Restitution Centers

Further Readings

Dobbs, Dan. *Dobbs Law of Remedies*, 2nd ed. St Paul, MN: West, 1993.

Garner, Bryan A. and Henry Campbell Black. *Black's Law Dictionary*. St. Paul, MN: Thomson West, 2009.

Hanokh, Dagan. *The Law and Ethics of Restitution*. New York: Cambridge University Press, 2004.

Siegel, Larry J. and Joseph J. Senna. *Essentials of Criminal Justice*. Belmont, CA: Wadsworth Cengage Learning, 2009.

Sims, Barbara. "Victim Restitution: A Review of the Literature." *Criminal Justice Studies*, v.13/3 (2000).

RESTITUTION CENTERS

Upon release from incarceration, certain offenders may require assistance to help facilitate a smooth reintegration into society, where they are expected to become both law-abiding and productive citizens in their communities and, depending on the offense committed, to pay restitution to the victims or other parties affected by their crimes. In order to prepare the offender for reentry to society and reduce the probability of recidivism, some facilities may provide counseling and life-training opportunities to offenders while they are serving their sentences, whereas others may provide ongoing assistance following release. Known as restitution centers, these facilities are highly structured community-based programs established to facilitate the completion of a restitution sentence in an environment conducive to rehabilitation and skills training, which also serve a punitive function. Some centers may require the offender to live in residence, while others allow offenders to live in the community—for example, with family members. In some cases, these centers may serve as a rehabilitative alternative for incarceration or as an option for some to complete the remainder of their sentence outside prison, while still protecting the community through supervision of the offender.

These programs are designed for certain offenders. As such, many restitutions centers have a rigorous screening process and specific eligibility requirements in order to identify a certain offending type—predominantly first-time offenders or newly released inmates convicted of minor or nonviolent offenses, such as property crime—who are more likely to complete the program successfully. Consequently, some offenders are rejected, namely, those who consistently recidivate, organized crime and white-collar offenders, and those capable of easily paying restitution. Eligible offenders also need to demonstrate good maturity and a genuine desire to participate in the program and be in good health—both mentally and physically—with no serious substance or alcohol problems, which may interfere in meeting obligations of the restitution program. Additionally, to make restitution, the offender should be employable and capable of learning new skills in order to make economic amends to the victim and others damaged through his or her crime.

Restitution centers operate on a rigid schedule for two purposes. In order help rehabilitate offenders, these programs provide assistance in locating employment through the links that counseling staff have developed with local community-based employers, while providing other services to offenders, such as budgeting and life skills, job training, counseling, group therapy, and adult education. They also serve a punitive function as they, like prisons, are secured facilities managed by state probation departments. However, restitution centers allow more freedom to offenders, with privileges to leave and return to the facility for work purposes or to fulfill other requirements of their restitution contract, such as unpaid community service, which usually takes place during evening and weekend hours. Some may require offenders to contribute a portion of their income to room and board expenses. The rigidity of these centers therefore interferes with the offender's criminogenic thoughts and activities, and serves as a diversion from other negative influences, such as associating with other offenders or engaging in risky pastime behavior. Typically, offenders stay in residence until their restitution sentence is completed, which gives a sense of accomplishment and has a motivating effect when they are able to make a positive change in their lives by securing work and paying off restitution.

Although many states have instituted restitution centers, only a few evaluations have been conducted on these programs. Founded in 1972 with a grant from the Law Enforcement Assistance Act and run by the Minnesota Corrections Authority, the Minnesota Restitution Center in Minneapolis YMCA was one of the early examples, which initially focused only on restitution, with no other rehabilitative services offered. Some 70 male offenders were admitted in 1974; however, only 26 successfully completed the program—21 offenders failed, 14 absconded, 6 committed new felonies and 3 violated parole. Restitution paid averaged $250 per offender, with an overall range from $15 to $2,000 on completion of a contract signed by the prisoner, victim or victims, two parole board members, and a center staff member. However, a follow-up study in 1976, after 16 months of release for 18 male property offenders matched to a parole group of similar characteristics, found that the restitution group had fewer convictions and were employed for a greater length of time, therefore offering hope in restitution centers as an alternative to incarceration. In 1993, an evaluation of the South Carolina Restitution Center Program concluded that the three- to six-month program was an ineffective alternative to incarceration, given the additional restrictions placed on offenders who would otherwise have received another type of non-prison sanction before the program was established in 1986. Overall, the recidivism rate was 44.4%, which was also an increase compared to a previous evaluation.

Today, a number of states operate restitution centers, which face challenges and concerns along with their advantages. Internally, a thorough evaluation needs to be conducted on eligible offenders in order to determine their suitability for the program, as well as any dangers they may pose by living in the community. For example, some may relapse back into crime by abusing the many privileges and freedoms provided by restitution centers, or may view these programs as a lighter alternative to incarceration, despite their otherwise demanding structure. Externally, citizens may not welcome the implementation of such programs in their communities, as they will undoubtedly bring more offenders to the locale, which may in turn bring safety concerns and potentially decrease property values. Even so, these centers provide many economic benefits to the community, with employers receiving tax breaks for providing jobs to offenders. Some offenders may be required to pay room and board expenses, which also makes these programs an inexpensive alternative while reducing costly reliance on public resources. The completion of a restitution program may bring closure or economic amends to the victim, unlike other types of sanctions administered. Overall, restitution centers provide many rehabilitative services for offenders, giving them a second chance to change their lives positively and effectively reintegrate themselves into the community.

Michael J. Puniskis
Middlesex University

See also Diversion Programs; Halfway Houses and Residential Centers; Reducing Prison Populations; Reentry Programs and Initiatives; Reintegration Into Communities; Residential Correctional Programs; Restitution

Further Readings

Heinz, J., B. Galaway, and J. Hudson. "Restitution or Probation: A Follow-Up Study of Adult Offenders." *Social Science Review*, v.50/1 (1976).

Jones, R. A. and C. Goff. *Study of the Costs and Benefits of the Washington County Restitution Center*. Washington, DC: National Institute of Justice, 1979.

Lawrence, R. "Diverting Offenders From Prison to Restitution Centers." *Journal of Crime and Justice*, v.13/1 (1990).

Serrill, M. S. "Minnesota Restitution Center." *Corrections Magazine*, v.1/3 (1975).

South Carolina State Reorganization Commission. *Follow-Up Evaluation of the South Carolina Department of Probation, Parole, and Pardon Services' Restitution Center Program*. Washington, DC: National Institute of Justice, 1993.

RESTORATIVE JUSTICE

Restorative justice, both in theory and in practice, puts special stress on the goal of repairing the variegated harms caused or revealed by criminal behavior. A restorative justice approach responds to crime by proactively identifying and taking steps to heal those harms, assigning a high priority to involving all stakeholders. Such an endeavor goes beyond the traditional response to criminal offenses—retribution—to find deeper solutions that heal broken interpersonal relationships. When the process succeeds, there is a transformation of the customary relationship between communities and their governments because on each side the perceptions of offenders and victims have drastically changed.

For victims, offenders, and community members, restorative justice initiates opportunities for affected parties to meet and to discuss the crime and its consequences. A basic expectation is that the offender will play an active role in repairing the harm that he or she may have caused. The restoration of both victims and offenders to the community as whole, contributing members is a substantial goal of restorative justice.

Assistance to victims is a key element of this process. Victims of crime are not only those immediately affected by the offense. Those indirectly affected—family members, friends of the family, and community members—are victims as well. The restorative justice process begins with giving proper attention to the social, emotional, and material needs of this broadly defined category of victims.

How is restorative justice carried out? Victim-offender mediation is one important program. This kind of mediation provides empowerment of victims as they participate in dialogue with offenders. Victims are active participants in the conversation that takes place, and they also play a role in sketching out the subsequent obligations and responsibilities of offenders. Offenders, too, are prompted to have an active voice in the mediation, to understand the harms they have caused and to take responsibility for their behavior. This means making an effort to "set things right" with the victim and to make amends for their violations. Offenders may commit to certain obligations, such as reparations, restitution, or community work. The ultimate goal of this arrangement is not revenge. Instead, it is to restore more or less normal, healthy relationships between individuals and to construct bridges of goodwill between offenders and the communities that have been most affected by their crimes. The reintegration of the offender back into the community is an important objective of restorative justice.

A second program of restorative justice is called circles or peacemaking circles. Circles have been used by communities for centuries to resolve disputes, but the recent practice is most common in the Native American cultures of the United States and Canada. In the 1980s, one of the first adaptations of circles to criminal justice occurred in the Yukon. First Nations peoples attempted to build closer relationships between the indigenous justice system and the larger community, and to this end, a judge introduced the sentencing circle as a tool for sharing the native justice process with the greater community.

An expanded version of circles is called conferencing. Conferencing brings more resources to the table; it is essentially a larger version of the circle that includes family members of the victim or offender, counselors, teachers, neighbors, and other significant community contacts. Involvement of a wider contingent of people can make conferencing a more productive experience than smaller circles. A sense of community is reinforced by such an experience.

Ex-offender assistance is another important element. These programs assist in developing in ex-inmates the capacities that allow them to function in the legitimate community. Assistance programs teach former inmates marketable skills that can be used in life after imprisonment and help smooth the transition from prisoner status to full membership in the community outside prison. Establishing or reestablishing the offender's connection with the community is a high priority.

Restitution is a strategy used in restorative justice, especially victim-offender mediation. It is based on the assumption that crimes are committed against real people and not the state. Thus, restorative justice programs encourage offenders to offer restitution to victims, rather than calling for retribution by the state against offenders. The purpose is to halt the cycle of violence and to restore relationships to a healthy state.

Offenders may be required to do community service as part of restorative justice. In the United States, such programs began with traffic offenders in California in the 1960s. The idea then spread through a series of local initiatives. One such project secured funding from the Indiana legislature to create workable alternatives to incarceration via community service. The legislators who sponsored the project believed that prison overcrowding could be alleviated if a portion of the prison population could be diverted to a series of community programs. Accordingly, nonviolent offenders who would otherwise have gone to prison were given the opportunity to provide community service or make restitution to their victims in lieu of incarceration. So much interest was generated by the new program that the Indiana budget for community service programs increased several fold in just five years during the 1980s.

Restorative justice may also be discussed in conjunction with efforts to prompt governments to engage certain constituencies in reparation negotiations pertaining to past wrongs committed by the government against its people. Governments often resist this process because the offenses typically took place long ago and at least some of the original wrongs have since been righted by progressive social legislation. Nonetheless, the pain and suffering emanating from the original offense still need to be addressed, and so does a perceived lack of remorse by the offending governments. African Americans and Native Americans, for example, are currently pursuing reparations from the U.S. government for past harms.

National reconciliation forums may employ restorative justice strategies in responding to severe human rights violations or cases of genocide. Such forums may require that governments confess past atrocities and uncover the extent to which victims have suffered. South Africa's Truth and Reconciliation Commission was an example of this type of assembly. Victims of gross human rights violations during apartheid were selected to testify in public hearings or to give statements about their experiences. In exchange for public testimony about their transgressions, perpetrators of violence could request amnesty from both civil and criminal prosecution.

Increasingly, restorative justice principles and practices are being applied in a growing number of settings entirely removed from juvenile and criminal justice: in schools, workplaces, faith communities, and national contexts to foster healing in the wake of violent conflicts within nations such as Northern Ireland, South Africa, and Liberia. What began as a mostly white, Eurocentric effort to change the juvenile and criminal justice systems has become a multipurpose, worldwide social movement.

Stan C. Weeber
McNeese State University

See also Circle Sentencing; Family Group Conferencing; Reintegration Into Communities; Restitution

Further Readings

Braithwaite, John. *Crime, Shame and Re-Integration*. New York: Cambridge University Press, 1989.

Braithwaite, John. "Restorative Justice: Assessing Optimistic and Pessimistic Accounts." In *Crime and Justice: A Review of Research*, Michael Tonry, ed. Chicago: University of Chicago Press, 1999.

Umbreit, Mark and Marilyn P. Armour. *Restorative Justice Dialogue: An Essential Guide for Research and Practice*. New York: Springer, 2010.

REVOCATION

In the United States, a revocable term of federal or state supervision almost always accompanies a criminal conviction. Generally, federal and state supervision, known collectively as community corrections, divides into two types: probation and parole. Probation is a form of supervision typically imposed in lieu of incarceration for misdemeanor convictions or low-level felony convictions. However, judges also routinely impose probation in addition to a period of incarceration. In such instances, probation can follow a term of imprisonment for any type of criminal offense. Parole is normally a term of supervision during which an offender serves the remainder of an imposed prison sentence outside prison. Like probation, however, parole can also follow a determinate period of incarceration. Both probation and parole require that criminal offenders abide by regulations designed to prevent potential criminal conduct. If a criminal offender fails to obey the regulations of supervised release, he or she may be subject to revocation. If a supervising agency initiates the revocation of an offender's probation or parole, that offender may face additional, more stringent supervision regulations or a period of incarceration.

Every U.S. jurisdiction employs probation as an alternative to incarceration or as an additional sanction. Parole, however, exists in only 34 states. The Sentencing Reform Act of 1984 eliminated parole in the federal criminal justice system. However, for federal offenders who committed an offense prior to November 1, 1987, parole is still available. Accordingly, probationers outnumber parolees nationally. In 2008, there were approximately 830,000 individuals on parole in the United States. That same year, almost 4.3 million individuals were on probation. Because prison overcrowding plagues most criminal justice systems, sentencing authorities often utilize probation as an alternative to incarceration for less serious criminal offenses. By doing so, sentencing authorities help to ease the financial and legal strains that arise when prison systems exceed capacity.

The regulations of parole and probation can vary jurisdictionally and among offenders. However, virtually every jurisdiction employs certain general supervision regulations for all offenders. For example, in accordance with such boilerplate restrictions, probationers and parolees must obey all laws, cannot travel more than certain designated distances from their residence, cannot associate with known criminals or gang members, cannot consume alcohol or use illegal drugs, cannot change residences without notifying supervising authorities, cannot own or possess firearms, must submit to drug tests, must maintain employment or schooling, must report to supervising agents regularly, and must submit to warrantless searches of their home or person. Some additional restrictions apply only to certain criminal offenders. For instance, probation and parole authorities usually require that sex offenders register with the municipality in which they live, participate in therapy tailored to their offense, and refrain from traveling near school zones and coming into contact with children. Research indicates that in recent years, boilerplate supervision restrictions have increased in number and variety. For example, researchers suggest that a national emphasis on reentry and offender supervision has led to an increase in boilerplate restrictions designed to treat and observe those under the watchful eye of supervising authorities.

When a probationer or parolee violates his or her supervision regulations (commits a technical violation) or commits a new crime, he or she is subject to revocation. Revocation is a process initiated by a supervising agent whereby a probationer or a parolee may receive additional sanctions as a result of violative conduct. In 1972, in *Morrissey v. Brewer*, the Supreme Court held that due process requires that a parolee receive a hearing before parole authorities prior to revocation. At a revocation hearing, a parolee may present evidence, call witnesses, and conduct cross-examinations. In 1973, in *Gagnon v. Scarpelli*, the Supreme Court granted similar rights to probationers facing revocation. The Supreme Court has also held that at probation and parole hearings, an alleged violator has the right to appointed counsel.

Penalties for probation and parole revocation vary. When a probationer or a parolee commits a technical violation, supervising authorities will generally refrain from imposing a term of incarceration. In such instances, supervising authorities may mandate that a violator receive substance abuse treatment, anger management counseling, or some other sanction less drastic than traditional imprisonment. In some cases, authorities will sanction a violator "halfway back," an expression used to describe sentences involving involuntary, secure treatment facilities. In cases involving repeat violators or violators who commit new criminal offenses, supervising authorities will normally impose a term of confinement.

An imposed prison sentence for a probation or parole violation can fluctuate, depending on the nature of the alleged violation. In situations in which a court initially sentences an offender to probation in lieu of prison, a technical violation of supervision regulations will sometimes warrant the imposition of the originally suspended sentence. However, in such cases, supervisory authorities possess the freedom to resentence an offender to less than the originally suspended term. Most jurisdictions employ similar sentencing schemes for technical parole violations. When a probationer or parolee commits a criminal offense during a term of supervision, supervising authorities will usually delay their revocation decision until after the disposition of the new offense in question. If a probationer or parolee is found guilty of committing a criminal offense while on supervised release, supervising authorities will typically impose a period of incarceration consecutive to or concurrent with the violator's sentence for his or her new criminal conviction.

James M. Binnall
University of California, Irvine

See also Parole Boards and Hearings; Probation: Administration Models; Probation: Early Termination; Probation and Parole: Intensive Supervision

Further Readings

Binnall, James. "Deterrence Is Down and Social Costs Are Up . . . : A Parolee Revisits *Pennsylvania Board of Probation and Parole v. Scott." Vermont Law Review*, v.32 (2007).

Branham, Lynn S. *The Law of Sentencing, Corrections, and Prisoners' Rights in a Nutshell.* St. Paul, MN: West Group, 2002.

Champion, Dean J. *Probation, Parole, and Community Corrections.* Upper Saddle River, NJ: Prentice Hall, 1999.

Hanser, Robert D. "Probationer and Parole Case Law Regarding Due Process During Revocation." In *Community Corrections.* Thousand Oaks, CA: Sage, 2010.

McBride, Elizabeth C. "Policing Parole: The Constitutional Limits of Back End Sentencing." *Stanford Law and Policy Review*, v.20 (2009).

RISK AND NEEDS ASSESSMENT INSTRUMENTS

The meaning of *assessment* is agreed upon in many literatures that serve to promote effective treatment; however, the literature is less clear on the distinction between *risk* and *needs* as these terms relate to risk and/or needs assessment instruments.

The prediction of future risk is one of the most difficult and controversial matters in the social sciences, particularly in the fields of law and criminal justice. The successful risk/needs assessment of violent behavior provides various benefits for the community as a whole and for its members. Risk/needs assessments are used across a wide range of correctional settings at some level in all states in the United

States, including pretrial, probation, parole, prison, and community corrections. The correction-based term *risk/needs assessment* refers to the process of conceptualizing various hazards in order to make judgments about their likelihood of occurring and the need for various preventive measures, such as who needs to receive treatment, what intermediate targets need to be set, and what is the best treatment for the target group, whether a program based on the principle of general or of specific responsivity. *General responsivity* refers to programs aimed at modifying an individual's general behavioral, social learning, and cognitive-behavioral strategies. *Specific responsivity*, by contrast, refers to programs that target services based on individual's demographic characteristics, such as age, gender, race, personality, motivation, and abilities.

Risk/needs assessment in the community correction context provides a measure of the probationer's or parolee's degree of dangerousness to the public and also measures the offender's tendency to engage in future criminal activity. Risk/needs assessment has been commonly used to classify offenders in order to place them in suitable levels of correctional treatment. The concerns underlying risk assessments relate to safeguarding against potential dangerousness in the community. The first risk assessment was introduced more than 80 years ago. Researchers during the 1920s and 1930s identified several risk factors: age, prior arrest, incarceration history, types of offense, types of disciplinary action during incarceration, and the offender's intelligence level. This effort concentrated on parole or release authorities to assist in identifying which offenders could be returned to the community; however, relatively little attention was paid to how to assess the risk until 1966. In that year, the landmark U.S. Supreme Court decision in *Baxstrom v. Herold* resulted in the release or transfer from maximum-security hospitals of 966 patients to the community or to lower-security interventions. Since this case, risk assessment has rapidly expanded; recently, risk assessment has incorporated a number of actuarial instruments to support, or sometimes to replace, the exercise of clinical judgment.

The first generation (1G) of assessments relied on interviewing the offender and using case-by-case anecdotal information to make unstructured professional judgments regarding the probability of offending behavior. Many studies, however, indicated that these predictions were highly inaccurate and consisted mainly of unstructured professional judgments of the probability of offending behavior. This approach is also called "structured clinical judgment" and is used in instruments such as the Historical, Clinical, and Risk Management Scheme (HCR-20).

Empirically based assessment tools were introduced in the second generation (2G) of assessment tools. The 2G assessments focus mainly on "static risk factors" related to previous behavior, which are inherent in the offender and are usually permanent. These include early age of onset of violent behavior, number of violent crimes committed, exposure to parental child abuse, trait characteristics such as psychopathy, and history of childhood behavioral problems, such as pyromania, animal abuse, stealing, hyperactivity, and lying. The analysis of these static risk factors guided probation and parole agencies in supervising offenders in the community. The 2G assessments include the Client Management Classification (CMC), the Wisconsin Client Management Classification, the Custody Rating Scale (CRS), the Static-99, the Statistical Inventory on Recidivism–Revised (SIR–R), and the Salient Factor Score (SFS).

Third-generation (3G) assessments measured both static and dynamic risk factors and were introduced in the 1970s and 1980s. These were known as "structured professional judgments" (SPJs) and were more explicit, empirically based, and theory-guided than 2G assessments, based on a broader selection of criminogenic factors. 3G assessments focused mainly on "dynamic risk factors," those characteristics that can change, are more or less influenced or controlled by the offender, and are highly correlated with the likelihood of recidivism. In many cases, dynamic factors, such as social, psychological, biological, or contextual factors, can be changed through treatment and rehabilitation programs. It helps to measure both positive and negative offender change over a period of time. 3G assessments focused on the informative value of prediction models for case management decision makers, such as parole officers, probation officers, parole boards, and forensic psychologists. The 3G assessments include the Sex Offender Needs Assessment Rating (SONAR), the Psychopathy Checklist Revised (PCL–R), the HCR-20, the Level of Service Inventory–Revised (LSI–R), the Structured Assessment of Violence Risk in Youth (SAVRY), and the Spousal Assault Risk Assessment (SARA).

The fourth generation (4G) of assessment tools consists of comprehensive and automated case-planning tools, which guide and follow service and supervision from intake through case closure. These 4G assessments are designed to be integrated into the process of risk or needs management with agency management information systems, selection of intervention modes and targets for treatment, and assessment of treatment progress. The 4G assessments also broaden the range of risk and needs factors (that is, content validity), broaden selection of explanatory theories, incorporate the strengths or resiliency perspective, apply more advanced statistical modeling, and apply assessment technologies, such as criminal justice database and Web-based implementations of assessment. 4G assessments identify areas of success within a case management plan designed to reduce risk. In addition, this can identify areas where strategies should be improved to maximize their potential for reducing risk. The 4G assessments include the original and classic Wisconsin system (now known as the Correctional Assessment and Intervention System, or CAIS), the Correctional Offender Management Profiling for Alternative Sanctions (COMPAS), and the Offender Intake Assessment (OIA) of Correctional Service Canada.

Efforts to develop solid risk assessments and needs assessments have been affected by the drift of policy in correctional settings over several decades. Risk/needs assessments in correctional settings have greatly improved since the use of unstructured risk/needs judgments. Many studies conclude that risk/needs assessments improve public protection by identifying the offenders who pose the greatest ongoing risk of recidivating with criminal behavior upon return to society. If the criminal justice system can identify the high-risk offender before returning that person to the community and provide an appropriate community-based correctional treatment that can reduce risk, the public can expect better protection. In addition, one of the major benefits of risk/needs assessment in community corrections is that the correctional system is better equipped to allocate resources more effectively. Adoption of risk/needs assessments by community corrections is rewarded by enhanced public protection, at least when assessments and services are conducted together.

Junseob Moon
Kean University

See also Actuarial Risk Assessment; Crime Control Model of Corrections; Crime Victims' Concerns; Effectiveness of Community Corrections; Evaluation of Programs; Goals and Objectives of Community Corrections; Hare Psychopathy Checklist; Long-Term Offender Designation; Offender Risks; Parole Boards and Hearings; Prediction Instruments; Recidivism; Risk Assessment Instruments: Three Generations; Wisconsin Risk Assessment Instrument

Further Readings

Baxstrom v. Herold, 383 U.S. 107 (1966).

Boer, D. P., S. D. Hart, P. R. Kropp, and C. D. Webster. *Manual for the Sexual Violence Risk–20: Professional Guidelines for Assessing Risk of Sexual Violence.* Vancouver: British Columbia Institute Against Family Violence, 1997.

Borum, R., P. Bartel, and A. Forth. *Manual for the Structured Assessment of Violence Risk in Youth (SAVRY): Version 2.* Tampa: University of South Florida, 2002.

Hare, R. D. *The Hare Psychopathy Checklist–Revised.* Toronto, ON: Multi-Health Systems, 1991.

Harris, G. T., M. R. Rice, and V. R. Quinsey. "Violent Recidivism of Mentally Disordered Offenders: The Development of a Statistical Prediction Instrument." *Criminal Justice and Behavior*, v.20 (1993).

Hart, S. D. et al. *The Risk for Sexual Violence Protocol (RSVP).* Burnaby, BC: Mental Health Law and Policy Institute, Simon Fraser University, 2003.

Hoffman, P. B. "Twenty Years of Operational Use of a Risk Prediction Instrument: The United States Parole Commission's Salient Factor Score." *Journal of Criminal Justice*, v.22 (1994).

Kropp, P. R., S. D. Hart, C. D. Webster, and D. Eaves. *Manual for the Spousal Assault Risk Assessment Guide*, 3rd ed. Toronto, ON: Multi-Health Systems, 1999.

McNiel, D. E. et al., eds. *Taking Psychology and Law Into the Twenty-First Century.* New York: Kluwer Academic, 2002.

Monahan, J. "The Prediction of Violent Behavior: Toward a Second Generation of Theory and Policy." *American Journal of Psychiatry*, v.141 (1984).

Motiuk, L. L. "Classification for Correctional Programming: The Offender Intake Assessment (OIA) Process." *Forum on Corrections Research*, v.9 (1997).

Van Voodhis, P., M. Braswell, and D. Lester. *Correctional Counseling and Rehabilitation*, 4th ed. Cincinnati, OH: Anderson, 2000.

Webster, C. D., K. S. Douglas, D. Eaves, and S. D. Hart. *The HCR-20: Assessing the Risk for Violence: Version 2.* Burnaby, BC: Mental Health, Law, and Policy Institute, Simon Fraser University, in Cooperation With the British Columbia Forensic Psychiatric Services Commission, 1997.

RISK ASSESSMENT INSTRUMENTS: THREE GENERATIONS

The criminal justice system supervises more than 7 million offenders of all ages, from diverse backgrounds, and with a variety of individual needs. A one-size-fits-all approach to correctional treatment would be ineffective and irresponsible. Consequently, the criminal justice system attempts to identify the risks and needs of every individual offender in order to determine the appropriate case management plan that will both protect the general public and reduce the likelihood that the offender will recidivate upon release from criminal justice supervision. This process of identifying an offender's risks and needs is known as offender risk assessment or offender classification. To date, scholars have identified three generations of risk assessment. The first generation of risk assessment tools was followed by subsequent generations that built upon the strengths of those tools while working to eliminate their weaknesses.

First Generation

First-generation risk assessments are based on practitioners' own professional and personal knowledge of the offender population and their ability to assess an offender's risk level. The first generation of risk assessments relies upon no standardized set of questions to be asked of each offender. Rather, the practitioner has the discretion to ask the offender as many or as few questions as he or she believes are appropriate. Moreover, classification decisions are based on the factors that each individual practitioner deems relevant in determining risk. Perhaps not surprisingly, the lack of structure in questioning offenders results in inconsistent classifications across criminal justice practitioners.

Another problem associated with first-generation assessments is that the absence of a standardized set of questions results in practitioners overclassifying offenders. In other words, the tendency of practitioners is to determine the offender to be higher-risk or more likely to recidivate than actually is the case. The tendency to overclassify offenders may be attributed to agencies holding their practitioners accountable for the assessments they conduct. If a practitioner underclassifies an offender and the offender recidivates, the practitioner who conducts the assessment can be scrutinized by his or her supervisor, as well as the general public, for incorrectly identifying the offender's risk level. As a result, it is in the best interest of the practitioner to err on the side of safety and overclassify an offender to ensure the public's protection.

Second Generation

The second-generation risk assessment relies on a standard set of theoretically driven questions that all offenders are asked. This greatly reduces the arbitrariness and potential for individual bias that exists in first-generation assessments, where all assessments were based on clinical judgment. Although second-generation instruments are an improvement over first-generation instruments, there are three identifiable problems with these instruments.

The first problem is resistance from the practitioners, who are expected to administer the assessments. Practitioners may be aggravated that they have to attend training on the instrument, may feel that it limits their professional discretion, and may feel as though they can do a better job of predicting an offender's risk level than can any instrument.

A second problem is that most instruments of this generation include only static factors. Static factors are those offender characteristics that cannot change (such as criminal history or age at first offense); hence, reassessment efforts are useless. The purpose of reassessing an offender is to determine whether or not the treatment has decreased the offender's risk level. However, second-generation risk assessments based on static factors prevent any conclusions regarding the effectiveness of treatment, because the offender's score will be the same or higher than it was on the offender's initial assessment.

A third problem is that second-generation assessments do not take into account responsivity factors.

Responsivity considers the individual characteristics or traits that may make an offender more or less amenable to change through certain treatment strategies and attempts to match offenders to treatment programs that will provide the greatest likelihood for success. Factors including, but not limited to, intelligence, gender, anxiety, and sexual abuse may limit the likelihood for success in certain treatment settings. Failure to take into account responsivity factors may hamper an offender's ability to succeed in a particular treatment program.

Third Generation

Third-generation risk assessments also incorporate a structured set of questions. However, third-generation risk assessments are based on dynamic factors and include only a few static factors, whereas second-generation assessment instruments rely almost entirely on static factors. The inclusion of dynamic factors is critical, because dynamic factors, unlike static factors, can be targeted for change through treatment.

An assessment instrument based on dynamic factors also allows for offender reassessment. Reassessing offenders informs practitioners whether or not treatment is working for the offender. If the reassessment suggests that the offender's risk level has changed, then the practitioner can modify the offender's case management plan accordingly.

Another strength of third-generation risk assessments is that they take into consideration responsivity factors. The opportunity to document responsivity factors improves the likelihood that criminal justice practitioners will properly match offenders to treatment programs that will maximize the offender's likelihood for success.

Conclusion

The evolution of the risk assessment instruments from one generation to the next is clear. First-generation assessments were led to classification based only on a practitioner's subjective judgment and instinct. Second-generation instruments provided a standardized set of questions but were not structured to assist in targeting treatment needs. Finally, third-generation assessments incorporate a standardized set of questions that identify an offender's criminogenic needs and responsivity factors.

This makes the third-generation risk assessment instruments an improvement over their predecessors when it comes to risk assessment and case management planning.

Brenda Vose
University of North Florida

See also Actuarial Risk Assessment; COMPASS Program; Hare Psychopathy Checklist; Offender Needs; Offender Responsivity; Offender Risks; Risk and Needs Assessment Instruments; Salient Factor Score; Wisconsin Risk Assessment Instrument

Further Readings

Andrews, Donald A., James Bonta, and J. Stephen Wormith. "The Recent Past and Near Future of Risk and/or Need Assessment." *Crime and Delinquency*, v.52 (2006).

Bonta, James. "Offender Risk Assessment Guidelines for Selection and Use." *Criminal Justice and Behavior*, v.29 (2002).

Clear, Todd R. and Kenneth W. Gallagher. "Probation and Parole Supervision: A Review of Current Classification Practices." *Crime and Delinquency*, v.31 (1985).

Gardner, William, Charles W. Lidz, Edward P. Mulvey, and Ester C. Shaw. "Clinical Versus Actuarial Predictions of Violence in Patients With Mental Illness." *Journal of Consulting and Clinical Psychology*, v.64 (1996).

Grove, William M. and Paul E. Meehl. "Comparative Efficiency of Informal (Subjective, Impressionistic) and Formal (Mechanical, Algorithmic) Prediction Procedures: The Clinical-Statistical Controversy." *Psychology, Public Policy, and Law*, v.2 (1996).

Grove, William M. et al. "Clinical Versus Mechanical Prediction: A Meta-Analysis." *Psychological Assessment*, v.12 (2000).

Sarbin, Theodore R. "A Contribution to the Study of Actuarial and Individual Methods of Prediction." *American Journal of Sociology*, v.48/5 (1943).

Schneider, Anne, Ervin L. Laurie, and Zoann Snyder-Joy. "Further Exploration of the Flight From Discretion: The Role of Risk/Need Instruments in Probation Supervision Decision." *Journal of Criminal Justice*, v.24 (1996).

SALIENT FACTOR SCORE

Parole risk instruments have become an integral part of the parole decision-making process. The majority of instruments follow a systematic format, collecting standard information about the offender. Generally, each risk item on the instrument is assigned a point value, and upon completion of the assessment, the offender is given a total risk score for future recidivism. Risk instruments also provide guidelines with recommendations about the specific amount of time to be served prior to release.

The Salient Factor Score (SFS) was created in the 1970s by the U.S. Parole Commission as a way of estimating an inmate's likelihood of recidivating following his or her release from prison. The SFS is an example of a second-generation parole risk instrument that is composed primarily of criminal-type variables with limited sociodemographic factors.

Development of the Salient Factor Score

The SFS is an empirically validated risk assessment tool incorporating an objective scale developed by the U.S. Parole Commission. The U.S. Parole Commission first used the SFS and parole guidelines in 1972. The SFS was not the first predictive instrument; other measures were available, but they did not have a strong effect on parole decisions. The U.S. Parole Commission was the first paroling agency to employ the use of a risk instrument in a way that clearly affected decisions regarding parole.

The original 1972 SFS was composed of eleven items. The SFS has been revised several times since then, and most of these revisions have resulted in a reduction in the number of factors considered predictive in the decision-making process. Items regarding noncriminal history, heroin dependency, and status have been deleted from updated versions of the SFS. Additionally, in 1998 the Parole Commission revised the SFS by increasing the weight given to prior commitments and age at offense and deleted the drug-use item. The revised SFS was designated as SFS 98.

The U.S. Parole Commission's version of the SFS 98 contains six items that are weighted according to their importance to the total risk score. These factors include the offender's prior convictions, previous commitments for more than 30 days, the offender's age at the time of the current offense in conjunction with prior commitments, the length of time without commitments prior to current offense, whether the offender was on probation, parole, confinement, or escape status at the time of the current offense, and whether the offender is considered older. Statistically, reducing the number of items on the instrument has not been detrimental to its predictive power. The benefits of using the SFS 98 are that the items are objective, easily scored, few in number, and unable to be manipulated by offenders.

SFS Components, Scoring, and Guidelines

The first component that the SFS 98 examines is the frequency of prior convictions as an adult or juvenile. Offenders can receive between zero and three points on this item, and scores range from 3 for none to 0 for four or more convictions. The SFS 98 then looks at prior commitments of more than 30 days. Scores range from 2 for none to 0 for three or more commitments. The third component examines the offender's age in conjunction with the number of previous commitments. There are four age categories: 19 and younger, 20–21 years, 22–25 years, and 26 and older. Scores range from 0 to 3, depending on the individual's age and prior commitments.

Another risk component that the SFS 98 examines is the period of time that the offender has not been incarcerated. Specifically, the SFS 98 looks to see if the offender has had another offense that resulted in a period of incarceration of more than 30 days within the three years prior to the current offense. Offenders who meet this offense requirement receive a score of 0, and those that do not receive a score of 1. The fifth component of the instrument examines whether the offender was on probation, parole, confinement, or escape status at the time of the current offense. Offenders who meet this offense requirement receive a score of 0, and those who do not receive a score of 1. The sixth item gives a score of 1 only to offenders who were 41 years of age or older at the time of the current offense.

Each one of these six items carries a different weight in the calculation of the total salient factor score. The SFS 98 is scored on a scale from 0 to 10, with a score of 10 indicating the lowest risk of recidivism and a score of 0 indicating the highest risk. The total score is then aggregated into four categories of risk: very good, good, fair, and poor. The offender's risk category is then examined on a grid with the seriousness of the current offense that provides a guideline range of total time to be served. This grid and its guidelines are provided only as proximities, thus enabling the parole board to consider other possible aggravating or mitigating factors.

Shamir Ratansi
Central Connecticut State University

See also Actuarial Risk Assessment; Level of Service Inventory; Parole Boards and Hearings; Risk and Needs Assessment Instruments

Further Readings

Bonta, James. "Offender Risk Assessment: Guidelines for Selection and Use." *Criminal Justice and Behavior*, v.29 (2002).

Hoffman, Peter. "Twenty Years of Operational Use of a Risk Prediction Instrument: The U.S. Parole Commission's Salient Factor Score." *Journal of Criminal Justice*, v.22 (1994).

Siegel, Larry J. and Joseph J. Senna. *Essentials of Criminal Justice*. Belmont, CA: Wadsworth Cengage Learning, 2009.

SANCTUARY

The term *sanctuary* generally refers to a historical practice whereby individuals accused of a criminal offense or other deviant act were able to alleviate, delay, avoid, or otherwise alter the penalty they were facing by entering into a specially designated location and requesting mercy. Once the individual had entered the designated location and had requested assistance, he or she could be provided with varying levels of consideration and protection.

The exact degree of protection or assistance that was provided to those requesting sanctuary depended on a number of factors. First, the protections afforded varied both geographically and across time. As a result, the individual benefits that accrued from requests for mercy were largely dependent upon when and where the individual sought sanctuary. Second, in order for sanctuary to be of any substantive value to an accused it must have been recognized to at least some degree by existing secular or religious authorities. In practice, this meant that the assistance afforded to individuals seeking sanctuary was dependent on the existing state of civil, criminal, and religious doctrines and laws. Third, only certain types of offenses or punishments made individuals eligible for sanctuary at any given point in time. This meant that only certain individuals could avail themselves to the protections linked to sanctuary, based upon either the type of offense they were alleged to have committed or the type of punishment that they were facing.

Over time, the practice of sanctuary also varied in regard to the type of location that was thought to justify a plea for mercy. In some of the earliest times, entire cities were set aside as areas where individuals could seek sanctuary. In later times, sanctuary was available to an individual only after that person had entered a specific type of building that was thought to be sacred or holy. Over time, sanctuary became more strongly associated with formal places of worship, such as churches, or facilities associated with those

The tradition of religious sanctuary dates back to ancient times, became a formalized practice in England by the 4th century, and was finally abolished in 1540. According to current U.S. law, religious institutions do not have permission to harbor criminals or protect them from the government. (Photos.com)

places of worship, such as monasteries, nunneries, and rectories. The idea that places of worship were especially sacred and therefore not subject to the direct control of governmental authorities may have had its roots in other concepts, such as the benefit of clergy, which held that religious officials themselves were not subject to the control of secular authorities.

In most instances, sanctuary did not necessarily provide a means through which individuals could avoid punishment altogether. Instead, in most European countries sanctuary typically provided individuals with a temporary reprieve while an alternative sanction was being identified and implemented. Frequently, these alternative sanctions stood in sharp contrast to the harsh physical punishments that otherwise would have awaited the individual seeking sanctuary. This may account for why the practice of sanctuary has alternately been viewed as a means of providing mercy and a means of carrying out punishment. In some instances, sanctuary would provide the accused individual with an opportunity to go into exile in a distant land, far away from where the original offense was alleged to have occurred. In other instances, the accused would be provided with protection from punishment until religious officials could reach a consensus regarding an appropriate alternative sanction. In still other circumstances, the accused individual might be required to make an admission of guilt in

exchange for an agreement among secular authorities to implement an alternative form of punishment from that originally proposed.

In America, the concept of sanctuary evolved to reflect a greater reliance on the provision of outright immunity from punishment. At the conclusion of the Middle Ages, sanctuary itself was no longer formally recognized in most European countries. In America, sanctuary never achieved the official status that it had achieved in other countries. Instead, other formally recognized practices, such as expungements and pardons, provided a means of judicial forgiveness for individuals convicted of criminal offenses. However, there were times in American history when sanctuary became a part of the legal and social fabric of the nation. At the same time, it should also be noted that sanctuary has tended to have an ephemeral history in America, emerging briefly only to fade away again shortly afterward.

During the time of slavery, sanctuary became one means whereby runaway slaves sought protection from the harsh penalties that almost certainly awaited them if they were returned to the locations from which they had originally fled. During the sanctuary movement that occurred during the latter part of the 20th century, many Central American immigrants fleeing civil conflicts sought refuge in American churches after being formally denied asylum by the United States. Events such as these may help explain why sanctuary has become increasingly associated with the contemporary practice of asylum. Today, individuals who claim that they are facing political, religious, or social persecution in their native countries may seek sanctuary in other countries while they negotiate the more permanent protections offered by asylum.

Jason R. Jolicoeur
Cincinnati State Technical and
Community College

See also Benefit of Clergy; Pardon and Restoration of Rights

Further Readings

Bau, Ignatius. *This Ground Is Holy: Church Sanctuary and Central American Refugees.* Mahwah, NJ: Paulist Press, 1985.

Cox, J. Charles. *The Sanctuaries and Sanctuary Seekers of Mediaeval England.* London: George Allen and Sons, 1911.

Duncan, Ann and Steven Jones, eds. *Church-State Issues in America Today: Religious Convictions and Practices in Public Life*. Westport, CT: Praeger, 2008.

Shoemaker, Karl. *Sanctuary and Crime in the Middle Ages, 400–1500*. Bronx, NY: Fordham University Press, 2011.

Second Chance Act

The Second Chance Act of 2007: Community Safety Through Recidivism Prevention was signed into law in 2008 to respond to the increasing numbers of people leaving prisons and jails. Each year, more than 700,000 people are released from prisons, and another 9 million leave jails, many more than once. The vast majority of them return to the communities from which they came and face a variety of challenges, including reconnecting with family and peers, finding housing and employment, and more generally avoiding criminal behavior. Recidivism rates among people leaving prison are high: Within three years of release, nearly two thirds of people are rearrested and more than half are reincarcerated. The Second Chance Act is a comprehensive bipartisan effort to address these reentry issues, primarily through grant authorizations and reforms to the Omnibus Crime Control and Safe Streets Act of 1968. The act identifies six main objectives, which focus on providing services to people leaving prisons, jails, and juvenile facilities, both while they are incarcerated and after release, with the goals of facilitating reentry and increasing public safety by reducing recidivism.

Key Provisions

Most of the objectives of the act are carried out through grants to state and local reentry demonstration projects, including reentry courts, and to nonprofit organizations for mentoring and other transitional services. In fiscal year 2009, $25 million was appropriated for programs under the act, and $114 million was appropriated in fiscal year 2010. Projects are encouraged to utilize evidence-based practices and programming, such as validated risk assessment tools, and are required to meet specific performance outcomes relating to the long-term goals of increasing public safety and reducing recidivism. These performance outcomes include reduction in recidivism rates, reduction in crime, increased employment and education opportunities,

The Second Chance Act was created to address issues surrounding prisoner reentry, increase public safety, and reduce recidivism. Services provided ranged from substance abuse treatment to family counseling to training on parenting skills for those with minor children. (Photos.com)

reduction in violation of conditions of supervised release, increased housing opportunities, reduction in drug and alcohol abuse, and increased participation in substance abuse and mental health services.

One of the main elements of the act is its emphasis on drug treatment. First, it aims to divert people from prison by providing grants to prosecutors at the state and local levels to develop or expand drug treatment programs as alternatives to incarceration. Second, the act authorizes grants to improve existing in-prison drug treatment, including drug treatment that continues after a person has been released from prison during any period of post-prison supervision that person is required to serve. Finally, the act increases the eligible pool of people for drug court admission by altering the definition of a "violent offender" so that people convicted of a violent offense punishable by less than one year of imprisonment are now eligible to participate in drug courts.

The act also recognizes the importance of family to the reentry process and accordingly authorizes grants for the development of family-based treatment programs in prisons and the community. The prison-based treatment programs would provide comprehensive services ranging from substance abuse treatment to family counseling and training in parenting skills for incarcerated parents of minor children. In addition, the act supports the creation of family-based substance abuse programs in the community as alternatives to incarceration.

The act calls for the establishment of a Federal Prisoner Reentry Initiative, a comprehensive reentry program for people leaving federal prisons. This initiative would provide pre-release planning services to help people apply for and obtain identification and federal and state benefits prior to release. The initiative also increases to 12 months the period of time that a person, at the discretion of the Bureau of Prisons, may spend in a community correctional facility prior to release. As part of the initiative, the act establishes a pilot program for the early release of certain nonviolent federal prisoners over the age of 65. People released under this provision would be placed on home detention or in a nursing home or other long-term residential care facility.

Research and Data Collection

The act emphasizes research, data collection, and evaluation. It authorizes the National Institute of Justice to conduct research on adult and juvenile reentry. Furthermore, grantees are required to collect data on their performance outcomes and, to be eligible for grant renewal, must demonstrate that they have measures in place to assess their progress to a 10 percent reduction in recidivism over two years. The act also establishes a National Adult and Juvenile Offender Reentry Resource Center to collect data and identify best practices in reentry, disseminate this information, and provide training and support.

Limitations

A number of existing federal laws impose significant obstacles to reentry in the form of collateral consequences of criminal convictions. These include prohibitions on the receipt of some public benefits and public housing eligibility restrictions. One of the main criticisms of the act has been its failure to address any of these restrictions. Furthermore, despite its emphasis on providing educational services in prisons, the act did not overturn the 1993 federal ban

on Pell grants for people in prison. Another criticism of the act is that its goal of reducing the recidivism rate for people released from prison is unrealistic. While existing successful reentry programs claim reductions in recidivism rates of between 5 and 20 percent, the act sets a goal of reducing recidivism by 50 percent.

Christine S. Scott-Hayward
New York University

See also Prisoner's Family and Reentry; Recidivism; Reintegration Into Communities

Further Readings

Henry, Jessica. "The Second Chance Act." *Criminal Law Bulletin*, v.45/3 (2009).

Jeffress, Robert. *Second Chance, Second Act: Turning Your Messes Into Successes*. Colorado Springs, CO: Waterbrook Press, 2007.

National Reentry Resource Center. "Reentry Facts." http://www.nationalreentryresourcecenter.org/facts (Accessed July 2011).

The Second Chance Act: Strengthening Safe and Effective Community Reentry. Hearing Before the Committee on the Judiciary, United States Senate, One Hundred Eleventh Congress, Second Session, July 21, 2010. Washington, DC: U.S. Government Printing Office, 2011.

Second Chance Act of 2007, Pub. L. 110-199, 122 Stat. 657 (2008).

SENTENCING GUIDELINES

Sentencing guidelines represent a system for structuring the punishments received by convicted offenders. Typically, sentencing guidelines will note both a minimum and a maximum recommended punishment that is based on the severity of the current offense, on the severity of the offender's prior record, or on both offense and prior record. Options for the sentencing judge may include community-based punishments, fines, and various types of incarceration with a range of recommended lengths. The judge making the sentencing decision is expected to follow the recommendation made within a guidelines structure but is not legally required to do so.

Sentencing guidelines differ from mandatory sentences in that a mandatory sentence legally prescribes both the type and the length of punishment for a specific type of crime. For example, many states have mandatory sentences for individuals convicted of drug crimes that may require the offender to serve a fixed amount of time in jail or prison. There is no option for the judge to reduce the sentence below the mandatory minimum, regardless of other information that may emerge about the nature of the crime or the offender.

A typical sentencing guidelines grid will use rows in a table to indicate information about the type or severity of the offense committed and will use columns to denote information about the offender's prior record. There is considerable variation in the specificity of guideline grids across jurisdictions that use them. Perhaps the most detailed grid is that used in the U.S. federal courts, where there are 43 levels of offense severity and six levels to represent gradations in the extensiveness and severity of the offender's criminal history. In contrast, Ohio's sentencing guidelines are limited to a single grid that relies on five offense levels and no information about the offender's prior record. Most states with sentencing guidelines rely on both offense and offender information.

Historical Background

As of 2011, 21 states and the U.S. federal government used some form of sentencing guidelines. The development and implementation of sentencing guidelines reflected a long-standing concern with criminal sentence reform. Throughout the 1960s and early 1970s, a growing body of social scientific research evidence indicated that offenders with similar backgrounds and convicted of similar crimes often received different punishments. The variations in punishment were the result of indeterminate sentencing practices, which meant that offenders received a range for a prison sentence, such as six to 24 months or two to five years. The rationale for such nonspecific—indeterminate—sentences was rehabilitation: Offenders could anticipate an early release if they behaved well while incarcerated. Research on punishment practices in the 1960s and 1970s illustrated that there were disparities in both the length of time sentenced to prison and the length of time kept in prison that varied by social and demographic characteristics of offenders, even after accounting for the types of crimes committed and the nature of the prior record.

Interestingly, efforts aimed at sentence reform came from two very different political viewpoints.

One broad group of reformers was concerned about the apparent effects that an offender's sex, race, or economic position had on the severity of the punishment received. Simultaneously, another broad group of reformers was concerned about punishments being too lenient for many offenders—that the early release of many offenders meant that punishments were not as harsh as some thought they should be. Consequently, from both sides of the political spectrum, sentencing guidelines, as well as a move to determinate sentencing, were seen as a means of making criminal punishments longer, but also more systematic and presumably fairer to convicted offenders.

In the 1970s, Minnesota and Pennsylvania were the first two states to enact sentencing guidelines. The purpose that sentencing guidelines were expected to serve in each state differed in important ways, however. In Minnesota, the guidelines were initially tied to the state's prison population and were aimed at trying to regulate the flow of persons in and out of prison. Pennsylvania's guidelines were less concerned with managing the number of state inmates and more focused on eliminating unjustified disparities in prison sentences.

The U.S. sentencing guidelines were developed in the 1980s and were primarily an attempt to make criminal sentences in the federal courts more systematic. The basis for constructing the range of sentences and punishment options in the U.S. sentencing grid was prior sentencing practices in the federal courts and existing federal laws designating punishments for certain crimes. The use of a large number of offense severity levels helped to ensure that the range of recommended sentences was small within each cell of the sentencing grid, which was expected to result in greater uniformity of sentencing decisions.

Using Sentencing Grids

In most states and the federal system, the sentencing grid is a table that uses rows to represent severity of the conviction offense and columns to represent the offender's criminal history. In those states that look only at the severity of the conviction offense (such as Ohio), there is effectively one column to the table and some number of rows to represent the different levels of offense severity.

Within each cell in the table, there will be a list of recommended punishments. These may include community-based punishments, fines, jail, and prison sentences. For punishments that require incarceration, there will also be a recommended range of sentence lengths, such as 12 to 18 months or 120 to 140 months. If the sentencing judge decides to incarcerate the offender, then the judge will need to choose an appropriate length of sentence from this range.

Many states also require judges to denote a minimum and a maximum sentence length. Again, the selected length of sentence, regardless of whether it is the minimum or the maximum sentence, needs to come from the recommended range in the guidelines grid. It is common for many judges to set the minimum and the maximum sentence to the same value.

Purpose of Sentencing Guidelines

Although there is variation in the phrasing that states and the federal government use in describing the purpose of their respective sentencing guidelines, three common reasons are given for the development and implementation of sentencing guidelines: (1) public safety, (2) equitable sentencing decisions, and (3) management of the prison population.

In regard to public safety, sentencing guidelines are viewed as a means of achieving a safer community by ensuring that sentences correspond to the severity of the offense and the relative risk that the offender may pose to the community. For example, offenders convicted of violent crimes will receive longer sentences than those convicted of property crimes, because of the magnitude of the negative consequences of violent crime and the perception that violent offenders pose a greater threat to public safety.

Sentencing guidelines are also focused on achieving equitable sentencing practices. The key mechanism for equity in sentencing is the restriction of the range of possible sentences that offenders could receive. What makes this mechanism so important is that it attempts to rationalize sentencing practices so that offenders who have committed similar crimes and who have similar criminal histories will receive similar punishments.

Fewer states have directly tried to link their guidelines grid to managing the prison population, but this has been a goal of several states (such as Minnesota) since the inception of sentencing guidelines. The expectation of state governments is that the punishments contained in a guidelines grid will also help the state to maintain a relatively stable prison population. Given their limited resources to house a fixed population of inmates safely, some states have tried to link their guidelines grids to the flow of inmates in and out of prison in a way that increases the predictability of state expenditures on corrections over time. In situations in which there has been a large and rapid increase in serious crime rates, this link is more tenuous, and prison populations will likely increase regardless of recommendations contained in a guidelines grid.

Role of Sentencing Commissions

Most of the states with sentencing guidelines as well as the federal government have sentencing commissions to provide oversight and monitoring in the use of the guidelines. There is no single model used by the states and the federal government for the configuration of and composition of their sentencing commissions. However, it is common for members of a sentencing commission to be judges (both sitting and retired), elected officials, and representatives from other state criminal justice agencies.

Many sentencing commissions have small research staffs that are responsible for daily collection of data on the administration of criminal punishments. Periodic reports from the research staff provide commission members with an overview of sentencing patterns and trends; these are crucial to effective oversight of the use of sentencing guidelines, particularly in the area of judicial compliance with the guidelines grid.

Departures From the Sentencing Guidelines and Appellate Review

There have been a number of legal challenges in both state and federal courts over the constitutionality of sentencing guidelines. Of particular concern has been whether the use of sentencing guidelines can be made mandatory. Through 2010, all guidelines systems, regardless of whether state or federal, were now voluntary for judges making sentencing decisions. The term used to describe this in the literature on sentencing guidelines is *presumptive*: There is the presumption that the sentencing judge will rely on the recommendations in the guidelines, but judges are not legally required to follow the recommendations.

To be sure, there are significant variations across states and the federal system in the degree of flexibility given to judges in making sentencing decisions. Nevertheless, judges in all jurisdictions may depart from the recommended sentence in the guidelines grid and sentence an offender to a punishment either more or less severe than the range included in the grid. Sentences that are more lenient than the lower threshold in the guidelines grid (that is, sentences resulting in less time in jail or prison) are referred to as "downward departures." A sentence that is severer than the upper threshold in the guidelines grid is referred to as an "upward departure." Historically, judges who have departed from the guidelines have been more inclined to punish offenders less severely than recommended.

Although departures from the recommended sentences included in the guidelines grid fall within the discretion of the sentencing judge, any kind of departure will open up the possibility of a legal challenge to the sentence, known as appellate review. Sentences that fall within the recommended range of the guidelines grid cannot be appealed by the offender or the prosecutor. Either the offender or the prosecutor may appeal any sentence that departs from the recommended range of sentences. Not surprisingly, offenders who have received sentences that are severer than the guidelines are likely to appeal. Conversely, prosecutors are more likely to appeal sentences that fall well below the recommended sentence, unless there is prior agreement with the judge and defense attorney. In all cases where a judge departs from the guidelines, there must typically be a good legal reason for the departure, since the sentence could be rejected upon appeal.

Impact of Sentencing Guidelines

Have sentencing guidelines had their proposed effects on sentencing? Little evidence allows experts to assess the impact of sentencing guidelines on all the three primary purposes for sentencing guidelines—public safety, equity in sentencing, and management of the corrections population. Perhaps the most difficult assessments concern the impact of sentencing guidelines on public safety. Because many sentencing guidelines grids were based on historical patterns of sentencing, there was neither an obvious increase in the severity of the punishment that could generate a deterrent effect nor an incapacitative effect of punishment. Following the initial implementation of many guidelines grids, states and the federal government have increased the severity of punishment for many forms of crime (especially drug crimes) through the use of mandatory minimum sentences. It is not clear that these severer sanctions have reduced crime rates,

but they do have the apparent effect of making the general public feel safer.

The analysis of sentencing decisions is perhaps one of the most thorough areas of research in the study of criminal courts in the United States. Much of the research published since the 1990s has relied on data collected by various sentencing commissions. There are two broad sets of findings to emerge from this research. First, research assessing pre- and post-guidelines sentencing patterns has shown less variation across judges, suggesting that there has been more consistency in how offenders are punished. Second, and despite the greater consistency in criminal punishments, there continue to be unwarranted disparities, where age, sex, race, ethnicity, and access to legal counsel (that is, private attorneys as opposed to public defenders) affect the severity of punishment, even after taking into account the severity of the conviction offense and of the offender's prior record as required by the guidelines grid.

The use of sentencing guidelines to manage corrections populations has not been successful. Starting in the mid-1980s, the number of people under some form of correctional supervision started to increase at a nearly exponential rate of growth and started to level off only by about 2010. If the states with sentencing guidelines grids had left sentencing policies to their sentencing commissions, then it may have been possible for those states to manage the sizes of their corrections population more effectively. It is not possible to know whether the guidelines would have been effective, since most guidelines grids have been superseded by a series of laws requiring mandatory minimum punishments for a subset of specific offenses, but particularly for drug crimes. These laws have had the effect of inflating the size of the corrections population in ways that were unanticipated during the original construction of most sentencing guidelines grids, which initially focused on longer prison terms for violent offenders.

Summary

The adherence to sentencing guidelines has been an attempt by a number of states and the federal government to introduce greater rationality into the sentencing of criminal offenders and a move away from indeterminate sentencing practices that were viewed by both sides of the political spectrum as problematic. To the extent that judges' sentencing decisions conform to those recommended in the guidelines grid—as they often do—criminal sentencing is a more rational and equitable process now than it was prior to the 1980s. This does not mean that the social and demographic characteristics of offenders no longer affect punishments, but the magnitude of these effects has decreased over time in those states with sentencing guidelines systems.

Chester L. Britt
Northeastern University

See also Attitudes and Myths About Punishment; Determinate Sentencing; Indeterminate Sentencing

Further Readings

Engen, Rodney and Sara Steen. "The Power to Punish: Discretion and Sentencing Reform in the War on Drugs." *American Journal of Sociology*, v.105/5 (2000).

Kauder, Neal and Brian Ostrom. *State Sentencing Guidelines: Profiles and Continuum.* http://www.pewtrusts.org/uploadedFiles/wwwpewtrustsorg/Reports/sentencing_and_corrections/NCSC%20Sentencing%20Guidelines%20profiles%20July%202008.pdf (Accessed March 2011).

Savelsberg, Joachim. "Law That Does Not Fit Society: Sentencing Guidelines as a Neo-Classical Reaction to the Dilemmas of Substantivized Law." *American Journal of Sociology*, v.97/5 (1992).

Simon, Jonathan. *Governing Through Crime: How the War on Crime Transformed American Democracy and Created a Culture of Fear.* New York: Oxford University Press, 2007.

Tonry, Michael. *Malign Neglect: Race, Crime, and Punishment in America.* New York: Oxford University Press, 1995.

Ulmer, Jeffery T. *Social Worlds of Sentencing: Court Communities Under Sentencing Guidelines.* Albany: State University of New York Press, 1997.

SERIOUS AND VIOLENT OFFENDER REENTRY INITIATIVE

The Serious and Violent Offender Reentry Initiative (SVORI) was developed and implemented by the U.S. Department of Justice (DOJ), Office of Justice Programs (OJP) in 2003, along with federal agency partners, in response to high rates of offender recidivism upon prison release resulting in subsequent incarceration. Data from examinations of rates of offender recidivism upon release from jail or prison indicate that roughly 66 percent of those released commit offenses that cause them to return to correctional facilities within three years. The commencement and implementation of the SVORI represented an unprecedented federal response geared toward collectively addressing the underlying causes of criminal offending and subsequent recidivism as a potential solution to addressing the increasing prison population. Federal funds were appropriated to assist states in expanding existing resources or developing concerted efforts to effectively link institutional and community correctional programs and services in order to prepare high-risk offenders for successful transition and community reintegration upon prison release. Included among the primary goals of the SVORI are a reduction in recidivism and an increase in public safety by meeting underlying needs of offenders as they are released from prison.

Juvenile and adult offenders who possess violent offense histories pose greater threats to public safety and are more likely to recidivate upon community reentry. The SVORI seeks to provide enhanced services and case-planning efforts to this population of offenders in an effort to address these issues. Among the initiation and implementation efforts associated with the SVORI, grantees at local and state levels were directed to utilize federal dollars to expand or improve upon their current reentry programming efforts for violent offender populations by providing additional training to staff, developing integrated supervision efforts, establishing or strengthening partnerships between institutional and community agencies, and creating innovative approaches to reentry for juveniles or adults within a specific area of each jurisdiction. SVORI funding requirements established that program participants must receive enhanced treatment and programming services throughout three specific phases: (1) prior to prison exit, (2) upon release to the community, and (3) several years following community release. The major organizational structure and goal of these programs involve providing a continuum of care that commences while the offender is incarcerated and continues to provide individuals with the assistance that they require at various stages of the reentry process. Such efforts require institutional and community corrections and state and local agencies to collaborate in effort to provide comprehensive services to program participants.

The collaboration of various agencies and organizations working to achieve intended goals is vital to the success of SVORI programs. Offender populations have a variety of needs and face several social and legal barriers to successful community reentry. These must be addressed as they exit prison and reenter the community. SVORI efforts recognize that this process is inherently difficult, and thus programming efforts focus on assessing offender needs and developing a reentry plan, prior to prison release, in order to become aware of these challenges and locate services that may assist this population with handling these challenges prior to prison release.

Federal agency partners that collaborated with the U.S. Department of Justice, Office of Justice Programs included the Department of Labor (DOL), the Department of Education (DOEd), the Department of Housing and Urban Development (DHUD), and the Department Health and Human Services (DHHS). The underlying goals associated with each of these agencies represent their ability to address many of the basic needs associated with offender populations, which are necessary for the facilitation of successful community reentry. SVORI programs have several goals, including, but not limited to, assisting the offender with finding and obtaining employment and housing, reconnecting with children and other family members, addressing substance abuse and mental health issues, improving physical health, and strengthening community relationships and bonds. Additionally, SVORI programs recognize that enhanced offender supervision is a vital component relating to the successfulness of the program. In sum, the effectiveness of this multifaceted program is dependent upon the ability of various agencies to collaborate in a collective effort focused on meeting the various needs of violent offender populations.

Research that has examined the effectiveness of SVORI efforts in various states has generally yielded findings in support of the comprehensive services provided to high-risk offenders during the three phases of the program's implementation. Evaluations of such programs in various states have indicated that SVORI participants participate in a greater number of correctional programs (in prison and upon prison exit), are more closely monitored and supervised upon community entry (thereby increasing public safety), are provided with services to meet many of their basic needs and facilitate community involvement, and are less likely to recidivate during the follow-up period. Additionally, several evaluations of SVORI programs have suggested that coordinated reentry efforts that connect institutional and community-based programming and case planning are effective for meeting the needs of high-risk offender populations.

Such programming efforts recognize that prison release is a process, whereby early case planning to address offender needs is orchestrated and implemented as a course of action throughout the transitional process, rather than an abrupt episode. More than 95 percent of the incarcerated population will eventually be released to the community, and while more research that examines the effectiveness of such programming efforts is needed, collaborative efforts by various state and community agencies, such as those encouraged by the SVORI, are crucial to the future effectiveness of institutional and community corrections, reducing rates of offender recidivism, and increasing public safety.

Lindsey Bergeron-Vigesaa
Nova Southeastern University

See also Recidivism; Reducing Prison Populations; Reentry Programs and Initiatives; Reintegration Into Communities

Further Readings

Bouffard, J. A. and L. E. Bergeron. "Reentry Works: The Implementation and Effectiveness of a Serious and Violent Offender Reentry Initiative." *Journal of Offender Rehabilitation*, v.44/2–3 (2006).

Petersilia, J. "Prisoner Reentry: Public Safety and Reintegration Challenges." *The Prison Journal*, v.81/3 (2001).

Seither, R. and K. Kadela. "Prisoner Reentry: What Works, What Does Not, and What Is Promising." *Crime and Delinquency*, v.49/3 (2003).

Taxman, F. S. et al. *From Prison Safety to Public Safety: Innovations in Prisoner Reentry*. Washington, DC: Department of Justice, 2002.

Travis, J. *But They All Come Back: Facing the Challenges of Prisoner Reentry*. Washington, DC: Urban Institute Press, 2005.

Sex Offender Registration

Since the early 2000s, every state has adopted some form of sex offender registration and community notification system. The sex offender registry is a mechanism used for tracking persons convicted of a sex offense after that person's reentry back into the community. The registry is also used to help criminal justice and law-enforcement personnel manage information and investigate new sex offenses that may occur in the area where a registered sex offender resides. Sex offender registry and notification systems were created and are used, in theory, to promote public safety and general deterrence. However, the effectiveness of sex offender registration and notification has been questioned. Collateral consequences experienced by convicted sex offenders and those who establish or maintain relationships with them after their release from prison have a profound impact on many facets of their lives.

The Sex Offender Registration and Notification Act (SORN), which is part of the Adam Walsh Child Protection and Safety Act of 2006, mandates a set of minimum standards for each state, district, U.S. territory, and Indian tribal government in which each jurisdiction must comply. The registration of convicted sex offenders allows for the notification of community members by providing access to information about certain classifications of convicted sex offenders. Every jurisdiction has a sex offender registry Website that can be accessed by members of the public. Community members are able to search information and receive e-mail notifications from the state about sex offenders living in their area. Some states provide an interactive map in addition to e-mail notification. Sex offender registration notification systems usually provide a photograph, a physical description including any scars or tattoos, and the home address, school address, work address, and vehicle information of individuals classified by the courts as moderate or high-risk sex offenders. Other jurisdictions may employ supplemental tactics to notify community members of persons convicted of sex offenses who reside in their area. In some areas, for example, when a convicted sex offender reenters the community, postcards are sent to anyone living in a three-block radius in urban areas and within a one-mile radius in rural areas to notify the residents of the offender and his or her address.

Current research questions the effectiveness of community notification statutes, which were created to protect the public from sexual abuse or exploitation. Some scholars assert that these statutes provide a false sense of security to community members because they overlook the fact that most perpetrators have some sort of relationship with their victim. Sex offender registration and notification statutes may actually reinforce myths about sexual assault (that is, the "stranger in the bushes" myth) instead of educating community members about the need to monitor relationships between children and adults who are close friends and family members.

Research conducted on convicted sex offenders whose information appears on registries has reported offenders' negative experiences attributed to the registries. These negative experiences include, but are not limited to, denial of residency, loss of employment, isolation from family members and support systems, and public harassment. More direct community notification methods, such as flyers passed out at schools or in the neighborhood, elicit more negative reactions from the community than do passive forms of notification, such as online registries.

Sex offender registration and notification can have major implications, or "collateral" (unanticipated) consequences, for both sex offenders reintegrating into the community and those who maintain ties with the offender, such as family members. The public, made aware of the offender's presence in their community, may react negatively, by isolating the offender socially, by inhibiting the offender's ability to secure housing and employment, and even by harassing and threatening the offender. After imprisonment, the person convicted of a sex offense may not be able to move back in with his or her family because of residential restriction laws. Additional difficulties arise when the homes of registered sex offenders are too close to a school, a day care center, or a school bus stop.

Although collateral consequences are most often experienced by the offender, evidence suggests that individuals, such as friends, romantic partners, and family members, who maintain relationships with the offender report experiencing "secondary" collateral consequences of the criminal sanctions. Like the sex offender him- or herself, people who maintain ties with sex offenders are often subjected to underemployment, lack of affordable housing, obstacles in maintaining parenting roles, and stigma. Family members who live with registered sex offenders often report experiencing physical and verbal harassment, assault, property damage, and emotional and psychological consequences. They also report having difficulties finding and maintaining employment.

Laura A. Rapp
University of Delaware

See also Sex Offenders in the Community; Sexual Predators: Civil Commitment

Further Readings

Laney, Garrione P. *Sex Offender Registration*. New York: Nova Science, 2009.

Office of Justice Programs. "National Guidelines for Sex Offender Registration and Notification." http://www.ojp.usdoj.gov/smart/pdfs/final_sornaguidelines.pdf (Accessed July 2011).

Prescott, J. J. and Jonah E. Rockoff. *Do Sex Offender Registration and Notification Laws Affect Criminal Behavior?* Cambridge, MA: National Bureau of Economic Research, 2008.

U.S. Department of Justice. *The National Guidelines for Sex Offender Registration and Notification*. Washington, DC: Author, 2008.

SEX OFFENDERS IN THE COMMUNITY

Sex offenders who reside in hometown communities are every parent's nightmare. Their close proximity to parks, schools, and neighborhood streets creates civic fear and disdain among citizens. One high-profile sex offender case still reverberates: the kidnapping of Polly Klaas from her own home. Polly's killer waited in her bedroom closet with a knife while two girlfriends joined Polly for an innocent sleepover. Another famous case was the abduction and murder of Amber Hagerman, a 9-year-old Texas girl riding her bike in her own neighborhood, which prompted the creation of the Amber alert: a critical missing child response program that utilizes law-enforcement and media resources to notify the public when children are kidnapped by predators.

Grieving families persist in their efforts to protect children from harm. Their vigilant campaigns focus on changing laws relevant to sex offenders. Numerous legal remedies and multifaceted/task-force approaches continue to emerge in the United States because of notorious high-profile sex offender cases. Risk assessment of sex offenders is an essential component in managing potentially dangerous offenders in the community.

Risk Assessment

Tracking sexual offenders involves the difficult task of risk assessment. Risk assessment provides essential information concerning the potential seriousness of the offender's sexual behavior. Evaluation attempts to determine the risk the offender might present to the community's children. Risk or dangerousness can vary in different social locations for sex offenders. Residing within close proximity to elementary schools and playgrounds elicits additional scrutiny.

Sex offenders represent every stratum of society. There are no scientific sex offender profiles; however, similarities exist in their methods of operation: (1) denial, (2) minimization concerning their offenses and behaviors, (3) multiple victims, and (4) predatory sexual behaviors. High-risk offenders require intense (also known as intensive) supervision.

The Legislative Approach

Megan's law was passed by the New Jersey legislature during a crusade led by the Kanka family in 1994. Seven-year-old Megan Kanka had been abducted, raped, and murdered by Jesse K. Timmendequas on July 27, 1994. Her parents were determined to help prevent sex offenders from sexually attacking and killing other children. The Kankas' efforts, along with the cooperation of the U.S. Congress, eventually led to establishing a federal sex offender registration and notification law in 1996, known today as Megan's law. Eventually, Megan's law became an amendment to the Jacob Wettering Crimes Against Children Act (CACA). The law required every state to develop procedures for notifying the public when a sex offender is released into the community. Megan's law authorizes local law-enforcement agencies to notify their communities about convicted sex offenders living, working, or visiting their localities.

The Adam Walsh Child Protection and Safety Act of 2006—named for Adam Walsh, a 6-year-old boy abducted from a Sears department store in Hollywood, Florida, in 1981 and found decapitated—targets sex offenders for failing to register when they cross state lines. Sex offender violators are subject to 10 years of imprisonment under this federal statute. The Walsh Act is directed at interstate travel; however, a related problem is homeless sex offenders who are mobile and difficult to track.

Multifaceted Approach

A multifaceted/task-force approach addresses sex offender compliance concerns. Sex offender laws are implemented differently in different jurisdictions. Agency partnership, collaboration, and cooperation share in the supervision of convicted sex offenders. Coordinated agencies develop guidelines for sharing information and coordinating their efforts.

Tracking sex offenders is very complex and requires informing communities about the presence of offenders. The most complex aspects concern compliance and enforcement of registration laws. Offenders who are no longer under correctional supervision represent a considerable concern to the community and to law enforcement. The benefits of a multifaceted approach are (1) increased cooperation, (2) enhanced supervision, and (3) accountability. In addition, the task-force team approach focuses on reducing recidivism and victimization.

The U.S. Marshals Service (USMS) coordinates the Sexual Predators Crime Branch and assists law-enforcement agencies in locating and apprehending noncompliant sex offenders. The National Center for Missing and Exploited Children (NCMEC) partners and coordinates with USMS and the Sexual Predators Branch. In addition, NCMEC serves as a central information and analysis center for assisting in the detection and apprehension of registered sex offenders. The Federal Bureau of Investigation (FBI), with state and local law-enforcement agencies, assist in identifying noncompliant registered sex offenders.

The Amber alert system is an important strategy and may prove decisive in cases of missing children kidnapped by sex offenders. When law-enforcement agencies have information that a child is under the threat of serious bodily harm or death, the Amber alert system is triggered. Activating the system notifies the broadcast media and provides some of the essential details of the case for the general public. Citizens listening to their car radios, observing turnpike road sign alerts, or viewing television become passive participants who provide the "eyes and ears of the police."

The National Alert Registry of all sex offender records incorporates various state registries. This system uses new technology and integrated strategies. The National Registry Act provides a single database with nationwide coverage that includes crime mapping and e-mail notification technologies.

Community Placement Obstacles

Balancing the rights of victims, communities, and offenders entails considerable obstacles to reintegration of sex offenders into communities. Community residents can, and often do, protest, lobby, and demonstrate against such reintegration. In addition, community notifications may encourage vigilantism, threats, and acts of violence. This makes it difficult for sex offenders to find housing and adjust to community life. The problems they face from community fears and emotional reactions have involved their relocation away from families, substandard housing, and relocation to rural areas where employment is more difficult to secure.

The Iowa County Prosecutor's Office has indicated that these restrictions might be counterproductive: The Iowa County Attorney's Association issued a position paper in 2006 opposing a 2,000-foot residency restriction against sex offenders from places where children congregate. Among many criticisms, the prosecutors noted the following:

Law enforcement has observed that the residency restriction is causing offenders to become homeless, to change residences without notifying authorities of their new locations, to register false addresses or to simply disappear. If they do not register, law enforcement and public do not know where they are living. The resulting damage to the reliability of the sex offender registry does not serve the interests of public safety.

Sex Offender Research

Considerable facts and fiction surround the topic of sex offenders. One myth is that sex offenders are dirty, old strangers who steal children from playgrounds. One Ohio prison research study found that only 2.2 percent of child molesters were strangers to their victims. Moreover, 89 percent had no prior convictions. In 2006, an Ohio sentencing commission report indicated that 93 percent of molestation victims were known to their sexual abusers. This 2006 report also revealed more than 50 percent of the victims were abused by close relatives.

Another myth is that treatment is a waste of money for sex offenders. For example, the Vermont Corrections Department tracked 190 offenders released a decade earlier. The arrest rate for these sex offenders was 3.8 percent for the people who had completed the sex offender program. The recidivism rate was 22.4 percent for those who had started the program but did not complete the program. Those sex offenders who never attended had a 27 percent recidivism rate.

Conclusion

The treatment of sex offenders should start in prison and continue after release. Treatment for this population of offenders is necessary for the prevention of recidivism and the protection of future victims. The legislative approach cannot be effective without excellent corrections and intensive supervision from law-enforcement and parole officers. The efforts of parole and law-enforcement officers represent the first-line efforts of those who function as the guardians and protectors of innocent potential victims of sex offenders. The multifaceted/task-force approach promises the collaboration and intervention that may prevent future sex offender offenses.

Thomas E. Baker
University of Scranton

See also Community-Based Vocational Networks; Sex Offender Registration; Sexual Predators: Civil Commitment

Further Readings

Dornin, Chris. "Facts and Fiction About Sex Offenders." 2010. http://www.corrections.com/articles/24500-Facts -And-Fiction-About-Sex-Offenders (Accessed July 2011).

International Association of Chiefs of Police. *Sex Offenders in the Community: Law Enforcement Prevention Strategies, for Law Enforcement.* Arlington, VA: Author, 2007.

Pollack, Joycelyn. *Prisons: Today and Tomorrow.* Sudbury, MA: Jones and Bartlett, 2005.

Sexual and Gender Minorities and Special Needs

Little is known about the impact of corrections on sexual and gender minority (SGM) persons. What is known comes primarily from research on adult males in prison. Learning from the challenges faced by incarcerated SGM persons, conclusions are drawn as to how community corrections may be especially beneficial to these populations.

Differentiating Sexual and Gender Minorities

A person's sexual orientation is to whom a person is emotionally, romantically, and sexually attracted. Gender identity is how a person self-identifies as a particular gender, regardless of physical sex characteristics. Corrections staff do not always recognize the distinction between sexual and gender orientations; some staff see those who identify as transgender as "gay" and vice versa.

Transgenderism describes the situation when a person is born a certain sex anatomically, but identifies, and wishes to live, as a different gender rather than as the sex the person's anatomy dictates. Sometimes, persons who identify as transgender are diagnosed with gender identity disorder (GID), a mental health condition represented by a conflict between a person's physical sex and the gender that person identifies as being. Treatment for GID is guided by the Harry Benjamin Standards of Care. However, some persons who identify as transgender wish to undergo either partial or no medical intervention.

Challenges of SGM Inmates

Both sexual and gender minorities encounter discrimination in the corrections system not only from fellow inmates but also from corrections staff. This discrimination is manifested through unequal treatment, unnecessary segregation, harassment, and violence toward SGM prisoners.

For those who are transgender, the gender-segregated organization of the corrections system is especially problematic. A person who is biologically male but identifies as female is often placed by the courts in a facility that corresponds with the person's anatomy rather than that person's identity. (Although persons who are biologically female but identify as male face a similar problem, there is no research to date on this population in corrections.) Such placement puts a transgender person at greater risk for assault, and the prison system at risk for liability. Transgender female inmates are disproportionately victims of sexual assault. To address this violence, some prisons have placed transgender persons in isolation, which not only does not guarantee protection but also subjects the victim to harsher conditions without due cause.

Some transgender prisoners are not allowed to be referred to by the gender-congruent name they prefer over their birth name because of prison regulations that restrict the use of aliases. The application of this law demonstrates disrespect toward the individual's gender status. Other prisoners are simply referred to by their birth name or pronoun out of disrespect or ignorance on the part of corrections staff.

Persons specifically diagnosed with GID are at risk for being denied proper medical care for their condition. Medical consensus states that persons receiving treatment for GID should continue to receive the Benjamin Standards of Care while incarcerated. However, because of bias, lack of medical expertise, lack of facilities, or a combination of these factors, such medical treatment is rare within the prison system.

Challenges of SGM Juvenile Offenders

SGM youths face discrimination not only from society at large but also directly from their families. Many youths become involved in the court system because of a breakdown in the parent-child relationship. More than one quarter of those who leave their families do so because of conflicts over their sexual orientation, and many become homeless; it is estimated that between 20 and 40 percent of homeless youths do not identify as heterosexual. Given their unstable family and living situations, sexual minority youths may be more likely to commit nonviolent survival crimes.

Additionally, sexual minority youths report higher rates of substance use, potentially a response to feelings of depression, social isolation, and ostracism caused by internal or external homophobia. SGM youths are also more likely to carry weapons—possibly as a precaution against assault, which they experience at extremely high rates. Disproportionate substance use or weapons possession, precipitated by reactions to discrimination and rejection, may result in higher rates of interactions with the justice system for SGM youths when compared to those of heterosexual youths. Indeed, sexual minority youths are more likely to report engaging in minor and moderate transgressions, but not violence.

Treatment within the system can be unjust and unsafe. It has been documented that, after controlling for rates of transgressions, sexual minority youths are more likely to be involved in police stops and in adult convictions. Incarcerated SGM youths, like adults, have been harassed or put in social isolation because of their gender identity; such actions violate a state's responsibility to provide a juvenile with safe conditions of confinement and to prevent unreasonable restrictive conditions.

Community Corrections

Although there is no literature directly addressing the impact of community corrections on SGM persons, several factors suggest that this system may benefit these populations. SGM individuals placed in community corrections may avoid many of the safety concerns that can arise from being incarcerated. Those who identify as transgender may especially benefit from community corrections by avoiding placement based on anatomy rather than identity. Being within the community may also allow a transgender person to be addressed by the person's preferred name and pronoun. For those diagnosed with gender identity disorder, it is possible that adherence to the Benjamin Standards of Care is easier within a community setting because of increased access.

However, gender-segregated programs and supports may still remain problematic for transgender persons. It has been recommended by a team of advocacy groups that includes the Transgender Law Center and the American Civil Liberties Union that all individuals in community corrections be screened for sexual orientation and transgender identity in order to prevent potential harassment as well as unnecessary limitations to program involvement. Additional recommendations include training in cultural competence issues related to SGM persons for all corrections staff.

Community corrections also appears promising for SGM youth offenders, as it allows those who have committed nonviolent "survival crimes" to remain integrated in a community where there are more possible supports. However, it is particularly important to identify supports that will accept their sexual and gender orientation and encourage healthy identity development.

L. Kris Gowen
Portland State University

See also Female Offenders and Special Needs; Offender Needs; Specialized Caseload Models

Further Readings

Brown, G. R. "Recommended Revisions to the World Professional Association for Transgender Health's Standards of Care Section on Medical Care for Incarcerated Persons With Gender Identity Disorder." *International Journal of Transgenderism*, v.11 (2009).

Davis, M. et al. "Preventing the Sexual Abuse of Lesbian, Gay, Bisexual, Trangender, and Intersex People in Correctional Settings: Comments Submitted in Response to Docket No. OAG-131; AG Order No. 3143–2010 National Standards to Prevent, Detect, and Respond to Prison Rape." 2010. http://www.nclrights.org/site/DocServer/PREA_Standards_Comments_-_ACLU__Lambda__NCLR__NCTE__TLC_.pdf?docID=7542 (Accessed September 2011).

Estrada, R. and J. Marksamer. "The Legal Rights of LGBT Youth in State Custody: What Child Welfare and Juvenile Justice Professionals Need to Know." *Child Welfare*, v.85 (2006).

Himmelstein, K. E. and H. Bruckner. "Criminal-Justice and School Sanctions Against Nonheterosexual Youth: A National Longitudinal Study." *Pediatrics*, v.127 (2010).

Mann, R. "The Treatment of Transgender Prisoners, Not Just an American Problem? A Comparative Analysis of American, Australian, and Canadian Prison Policies Concerning the Treatment of Transgender Prisoners and a 'Universal' Recommendation to Improve Treatment." *Law and Sexuality*, v.15 (2006).

SEXUAL PREDATORS: CIVIL COMMITMENT

Currently there are about 636,000 registered sex offenders, and an additional 234,000 sex offenders are under correctional supervision, including prisons, jails, probation, and parole. Each year, between 9,000 and 10,000 of these offenders are released into the community. All of these offenders are violent offenders, because they were incarcerated for violent sex offenses. Some offenders may continue to commit violent sex offenses, and thus many states have implemented civil commitment statutes that allow the state to hold dangerous offenders in custody after they have finished serving their sentences. The main purpose of civil commitment of sexual predators is to protect the public.

Civil commitment of sex offenders has, however, become an increasingly controversial issue since the 1990s, when several child abduction cases led to a public outcry and a demand for harsher sentences. The debate about civil commitment mainly revolves around the questions of whether civil commitment is a form of punishment and whether it violates civil liberties. These questions were brought before the U.S. Supreme Court in *Kansas v. Hendricks* (1997) for state statutes and in *United States v. Comstock* (2010) for federal statutes. In both cases, the Court decided that sexual predators may be held in custody after the end of their sentences if they are "sexually dangerous" to others and suffer from a "mental abnormality" that leads to a lack of control of their sexual urges.

Development of Civil Commitment

Civil commitment of sexual predators has a long history within the United States. The first civil commitment statutes in the United States can be traced to the 1900s. These statutes, however, were used only sporadically and in a few states. Civil commitment became more widespread between 1936 and 1955. During this period, 26 states implemented "sexual psychopath" laws, which allowed the courts to admit sex offenders to mental hospitals for treatment. Most of these statutes were struck down by the courts as unconstitutional. In the 1990s, several states began to reenact civil commitment statutes in response to several murders of children committed by sexual predators. One of the best-known cases is that of Megan Kanka, a 7-year-old girl who was abducted, raped, and murdered by Jesse K. Timmendequas on July 27, 1994. Timmendequas was a repeat sex offender who had been convicted twice before for sex offenses against children. The public demanded that sex offenders receive harsher punishments, and legislatures in all states enacted laws that would keep sexual predators in prison longer, register them as sex offenders after release, and inform the public about released sex offenders, including making their home addresses public.

Registration of sex offenders by itself, however, did not solve the problem that some of these offenders committed new violent sex crimes. Recidivism rates of sex offenders are about 5.3 percent within three years of release from prison. Of all sex offenders, child molesters had the highest recidivism rate within three years, according to a 2003 report of the Bureau of Justice Statistics. In response to these violent repeat offenders, states have implemented civil commitment procedures that allowed them to keep dangerous sexual predators locked up. Civil commitment statutes are now being used in 20 states and by the federal government to confine sex offenders who are believed to be dangerous to the public. The procedures used for civil commitment are similar across states. In order to hold a sex offender in preventive detention, the prosecutor must prove in a court hearing that the offender will be dangerous if released to the community. Depending on the state, either a judge or a jury decides whether the offender will be civilly committed.

Legal Basis of Civil Commitment

The legal basis for the current civil commitment statutes was set in *Kansas v. Hendricks* (1997), where the U.S. Supreme Court upheld the statute arguing that sex offenders who have a mental abnormality and have engaged in violent sexual behavior may be held at a state detention facility after the conclusion of their sentence until they are no longer a danger to the community. Similarly, in *United States v. Comstock* (130 S. Ct. 1949, 2010) the U.S. Supreme Court upheld the right of the federal government to civilly commit violent sex offenders suffering from a mental abnormality by stating that civil commitment of sex offenders falls under the mental healthcare proceedings and that commitment and treatment for a mental illness do not constitute punishment. In accordance with the judgment, the incarcerated individuals must receive regular psychiatric evaluations and have the right to judicial review every six months. Offenders must receive adequate treatment aiming to cure the mental illness of the individual and working toward release. Because of the fact that the U.S. Supreme Court has not formulated any specific requirements about what "adequate treatment" means, all states and the federal government have their own treatment standards. The absence of specific treatment requirements is problematic, because the release of an offender depends on his or her progress, and if treatment is inadequate, progress and, as a result, release are less likely.

Legal Issues of Civil Commitment

Several legal issues surrounding sexual predators are being discussed by legal and clinical professionals.

First, opponents argue that the civil commitment statutes violate the substantive due process rights of individuals because the state may not limit individuals' constitutional rights unless the state demonstrates that there is a compelling state interest. States have responded to this argument by asserting that the state has an obligation to protect its citizens from harm, and violent sex offenders constitute a danger to the public. Also, supporters argue that these statutes provide an opportunity to treat the mental issues of these individuals and possibly reintegrate them into society.

Second, critics believe that civil commitment statutes are also a violation of procedural due process rights, because the statutes are overly broad. The main argument is that sexual predators do not suffer from a mental illness per se but rather from a mental abnormality. A "mental abnormality" is a very broad notion that can be abused to include anyone who is different from the average citizen.

Third, opponents criticize the statutes for violating the Sixth Amendment rights against double jeopardy. An offender should not be punished twice for the same crime. The states have responded to this argument by noting the sex offenders are treated as mentally ill persons and that treatment of a mental illness is not punishment.

Finally, as mentioned above, opponents claim that civil commitment statutes violate the rights of sex offenders as mentally ill people because the commitment of the individual is not directly bound to a treatment program.

Janine Kremling
California State University, San Bernardino

See also Risk Assessment Instruments: Three Generations; Sex Offender Registration; Sex Offenders in the Community

Further Readings

Gillespie, Anne G. "Note: Constitutional Challenges to Civil Commitment Laws: An Uphill Battle for Sexual Predators After *Kansas v. Hendricks*." *Catholic University Law Review*, v.47 (1998).

Kansas v. Hendricks, 521 U.S. 346 (1997).

Smith, Douglas G. "The Constitutionality of Civil Commitment and the Requirement of Adequate Treatment." *Boston College Law Review*, v.43 (2008).

Spierling, Sarah. "Notes and Comments: Lock Them Up and Throw Away the Key: How Washington's Violent

Sexual Predator Law Will Shape the Future Balance Between Punishment and Prevention." *Journal of Law and Policy*, v.9 (2001).

United States v. Comstock, 130 S.Ct. 1949 (2010).

U.S. Bureau of Justice Statistics. *Recidivism of Sex Offenders Released From Prison in 1994*. http://bjs.ojp .usdoj.gov/content/pub/pdf/rsorp94.pdf (Accessed July 2011).

Velazquez, Tracy. *The Pursuit of Justice: Sex Offender Policy in the United States*. New York: Vera Institute of Justice, 2008. http://www.vera.org/download?file=1801/ Sex_offender_policy_with_appendices_final.pdf (Accessed July 2011).

Shock Probation

Shock probation, sometimes referred to as "judicial review" or "shock incarceration," is a court disposition characterized by a brief period of incarceration followed by a period of probation, parole, or community supervision. Shock probation is often used interchangeably with "split probation"; however, the two sentences differ in at least two regards. Shock probation requires the defendant to be sentenced to a period of incarceration unaware that he or she will receive an early release. Release from incarceration comes only after judicial review. The probationer receiving a split probation sentence, by contrast, is aware of the length of incarceration at sentencing; further judicial review is unnecessary.

Guidelines for granting shock probation are governed by statute, and shock probation is generally considered a privilege rather than an entitlement. Philosophically, shock probation is a form of specific deterrence and is considered a close relative of the "scared straight," "wilderness experience," and "boot camp" sentencing strategies. Typically, the defendant is sentenced to a period of incarceration. It then becomes incumbent upon the defense to petition the court to initiate a court review to determine eligibility for shock probation within a specific time frame, usually within 30 to 120 days after sentencing. Offenders deemed ineligible for shock probation may apply for parole. Shock probation is typically reserved for youthful, first-time offenders who have committed nonviolent crimes. However, in some states, conviction for drug offenses and or burglary will disqualify the offender from eligibility for shock probation. The first shock probation legislation was passed in Ohio in 1965. Currently, 25 states have legislation authorizing shock probation.

One of the primary benefits of shock probation is grounded in the belief that the deterrent effect of prison confinement occurs early in the period of incarceration and the beneficial effects of incarceration rapidly deteriorate after 30 to 120 days. Shock probation allows the defendant to receive the early, deterrent effect of incarceration and provides a mechanization to allow return to the community before the detrimental effects of imprisonment take hold. Presumably, the defendant is "shocked" by the prison experience and returns to the community more motivated to take advantage of community rehabilitative resources. Proponents of shock probation cite additional benefits, including a reduction in prison overcrowding, a reduction in the costs of incarceration, and increased flexibility in

Shock probation is typically used on young, nonviolent offenders who have committed a crime for the first time. The defendant is sentenced to a period of incarceration and may be granted an early release after judicial review, however this fact is not revealed to the offender and the hope is that he or she will be "scared straight" by the experience in prison. (Photos.com)

sentencing through an additional plea-bargaining tool. Proponents also maintain that the inherent court review process increases judicial oversight.

Opponents of shock probation express concern that reducing terms of incarceration undermines the deterrent effect of sentencing by holding out hope for defendants that their sentences will be reduced. Opponents also argue that shock probation is perceived by defendants as a sign of weakness in the judicial system and thereby further serves to undermine the deterrent effect of sentencing. Additionally, critics fear that subjective interpretation of shock probation statutes and overreliance on shock probation may lead to inconsistent sentencing and other abuses of judicial discretion. Finally, opponents argue that shock probation denies victims a measure of closure and a sense that justice has been done, and that the offender's quick return to the community undermines public confidence in the criminal justice system.

Much early literature on shock probation is largely anecdotal. Early shock probation programs were warmly embraced by criminal justice practitioners, who were buoyed by the initial attitude changes observed in some persons recently returned from prison. Attempts to evaluate the long-term effectiveness of shock probation have been plagued by questionable data and research designs. It is no surprise that empirical investigation of the effectiveness of shock probation has produced mixed results. Some early studies found that recidivism rates for persons on shock probation were significantly lower than recidivism rates for probationers under more traditional forms of supervision. Later investigations found no significant difference in recidivism rates between individuals on shock probation and individuals on other forms of probation. Most recent studies have concluded that shock probation has little effect in reducing recidivism.

Scholars have identified several factors believed to be related to the effectiveness of shock probation in reducing recidivism rates. Factors considered important in increasing the effectiveness of shock probation are (1) the length of the incarceration (less than 30 days being the optimum, although some scholars advocate prison stays of only one or two weeks); (2) the defendant's expectations with regard to incarceration (offenders expecting traditional probation are likely to view the prison portion of the sentence as excessive); and (3) the offender's lack of any previous incarceration experience that might erode the "shock" of the prison portion of the sentence.

James A. Brecher
Nova Southeastern University

See also Boot Camps; Split Sentencing and Blended Sentencing; Wilderness Experience

Further Readings

Boudouris, James and Bruce W. Turnbull. "Shock Probation in Iowa." *Journal of Offender Counseling, Services, and Rehabilitation*, v.9/4 (1985).

Kempinen, Cynthia A. and Megan C. Kurlychek. "An Outcome Evaluation of Pennsylvania's Boot Camp: Does Rehabilitative Programming Within a Disciplinary Setting Reduce Recidivism?" *Crime and Delinquency*, v.49 (2003).

MacKenzie, Doris Layton. *What Works in Corrections: Reducing Recidivism*. New York: Cambridge University Press, 2006.

MacKenzie, Doris Layton et al. "Characteristics Associated With Successful Adjustment to Supervision: A Comparison of Parolees, Probationers, Shock Participants, and Shock Dropouts." *Criminal Justice and Behavior*, v.19/4 (1992).

Parent, James G. *Shock Incarceration: An Overview of Existing Programs*. Washington, DC: U.S. Government Printing Office, 1989.

Petrosino, Anthony et al. "Well-Meaning Programs Can Have Harmful Effects! Lessons From Experiments of Programs Such as Scared Straight." *Crime and Delinquency*, v.46/3 (2000).

Sims, T. C. "Shock Probation—Background, Issues, and Trends." *Texas Journal of Corrections*, v.5/5 (1979).

Vito, Gennaro F. et al. "The Effect of Shock and Regular Probation Upon Recidivism: A Comparative Analysis." *American Journal of Criminal Justice*, v.9/2 (1985).

SMART Partnership

With recidivating offenders garnering national media attention, concerns of community safety, and knowledge that supervised offenders are at risk for reoffending, both local police departments and corrections officials are developing methods to enhance the supervision of offenders in the community. In response to such concerns, many cities are beginning to implement strategic plans between police departments and state corrections departments to improve their supervision of these offenders in the community. In 1992, the Redmond Police Department, located in Redmond, Washington, a suburb of Seattle 16 miles to the east, collaborated with the Washington State Department of Corrections in Bellevue, Washington, another east-side suburb, and launched the Supervision, Management, and Recidivist Tracking (SMART) Partnership. The SMART Partnership program had the strategic goal of ensuring the safety of community members through enhanced supervision of offenders.

In 2008, according to the Washington State Department of Corrections (WA DOC), there were 18,623 offenders under some form of incarceration: prison, work release facilities, rented in-state beds, or rented out-of-state beds. The majority of WA DOC offenders are male, and the average age of all offenders under supervision is 36.9 years of age. Additionally, the majority of those who are incarcerated are serving sentences of two to five years, with a five- to 10-year sentence being the second most common time being served by offenders. Moreover, WA DOC reports that their readmission rate is 37 percent.

This recidivism rate is well below that of other states in the nation, which have recidivism rates that fall between 50 and 70 percent. In terms of those under community supervision in King County, the counties in which Redmond and Bellevue are located, WA DOC (2008) reports that there are approximately 14,000 individuals. When these offenders harm the public and government officials in Washington State while under community supervision, the demand by the public for protection from these offenders is high. To help alleviate these concerns over supervised offenders' recidivating, a unique crime-fighting tool, the SMART Partnership, was developed in Washington State.

The SMART Partnership started as a collaboration between Redmond, Washington, police officers and Bellevue, Washington, community corrections officers (CCOs). It was implemented in 1992 to increase the supervision of offenders who reside in, or frequently visit, Redmond. The SMART Partnership program is a two-part program in which police officers and CCOs assist one another in the supervision of offenders under a community corrections sentence.

T. Morgan described the program in a 2002 report in the *FBI Law Enforcement Bulletin*. In the first part of the SMART program, Redmond police officers assist CCOs in the monitoring of offenders who reside in their patrol areas. In conjunction with WA DOC Bellevue CCOs, Redmond police officers are assigned from one to two offenders to supervise. The CCOs provide the officers with information such as to where the offender resides in Redmond and the conditions of supervision that the offender is required to follow. During routine patrols, the assigned Redmond police officer and a partner may stop by the residence of an offender under supervision once or twice per month to determine if the offender is indeed home during curfew hours. Following the random check-in, the officer documents the visit on a form and provides it to the offender's CCO. If the officer observes any illegal activity, the officer will take normal law-enforcement actions.

In the second part of the SMART program, Redmond police officers document any contact that they may have with a WA DOC supervised offender in their jurisdiction. Thus, when an officer runs a name through a computer in his or her cruiser, it will inform the officer whether that individual is someone under WA DOC supervision. If a Redmond police officer comes into contact with a WA DOC offender via a traffic stop or an arrest, the officer forwards these contacts to WA DOC, Bellevue Office, on a weekly basis via a field interview report (FIR). The FIR provides a detailed account of the contact, including the time, date, and location of contact as well as a summation of the nature of the encounter, such as a traffic stop or domestic disturbance call. When WA DOC in Bellevue receives the FIR, the agency forwards that information to the assigned CCO for that offender. Prior to the creation of the SMART system, such communication did not take place on a consistent basis in a uniform manner, and sometimes it did not take place at all.

Morgan reports that, since 1992, more than 70 additional police departments and correctional field offices in Washington State have implemented SMART Partnership programs, including the city of Seattle. The SMART Partnership was deemed to be so useful that, in 1998, Washington State formally linked its Homicide Investigative Tracking System (HITS) with the SMART system. The HITS system had been developed in the Criminal Division Unit of the Washington State Attorney General's Office in 1987 as a method for tracking homicides.

The database includes information about the victim, offender, and modus operandi. It was expanded in 1991 to track all violent crimes, including sex crimes; within the database, it now also contains information for all registered sex offenders. With the HITS and SMART systems linked in an electronic database, all FIRs are now sent to the new system, which is accessible to all law-enforcement investigators, the attorney general, and corrections officials.

Clearly, by linking WA DOC officials in Bellevue with Redmond police officers, the SMART Partnership program has the ability to enhance the monitoring and supervision of offenders under community corrections sentences. In addition to enhancing surveillance of offenders, this partnership allows the agencies to pool their resources and offers the public a cost-effective method of doing so. The SMART Partnership program is a unique and effective crime-fighting tool, and with the HITS/SMART systems combined, the supervision of offenders is more streamlined.

Elaine Gunnison
Seattle University

See also Correctional Case Managers; Offender Supervision; Recidivism

Further Readings

Morgan, T. "HITS/SMART Washington State's Crime Fighting Tool." *FBI Law Enforcement Bulletin*, v.71/12 (2002). http://findarticles.com/p/articles/mi_m2194/is_2_71/ai_83794804 (Accessed July 2011).

Petersilia, Joan. *Community Corrections: Probation, Parole, and Intermediate Sanctions.* New York: Oxford University Press, 1998.

SPECIALIZED CASELOAD MODELS

Community corrections offer alternatives to incarceration and long-term imprisonment. A specialized caseload approach provides the means for addressing an offender's individual needs for rehabilitation, and correctional efforts have recently focused on improved specialized caseload models. Counseling and support services can improve offenders' reintegration opportunities and sustain significant intervention goals. The rationale behind this model is that it enhances offenders' chances for successful rehabilitation, including their compliance with the law and societal norms. Correctional administration innovations necessitate improving offender intervention methods, case management practices, and treatment programs. Innovative correctional and counseling strategies require vision and mission changes. Contemporary services will, one would hope, inspire offenders to adopt behaviors that lead to an improved life, avoid recidivism, and contribute to the successful realization of the community corrections movement.

Community corrections models offer two basic types of interventions: administrative interventions and therapeutic interventions. The administrative intervention model primarily involves surveillance and supervisory control; therapeutic interventions or specialized caseload models, on the other hand, emphasize counseling and social work. Individual jurisdictions in the United States frequently embrace overlapping models.

Administrative Interventions

The American Correctional Association urges correctional agencies to develop and adopt procedures for the early identification of special-needs inmates. The administrative intervention model, however, emphasizes discipline, power, and control; in this model, offender rehabilitation is not considered as high a priority as community protection. The administrative model focuses on using sanctions and supervision to monitor and control offender status, rarely applying therapeutic interventions or remedies. Administrative offender categories include intensive supervision and home detention, for example, to manage offenders who have been convicted of driving under the influence (DUI) of sex offenses.

For example, sex offenders can be managed with therapeutic or administrative interventions, depending on the jurisdiction's emphasis regarding compliance or administrative control. Under the administrative model, management of sex offenders focuses on technical compliance rather than treatment, and the officers who supervise these offenders do not emphasize rehabilitation. External, private therapeutic interventions are not generally accepted as a module in administrative programs.

Therapeutic Interventions

In contrast to the administrative model, the therapeutic, or social work, model sets the essential foundation for a specialized caseload model. Model blending seeks to address and treat client issues or disorders that have led to dysfunctional criminal behaviors. For example, clients are mandated to participate in therapeutically oriented programs that address alcohol and drug abuse, sex offenses, and other problematic behaviors that gave impetus to their crimes.

Mentally ill probationers are described as more noncompliant than other groups. Supervisors of mentally ill offenders identify them to be their most difficult cases. Among the challenges that mentally ill probationers pose for supervisors are the coordination of their treatment sessions and ensuring that they take their medications.

The Specialized Caseload Approach

Probation officers and probation counselors who use specialized caseload models emphasize counseling and treatment modalities. The approach is individual and strives for enhanced rapport with the offender. The purpose is to establish the change necessary for psychological adjustment to community life. The probation officer or counselor applies social work strategies and individualized casework methods to provide the necessary support for adjustment.

A risk assessment approach enhances supervision and intervention. The staffing process and classification of offenders by type of offense are established methods of managing specialized caseload assignments. In addition, case supervision and client management strategies may result from officer referral or court or parole board orders. Some specialized case counseling programs materialize from statutory law. At present, there is no ideal or perfect approach to assigning specialized cases.

Specialized caseloads involve careful supervision of offenders who represent high-risk profiles, including gang members, sex offenders, mentally impaired clients, chronic drug abusers, and others who require frequent home and field contacts. The related counseling process attempts to ensure compliance with court-ordered recommendations. Offenders are grouped according to similar attributes and assigned to professionals who are specifically trained to meet their risk assessment needs. Dividing caseloads among staff with related expertise acknowledges the need for individualized treatment.

Moreover, the development of specialized caseload expertise among staff may encourage a sense of professionalism and reduce role conflict by allowing probation officers and counselors to focus on a particular area of responsibility. Staff are given opportunities to develop their skills by specializing and focusing on a particular clientele and treatment modality.

The specialized caseload model emphasizes active listening skills as opposed to telling; it requires feedback and exchange. This practice of social work interviewing and probation counseling requires clients to move beyond their personal problems in order to realize their future potential. The counseling addresses human development and life skills; however, confrontation and the examination of personal discrepancies help maximize client potential.

The effective probation officer or counselor has the ability to suggest incongruities or mixed messages in the client's verbal expressions and related behaviors. This implies the ability to draw the offender into a meaningful dialogue about his or her mind-set. It facilitates resolution between thoughts, verbal expression, and personal commitment to positive change. The offender's limited life script defines the mental "inner prison" that prevents adequate adjustment to community-based corrections programs. Some client deficits include illogical thinking and failure to define meaningful life goals and objectives. This process takes considerable time and a sincere effort on the part of both counselor and client.

Conclusion

A growing population of offenders presents special needs. This population will continue to require specific counseling interventions as special needs clients, not simply criminal offenders. The specialized caseload model can provide services that respond to these special needs, monitoring and evaluating the delivery of services in community as well as institutional settings. These interventions target and assess individual offender risks and needs by matching clients with available resources.

The specialized caseload model therefore represents the wave of the future. Specialized interventions acknowledge the need for and roles of counseling and individualized supervision, making up for many of the deficiencies posed by purely administrative interventions. Advocates of the specialized caseload approach assert that individualized treatment offers enhanced opportunities to expand supportive relationships among offenders, parole officers, and community representatives.

Thomas E. Baker
University of Scranton

See also Disabled Offenders; Diversity in Community Corrections; Drug- and Alcohol-Abusing Offenders and Treatment; Elderly Offenders; Female Offenders and Special Needs; Juvenile and Youth Offenders; Offender Needs; Sexual and Gender Minorities and Special Needs

Further Readings

Alarid, Leanne Fiftal and Rolando V. del Carmen. *Community-Based Corrections,* 8th ed. Belmont, CA: Thomson Wadsworth, 2011.

Hanser, Robert D. *Community Corrections.* Thousand Oaks, CA: Sage, 2009.

Stohr, Mary, Anthony Walsh, and Craig Hemmens. *Corrections: A Text/Reader.* Thousand Oaks, CA: Sage, 2009.

SPLIT SENTENCING AND BLENDED SENTENCING

Two alternative forms of judicial sanctions are blended sentences and split sentences. They are quite different from each other, although both of them have two phases, and each phase provides incentives for rehabilitation.

Split Sentences

Today, most state courts as well as the federal court system employ an intermediate sanction called split sentencing. Although there is variation across jurisdictions, a split sentence generally refers to a mandatory period of incarceration (in jail or prison), followed by probation or parole. The incarceration portion of the sentence is usually considerably shorter than one given under traditional sentencing. Split sentencing is also unique in allowing judges to mandate probation or parole, rather than leaving that decision up to a parole board or other agency. Depending on the state, the probation or parole period involves some combination of monitoring,

If a defendant's crime qualifies under the Federal Sentencing Table, up to half of his or her term of imprisonment can be served in a setting other than a prison. Blended sentences are fairly new to the criminal justice system and allow judges to combine juvenile and adult sanctions in cases originating in juvenile court. (Photos.com)

programming, and restrictions. If an offender violates these terms, he or she is returned to a correctional facility for the length of the original sentence. A few states also have reverse split sentencing, requiring offenders to complete a period of probation followed by incarceration. Split sentencing is similar to shock parole but does not require a second judicial or parole board hearing between incarceration and probation. In both types of sentencing, however, the relatively short period of incarceration is used primarily to provide a wake-up call for offenders.

Advocates argue that split sentencing offers the possibility of cost savings and helps to reduce overcrowding in correctional facilities. On the other hand, its availability can have the opposite effect if judges impose split sentences in cases in which they would previously have opted only for probation. Because some split sentencing legislation requires offenders to serve time in local jails instead of state prisons, this form of sentencing may simply shift costs. Critics of split sentencing argue that it gives judges too much discretion and may result in shorter terms of incarceration, possibly jeopardizing public safety. In some cases, however, people with split sentences serve more time than those with traditional sentences, as they are usually ineligible for early release. For this reason, advocates say that this type of sentencing is consistent with the principle of truth in sentencing. Unfortunately, little solid research has been conducted on the effects of split sentencing.

Blended Sentences

Blended sentencing is a relatively new form that allows judges to combine juvenile and adult sanctions in cases originating in juvenile court. The goal is to impose strict sentences on youthful offenders while providing for leniency in the event of rehabilitation. Blended sentences have become increasingly common in the last 20 years, and today about half of the states employ them.

Under the most common type of blended sentencing, an "inclusive blend," a juvenile is given both a juvenile and an adult sentence. At the conclusion of the juvenile sentence, a judge holds a hearing to determine whether the youth has been rehabilitated. If the judge concludes that the youth has made progress, he or she can suspend the adult portion of the sentence and the youth can leave the juvenile correctional facility without serving any adult time. Those who have behaved badly in prison or who have not provided evidence of rehabilitation are required to serve the adult portion of the sentence.

A second type of blended sentence, called a "contiguous blend," allows juvenile court judges to sentence youths past the state's upper age limit. For example, in many states youths can remain incarcerated or under supervision in the juvenile system only until their 21st birthday. A contiguous blended sentence allows a juvenile court judge to sentence youths past this age. Once they reach the maximum age for juvenile court jurisdiction, however, youths with contiguous sentences are transferred to an adult facility.

A third type of blended sentence, known as an "exclusive blend," gives a juvenile court judge the option to order an adult sentence or a criminal court judge to order a juvenile sentence.

Advocates argue that blended sentences provide an incentive for incarcerated youths to behave well and participate in rehabilitative programming. Critics point out, however, that there are ethical problems associated with blended sentences. In some states, youths receive a blended sentence in a juvenile court, where there are fewer legal protections than in an adult court. As a result, some youths are sentenced to adult time without adult legal protections.

Anne M. Nurse
College of Wooster

See also Probation: Early Termination; Sentencing Guidelines; Shock Probation

Further Readings

Cheesman, Fred and Nicole L. Waters. *Who Gets a Second Chance? An Investigation of Ohio's Blended Juvenile Sentence*. Washington, DC: National Center for State Courts, 2008. http://www.ssrn.com (Accessed January 2011).

Shear, G. E. "The Disregarding of the Rehabilitative Spirit of Juvenile Codes: Addressing Resentencing Hearings in Blended Sentencing Schemes." *Kentucky Law Journal*, v.99/1 (2011).

Siegal, Larry. *Essentials of Criminal Justice*. Belmont, CA: Thomson Wadsworth, 2009.

Trulson, C. R., D. R. Haerle, M. DeLisi, and J. W. Marquart. "Blended Sentencing, Early Release, and Recidivism of Violent Institutionalized Delinquents." *Prison Journal*, v.91/3 (2011).

TEEN COURTS

Teen courts originated from a number of programs beginning in the late 1960s and as of 2010 numbered about 1,200 in the United States. The basic idea informing these programs is that young offenders will benefit by having creative, thoughtful or unique dispositions ("sentences," in the terminology of juvenile courts) imposed by a panel of peers. The underlying philosophy is the notion that desire to gain peer approval and avoid peer disapprobation among young people will make such a process more germane to youthful offenders. Conformist peers, it is assumed, will make a more effective court than will an often austere and seemingly remote and removed adult judge. At intake, teen court defendants have to admit culpability before being diverted from the more formal juvenile court process and must agree to accept the jurisdiction and disposition imposed by the teen court.

In this process, evidence and the charges are reviewed, a hearing is held, and a disposition is imposed by a panel of youths. In theory, all roles are held by and functions are mediated and performed by a panel of young people. Adults act in supervisory and administrative roles and function as probation officers to coordinate any community service disposition imposed by the court. In practice there are different teen court formats.

Teen courts are seen as offering a number of benefits: timeliness, accountability, cost savings, and promoting community cohesion. Generally teen court cases are heard within days or weeks of the instant offense, and generally only minor offenses are heard by this tribunal. Thus an offense that might be regarded as minor by adult juvenile court personnel might be acted upon with more severity if seen as significant by peers. Because most teen court participants are volunteers and are from the community, savings and respect for the law by the general public and juvenile audience are supposedly enhanced by this program.

Most teen courts are affiliated with traditional courts, although some are moderated and administered through law-enforcement agencies. Private agencies working under grants operate about 25 percent of these programs. These programs receive referrals from juvenile courts.

Most teen court defendants are first-time, younger offenders. Many programs accept only first-time offenders and accept no defendants with prior felony arrests or prior juvenile records. Offenders most often referred to the teen court are those accused of theft, simple assault, alcohol offenses, disorderly conduct, and vandalism.

Teen courts generally attempt to impose dispositions that are restorative in nature. That is, they try to convince the youthful offender to repair that which he or she has destroyed or to see the point of view of those against whom he or she has transgressed. Typically, a vandal might have to work in the yard of someone whose property he has vandalized and perhaps also write a letter of apology to the victim. Sometimes classes in anger management or decision making might be part of the disposition.

An interesting and unique feature of this convention is that offenders are expected to serve on future teen court panels. This is seen as enhancing prosocial interactions and increase awareness of victim impact. That notwithstanding, community service is the most frequent sanction imposed, followed by apology letters, essays, and teen jury service. Attendance in specialized classes is a common outcome, as is restitution.

The most common format used in teen court is that which retains an adult judge. In this model, the jury recommends a disposition that the judge is free to use or disregard. Youth attorneys participate, but the ultimate authority resides with the judge. A smaller number of courts employ a youth judge, and some use a three-panel youth tribunal in place of a judge and jury. In a peer jury model, an adult judge has a limited role and the jury may question the defendant. The jury then recommends a disposition, as is the practice in other teen courts.

Interestingly, directors of teen courts see juvenile court judges as having a high degree of support for the teen court concept. Police agencies are similarly seen as generally supportive, as are juvenile court intake and probation officers. As a whole, both media and parent groups are also numbered as supporters of teen courts by teen court directors. Most elected officials pay lip service to the concept as well. The least supportive component of the possible audience, as viewed by teen court coordinators, is the business community. Even so, all segments of the community are seen, by admittedly biased and self-interested teen court directors, as generally supportive.

Teen courts face a number of problematic issues. Funding, not unexpectedly, is a serious problem. Even the modest expenditures of administering the program may strain severely already stretched municipal budgets. Recruiting adult volunteers and keeping them involved is another continuing problem. Teenagers often have busy schedules, conflicting priorities, and transportation problems; retaining youth volunteers is a persistent difficulty. Recruiting prosocial youthful volunteers may prove to be a challenge in some communities as well. Teen courts also report problems with delays between intake and referral, internal juvenile court politics, lack of judicial support, and too many referrals.

Recidivism research—that is, studies on the rate of juvenile reoffending after a teen court disposition—reveals some interesting findings. Generally, the teen courts with the most juvenile participation have the least recidivism. This means that juvenile offenders may be reacting favorably to participating in a process in which they see other young people in meaningful and responsible roles. This would tend to affirm the underlying principles of the utility and relevance of peer involvement as a critical component of this process. As a rule, those who have been through teen courts of any type are somewhat less likely to reoffend. Involved youths and parents report satisfaction with the teen court experience. As long as funding can be found, it is anticipated that the teen court concept will spread and manifest more diversity in form.

Francis Frederick Hawley
Western Carolina University

See also Juvenile and Youth Offenders; Juvenile Probation Officers; Predispositional Reports for Juveniles; Pre-Sentence Investigation Reports; Therapeutic Jurisprudence

Further Readings

Butts, J. and J. Buck. *Teen Courts: A Focus on Research.* Washington, DC: Juvenile Justice Bulletin, U.S. Department of Justice, Office of Juvenile Justice and Delinquency Prevention, 2000.

Butts, J., J. Buck, and M. Coggeshall. *Teen Courts.* Washington, DC: Urban Institute, 2002. http://www .urban.org/uploadedpdf/410457.pdf (Accessed July 2010).

Sanborn, J. and A. Salerno. *The Juvenile Justice System: Law and Process.* Los Angeles: Roxbury, 2005.

TEMPERANCE MOVEMENT

Benjamin Rush—patriot, physician, intellectual, and professor of medicine—was among the first influential Americans systematically to illustrate the negative aspects of alcohol in the late 1700s. Indeed, prior to that time alcohol was thought to be a healthful tonic and effective panacea. In the absence of opiates, which were not much used at that time in America, alcohol was about the only painkiller available to both doctors and laypersons. Rush was reacting to a large growth of drunkenness that followed the American Revolution. Old verities and authorities had fallen by the wayside after the war, and the use of spirituous liquors rose precipitously. For example, whiskey was used as currency in the backcountry, and taverns were full of common workers and artisans, many of whom customarily drank to excess on a daily basis. This, coupled with the almost universal practice of employers giving alcohol to apprentices and journeymen as part of their wages, led to a besotted working class. In fact, for many workers there were two drinking breaks during the workday until the 1830s. After work, men frequently repaired to neighborhood taverns, preserves of masculinity where they were encouraged to gamble and consort with prostitutes; there they continued drinking to excess and squandering their substance. Violence, riot, and crime in the city streets were often alcohol-fueled, and drunken gangs ranged urban streets well into the late 1850s. Farmers typically supplied alcohol to workers during harvest and that harvest time often degenerated into drunken affrays in rural areas, as well. Elections were periods of high drunkenness; politicians plied voters with copious amounts of liquor and punch. The upper classes also partook of large amounts of spirituous liquors, as writings of the day reveal. For example, 55 delegates to the Constitutional Convention at a party in 1787 drank 114 bottles of wine, 34 of beer and porter, eight of whiskey, eight of hard cider, and seven bowls of alcohol-laced punch. The use of spirituous liquors and wine was seen as a normal accompaniment to the business of the day and was frequent at festivals and celebrations of all types. However, for people of all classes, excessive use of alcohol frequently resulted in disease, dissipation, and financial ruin.

Rush and the early temperance advocates noted this and proposed that among some people chronic drunkenness had more in common with a disease than merely being a manifestation of lack of character or stamina. By the 1820s, a movement promoting temperance—which at that time meant refraining only from drinking spirituous (hard) liquor—came into being. The word *temperance* simply means moderation, and the hope was to change drinking habits from imbibing hard liquor to drinking moderate amounts of less harmful beer and wine. However, as soon as the movement gathered momentum, the focus shifted, and temperance came to mean abstinence from all alcoholic beverages, or teetotalism. Many of the founders of the early movement were members of the Federalist aristocracy.

They were appalled by the rise of the common man as exemplified by Jeffersonian and Jacksonian democracy. To many in the movement, temperance meant encouraging the lower orders to modify their behavior and manifest more middle-class norms of moderation and reputability. Temperance was a way of asserting real and symbolic control over the behavior and aspirations of the lower classes.

The south has been ignored as a hotbed of temperance agitation in the period, but southern chapters of temperance groups were large and included many upper-class members. The spread of temperance ideology was helped in large part by Protestant ministers and churchwomen. Moreover, although temperance was often linked to causes such as abolitionism, populism, and women's suffrage, this was generally not the case in the south. In the north, however, temperance and progressive causes were often joined; the Republican Party included temperance in its 1854 platform (although dropping it upon realizing that it would offend too many German-American voters). Later in the century, linkage by an activist leadership cohort to radical political movements would cause a structural schism in the most influential group, the Woman's Christian Temperance Union (WCTU).

Initially, the WCTU and other groups attempted to change the lower-class man's behavior on a collective basis. The hope was that he would voluntarily abstain and moderate his behavior, become a good employee, and become a good, middle-class citizen. When working-class males continued to adhere to a hard-drinking lifestyle, continued to frequent urban saloons, and resisted efforts at assimilative change, the temperance movement gradually shifted to more coercive strategies and worked for prohibitionist change on the state level. Fourteen states had restrictive laws that restricted alcohol by the outbreak of the Civil War, the most celebrated being Maine, in which alcohol was completely prohibited. Notwithstanding, alcohol, in the form of whiskey and hard cider, was prized in the military camps of both the Union and the Confederacy during that protracted and cruel war.

After the war, alcohol use increased yet again, which prompted different organizations within the temperance movement to move to a more confrontational stance and an even more restrictive expediency, national Prohibition. The Anti-Saloon League, founded in 1893, used confrontational tactics in order to draw attention to what its members viewed as an unsavory and debasing institution. Some extremists, led by Carrie A. Nation, destroyed saloons with axes. However, legislative action and effective lobbying by Protestant groups and progressives was manifested in the Eighteenth Amendment, which was in effect from 1920 to 1933.

This constitutional amendment banned the manufacture, sale, and transport of alcohol in the United States. However, the "noble experiment" came to be recognized as a gross failure, because it prompted a period of lawlessness that involved otherwise law-abiding citizens in illegal purchase and consumption of alcohol and helped establish organized crime in the United States, which found a lucrative black market in illegal importation and distribution of liquor and other alcoholic beverages. As a result, organized crime became entrenched in mainstream American life. Criminal groups manufactured alcohol and imported large amounts from Cuba, Canada, and Mexico. Speakeasies, informal bars run by organized crime, sprang up across the country. Local officials became subject to corruption, and some cities became virtually Mob strongholds. Additionally, many who drank moderately before Prohibition continued to drink during Prohibition; thus, the Eighteenth Amendment fostered disrespect for the law and cynicism among many normally law-abiding citizens. Alcohol developed a mystique in the minds of many, particularly the young.

It should be noted that most alcohol-related health problems fell dramatically during the period of Prohibition. However, a more pressing motivation for repeal was that alcohol excise taxes, which had become nonexistent during Prohibition, forced wealthy Americans to pay more taxes. Therefore, the upper classes, who had previously supported temperance, began to withdraw their support, leave the movement, and argue for repeal of Prohibition in order to lower their tax burden. Although the Anti-Saloon League, the WCTU, and other, mainly religious, groups fought heavily against repealing the Eighteenth Amendment, the election of Franklin Delano Roosevelt sealed its demise. On December 5, 1933, the Twenty-first Amendment repealed the Eighteenth.

Today the WCTU and other organized groups advocating temperance have fallen upon lean times and are viewed as irrelevant to law and criminal justice policy. However, the notion of temperance, in the sense of moderation in drinking, has found a place in the "harm reduction" view of dealing with drug and alcohol use.

Francis Frederick Hawley
Western Carolina University

See also Addiction-Specific Support Groups; Drug- and Alcohol-Abusing Offenders and Treatment; Drug Testing in Community Corrections; Political Determinants of Corrections Policy

Further Readings

Carlson, D. "'Drinks He to His Own Undoing': Temperance Ideology in the Deep South." *Journal of the Early Republic*, v.18/4 (Winter 1998).

Gusfield, J. *Symbolic Crusade: Status Politics and the American Temperance Movement*. Chicago: University of Illinois Press, 1976.

Katcher, B. "Benjamin Rush's Educational Campaign Against Hard Drinking." *American Journal of Public Health*, v.83/2 (February 1993).

THERAPEUTIC COMMUNITIES

Therapeutic communities (TCs) are long-term, drug-free, group-based community facilities offering group counseling and psychotherapy to drug and alcohol abusers, as well as sex offenders and those with personality disorders, to improve the health and well-being of TC users. In the United States, TCs can take two forms, prison-based and community-based, and are voluntary for offenders following conviction. Increasingly, TCs are becoming widely used to detoxify individuals with severe drug dependencies, with clients typically in residence from a year to 18 months, followed by a period of aftercare to help clients make the transition to society and to prevent relapse caused by life stressors. Offenders are screened in order to determine their suitability for treatment in TCs. Akin to a supportive family, counselors typically live with substance abusers for the duration of their treatment with the goal to modify the behavior, attitudes, and thoughts that may lead a person to substance abuse, through group confrontation, individual counseling, and community meetings.

TC clinicians are also recovering substance abusers who were rehabilitated in TCs and therefore function as role models who are in a position to identify and mentor clients in a unique way. The holistic treatment model focuses on the person, rather than the drug, as the main problem, and the addiction as the symptom of the disorder. Drug testing of TC clients is conducted regularly. Recovery is facilitated through positive and negative pressures to change whereby counselors work with clients to build relationships and provide opportunities for individual reflection, self-improvement, and respect for authority. They use hierarchies of increasing responsibility and step programs, similar to that of Alcoholics Anonymous, which can be achieved through good behavior, successful progress, and completion of chores. Each TC establishes rules and regulations, including rewards systems, which are enforced by residents in order to guide and encourage positive behavior and provide safe and structured communities conducive to helping clients achieve a more responsible and drug-free lifestyle. Violations may lead to extra chores or group shaming.

In the United States, the history of TCs dates back to the late 1960s. While variations were in operation in other countries, such as the United Kingdom, which adopts a more psychologically and psychiatrically informed approach, the idea for TCs in the United States was sparked by the Synanon organization. This was a drug rehabilitation program founded by recovering alcoholic Charles Dederich in 1958 in Santa Monica, California, to provide a type of alternative community to help recovering addicts and former offenders improve their lives through group therapy, activities, discussions, and constructive confrontation to help foster self-examination in the search for and creation of a better lifestyle. It became known as the cult-like "church of Synanon" in the 1970s, and it eventually ceased in 1989 over charges of tax evasion and other problems. However, the foundational principles for the establishment of other TCs had been laid, and the first model TC program opened in 1969, based in the federal penitentiary in Marion, Illinois. Developed by prison psychiatrist Dr. Martin Groder, this program combined psychiatric techniques with group therapy—known as the Asklepieion model, named after the Greek god of healing—using the community and groups as a vehicle for change. Like Synanon, this model program laid the foundation for more prison-based TCs developed in the 1970s through funds provided by the federal Law Enforcement Assistance Administration.

The 1970s and 1980s saw the implementation of a number of prison-based TCs around the

The group-based approach of therapeutic communities are becoming more popular, to the degree that modified therapeutic communities have been created in several U.S. correctional facilities for substance abuse treatment. Clients may reside in this setting for up to 18 months and receive aftercare to for their transition to society. (Photos.com)

country, all with varying degrees of success. In South Carolina, another TC, started in 1975, lasted only four years because of overcrowding and contraband drugs facilitated through corruption and inadequate staffing. Another TC in Virginia, called House of Thought, experienced similar problems until its relocation to the Powhatan Correctional Center in 1980, where it closed in 1982 because of declining state funding. The successful Stay'n Out program was launched in 1977 in New York; it has five units treating 180 males located at the Arthur Kill Correctional Facility and 40 females at the Bayview Correctional Facility. As of 1998, the costs per inmate averaged $3,000. The Cornerstone program in Oregon was established in 1975 as a 32-bed TC similar to Stay'n Out; however, it closed in 1996. Unlike traditional TCs, Cornerstone employed a number of professional staff and correctional officers, therefore costing clients nearly $39 per day (or $14,235 per year). In many of these cases, new TCs replaced closed ones.

Like other community-based initiatives, TCs face a number of criticisms and challenges. They have been faulted for using inhumane shaming methods and public humiliation for clients who violate rules or fail to participate. Some of the sanctions, such as wearing signs around the facility, have been criticized for being counterproductive in the treatment of clients. TCs have also seen high program failure rates because of relapses, with as many as 85 percent of new clients failing before 30 days, according to one 1993 study. This may be amended through a better screening process in order to identify offenders more likely to benefit from TC programs.

Michael J. Puniskis
Middlesex University

See also Addiction-Specific Support Groups; Drug- and Alcohol-Abusing Offenders and Treatment; Family Therapy; Offenders With Mental Illness; Therapeutic Jurisprudence

Further Readings

Campling, Penelope and Rex Haigh. *Therapeutic Communities: Past, Present, and Future.* London: Jessica Kingsley, 1999.

Cullen, Eric, Lawrence Jones, and Roland Woodward. *Therapeutic Communities for Offenders.* New York: Wiley, 1997.

Lipton, D. S. "Therapeutic Community Treatment Programming in Corrections." In *Handbook of Offender Assessment and Treatment*, Clive R. Hollin, ed. London: John Wiley and Sons, 1998.

THERAPEUTIC JURISPRUDENCE

Therapeutic jurisprudence is an approach to legal scholarship that examines whether the legal system has a therapeutic or antitherapeutic effect on individuals. It draws from the fields of psychology, psychiatry, social work, criminal justice, public health, and others to examine, and advocate for changes in, laws and legal practices that will result in more therapeutic outcomes. It critically evaluates the impact of laws, courtroom practices, and legal actors on the well-being of offenders. Originally, therapeutic jurisprudence scholars focused mostly on mental health law. For example, they asked how the insanity defense, civil commitments (the involuntary incarceration of the mentally ill in mental institutions), and other legal arrangements could be reformed to better benefit the mentally ill. With

regard to competence to consent to hospitalization, for example, some scholars suggested a restructuring of the legal standard of competence based on the psychology literature.

Therapeutic jurisprudence has expanded to affect many other areas of law. For instance, therapeutic jurisprudence is prevalent in the "problem-solving courts," such as drug courts, mental health courts, teen courts, domestic violence courts, and reentry courts. Drug courts are understood to be the first criminal justice institution to rely on and consistently use the ideas of therapeutic jurisprudence scholars. These courts rely on techniques such as government "wagers" and "behavioral contracting" (getting patients to agree to comply with a suggested therapeutic course). These techniques draw on cognitive behaviorial therapies to persuade offenders, referred to as "clients," to examine and modify their own behavior. Drug courts can replace direct criminal sanctions; through them, the government "bargains" with drug addicts to change and to comply with the law. Another example of a therapeutic jurisprudence is found in teen courts, where youths take an active role in judicial proceedings—for example, by serving as attorneys for victims. Through this practice, teen courts try to engender more empathy in delinquent youths for those whom they have offended.

Historical Context

Therapeutic jurisprudence emerged as a theoretical perspective and field of study primarily as a result of the work of two law professors, David B. Wexler and Bruce J. Winick, who coauthored *Essays in Therapeutic Jurisprudence*, published in 1991. Earlier, in the 1960s and 1970s, during the era of the Supreme Court of Chief Justice Earl Warren, mental health law focused primarily on due process rights. Debates centered on such issues as the appropriate legal test to determine insanity, the necessary standard of proof for civil commitment, and whether the right to counsel and a jury trial should apply to the mentally ill. The courts had determined that mental health laws should protect the mentally ill in the same way that other laws protect the rights of criminal defendants.

Therapeutic jurisprudence, however, diverged from traditional rights-based legal approaches by focusing on individuals' perceptions of these laws and analyzing the psychological effects that laws and courtroom practices had on individuals. While proponents of therapeutic jurisprudence acknowledge the importance of citizens' rights and the equal application of the law, they expand traditional notions of law to ask how the legal system can serve proactively as a therapeutic agent.

In the last 20 years, therapeutic jurisprudence has influenced the judicial system so profoundly that some legal scholars claim it has introduced an entirely new juridical model. They ask whether therapeutic jurisprudence oversteps citizens' rights and to what extent it has redefined the meaning and basic principles of justice.

Therapeutic Jurisprudence and Drug Courts

The discipline of therapeutic jurisprudence proposes some important reforms by shifting the focus of legal study. It does this by assessing the therapeutic consequences of laws and courtroom and social worker practices on the well-being of individuals and groups such as mental health patients, drug users, delinquent teens, perpetrators of domestic violence, and other groups. It has spearheaded many of the legal changes and innovations found in the problem-solving courts. Of particular importance is the fact that therapeutic jurisprudence offers judges and other legal actors a viable alternative to punishing offenders. This approach to law has presented a vastly different perspective on legal scholarship from that offered by approaches that focus primarily on constitutional rights.

However, scholarly critiques of the therapeutic jurisprudence approach have pointed out that assessing laws and legal practices based on their therapeutic or antitherapeutic consequences can have unintended effects, such as promoting new forms of social control under the guise of "therapy." Therapeutic jurisprudence uncritically accepts the normative function of the psychology field. Some legal scholars argue that by combining legal with therapeutic practices, power over offenders or "clients" is spread out over more actors, creating a kind of net-widening effect of control. For example, in drug courts, in addition to judges and lawyers, an array of psychological actors—counselors, therapists, social workers, and other case managers—can wield control over offenders. One must ask if more therapy results in more justice when the psychology field becomes allied with the coercive power of the criminal justice system.

While scholars of therapeutic jurisprudence would agree that criminalizing drug addicts is an antitherapeutic outcome of current laws, drug court practices such as behavioral contracting with drug users are seen by many as also antitherapeutic and coercive. Behavioral contracts often accompany a highly structured, court-mandated style of drug treatment that can carry the consequence of imprisonment if a client fails. Moreover, therapeutic jurisprudence, despite its psychological and mental health focus, does not remove drug users or the mentally ill from the purview of the criminal justice system. Many claim that these populations need social services and would be better off in noncoercive treatment settings. The strengths and promise of the innovative therapeutic jurisprudence approach must be balanced against the potential for social control.

Julie A. Beck
California State University, East Bay

See also Drug Courts; Net Widening; Teen Courts

Further Readings

Diesfeld, Kate and Ian Freckelton, eds. *Involuntary Detention and Therapeutic Jurisprudence: International Perspectives on Civil Commitment.* Burlington, VT: Ashgate, 2003.

Hora, Peggy Fulton and William G. Schma. "Therapeutic Jurisprudence and the Drug Treatment Court Movement: Revolutionizing the Criminal Justice Systems' Response to Drug Abuse and Crime in America." *Notre Dame Law Review*, v.74 (1999).

Nolan, James L. *Reinventing Justice: The American Drug Court Movement.* Princeton, NJ: Princeton University Press, 2001.

Wexler, David B. and Bruce J. Winick. *Essays in Therapeutic Jurisprudence.* Durham, NC: Carolina Academic Press, 1991.

Winick, Bruce J. and David B. Wexler, eds. *Judging in a Therapeutic Key: Therapeutic Jurisprudence and the Courts.* Durham, NC: Carolina Academic Press, 2003.

THINKING FOR A CHANGE

In 1997, the "Thinking for a Change" program was developed by Jack Bush, Barry Glick, and Juliana Taymans in cooperation with the National Institute of Corrections. Thinking for a Change is an integrated cognitive behavioral change program that includes cognitive restructuring, social skills development, and the development of problem-solving skills. The program was designed to be used with offender populations in prisons, jails, community corrections, probation, and parole settings.

Program Description

Bush, Glick, and Taymans have noted that the major impetus to developing this program was founded on the experience that criminal behavior was more susceptible to positive social change when offenders were able to implement and to incorporate both cognitive-restructuring and cognitive skills programs. Generally, cognitive behavioral therapies administered to offender populations have been designated as cognitive-restructuring, coping-skills, or problem-solving therapies. Cognitive restructuring focuses on the makeup of an offender's thinking in an effort to change those core attitudes and beliefs that can lead to criminal behavior. The coping-skills therapy approach emphasizes attempts to improve an individual's inability to adapt to demanding and difficult situations involving interpersonal skills and critical reasoning. Problem-solving approaches assist offenders in how to think, solve problems, and engage in prosocial behavior. Most cognitive behavioral therapies for offenders incorporate some combination of these three approaches.

The Thinking for a Change program consists of 22 lessons generally delivered over an eleven-week period. Each lesson is approximately two hours in length. Essentially, each lesson is similarly formatted, beginning with a summary and rationale portion; the beginning section covers the scope, breadth, and reason for teaching the lesson. Next, the lesson presents concepts and definitions, followed by lesson objectives and major activities. For instance, one activity uses role-play to illustrate an escalating conflict between an offender and someone in authority, such as a probation officer, a correctional officer, or a police officer. One suggested example provided for program trainers is the following: A correctional officer keeps an inmate waiting at the door of his living unit while the officer finishes a conversation with another officer about the duty schedule for the next work shift. The inmate expresses irritation with sarcasm ("Take your own sweet time"). The officer expresses irritation at this by asserting his authority in a gruff tone ("Jones, you stand behind that line until this door is open and you're clear to pass"). He

points to a line on the floor some feet behind where the inmate is standing.

Participants are instructed that neither side is completely right or wrong. The point is to demonstrate two different viewpoints in a conflicting situation. Next, the participants are asked what they think each person is thinking and feeling.

Specifically, Sessions 1 to 9 focus on the cognitive-restructuring approach. These lessons teach offenders to self-reflect on their attitudes, beliefs, and feelings. Offenders are also taught, and practice, the objective observation of these thoughts, feelings, and attitudes. Next, the sessions focus on helping offenders recognize those cognitive processes that led them to maladaptive behavior, followed by helping them find more adaptive forms of thinking and acting.

Sessions 10 to 12 focus on social skills training. These sessions strengthen and emphasize those lessons introduced in the cognitive-restructuring portion while building such social skills as empathy and "perspective taking." For instance, participants are instructed on how to enhance their understanding of others' feelings as well as their responses to those feelings. Furthermore, participants are taught how to manage and respond to anger as well as the potential consequences of acting out on those feelings of anger, even when faced with accusations of wrongdoing, whether true or not.

Sessions 13 to 22 incorporate aspects associated with problem solving. In these sessions, the cognitive restructuring and social skills taught in the previous sessions are integrated into the problem-solving portion. Starting in Session 17, participants are taught six problem-solving steps: (1) stop and think, (2) describe the problem, (3) get information to set a goal, (4) consider choices and consequences, (5) choose-plan-do, and (6) evaluate.

Evaluation of Thinking for a Change

In 2006, Lori Golden, Robert Gatchel, and Melissa Cahill evaluated the effectiveness of the Thinking for a Change program. The study included 100 male and 42 female probationers. Those probationers assigned to the Thinking for a Change program were matched with other probationers not assigned to the program (the comparison group). Various measures were used to evaluate program effectiveness, including interpersonal problem-solving skills (both before and after the program) and recidivism at three months to one year after the program's completion.

The results of this evaluation revealed that, compared to those probationers who did complete the program (completers), 33 percent of those probationers who did not complete the program (dropouts) committed a new offense during the one-year follow-up. Probationer dropouts had a significantly higher number of technical violations compared with probationer completers. Furthermore, when the researchers compared the pre-program and post-program measures, they found that program completers significantly improved on interpersonal problem-solving skills. The program dropouts, however, did not report such improvements. The researchers concluded that these skills may subsequently deter offenders from future criminal activity. They also noted that future research might consider exploring whether "booster sessions," such as an aftercare group or other relapse prevention measures, could further deter future criminal behavior.

In 2009, Christopher Lowenkamp, Dana Hubbard, Matthew Makarios, and Edward Latessa reported on the quasi-experimental evaluation of the Thinking for a Change program. The evaluation comprised a total of 217 participants who were placed on probation for a felony offense. Of this total, 121 were referred to the program, while the remaining 96 probationers were not referred to the program. The results revealed that those probationers in the treatment group had a significantly lower rearrest rate (23 percent of the treatment group recidivated), compared with those in the control group (36 percent of the control group recidivated). The researchers concluded, however, that no one study in the social sciences is definitive. Thus, they emphasized the importance of conducting additional research to examine the effects of the Thinking for a Change program. They also stressed that such further research should examine the effectiveness of the program on various types of offenders, not just probationers.

Pamela J. Schram
California State University, San Bernardino

See also Counseling; Goals and Objectives of Community Corrections; Offender Needs

Further Readings

Bush, Jack, Barry Glick, and Juliana Taymans. *Thinking for a Change: Integrated Cognitive Behavior Change Program*. Washington, DC: National Institute of Corrections, U.S. Department of Justice, 1997.

Golden, Lori. *Evaluation of the Efficacy of a Cognitive Behavioral Program for Offenders on Probation: Thinking for a Change*. Doctoral Dissertation. University of Texas Southwestern Medical Center, Dallas, 2002.

Golden, Lori, Robert Gatchel, and Melissa Cahill. "Evaluating the Effectiveness of the National Institute of Corrections' 'Thinking for a Change' Program Among Probationers." *Journal of Offender Rehabilitation*, v.43 (2006).

Lowenkamp, Christopher, Dana Hubbard, Matthew Makarios, and Edward Latessa. "A Quasi-Experimental Evaluation of Thinking for a Change: A 'Real-World' Application." *Criminal Justice and Behavior*, v.36 (2009).

THREE STRIKES AND YOU'RE OUT

Three-strikes laws, a particularly punitive type of recidivist statute (a law that increases punishments for repeat offenders), exist in about half the states and are often enacted by the voters via the initiative process. As in baseball, on the third "strike" (usually a serious or violent felony), the offender is "out," often meaning he or she is sentenced to an indeterminate life sentence and may in fact serve the rest of his or her life in prison.

These laws are therefore controversial. Supporters claim the laws have substantially lowered the crime rate and better protect society from the most dangerous of repeat offenders. Opponents dispute the causal link to the crime rate and lament the substantial resources devoted to increased incarceration. The effect of three-strikes laws has been most scrutinized in California, which has the most famous and draconian version of the law. The U.S. Supreme Court has upheld the law against a constitutional challenge, ruling that it does not violate the Eighth Amendment's prohibition against cruel and unusual punishment. In some states, a liberal use of three-strikes laws contributes to prison overcrowding, since offenders serve longer sentences than previously for the same type of crime. This overcrowding may, by necessity, encourage development of community-based corrections for other offenders as an alternative to incarceration.

Origin of the Laws

While recidivist statutes have existed for many years, the first of the laws known as "three strikes and you're out" was passed by Washington State voters in 1993. California followed shortly thereafter, with both the legislature and the voters passing three-strikes provisions in 1994. This version of "tough-on-crime" legislation proved popular, with 24 states and the federal government enacting three-strikes laws between the years of 1993 and 1995. Supporters of the laws rely on two primary punishment justifications: specific deterrence (the logic being that perhaps a two-strikes offender will not commit another felony, knowing that life imprisonment could be the consequence) and incapacitation (the logic being that, if a felon does reoffend, he or she is now removed from society for a longer period of time). During this period, in the mid-1990s, crime rates were falling, but media coverage of certain violent crimes (especially those involving children or female victims) intensified, and the public felt increasingly at risk. Particularly vivid cases galvanized support for three-strikes laws. In California, a recent parolee with a violent past kidnapped 12-year-old Polly Klaas from her home in 1993, sexually assaulting and murdering her. The case received extensive media coverage and is cited as a catalyst for three-strikes laws, which were passed across the country, both by initiative process and by constituent pressure upon legislators.

While the three-strikes laws vary, they commonly provide that an offender is sentenced to life in prison after a third conviction for a violent crime. California's law differs significantly in that, while the prior strikes must be crimes described under the law as either "serious" or "violent," the third crime need be only a felony. Further, with one strike, the sentence for a second felony is doubled. This broad statutory scheme constitutes the best-known and most controversial three-strikes law in the country. The largest number of offenders serving time under three-strikes laws are in California. For all of these reasons, much of the national debate about three-strikes laws has centered on California's law.

Criticism and Challenges

Critics of the California law denounce the increase in incarceration brought by three strikes, in a state already known for its high rate of incarceration. By 2005, almost 90,000 inmates had been sentenced under the law, with the majority serving time on a second strike. Those sentenced under this law

constitute about 25 percent of the ongoing prison population. Inmates over the age of 50 often cost two to three times more to incarcerate than younger inmates because of increased medical care costs; the number of those inmates tripled in the 10 years after passage of three strikes. Critics also aver that the variance in three-strikes enforcement across counties is unfair, resulting in significantly disparate sentences for the same offenses. Prosecutors may choose when to charge cases under three strikes, and policies vary significantly from county to county. Opponents argue that three strikes has had little effect on a crime rate that was already dropping by 1994, whereas supporters claim that three strikes is pivotal in crime reduction.

Opponents of California's three-strikes law mounted two major challenges to the law, one through the courts and the other through the initiative process. In a pair of rulings in 2003, *Ewing v. California* and *Lockyer v. Andrade*, the U.S. Supreme Court declared that the California scheme did not violate the Eighth Amendment's prohibition against cruel and unusual punishment. In both cases, the third strike was a theft, a nonviolent, nonserious crime, chargeable as a misdemeanor or a felony. The closely divided (5–4) Court deferred to the state's penological goals, observing that the three-strikes law sought to deter and then to incapacitate recidivists. The Court announced that life imprisonment is not a constitutionally disproportionate sentence, for it does not punish only the current felony but also the offender's criminal record. In the second challenge, a 2004 ballot measure sought to modify the law to require that the third felony be either serious or violent. The voters rejected that change.

Three-strikes laws, initiated by the public, remain popular. Thus, these laws are likely to remain part of American jurisprudence for the foreseeable future.

Kimberlee Candela
California State University, Chico

See also Attitudes and Myths About Punishment; Indeterminate Sentencing; Prison Overcrowding; Recidivism

Further Readings

Chen, Elsa Y. "Impacts of 'Three Strikes and You're Out' on Crime Trends in California and Throughout the United States." *Journal of Contemporary Criminal Justice*, v.24 (2008).

Clark, J., J. Austin, and D. A. Henry. *Three Strikes and You're Out: A Review of State Legislation.* Washington, DC: National Institute of Justice, 1997.

Domanick, Joe. *Cruel Justice: Three Strikes and the Politics of Crime in America's Golden State.* Berkeley: University of California Press, 2005.

Shichor, David and Dale K. Sechrest, eds. *Three Strikes and You're Out: Vengeance as Social Policy.* Thousand Oaks, CA: Sage, 1996.

Walsh, Jennifer. *Three Strikes Laws.* Santa Barbara, CA: Greenwood Press, 2007.

Zimring, Franklin E., Gordon Hawkins, and Sam Kamin. *Punishment and Democracy: Three Strikes and You're Out in California.* New York: Oxford University Press, 2001.

TRUTH-IN-SENTENCING PROVISIONS

The term *truth in sentencing* (TIS) alludes to a variety of sentencing guidelines and restrictions that serve to reduce uncertainty associated with the length of time that convicted offenders must serve in prison. Although truth-in-sentencing provisions vary widely by jurisdiction, common elements include the elimination or restriction of parole eligibility and good-time credits, the use of sentencing guidelines and mandatory minimum sentences, and notably, the requirement that inmates serve at least 85 percent of their prison sentence prior to becoming eligible for supervised or unconditional release back into society. Truth-in-sentencing efforts have been undertaken primarily with the intention of ending or limiting early release mechanisms to keep violent offenders in prison, while exacting "just deserts" by reducing common disparities between the length of court-ordered prison sentences and the actual time inmates serve in prison.

Truth in sentencing became one of the most prominent determinate sentencing reforms of the 1980s and 1990s, because the actual amount of time convicted offenders were generally spending in prison was significantly less than the judicially imposed sentence handed down by courts. Indeterminate sentencing made this, and the release of a prisoner prior to the expiration of his or her court-imposed sentence, a likely possibility. As a result, various criticisms had been leveled at indeterminate sentencing practices, which were pervasive prior to this period. TIS proponents argued that disparities between prison sentences and actual time served could undermine public confidence in the legitimacy of the criminal justice system. It has also been argued that early release could attenuate the goal of deterring criminal behavior by attaching a level of uncertainty to a prison sentence. Finally, it was believed the full effects of incapacitation could not be achieved with early release still existing as a possibility.

As a result, many states and the federal government began adopting various determinate and truth-in-sentencing protocols, which require convicted offenders to serve a substantial and more clearly specified portion of their given prison sentence prior to becoming eligible for release. Washington became the first state to enact a truth-in-sentencing law, in 1984, with many states, as well as the federal government, following closely behind. Congress quickly began reacting to changing attitudes about sentencing and corrections by mandating TIS provisions at the federal level through the Sentencing Reform Act of 1984. The subsequent development of the federal truth-in-sentencing program continued to reflect the attitudes, sentencing reforms, and practices taking shape in many states across the country.

Ten years later, Congress responded again by authoring the Violent Crime Control and Law Enforcement Act of 1994. This legislation created violent offender incarceration and truth-in-sentencing (VOI/TIS) incentive grants, designed to help states reduce the number of violent offenders in communities. Grants were initially made available to determinate sentencing states that wished to build new or expand existing correctional facilities in order to provide more bed capacity to house violent offenders. The Violent Crime Control and Law Enforcement Act of 1994 was later amended in 1996 to allow for the possible inclusion of states exercising indeterminate sentencing policies.

In addition to a focus on violent offenders, VOI/TIS funds have been used to expand housing for convicted nonviolent offenders and illegal aliens, as well as increase available funding for drug testing and treatment programs. To qualify for VOI/TIS federal funds, states have been required either to implement various TIS laws that require persons convicted of specific violent offenses (Part I) to serve not less than 85 percent of the judicially imposed sentence or to prove that they have already been requiring convicted violent offenders to serve at least 85 percent of the sentence.

Although truth in sentencing reached widespread prominence as a sentencing reform in the United States during the 1990s, many objections have been levied against these policies and practices. Critics argue that truth in sentencing results in significant increases in prison populations, as well as increased expenditures and correctional costs associated with larger numbers of inmates. It is also believed that TIS may exacerbate prison conditions and produce more dangerous institutions. This may be because of the presence of a greater proportion of violent offenders and inmate populations who are less inclined to follow prison rules, because their release dates are not contingent on institutional behavior. In addition, it is possible that lengthy prison terms resulting from TIS policies may heighten difficulties associated with maintaining social ties to family and communities and may serve to intensify the effects of prison institutionalization, making it more difficult to make the transition from incarceration to life in the community. Despite these criticisms, most state and federal truth-in-sentencing provisions remained in effect as of 2010.

William Stadler
University of Missouri, Kansas City

See also Determinate Sentencing; Sentencing Guidelines

Further Readings

Ditton, Paula M. and Doris J. Wilson. *Truth in Sentencing in State Prisons.* Washington, DC: U.S. Department of Justice, Bureau of Justice Statistics, 1999.

Sabol, William J. et al. *The Influences of Truth-in-Sentencing Reforms on Changes in States' Sentencing Practices and Prison Populations.* Washington, DC: Urban Institute, 2002.

Travis, Lawrence F. "Sentencing in the United States." In *Correctional Contexts: Contemporary and Classical Readings,* 4th ed., E. Latessa and A. Holsinger, eds. New York: Oxford University Press, 2005.

U.S. Department of Justice. "Report to Congress: Violent Offender Incarceration and Truth-in-Sentencing Incentive Formula Grant Program." http://www.ojp.usdoj.gov/ BJA/pdf/VOITISreport.pdf (Accessed February 2011).

VICTIM IMPACT STATEMENTS

A victim impact statement (VIS) is an oral allocution or written or recorded statement created by an individual who has been impacted by a criminal victimization. The VIS is a conduit through which information, which may not have been introduced or admissible during the trial, is presented to the decision makers. The VIS generally contains information about the physical, financial, psychological, social, spiritual, or emotional harms brought about by the criminal or delinquent behavior of a juvenile or adult. Sometimes the VIS can also include a recommendation for the appropriate sentence that the offender should receive or a reaction to a proposed sentence if the offender is found guilty of committing the crime. In the case of homicides, personal information is given about the deceased. This personal information could, for example, be about the type of parent, spouse, sibling, worker, or community member that the deceased was. Additionally, the surviving family members might present information about the ways in which their lives have changed as a result of the homicide. The VIS can be presented by the victim, the victim's family or loved ones, the victim's colleagues, or other members of the community.

The use of the VIS exemplifies the dramatic changes that have taken place over the past 50 years in regard to the relationship between victims of crimes and the criminal justice system. The victims' rights movement began in earnest in the 1970s, when victims of crime started to voice dissatisfaction with the way in which they were treated by the criminal justice system. Their dissatisfaction stemmed from their belief that they were not respected by the criminal justice system. Also dissatisfied at that time were prosecutors, who were frustrated by the failure of crime victims to participate fully in the criminal process because of their dissatisfaction with the system.

In response to this dissatisfaction, President Ronald Reagan ordered the formation of the President's Task Force on Victims of Crime to investigate the experiences of crime victims and to make recommendations that would improve their interactions with and participation in the criminal justice system. Their report, made public in 1982, outlined 68 recommendations. Among their recommendations was the suggestion that an amendment to the Sixth Amendment should be made that would afford the victim of a crime the right to be present and heard during critical stages of the criminal trial and sentencing processes. The concept embodied in this recommendation was not new; the first victim impact statement had already been created in California in 1976. While the constitutional amendment was never enacted, the spirit of this recommendation became practice in 1982.

Consistent and widespread use of the VIS started in the federal court system following the passage of the Victim and Witness Protection Act of 1982, which required that a VIS be given to federal district court judges to consider prior to sentencing. States began to follow suit, and the use of the VIS began to spread. Today, all states allow its use to determine the appropriate sentence that a defendant will be given in noncapital cases. Noncapital cases are those in which punishment cannot be the death sentence.

A victim impact statement can allow the those directly affected by a crime to address the court during the sentencing decision-making process. These statements can include details of the direct trauma they have suffered as a result of the crime and recommendations for sentencing if the defendant is found guilty. (Photos.com)

One of the primary resources that judges use to determine the appropriate sentence for a particular defendant is the pre-sentence investigation (PSI), which includes information about the defendant's prior convictions, employment, family or other social support, and addiction issues. The VIS is now routinely included in the PSI so that judges will have the victim's input in the sentencing decision. The VIS is also a valuable resource for calculating the appropriate restitution order. Additionally, the VIS can be introduced in the sentencing phase of the trial and can be presented to the court orally or by means of a written copy presented to the judge. Research on the impact of the VIS on sentencing suggests that it does not lead to substantially longer sentences but may impact the decision to grant probation or sentence the defendant to incarceration. Research also indicates that victim satisfaction with the criminal justice system increases when the VIS is used in this manner. The VIS is also frequently used when an incarcerated individual is considered for parole. Recent research indicates that when a parole board is presented with either an oral or a written VIS, it is more likely to deny the prisoner parole.

The most controversial use of the VIS is in capital murder trials. The Supreme Court of the United States in two cases, *Booth v. Maryland* (1987) and *South Carolina v. Gathers* (1989), ruled that use of the VIS, when determining whether a defendant should be sentenced to death, violated the Eighth Amendment, because it could introduce arbitrariness and capriciousness into the decision process. However, in the case of *Payne v. Tennessee* (1991), the Court overturned those decisions and ruled that the VIS may be used in capital murder sentencing trials. The Court leaves to the states the decision of whether or not the VIS should be used in capital sentencing trials. The only restriction still placed on the VIS is that it cannot make a recommendation to the judge or jury regarding a sentence of life or death.

Additional reinforcement of the rights of victims to present a VIS in federal court is provided for in the 2004 Crime Victims' Rights Act (CVRA), which grants standing to victims when their right to be heard has been denied. Standing entitles the victim to sue to have the sentence vacated (eliminated) and to request a new sentencing hearing.

Patti Ross Salinas
Missouri State University
Tana M. McCoy
Roosevelt University

See also Attitudes and Myths About Punishment; Parole Boards and Hearings; Predispositional Reports for Juveniles; Pre-Sentence Investigation Reports; Victim-Offender Reconciliation Programs

Further Readings

Boland, Mary L. and Russell Butler. "Crime Victims' Rights: From Illusion to Reality." *Criminal Justice*, v.24/1 (2009).
Booth v. Maryland, 482 U.S. 496 (1987).
Paternoster, Ray and Jerome Deise. "A Heavy Thumb on the Scale: The Effect of Victim Impact Evidence on Capital Decision Making." *Criminology*, v.49/1 (2011).
Payne v. Tennessee, 501 U.S. 808 (1991).
Smith, Brent L., Erin Watkins, and Kathryn Morgan. "The Effect of Victim Participation on Parole Decisions: Results From a Southeastern State." *Criminal Justice Policy Review*, v.8/1 (1997).
South Carolina v. Gathers, 490 U.S. 805 (1989).

Victim Services

Today, a multitude of services are available to victims of crime, but this has not always been the case. In the 1970s, victims of crime and their families and friends began to unite to draw attention to the problems that they felt existed. At about the same time, women's rights advocates began to draw attention to the plight of rape and domestic violence victims, and women's groups began to form to assist victims and to demand that change occur. Nearly simultaneously, prosecutors experienced frustration at the difficulty they were having in getting crime victims to participate in criminal trials, because crime victims perceived that they were not being treated with the respect that they deserved. In response, states began to legislate change, and in the early 1980s the federal government followed suit.

At the federal level, one of the first laws passed was the 1982 Victim and Witness Protection Act, which recognized the importance of keeping victims and witnesses informed about important actions involving the people who were being tried for the crime or who had been convicted of the crime. Important actions would include trials, sentencing, hearings for probation or parole, and scheduled dates of release. Shortly thereafter, Congress passed the Victims of Crime Act (VOCA), which is arguably the most important piece of legislation for victims of crime. Under VOCA, the Office for Victims of Crimes (OVC) was created to provide assistance and to fund compensation programs, which are operated by the states. Today, compensation programs reimburse victims of violent crime for expenses that are not covered by insurance. Although there is variation among the types of expenses that can be covered, all states reimburse for medical and psychological treatment, lost wages, and funeral expenses, and many pay for the expenses incurred in relocation following domestic assault.

In 1994, the Violence Against Women Act (VAWA) was passed and the Office on Violence Against Women was created. The purpose of this law was to direct national attention to crimes of violence that have a negative impact on women, such as sexual assault, stalking, and domestic violence. Because various states have added crime victims' bills of rights to their state constitutions, several attempts have been made to add similar provisions to the U.S. Constitution. Although none of these attempts has been successful, in 2004 a federal law was passed that incorporates most of the rights that have been provided by the states. Some of the rights included are the right to be reasonably protected from the accused, the right to restitution, the right to be heard at public proceedings, and the right to be treated with fairness and dignity. Finally, victims are granted the authority to sue in civil court for damages that they have suffered as a result of the crime.

To ensure that crime victims are afforded the rights they have been granted either by law or by constitutional amendment, most states and counties have created an office to assist crime victims. The assistance offered to the victim begins immediately after the crime has occurred when a crisis counselor makes contact with the victim and helps that victim to get the services that he or she needs. The services that the victim may need are sometimes dependent on the type of victimization that has occurred. For example, victims of domestic violence may need a safe place to stay in both the short and long terms, diapers and formula for an infant, food and clothes for themselves and their children, replacement documents such as birth certificates or social security cards, help completing forms necessary for compensation, or counseling. Additionally, an advocate can be assigned to the victim. The advocate is there to provide emotional support to the victim and to assist the victim in understanding and navigating the criminal process. The advocate can also assist the victim in getting an order of protection from the court. While many of the services needed by the victim are provided by funded agencies, other services are provided by grassroots volunteers.

Volunteers have always been an integral part of the services provided to victims. Today, one of the functions of funded agencies is to provide quality training to those who have donated their time to service. Additionally, there has been a concerted effort to increase the professionalism of those working in the field. The Internet is now being used to offer high-quality, evidence-based, standardized training in the online format, so that certification and continuing education are available to individuals living in both rural and urban areas.

Despite the variety of services available to victims of crime, the percentage of victims who take advantage of the services still remains extremely low. This is particularly evident when one examines the number of people who take advantage of compensation programs. This low percentage has been attributed to various factors, but the primary culprit appears to be a lack of knowledge about the services available, even in states where law-enforcement officers are required by law to notify victims of the services that are available to them.

Research that has studied crime victims indicates that, overall, those individuals who use some of the services offered appreciate the services and are grateful that they are available. What has not been established is whether or not services are successful in helping victims overcome their trauma in the long term. Overall, great strides have been made in the past 50 years in regard to the provision of services to victims of crime, but there is considerable progress to be made.

Patti Ross Salinas
Missouri State University

See also Crime Victims' Concerns; Restorative Justice; Victim-Offender Reconciliation Programs; Victims of Crime Act of 1984

Further Readings

Doerner, William and Steven Lab. *Victimology*, 3rd ed. Cincinnati, OH: Anderson, 2002.

Karmen, Andrew. *Crime Victims: An Introduction to Victimology*, 7th ed. Belmont, CA: Thomson Wadsworth, 2010.

Moriarty, Laura J. *Controversies in Victimology*, 2nd ed. Newark, NJ: Bender, 2008.

Sims, Barbara, Berwood Yost, and Christina Abbott. "The Efficacy of Victim Services Programs: Alleviating the Psychological Suffering of Crime Victims?" *Criminal Justice Policy Review*, v.17 (2006).

VICTIM-OFFENDER RECONCILIATION PROGRAMS

Victim-offender reconciliation programs (VORPs) constitute one of several types of victim-offender interventions employed within the larger philosophical and applied approach to crime and conflict called "restorative justice." The specific attributes of restorative justice interventions and programs vary. However, as pioneer in the field of restorative justice Howard Zehr has argued, most restorative justice interventions (including VORPs) share at least four assumptions:

- Crime can be better understood as harms and violations of relationships than as a breaking of the law.

- The focus of justice systems should be primarily on identifying the needs of victims and the obligations of offenders to make things right.
- Victims (and not the state) should be the central party defining the harms caused to them, and victims should be provided an opportunity to define and address these harms directly to offenders, when requested and when possible.
- When offenders are amenable and able, they should be provided an opportunity to make amends and to repair harms caused to victims and to be accepted back into their communities upon restoration of harms caused.

Following these assumptions, restorative justice interventions seek to bring offenders and victims together to meet in order to achieve these goals. In the case of VORPs, such meetings generally employ the use of volunteers or professionals trained in conflict resolution and mediation. Some VORPs are conducted without any prior contact between the mediator and the victim or offender, but this is perhaps less common today than it once was, in that the mediator often has an initial meeting with one or both parties to explain the VORP process and to address concerns or questions from either party.

VORPs usually begin with the mediator or volunteer explaining the purpose of the meeting and the processes and guidelines that each party is expected to follow. Although these processes and guidelines vary, there has been an extensive development of "best practice" research on the use of VORPs and victim-offender mediations (VOMs) since the 1980s. Following this research and the experience of practitioners, VORPs are generally designed to move through a process of explanation, clarification and discussion, and (when possible) agreement. Each party is provided an opportunity to speak without interruption on the event or harm as that party sees it. For victims, this frequently entails a description of the effects of the harms caused to them, as well as other concerns immediate to their well-being or sense of mind. For offenders, this frequently includes an explanation of why they did what they did, reassurances to the victim, and even justifications for the offense.

Clarification and discussion involve both the opportunity to ask questions of either party and dialogue regarding motives and intent (on the part of the offender) and further explanation or elucidation of harms and concerns (on the part of the victim). Offenders often make apologies for their actions, either in the explanation or the clarification phase, but VORPs are also structured in a way that ideally moves the offender past mere apology into a conversation with the victim about concrete ways he or she can make amends. Agreements, however, are not the only goals of VORPs, and they are seen as desirable only when offenders and victims reach them willingly. Once an agreement has been reached, it is usually entered into a contract with conditions that may include the possibility of further charges if the agreement is not completed by the offender or, alternatively, no charges or the dropping of charges when the agreement is completed.

The first use of VORPs is generally thought to have taken place in Ontario, Canada, in 1974. Two youths who had vandalized several family properties were taken to these homes to meet with victims and decide upon appropriate restitution. The outcome of this and similar interventions led to the creation of the Victim Offender Reconciliation Program (VORP) in Kitchener, Ontario, in 1976. A similar program was established in Elkhart, Indiana, in 1978. In Canada and the United States, the development of VORPs in the 1970s and 1980s was closely tied to the influence and participation of religious communities, especially Mennonite, Quaker, and Christian communities rooted in the use of exchange and dialogue for conflict resolution. Along with their religious affiliations, VORP and VOM interventions, at their inception, were largely informal, working either as alternatives to courts or as alternatives within courts. Most mediation or reconciliation staff from the late 1970s through the early 1990s were not employed directly by justice agencies, but rather came from conflict resolution or civil mediation backgrounds. Since the 1990s, however, mediators have increasingly been trained specifically in mediation for criminal offenses, often within justice agencies themselves.

By the 1980s, dozens of VORPs, as well as VOM programs, existed in North America. Beginning in the 1980s, the use of the term VOM began to replace VORP in some cases, particularly where programs were developed outside the context of religiously based mediation practices. However, the two terms are still used today, mostly interchangeably.

A national survey in 1997 found more than 300 such programs in the United States, and by the turn of the century there were more than 1,000 VORP and/or VOM programs in use in the United States. Research on the effectiveness of VORPs and VOMs since the 1990s has found significant support for increased victim involvement and satisfaction, as well as moderate support for the reduction of offender recidivism.

William R. Wood
University of Auckland

See also Effectiveness of Community Corrections; Goals and Objectives of Community Corrections; Juvenile and Youth Offenders; Mediation; Recidivism; Reintegration Into Communities; Restorative Justice

Further Readings

Coates, Robert B. and John Gehm. *Victim Meets Offender: An Evaluation of Victim-Offender Reconciliation Programs.* Valparaiso, IN: Pact Institute of Justice, 1985.

Davis, Robert C., Arthur J. Lurigio, and Wesley G. Skogan. *Victims of Crime.* Thousand Oaks, CA: Sage, 1997.

Taylor, Susan C. "Victim-Offender Reconciliation Program: A New Paradigm Towards Justice." *University of Memphis Law Review*, v.26 (Spring 1996).

Umbreit, Mark, Robert B. Coates, and Boris Kalai. *Victim Meets Offender: The Impact of Restorative Justice and Mediation (Evaluation of Four Programs in the United States).* Monsey, NY: Criminal Justice Press, 1994.

Zehr, Howard. *The Little Book of Restorative Justice.* Intercourse, PA: Good Books, 2002.

Victims of Crime Act of 1984

The Victims of Crime Act of 1984 (VOCA), or federal statute 42 U.S. Code 10601, was passed in 1984 by the U.S. Congress with the backing of citizens and lobby groups. Supporters of the bill held that the current system of criminal adjudication and existing victim compensation programs were inadequate to compensate crime victims. VOCA grew directly out of a congressional task force established in 1982. The act has two main provisions: a Victim Assistance Program and a Victim Notification System. Victim/witness assistance programs offer economic, social, and psychological assistance to victims of crime and those who have witnessed a crime that has caused physical, psychological, or economic injury. The Victim Notification System grants crime victims new rights during the criminal prosecution process. While the main focus is on violent crime, nonviolent felonies and misdemeanors are included in the category of crime.

Victim Assistance and Compensation

Through a federal Crime Victims Fund, established by VOCA, crime victims can now receive restitution in the form of monetary compensation. This fund is a nontaxpayer source of monies that are drawn to finance various programs for adult and child crime victims. (The fund is supported through fines and penalties that convicted federal felons may be required to pay, special assessments collected for certain federal crimes, federal bonds such as bail bonds, any collateral collected, or private donations or gifts made to the fund.) These funds provide compensation to victims of crimes resulting in serious injury and are distributed to victims' compensation programs, which exist in all 50 states. Victim assistance also includes social services for crime victims that include psychological counseling, crisis intervention, mediation and emergency services (such as medical care and shelter), and sometimes legal or paralegal counsel.

Victim Notification

VOCA also has a direct impact on the judicial system. Its mandate of a victim notification system greatly expands the role of crime victims in all stages of the criminal adjudication process. Crime victims now receive notification of a defendant's arrest and initial court appearance, and almost all states require advance notification of all court appearances and notification of proceedings in the prosecution of the accused. Most states also require that a victim be notified if the defendant is released on bail or granted probation or parole. Crime victims are also given a consulting role in plea bargaining and are notified when a plea bargain is struck. Moreover, VOCA grants crime victims the right to testify at sentencing hearings and sometimes allows them to make statements in court. Prior to sentencing, the federal and many state systems now require that the trial judge read a "victim impact statement,"

included in the court's pre-sentence report, in which the victim describes how the crime affected his or her physical, mental, and financial health and that of his or her family.

Political Context of VOCA

The granting of special rights to crime victims (which extend beyond the protection the state provides by criminal prosecuting offenders) is a new concept. Calls for victims' rights began in the 1980s with the rise of a national victims' rights movement. The social and political context of the victims' rights movement was the conservative backlash in the late 1970s and 1980s and the government's "war on crime." The backlash included a directed effort to undo the liberal Warren Court's procedural law revolution, which had expanded the due process rights of defendants.

Victims' rights claims and legislation were aimed at expanding the power of crime victims in the judicial system and reducing the rights of defendants. The very concept of victims' rights has been a controversial and evolving "right": U.S. Supreme Court decisions in the past did not always support the concept of restitution for victims of crimes or of victims' rights. However, by the mid-1990s, more than 30 states had legislation providing victims' rights, including a Victims' Bill of Rights, and about 20 states had constitutional amendments that upheld victims' rights.

Ethical and Legal Considerations

VOCA has produced some beneficial outcomes for crime victims. It expands social service provisions to victims of crimes, including to survivors of domestic violence and child abuse. Nearly half of those receiving services are domestic violence and sexual assault victims, and child-abuse prevention and treatment programs have been slated to receive the first $10 million in the federal Victim Compensation Fund. The fund has also expanded to set aside $50 million as an emergency reserve for potential victims of terrorism. The personalizing of the criminal prosecution process for crime victims has made it possible for those affected most directly by violent crime to have a voice in the criminal adjudication process.

On the other hand, the legislating of specific rights for individual crime victims has resulted in what some legal scholars believe to be a detrimental merging of public law (criminal law) and private law (civil law). They warn that victims' rights laws undermine the state's role to prosecute the accused with judicial impartiality. Prosecution risks becoming a matter of personal vengeance rather than of protecting the public from crimes committed against society. The legislation of victims' rights also raises concerns about due process, which protects the rights of the accused by curbing governmental power. California voters' passage of Proposition 9 in 2009 in the name of victims' rights, for example, sharply curtailed the chances that "lifers" (those serving 25 years to life with the possibility of parole) would ever have a chance of being paroled. Most offenses and offenders are nonviolent, but victims' rights laws highlight violent crime, and many states have victims' bills of rights that restrict plea bargaining and other options. Significantly, studies have found that VOCA does not make crime victims feel safer. Strengthening governmental power through eroding due process and legislating tougher crime policies, many scholars claim, ultimately undermines the rights of all citizens.

Julie A. Beck
California State University, East Bay

See also Crime Victims' Concerns; Victim Impact Statements; Victim Services; Victim-Offender Reconciliation Programs

Further Readings

Beck, Julie A. "Victims' Rights and Public Safety? Unmasking Racial Politics in Crime Discourses Surrounding Parole Revocation for 'Lifers' in California." *Western Criminology Review*, v.11/1 (2010). http://wcr.sonoma.eduv11n1/Beck.pdf (Accessed July 2011).

Elias, Robert. *The Politics of Victimization: Victims, Victimology, and Human Rights*. New York: Oxford University Press, 1986.

Moriarty, Laura J. and Robert A. Jerin, eds. *Current Issues in Victimology Research*. Durham, NC: Carolina Academic Press, 1998.

Schneider, H. J. "Victimological Developments in the World During the Past Three Decades (I): A Study of Comparative Victimology." *International Journal of Offender Therapy and Comparative Criminology*, v.45 (2001).

West Group. "Victims of Crime Act of 1984." In *West's Encyclopedia of American Law*. St. Paul, MN: Author, 1998. http://www.enotes.com/wests-Law-Encyclopedia/victims-Crime-Act (Accessed August 2010).

VIOLENT OFFENDER RECONCILIATION PROGRAMS

Violent offender reconciliation programs originate from the restorative justice paradigm and are designed to assist victims of such crimes as murder, armed robbery, homicide, vehicular homicide, and sexual assault. The American criminal justice system is rooted in adversarial interactions, retribution, and the due process rights of criminal defendants. Victims of violent crime may have little or no control over judicial proceedings concerning the crimes perpetrated against them. Rather, the state maintains the power position in the criminal justice system. More precisely, a violent crime is viewed as a violation against the state, and punitive measures are used to address this violation. In contrast, restorative justice makes the victim a priority and is community-centered. Moreover, restorative justice is contingent upon an understanding and appreciation of both shared interests and shared relations. Since the 1970s, victim advocate groups have struggled to meet the needs and protect the rights of victims. Generally, violent offender reconciliation programs are not used in place of the criminal justice system. Rather, these programs are used along with the criminal justice system to directly address and acknowledge the interests of victims. Since the rights of a criminal defendant are of paramount concern in the U.S. judicial system, victims of violent crime often feel ignored, disempowered, and even revictimized by the criminal justice system.

Originally, the vast majority of victim-offender mediation programs primarily accepted cases involving minor assaults and property crimes. However, the success of victim-offender mediation in dealing with nonviolent crimes, as well as growing dissatisfaction with the treatment and role of victims in the criminal justice system, has led to the use of violent offender reconciliation programs. Ideally, as a result of the reconciliation, violent offenders are made aware of and gain an appreciation for the consequences of their actions. Specifically, violent offender reconciliation programs allow offenders to conceptualize the impact of their actions from the intimate perspective of their victims' suffering. Moreover, the process provides victims with the opportunity to comprehend their offenders, as well as the factors that might have served as a catalyst for the offender's violent act.

In most instances, violent offender reconciliations are started with a request from the victim. The offender's participation is voluntary, and either party may terminate the process at any time. Generally, prior to the reconciliation, the offender has admitted his or her guilt. Hence, these programs aspire to foster constructive dialogue between the victim and the offender. During the process, the victim may gain validation via an apology, or the offender may gain forgiveness. An in-depth screening process, which may take up to a year or more, is utilized to confirm that a case is appropriate for a violent offender reconciliation program. The objective of the screening process is to maintain the safety of all parties involved, as well as the integrity of the reconciliation. Additionally, prior to the reconciliation, the mediator meets with each party individually to address questions and concerns. Often in violent offender reconciliation programs, this stage is vital in establishing the parameters of the reconciliation, including particular topics to be discussed. Additionally, this stage is important in addressing and accessing expectations of both parties participating in the reconciliation.

Violent offender reconciliations usually take place in a prison. Friends and family members of the victim may also be involved in the process. An appropriately trained mediator is crucial in a violent offender reconciliation. The trained mediator is present at all times during the reconciliation and is responsible for maintaining a safe and controlled environment. Moreover, during the reconciliation, the mediator acts as a facilitator but refrains from actively participating in the dialogue between the victim and the offender. Specifically, the mediator may encourage brainstorming, may actively and or reflectively listen, may refocus or reframe the dialogue, may confirm feelings, may refocus the discussion, and may recast the participant's positions into needs. It should be noted that the experience and concerns may differ when the family of a violent crime victim in a murder or homicide case is involved, as opposed to the individual who was the victim of the violent crime (in a robbery or sexual assault case). Generally, the victim will speak first about his or her experience of the crime. Following this, the offender will describe how he or she experienced and perceived the crime. Both parties are encouraged to fully express their feelings surrounding the incident and its impact. Because only a few people are involved in the reconciliation, there is an opportunity for great emotional intensity, which promotes open communication and empathy. It is crucial, however, that the parties are properly prepared prior to the mediation.

Some opponents of violent offender reconciliations argue that the crimes involved are too personal and complex for reconciliations. Specifically, opponents argue that participants face an array of risks in violent offender reconciliations because of these complexities and the inherent limitations of the process. For example, the victim may leave the reconciliation feeling that the offender lacked remorse for the crime or that the offender offered excuses rather than accepting responsibility. However, proponents of violent offender reconciliations feel that the potential benefits of properly conducted violent offender reconciliations substantially outweigh the risks. Additionally, some proponents of violent offender reconciliation programs have argued that these programs may be useful in place of the criminal justice system or before the sentencing phase. However, opponents argue that victims of violent crime may be exploited by the use of the reconciliation prior to criminal adjudication to determine appropriate punishment. Another policy debate surrounding violent offender reconciliation programs is whether participation in the reconciliation should affect the offender's post-conviction prison, parole, or probation status. The Texas Department of Criminal Justice has instituted a program allowing for victims of violent crimes to meet with offenders. Participation in the program generally does not affect the offender's prison, parole, or probation status.

Neil Guzy
University of Pittsburgh, Greensburg

See also Public Shaming as Punishment; Restorative Justice; Victim Impact Statements; Victim Services; Victim-Offender Reconciliation Programs

Further Readings

Cayley, David. *The Expanding Prison: The Crisis in Crime and Punishment and the Search for Alternatives.* Toronto, ON: House of Anansi, 1998.

Mika, Harry. "The Practice and Prospect of Victim-Offender Programs." *SMU Law Review*, v.46 (1993).

Rendon, Josefina Muniz. "Mediation in the Criminal Courts." *Houston Lawyer*, v.35 (1998).

Umbreit, Mark S. *Victim Meets Offender: The Impact of Restorative Justice and Mediation*. Monsey, NY: Criminal Justice Press, 1994.

Umbreit, Mark S. and Jean Greenwood. "National Survey of Victim-Offender Mediation Programs in the United States." *Mediation Quarterly*, v.16/3 (1999).

VOLUNTEERS AND COMMUNITY CORRECTIONS

Although the field of corrections has used volunteers to provide religious counseling and tutoring services for inmates incarcerated in prisons and jails and for offenders under correctional supervision in the community (probation and parole), today there is much more attention to the role of volunteers in reentry and community corrections. Volunteerism involves building strategic alliances, or partnerships, between departments of corrections' probation and parole divisions and community stakeholders. Volunteerism can help county probation officers and state parole agents with goals related to offender reform and community restoration, as long as the purpose and goals of the programs are clear.

In the 1990s, the loss of support for "get tough" crime control policies and practices and the over-reliance on incarceration led to an interest in using community placements as means of helping with offender reintegration. The U.S. Department of Justice is interested in the successful implementation of the reentry and community corrections laws that require day reporting, work release, halfway houses, therapeutic residential programs, probation, parole, and agents of government providing correctional services to work with the community stakeholders to help offenders achieve expectations upon reintegration. Examples include the Kansas Department of Corrections, which works with volunteers to operate the JEHT Foundation's intensive supervision program to help offender reentry; the sex offender management training program developed by Massachusetts in conjunction with the Parole Authority to improve the decision-making process and minimize risk upon release of sex offenders; and work with partners in Ramsey County, Minnesota, to help juveniles become successful during probation. U.S. Department of Justice statistics indicate that 44 to 70 percent of offenders released from incarceration back into the community are rearrested within one to three years. Minority and younger offenders have disproportionately higher recidivism rates. Some believe that community programs and volunteerism are appropriate for nonviolent offenders. Others believe that corrections is sufficiently challenged to meet its mission and goals without including community volunteers. If used correctly, however, volunteers can be an important resource.

Types of Volunteers

Volunteers are typically stakeholders in the community and can include the family, friends, and guardians of offenders, as well as members of civic, faith-based, nonprofit, and private business organizations and even former victims eager to ensure that offenses similar to those they experienced do not occur in the future. Volunteers can advocate for improvements in correctional services and become involved as mentors, tutors, teachers, job trainers, and helpers in drug rehabilitation programs, juvenile courts, and police athletic leagues (PALs). Statistics indicate that in St. Louis, some 17,000 offenders return to the community yearly, and 53 percent are unemployed and return to custody (or recidivate) within a year after release. Private companies work with the probation offices and parole divisions for altruistic reasons—that is, everyone must get a second chance.

The U.S. Department of Justice provided funding to states for reentry programs, and there was a volunteer component incorporated into each program. In St. Louis, the departments of corrections

Experienced probation and parole officers partner with community volunteers to ensure that safety and security is maintained during the corrections volunteer process. (Photos.com)

developed a model to cross-train probation and parole officers so that they learned special skills to work with private business partners and help the offenders with employment. A position known as case management specialist was created; people in this position are trained to find jobs and work interdependently with employers to hire offenders. Corrections professionals recognize that lack of work and poor literacy are the greatest challenge to the successful reintegration of offenders under correctional supervision in the community.

In 2004, as an outgrowth of the Prisoner Reentry Summit in Los Angeles, empirical research found that female offenders, many the breadwinners in the family, have a difficult time with employment. The Department of Labor's Ready4Work Project aims to use volunteerism and innovative programs to help meet the needs of females leaving prison and returning home. Work preparation programs can reduce recidivism rates by participants. Models for prisoners reentering society after release from prisons find they need the services of volunteers. Leadership from not-for-profit, private, and public organizations to devise strategies to help offenders is necessary for the effective implementation of volunteerism in the field of corrections. The restorative justice model places emphasis on civic engagement and encourages community service to help transform the offender and the community. In general, corrections departments are now considering the community as a resource and support, rather than an obstacle, for effective and efficient implementation of the corrections mission.

Regardless of the benefits of using volunteers in community corrections programs and services, there are noteworthy pros and cons that must be addressed by policy makers and corrections professionals before volunteers can be used successfully.

Pros

In general, governments cannot work alone to help the corrections population, and many people express an interest in volunteer service as a way to serve their community. Probation and parole offices see volunteerism as a cost-efficient way to provide services. In order for volunteerism to work well, instructions to volunteers must be clear with regard to the corrections environment and population, and there must be sufficient training. Experienced probation officers should be assigned to partner with community volunteers to ensure that safety and security goals are met. Likewise, juvenile court volunteers require special training and must honor their volunteer commitments. Volunteers must also acknowledge the special nature of corrections; for example, volunteers must meet certain standards of confidentiality and professionalism.

In Alabama, there is a volunteer call center that coordinates volunteer activities and works closely with the courts and probation. The United Way Elder Volunteer Program works with correctional agencies in training volunteers as reading tutors, and private organizations have volunteer opportunities for people to help disabled persons in community corrections programs. Police athletic leagues (PALs) work with juvenile probation departments as a delinquency prevention and intervention strategy, and state departments of education offer funding to such libraries, community colleges, and civic organizations to work with probation and parole authorities in an effort to provide adult literacy programs to illiterate offenders returning to the community.

In Los Angeles, probation partners with the California State University system to work with juveniles so that they can complete their general equivalency diplomas (GEDs) and look ahead to college. Faith-based community initiatives have received $25 million in federal funds to help the 650,000 offenders released yearly from prisons back into the community with literacy and job skills.

Multicultural volunteers are particularly important to corrections because they represent the diversity in the community to which the offender returns under correctional supervision and often enhance offender-volunteer relatability. Volunteers may range in age, ethnicity, gender, and skill set; those who have special skills—whether in painting, photography, or computers—can teach those skills to both adults and juveniles. With a diverse range of volunteers, the chances of matching volunteers' abilities with offenders' needs is enhanced, and so is safety in the community.

Cons

A high rate of volunteer turnover can occur when volunteers cannot adapt to the correctional environment. There can be trouble with the training and frustration with the progress of the offender population. Departments of corrections often do not have well-designed volunteer programs, which may offer no volunteer training or may mismatch volunteers and clients. Volunteers, by definition, must work hard for no monetary compensation, and they may become discouraged because of a lack of recognition and praise. Moreover, the victims of crime can often be opposed to volunteerism, fearing that justice is being denied to them while the community appears more interested in serving the offender. Public safety and fear, if improperly addressed, can also generate opposition to volunteerism. Not having the support of top-level management is a problem as well.

Conclusion

The crime control and corrections model that over-relies on incarceration is incongruent with the community corrections model and volunteerism. However, financial constraints and employee layoffs motivate managers in corrections to find ways to offer correctional services and achieve their mission and goals. Volunteerism can help meet these needs: Volunteers can work with communities to ensure offender accountability and restoration of neighborhoods. It is difficult to design programs so that there is "ownership" of justice linked to offenders, victims, and the community and assuage citizens' concerns about the value of programs that claim to change the behavior and actions of offenders. Community partnerships with departments of corrections involve explicit program goals, recruitment, training, sensitivity for victims, and knowledge of the family and community. Volunteers can be instrumental in this process.

Kimberley Garth-James
California State University, Sonoma

See also Attitudes of Offenders Toward Community Corrections; Faith-Based Initiatives; Reparation Boards; Teen Courts; Victim Services

Further Readings

Center for Community Corrections. "Reentry and Employment in St. Louis: A Model for Business, Community and Workers." 2007. http://www .centerforcommunitycorrections.org (Accessed July 2011).

Lindsay, Diane and Margot Robinson. *Volunteers: How to Find, Train, and Manage Them.* Washington, DC: U.S. Department of Justice, 2000.

Stevenson, Phillip and Jessica Ashley. *Implementing Balanced and Restorative Justice: A Guide for Juvenile Corrections.* Chicago: Illinois Criminal Justice Information Authority, 2006.

"WHAT WORKS" APPROACH AND EVIDENCE-BASED PRACTICES

"What works" is not a program or an intervention, but a body of knowledge based on more than 30 years of research that has been conducted by numerous scholars in North America and Europe. Also referred to as evidence-based practice, the "what works" movement demonstrates empirically that theoretically sound, well-designed correctional programs that meet certain conditions can appreciably reduce recidivism rates for offenders. Through the review and analysis of hundreds of studies, researchers have identified a set of principles that should guide these programs.

The Risk Principle

The first is the risk principle, or the "who" to target: those offenders who pose the higher risk of continued criminal conduct. Risk in this context refers to those offenders with a higher probability of recidivating. This principle states that the most intensive, structured correctional treatment and intervention programs should be reserved for higher-risk offenders. Why waste programs on offenders who do not need them? More important, research has clearly demonstrated that when lower-risk offenders are placed in highly structured programs, their failure rates tend to increase (and thus the overall effectiveness of the program is decreased). There are several reasons this occurs. First, placing low-risk offenders with higher-risk offenders only serves to increase the chances of failure for those at low risk. For example, a teenager who got into some trouble with the law but did not use drugs would not benefit from being placed in a program or group with heavy drug users; it is more likely that the higher-risk, drug-using youths would influence the non-drug-using teen rather than the other way around.

Second, placing low-risk offenders in these programs also tends to disrupt their prosocial networks; in other words, the very attributes that make them low risk—such as school, employment, and family—become interrupted. (If they do not have these attributes, it is unlikely that they are low risk to begin with.) The risk principle can best be seen from a 2002 study of offenders in Ohio who were placed in a halfway house or community-based correctional facility (CBCF). The study found that the recidivism rate for higher-risk offenders who were placed in a halfway house or CBCF was reduced, whereas the recidivism rates for the low-risk offenders who were placed in the programs actually increased. This study was later replicated with more than 20,000 offenders and once again saw the same effect; overall, there was a 3 percent increase in recidivism rates for low-risk offenders and a 14 percent reduction for high-risk offenders.

The Need Principle

The second principle is referred to as the need principle, or the "what" to target: criminogenic factors that are highly correlated with criminal conduct. The need principle states that programs should target crime-producing needs, such as antisocial attitudes, values, beliefs, and peer associations, as well as substance abuse, lack of problem-solving and self-control skills, and other factors that are highly correlated with criminal conduct. Researchers such as D. A. Andrews, James Bonta, and Paul Gendreau have identified a major set of risk factors:

1. Antisocial and procriminal attitudes, values, beliefs, and cognitive emotional states

2. Procriminal associates and isolation from anticriminal others

3. Temperamental and antisocial personality patterns conducive to criminal activity, including the following:

   - Weak socialization
   - Impulsivity
   - Adventurousness
   - Restlessness and aggressiveness
   - Egocentrism
   - A taste for risk
   - Weak problem-solving, self-regulation, and coping skills

4. A history of antisocial behavior

5. Familial factors that include criminality and a variety of psychological problems in the family of origin, including the following:

   - Low levels of affection, caring, and cohesiveness
   - Poor parental supervision and discipline practices
   - Outright neglect and abuse

6. Low levels of personal, educational, vocational, or financial achievement

7. Low levels of involvement in prosocial leisure activities

8. Substance abuse

Although these eight domains constitute the major set, the first four are considered the most important and are often referred to as the "big four." If these four can be successfully targeted and changed, the others often follow.

A study conducted by the Pennsylvania Department of Corrections confirms the importance of these risk factors. This study examined men and women on parole and looked at who failed and who succeeded: Those who failed exhibited the following characteristics and attitudes:

- Were more likely to hang around with individuals with criminal backgrounds
- Were less likely to live with a spouse
- Were less likely to be in a stable, supportive relationship
- Were less likely to identify someone in their life who served in a mentoring capacity
- Were less likely to have job stability
- Were less likely to be satisfied with employment
- Were less likely to take a low-end job and work up
- Were more likely to have negative attitudes toward employment and unrealistic job expectations
- Were less likely to have a bank account
- Were more likely to report that they were "barely making it" (yet the success group reported more than double the median debt)
- Were more likely to report use of alcohol or drugs while on parole (but with no difference in prior assessment of dependency problems, and poor management of stress was a primary contributing factor to relapse)
- Had unrealistic expectations about what life would be like outside prison
- Had poor problem-solving or coping skills
- Did not anticipate long-term consequences of behavior
- Failed to utilize resources to help themselves
- Acted impulsively to immediate situations
- Felt they were not in control
- Were more likely to maintain antisocial attitudes
- Viewed violations as an acceptable option in reacting to a situation
- Maintained general lack of empathy
- Shifted blame or denied responsibility

Interestingly, those who succeeded and those who failed faced no more or less difficulty in finding a place to live after release and were equally likely to report eventually obtaining a job. The most important factors centered on attitudes, whether they be about work, behavior, social support systems, or peers, and temperament and skill deficiencies.

It is also important to remember that programs need to ensure that the vast majority of their interventions are focused on these factors. Noncriminogenic factors such as self-esteem, physical conditioning, understanding one's culture or history, and creative abilities will not have much effect on recidivism rates. An example of a program that tends to target noncriminogenic factors can be seen in offender-based military-style boot camps. These programs tend to focus on noncriminogenic factors, such as drill and ceremony, physical conditioning, discipline, self-esteem, and bonding offenders together. Because they tend to focus on noncrime-producing needs, most studies show that boot camps have little impact on future criminal behavior. It is also important to remember that high-risk offenders have multiple risk factors, which is why programs that tend to be one-dimensional are much less effective than programs that target multiple risk factors.

The Treatment Principle

The third principle is the treatment principle, or the "how"—the ways in which correctional programs should target risk and need factors. This principle states that the most effective programs are behavioral in nature. Behavioral programs have several attributes. First, they are centered on the *present* circumstances and risk factors that are responsible for the offender's behavior. Hanging around with the wrong people, not going to work or school, and using drugs or alcohol to excess are examples of current risk factors, whereas focusing on the past is not very productive, mainly because one cannot change the past. Second, behavioral programs are *action*-oriented rather than talk-oriented.

In other words, successful programs focus on offenders doing something about their difficulties rather than just talking about them. These approaches are used to teach offenders new, pro-social skills to replace the antisocial ones (such as stealing, cheating, and lying) through modeling, practice, and reinforcement. Examples of behavioral programs would include structured social learning programs that teach new skills and behaviors, in which positive attitudes are consistently reinforced; cognitive behavioral programs that target attitudes, values, peers, substance abuse, anger, and the like; and family-based interventions that train family on appropriate behavioral techniques. Interventions based on these approaches are very structured and emphasize the importance of modeling and behavioral rehearsal techniques that engender self-efficacy, challenge cognitive distortions, and assist offenders in developing good problem-solving and self-control skills. These strategies have been demonstrated to be effective in reducing recidivism.

Nonbehavioral interventions that are often used in programs would include drug and alcohol education, fear tactics and other emotional appeals, talk therapy, nondirective client-centered approaches, having offenders read books, shaming offenders, lecturing them, milieu therapy, and self-help. In addition, programs (regardless of the model) that cannot maintain fidelity (that is, those with constant staff turnover) or are vague and unstructured (that is, whose counseling is designed for everyone) are also ineffective. There is little empirical evidence that these approaches will lead to long-term reductions in recidivism.

The Responsivity Principle

Finally, a host of other considerations will increase correctional program effectiveness. These include targeting responsivity factors, such as a lack of motivation or other barriers that can influence someone's participation in a program. Effectiveness depends on program managers making sure they have well-trained and interpersonally sensitive staff, providing close monitoring of offenders' whereabouts and associates, assisting with other needs that the offender might have, ensuring through quality assurance processes that the program is delivered as designed, and providing structured aftercare. These program attributes all enhance correctional program effectiveness.

Together, the proper management of these three principles—the who, the what, and the how—add up to effective correctional intervention, also known as "what works."

Edward J. Latessa
University of Cincinnati

See also Classification Systems; Martinson, Robert; Parole; Political Determinants of Corrections Policy; Public Safety and Collaborative Prevention; Public Shaming as Punishment

Further Readings

Andrews, D. A. and J. Bonta. *The Psychology of Criminal Conduct,* 5th ed. Cincinnati, OH: Anderson, 2010.

Bayens, Gerald J. and John Ortiz Smykla. *Probation, Parole, and Community-Based Corrections: Supervision, Treatment, and Evidence-Based Practices.* New York: McGraw-Hill, 2012.

Carter, Madeline M. *Increasing Public Safety Through Successful Offender Reentry: Evidence-Based and*

Emerging Practices in Corrections. Silver Spring, MD: Center for Effective Public Policy, 2007.

Gendreau, P., T. Little, and C. Goggin. "A Meta-Analysis of the Predictors of Adult Offender Recidivism: What Works!" *Criminology*, v.34/4 (1996).

Johnson, Shelley, Dana Jones Hubbard, and Edward J. Latessa. "Drug Courts and Treatment: Lessons to Be Learned From the 'What Works' Literature." *Corrections Management Quarterly*, v.4/4 (Fall 2000).

Lowenkamp, Christopher T. and Edward J. Latessa. "Developing Successful Reentry Programs: Lessons Learned From the 'What Works' Research." *Corrections Today*, v.67/2 (April 2005).

Martinson, Robert. "What Works: Questions and Answers About Prison Reform." In *Correctional Contexts: Contemporary and Classical Readings*, Edward J. Latessa et al., eds. Los Angeles: Roxbury, 2001.

Taxman, Faye S. and Steven Belenko. *Implementing Evidence-Based Practices in Community Corrections and Addiction Treatment*. New York: Springer, 2011.

WILDERNESS EXPERIENCE

The wilderness experience, commonly delivered in a corrections context as a wilderness program, is considered a therapeutic intervention for juvenile offenders. Wilderness programs provide residential placement, education, and a therapeutic component for delinquent youths that are alternative to the more conventional, secure detention institutions of juvenile corrections. These programs, described as rigorous outdoor activity–based programs, combine residential living with outdoor adventure–based programs to engage youths in a series of physically challenging activities that use a group approach to problem solving. Teamwork is often necessary for day-to-day success. Some wilderness programs offer youths an alternative to arrest or a diversion from formal court oversight by intervening at the preadjudication stages. Because of this approach, wilderness programs operate under both a community corrections model (such as focusing on reintegration of the youth into the community) and a residential placement model (such as focusing on prevention of recidivism).

History of Wilderness Programs

In the 1930s, forestry camps were established with the intention of rehabilitating male youth offenders

Therapeutic wilderness programs involve rigorous outdoor activity, residential living, and physically challenging activities in a group setting with the goal of reducing recidivism among juvenile delinquents by improving self-esteem. (Photos.com)

in Los Angeles County, California. The original programs recruited delinquent youths to work on community-based, outdoor projects. For example, youths worked to preserve nature (such as developing parks in the community) or provide other benefits to the community (such as constructing roads).

During the 1960s, the Outward Bound model, a different program but also based outdoors, was introduced to the United States. This program was originally intended to teach soldiers in Europe military survival skills during war. The fundamental tenet of the program was to build cohesion among soldiers and instill in them the self-discipline necessary for survival. When Outward Bound came to the United States, the program was redesigned to serve the general public rather than the military.

Purpose of the Programs

One important goal of wilderness programs is to reduce recidivism among youths by providing therapeutic programs for nonviolent juvenile offenders.

Treatment is based on experiential learning, that is, learning through active involvement, with the intention of developing a stronger self-concept for the youth. Specifically, wilderness programs are designed for youths who tend to have poor decision-making skills, low self-esteem, lack of self-control, and uncooperative behavior when working with others. The programs operate under the philosophy that youths will learn responsible and competent behavior when faced with physical challenges. Team leaders and peers provide the young participants with both guidance and support in completing activities. The philosophy further argues that, because youths have been removed from hostile, isolating environments that have labeled them with negative identities, youths will develop more positive attitudes and reduce the risk-taking behaviors associated with delinquency and status offenses. Interpersonal conflict is immediately addressed by staff, and youths are expected to accept responsibility for resolving conflict. Because the program specifically teaches the skills necessary for these young people to be productive members of their families and communities, these newly developed attitudes, behaviors, and skills should transition with the youths when they are returned to their communities of origin.

How Wilderness Programs Work

Most wilderness programs include different components of skill-building: academics, vocation, and personal. The personal skills developed include interpersonal communication and building positive peer relationships. The development of these skills occurs through a variety of means, including individual physically challenging outdoor activities (such as backpacking or rock climbing) and small-group activities requiring teamwork in order to complete the task (such as meal preparation). Wilderness programs are intended to offer youths an outdoor experience that teaches them how to meet their basic physical needs without reliance on modern conveniences, such as electricity. The programs also aim to appeal to a desire for excitement but in a safe, socially acceptable manner.

Most programs also offer a therapeutic component to address individual mental health needs. Part of the therapeutic component is having a small staff-to-youth ratio. One staff tends to be assigned to a small group of youths. Further, many of the staff will have specialized skills in a specific outdoor activity (such as mountain climbing). Wilderness programs may last between three days and three months. The staff are expected over time to become the youth group's role models, through their interactions with the youths and by demonstrating behavioral expectations for them.

Variation among programs is common. However, in general, wilderness programs tend to focus on incremental improvements in mastering physically difficult tasks (such as canoeing and rock climbing) and learning to engage in teamwork. These programs provide the opportunity to build self-respect in young people who have not previously experienced success in their lives (such as academic achievement and good peer relationships).

Benefits

Wilderness programs claim to reduce recidivism among juvenile delinquents through the improvement of the young person's self-concept and self-esteem. Proponents of these programs argue that the challenges offered to youths may increase problem-solving skills by teaching them to be self-reliant. These programs offer opportunities for peer interaction and personalized interaction with staff during their residence in the wilderness program, so that youths may experience less social alienation while also benefitting from the influence of positive role models. At the same time, many programs offer a therapeutic component for both the youths and their parents in an attempt to reduce parent-child conflict in the home and improve communication. Proponents of wilderness programs argue that another key benefit of this alternative to traditional juvenile corrections is the cost savings.

Risks

However, research tends to show only some short-term effects in reducing recidivism, usually within the first three months of exiting the program. Overall, wilderness programs seem to have little long-term effect on reducing delinquency and recidivism. Wilderness programs, like other social services programs, tend to have low-paid staff. Staff undertake a 24-hour-per-day work model, residing with and being responsible for the youths in the program continuously, and burnout rates can therefore be high, leading to high staff turnover. High turnover rates can interrupt the bonding process between staff and the residents. This may then interfere with the development of reliable, positive role models. Furthermore, given the physical challenges of the program, staff inattentiveness or inability to supervise a youth group fully can result in serious injuries or even accidental death. There is also the risk of a staff member misusing his or her position of authority and power to the extent that an abusive situation might occur.

Overall, evaluation of wilderness programs is limited. More research is necessary if the effectiveness of these programs, including their impact on delinquency and recidivism, is to be understood completely.

Aimée Delaney Lutz
University of New Hampshire

See also Community Corrections as an Alternative to Imprisonment; Diversion Programs; Family Therapy; Juvenile and Youth Offenders; Residential Programs for Juveniles

Further Readings

Friese, Greg, John C. Hendee, and Mike Kinziger. "The Wilderness Experience Program Industry in the United States: Characteristics and Dynamics." *Journal of Experiential Education*, v.21/1 (1998).

Harris, Patricia M. et al. "A Wilderness Challenge Program as Correctional Treatment." *Journal of Offender Rehabilitation*, v.19/3 (1993).

Roberts, Albert R. "Wilderness Programs for Juvenile Offenders: A Challenging Alternative." *Juvenile and Family Court Journal*, v.39/1 (1988).

Wilson, Sandra Jo and Mark W. Lipsey. "Wilderness Challenge Programs for Delinquent Youth: A Meta-Analysis of Outcome Evaluations." *Evaluation and Program Planning*, v.23 (2000).

Wisconsin Risk Assessment Instrument

Community corrections agencies across the United States utilize risk assessment instruments to better predict the threat of reoffending (that is, recidivism) by probationers and parolees. The information gained from these risk assessments is used to categorize offenders based on their predicted probability of recidivism and hence to allocate resources more efficiently. One of the first risk assessment scales, known as the Wisconsin Risk Assessment Instrument (WRAI, also referred to as form DOC-502 by the Wisconsin Department of Corrections), was developed in the late 1970s as part of the Wisconsin Case Classification and Staff Deployment Project. The instrument was created using a three-step process. First, data relevant to offender risk of recidivism were gleaned from approximately 250 randomly chosen probationers and parolees. Second, experts provided feedback regarding additional variables that could be used to predict recidivism. Third, the instrument was validated with a new sample and risk categories with score cutoffs were determined.

The WRAI was first evaluated by Christopher Baird, Richard Heinz, and Brian Bemus in 1979 as part of the Wisconsin Case Classification and Staff Deployment project. This early evaluation indicated that classification of offenders based on the scores obtained from the WRAI resulted in more intensive levels of supervision for high-risk clients, which in turn decreased future convictions, revocations, and rules violations. Furthermore, the less intensive supervision received by those identified as low risk did not appear to result in undesirable outcomes (that is, higher recidivism rates). In short, the WRAI appeared to be a valid and reliable tool.

Based on these early findings, the National Institute of Corrections (NIC) declared the WRAI a "model approach" and advocated for its adoption in community corrections agencies nationwide. Many states followed this recommendation; results from a national survey conducted by Dana Jones Hubbard and her colleagues in 1999 indicated that roughly 27 percent of U.S. probation and parole agencies were utilizing the WRAI. Around this time, however, academic scholars began to raise questions about the use of a specific risk assessment instrument on populations for which it had not been designed. In 1984, Kevin Wright, Todd Clear, and Paul Dickson assessed the validity of the WRAI for probationers in New York City. Their evaluation revealed that several items of the WRAI did not adequately predict the threat of reoffending. Similar concerns were subsequently raised with the use of the WRAI for probationers in Hawaii and Texas.

At the request of the Wisconsin Department of Corrections, the Council of State Governments' Justice Center conducted a comprehensive validation of the WRAI on Wisconsin probationers in 2009. This evaluation revealed three main problems. First, a vast majority of the probationers and parolees were being categorized as high risk. This defied the objective of the assessment, which was to rank offenders based on their recidivism risk in order to assign more funds and caseworkers to those who posed the highest risk. Second, the evaluation revealed that probationers and parolees classified at the same risk level did not display the same rates of reoffending. For example, only 18 percent of probationers with no prior felony convictions reoffended within three years of release compared to 30 percent of parolees with no prior felony convictions. Third, researchers realized that the WRAI did not take into consideration that misdemeanor probationers had lower reoffending rates than felony probationers. Based on these findings, the research group recommended that new weightings be assigned for selected items in the instrument, some definitions of risk factors be revised, the assaultive history item be removed, and a new variable measuring the offender's age at placement on community supervision be added. Additionally, the researchers proposed that there be four risk levels of supervision and that probationers and parolees be considered separately when being assigned to these risk levels.

Following the recommendations of the Wisconsin validation study, the WRAI was last revised in August 2009. The most current version of the WRAI includes 11 items that tap various domains, such as the client's residency status, employment history, substance abuse problems, and perceived demeanor. The scale also includes items pertaining to the client's prior conviction and community supervision history.

In conclusion, the development of the WRAI has been an important step toward a more objective and quantifiable prediction of the recidivism risk posed by offenders released to the community. The underlying rationale of the WRAI is to afford corrections departments a tool that can assist in more effectively allocating resources to high-risk offenders. However, to realize this goal, it has proven vital to revisit the validity of the instrument periodically through empirical studies. It is especially important to evaluate the applicability of the WRAI with appropriate populations before its adoption by out-of-state community corrections agencies.

Henriikka Weir
J. C. Barnes
University of Texas, Dallas

See also Classification Systems; Offender Risks;
    Prediction Instruments; Recidivism; Risk and Needs
    Assessment Instruments

Further Readings

Baird, Christopher, Richard Heinz, and Brian Bemus. *The Wisconsin Case Classification/Staff Deployment Project: A Two-Year Follow-Up Report.* Madison, WI: Health and Social Services Department, 1979.

Eisenberg, Mike, Jason Bryl, and Tony Fabelo. *Validation of the Wisconsin Department of Corrections Risk Assessment Instrument.* New York: The Council of Governments Justice Center, 2009. http://www.wi-Doc.com/PDF_Files/WIRiskValidation_August%202009.pdf (Accessed at January 2011).

Henderson, Howard. "The Predictive Utility of the Wisconsin Risk Needs Assessment in a Sample of Texas Probationers." *Dissertations Abstracts International,* v.68/2 (2007).

Jones Hubbard, Dana, Lawrence F. Travis, and Edward J. Latessa. *Case Classification in Community Corrections: A National Survey of the State of the Art.* Cincinnati, OH: Center for Criminal Justice Research, Division of Criminal Justice, University of Cincinnati, 2001.

University of Hawaii at Manoa Center for Youth Research. *Hawaii Risk Assessment Instrument: A Preliminary Report.* Rockville, MD: National Institute of Justice, 1986.

Wisconsin Department of Health and Social Services. *Development of the Wisconsin Risk Assessment Scale.* Rockville, MD: National Institute of Justice, 1976.

Wright, Kevin, Todd Clear, and Paul Dickson. "Universal Applicability of Probation Risk Assessment Instruments." *Criminology,* v.22/1 (1984).

WOMEN IN COMMUNITY SERVICE PROGRAMS

The idea of community service as an alternative sanction to incarceration began in the United States in the 1960s. Since its inception, the community service sanction has spread all over the country and is used for a variety of violations, including, but not limited to, "white-collar" crimes, juvenile delinquency, and other forms of minor crime. Such sanctions are usually withheld from violent offenders, repeat offenders, and the poor. Community service sentences are defined as sentences that mandate work to be performed by offenders for a specific number of hours for public or nonprofit agencies, under the jurisdiction of the court, without pay. In the United States, these sentences, generally ranging from 40 to 240 hours, can stand alone or be used in conjunction with other penalties, such as fines, probation, or incarceration. Conversely, community service sentences in Europe and Asia are generally ordered as alternatives to incarceration and stand alone.

Research has shown that community service can be an effective sanction in terms of lowering recidivism when applied to certain types of offenders in lieu of other punishments. For instance, people who are more educated, white or Asian, and engage in less serious crimes tend to respond to community service orders, recidivating less often compared to other types of offenders. Additionally, evidence shows that issuing community service orders as alternative sanctions can benefit the community by providing unpaid labor and saving money on incarceration costs.

Females and the Community Service Sentence

Beginning in Alameda County, California, in 1966, community service sentences were issued to women who were "driving under the influence" (DUI) offenders. Several reasons for this decision exist. Many of these women were young, poor, first-time offenders with dependents. Unable to pay their monetary fines, these women were winding up in jail. Not wanting to separate these mothers from their children, the courts began to look for an alternative to the traditional DUI sanction (a monetary fine). Community service appeared as a logical alternative.

The number of women in prisons and jails has been growing at an exceedingly fast rate. Community service, as an alternative sanction, has become an attractive alternative for female (and male) offenders because of its cost-saving benefits. The use of community service, as an alternative to incarceration, reduces costs, as it does not require the hiring and paying of more wardens, corrections officers, and healthcare professionals needed in order to run and maintain a prison. Furthermore, if offenders with dependents are sentenced to community service, as opposed to jail, the state does not incur the cost of caring for female offenders' children while their mothers serve an incarceration sentence.

Effectiveness

In terms of gender-differentiated research, no published research studies originating in the United States specifically examine the impact of community service orders on recidivism rates among female offenders. Fortunately, a few research studies in Europe have looked at this area. Overall, research indicates that community service sentences, as an alternative form of punishment, are at least as effective as other forms of punishment, including fines and short-term incarceration sentences. Furthermore, community service sentences appear to have an equivalent, if not a greater, effect in terms of lowering recidivism among offenders, including female offenders. For example, Lena Dominelli, in her examination of all community service sentences ordered in West Yorkshire, England, between 1976 and 1981, found that while male and female offenders were equally likely to complete their community service sentences, female offenders were less likely to recidivate than male offenders.

Benefits

In addition to reductions in recidivism, there appear to be other benefits of utilizing community service sentences as an alternative sanction with respect to female offenders, even though research examining such issues is limited. For example, it has been suggested that because female offenders are likely to be young, to have children, and to have committed minor, nonviolent crimes, community service orders are well suited for female offenders.

Community service sentences also divert offenders out of jail and prison. This is especially salient for female offenders because of their familial responsibilities. Rather than having to suffer the distress of being separated from their children if these offenders were to be incarcerated, community service sentences allow female offenders the opportunity to remain in the home and care for their children while completing their court order, while still holding the offender accountable for the crime she committed. It is also important to note that by keeping female offenders out of the system, labeling is avoided. This is critical because labels tend to degrade people and increase recidivism. This is especially important because females may be more sensitive to criminal justice labels than males.

In addition to the benefits the community service sentence provides female offenders, the community as a whole can benefit from the community service order. First, the community reaps economic remuneration through the use of unpaid labor. Research has shown that the unpaid labor resulting from community service sentences can produce up to twice as much revenue for the community than the revenue that would be generated were these offenders simply fined for their crimes. Furthermore, by diverting these offenders from incarceration, taxpayers save more money on prison facility costs, healthcare for prisoners, and other costs that go toward imprisoned offenders. Also, the public is able to see offenders working for the community in order to make up for their crimes. As a result, the community may view offenders in a more positive light than it would were these offenders sentenced to jail.

Finally, the community service order taps into aspects of restorative justice. The principle of restorative justice refers to money paid by the offender to the victim or to the service an offender provides to the community, known as symbolic restitution. The latter part of this principle means that harm caused by the illegal act is repaired through a cooperative process involving the offender, the government, and the victim if there is one present. The offender is actively working in the community to make amends for the crime committed, while the government monitors and ensures that the sentence is carried out. The victim is provided restitution in the form of unpaid labor that benefits the community in which the victim resides.

Conclusion

Although community service sanctions for female offenders have been utilized for the past 50 years in the United States, there appears to be relatively little research on these programs. Researchers have paid far greater attention to studying either imprisonment or various probation programs. Many of the available studies on community service and the female offender have been done outside the United States. This research indicates that, although young males were much more likely to receive a community service sentence, women receiving the same sentence actually respond more positively and recidivate at lower rates than men.

Lisa R. Muftić
Christian Dane
Georgia State University

See also Community Service Order; Diversity in Community Corrections; Female Offenders and Special Needs; Restorative Justice

Further Readings

Bouffard, Jeffrey and Lisa Muftić. "The Effectiveness of Community Service Sentences Compared to Traditional Fines for Low-Level Offenders." *The Prison Journal*, v.87/2 (2007).

Caputo, Gail. "Why Not Community Service?" *Criminal Justice Policy Review*, v.10/4 (1999).

Dominelli, Lena. "Differential Justice: Domestic Labour, Community Service and Female Offenders." *Probation Journal*, v.31/3 (1984).

McIvor, Gill. "Jobs for the Boys? Gender Differences in Referral to Community Service." *Howard Journal of Criminal Justice*, v.37/3 (1998).

Tonry, Michael. *Sentencing Matters*. New York: Oxford University Press, 1996.

WORK/STUDY RELEASE PROGRAMS

As early as the 1920s, American departments of corrections implemented work release programs to reduce the employability risk factors (ERFs) of offenders released from the prison and back into society. The Bureau of Justice Statistics shows that about 500,000 offenders return home each year, and about 60 percent of them will violate their terms of release. Study release programs involving basic education and secondary education (to gain a general equivalency diploma, or GED) help offenders with reentry. In the 1960s and 1970s, work/study release programs offered an alternative to traditional incarceration. State departments of corrections authorized work/study release as part of community corrections and the focus on rehabilitation for offenders committed to prisons for nonviolent crimes, as shown in national statistics. Violent offenders are ineligible for work/study release.

Why Work/Study?

In the 1970s, the goals of rehabilitation and community reintegration were embraced and the federal Law Enforcement Assistance Administration (LEAA) provided state funds for work/study release to assist soon-to-be-released offenders with the opportunity to gain work and work-related literacy skills as well as experience outside the correctional facility. The focus on a *transition* from prison to community includes job retention, management of finances, familial support, and a GED education. Some believe that corrections departments operate inefficiently, given offender recidivism rates (measured three years after release from prison) as high as 60 percent. High costs of prison beds versus work release beds were motives to create work release under community corrections policies. Others argue that ethics is an incentive for correctional

An alternative to traditional incarceration, work/study release may be granted only to nonviolent offenders. Security measures like electronic monitoring may be used to ensure public safety while an offender is at the work site. (Photos.com)

work/study release programs; humane treatment of offenders inside and outside prisons (and jails) includes employment preparation, educational and literacy attainment (GEDs), and experience while under correctional supervision. The highest participation in work/study release programs was in the 1970s, when arguments of cost savings and intentions to lower recidivism rates were popular with state departments of corrections.

Program Expectations

Select offenders who are close to completion of their terms of incarceration or in halfway houses are supervised in the community as they go to work. They learn and refine social and living skills, such as riding the bus, going to the grocery store, and managing their personal finances—all while under supervision. The Bureau of Justice Assistance indicates that meritorious good time is a popular incentive for offenders who participate in work/study release programs and a way to reduce the participants' sentences. The programs are an opportunity for self-improvement and help offenders to create a safe and productive lifestyle that can be sustained upon release. Offender accountability and rules are built into the work/study release programs. Participants must search for and retain employment, take adult education classes, and submit to monitoring by the department of corrections to ensure compliance. Offenders must also submit to frequent tests for substance abuse and comply with

requirements for classes, treatment, counseling, and family visits; their accountability is important, and failure to comply will result in explicit penalties and/or termination from the program.

Cost Savings and Offender Reentry

Are work/study release programs a cost-effective community alternative to traditional lock-up? Few research studies on the cost-effectiveness of work/study release programs and their effect on recidivism exist. Susan Turner and Joan Petersilia studied work release programs and discovered that in 1970, 45 U.S. state departments of corrections operated programs under community corrections; by 1990, fewer than 15 states had programs. Washington State's department of corrections is often cited in research on work/study release programs related to cost-savings and recidivism. It established rules for offender selection and screening for entry into the program; identified the types of employment, literacy skills, and training necessary; and picked the private and not-for-profit partners to provide work/study release services to offenders, using security measures (electronic monitoring) to ensure public safety while participants were outside the prison at work/study during the day. At night, they returned to the custodial supervision of the department of corrections or a halfway house. Washington's program held participants' arrests to less than 50 percent; only 5 percent committed crimes. Cost-efficiency was less promising and did not meet expectations.

Studies indicate that work release should focus on offenders' *transition* from prison back into the community as a key aspect of community corrections. Outcomes can be better for low-risk offenders convicted of driving while intoxicated (DWI), property crimes, drug crimes, or short-term nonviolent offenses. The use of global positioning system (GPS) monitoring adds to the success of work release participants.

Observations and Implications

Work/study release programs can be an alternative to traditional incarceration when there are concerns about offender transition from the correctional facility to the community. Most agree that ERFs interfere with offenders' job security. The national decline of work/study release programs operated by corrections reflects decreases in federal funding and loss of interest in the "rehabilitative ideal" described by researcher Francis Cullen, which has come to seen as "soft" rather than "tough" on crime.

That there are few effectiveness assessments on work/study release outcomes reflects a broader problem in the field of corrections. Decision makers need evidence of the benefits relative to costs of the programs, yet there are methodological issues concerning nonstandardized definitions of work/study release, difficulty in correlating aspects of work/study services with changes in criminal behavior, and issues regarding claims of offender preselection. Moreover, the disabled are underrepresented in work/study release programs. In 2008, 2 percent of offenders participated in these programs. Offenders who abide by program rules and fulfill sentencing conditions may address the political and public concerns about recidivism and high costs of corrections related to work/study release.

Kimberley Garth-James
California State University, Sonoma

See also Community Corrections and Sanctions; Community Corrections as an Add-On to Imprisonment; Community Corrections as an Alternative to Imprisonment

Further Readings

Berk, Jillan. *Does Work Release Work?* Unpublished Manuscript, Brown University, 2008.

Cullen, Francis T. "The Twelve People Who Saved Rehabilitation: How the Science of Criminology Made a Difference." *Criminology,* v.43 (2005).

Garth, Kimberley. *Public-Private Partnerships: The Free Venture Program Operating in the California Youth Authority.* Doctoral Dissertation, Golden Gate University, 1994.

Public Policy Forum. *Summary of Public Policy Research on Work Release and Global Positioning System Technology.* http://www.publicpolicyforum. org/pdfs/CJC_WorkRelease.pdf (Accessed November 2010).

Turner, Susan and Joan Petersilia. "Work Release in Washington: Effects on Recidivism and Corrections Costs." *Prison Journal,* v.76 (June 1996).

Waldo, Gordon and Theodore Chircos. "Work Release and Recidivism: An Empirical Evaluation of Social Policy." *Evaluation Review,* v.1 (1977).

Glossary

Absconding: Failing to appear for a court date without having a legitimate reason for the absence.

ACA: The American Correctional Association (formerly the American Prison Association), the oldest association (founded in 1870) for people working in the correctional facilities. In 2011, the ACA had approximately 20,000 active members.

Adam Walsh Child Protection and Safety Act: A 2006 federal law that created a national sex offender registry, with reporting requirements varying according to the severity of the offense.

Administrative remedy process: A system created within the U.S. Federal Bureau of Prisons in the 1970s and later adopted by many state and international corrections systems to address inmate grievances and concerns.

Aftercare: Similar to parole for juvenile offenders, a form of supervised release to the community following a period of incarceration.

Aggravating factors: Elements present in the commission of a specific crime, which a judge may consider when setting a sentence for an individual.

Attica Correctional Facility: A prison in New York State most famous for an inmate uprising in 1971 that led to the deaths of 11 prison employees and 32 prisoners.

Bail: An amount of money, as determined by a judge, that a person awaiting trial must post as a precondition for release. If the person does not appear in court on the appointed date, the bail is forfeited; hence, posting bail is meant to ensure the timely appearance in court of the accused.

Balanced model: A model of corrections that replaced the medical model in the 1970s and that states that punishment, deterrence, incapacitation, and rehabilitation are all worthwhile goals in the prison system.

Boot camp: A type of rehabilitation program, most often used with young offenders, that mimics aspects of military basic training, including rigorous discipline and physical conditioning.

CEA: The Correctional Education Association, an international organization founded in 1930 by and for professionals who provide education in adult and juvenile correctional and justice facilities.

Civil disabilities: Legal restrictions placed on convicted felons, such as removing their right to vote and hold office, engage in certain occupations, and associate with other offenders.

Classical criminology: An approach to criminology that emphasizes that behavior stems from free will, that perpetrators should be held responsible for their behavior, and that punishment is valuable as a deterrent.

Client-specific planning: A method of developing a sentence for an individual that takes into account factors such as the crime committed, the risk the individual poses to the community, and the specific needs of the individual; generally the plan is created by the defendant's lawyer and submitted to a judge for approval.

Community correctional center: A group living facility for offenders, often for those recently released from prison.

Community court: A type of court first created in New York City to speed up adjudication of minor offenses and provide restitution and supervision of offenders.

Community justice: A philosophy that emphasizes providing reparation to the community and to individual victims of crime, as well as involving citizens in crime prevention.

Community service: The requirement that, as a term of probation, an offender work (for instance at a hospital, in a nursing home, or picking up litter in parks) for a set numbers of hours to provide reparation to the community.

Comprehensive Crime Control Act of 1984: A law that established many new federal crimes and made other changes, including abolition of parole and establishment of sentencing guidelines that led to a substantial increase in the inmate population of the U.S. federal prison system.

Conditions of release: Legally binding restrictions on conduct that must be obeyed by individuals on parole.

Confrontation therapy: A type of therapy that forces an offender to acknowledge the consequences of his or her crime to the victim and/or to society.

Congregate system: A type of penitentiary system developed in Auburn, New York, in which inmates worked together during the day, under a rule of silence, and were held in isolation at night. It was developed by warden Elam Lynds, who also mandated that prisoners wear striped clothing, be addressed by their numbers rather than their names, and move in lockstep.

Contract labor system: The practice of selling the use of inmates' labor to private employers; inmates worked within the prison, using equipment and materials provided by the employer, to produce marketable goods.

CTU: The Counter-Terrorism Unit of the Federal Bureau of Prisons, established in 2006 to help monitor the activities of inmates suspected of terrorist activity and to improve collaboration among the bureau, other correctional agencies, and the law-enforcement and intelligence communities.

Day reporting center: A facility providing activities such as employment training, social skills training, and substance abuse counseling, often included in a type of intermediate sanction that requires offenders to report on a regular basis to the day reporting center.

Deinstitutionalization: Releasing mental patients from large facilities, such as state mental hospitals, and returning them, usually with supportive services, to the community.

Depo-Provera: The brand-name for the generic drug depot medroxyprogesterone acetate, a drug sometimes administered to male sex offenders because it removes their ability to respond sexually.

Determinate sentence: A fixed period of incarceration, imposed by a court and reflecting a philosophy of retribution for a crime.

Drug court: A court provided specifically to deal with substance abusers that takes a nonadversarial approach in the hope of breaking the cycle of addiction and crime; typically, an offender must frequently appear before the judge, undergo treatment, and submit to regular drug testing and other constraints.

Electronic monitoring: A method of providing community supervision, sometimes in conjunction with house arrest, in which an offender wears an electronic monitoring device, such as an anklet, that will set off an alarm if he or she leaves a specified area.

Evidence-based practice: Correctional methods that have been demonstrated in well-designed research studies to be effective.

Expiration release: The release of an inmate from incarceration without the threat that he or she can be returned to prison to serve the remainder of the sentence.

FPI: Federal Prison Industries, also known as UNICOR, established in 1934 as a government corporation to help inmates learn work skills that will facilitate their adjustment to life outside prison.

Furlough: The temporary release of an inmate, usually for one to three days, to allow a home visit intended to strengthen family ties and prepare the inmate for eventual release.

Good time: Discretionary reduction in a prison sentence as a reward for good behavior, such as participation in a treatment program.

Great Law: A principle adopted in Pennsylvania in 1682, drawing on Quaker principles that emphasized hard labor as punishment for most crimes, with the death penalty imposed only for premeditated murder.

Habeas corpus: Literally "produce the body," a judicial order requiring that a prisoner be shown (as opposed to keeping people incarcerated in secret) and that reasons be supplied for their confinement.

Halfway house: A place where offenders reside during an intermediate stage intended to bridge the gap between incarceration and complete reintroduction into the community, typically a community-based facility in which active rehabilitation and counseling are provided while residents are allowed to work or otherwise engage in life in the community.

House arrest: A punishment in which an offender is confined to his or her home, except for specified court-approved activities such as working or attending school; it may be combined with electronic monitoring.

Incapacitation: Taking away an offender's ability to commit further crimes, often by incarceration in a penal institution.

Inmate balance theory: A theory of prison governance that advocates that officials tolerate small infractions, relax security measures, and incorporate inmate leadership in their efforts to maintain control of the prison.

Intermediate sanctions: Punishments that exist on a continuum between prison and probation, including methods such as electronic monitoring and day reporting centers.

Justice reinvestment: A community development strategy that uses funds that would otherwise be spent on prisons to create and support community safety projects.

LCP: The Life Connections Program, established in 2002 as the first residential multi-faith-based program in the federal prison system.

Lease system: A system in which inmates were provided to contractors who were entitled to their labor (for instance, in agricultural work), who in turn provided the inmates with food and clothing.

Least restrictive methods: The principle that when choosing among methods used to ensure a legitimate state interest, such as security, the preferred method should make the least infringement possible on a prisoner's rights.

Mala in se: Offenses that are considered wrong by their nature.

Mala prohibita: Offenses that are not wrong by their nature but are prohibited by law.

Mandatory sentence: A type of sentence that imposes a minimum punishment (such as a term of incarceration) for a given crime, without regard to

circumstances and without allowing a judge to override this minimum punishment.

Marks system: A method of classifying prisoners based on the severity of their crime, which offers prisoners the opportunity to reduce their sentence terms through good behavior, educational achievement, and labor.

Mediation: A process sometimes used to divert offenders from criminal prosecution or to resolve civil disputes; it provides a neutral third party (the mediator) to help disputants reach an agreement, which often focuses on restitution and future behavior.

Medical model: A theory of criminology that viewed criminal behavior as a disease that could be diagnosed and treated through rehabilitative programs.

Megan's laws: An informal name for laws in the United States that differ from one state to the next but that require information about sex offenders (such as name, photograph, and address) to be released to the public; the first such law was passed in 1992 in New Jersey, following the rape and murder of a 7-year-old girl, Megan Kanka, by a known sex offender.

Mitigating factors: Elements of a crime that a judge may use in lowering the sentence for a defendant.

National Capital Revitalization and Self-Government Improvement Act: A 1997 law that required the Federal Bureau of Prisons system to absorb felons from the District of Columbia.

National Committee on Community Corrections: A public-private coalition created in 1987 in Washington, D.C., to promote community-based sanctions.

National Institute of Corrections: An agency of the U.S. Department of Justice created in 1974 and charged with assisting federal, state, and local corrections agencies.

National Reentry Affairs Branch: An entity created within the U.S. federal prison system in 2003 by Harley G. Lappin to coordinate release preparation and reentry efforts; it was originally called the Inmate Skills Development Branch.

New York House of Refuge: The first institution for juvenile delinquents, opened in 1825.

Parens patriae: Literally "parent of the nation," the power of the state to act on the behalf of a child—for instance, by removing a child from the custody of an abusive parent.

Parole: Release of an inmate from incarceration to the community, under supervision, after the inmate has served part of his or her sentence.

PINS: A person in need of supervision, which may include a juvenile status offender or a youth believed to be on the brink of getting into trouble.

Pre-sentence report: A report, prepared by a probation officer in order to advise a judge on sentencing, that includes information about a convicted individual's background.

Presumptive sentence: A sentence with a specified minimum and maximum range of time that allows a judge to set an individual's sentence within that range.

Pretrial diversion: A method of avoiding adjudication in that a defendant agrees to specified conditions (such as entering a drug rehabilitation program or submitting to regular drug monitoring) in exchange for the charges against him or her being dropped.

Prison Rape Elimination Act: A 2003 federal law intended to curb prison rape, in part by creating the National Prison Rape Elimination Commission to study the problem and mandating that the Department of Justice make elimination of rape in prison a high priority.

Private prison: A prison (or detention center or jail) operated by a third party under contract to a governmental agency in return for a specified daily or monthly fee per prisoner.

Probation: A sentence that allows a convicted offender to live in the community, generally with supervision, while serving his or her sentence.

PSI: A pre-sentence investigation, a report on a convicted offender's background for the purpose of helping the judge determine an appropriate sentence.

Recidivism: The return of former prisoners to criminal behavior, often followed by repeated incarceration; recidivism is often reported as the percentage of former criminals who return to crime after serving their sentences.

Recognizance: The obligation by an offender to perform specific acts (such as pay a debt or keep a court date) as a condition of being allowed to live in the community.

Reentry court: A court established to facilitate a released prisoner's adjustment to his or her life in the community.

Reformatory: An institution for juvenile offenders that emphasizes training, use of the marks system, and indeterminate sentences.

Rehabilitation model: A philosophy of corrections that emphasizes reforming offenders through provision of appropriate treatment programs.

Reintegration model: A philosophy of corrections that emphasizes maintaining a prisoner's ties with the community and his or her family in order to facilitate a successful return to the community.

Restitution: Providing money or services to a victim, often required from an offender as a condition of probation.

Restorative justice: A type of punishment that attempts to compensate victims or repair damage resulting from a criminal act; it is based on the philosophy that a crime is an offense not merely against the state but also against a victim and a community.

Retribution: A philosophy of justice that states that criminals who have infringed on the rights of others should be penalized, with the severity of the penalty appropriate to the severity of the crime.

ROR: Release on own recognizance, a type of pretrial release granted if a judge believes the defendant has sufficient ties to the community to guarantee that he or she will appear in court on the specified day.

Selective incapacitation: A method intended to make the best use of scarce prison resources by determining who, among the population of convicts subject to incarceration (and hence incapacitation), will most reduce the risk of further crime to society by actual incarceration.

Sentencing guidelines: A set of guidelines developed for judges, which indicates typical sanctions imposed in the past for particular offenses.

Separate confinement: A penitentiary system developed in Pennsylvania in which each inmate is housed separately in a cell and isolated from other inmates, including during work periods.

Shock incarceration: Imposition of a shock in the form of a short period of incarceration followed by a reduction in sentence.

SORNA: The Sex Offender Registration and Notification Act, another name for the Adam Walsh Child Protection and Safety Act, which established a national sex offender registry in the United States in 2006.

Spatial concentration: A phenomenon noted in some communities in which certain areas or neighborhoods have a high number of arrests and incarcerations compared to other areas.

Status offense: An act committed by juveniles that would not be a crime if committed by adults (for instance, alcohol consumption).

Technical violation: Failure of an individual on probation to abide by the rules and conditions of his or her probation, as specified by a judge; a technical violation may result in revocation of probation.

Therapeutic justice: A philosophy of justice that emphasizes rehabilitation rather than the punitive aspects of incarceration.

Three Prisons Act: An act of the U.S. Congress, passed in 1891, that established the federal prison system with three branches, in Leavenworth, Kansas; Atlanta, Georgia; and McNeil Island, Washington State. These were operated with limited oversight from the Department of Justice.

Unsupervised probation: A period of time specified by a court during which a released convict must abide by certain conditions but is not subject to probation monitoring; also called administrative probation.

Utilitarianism: A philosophy based on the principle that an action should be judged by its ability to maximize utility (variously defined as pleasure or preference), which, when applied to corrections, states that punishment must achieve sufficient good to outweigh the pain it inflicts.

Victims' services: Support provided, often by a district attorney's office, to assist victims and witnesses and help coordinate their testimony.

Violent Crime and Law Enforcement Act: A 1994 law that reduced the sentences of inmates who participated in drug treatment programs.

Work release center: A facility created to allow offenders to work in the community during the day while living in the center during nonworking hours.

Sarah E. Boslaugh
Kennesaw State University

Resource Guide

Books

Abramsky, Sasha. *American Furies: Crime, Punishment, and Vengeance in the Age of Mass Imprisonment.* Boston: Beacon Press, 2007.

Armstrong, Troy L., ed. *Intensive Interventions With High-Risk Youths: Promising Approaches in Juvenile Probation and Parole.* Monsey, NY: Criminal Justice Press, 1991.

Beccaria, Cesare. *On Crimes and Punishments*, Henry Paolucci, trans. Englewood Cliffs, NJ: Prentice Hall, 1963.

Bentham, Jeremy. *The Principles of Morals and Legislation.* New York: Hafner Press, 1948.

Berman, Greg and John Feinblatt. *Good Courts: The Case for Problem-Solving Justice.* New York: The New Press, 2005.

Bilchik, Shay. *Promising Strategies to Reduce Gun Violence.* Washington, DC: U.S. Department of Justice, 1998.

Braithwaite, John. *Crime, Shame and Re-Integration.* New York: Cambridge University Press, 1989.

Bynum, Tim and Scott H. Decker. *Project Safe Neighborhoods: Strategic Interventions.* Chronic Violent Offenders Lists, Case Study 4. Washington, DC: U.S. Department of Justice, 2006.

Byrne, James M., Arthur J. Lurigio, and Joan Petersilia. *Smart Sentencing: The Emergence of Intermediate Sanctions.* Thousand Oaks, CA: Sage, 1992.

Byrnes, Michelle, Daniel Macallair, and Andrea D. Shorter. *Aftercare as Afterthought: Reentry and the California Youth Authority.* San Francisco: Center on Juvenile and Criminal Justice, 2002.

Campbell, Donald T. and Julian C. Stanley. *Experimental and Quasi-Experimental Designs for Research.* Dallas: Houghton Mifflin, 1963.

Carlson, Peter and Judith Garrett. *Prison and Jail Administration: Practice and Theory*, 2nd ed. Sudbury, MA: Jones and Bartlett, 2008.

Champion, Dean J. *Corrections in the United States: A Contemporary Perspective*, 3rd ed. Upper Saddle River, NJ: Prentice Hall, 2001.

Clear, Todd R., George F. Cole, and Michael D. Reisig. *American Corrections*, 9th ed. Belmont, CA: Thomson Wadsworth, 2010.

Cook, Phillip and Jens Ludwig. *Gun Violence: The Real Costs.* New York: Oxford University Press, 2000.

Ekirch, A. *Bound for America: The Transportation of British Convicts to the Colonies, 1718–1775.* New York: Oxford University Press, 1987.

Enos, Richard and Stephen Southern. *Correctional Case Management.* Cincinnati, OH: Anderson, 1996.

Foucault, Michel. *Discipline and Punish*, Alan Sheridan, trans. New York: Pantheon Books, 1977.

Glaser, Daniel. *The Effectiveness of a Prison and Parole System.* Indianapolis, IN: Bobbs-Merrill, 1964.

Glaze, Lauren E. and Thomas P. Bonczar. *Probation and Parole in the United States 2008.* Washington, DC: U.S. Department of Justice, 2009.

Gray, M. *The Business of Captivity: Elmira and Its Civil War Prison.* Kent, OH: Kent State University Press, 2001.

Greenfeld, Lawrence A. and Marilyn W. Zawitz. *Weapons Offenses and Offenders.* Washington, DC: U.S. Department of Justice, Office of Justice Programs, 1995.

Greenwood, Peter W. *Selective Incapacitation.* Santa Monica, CA: RAND, 1982.

Hanser, Robert D. *Community Corrections.* Los Angeles: Sage, 2010.

Heeley, Kerry. *Case Management in the Criminal Justice System.* Washington, DC: National Institute of Justice, 1999.

Howell, J. *Preventing and Reducing Juvenile Delinquency: A Comprehensive Framework*, 2nd ed. Thousand Oaks, CA: Sage, 2009.

Hughes, R. *The Fatal Shore: The Epic of Australia's Founding.* New York: Vintage, 1988.

Jones, R. A. and C. Goff. *Study of the Costs and Benefits of the Washington County Restitution Center.* Washington, DC: National Institute of Justice, 1979.

Kant, Immanuel. *The Philosophy of Law*, W. Hastie, trans. Edinburgh: T. and T. Clark, 1887.

Korn, Richard R. and Lloyd W. McCorkle. *Criminology and Penology*. New York: Holt, Rinehart and Winston, 1959.

Lamb, H. Richard and Linda E. Weinberger. *Deinstitutionalization: Promise and Problems*. San Francisco: Jossey-Bass, 2001.

Lombroso, Cesare. *Criminal Man*, Nicole Rafter, ed. Durham, NC: Duke University Press, 2006.

Marion, Nancy E. and Willard M. Oliver. *The Public Policy of Crime and Criminal Justice*. Upper Saddle River, NJ: Pearson Prentice Hall, 2006.

Martin, Gus. *Juvenile Justice: Process and Systems*. Thousand Oaks, CA: Sage, 2005.

Mauer, Marc and Meda Chesney-Lind. *Invisible Punishment: The Collateral Consequences of Mass Imprisonment*. New York: New York Press, 2002.

Mays, G. Larry and L. Thomas Winfree, Jr. *Essentials of Corrections*, 4th ed. Belmont, CA: Thomson Wadsworth, 2009.

Morris, N. and D. Rothman. *The Oxford History of the Prison: The Practice of Punishment in Western Society*. New York: Oxford University Press, 1995.

Morris, Norval. *The Future of Imprisonment*. Chicago: University of Chicago Press, 1974.

Murphy, Jeffrie G. *Punishment and Rehabilitation*, 2nd ed. Belmont, CA: Thomson Wadsworth, 1985.

O'Brien, Patricia. *Making It in the Free World: Women in Transition From Prison*. Albany: State University of New York Press, 2001.

Packer, Herbert L. *The Limits of the Criminal Sanction*. Stanford, CA: Stanford University Press, 1968.

Parent, Dale. *Day Reporting Centers for Criminal Offenders: A Descriptive Analysis of Existing Programs*. Washington, DC: U.S. Department of Justice, 1990.

Petersilia, Joan. *When Prisoners Come Home: Parole and Prisoner Reentry*. New York: Oxford University Press, 2003.

Phillipson, Coleman. *Three Criminal Law Reformers: Beccaria, Bentham, Romilly*. Montclair, NJ: Patterson Smith, 1970.

Pisciotta, A. W. *Benevolent Repression: Social Control and the American Reformatory-Prison Movement*. New York: New York University Press, 1994.

Roberts, John W. *Reform and Retribution: An Illustrated History of American Prisons*. Lanham, MD: American Correctional Association, 1997.

Robinson, Paul H. *Distributive Principles of Criminal Law: Who Should Be Punished, How Much?* New York: Oxford University Press, 2008.

Sanborn, J. and A. Salerno. *The Juvenile Justice System: Law and Process*. Los Angeles: Roxbury, 2005.

Schneider, Richard D., Hy Bloom, and Mark Heerema. *Mental Health Courts: Decriminalizing the Mentally Ill*. Toronto: Irwin Law, 2006.

Simon, Jonathan. *Poor Discipline: Parole and the Social Control of the Underclass, 1890 to 1990*. Chicago: Chicago University Press, 1993.

Solzhenitsyn, Alexander. *The Gulag Archipelago*. New York: Harper and Row, 1973.

Tonry, Michael and Kate Hamilton, eds. *Intermediate Sanctions in Overcrowded Times*. Boston: Northeastern University Press, 1995.

Travis, Jeremy. *But They All Come Back: Facing the Challenges of Prisoner Reentry*. Washington, DC: Urban Institute Press, 2005.

Tyler, Tom. *Why People Obey the Law*. New Haven, CT: Yale University Press, 1990.

Umbreit, Mark and Marilyn P. Armour. *Restorative Justice Dialogue: An Essential Guide for Research and Practice*. New York: Springer, 2010.

von Hirsch, Andrew. *Censure and Sanctions*. New York: Oxford University Press, 1993.

Zimring, Franklin E. and Gordon Hawkins. *Incapacitation: Penal Confinement and the Restraint of Crime*. New York: Oxford University Press, 1995.

Journals

American Journal of Criminal Justice
American Journal of Family Therapy
American Journal of Legal History
American Historical Review
Annals of the American Academy of Political and Social Science
Archives of General Psychiatry
Child Welfare
Community College Journal of Research & Practice
Corrections Management Quarterly
Corrections Today
Crime and Delinquency
Crime and Justice: A Review of Research
Criminal Justice and Behavior
Criminology and Public Policy
Critical Social Policy
Fordham Urban Law Journal
Hofstra Law Review
International Journal of Drug Policy
International Journal of Law and Psychiatry
International Journal of Offender Therapy and Comparative Criminology
Journal of British Studies
Journal of Contemporary Criminal Justice

Journal of Contemporary Health Law and Policy
Journal of Crime and Justice
Journal of Criminal Justice
Journal of Criminal Justice and Popular Culture
Journal of Criminal Law, Criminology, and Police Science
Journal of Negro History
Journal of Offender Rehabilitation
Journal of Substance Abuse Treatment
Journal of the American Medical Association
Justice Policy Journal
Justice Quarterly
Juvenile and Family Court Journal
Law and Contemporary Problems
Law and Human Behavior
Law and Inequality Journal
Law and Society Review
Legal and Criminological Psychology
Michigan Historical Review
National Drug Court Institute Review
National Institute of Justice Journal
New England Journal on Criminal and Civil Commitment
NIJ Journal
Perspectives on Policing
The Prison Journal
Psychology, Public Policy, and Law
The Public Interest
Reviews in American History
Social Justice
Social Science Review
Stanford Law and Policy Review
Substance Use and Misuse
University of Chicago Law Review
University of Toronto Law Journal
Vermont Law Review
Victims and Offenders
William and Mary Law Review
Youth Violence and Juvenile Justice

Internet

Boot Camps for Teens: http://www.bootcampsforteens.com
California Department of Corrections and Rehabilitation: http://www.cdcr.ca.gov
Canadian Addiction Research Foundation: http://www.peele.net/aab/arf.html
Centre for the Study of Violence and Reconciliation: http://csvr.org.za
Corrections.com: http://www.corrections.com
Criminal Watch: http://www.criminalwatch.com
Family Violence Prevention Fund: http://www.endabuse.org
Federal Justice Statistics Resource Center: http://fjsrc.urban.org
Institute for the Study and Prevention of Violence: http://dept.kent.edu/ispv
International Law Enforcement: http://www.copnet.org
Juvenile Justice Trainers Association: http://www.jjta.org
Military School Alternatives: http://www.militaryschoolalternatives.com
Most Wanted Criminals and Fugitives: http://www.ancestorhunt.com/most-wanted-criminals-and-fugitives.htm
National Crime Prevention Council: http://www.ncpc.org
National Institute of Corrections: http://www.nicic.gov
National Rifle Association: http://home.nra.org
Police: The Law Enforcement Magazine: http://www.policemag.com
Policeguide.com: http://www.policeguide.com
PoliceWorld: http://www.policeworld.net
Probation Information: http://www.probationinfo.com
Quick Facts About the Bureau of Prisons: http://www.bop.gov/about/facts.jsp
Sexual Abuse Treatment: http://www.stopoffending.com
Teen Boot Camps: http://www.teenbootcamps.net
U.S. Parole Commission: http://www.justice.gov/uspc

Appendix

The following selected Websites, along with editorial commentary, are provided for further research in community corrections.

CEP: European Organisation for Probation

http://www.cep-probation.org

The CEP, an organization supported by the Directorate-General for Justice of the European Union, "aims to promote the social inclusion of offenders through community sanctions and measures such as probation, community service, mediation and conciliation. The CEP is committed to enhance the profile of probation and to improve professionalism in this field, on a national and a European level," according to its Website. The CEP membership is composed of individuals and organizations working in or having an interest in probation and criminal justice. The CEP promotes cooperation among European countries on these matters by organizing conferences and publishing reports of those conferences as well as a newsletter and also acts as the "voice of probation" to the European Union and the Council of Europe. Organizations within 32 European countries are members of the CEP, and an interactive map provides links to the Websites of member organizations within each country as well as a summary of the probation system in each country. The CEP Website is written in English and French, and some CEP publications are also available in other European languages.

The "Knowledgebase" (http://www.cepprobation .org/page/58/knowledgebase) section of the CEP Website is a database that includes fact sheets (drawn from the comprehensive 2008 survey *Probation in Europe* by Anton van Kalmthout and Ioan Durnescu) that describe the probation systems in most European countries (including statistics and lists of relevant Websites), texts of European probation regulations, relevant articles, and presentations given at CEP events. Information within the "Knowledgebase" may be accessed by country or by keyword text search.

One section of the CEP Website is devoted to the Special Interest Group on Foreign National Prisoners, defined as "European citizens imprisoned outside their country of residence." The purpose of this group, which is an umbrella organization comprised of member organizations, is to promote the welfare and interests of these individuals and facilitate their social reintegration. This section of the CEP Website (http://www .cepprobation.org/page/79/foreign-national-prisoners) explains the priorities of the Special Interest Group, lists members and their contact information, and includes a link to a downloadable copy (in PDF format) of the *Good Practice Guide: Developing Services for European Citizens Detained Abroad*, published by the CEP's Expert Group on Foreign Nationals.

The CEP publishes a newsletter that can be subscribed to through the Website. Links are provided on the Website to two other publications concerned with European probation issues: the *European Journal of Probation* and *EuroVista: Probation and Community Justice*. Articles from the *European Journal of Probation* may be downloaded for free, but articles from *EuroVista* must be purchased. The Website also contains information about CEP events (including four to five conferences held each year), links to funding programs relevant to European probation issues, a register of experts and training consultants in the field, and links to journals and organizations working in this field.

Corrections and Public Safety (Pew Center on the States)

http://www.pewcenteronthestates.org/topic_
category.aspx?category=528

The Pew Charitable Trusts is a nonprofit, research-focused organization dedicated to improving public policy, informing the public, and stimulating civic life. According to its Website, the Pew Center on the States (PCS), a division of the Pew Charitable Trusts, "works to advance state policies that serve the public interest. PCS conducts credible research, brings together diverse perspectives, and analyzes states' experiences to determine what works and what does not. We work with a wide variety of partners to identify and advance nonpartisan, pragmatic solutions for pressing problems affecting Americans." Corrections and public safety is one of the major areas of concern for the PCS (others include government performance, elections, voluntary home visiting, pre-K education, and children's dental health).

The Corrections and Public Safety Website is organized into four areas: reports, experts, related research, and related initiatives. The reports section includes downloadable, full-text documents of Pew Center reports (in PDF format) in five categories: prison population, community supervision, probation and parole, fiscal impact, and sentencing and courts. Calling up one of these reports on the Website often provides links to related information and research tools as well. For instance, on April 13, 2011, Pew published the report "State of Recidivism: The Revolving Door of America's Prisons," which may be downloaded from the Website. Additional materials supplied with this report include a press release, a summary of key findings, an interactive map that allows readers to examine recidivism data by state, links to news media coverage of the report, a video, and a link to a biography of the director of Pew's Public Safety Performance Project. The experts section of the Website includes links to biographies of Pew staff members who have expertise in the area of public safety and corrections (as of 2011, these were Adam Gelb, Richard Jerome, and Jake Horowitz) and information about how to contact them. The final two sections include links to other Pew publications and initiatives related to public safety and corrections as well as links to related press releases and coverage of Pew reports in the news media.

Information on the PCS Website may be retrieved in several ways. These include a site-wide search engine, a site map, and a resource library that may be searched or browsed by category. Advanced searches may be limited by topic, state, resource type (e.g., fact sheet, report, press release, or news article), date, and keyword. Additional resources on this Website include a calendar of events, a general introduction to the Pew Center and its goals, and sections devoted to Pew initiatives (including the Public Safety Performance initiative).

National Drug Court Institute

http://www.ndci.org/ndci-home

The National Drug Court Institute (NDCI), a nonprofit 501(c)(3) organization that began operation in 1998, is a professional services branch of the National Association of Drug Court Professionals (NADCP). The NDCI is supported by the White House Office of National Drug Control Policy and several entities within the U.S. Department of Justice and the U.S. Department of Health and Human Services. It performs and supports three main activities: education, research, and publication. In the realm of education the NDCI provides four tiers of training: Drug Court Planning Initiative training for local jurisdictional teams planning to implement a DWI (driving while intoxicated) or adult or family drug court; Comprehensive Drug Court Practitioner training, discipline-specific instruction for key drug court professionals, including judges, attorneys, treatment providers, law enforcement professionals, and individuals working in the fields of probation and parole; advanced subject-matter training, which addresses aspects of drug court operations such as long-term sustainability and responses to client behavior; and on-site and office-based technical assistance. In the area of research, the NDCI supports projects intended to help develop more effective procedures for drug courts and problem-solving courts. In the realm of publications, the NDCI disseminates publications aimed at improving drug court operations.

Information on the NDCI Website can be accessed in several ways. One is by the function of the person seeking information: An interface allows the user to select among 10 roles (case manager, defense attorney, probation officer, etc.) and be taken to information relevant to that role. Information is also organized into the categories of training, research, publications, and law. An interactive map on the Website allows users to search for drug courts in their state and provides local contact information. Several NDCI research reports are available for free download (in PDF format) from the Website, as are a number of brief fact sheets addressing topics such as synthetic cannabinoids and the application of the drug court model to cases of child maltreatment. Issues of the *Drug Court Review*, a professional journal published by the NDCI, are available for free download as well, and author guidelines and submission requirements are listed on the Website. Publications in the NDCI monograph series are also available for free download from the NDCI Website, as are issues of *Painting the Current Picture: A National Report on Drug Courts and Other Problem Solving Court Programs in the United States*, which has been published irregularly since 2004. The "Law" section of the Website includes a summary of judicial decisions relevant to drug courts, with links to the official record for each decision.

Office of Faith-Based and Neighborhood Partnerships (White House)

http://www.whitehouse.gov/administration/
eop/ofbnp

The Office of Faith-based and Neighborhood Partnerships is part of the executive branch of the U.S. federal government; it was established in 2001 by President George W. Bush. The purpose of this office, according to its Website, is "to build bridges between the federal government and nonprofit organizations, both secular and faith-based, to better serve Americans in need." These goals are achieved primarily by working through 12 agency centers located in different branches of the federal government: the Department of Health and Human Services, the Department of Congress, the Department of Housing and Urban Development, the Department of Veterans Affairs, the Department of Agriculture, the Department of Homeland Security, the Agency for International Development, the Department of Education, the Small Business Administration, the Department of Labor, the Department of Justice, and the Environmental Protection Agency. Contact information, including Web links, for each of these agency centers is provided on the Office of Faith-based and Neighborhood Partnerships Website. This office also coordinates the President's Advisory Council on Faith-based and Neighborhood Partnerships, a group of 25 leaders of nonsectarian and faith-based organizations that makes recommendations on ways the federal government can partner with community organizations.

The policy priorities of the office, according to its Website, are "strengthening the role of community organizations in the economic recovery; reducing unintended pregnancies, supporting maternal and child health, and reducing the need for abortion; promoting responsible fatherhood and strong communities, and promoting interfaith dialogue." The Website includes sections that highlight activities focused on each of these priorities, with links to other state and federal initiatives with similar concerns. Although the office does not administer or manage grant programs, the Website includes links to federal grant programs that may be relevant to faith-based and neighborhood partnership programs. The office maintains a blog on its Website that includes reports of specific activities of the agency centers and their community partners, often containing video and links to related stories.

More information about faith-based and community initiatives within the Department of Justice (DOJ) can be found within the DOJ Website (http://www.justice.gov/archive/fbci/index.html), which outlines the history of the program and the efforts of the DOJ's Task Force for Faith-based and Community Initiatives. The mission of the DOJ task force, according to its Website, is "to coordinate efforts to eliminate regulatory, contracting, and other programmatic obstacles to the participation of faith-based and other community organizations in the provision of social services." Currently there are four areas of focus for the DOJ task force: at-risk youth and gang prevention, domestic violence, prisoners and prisoner reentry, and victims of crime. The Website includes information about these areas of focus, funding opportunities, and conferences and events; it also includes links to a number of downloadable publications reporting on specific programs associated with the DOJ's Faith-based Task Force and offering advice about applying for partnership programs.

United States Department of Justice, Bureau of Justice Statistics

http://bjs.ojp.usdoj.gov

The Bureau of Justice Statistics (BJS), part of the Office of Justice Programs within the U.S. Department of Justice, was established in 1979. The mission of the BJS, according to its Website, is "To collect, analyze, publish, and disseminate information on crime, criminal offenders, victims of crime, and the operation of justice systems on all levels of government. These data are critical to federal, state, and local policymakers in combating crime and ensuring that justice is both efficient and evenhanded." The BJS publishes annual data on criminal victimization, correctional populations and federal offenders, and case processing; it also publishes a number of periodic data series on topics such as characteristics of correctional populations, prosecutorial practices and policies, expenditures and employment in the field of criminal justice, state processing of civil cases, and other criminal justice topics. The BJS Website includes an interface that allows the user to subscribe, through e-mail or RSS, to a service that sends notification when new crime and justice statistical materials from the BJS, the Federal Bureau of Investigation (FBI), and the Office of Juvenile Justice and Delinquency Prevention (OJJDP) are available.

BJS information is not copyrighted and may be freely distributed, copied, and reprinted. Many BJS publications and other products (e.g., press releases, data tables) are available for free download from the Website. These publications can be searched, viewed by product type or topic, or browsed alphabetically. A list of forthcoming publications and products is also available on the BJS Website. Graphs and data tables that clearly present basic historical statistics about topics of common interest (e.g., the number of adults incarcerated in the United States, the number of executions) are available in the "Key Facts" section of the Website (http://bjs.ojp.usdoj.gov/index.cfm?ty=kfa).

Many BJS data sets are available for download from the Website. They are organized into eight categories: corrections, courts, crime type, Criminal Justice Data Improvement Program, employment and expenditure, federal, law enforcement, and victims. Each data set is accompanied by ancillary information such as status of the project, collection period, questionnaires used, related documentation and other publications, methodology used to collect the data, changes over time (for recurring data series), and links to related topics. For example, the Annual Probation Survey and Annual Parole Survey is an active project that has been conducted annually since 1980 (except 1991), with 2009 the latest year available. The information in this survey is collected from probation and parole agencies and is available at both the national and state level. The annual reports are available for download (in PDF format) for 1998 through 2009; for earlier years, the reports are available in paper format only. The BJS Website also includes several data analysis tools, some of which allow users to perform calculations and/or to create customized tables and graphs without needing to download data and analyze it in a spreadsheet or statistical program. Data sets that can be accessed this way include those from the FBI's Uniform Crime Reporting Program, those from a BJS study on state prisoner recidivism, and various data from the Office of Juvenile Justice and Delinquency Prevention.

Sarah E. Boslaugh
Kennesaw State University

Index

Entry titles and their page numbers are in bold.